NEW HORIZON
FACTFINDER

NEW HORIZON
FACTFINDER

Edited by Michael W. Dempsey

PARRAGON

Contributors and Consultants
Norman Barrett
Arthur Butterfield
Jean Cooke
Andrew Ewart
Lionel Grigson
Andrew Johnson
Robin Johnson
Ann Kramer
Mark Lambert
Keith Lye
Ruth Midgley
James Muirden
Ian Ridpath
Avril Rodway
Theodore Rowland-Entwistle
Ron Taylor
Christopher Tunney
Brian Williams

This edition produced especially for Parragon in 1993 by Grisewood & Dempsey Ltd, Elsley House, 24–30 Great Titchfield Street, London W1P 7AD

10 9 8 7 6 5 4 3 2 1

Originally published in 1991

© Grisewood & Dempsey Ltd 1982, 1988, 1991

ISBN 1 85813 353 6

Printed and bound in Slovenia

Contents

Ideas and Beliefs 134–145

Glossary of Terms, Major Religions, Patron Saints, Biblical Characters, Prophets, Mythology, Roman-Greek Equivalents, Twelve Labours of Hercules, The Nine Muses

The Arts 146–169

Architectural Terms, Architects, Periods of Architecture, Literary Forms, Poets Laureate, Theatre, Cinema, Academy Awards, Musical Terms, Symbols and Notation, Tonic Sol-Fa, Operatic Terms, Ballet, Popular Music, Glossary of Painting, Glossary of Sculpture, Pottery Terms, Chinese Dynasties, Historic Pottery and Porcelain Factories

World History 170–229

Chronology of World History, Major Battles, Exploration and Discovery, British Rulers, British Prime Ministers, American Presidents, Popes, Holy Roman Emperors, Historic Assassinations

Science and Technology 230–255

Glossary of Science, Alloys, Carbon Compounds, Electrochemical Series, Chemical Elements, Elementary Particles, Metals and Ores, Equations of Motion, Physical Constants, SI units, Specific Gravities, Computer Terms, Glossary of Invention and Discovery

The Living World 256–271

Biological Terms, Animals: Longevity and Specialized Names, Animal Speed Records, Classification of Plants and Animals

Medicine 272–281

Medical Terms, Nutrition: Calories, Calorific Value, Vitamins

Prominent People 282–323
Brief Biographies of Famous People Past and Present, including Life Dates

Sport 324–337
Personalities in Sport, Olympic Games, Winter Olympics, Commonwealth Games, Association Football, Athletics, Badminton, Baseball, Basketball, Billiards and Snooker, Bowls, Boxing, Chess, Cricket, Croquet, Cycle Racing, Equestrian Sports, Fencing, Football (American, Australian, Gaelic), Golf, Gymnastics, Handball, Hockey, Horse Racing, Lacrosse, Modern Pentathlon, Motor Sport, Motorcycling Sport, Netball, Rowing, Rugby League, Rugby Union, Speedway, Squash, Swimming and Diving, Table Tennis, Tennis, Tenpin Bowling, Volleyball, Water Polo, Water Skiing, Weightlifting, Winter Sports

General Information 338–365
Nobel Prizewinners, Civil Aircraft Markings, Motor Cars: International Identification Letters, Notable Disasters (Air, Sea, Rail), Longest Bridge Spans, Longest Tunnels, Tallest Structures, Cooking Terms, Useful Measures, Oven Temperatures, Wine Glossary, Alcohol Content Proof Systems, Vintage Gradings, World Consumption, Which Wine?, Traditional Anniversary Names, Birthstones, Seven Wonders of World, Chess Notation, Languages of the World, Derivation of Days and Months, Alphabets, Abbreviations, Measurement and Number

Index 366–384

Astronomy

GLOSSARY OF ASTRONOMY

Absolute magnitude – see MAGNITUDE

Albedo is a measure of how much light a body, such as a planet, reflects. A perfectly white body reflects all the light that hits it, and has an albedo of 1; a completely black body, which reflects no light, has an albedo of 0.

Aldebaran is a RED GIANT star 68 light-years away in the constellation TAURUS. It is about 40 times the diameter of the Sun.

Algol is a star 82 light-years away in the constellation PERSEUS which periodically changes in brightness. The variability is caused by a second star which eclipses it every 2.87 days.

Alpha Centauri is the nearest bright star to the Sun, 4.28 light-years away; it lies in the southern hemisphere constellation CENTAURUS. Actually, it is a group of three stars, one of which, PROXIMA CENTAURI, is slightly closer than the others.

Altair A bright white star about 16 light-years away in the constellation Aquila, the eagle.

Altazimuth mounting A simple form of mounting for a telescope or binoculars which allows the instrument to swivel freely up and down (in altitude) and from side to side (in azimuth).

Andromeda is a major constellation of the northern hemisphere of the sky, representing a princess of Greek mythology. It is best seen during autumn evenings.

Andromeda galaxy A spiral-shaped galaxy of about 300,000 million stars visible to the naked eye as a fuzzy patch in the constellation ANDROMEDA. It lies about 2.2 million light-years away.

Anglo-Australian Observatory is an astronomical observatory at Siding Spring, New South Wales, jointly operated by the UK and Australian governments. Its main telescope is the 3.9-metre (154-inch) Anglo-Australian reflector, opened in 1974.

Antares is a red giant star about 400 light-years away in the constellation SCORPIUS. It is about 100 times the diameter of the Sun.

Aperture synthesis is a technique used in radio astronomy to synthesize the performance of a very large radio telescope by combining the output of several smaller telescopes. The technique was developed at the Mullard radio observatory, Cambridge, by Sir Martin Ryle, who was awarded the Nobel prize in 1974 for the advance.

Aphelion is the farthest point from the Sun that a body such as a planet reaches in its orbit.

Apogee is the farthest point from the Earth that a body such as an artificial satellite reaches in its orbit.

Left: The Andromeda galaxy, with its two small companions, is hundreds of times more remote than the foreground stars, which belong to our own galaxy.

Apollo project was the American man-on-the-Moon programme. A total of 12 American astronauts landed on the Moon in the Apollo project between July 1969 and December 1972. The astronauts were launched into space in the three-man Apollo command module; two of them later transferred into the spidery lunar module to make the Moon landing. Apollo capsules were also used to ferry astronauts to the SKYLAB space station, and for the link-up in July 1975 with a Soviet SOYUZ.

Apparent magnitude – see MAGNITUDE

Aquarius, the water carrier, is a constellation of the zodiac, lying in the equatorial region of the sky. The Sun passes in front of Aquarius in late February and early March.

Arcturus is a red giant star 37 light-years away in the constellation Bootes, the herdsman. It is 27 times the diameter of the Sun.

Arecibo Radio Observatory, in Puerto Rico, is the location of the world's largest radio astronomy dish, 305 m (1000 ft) in diameter. The Arecibo radio telescope is slung from towers in a natural hollow in the hills.

Ariel satellites are a series of UK scientific satellites, launched by the United States. Most famous of the series was the X-ray satellite Ariel 5, launched in 1974.

Aries, the ram, is a faint constellation of the zodiac lying in the northern hemisphere of the sky. The Sun passes in front of Aries from late April to mid-May.

Asteroids are irregular rocky bodies orbiting the Sun. They are also known as minor planets. Asteroids range in size from about 1000 km (620 mi) down. As many as 100,000 asteroids may be visible in the largest telescopes. The first asteroid to be discovered was CERES.

THE LARGEST ASTEROIDS

	Diameter in km (mi)	Distance from Sun in millions km (mi)
Ceres	1003 (623)	414 (257)
Pallas	608 (378)	414 (257)
Vesta	538 (334)	353 (219)
Hygeia	450 (280)	471 (293)
Euphrosyne	370 (230)	473 (294)

Astronomical unit is the average distance between the Earth and Sun; it is often abbreviated a.u. One a.u. is about 150,000,000 km (93,000,000 mi).

Atlas rocket A rocket used for launching American satellites and space probes, either with an Agena or a Centaur upper stage. Atlas rockets were used to launch American astronauts into orbit in the MERCURY PROJECT.

Aurora A display of coloured light in the sky near the Earth's north or south pole. Charged particles from the Sun are attracted to the poles. When the particles enter the upper atmosphere, they make the gas there glow. In the northern hemisphere, this effect is called the aurora borealis, or northern lights. In the southern hemisphere, it is known as the aurora australis, or southern lights.

Background radiation is a slight warmth in the universe, detectable at short radio wavelengths, which is believed to be energy left over from the BIG BANG. From an initial temperature of thousands of millions of degrees when the universe formed, it has now fallen to 2.7 degrees above absolute zero.

Baikonur – see TYURATAM

Barnard's star is a red dwarf, and the second closest star to the Sun. It lies 6 light-years away in the constellation Ophiuchus, the serpent bearer, but is too faint to be seen without a telescope. Barnard's star is believed to have planets.

Barred spiral galaxy A galaxy in which the stars and gas near the centre are arranged into a long, straight bar. Spiral arms curve from the ends of the bar.

Betelgeuse is a red giant star, about 650 light-years away in the constellation ORION. Betelgeuse varies in size between about 300 and 500 times the diameter of the Sun.

Big Bang is the name given to the giant explosion which is believed to have marked the origin of the universe as we know it. The Big Bang is estimated to have occurred about 20,000 million years ago, and the universe has been expanding ever since.

Binary star A pair of stars orbiting around a common centre of gravity. Some binaries can be seen as double in a telescope, but others are so close together that they can only be identified as binaries by analysis of their light; these are known as spectroscopic binaries. In some binaries, such as ALGOL, the stars eclipse each other; these are known as eclipsing binaries.

Black hole An area of space in which the pull of gravity is so strong that nothing can escape, not even light. Black holes are believed to form when giant stars collapse at the ends of their lives. Giant black holes may exist at the centres of galaxies, where they provide the power source for objects such as QUASARS.

Callisto is Jupiter's second largest satellite, 4820 km (2995 mi) in diameter. It orbits Jupiter every 16.69 days at an average distance of 1.9 million km (1.2 million mi).

Cancer, the crab, is a faint constellation of the northern sky. The Sun passes through it from late July to mid-August.

Canopus is the second brightest star in the sky. It lies about 110 light-years away in the southern hemisphere constellation of Carina, the keel, and is approximately 25 times the diameter of the Sun.

Cape Canaveral, in Florida, is the main site used by the United States for space launchings. It was temporarily renamed Cape Kennedy from 1963 to 1973.

Capella is a bright yellow star, 46 light-years away in the constellation Auriga, the charioteer.

Capricornus, the sea goat, is a constellation of the southern hemisphere of the sky. The Sun passes in front of it in late January to mid-February.

Cassegrain telescope is a popular design of reflecting telescope, named after the French physicist N Cassegrain who invented it in 1672. Light collected by the main mirror is reflected onto a secondary, which reflects it back through a hole in the main mirror to a final focus.

Cassiopeia is a famous constellation of the northern sky, representing a queen of Greek mythology. Cassiopeia has a distinctive W shape.

Castor is a bright white star 45 light-years away in the constellation GEMINI. Castor is actually a system of six stars linked by gravity.

Centaurus, the Centaur, is a constellation in the southern hemisphere of the sky, containing the closest star to the Sun, PROXIMA CENTAURI.

Cepheid variable is a type of star that cyclically expands and contracts in size, changing in brightness as it does so.

Ceres is the largest asteroid, 1003 km (623 mi) in diameter, and the first to be discovered, by Giuseppe Piazzi in 1801. Ceres orbits the Sun every 4.6 years between the orbits of Mars and Jupiter.

Chromosphere A layer of hot gas about 16,000 km (10,000 mi) deep surrounding the visible surface of the Sun (the PHOTOSPHERE). The chromosphere is only visible in special instruments or at total solar eclipses when the Moon blocks out the dazzling light from the photosphere. The chromosphere is then visible as a red circle of light, from which it takes its name meaning 'colour sphere'.

Comet A body a few kilometres across, consisting of powdery rock and ice. Comets orbit the Sun on elongated paths. When closest to the Sun, the ice vaporises and dust particles are released, producing a flowing tail. Small particles released from comets burns up in the atmosphere to produce METEORS.

FAMOUS COMETS

Name	First seen	Orbital period (years)
Halley's Comet	240BC	76
Biela's Comet	1772	6.7
Encke's Comet	1786	3.3
Great Comet of 1811	1811	3,000
Pons-Winnecke Comet	1806	6.3
Great Comet of 1843	1843	512.4
Donati's Comet	1858	2,040
Schwassmann-Wachmann Comet	1925	15
Arend-Roland Comet	1957	10,000
Ikeya-Seki Comet	1965	880
Kouhoutek's Comet*	1975	
Comet West	1976	

*observed from Skylab and Soyuz spacecraft

Conjunction is an alignment of celestial bodies, commonly referring to a planet lying on the far side of the Sun. In the case of Mercury and Venus, astronomers distinguish between INFERIOR CONJUNCTION, when they are on the near side of the Sun, and SUPERIOR CONJUNCTION, on the far side of the Sun.

Constellation A pattern of stars in the sky. A total of 88 constellations covers the entire sky, many of them representing figures from ancient mythology.

THE CONSTELLATIONS

Latin name (English name)
Andromeda (Andromeda)
Antlia (Air Pump)
Apus (Bird of Paradise)
Aquarius (Water Bearer)
Aquila (Eagle)
Ara (Altar)
Aries (Ram)
Auriga (Charioteer)
Bootes (Herdsman)
Caelum (Chisel)
Camelopardus (Giraffe)
Cancer (Crab)
Canes Venatici (Hunting Dogs)
Canis Major (Great Dog)
Canis Minor (Little Dog)
Capricornus (Sea-Goat)
Carina (Keel—of Argo)
Cassiopeia (Cassiopeia)
Centaurus (Centaur)
Cepheus (Cepheus)
Cetus (Whale)
Chamaeleon (Chameleon)
Circinus (Pair of Compasses)
Columba (Dove)
Coma Berenices (Berenice's Hair)
Corona Australis (Southern Crown)
Corona Borealis (Northern Crown)
Corvus (Crow)
Crater (Cup)
Crux (Cross)
Cygnus (Swan)
Delphinus (Dolphin)
Dorado (Swordfish)
Draco (Dragon)
Equuleus (Little Horse)
Eridanus (River Eridanus)
Fornax (Furnace)
Gemini (Twins)
Grus (Crane)
Hercules (Hercules)
Horologium (Clock)
Hydra (Sea-Serpent)
Hydrus (Watersnake)
Indus (Indian)
Lacerta (Lizard)
Leo (Lion)
Leo Minor (Little Lion)
Lepus (Hare)
Libra (Scales)
Lupus (Wolf)
Lynx (Lynx)
Lyra (Lyre)
Mensa (Table)
Microscopium (Microscope)
Monoceros (Unicorn)
Musca (Fly)
Norma (Rule—straight-edge)
Octans (Octant)
Ophiuchus (Serpent Bearer)
Orion (Orion—hunter)
Pavo (Peacock)
Pegasus (Pegasus—winged horse)
Perseus (Perseus)
Phoenix (Phoenix)
Pictor (Painter or Easel)
Pisces (Fishes)
Piscis Austrinus (Southern Fish)
Puppis (Poop—of Argo)
Pyxis (Mariner's Compass)
Reticulum (Net)
Sagitta (Arrow)

Sagittarius (Archer)
Scorpius (Scorpion)
Sculptor (Sculptor)
Scutum (Shield)
Serpens (Serpent)
Sextans (Sextant)
Taurus (Bull)
Telescopium (Telescope)
Triangulum (Triangle)

Triangulum Australe (Southern Triangle)
Tucana (Toucan)
Ursa Major (Great Bear or Plough)
Ursa Minor (Little Bear)
Vela (Sails—of Argo)
Virgo (Virgin)
Volans (Flying Fish)
Vulpecula (Fox)

Corona The thin gaseous atmosphere of the Sun, visible as a pearly glow around the Sun at a total eclipse. It consists of gas expelled from the Sun's surface.

Crab nebula, 6000 light-years away in TAURUS, is the remains of a star which was seen by Oriental astronomers to flare up as a SUPERNOVA in AD 1054.

Crater A roughly circular depression on the surface of a planetary body, usually caused by the impact of a smaller solid projectile.

Crux, the southern cross, is the smallest constellation in the sky.

Cygnus, the swan, is a constellation of the northern sky often called the northern cross because of its shape. Its brightest star is DENEB.

Declination A coordinate for locating objects in the sky, the celestial equivalent of latitude.

Deimos is the smaller and more distant moon of Mars, roughly 12.5 km (7.8 mi) in diameter, orbiting Mars every 1.26 days at an average distance of 23,500 km (14,600 mi) from the planet's centre.

Deneb is a white star 1630 light-years away in the constellation CYGNUS.

Doppler effect The change in wavelength of light from an object, caused by the object's motion. If the object is receding, then its light is lengthened (reddened) in wavelength. The RED SHIFT of light from galaxies shows that the universe is expanding.

EARTH	
Equatorial diameter:	12,756 km, 7926 mi
Polar diameter:	12,714 km, 7900 mi
Surface area:	5.1×10^8 sq km
	1.97×10^8 sq mi
Volume:	1.08×10^6 cu km,
	0.26×10^6 cu mi
Mean density:	5.52 (water=1)
Mass:	5.98×10^{21} tonnes
Acceleration	981 cm/sec/sec.
due to gravity:	32.2 ft/sec/sec
Mean distance	149,600,000 km
from Sun:	92,960,000 mi
Aphelion:	152,100,000 km,
	94,510,000 mi
Perihelion:	147,100,000 km,
	91,400,000 mi
Mean solar day:	24 hours
Spins on axis in:	23 h 56 min 4 sec
Orbits Sun in	365 days
(sidereal period):	6 h 9 min 10 sec
Velocity in orbit:	29.8 km/sec,
	18.5 mi/sec
Equatorial rotation	0.5 km/sec,
velocity:	0.3 mi/sec
Escape velocity:	11.2 km/sec,
	7.0 mi/sec

Earth is the third planet from the Sun, and the only one with large amounts of water on its surface and free oxygen in its atmosphere. Once cratered like the Moon, almost all traces of these ancient features have been destroyed by later crustal movements. Its original carbon dioxide atmosphere has been cleared by the photosynthesis of plants.

Eclipse This occurs when the Earth and Moon enter each other's shadow. When the Moon passes in front of the Sun, a solar eclipse is seen in those areas on which the Moon's shadow falls. When the Moon enters the Earth's shadow, a lunar eclipse ensues. On average, two to seven eclipses occur each year.

Eclipsing binary – see BINARY STAR

Ecliptic The path followed by the Sun around the sky each year. It gets its name because only when New Moon or Full Moon occurs on or near this line can eclipses occur.

Effelsberg Radio Observatory, near Bonn, West Germany, is the site of the world's largest fully steerable radio dish, 100 m (330 ft) in aperture.

Elements, chemical The most abundant element in the universe is hydrogen, comprising about 90 per cent of all matter. Helium accounts for another 19 per cent. All other elements, which astronomers term the heavy elements, make up only about 1 per cent of the universe. Originally, the universe is believed to have contained only hydrogen and helium, formed in the BIG BANG. The heavier elements have been built up by nuclear reactions inside stars, and distributed through space by SUPERNOVAE.

Elliptical galaxy A galaxy made of old stars, with no spiral arms. Elliptical galaxies range in shape from almost globular to a cross-sectional shape like that of a rugby ball.

Elongation is the angle of Mercury or Venus from the Sun as seen at any given time. Greatest elongation is the time of maximum angular separation.

Encke's comet is the comet of shortest known orbital period, 3.3 years. The comet was discovered in 1818 by the French astronomer Jean Louis Pons, and had its orbit calculated by the German astronomer Johann Franz Encke (1791–1865).

Equatorial mounting A form of mounting for telescopes. One axis of the mount is aligned parallel with the axis of the Earth; by turning this axis, the rotation of the Earth can be counteracted, so that the image stays still in the telescope's field of view.

Equinox is the instant when the Sun crosses the celestial equator. At the equinoxes, which occur in late March and September, the Sun is overhead on the equator at noon, and everywhere on Earth has equal day and night; the name 'equinox' means 'equal night'.

Europa is the smallest of the four main moons of Jupiter, 3100 km (1926 mi) in diameter. It orbits Jupiter every 3.55 days at an average distance of 670,000 km (416,000 mi).

European Space Agency is an organization of European countries involved in space research. ESA is involved in satellite projects both on its own and in conjunction with NASA.

Explorer satellites are a continuing series of American scientific satellites. The first American satellite was Explorer 1, launched on January 31, 1958.

Flare A brilliant outburst on the surface of the Sun, caused by a local eruption of energy, usually near a SUNSPOT. Flares eject atomic particles into space which cause radio interference on Earth.

Galaxy A collection of stars bound together by gravity. The smallest galaxies contain about a million stars, whereas the largest contain a million times more. Most galaxies are elliptical in shape, but about one in five is a spiral like our own, while some are irregular.

Ganymede is the largest moon of Jupiter, 5270 km (3275 mi) in diameter. Ganymede orbits Jupiter every 7.15 days.

Gemini, the twins, is a famous constellation of the northern hemisphere of the sky. Its two brightest stars are POLLUX and CASTOR.

Gemini project was a series of American space flights in the two-man Gemini capsule. During the Gemini programme, in 1965 and 1966, astronauts learned the techniques of rendezvous and docking of spacecraft and space walks that were vital to the APOLLO PROJECT.

Geosynchronous orbit is an orbit used by artificial satellites, particularly communications satellites, 35,900 km (22,300 mi) above the equator. At this height the satellite moves at the same rate as the Earth spins, and thus appears to hang stationary over a point of the equator.

Globular cluster A ball-shaped group of stars found around the centre of a galaxy. There are about 500 globular clusters arranged in a halo around our own Galaxy, each containing between about 100,000 and a million stars.

Gravity is the general force of attraction between bodies in the universe. It does not operate within atoms, whose particles are controlled by nuclear forces.

Hale Observatories is the name given since 1970 to the astronomical observatories on Mount Wilson and Mount Palomar in California, both founded by George Hale. Mount Wilson contains the famous 2.5-metre (100-inch) reflector opened in 1917. On Mount Palomar is the 5-metre (200-inch) Hale reflector, which was the world's largest until surpassed by a large telescope at the ZELENCHUKSKAYA OBSERVATORY, USSR.

Halley's comet orbits the Sun every 76 years.

Hercules is a major constellation of the northern hemisphere of the sky, named after a hero from Greek mythology.

Hertzsprung-Russell diagram is a graph in which the temperature of stars is plotted against their brightness. A star's position on the H-R diagram shows whether it is a normal star (on the MAIN SEQUENCE), a red giant (large but cool) or a white dwarf (small but hot).

Hubble constant A figure that shows how fast the universe is expanding, and thus how long ago the BIG BANG took place. According to latest measurements, galaxies move at about 16 km (10 miles) a second for every million light-years they are apart.

Hubble Space Telescope was launched in 1990 to orbit the Earth; despite some defects, it enabled astronomers to see further than ever before.

Hyades is a cluster of about 200 stars, 148 light-years away in the constellation TAURUS.

Hydrogen in space Hydrogen is the simplest and most abundant of all the ELEMENTS in space. Stars are made mostly of hydrogen, as are the glowing clouds of gas such as the ORION NEBULA. Hydrogen emits radio waves at 21 centimetres (see TWENTY-ONE CENTIMETRE RADIATION).

Inclination The angle of a planet's orbit to the Earth's orbit, or of a satellite to the Earth's equator.

Inferior conjunction is the instant when Mercury or Venus is in line between the Earth and Sun.

Infra-red astronomy is the study of the universe at wavelengths longer than those of red light. These studies reveal objects such as gas clouds and forming stars which are too cool to emit visible light, and brilliant objects such as the centres of galaxies that are otherwise obscured by dust.

Intelsat is the name of the communications satellites that provide a global telephone, radio, and TV network. Early Bird, the first, was launched in 1965. The current Intelsat IV A series can each carry 6000 telephone calls.

Interstellar molecules are molecules in space, usually detected by the radio waves they emit. Over 30 interstellar molecules of varying complexity are known, including water, ammonia and formaldehyde. Their presence indicates the existence of dense gas clouds, such as those from which stars form.

Io is the nearest of the four main satellites of Jupiter, orbiting every 1.77 days at an average distance of 422,000 km (262,000 mi). Io is 3630 km (2255 mi) in diameter.

Jodrell Bank is the location near Macclesfield, Cheshire, of the radio observatory of the University of Manchester. Its main instrument is the famous 76-metre (250-foot) diameter dish.

Juno was the third known asteroid, discovered in 1807. It is about 230 km (143 mi) in diameter and orbits the Sun every 4.36 years between the orbits of Mars and Jupiter.

Jupiter is the largest planet of the solar system. It is mainly hydrogen, similar in composition to the Sun, but may have a central rocky core. The visible surface is not solid, but consists of swirling, multi-coloured clouds, the only permanent feature of which is the red spot, apparently the top of a cyclonic feature.

JUPITER	
Diameter, equator:	142,800 km, 88,700 mi
Volume:	1316 Earth's volume
Mean density:	1.34 (water=1)
Mass:	317.8 Earth's mass
Gravity:	2.64 Earth's gravity
Mean distance from Sun:	778,000,000 km, 484,000,000 mi
Spins on axis in:	9 h 50 min
Orbits Sun in:	11.9 years
Velocity in orbit:	13.1 km/sec, 8.1 mi/sec
Escape velocity:	61 km/sec, 38 mi/sec
Satellites:	16, plus one ring

Kepler's laws are the three laws of planetary motion calculated by Johannes Kepler. The first, and most important law, is that planets orbit the Sun in elliptical paths (not circular paths as had always been assumed previously). Secondly, the planet moves fastest when it is nearest to the Sun. These two laws were published in 1609. The third law, published in 1619, notes that there is a direct connection between a planet's orbital period and its distance from the Sun.

Kitt Peak Observatory is an astronomical observatory near Tucson, Arizona, containing the largest collection of telescopes in the world.

13

MARS	
Diameter, equator:	6794 km, 4222 mi
Volume:	0.15 Earth's volume
Mean density:	3.95 (water=1)
Mass:	0.11 Earth's mass
Gravity:	0.38 Earth's gravity
Mean distance from Sun:	228,000,000 km, 142,000,000 mi
Spins on axis in:	24 h 37 min
Orbits Sun in:	687 days
Velocity in orbit:	24.1 km/sec, 15.0 mi/sec
Escape velocity:	5.0 km/sec, 3.1 mi/sec
Satellites:	2

MERCURY	
Diameter, equator:	4878 km, 3031 mi
Volume:	0.054 Earth's volume
Mean density:	5.4 (water=1)
Mass:	0.055 Earth's mass
Gravity:	0.37 Earth's gravity
Mean distance from Sun:	58,000,000 km 36,000,000 mi
Spins on axis in:	59 days
Orbits Sun in:	87.97
Velocity in orbit:	47.9 km/sec, 29.8 mi/sec
Escape velocity:	4.2 km/sec, 2.6 mi/sec
Satellites:	None

Landsat is the name of two American satellites for surveying the Earth. Their photographs are used to make maps of remote countries, identify locations of new mineral resources, detect areas of crop disease and monitor pollution.

Leo, the lion, is a constellation of the equatorial region of the sky. The Sun passes in front of Leo from mid-August to mid-September. The brightest star in Leo is REGULUS.

Libra, the scales, is a faint constellation of the southern hemisphere of the sky. The Sun passes in front of Libra during November.

Lick Observatory is the astronomical observatory of the University of California, on Mount Hamilton.

Light-year The distance travelled by a beam of light in one year. It is equivalent to 9.5 million million km (6 million million mi).

Local group The cluster of over 20 known galaxies of which our own Galaxy is the second largest member. The largest member of the local group is the ANDROMEDA GALAXY.

Lowell Observatory An astronomical observatory at Flagstaff, Arizona, founded in 1894 by Percival Lowell.

Luna probes are a series of Soviet Moon probes, members of which have photographed the Moon and landed on its surface. Two automatic Moon rovers have been delivered by Luna probes, and others have automatically brought lunar samples back to Earth.

Lunik spacecraft, launched from the USSR in 1959, were the first probes to strike the Moon and photograph its averted side.

Lyra, the lyre, is a small but prominent constellation of the northern sky. Its brightest star is VEGA.

Magellanic clouds are two satellite galaxies of our own Milky Way. They are each about 160,000 light-years away, and are about 1/30 and 1/200 the size of the Milky Way.

Magnitude is a scale that measures a star's brightness. The faintest stars visible to the naked eye are called magnitude 6; they are 100 times fainter than the first magnitude stars. Objects even brighter are given negative (minus) magnitudes. Objects fainter than magnitude 6 are given progressively larger positive magnitudes.

Main sequence is the classification given to stars in the healthy prime of their lives, when they are burning hydrogen at their centres to create energy, as is the Sun. Main-sequence stars form a band across the HERTZSPRUNG-RUSSELL DIAGRAM.

Mare (plural **maria**) is the name given to the large, dark plains which extend over much of the Earth-turned hemisphere of the Moon.

Mariner spacecraft are a series of American planetary probes. Mariner 9 made a complete photographic map of Mars in 1971–72, and Mariner 10 took the first close-up photographs of Mercury and Venus in 1974.

Mars is the fourth planet in line from the Sun. It is known as the red planet, because of the distinctive colour of its surface rocks, caused by extensive amounts of iron oxide. There is little air or water on Mars, and temperatures are frigid. Despite searches by the VIKING PROBES, there is no sign of life on Mars.

Mercury is the nearest planet to the Sun, not much larger than our own Moon. Its surface is lunar-like, covered with craters presumably formed by meteorites. Mercury has no appreciable atmosphere.

Mercury project was the first American attempt to fly men in space, in the one-man Mercury capsule. The programme lasted from May 1961 to May 1963, during which time a total of 6 astronauts were launched into space, the longest flight lasting 34 hours.

Meteor A dust particle from space, seen as it burns up in the atmosphere. Meteors are believed to be

---

METEOR SHOWERS

On an average night during the year about five or six meteors can be seen every hour. There are rather more after midnight, when the Earth's atmosphere encounters the meteoroid particles head on. At the time of meteor showers, however, the hourly rate may increase sharply to tens and very occasionally to hundreds. The showers occur regularly every year on or around the same dates and are caused by the Earth passing through the debris of broken-up comets. Because of perspective, the meteors in a shower all appear to originate from a point in the sky, which is termed the *radiant*. A shower is named after the constellation in which the radiant is located. Interesting showers include:

Quadrantids	Jan 1–5
April Lyrids	Apr 19–24
Aquarids	May 1–8
June Lyrids	June 10–21
Perseids	Jul 25–Aug 18
Cygnids	Aug 18–22
Orionids	Oct 16–27
Taurids	Oct 10–Dec 5
Leonids	Nov 14–20
Geminids	Dec 7–15

MILKY WAY

Diameter:	100,000 light-years
Thickness at the centre:	20,000 light-years
Thickness at the edge:	7000 light-years
Total mass of the system:	100,000 solar masses
Density in solar neighbourhood:	1200 Earth masses per cubic light-year
Absolute magnitude (from above the galactic pole):	−20.5
Total number of stars:	100,000
Total number of globular clusters:	500
Total number of open clusters:	18,000
Total number of stellar associations:	800
Distance of Sun from galactic centre:	32,000 light-years
Distance of Sun from galactic plane:	30 light-years 'north'
Rotational velocity near the Sun:	250 km/sec, 155 mi/sec
Rotational period near the Sun:	225 million years
Age of Galaxy:	12,000 million years

NEPTUNE

Diameter, equator:	48,400 km, 30,075 mi
Volume:	44 Earth's volume
Mean density:	2.30 (water = 1)
Mass:	17.2 Earth's mass
Gravity:	1.4 Earth's gravity
Mean distance from Sun:	4,497,000,000 km, 2,794,000,000 mi
Spins on axis in:	18 h
Orbits Sun in:	164.8 years
Velocity in orbit:	5.4 km/sec, 3.4 mi/sec
Escape velocity:	25 km/sec, 16 mi/sec
Satellites:	8 plus rings

dust from comets. When the Earth crosses the orbit of a comet, as happens several times a year, a meteor shower is seen. Most meteors are about the size of a grain of sand, and burn up long before reaching the Earth's surface.

Meteorite A lump of rock or metal from space that penetrates the atmosphere to reach the Earth's surface. If a meteorite is large enough it will blast a crater, like the 1-kilometre crater in Arizona.

Milky Way is the faint band of starlight seen crossing the sky on clear, dark evenings. The Milky Way is actually the plane of our Galaxy seen from inside, therefore our Galaxy is also known as the Milky Way. There are about 100,000 million stars in the Milky Way Galaxy, which is 100,000 light-years in diameter.

Minor planet – see ASTEROID

Mir Space Station was launched by the USSR in 1986; in 1987–8 two cosmonauts aboard *Mir* set a record of 366 days in space.

Moon The Earth's nearest natural neighbour in space. It is a rocky band pitted with countless craters believed to have been formed by meteorite impacts. In some places, volcanic eruptions have produced the dark lava plains known as maria

MOON

Diameter, equator:	3476 km, 2160 mi
Volume:	1/49 Earth's volume
Mean density:	3.34 (water = 1)
Mass:	1/81 Earth's mass
Gravity:	1/6 Earth's gravity
Perigee:	356,400 km, 221,460
Apogee:	406,697 km, 252,716 mi
Mean distance from Earth:	384,400 km, 238,860 mi
Spins on axis in:	27⅓ days
Orbits Earth in (sidereal month):	27⅓ days
Synodic month (new Moon – new Moon):	29½ days
Escape velocity:	2.4 km/sec, 1.5 mi/sec

('seas'). The Moon turns on its axis in the same time as it takes to orbit the Earth, so that it keeps one face permanently turned towards us. The Moon is airless, waterless and lifeless.

Mount Wilson and Palomar Observatories – see HALE OBSERVATORIES

Mullard Radio Observatory, át Cambridge, England, is the site of two large APERTURE SYNTHESIS radio telescopes, the One Mile and the Five Kilometre instruments (the names signify their length). PULSARS were discovered at the observatory, which is operated by the University of Cambridge.

NASA, the National Aeronautics and Space Administration, is the American government agency for civilian space flight, founded in 1958.

Nebula (plural **Nebulae**) is a mass of gas and dust in space. Some are believed to be the sites of star formation, such as the ORION NEBULA. Some nebulae are made to glow by the light of stars inside them, others shine by reflection, but others are dark and invisible.

Neptune is the eighth planet in average distance from the Sun, discovered in 1846 by J G Galle. Neptune has a deep gaseous atmosphere, underneath which is believed to be a core of rock and ice. The planet appears as nothing more than a greenish disc in even a large telescope.

Neutron star A small, highly compressed star about 10 to 20 km (6–12 mi) diameter, left behind after the death of a star more massive than the Sun. In a neutron star, gravity has compressed the electrons and protons of the star's atoms to form the atomic particles called neutrons. See also PULSARS.

NGC is an abbreviation for the New General Catalogue of star clusters and nebulae, compiled in 1888 by the Danish astronomer J L E Dreyer and widely referred to by astronomers.

Nova A stellar outburst caused by the transfer and ignition of gas between two stars in a binary system. The star that causes the outburst is a WHITE DWARF, on to the surface of which gas flows from a normal companion, and then erupts in a nuclear explosion.

Nutation is a slight nodding of the Earth's axis caused by the uneven gravitational pulls of the Sun and Moon. Nutation slightly alters the Earth's tilt in space every 18.6 years.

Object glass is the main lens at the front of a refracting telescope.

Occultation is the covering of a celestial body by the Moon. The occultation of stars by the Moon is used to track the Moon's orbit around the Earth.

15

Olbers' paradox asks why, if the universe is infinite, the night sky is dark. The German astronomer Heinrich Wilhelm Olbers (1758–1840) argued that light from distant stars should combine to make the night sky bright. The answer is that the galaxies, in which the distant stars are contained, are moving away as the universe expands, so that their light is weakened by the RED SHIFT.

Opposition is the instant when a planet is opposite in the sky to the Sun. At opposition, a planet is seen due south at midnight.

Orbit The path in space of one body around another. Orbits are usually elliptical in shape, although the orbits of the planets scarcely depart from circles.

Orbiter spacecraft, 5 of which were launched from the USA in 1966 and 1967, orbited the Moon at heights of a few hundred kilometres and took detailed photographs of practically the whole surface, showing details down to a metre across.

Orion is a major constellation in the equatorial region of the sky, representing a figure from Greek mythology. Its two brightest stars are RIGEL and BETELGEUSE, and it also contains the ORION NEBULA.

Orion nebula is a glowing mass of gas about 1500 light-years away in the constellation ORION. New stars are forming inside the nebula, and it is their light which makes it glow. A whole cluster of stars will probably be formed from the Orion nebula.

Oscillating universe is the theory which says that the current expansion of the universe will eventually slow, stop, and be reversed, so that the universe collapses again to another BIG BANG. According to this theory, the universe continues in endless cycles of expansion and contraction. However, astronomers do not presently believe that the expansion of the universe will be halted.

Ozone Triatomic oxygen (O_3)

Pallas is the second largest asteroid, 610 km (379 mi) in diameter, and the second to be discovered, by Wilhelm Olbers in 1802. Pallas orbits the Sun every 4.6 years between the orbits of Mars and Jupiter.

Parallax The slight shift in position of a nearby star when viewed from opposite sides of the Earth's orbit. The amount of parallax shift reveals the star's distance. Stars beyond about 100 light-years distance have parallaxes too small to be accurately measured.

Parsec A unit of distance in astronomy, equivalent to 3.26 LIGHT-YEARS. It is the distance at which a star would show a PARALLAX of 1 second of arc, although no star is actually quite this close.

Pegasus is a large constellation of the northern hemisphere of the sky, representing the winged horse of Greek mythology. Its main feature is a great square marked out by four stars.

Perigee is the nearest point to the Earth that a body such as an artificial satellite reaches in its orbit.

Perihelion is the nearest point to the Sun that a body such as a planet reaches in its orbit.

Perseus is a constellation of the northern sky, representing a figure from Greek mythology. Its most famous star is ALGOL.

Phobos is the larger and nearer of the two moons of Mars, 22.5 km (14 mi) in diameter, orbiting every 7.65 hours 9350 km (5810 mi) from the planet's centre.

Photon A 'packet', or quantum, of light radiation.

Photosphere is the visible surface of the Sun, a layer of gas at a temperature of about 6000°C.

Pioneer probes are a series of American craft to investigate the solar system. Pioneers 10 and 11 took remarkable close-up photographs of Jupiter in 1973 and 1974.

Pisces, the fishes, is a constellation of the equatorial region of the sky. The Sun passes in front of Pisces from mid-March to mid-April.

Planet A large non-luminous body in orbit around a star, which can be made of rock or gas. Planets are not large enough to generate energy at their centres by nuclear reactions, as do stars.

Planetary nebula A shell of gas ejected from a red giant at the end of its life, leaving the star's hot core as a central WHITE DWARF. Planetary nebulae are so named that they superficially resemble a planet's disc when seen through a small telescope.

Pleiades A group of 200 stars about 400 light-years away in the constellation TAURUS.

Plough – see URSA MAJOR

Pluto is the planet with the greatest average distance from the Sun, discovered in 1930 by Clyde Tombaugh. Actually, its orbit is so eccentric that from 1979 to 1999 it comes closer to the Sun than Neptune. Many astronomers think that Pluto is an escaped satellite of Neptune. Latest measurements suggest that it is the smallest planet of the solar system.

PLUTO

(Only limited data are given because there is doubt about the planet's diameter)

Diameter, equator:	3000 km, 1800 mi
Mass:	0.17 Earth's mass
Mean distance from Sun:	5,900,000,000 km, 3,670,000,000 mi
Spins on axis in:	153 hours
Orbits Sun in:	247.7 years
Velocity in orbit:	4.7 km/sec, 2.9 mi/sec
Satellites:	1

Polaris, the pole star, lies approximately 400 light-years away in the constellation URSA MINOR.

Pollux is an orange giant star, 36 light-years away in the constellation GEMINI, of which it is the brightest star.

Precession is a wobbling of the Earth on its axis every 26,000 years like a spinning top, caused by the gravitational pulls of the Sun and Moon.

Procyon is the brightest star in the constellation Canis Minor, 11.4 light-years away. It has a WHITE DWARF companion.

Prominences are eruptions of gas from the surface of the Sun, often associated with SUNSPOTS.

Proper motion is a change in a star's position over time caused by its movement around the Galaxy. The proper motions of stars are not noticeable to the naked eye, but over thousands of years they slowly change the shapes of the constellations.

Proxima Centauri is a red dwarf star 4.3 light-years away, the closest member of the ALPHA CENTAURI triple system.

Pulsar A rapidly rotating NEUTRON STAR that emits a radio or optical pulse as it spins. Pulsars were discovered by Cambridge radio astronomers in 1967. The fastest pulsar, at the centre of the CRAB

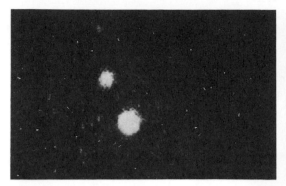

*This pulsar, in the Crab Nebula, is the spinning
remains of a supernova. It flickers into visibility
(left) and disappears (right) as its beam of
radiation passes over the Earth.*

NEBULA, flashes 30 times a second; the slowest
ones flash every 3 seconds or so.

Quasar A small but brilliant object far off in space.
Quasars can give out the energy of hundreds of
galaxies from a space not much larger than our
own solar system.

Radio astronomy is the study of the universe in
radio waves, emitted naturally by many objects in
space. Radio astronomy has led to the discovery of
objects such as QUASARS and PULSARS, and has also
helped astronomers map the structure of our own
Galaxy through the TWENTY-ONE CENTIMETRE
RADIATION of hydrogen.

*This radio telescope at Parkes Observatory, NSW,
Australia has a collecting dish 64 metres (210 feet)
across. This dish reflects radio emissions on to a
receiver, which is held at the focus by the large
tripod.*

Radio galaxy A galaxy that emits considerable
radio energy, both from a central point and from
lobes either side of the galaxy that seem to have
been ejected in explosions. Radio galaxies are
closely related to QUASARS.

Radio telescope A device for collecting radio waves
from space. Most radio telescopes are like reflecting telescopes in design, but because radio waves
are so much longer than light waves, radio telescopes have to be correspondingly larger to see
the sky in as much detail. One solution is the
APERTURE SYNTHESIS design.

Red dwarf A faint star that is smaller and cooler
than the Sun.

Red giant A large star with a cool surface, which
has swelled up towards the end of its life. In about
5000 million years, our Sun will become a red
giant like ARCTURUS.

Red shift is the lengthening in the wavelength of
light from a receding object, such as a galaxy. The
amount of red shift, which is caused by the
DOPPLER EFFECT, reveals how fast the object is
receding.

Reflecting telescope A telescope that uses a mirror
to collect and focus light. The first reflector was
built in 1668 by Isaac Newton, but the idea had
previously been proposed in 1663 by the Scottish
scientist James Gregory.

Refracting telescope is a telescope that uses lenses
to collect and focus light. The invention of the
refractor is attributed to the Dutch optician Hans
Lippershey in 1608, although he was almost
certainly not the first to make one.

Regulus is a blue-white star about 85 light-years
away in the constellation LEO, of which it is the
brightest star.

Rigel is a blue giant star 850 light-years away, the
brightest star in ORION.

Right ascension is a coordinate for locating objects
in the sky, the celestial equivalent of longitude.

Royal Greenwich Observatory was set up in 1675.
In 1958 it moved from Greenwich to Herst-
monceux, East Sussex; in 1990 it was transferred to
Cambridge; its main telescopes are now in Las
Palmas, in the Canary Islands.

Sagittarius, the archer, is a constellation of the
southern hemisphere of the sky. The Sun passes in
front of Sagittarius from mid-December to mid-
January.

Salyut is a Soviet space station, smaller than the
American SKYLAB. The first of the Salyut series was
launched in 1971.

Lift-off for Soyuz 11 in May 1971; the launcher has four wrap-round boosters. After 24 days in orbit in the Salyut space station the cosmonauts were killed during re-entry.

Satellites are any bodies that move in an orbit around another, more massive body. The planets, for example, are satellites of the Sun. And the Moon is a satellite of the Earth. Many other artificial, or man-made, satellites orbit the Earth, too. They are used for such purposes as radio and television communications, and for gathering information on the Earth and the weather.

Saturn is the sixth planet from the Sun and closely resembles Jupiter. Saturn's most interesting feature is its rings, 272,000 km (169,000 mi) in diameter, made of tiny icy fragments.

SATURN	
Diameter, equator:	120,200 km, 74,700 mi
Volume:	755 Earth's volume
Mean density:	0.70 (water=1)
Mass:	95.2 Earth's mass
Gravity:	1.2 Earth's gravity
Mean distance	1,427,000,000 km,
from Sun:	887,000,000 mi
Spins on axis in:	10 h 14 min
Orbits Sun in:	29.5 years
Velocity in orbit:	9.6 km/sec, 6.0 mi/sec
Escape velocity:	37 km/sec, 23 mi/sec
Satellites:	23

Saturn rockets are two related rockets designed for manned launchings. The smaller Saturn 1B was used for launching Apollo capsules into Earth orbit; the larger Saturn V was used to launch the Apollo Moon missions.

Schmidt telescope A wide-angle photographic telescope using both lenses and mirrors, designed in 1930 by the Estonian optician Bernhard Schmidt.

Scorpius, the scorpion, is a constellation of the southern sky whose brightest star is ANTARES. The Sun passes across part of Scorpius at the end of November.

Seeing is a term used to describe the steadiness of the atmosphere, which affects the quality of an image during astronomical observations.

Seyfert galaxy A galaxy with a brilliant core, rather like a scaled-down QUASAR. Astronomers think that Seyfert galaxies are closely related to quasars.

Shooting Star – see METEOR

Sidereal period is the time take for an object such as a planet or satellite to complete one orbit relative to the stars.

Sirius is the brightest star in the sky, 8.8 light-years away in the constellation Canis Major. It has a WHITE DWARF companion.

Skylab was an American space station made from a converted Saturn V upper stage. Astronauts spent up to 84 days in Skylab in 1973–74.

Solar day is the time taken for an object to complete one axial rotation relative to the Sun.

Solar system The collection of planets and other objects orbiting the Sun.

Solar wind A stream of electrically charged particles given off by the Sun. Some of these particles enter the Earth's atmosphere in the polar regions, where they give rise to AURORAS.

Solstice is the time in late June and late December when the Sun is at its farthest north or south of the equator.

Southern Cross – see CRUX

Soyuz is a Soviet spacecraft capable of holding two or three men. Soyuz capsules can fly on their own, or are used to ferry cosmonauts to SALYUT space stations.

Space shuttles are reusable space planes for launching men and satellites into orbit. The first was successfully launched in 1981, and there have been many flights since; on the 25th mission, in 1986, the shuttle *Challenger* exploded on launching.

Spacelab is a European-built space station which flies in the cargo bay of the SPACE SHUTTLE.

Spectrum The band of colours obtained when the light from a body is split into its various wavelengths. This is usually done by a spectrograph, which photographs the spectrum. A spectrum gives information about the temperature of a body and the materials composing it.

Spica is a blue-white star 260 light-years away.

Spiral galaxy An important type of galaxy in space. Old stars are arranged in a central bulge, while newer stars form spiral arms around it. Our MILKY WAY galaxy is a spiral.

Sputnik was a series of early Soviet satellites. Sputnik 1, launched on October 4, 1957, was the first artificial satellite.

Star A glowing ball of gas that produces energy by nuclear reactions at its centre, unlike a planet which shines only by reflecting light.

Steady state theory says that the universe never had a single beginning like the BIG BANG, but instead that matter is continually created in space. The theory is not widely supported.

Three different types of spiral galaxy. Left: Type Sa, with a large nucleus and faint arms. Centre: Type Sc, with loose, prominent arms. (The Milky Way is of intermediate type, Sb, resembling the Andromeda galaxy shown on page 8.) Right: A barred spiral with loose arms (type SBc).

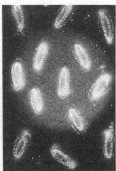

The Steady State theory suggests that, as galaxies fly apart, new material comes into existence, forming fresh galaxies to fill the gaps.

THE NEAREST STARS

	Distance (light-years)	Proper motion ("/yr)	Visual magnitude	Abs magnitude	Spectral Type
Proxima Centauri	4.28	3.85	11.05	15.45	M5
α-Centauri A	4.37	3.68	−0.01	4.35	G2
α-Centauri B	4.37	3.68	1.33	5.69	K5
Barnard's Star	5.8	10.31	9.54	13.25	M5
Wolf 359	7.60	4.71	13.53	16.68	M8
Lalande 21185	8.13	4.78	7.50	10.49	M2
Sirius A	8.7	1.33	−1.45	1.41	A1
Sirius B §	8.7	1.33	8.68	11.66	A
Luyten 726–8A	8.88	3.36	12.45	15.27	M5
UV Ceti	8.88	3.36	12.95	15.80	M6
Ross 154	9.44	0.72	10.60	13.30	M4
Ross 248	10.28	1.59	12.30	14.80	M6
ε-Eridani	10.76	0.98	3.73	6.13	K2
Luyten 789–6	10.76	3.26	12.18	14.60	M7
Ross 128	10.83	1.37	11.10	13.50	M5
61 Cygni A	11.09	5.21	5.22	7.58	K5
61 Cygni B	11.09	5.21	6.03	8.39	K7
ε-Indi	11.20	4.69	4.68	7.00	K5
Procyon A	11.40	1.25	0.35	2.65	F5
Procyon B §	11.40	1.25	10.70	13.00	F
Struve 2398 A	11.52	2.30	8.90	11.15	M4
Struve 2398 B	11.52	2.28	9.69	11.94	M5
§ White dwarf					

THE BRIGHTEST STARS

Name	Designation	Visual magnitude	Abs magnitude	Spectral Type	Distance (light-years)
Sun	—	−26.74	4.83	G2	—
Sirius	α-Canis Majoris	−1.45	1.41	A1	8.7
Canopus	α-Carinae	−0.73	−4.70	F0	1200
Rigil Kent	α-Centauri	−0.10	4.35	G2	4.37
Arcturus	α-Boötes	−0.06	−0.20	K1	36
Vega	α-Lyrae	0.04	0.50	A0	26
Capella	α-Aurigae	0.01	−0.60	G0	42
Rigel	β-Orionis	0.11	−7.00	B8	900
Procyon	α-Canis Minoris	0.38	2.65	F5	11.4
Achernar	α-Eridani	0.46	−2.20	B5	85
Agena	β-Centauri	0.61	−5.00	B1	460
Altair	α-Aquilae	0.77	2.30	A7	16
Betelgeuse	α-Orionis	1.00	−6.00	M2	310
Aldebaran	α-Tauri	0.85	−0.70	K5	68
Acrux	α-Crucis	0.90	−3.50	B1	360
Spica	α-Virginis	0.96	−3.40	B1	261
Antares	α-Scorpii	1.00	−4.70	M1	330
Pollux	β-Geminorum	1.14	0.95	K0	36
Fomalhaut	α-Piscis Austrini	1.16	1.90	A3	22
Deneb	α-Cygni	1.25	−7.30	A2	1800
Mimosa	β-Crucis	1.26	−4.70	B0	425
Regulus	α-Leonis	1.35	−0.60	B7	85

Stellar spectroscopy is the analysis of light from stars. It reveals the star's composition, its temperature, and whether it is a dwarf or a giant.

Stonehenge is a monument on Salisbury Plain, England, which some astronomers believe embodies advanced astronomical knowledge. The oldest parts of it date back 4500 years.

Sun The Sun is our nearest star, 1.39 million km (865,000 mi) in diameter. It is believed to have been born, along with the rest of the solar system, 4600 million years ago. It keeps hot by nuclear reactions at its centre which turn the hydrogen of which it is mostly made into helium.

SUN	
Diameter, equator:	1,392,000 km
	865,000 mi
Volume:	1,303,600 Earth's
	volume
Mean density:	1.41 (water=1)
Mass:	333,000 Earth's mass
Gravity:	28 Earth's gravity
Mean distance	149,600,000 km,
from Earth:	92,960,000 mi
Escape velocity	618 km/sec
	384 mi/sec
Surface temperature:	6000°C
Core temperature:	circa 15,000,000°C
Spins on axis in:	25.38 days
Orbits galaxy in:	225 million years
Velocity in orbit:	2,150 km/sec,
	1,336 mi/sec
Distance from	
galactic centre:	30,000 light-years
Spectral type:	G2
Absolute magnitude	+4.83
Apparent magnitude:	−26.74

Sunspot An area on the Sun's surface about 1500°C cooler than its surroundings, so that it appears darker by contrast. Sunspots are believed to be caused by strong magnetic fields which block the outward flow of heat from the Sun's interior.

Superior conjunction is the instant when Mercury and Venus are on the far side of the Sun from Earth.

Supernova is the nuclear explosion of a giant star at the end of its life. The CRAB NEBULA is the remnant of a supernova.

Surveyor probes were a series of American spacecraft which in 1966–68 automatically soft landed on the Moon.

Synodic period is the time taken for the Moon or a planet to return to the same position relative to the Sun.

Taurus, the bull, is a major constellation of the equatorial region of the sky. Its brightest star is ALDEBARAN, and it also contains the CRAB NEBULA, the HYADES, and the PLEIADES. The sun passes in front of Taurus from mid-May to late June.

Telescope A device for collecting and focusing light, thereby revealing faint objects and fine detail otherwise invisible to the naked eye. The most important statistic about a telescope is its aperture, rather than its magnification.

Titan is the largest satellite of Saturn, 5120 km (3180 mi) in diameter. It orbits Saturn every 15.95 days at a distance of 1.2 million km (746,000

mi). It is the only satellite known to have a substantial atmosphere.

Titan rocket is an American space launcher used in various designs to orbit GEMINI PROJECT astronauts, Earth satellites, and planetary probes.

Transit The passage of a solar system body across the face of the Sun, or of a celestial object across an observer's north-south meridian or of a marking across a planet's north-south meridian.

Triton is the largest moon of NEPTUNE; its estimated diameter is 3700 km (2300 mi). Triton orbits Neptune every 5.88 days at a distance of 355,000 km (208,000 mi).

Twenty-one centimetre radiation is emitted naturally by hydrogen gas in space. It is detected by radio astronomers who have used it to trace the spiral shape of our Milky Way Galaxy.

Tyuratam is the main Soviet launch site, their equivalent of Cape Canaveral, north-east of the Aral Sea.

Ultraviolet astronomy is the study of the universe at wavelengths shorter than those of visible light. Ultraviolet radiation is emitted strongly by very hot stars and gas and thus provides information on energetic processes in the universe.

URANUS	
Diameter, equator:	52,000 km, 32,300 mi
Volume:	52 Earth's volume
Mean density:	1.58 (water=1)
Mass:	14.5 Earth's mass
Gravity:	1.1 Earth's gravity
Mean distance	2,870,000,000 km,
from Sun:	1,783,000,000 mi
Spins on axis in:	17 h
Orbits Sun in:	84.0 years
Velocity in orbit:	6.8 km/sec, 4.2 mi/sec
Escape velocity	22 km/sec, 14 mi/sec
Satellites	15, plus rings

Uranus is the seventh planet from the Sun, made mostly of hydrogen but probably with a rocky core. For reasons unknown, its rotation axis is tilted almost in the plane of its orbit. In 1977, astronomers found at least five rings of debris around Uranus.

Ursa Major, the great bear, is a famous constellation in the northern sky. Seven of its stars make up the familiar saucepan shape, also known as the Big Dipper or the Plough.

Ursa Minor, the lesser bear, is a constellation at the north pole of the sky. Its brightest star is POLARIS.

Variable stars change in brightness because of variations in the size of the star itself as in a CEPHEID VARIABLE, because one star in a binary eclipses the other, as with ALGOL, or even because of gas passing between two close stars, as in a NOVA. Over 25,000 variable stars of all types are known.

Vega is a white star, 26 light-years away in the constellation LYRA.

Venus is the second planet from the Sun, and the brightest object as seen from Earth after the Sun and Moon. The brightness of Venus is partly caused by its unbroken layer of white clouds.

VENUS	
Diameter, equator:	12,104 km, 7,521 mi
Volume:	0.88 Earth's volume
Mean density:	5.2 (water=1)
Mass:	0.82 Earth's mass
Gravity:	0.88 Earth's gravity
Mean distance	108,000,000 km,
from Sun:	67,000,000 mi
Spins on axis in:	243 days
Orbits Sun in:	224.7 days
Velocity in orbit:	35.0 km/sec
	21.7 mi/sec
Escape velocity	10.3 km/sec, 6.4 mi/sec
Satellites	None

Below the clouds, its dense atmosphere of carbon dioxide is too hot for life, producing temperatures up to 480°C. For reasons unknown, Venus rotates back to front (east to west) very slowly.

Vernal equinox is the moment when the Sun moves into the northern hemisphere of the sky, on or around March 21 each year.

Very Large Array is the world's largest radio astronomy instrument, completed in 1980 near Socorro, New Mexico. VLA uses the technique of APERTURE SYNTHESIS to produce the performance of a single dish 21 km (13 mi) in diameter.

Vesta is the third largest asteroid, 538 km (334 mi) in diameter, and the fourth to be discovered by Wilhelm Olbers in 1807. Vesta orbits the Sun every 3.6 years between the orbits of Mars and Jupiter.

Viking probes were two American spacecraft sent to look for life on Mars in 1976. Though both landed successfully, no sure signs of Martian life were detected.

Virgo, the virgin, is a constellation of the equatorial region of the sky, whose brightest star is SPICA. The Sun passes in front of Virgo from mid-September to early November.

Voskhod was a Soviet VOSTOK spacecraft modified to hold two or three men.

Vostok was a Soviet one-man capsule, a sphere 2.3 m (7.5 ft) in diameter, in which Yuri Gagarin made the first manned spaceflight. A total of six cosmonauts made flights in Vostoks, the longest lasting five days.

Voyager probes are two American spacecraft launched in 1977 to examine the outer reaches of the solar system.

White dwarf is a small, hot star about the size of the Earth, all that remains after a star such as the Sun runs out of fuel at the end of its life.

X-ray astronomy is the study of X-rays from the universe, produced by energetic processes involving super-hot gas. Some X-ray sources are believed to be caused by gas falling into BLACK HOLES.

Yerkes Observatory is the astronomical observatory of the University of Chicago, at Williams Bay, Wisconsin.

Zelenchukskaya Observatory is the location in the Caucasus mountains of Russia of the world's largest optical telescope, the 6-m (236-inch) reflector opened in 1976.

Zodiac is the band of 12 constellations in front of which the Sun moves during a year.

CHRONOLOGY OF SPACE EXPLORATION

1865 Publication of Jules Verne's novel *From the Earth to the Moon* inspires serious thought about space travel.

1898 Konstantin Tsiolkovsky, a Russian schoolmaster, first to suggest use of liquid-fuelled rockets for interplanetary travel.

1924 Publication of Hermann Oberth's *The Rocket into Interplanetary Space*, first serious technical study of rocket principles.

1926 Robert H Goddard (US) launches first (small) liquid-fuelled rocket; it travels 184 ft (56 m) in 2.5 sec.

1927 Formation in Germany of VfR, Society of Space Travel, for rocket research.

1943 German V-2 rocket, launched at Peenemünde, in the Baltic, travels 122 mi (196 km).

1945 Americans establish White Sands Proving Ground in New Mexico.

1946 First successful launching of German V-2s from White Sands, reaching record altitude of 114 mi (183 km).

1949 Americans establish Cape Canaveral (*later Cape Kennedy*) launching site in Florida.

1957 First artificial Earth satellite: Russians launch *Sputnik 1* on 4 October, heralding Space Age; weighing 184 lb (83 kg) and transmitting for 21 days, it remains in orbit until 4 January 1958.

On 3 November, Russians launch *Sputnik 2*, containing dog Laika, first mammal in space; Laika dies long before craft is destroyed on re-entry (14.4.58).

1958 On 31 January, Americans launch their first satellite, *Explorer 1*, from Cape Canaveral.

1959 Russians launch *Lunik 1* (first probe to go near Moon), *Lunik 2* (first to crash-land on Moon), and *Lunik 3* (first photographs of hidden side of Moon).

1960 *Lunik 1* becomes first artificial satellite of Sun, having missed Moon. On 1 April, US launch *Tiros 1*, first weather satellite (clear photographs of Earth's cloud cover). US satellite *Discoverer 13* ejects capsule on 17th orbit, first object recovered from orbit (Pacific Ocean). US launch 100-ft (30-m) diameter balloon *Echo 1* into orbit (passive communications satellite). Russian dogs Belka and Strelka become first animals recovered from orbit (from returned capsule of *Sputnik 5*).

1961 First man in space: Russian cosmonaut Yuri Gagarin makes one orbit in *Vostok 1* on 12 April. First American astronaut Alan Shepard makes sub-orbital flight on 5 May to height of 116 mi (187 km). On 6 August, second Russian spaceman, Gherman Titov, begins 17-orbit, 24-hour flight in *Vostok 2*.

1962 First American in orbit, John Glenn makes 3 orbits on 20 February in *Friendship 7* (Mercury craft). On 26 April, *Ranger 4* becomes first US craft to reach Moon. First commercial communications satellite, *Telstar 1*, launched on 10 July; begins relaying TV programmes across Atlantic. *Vostok 3* (launched 11 Aug) and *Vostok 4* (12 Aug) come within 4 mi (6½ km) of each other, piloted by Andriyan Nikolayev and Pavel Popovich, respectively. Russians launch first Mars probe, but contact lost. US probe *Mariner 2* (launched 26 Aug) returns close-range information of Venus.

1963 First woman in space: Russian cosmonaut Valentina Tereshkova, on 16 June.

1964 Russians launch *Voskhod 1* (12 Oct) with Vladimir Komarov, Boris Yegorov, and Konstantin Feoktistov aboard, first craft with more than one spaceman (made 16 orbits).

1965 First space walk: Alexei Leonov 'walked' for 10 min (18 March) from *Voskhod 2*. First manned Gemini test flight, astronauts Gus Grissom and John Young making 3 orbits in *Gemini 3*. Ed White makes first American space walk (3 June), from *Gemini 4*. **First space rendezvous:** Wally Schirra and Tom Stafford in *Gemini 6* come within 1 ft (30 cm) of *Gemini 7* on 16 December.

1966 Russia's *Luna 9* makes soft landing on Moon and returns TV pictures from Ocean of Storms (31 Jan). Russian probe *Venera 3* (launched 16.11.65) impacts on Venus (1 March), failing to soft-land. **First 'docking' in space:** Neil Armstrong and Dave Scott, in *Gemini 8*, dock with unmanned Agena rocket (16 March). First American soft landing on Moon (30 May) by *Surveyor 1* highly successful, over 11,000 pictures returned.

1967 First space disasters: on 27 January, three American astronauts (Ed White, Gus Grissom, Roger Chaffee) are killed in *Apollo 1* launch-pad fire; on 24 April, Vladimir Komarov is killed when *Soyuz 1* crashes on Earth after parachute failure. Russian Venus probe *Venera 4* (launched 12 June) reaches planet 17 October and transmits information.

1968 First recovery of unmanned lunar probe, Russian *Zond 5*, from Indian Ocean on 21 September. First manned lunar flight: *Apollo 8* (Frank Borman, James Lovell, William Anders) completes 10 orbits.

1969 First docking of two manned spacecraft (15 Jan), with exchange of cosmonauts by space walk (*Soyuz 4* and *5*). In March, Americans make first manned flight of lunar module, James McDivitt, David Scott, and Russell Schweickart in *Apollo 9*; and in May *Apollo 10* (Thomas Stafford, Eugene Cernan, John Young) descends to within 6 mi (10 km) of Moon's surface. Russian probes *Venera 5* and *6* (launched Jan) land on Venus 16 and 17 May, returning data. **First man on Moon:** on 21 July, American astronaut Neil Armstrong becomes first man to walk on Moon; *Apollo 11* (launched 16 July) sends Armstrong and Edwin 'Buzz' Aldrin in lunar module to Moon, while Michael Collins remains in orbiting command module; astronauts stay 21 hr 36 min 21 sec on Moon, collecting 48.5 lb (22 kg) of soil and rock samples and leaving experiments on Moon's surface during their moonwalks; on 21 July, lunar module *Eagle* blasts off and docks with command

The second man on the Moon, Edwin Aldrin, photographed by the first man, Neil Armstrong, after the Apollo II *landing on 21 July 1969.*

and service module *Columbia*, which makes successful splash-down (24 July) in Pacific; astronauts go into 21-day quarantine. In October, Russians make first triple launching: *Soyuz 6*, *7*, and *8* complete rendezvous but do not dock; Valery Kubasov (in *Soyuz 6*) makes first welding of metals in space. Second Moon landing made on 14 November: Charles Conrad, Alan Bean, and Richard Gordon in *Apollo 12*, module with Conrad and Bean landing in Ocean of Storms; they make moonwalks.

1970 Russians soft-land unmanned *Luna 17* on Moon's Sea of Rains (17 Nov) and use 8-wheeled *Lunokhod 1*, first propelled vehicle on Moon (operated, with 3-sec delay, from Earth), for exploration and experiments. Russian probe *Venera 7* lands on Venus (15 Dec) and transmits data back.

1971 *Apollo 14* (Alan Shepard, Stuart Roosa, Edgar Mitchell) launched, Shepard and Mitchell making 3rd Moon landing (Jan/Feb). Russians launch *Salyut* space station and three *Soyuz 10* cosmonauts dock with it, but abort mission after 5½ hr (24 April). Three cosmonauts (Georgi Dobrovolsky, Vladislav Volkov, Viktor Patsayev) make longest space flight to date (23 days 17 hr 40 min), docking with *Salyut* space station (orbiting Earth for 23 days); crew die in *Soyuz 11* on re-entry, due to loss of pressurization. *Apollo 15* launched, with David Scott, James Irwin, and Alfred Worden aboard; Scott and Irwin make 4th lunar landing, use first lunar rover; first live pictures of lunar module lift-off, and longest exploration (18 hr) of Moon's surface. On 14 November, US probe *Mariner 9* becomes first artificial satellite of Mars. On 21 November, first man-made object lands on surface of Mars, when capsule from Russian probe *Mars 2* crashes.

1972 Americans launch *Pioneer 10* (3 March) on 21-month mission to Jupiter; 620-million-mi (1000-million-km) flight path passes through asteroid belt and passes Jupiter (3 Dec), transmitting pictures and other information; scheduled to cross orbits of Saturn, Uranus, Neptune, and Pluto, and eventually become first man-made object to escape Solar System (1986). *Apollo 16* completes 5th lunar landing mission in April, Chárles Duke and John Young landing and exploring Moon for 20 hr 14 min; Thomas Mattingly makes space walk of 1 hr 23 min on mission. Sixth and last **Apollo mission to Moon:** *Apollo 17* (Eugene Cernan, Ronald Evans, Harrison Schmitt) launched on 7 December, Cernan and Schmitt landing and making record 75-hr stay and collecting 243 lb (110 kg) of lunar samples (returned to Earth 19 Dec).

1973 *Pioneer 11* launched (6 April) towards Jupiter, scheduled to pass three times nearer than *Pioneer 10*, i.e. about 25,000 mi (40,000 km). On 14 May, Americans launch *Skylab 1*, unmanned portion of their first manned orbiting space station, including workshop and telescope mount. *Skylab 2, 3,* and *4* missions (launched 25 May, 28 July, 16 Nov), each with three astronauts.

1974 *Skylab 4* returns (8 Feb) to Earth after 84 days 1 hr 16 min 30 sec. *Mariner 10* (launched by US 3.11.73) passes Venus (5 Feb) and then within 451 mi (726 km) of Mercury (29 March) for man's first close-up look; first time gravity of one planet (Venus) used to send craft towards another; craft scheduled to take further looks at Mercury. Russians launch another *Salyut* space station (25 June) and follow up with two-man visit from *Soyuz 14*, but *Soyuz 15* fails to dock and has to return, Gennady Sarafanov and Lev Demin making first night landing.

1975 First joint Russian-American mission in space: *Soyuz 19* (launched 15 July) and *Apollo 18* (launched 7½ hr later) dock while orbiting Earth at about 140 mi (225 km) on 17 July. Astronauts Thomas Stafford, Donald Clayton (aged 51), and Vance Brand and cosmonauts Alexei Leonov and Valeri Kubasov carry out exchange visits and experiments. The Russian probes *Venera 9* and *Venera 10* soft-land on Venus (22 and 25 Oct) providing further data of importance in the study of Venusian geology. Pictures sent back suggest volcanic activity.

1976 On 16 April, *Helios B*, a research spacecraft carrying American and German instrumentation, comes within 27 million mi (43.4 million km) of the Sun. In June, data and pictures from the US spacecraft *Viking I* on Mars produce a wealth of new geological information, but no trace of organic compounds; yet the evidence of one of the instruments still seems to favour the existence of life and new investigations are planned to test these strange results. *Viking II* goes into orbit around Mars. The Soviet spacecraft *Luna 24* makes a soft landing on the surface of the Moon (18 Aug) near the south-east part of the Sea of Crises, to take soil samples with automatic scoop.

1977 The Soviet craft *Soyuz 24* docks successfully with orbiting *Salyut 5* space laboratory one day after launch (8 Feb). The US launch two *Voyager* spacecraft to fly to Jupiter (arriving 1979) and Saturn (arriving 1980), in order to investigate their satellites and interplanetary gas.

1978 Two Soviet spacecraft dock with the orbiting *Salyut* space laboratory (11 Jan) thus achieving the first triple link-up in space. On 24 January, a Soviet surveillance satellite, *Cosmos 954*, disintegrates in the atmosphere and falls to Earth in the New Territories of Canada. Russian cosmonauts Yuri Romanenko and Georgy Grechko return to Earth on 3 March after spending 84 days in *Salyut 6*. The Russians launch *Soyuz 29* on 15 June carrying cosmonauts Vladimir Kovalyonok and Aleksandr Ivanchenko to the *Salyut 6* space laboratory. *Soyuz 30* launched on 27 June also links with *Salyut 6*. Kovalyonok and Ivanchenko subsequently spent more than 139 days in space, having travelled more than 56 million mi (90 million km). It is reported that they experienced some difficulties adjusting back to the Earth's gravity from 'weightlessness', and had to relearn how to walk and pick up a cup of tea.

1979 Soviet spacecraft is launched on 25 February with two cosmonauts on board – Valery Ryumin and Vladimir Lyakhov – who go on to spend a record 175 days in space aboard the *Salyut-Soyuz* orbital research station, returning to Earth on 19 August. The American *Skylab I* falls to Earth on its 34,981st orbit on 11 July, strewing pieces over the Western Australian desert and coast. *Voyager 1* passes within 172,000 mi (277,000 km) of Jupiter, revealing three new satellites (making 16 in all) and taking close-up photographs. Western Europe's *Ariane* rocket, designed as commercial satellite launcher, makes first test flight.

1980 *Voyager 1* flies past Saturn, within 78,000 mi (126,000 km) of the surface. Its instruments reveal that Saturn's rings are more numerous and complex than had been thought, with 'braids' and 'shepherd moons' within the rings. Soviet cosmonauts Valery Ryumin and Leonid Popov extend the space endurance record to 185 days aboard *Salyut 6*. Ryumin's personal record becomes 362 days in space. During several manned visits to the orbiting *Salyut* station, the Soviets test an improved T-2 model of the *Soyuz* spacecraft. The American *Pioneer/Venus* orbiter completes two Earth years (730 orbits) studying Venus: having mapped 93 per cent of the planet and measured the highest peak, Maxwell Montes, at 34,980 ft (10,600 m). On Mars, the *Viking 2* lander finally closes down, but *Viking 1* continues to send weekly messages back to Earth.

1981 The US space shuttle *Columbia* makes first test flight of 54¼ hr, orbiting the Earth and gliding back to a perfect soft landing.

1984 US space shuttle astronauts Bruce McCandless and Robert Stewart, wearing special backpacks, achieve untethered space flight.

1985 American astronauts James van Hoften and William Fisher take spacewalks, capture a crippled communications satellite, repair and relaunch it.

1986 American space shuttle *Challenger* explodes just after take-off, killing all seven crew. *Voyager 2* passes within 50,679 mi (81,560 km) of Uranus, photographing its rings and 15 moons.

1989 *Voyager 2* passes within 3,100 mi (5,000 km) of Neptune, discovering its storms and photographing its moons.

23

Planet Earth

GLOSSARY OF EARTH SCIENCES

Aa is a Hawaiian word (pronounced ah-ah) for a type of LAVA which, when it solidifies, has a rough and jagged surface. See also PAHOEHOE.

Ablation means removal. Geographers use the term when describing how ice is lost from a GLACIER by melting, evaporation or the calving (breaking away) of ICEBERGS along coasts.

Abrasion The wearing away of the land by eroded fragments of rock as they are carried along by ice, rivers or wind. For example, wind-blown sand abrades rocks.

Abyss is the name for the deep parts of the oceans, below the CONTINENTAL SLOPES. The abyss was once thought to be flat, but it contains volcanic mountains, long, high ridges and deep trenches.

Air is a mixture of gases which forms the ATMOSPHERE. The three main gases in air, making up 99.97 per cent of the total, are nitrogen (78.09 per cent), oxygen (20.95 per cent) and argon (0.93 per cent). The remaining 0.03 per cent is made up of minute amounts of carbon dioxide, helium, hydrogen, krypton, methane, neon, ozone and xenon. Carbon dioxide is important because plants use it for photosynthesis. Air also contains water vapour and specks of dust and salt (from sea spray).

Air mass A body of air whose characteristics are roughly the same over large areas. Hence, such areas have similar weather conditions. One air mass is separated from another by a FRONT.

Alluvium consists of material (SAND, SILT and MUD) which is deposited by rivers. Alluvial plains or deltas are among the world's most fertile regions.

Altitude is the height of a place above mean sea-level.

Andesite is a fine-grained extrusive igneous rock. It is named after the Andes mountains of South America, where large masses occur. Andesite forms from lava ejected during volcanic eruptions in continental, not oceanic, areas.

Anemometer An instrument which measures wind speeds and, often, wind directions. One type, the cup anemometer, has three or four cups mounted on a vertical spindle. As the wind blows the cups around, the spindle rotates. Wind speeds are shown on an indicator.

Antarctic The part of the Earth which lies south of the Antarctic Circle (latitude 66½° South). It contains the icy continent of Antarctica which is surrounded by the Antarctic Ocean.

Anticline An upfold, or arch-like structure in rocks, caused by lateral (sideways) pressure. An anti-clinorium is a complex anticline, in which a large arch contains many small folds.

Anticyclone A region of high air pressure, the highest pressures occurring in the centre. In anticyclones, weather conditions are fairly stable. Winds circulate in a clockwise direction around anticyclones in the northern hemisphere and in an anti-clockwise direction in the southern hemisphere.

Antipodes are places on opposite sides of the Earth. The name comes from Antipodes Island, near New Zealand, which is roughly 180° away from London in England. In Britain, people sometimes refer to Australia and New Zealand as the Antipodes.

Aquifer A layer of rock through which GROUND WATER percolates. This water may be tapped by wells. If the aquifer outcrops at the surface, SPRINGS appear.

Archaeozoic era The middle of the three eras into which the PRE-CAMBRIAN is divided. It followed the AZOIC ERA and ended about 1850 million years ago. Archaeozoic means 'ancient life'.

Archipelago is a sea containing many islands, such as the Aegean Sea between Greece and Turkey. The term is also used to mean a group of islands.

Arctic The part of the Earth which lies north of the Arctic Circle (latitude 66½° North). It contains the icy Arctic Ocean and the northernmost parts of Asia, Europe and North America.

Arête A knife-edged ridge caused when GLACIERS wear away two CIRQUES back to back.

Artesian well A WELL in which water usually rises under pressure. The pressure occurs because the AQUIFER is tilted and so the source of the water is at a higher level than the well.

Ash cone A steep-sided volcano composed of fine ash erupted from the volcano. Cinder cones, consisting of coarser material, are usually even steeper. Composite cones contain layers of ash and cinders alternating with layers of LAVA.

Atmosphere The layer of air which surrounds the Earth.

Atoll A low-lying CORAL island which is usually circular or horseshoe-shaped, surrounding a LAGOON.

Attrition is the wearing down of eroded rock fragments into smaller and smaller pieces while they are being transported by ice, rivers or the wind.

Aurorae are lights and colours in the sky, seen particularly in polar regions. They occur in the IONOSPHERE when streams of charged particles from the Sun collide with molecules of air in the upper atmosphere and are deflected towards the MAGNETIC POLES. The collisions cause the particles to change their electric charge and glow, like particles in a neon tube, causing the *aurora borealis* in the northern hemisphere and the *aurora australis* in the southern. Aurorae are often accompanied

---

Left: The Alps of southern Switzerland contain all the features associated with glaciated scenery, including the pyramidal Matterhorn in the background, arêtes and a valley glacier.

The horns of crescent-shaped barchans (sand dunes) point in the direction of the prevailing wind.

by magnetic storms (disturbances in the Earth's magnetic field), when COMPASS needles swing about violently and radio communications are interrupted.

Avalanches occur when a mass of snow, ice and rock crashes down a mountainside under its own weight. Most avalanches occur in spring when the snow stars to melt. But some are triggered off by earthquakes or even by pistol shots. One avalanche in Peru, in 1941, killed 5000 people.

Axis The line about which a body rotates. The axis of the Earth, about which our planet rotates, is an imaginary line joining the North Pole, the centre of the Earth and the South Pole. The Earth's axis is tilted at $66\frac{1}{2}°$ to the plane of the Earth's orbit.

Azoic era is the first era in Earth history. Azoic means 'without life'.

Bar has two geographical meanings. First, a bar is an accumulation of sand, gravel and pebbles deposited along some coasts. A bar is also a unit of atmospheric pressure, equivalent to 750.1 mm of mercury at 0°C in latitude 45°. Millibars are equal to one-thousandth of a bar. Hence, an atmospheric pressure of 1000 millibars is the equivalent of 750.1 mm of·mercury.

Barchan A crescent-shaped sand DUNE.

Barometer A name for several instruments used to measure atmospheric pressure. *Mercury barometers* consists of a tube filled with mercury, sealed at one end and placed in a trough of mercury. The level of the mercury in the tube will vary according to the changing atmospheric pressure acting on the mercury in the trough. *Aneroid barometers*, including many used in homes to indicate the weather, contain a metal capsule from which all

the air has been removed. The changing atmospheric pressure makes the sides of the capsule move in and out. These movements are recorded on a scale. *Hypsometers* are barometers often used by mountaineers to discover their height. These instruments are based on the principle that the temperature at which water boils varies according to the atmospheric pressure.

Basalt is a fine-grained, heavy igneous rock which is usually dark grey or black in colour. It is the most common rock formed from lava flows.

Basin A region where the land dips down towards the centre. For example, SYNCLINES are often called basins. A river basin is a region drained by a river and all its TRIBUTARIES. River basins are bounded by WATERSHEDS.

Batholith A dome-shaped mass of IGNEOUS ROCK, which has cooled underground. Often consisting of GRANITE, batholiths appear on the surface when the overlying rocks are worn away.

Bathyscaphe A submersible chamber used in deep-sea research. Bathyscaphes float because they have air chambers and other chambers filled with a liquid which is lighter than water. To descend, the air chambers are flooded with water and heavy iron shot causes the bathyscaphe to sink. To ascend, the iron shot is released. August Piccard's bathyscaphe descended 10,917 m (33,260 ft) in 1960.

Beach The land bordering the sea. It may be covered by mud, pebbles or sand.

Beaufort scale was devised by the British Rear Admiral Sir Francis Beaufort to classify winds. The scale is numbered from 0 to 12. A wind with Beaufort number 0 blows at less than $1\frac{1}{2}$ km (0.9 mi) an hour. Beaufort number 12 is a hurricane-force wind, blowing at more than 120 km (75 mi) an hour.

Bedding plane Surface or plane that separates two distinct layers of SEDIMENTARY ROCK.

Bedrock is the solid rock which underlies the soil or any other loose rock fragments on the surface.

Bergschrund A deep and wide CREVASSE which occurs near the head of a GLACIER, around the point where it descends steeply into a CIRQUE and the ice pulls away from the rock. It is an obstacle to climbers.

Biogeography is the study of the world distribution of plants and animals. It is divided into plant geography (phytogeography) and animal geography, which is called zoogeography.

BEAUFORT SCALE				
No.	Wind force	Mph	km/h	Observable effects
0	calm	<1	<1.6	smoke rises vertically
1	light air	1–3	1.6–4.8	direction shown by smoke
2	slight breeze	4–7	6.4–11.3	felt on face; wind vanes move
3	gentle breeze	8–12	12.9–19.3	leaves, twigs move; flags extended
4	moderate breeze	13–18	20.9–29.0	dust, paper, small branches move
5	fresh breeze	19–24	30.6–38.6	small trees sway; flags ripple
6	strong breeze	25–31	40.2–50.0	large branches move; flags beat
7	moderate gale	32–38	51.5–61.2	whole trees sway; walking difficult
8	fresh gale	39–46	62.8–74.0	twigs break off; walking hindered
9	strong gale	47–54	75.6–86.9	slight damage – chimney-pots, slates
10	whole gale	55–63	88.5–101.4	severe damage; trees uprooted
11	storm	64–72	103.0–115.9	widespread damage
12	hurricane	>73	>115.9	devastation

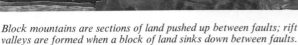

Block mountains are sections of land pushed up between faults; rift valleys are formed when a block of land sinks down between faults.

Caves and blowholes are features of coastal erosion.

Biosphere That part of the Earth occupied by living things. It therefore penetrates the three main zones of the Earth: the ATMOSPHERE, the HYDROSPHERE and the LITHOSPHERE.

Black earth is black or dark brown soil containing a large amount of humus, mostly derived from decayed grass. These fertile soils are also called by a Russian word, chernozems, and they cover much of the steppes of the southern USSR. They also occur in the prairies of North America and the pampas of Argentina.

Blizzard A storm which occurs when fierce winds drive loose snow across the land.

Block mountains are blocks of land raised up by vertical movements between faults in the Earth's crust. Long, ridge-like block mountains are called HORSTS.

Blow-hole A hole in the roof of a sea CAVE, so-called because spray from waves is blown through the hole on to land at high tide.

Bore A tidal flood which occurs in funnel-like river estuaries during high tides. At spring tides, the water rises in height as it advances up a narrowing estuary and sometimes surges upstream in a wall-like flood. Bores are also called eagres.

Boulder clay is a mixture of rocks, sand and clay deposited by GLACIERS and ICE SHEETS. It occurs widely in regions covered by ice during the ICE AGE. Boulder clay is sometimes called till.

Breccia is a rock consisting of angular fragments, cemented together by finer material.

Brown earth is an important agricultural soil which developed in moist, temperate regions which were once under deciduous forest. For example, it occurs in southern England, France and the North Island of New Zealand.

Butte An isolated, flat-topped and steep-sided hill. Similar to the larger MESAS, buttes are remnants of a former PLATEAU landscape.

Caldera A deep, steep-sided CRATER in the top of a VOLCANO. It often contains a lake.

Calendar A system of dividing time. The present Christian calendar is called the Gregorian. One year on this calendar is, on average, only 26 seconds longer than one solar year.

Cambrian period began about 570 million years ago and ended 530 million years ago. Cambrian rocks are rich in FOSSILS, whereas there are very few in older, PRE-CAMBRIAN rocks. All the living creatures were marine invertebrates (animals without backbones) but many, such as brachiopods and trilobites, had hard parts which fossilized in sedimentary rocks.

Canyon A deep, steep-sided valley, usually cut by a river in an arid area. As a result, WEATHERING and rain-water do not broaden the river valley.

Carbonation is the chemical process which occurs when rain-water, containing dissolved carbon dioxide, reacts with limestone, to form such features as limestone caves.

Carboniferous period began about 345 million years ago and ended 280 million years ago. This period is divided, in the United States, into the Mississippian period (the first 20 million years) and the Pennsylvanian period (the last 45 million years). The Upper Carboniferous, or Pennsylvanian, rocks contain important coal measures.

Cartography is the art of drawing MAPS.

Cataract A series of waterfalls. The term is sometimes used for RAPIDS.

Catchment area Area from which river or reservoir draws its water supply; also called drainage area.

Cave A hollow in the Earth. There are several kinds of caves, including sea caves and LAVA caves. But the most spectacular caves occur in carbonate rocks – that is, LIMESTONE and DOLOMITE.

Cenozoic era covers the last 63 to 64 million years of the Earth's history. It is divided into two periods, the TERTIARY and the QUATERNARY. Cenozoic, also spelled Cainozoic or Kainozoic, means 'new life'. The era saw the rise of mammals and, towards the end of the era, the emergence of Man.

Chalk is a form of LIMESTONE, largely composed of the remains of tiny sea creatures. It should not be confused with 'blackboard chalk', which is made from gypsum and 'French chalk', which is talc.

Chernozem – see BLACK EARTH

Chestnut-brown soil is characteristic of extremely dry grasslands, such as those which occur south of the steppes in the USSR and in dry parts of the pampas of Argentina, the veld of South Africa and the High Plains of the United States. The soil is coloured by humus, formed from decayed grass. The humus is not LEACHED because the rainfall is so low.

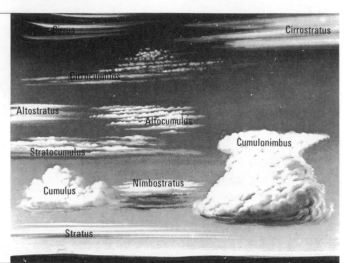

Broadly, there are two types of clouds: cumuliform or 'heap' clouds and stratiform or 'layer' clouds. The main clouds that form below about 2500 metres (8200 ft) are stratus, cumulus, cumulonimbus or thunderclouds, nimbostratus and stratocumulus. Between 2500 and 6100 metres (8200–20,000 ft) are altostratus and altocumulus. Above 6100 metres (20,000 ft), the high clouds are cirrocumulus, cirrostratus and cirrus.

Chinook A wind which blows down the eastern side of the Rocky Mountains in North America, mostly in winter and spring. The wind loses most of its moisture on the western flanks of the Rocky Mountains and so the chinook is a dry wind. It is also warmed as it descends, melting winter snows and exposing pasture for livestock.

Chronometer An extremely accurate clock, invented so that navigators could find their longitude.

Cirque A round, armchair-shaped depression worn out by glaciers in mountain regions. Lakes, or tarns, are often found in cirques. Cirques are also called corries or cwms.

Clastic rock is composed of worn fragments of other rocks. There are three main kinds of clastic rocks: argillaceous, arenaceous and rudaceous. Argillaceous rocks, such as siltstones and marls, contain particles measuring between $\frac{1}{256}$th and $\frac{1}{16}$th of a millimetre across, although CLAYS are even finer. Arenaceous rocks, such as SANDSTONE, have particles ranging in size from $\frac{1}{16}$th to 2 mm across. Rudaceous rocks, such as BRECCIAS and CONGLOMERATES, have particles which are more than 2 mm across.

Clay is a soft rock composed of extremely fine grains less than $\frac{1}{256}$th mm across. It is often formed from igneous rocks by weathering and mostly consists of silicates of alumina. One form of clay, kaolin, is used to make fine porcelain. Other clays are used to make bricks, paper and pottery.

GREAT CITIES

City	Population	City	Population
Athens (Greece)	3,027,000	Mexico City (Mexico)	15,505,000
Baghdad (Iraq)	3,206,000	Milan (Italy)	4,000,000
Bangkok (Thailand)	5,154,000	Moscow (USSR)	8,099,000
Beijing (China)	9,330,000	New Delhi (India)	5,729,000
Berlin (Germany)	3,063,000	New York City (USA)	7,322,564
Bogota (Columbia)	3,983,000	Paris (France)	8,550,000
Bombay (India)	8,227,000	Pusan (S. Korea)	3,160,000
Buenos Aires (Argentina)	9,927,000	Rio de Janiero (Brazil)	5,395,000
Cairo (Egypt)	5,875,000	Rome (Italy)	3,700,000
Calcutta (India)	9,194,000	Santiago (Chile)	4,225,000
Canton (China)	3,160,000	Sao Paulo (Brazil)	8,408,00
Caracas (Venezuela)	3,508,000	Seoul (S. Korea)	9,646,000
Chengdu (China)	2,510,000	Shanghai (China)	11,940,000
Chungking (China)	2,690,000	Shenyang (China)	4,080,000
Djakarta (Indonesia)	6,506,000	Sydney (Australia)	3,193,000
Ho Chi Minh City (Vietnam)	3,500,000	Taipai (Taiwan)	3,050,000
Karachi (Pakistan)	3,499,000	Tehran (Iran)	5,734,000
Leningrad (USSR)	4,638,000	Tianjin (China)	7,850,000
Lima (Peru)	4,608,000	Tokyo (Japan)	11,695,000
London (UK)	6,696,000	Toronto (Canada)	2,803,000
Madras (India)	4,289,000	Wuhan (China)	3,280,000
Madrid (Spain)	4,731,000	Yangon (Myanmar)	3,973,872

Climate is the typical WEATHER of a place, based on average conditions over a period of years.

Clint is an area of bare limestone rock, which is bounded by fissures called GRIKES.

Cloud is a mass of tiny water droplets or ice crystals formed when WATER VAPOUR in the air condenses.

Coasts are strips of land which border large areas of water, such as lakes and seas.

Col A depression or pass in a range of mountains or hills. The term is also used in meteorology for the region between two DEPRESSIONS or two ANTI-CYCLONES. It is so used because the shape of the ISOBARS on a weather map resembles the shapes of CONTOURS which show cols on topographical maps.

Compass An instrument used to measure directions. Magnetic compasses contain a magnetized needle which points to the North MAGNETIC POLE. Mariners' compasses contain a compass card which has strips of magnetized metal stuck to its underside. The card is usually mounted in alcohol to stop it swinging around. Radio compasses, used by aircraft pilots, contain a rotating antenna which points in the direction of radio signals sent by a transmitter on the ground, whose position is known.

Condensation is a state of change. It occurs when a gas or vapour turns into a liquid. For example, steam changes into water when the steam cools below 100°C. WATER VAPOUR, which is invisible, condenses into water droplets in the air when the air is cooled and reaches DEW POINT.

Conglomerate is a rock containing large, rounded fragments of other rocks, cemented together by finer material.

Continental drift is the name for the theory that the continents have moved, and are still moving, around the Earth's surface. The latest theories suggest that the Earth's crust is split into a number of 'plates' which support the continents. These plates are moved around by ocean spreading (the addition of new crustal rock along mid-oceanic ridges) and by convection currents in the rocks of the Earth's MANTLE, beneath the crust. This theory has helped to explain how FOLD and BLOCK MOUN-TAINS, VOLCANOES and EARTHQUAKES occur.

Continental shelf is the name for the gently-sloping sea-bed around continents. Although it is covered by shallow seas, it is really part of the continent.

Continental slope is the steep slope which occurs at the edge of the CONTINENTAL SHELF. The continental slope plunges down to the ABYSS and is the real boundary between the continents and the oceans.

Contour A line on a map, joining places with the same height. Contours, usually shown by brown lines, depict the general relief of the land.

Convection currents are the means by which heat moves from one place to another in gases or liquids. When a gas or liquid is heated, particles near the heat expand and become lighter (less dense). As a result, they rise towards the top of the gas or liquid. But, as they rise, they cool and spread out. Finally, they become dense enough to sink again. Convection currents occur in the ATMOSPHERE. In equatorial regions, the hot ground heats air near the surface. This hot air rises and, eventually, spreads out north and south. It finally

CONTINENTAL DRIFT

200 million years ago

180 million years ago

135 million years ago

65 million years ago

Today

29

sinks back to Earth around the HORSE LATITUDES and some of it flows back towards the equator. Convection currents occur also in the semi-fluid rocks underlying the Earth's crust. The outward-spreading of these rocks may help to move the plates in the Earth's crust, causing CONTINENTAL DRIFT.

Conventional symbols are drawn on maps to show land features. By using symbols, map-makers can get a lot of information on a map.

Coral polyps are small, jelly-like creatures which live in warm, clear seas. They secrete calcium carbonate to build hard, cup-like external skeletons around themselves. These hard parts accumulate to form coral islands and REEFS.

Cordillera is the name for a series of roughly parallel mountain chains which are separated by basins and plateaux, such as the Andes in South America.

Core, Earth's The Earth's core has a diameter of about 6920 km (4300 mi). The inner core is dense and probably solid. It is surrounded by a liquid outer core.

Coriolis force is caused by the Earth's rotation on its axis from west to east. It causes winds and ocean currents in the northern hemisphere to deflect to the right of the direction in which they are moving. The opposite occurs in the southern hemisphere.

Corrasion is erosion caused when rivers or winds move loose fragments of rock over the land. It should not be confused with corrosion, which is the wearing away of rock by chemical action or by solution.

Crag-and-tail A land feature formed when a moving body of ice is obstructed by a crag (mass of rock), such as a tough VOLCANIC PLUG. The up-stream side of the crag is cliff-like, but the down-stream side, or 'tail' has a gentle slope covered by eroded material.

Crater The hollow within the cone of a volcano. Meteorites which strike the Earth can cause craters.

Cretaceous period began about 136 million years ago and ended between 63 and 64 million years ago. The end of this period was marked by the mysterious extinction of the dinosaurs and great reptiles which had dominated the Earth throughout the MESOZOIC ERA. *Creta* is the Latin word for CHALK and thick chalk formations are common Cretaceous rocks.

Crevasse A deep, open crack in the surface of a glacier.

Crust Outer shell of the Earth, between 16 and 48 km (10–30 miles) thick.

Current, Ocean An ocean current is a distinctive flow of water in the oceans. Surface currents are caused mostly by winds or by density differences in the water. Some currents flow well beneath the surface, often in the opposite direction to surface currents.

Cyclone A region of low air pressure associated with stormy weather. It is sometimes used to mean a DEPRESSION. Tropical cyclones are also called HURRICANES or TYPHOONS.

Dating rocks according to their absolute age was not possible until the discovery of radioactivity. Because radioactive elements in rocks break down,

or decay, at a constant rate, scientists can date these substances, and hence the rocks in which they are found, by measuring the amount of decay. A similar method of dating objects up to 45,000 years old is radiocarbon dating. Other methods for dating the recent past include tree ring and pollen-count dating.

Day The time taken by the Earth to complete one turn on its AXIS. It varies slightly, but the mean, or average, solar day is 24 hours.

Delta An area of land at the outlets of some rivers. They contain sediments deposited by the river.

Denudation means the wearing away of the land by the forces of erosion.

Deposition means the laying down of eroded material which has been transported by water, winds or ice.

Depression A region of low air pressure, associated with stormy, unsettled weather. Depressions form along the polar FRONT, where cold, dense polar air meets warm, light air from sub-tropical regions. Warm air flows into waves in the polar front and cold air flows in behind it, setting up a rotating air mass with the lowest pressure at its centre. Clouds and rain occur along the cold and warm fronts.

Desert Any large area of land with little rainfall – less than 10 in (250 mm) a year – and, as a result, scanty vegetation. Deserts may be hot (e.g. Sahara) or cold (e.g. the Antarctic).

Devonian period began about 410 million years ago and ended about 345 million years ago. Its name comes from Devon, an English county, where rocks of this period were first studied. Bony fishes were abundant in Devonian seas and amphibians began to evolve from air-breathing fishes at the end of the period.

Dew is moisture deposited on such objects as blades of grass and stones by condensation. The moisture comes from water vapour in the air.

Dew point is the temperature at which the air is completely saturated by WATER VAPOUR. When the temperature falls below dew point, CONDENSATION occurs and water vapour is converted into water droplets. The temperature of dew point varies,

A depression or cyclone is an area of low air pressure. This satellite photograph shows a hurricane, a severe tropical cyclone.

THE EARTH: BASIC FACTS

Circumference
 – equatorial 40,075 km (24,902 mi)
 – polar 40,007 km (24,860 mi)
Diameter
 – equatorial 12,757 km (7927 mi)
 – polar 12,714 km (7900 mi)
Mass 5976 million million million tonnes
Average density 5.52

INSIDE THE EARTH

	Density	Temp. (°C)	State
Sial	2.8	<500	solid
Sima	2.9	<1100	solid
Upper mantle	4.3	1400	probably molten
Lower mantle	5.5	1700	solid
Outer core	10.0	2300	molten
Inner core	13.6	2500	solid

Thickness of sial	0–30 km (0–18 mi)
Thickness of sima	10–50 km (6–30 mi)
Thickness of upper mantle	700 km (430 mi)
Thickness of lower mantle	2200 km (1370 mi)
Thickness of outer core	2250 km (1400 mi)
Radius of inner core	1300 km (800 mi)

EARTH EXTREMES

Hottest shade temperature recorded: 57.7°C (136.4°F) at Al 'Aziziyah, Libya, on 13.9.22
Coldest temperature recorded: −88.3°C (−126.9°F) at Vostok, Antarctica, on 24.8.60
Highest annual average rainfall: 11,680 mm (460 in) at Mt Waialeale, Hawaii
Most rain in one month: 9300 mm (366.14 in) at Cherrapunji, India, in July 1861
Driest place on earth: Arica, Chile, averages 0.76 mm (0.03 in) of rain per year
Most snow in one year: 31,102 mm (1224.5 in) on Mt Rainier, Washington State, USA, 1971–2
Greatest ocean depth: 11,033 m (36,198 ft) Marianas trench, Pacific Ocean
Greatest tides: 16.3 m (53.5 ft) Bay of Fundy, Nova Scotia, Canada
Strongest surface wind recorded: 372 km/h (231 mph) at Mt Washington, N.H., USA, in 1934
Deepest gorge: 2400 m (7874 ft) Hells Canyon, Idaho, USA
Longest gorge: 349 km (217 mi) Grand Canyon, Arizona, USA
Highest navigated lake: Titicaca, Peru/Bolivia, 3810 m (12,500 ft) above sea level
Deepest lake: Baykal, Siberia, USSR, 1940 m (6365 ft)

---

because warm air can hold more water vapour than cold air.

Doldrums is a low-air-pressure region around the equator towards which TRADE WINDS are drawn. The region is marked by calms and so sailing ships tried to avoid the area.

Dolerite is a medium-textured intrusive igneous rock, which often occurs in DYKES and SILLS. Chemically, dolerite is similar to basalt and gabbro.

Dolomite is a mineral which forms a rock similar to LIMESTONE.

Drumlin A low, oval-shaped hill formed from BOULDER CLAY, deposited and moulded by moving ice.

Dune A wind-moulded mound or ridge of sand. Kinds of dunes include crescent-shaped BARCHANS and ridge-like SEIF DUNES. Dunes occur in hot deserts and along some coastlines.

Dust devil A whirling column of rotating air and dust, which is only a few metres across.

Duststorm An unpleasant storm in desert regions, caused by strong winds which drive dust into the air. Visibility is greatly reduced up to heights of 3000 m (10,000 ft) or more.

Dyke In geology, a vertical or steeply-inclined sheet of MAGMA which solidified underground.

Earthquake Shaking or rolling of Earth's crust caused by underground volcanoes or slipping movement of a weak part of the Earth.

Eocene epoch is part of the TERTIARY PERIOD. The Eocene epoch began about 54 million years ago and ended 38 million years ago. During this epoch, the ancestors of some modern mammals first began to evolve. For example, the first member of the horse family (*Eohippus*) evolved during the Eocene epoch.

Epicentre is a point on the Earth's surface which is directly above the focus, or point of origin, of an earthquake.

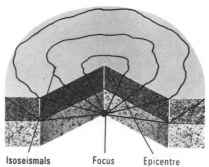

Left: The 1906 San Francisco earthquake was caused by a movement along the San Andreas Fault. Below: The epicentre of an earthquake lies directly above the focus, or point of origin.

Isoseismals   Focus   Epicentre

31

Equator An imaginary line around the Earth, midway between the North and South Poles. It is 0° latitude. The equator is 40,075 km (24,900 mi) long. It is divided into 360° of longitude, so one degree of longitude on the equator is about 111.3 km (69.2 mi).

Equinox is the name for two occasions which occur every year when the Sun is directly overhead at the equator. The vernal (spring) equinox occurs about March 21 and the autumnal equinox about September 23. The word equinox means 'equal night', because everywhere on Earth has 12 hr of daylight and 12 hr of night at the equinoxes.

Erg A desert covered by sand dunes.

Erosion is the process by which natural forces, such as weathering, rivers, glaciers and ice sheets, winds and the sea, are constantly wearing down the land.

Erratic A boulder which was transported by ice and dropped somewhere where the surrounding rocks are different from those in the boulder. The study of erratics first convinced scientists of the power of ice to transport rock and also of the vast area covered by ice during the last ICE AGE.

Esker A long, narrow ridge formed from ice-eroded material by streams which once flowed beneath or within glaciers and ice sheets.

Estuary The part of the mouth of a river which is affected by tides, so that river and sea-water mix.

Evaporation is a change of state, opposite to CONDENSATION, which occurs when a liquid becomes a vapour or a gas. For example, heat evaporates water to form WATER VAPOUR in the air.

Exosphere The outermost part of the ATMOSPHERE. There, the air is extremely rarefied.

Fathom is a measurement used by sailors for depths of water. One fathom is six feet or 1.828 m.

Fault A fracture or break in rocks in the Earth's crust, along which the rocks have been displaced.

Fiord A deep, steep-sided and long inlet of the sea. Fiords were eroded by valley glaciers. They occur in such places as Greenland, South Island in New Zealand and in Norway.

Fissure A narrow opening in the ground from which lava wells.

Flood plains occur when rivers are in their 'old age' stage. The plains consist of layers of sediment carried by the river but spread over the land during periodic floods. Features of flood plains are LEVEES, MEANDERS and OX-BOW LAKES.

Focus is the point of origin, inside the Earth, of an earthquake. See also EPICENTRE.

Fog consists of a mass of tiny water droplets in the air. These droplets form as the air cools below DEW POINT and WATER VAPOUR condenses. Fog is therefore similar to cloud, but fog occurs on the ground. Fog mixed with soot, smoke and gases from factory chimneys is called smog. Internationally, fog is defined as a visibility of less than one kilometre (0.62 mi).

Föhn winds are similar to CHINOOKS. Föhn winds are drawn into the valleys of the northern Alps by low-pressure air systems. These winds originate in the south, but they lose most of their moisture as they ascend the southern slopes of the Alps and they are warmed as they descend to the north. Föhn winds in spring melt the snow, uncovering pasture.

Fold mountains are caused by lateral pressure in the Earth's crust. Horizontal layers of rock are compressed into great loops or folds.

Fossils are evidence of ancient life. They are found in sedimentary rocks and were formed in several ways.

Front A boundary between two bodies of air with quite different properties. In depressions, the warm front is the leading edge of the warm, light air at ground level. Behind, the cold front is the leading edge of the cold, dense air. When the cold front overtakes the warm front, the warm air is pushed above ground level, forming an occluded front or OCCLUSION. Cold and warm fronts bring cloudy, rainy weather. Cloud and rain persist for a while along occlusions.

Frost consists of frozen moisture. Hoar frost is condensed from the air as solid ice crystals on window-panes when the temperature of the air falls below freezing point. Glazed frost consists of thick coatings of ice which form on surfaces that are below freezing point. Rime, a mass of ice crystals on grass and other surfaces, is formed from supercooled water droplets which freeze on contact with any surface.

GEMSTONES

Mineral	Colour	Moh's hardness
Agate	brown, red, blue, green, yellow	7.0
Amethyst	violet	7.0
Aquamarine	sky blue, greenish blue	7.5
Beryl	green, blue, pink	7.5
Bloodstone	green with red spots	7.0
Chalcedony	all colours	7.0
Citrine	yellow	7.0
Diamond	colourless, tints of various colours	10.0
Emerald	green	7.5
Garnet	red and other colours	6.5–7.25
Jade	green, whitish, mauve, brown	7.0
Lapis lazuli	deep blue	5.5
Malachite	dark green banded	3.5
Moonstone	whitish with blue shimmer	6.0
Onyx	various colours with straight coloured bands	7.0
Opal	black, white, orange-red, rainbow coloured	6.0
Ruby	red	9.0
Sapphire	blue, and other colours	9.0
Serpentine	red and green	3.0
Soapstone	white, may be stained with impurities	2.0
Sunstone	whitish-red-brown flecked with golden particles	6.0
Topaz	blue, green, pink, yellow, colourless	8.0
Tourmaline	brown-black, blue, pink, red, violet-red, yellow, green	7.5
Turquoise	greenish-grey, sky blue	6.0
Zircon	All colours	7.5

GEOLOGICAL TIME SCALE

Eras	Periods	Epochs	Millions of years ago	Life forms
CENOZOIC	Quaternary	Holocene (recent)		(End of ice age)
		Pleistocene	0.01	(Ice ages) Mammoths, woolly rhinoceroses. Development of modern man
	Tertiary	Pliocene	2	Mammals spread; earliest men
		Miocene	7	Whales and apes
		Oligocene	26	Modern types of mammals
		Eocene	38	First horses and elephants
		Palaeocene	54	Early mammals
MESOZOIC	Cretaceous		64	End of dinosaurs; flowering plants spread
	Jurassic		136	Giant dinosaurs; first birds
	Triassic		195	Small dinosaurs; first mammals
PALAEOZOIC	Permian			Rapid increase in reptiles
	Carboniferous (Pennsylvanian and Mississippian)		280	Forests formed coal; first reptiles; first insects
	Devonian		345	First forests and land animals, amphibians. Age of fishes
	Silurian		410	First land plants. First jawed fishes
	Ordovician		440	First vertebrates—armoured fish—appear in the sea
	Cambrian		530	Fossils abundant in rocks. All major groups of invertebrates represented
PRE–CAMBRIAN	Proterozoic		570	Sea animals without backbones; seaweeds
	Archaeozoic		1,850	First primitive plants and animals
	Azoic		4,000 / 4,500	(Earliest known rocks) (Earth formed)

Fumarole A hole in the ground, usually in volcanic regions, from which steam and gases are ejected.

Gabbro is a coarse-grained, intrusive igneous rock. It is a plutonic rock – that is, a rock formed at great depths.

Geodesy Branch of mathematics that deals with measurement of size, shape, and curvature of the Earth or of large parts of it.

Geography is the study of the Earth's surface. It includes physical features, climate and vegetation, soils, the oceans, the Earth's peoples and how they live and work, the Earth's resources, production of food, minerals, fuels and manufactures, and so on. Geographers are specially interested in the distribution of all these features.

Geographic and Magnetic Poles The Earth acts like a giant magnet. Like any magnet, the Earth has two magnetic poles. These poles are places where magnetism seems to be concentrated. The magnetic poles are situated near the geographic poles – points on the Earth's surface at the ends of the Earth's tilted axis. The magnetic North Pole is about 1600 km (1000 mi) from the geographic North Pole. The magnetic South Pole is about 2400 km (1500 mi) from the geographic South Pole. The magnetic poles are useful in navigation, because magnetic compass needles point towards them, showing the direction of north and south. Earth magnetism may be caused by electricity which is generated by movements in the Earth's liquid outer core.

Geology is the study of the composition and structure of the Earth and its history.

Geophysics Science that deals with physics of the Earth; it includes atmosphere, water, earthquakes, and magnetism.

Geosyncline A large downfold (SYNCLINE) or trough in the Earth's crust.

Glaciation is the action of ice on the landscape, including EROSION and DEPOSITION.

Glacier A body of ice formed from compressed snow above the snow-line. It moves downhill along valleys under the force of gravity.

Glacio-fluvial deposits are deposits of eroded material laid down by streams flowing from glaciers. See also OUTWASH PLAIN.

Gneiss is a banded metamorphic rock. Granite gneiss contains the same minerals as granite, but the minerals have been recrystallized by heat and pressure.

Gondwanaland was the southern part of the ancient land mass of PANGAEA. It contained South America, Africa, India, Australia and Antarctica.

Gorge A deep, narrow valley.

Granite is a common, hard and coarsegrained intrusive igneous rock. Formed usually in large underground masses, granites are exposed on the surface when the overlying rocks are worn away. Its colour ranges from pink to dark grey.

Gravimeter An instrument used by prospectors to measure the density of rocks.

Great circle Any circle around the Earth whose plane passes through the Earth's centre. Hence, the EQUATOR is a great circle. Like other great circles, it divides the Earth into two hemispheres. The shortest distance between any two points on the Earth's surface is the great circle linking those points.

Greenwich mean time (GMT) is the standard time in Britain and western Europe. Greenwich, in London, lies on longitude 0° – the PRIME MERIDIAN. TIME ZONES east of Greenwich are ahead of GMT and time zones west of Greenwich are behind GMT.

Grike A joint dissolved by rain-water into an open fissure in the surface of a LIMESTONE outcrop.

Ground water is water which percolates through rocks beneath the Earth's surface.

Gulley A small channel worn by a stream, usually on sloping land. Gully erosion is a form of SOIL EROSION.

Haff is a German word for a shallow LAGOON which lies behind a sand BAR or SPIT.

Hail consists of ice pellets which fall from clouds, often during thunderstorms. The pellets do not melt and become rain, because the air near the ground is cold. The heaviest known hailstone weighed 750 gm (26.5 oz).

Hammada is a desert landscape consisting of bare rock, without any sand or gravel.

Hanging valleys occur in glaciated regions when valley glaciers deepen a main valley into a U-shape. Tributary valleys are left 'hanging' above the U-shaped trough. Streams from hanging valleys descend in rapids or waterfalls.

Harmattan A hot, dry wind which blows from the Sahara onto the coastlands of West Africa between December and February.

Holocene epoch, also called Recent epoch, includes the last 10,000 to 25,000 years of the Earth's history. Holocene deposits include sands, silts and clays which have been laid down since the end of the PLEISTOCENE EPOCH and the last retreat of the ice which covered much of the northern hemisphere.

Hornfels is a fine-grained metamorphic rock created

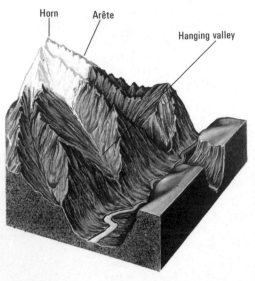

This diagram shows features of glaciated mountain scenery. Horns are pyramidal peaks formed at the meeting point of several adjacent cirques which are separated by steep arêtes. Hanging valleys are left above the deep U-shaped troughs that have been gouged out by valley glaciers.

by heat, which usually comes from intrusions of magma.

Horse latitudes is the name for high-pressure regions around latitudes 30° North and 30° South, between the TRADE WIND belt and the WESTERLIES. The horse latitudes move north and south with the seasons. Calm weather conditions prevail in these regions. The name may come from the fact that becalmed ships carrying horses to the Americas often ran out of fresh water and some horses were thrown overboard.

Horst A ridge-like BLOCK MOUNTAIN. Examples of horsts are the Vosges and Harz mountains.

Humidity is a measure of the amount of WATER VAPOUR in the air. Absolute humidity is a measure of the actual amount of water vapour in air in grams per cubic metre. Relative humidity is a measure of the amount of water vapour in the air compared with what the air could hold if it were saturated – a quantity which varies according to the temperature. Relative humidity is usually expressed as a percentage – 100 per cent relative humidity being the same as DEW POINT.

Hurricane is a severe tropical CYCLONE. Fast spiralling winds in hurricanes do much damage. Hurricane-force winds are classed as 12 on the BEAUFORT SCALE.

Hydrology is the study of water on Earth.

Hydrolysis is a chemical reaction caused in some rocks by water. The chemical reactions decompose, or rot, the rocks, producing new compounds. Hydrolysis is a form of chemical WEATHERING.

Hydrosphere is all the water on Earth, about 97.2 per cent of which is in the oceans; 2.15 per cent is ice; 0.625 per cent is ground water; 0.0171 per cent is in rivers and lakes; and 0.001 per cent is water

During the Ice Age in the Pleistocene epoch, ice spread over much of North America and northern Europe, with large outliers of ice in mountain regions. The map shows the maximum extent of ice coverage; the ice advanced and retreated several times in a series of glacial and interglacial ages. The southernmost extent of the ice has been identified by the study of glacial moraine – rock fragments eroded, transported and finally dumped by the ice. Some meteorologists have recently speculated that another glacial age may be near.

vapour in the atmosphere. The term hydrosphere is used to distinguish the water on Earth from the other main zones, the ATMOSPHERE and the LITHO-SPHERE.

Hygrometer is an instrument used to measure relative humidity. Psychrometers are kinds of hydrometers. They contain a 'dry bulb' thermometer to record the temperature of the air, and a 'wet bulb' thermometer – the bulb of which is wrapped in cloth which is soaked in water. As the humidity decreases, more and more moisture is evaporated from the cloth. This makes the temperature reading on the wet-bulb thermometer fall. The difference between the readings on the two thermometers is used to discover the relative humidity. Other hygrometers are self-recording hygrographs and electrical hygrometers.

Ice is frozen water. It has a lower density than water, upon which it floats, and it occupies a greater volume than the water from which it forms. It occurs in GLACIERS, ICE SHEETS and in FROST, HAIL and SNOW.

Ice Ages are ages in the Earth's history when ICE SHEETS have spread over areas which now have warm or temperate climates. One great Ice Age began in the late CARBONIFEROUS period and continued into the PERMIAN period. Ice then covered southern Africa, India and parts of South America and Australia. During the PLEISTOCENE Ice Age, ice covered much of the northern hemisphere. In fact, the Pleistocene Ice Age consisted of four glacial ages when the ice advanced and three interglacial ages when it retreated. We may now be living in a fourth interglacial age and a fifth glacial age may follow.

Iceberg A floating body of ice in the sea, about eight-ninths of which is hidden beneath the surface.

Ice cap is a small ICE SHEET.

Ice sheet A vast, thick body of ice. The world's two ice sheets cover Antarctica and Greenland.

Igneous rock is a rock formed from solidified MAGMA, either on the surface from LAVA, or underground.

Inselberg is a German word meaning 'island mountain'. It is used, in geography, for isolated mountains which are remnants of an earlier land surface which has mostly been removed by erosion.

Insolation is the energy which the Earth gets from the Sun. Insolation is most effective at the equator and least effective at the poles.

International date line is an imaginary line around longitude 180° West. When travellers cross this line from west to east, they gain one day. Crossing from east to west, however, they lose one day. This happens because time is measured from GREEN-WICH MEAN TIME, the standard time at Greenwich, London. Going eastwards from Greenwich, 180° of longitude represents a gain of 12 hr (15° longitude = 1 hr), so that the time is 12 hr ahead of GMT. But westwards from Greenwich, 180° of longitude represents a loss of 12 hr, so that the time is 12 hr behind GMT. As a result, at longitude 180° West (which is the same as 180° East), there is a difference of 24 hr, or one day.

Ionosphere is the layer of the ATMOSPHERE between 80 and 500 km (50 and 300 mi) above the Earth.

LARGEST ISLANDS		
	sq km	sq mi
Greenland (N. Atlantic)	2,175,600	840,050
New Guinea (SW. Pacific)	794,090	306,600
Borneo (SW. Pacific)	751,078	289,993
Madagascar (Indian Ocean)	587,041	226,670
Baffin I. (Canadian Arctic)	476,066	183,810
Sumatra (Indian Ocean)	431,982	166,789
Great Britain (N. Atlantic)	229,522	88,619
Honshu (NW. Pacific)	226,087	87,293
Ellesmere (Canadian Arctic)	198,393	76,600
Victoria I. (Canadian Arctic)	192,695	74,400

Isobar A line on a weather map which joins places with the same atmospheric pressure.

Isotherm A line on a map joining places with the same temperature.

Isthmus A narrow land bridge, usually joining two large land areas.

Jet stream A powerful wind which blows around the TROPOPAUSE in the atmosphere. Wind speeds are mostly around 160 km/h (100 mph), but sometimes jet streams reach speeds of nearly 500 km/h (300 mph). Aircraft pilots sometimes fly in jet streams to increase their speed and reduce their fuel consumption.

Joints are cracks in rocks, at right angles to bedding planes, along which movement does not normally occur, as in FAULTS.

Jurassic period began between 190 and 195 million years ago and ended 136 million years ago. It was the middle period of the MESOZOIC ERA. Great reptiles, including dinosaurs, dominated the land. The name of the period comes from the Jura mountains where Jurassic rocks were first studied.

Kames are mounds of sand and gravel deposited by streams which flow from the snouts of glaciers.

Karst scenery is so-called after the Karst district of the Dinaric Alps in Yugoslavia. This region is a LIMESTONE upland, largely covered by a bare limestone platform, whose surface is pitted with CLINTS, GRIKES and SWALLOW HOLES, which lead down to underground caves.

Kettle hole A small depression formed when ice is left embedded in BOULDER CLAY or gravel after an ice sheet or glacier has retreated. When the buried ice melts, the ground slumps down to form a hollow.

Khamsin A hot, dusty wind which blows into Egypt from the south in spring and early summer. It is similar to the SIROCCO of North Africa.

Laccolith A body of IGNEOUS ROCK which solidified underground. Smaller than a BATHOLITH, a laccolith usually has a flat base and a domed upper surface.

Lagoon A body of shallow water separated from the sea by a small strip of land, such as a BAR, REEF or SPIT. See also HAFF.

Lahar A landslide of volcanic debris, caused when melting snow, rain, or water from volcanic steam or from a crater lake mix with ash or volcanic fragments on the sides of a volcano. The Roman town of Herculaneum was probably destroyed in AD 79 by a lahar on Mount Vesuvius.

LARGEST LAKES

	sq km	sq mi
Caspian Sea (USSR/Iran)	438,695	169,390
Superior (USA/Canada)	82,409	31,820
Victoria Nyanza (Africa)	69,484	26,828
Huron (USA/Canada)	59,570	23,000
Michigan (USA)	58,016	22,400
Aral Sea (USSR)	40,000	15,000
Baykal (USSR)	34,180	13,197
Tanganyika (Africa)	31,999	12,355
Great Bear (Canada)	31,598	12,200
Malawi* (Africa)	28,490	11,000

*Also called Lake Nyasa

Landslides are movements of masses of loose rock and soil down steep slopes. They may occur because of earthquakes or because heavy rain has lubricated the soil and the rocks.

Lapilli, or cinders, are small lumps of lava which are thrown from an erupting volcano.

Laterite is the material which makes up LATOSOLS, soils which occur over large areas in humid, tropical regions. Laterites are heavily leached, but insoluble substances, including iron (which colours laterites red), bauxite and manganese, remain. Laterite bakes hard and is often used in building.

Latitude and longitude Lines of latitude are measured north and south of the equator, which is 0° latitude. The North Pole is 90° North and the South Pole is 90° South. The latitude of any place between the equator and the poles is the angle formed at the centre of the Earth between that place and the equator. Lines of longitude are measured from the prime meridian eastwards for 180° and westwards for 180°. Degrees of latitude and longitude are divided into minutes and seconds.

Latosol is a leached soil in humid tropical regions. It consists of material called LATERITE.

Laurasia was the northern part of the ancient continent of PANGAEA. It consisted of North America and Eurasia (but not India).

Lava is MAGMA (molten rock) which appears on the surface during volcanic eruptions. When lava hardens, it forms IGNEOUS ROCKS.

Leaching occurs when rain-water dissolves various substances out of the top layer, or A horizon, of a soil. The dissolved substances may be removed entirely or deposited lower down in the B horizon.

Leap years are years with 366 days. Nearly all years divisible by four, such as 1980 and 1984, are leap years. But, although century years are divisible by four, only those divisible by 400 are leap years. Hence, 1700, 1800 and 1900 were not leap years, but 2000 will be a leap year. Leap years are necessary to adjust the calendar, because one year consists of 365 days, 5 hr, 48 min and 46 sec.

Levee is a river embankment. Some are natural and form when a river overflows its banks and piles up material along its edges. Others are man-made, to prevent flooding.

Lightning consists of huge sparks of electricity in clouds or between clouds and the ground.

Limestone is a sedimentary rock, consisting mainly of calcium carbonate. Chalk is the purest form. Some limestones are composed mainly of the remains of dead sea creatures. Coral growth, for example, creates limestones. Some limestones are precipitated from sea-water, which contains calcium carbonate. Oolitic limestone consists of small spherical grains of calcium carbonate which have formed around tiny nuclei.

Lithosphere is the outer layer of the Earth, comprising the CRUST and the uppermost part of the MANTLE.

Loam is fertile soil, consisting of almost equal amounts of CLAY, SAND and SILT.

Loess is a fine, usually wind-deposited soil which reaches great thicknesses in northern China and colours the Yellow Sea and Yellow River.

Longitude – see LATITUDE AND LONGITUDE

Magma is molten rock which, when it solidifies, becomes IGNEOUS ROCK.

Magnetic poles The Earth is a like a giant magnet, with magnetic north and south poles.

Magnetometers are instruments which measure variations in the intensity of the Earth's magnetic field. They are used to locate iron ore deposits.

Mantle The part of the Earth between the CRUST and the CORE. It is 2900 km (1800 mi) thick. Near the top, some of the rocks are semi-fluid and probably move in CONVECTION CURRENTS.

Map A representation, drawn to SCALE, of all or part of the Earth's surface. Maps are the essential tools of people who study GEOGRAPHY, because maps summarize much information about the Earth and show how particular features are distributed.

Map projections are ways of depicting the curved surface of the Earth on a flat surface. Most projections are derived by mathematics.

Marble is a metamorphic rock formed by the action of heat on limestones and dolomite. Pure marble is snow-white in colour, and has been widely used by sculptors. Many kinds of marble are coloured by impurities.

Meander A bend in a river. Meanders occur in a river's mature and old age stage. Meanders grow in size because rivers undercut the bank on the outside of the bend, while depositing alluvium on the inside of the bend. The bends may grow until the channels of two meanders meet, cutting off a large loop of the river, which forms an OX-BOW LAKE.

Meridian is another name for a line of longitude. See LATITUDE AND LONGITUDE.

Mesa A flat-topped upland, the word mesa being Spanish for 'table'. The hard rocks which cap the mesas are parts of an original land surface which has been eroded. Mesas are eventually worn down into smaller features called BUTTES.

Mesozoic era began 225 million years ago and ended between 63 and 64 million years ago. It consisted of the TRIASSIC, JURASSIC and CRETACEOUS periods. Mesozoic means 'middle life' and this era is also known as the 'age of reptiles', because reptiles, including dinosaurs, dominated the Earth.

Metamorphic rocks are either IGNEOUS or SEDIMENTARY ROCKS which have been changed by great heat, pressure or chemical reactions in the Earth's crust. For example, contact metamorphism is caused mainly by heat from pockets of MAGMA. This heat bakes and hardens surrounding rocks. Chemical changes may also take place, because the heat often releases the gas carbon dioxide from the surrounding rocks, so changing their chemical composition. Heat and pressure combined can change limestone into marble. Chemical changes often occur when gases and liquids are released into other rocks from pockets of magma.

Meteorology is the science which involves the study of the air, its properties and the WEATHER.

Midnight Sun Because of the tilt in the Earth's AXIS, the Sun never sets at the North Pole between about March 21 and September 21. The South Pole has continuous daylight between September 21 and March 21. Away from the poles, the number of days when the Sun shines at midnight decreases. At the Arctic Circle, it is seen on only one night, on June 22. At the Antarctic Circle, it is seen on December 21.

MAP PROJECTIONS

Azimuthal projection

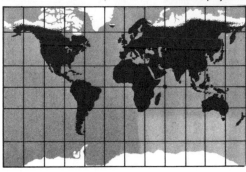

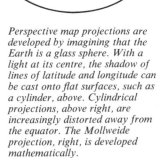

Perspective map projections are developed by imagining that the Earth is a glass sphere. With a light at its centre, the shadow of lines of latitude and longitude can be cast onto flat surfaces, such as a cylinder, above. Cylindrical projections, above right, are increasingly distorted away from the equator. The Mollweide projection, right, is developed mathematically.

Mollweide's projection

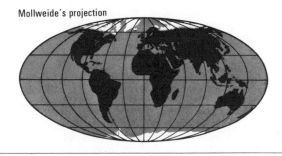

HIGHEST MOUNTAINS		
Asia	m	ft
Everest (Himalaya-Nepal/Tibet)	8848	29,028
Godwin Austen (Pakistan/India)	8611	28,250
Kanchenjunga (Himalaya-Nepal/ Sikkim)	8579	28,146
Makalu (Himalaya-Nepal/Tibet)	8470	27,790
Dhaulagiri (Himalaya-Nepal)	8172	26,810
Nanga Parbat (Himalaya-India)	8126	26,660
Annapurna (Himalaya-Nepal)	8075	26,492
Gasherbrum (Karakoram-India)	8068	26,470
Gosainthan (Himalaya-Tibet)	8013	26,291
Nanda Devi (Himalaya-India)	7817	25,645
South America		
Aconcagua (Andes-Argentina)	6960	22,835
North America		
McKinley (Alaska-USA)	6194	20,322
Africa		
Kilimanjaro (volcanic-Tanzania)	5895	19,341
Europe		
Elbruz (Caucasus-USSR)	5633	18,481
Mont Blanc (Alps-France)	4810	15,781
Antarctica		
Vinson Massif	5139	16,860
Oceania		
Wilhelm (Bismarck Range- New Guinea)	4694	15,400

Mount Everest, the highest peak in the Himalayas, was formed when a plate collision squeezed up rocks on an ancient seabed into huge folds.

Miocene epoch began about 26 million years ago and lasted 19 million years. It is part of the TERTIARY PERIOD and most Miocene animals belonged to families which are represented today.

Mist consists of tiny droplets of moisture in the air, caused by CONDENSATION OF WATER VAPOUR.

Mistral A cold wind which blows mostly in winter in the north-western Mediterranean lands. It comes from the north or north-west, blowing outwards from high-air-pressure systems.

MOH'S HARDNESS SCALE*		
Mineral	Simple hardness test	Moh's hardness
Talc	Crushed by finger nail	1.0
Gypsum	Scratched by finger nail	2.0
Calcite	Scratched by copper coin	3.0
Fluorspar	Scratched by glass	4.0
Apatite	Scratched by a penknife	5.0
Feldspar	Scratched by quartz	6.0
Quartz	Scratched by a steel file	7.0
Topaz	Scratched by corundum	8.0
Corundum	Scratched by diamond	9.0
Diamond		10.0

*Used for testing hardness of materials, by comparing them with the 10 standard minerals

Monsoon is a term used to describe a wind system in which the directions of PREVAILING WINDS are reversed from one season to another. For example, over continents, cold winter temperatures create high-pressure air masses from which winds blow outwards. But, in summer, rapid heating creates low-pressure air masses which draw in winds.

Month Astronomically, a month is the time taken for the Moon to revolve once around the Earth – about 29.5 days. But the lunar month is unsuitable for our CALENDAR because 12 months of $29\frac{1}{4}$ days is only 354 days, 11 less than one year. Hence,

the 12 calendar months vary in length and total 365 days (or 366 in LEAP YEARS).

Moraine consists of fragments of eroded rock carried and finally dumped by glaciers and ice sheets. Loose rocks on the sides of glaciers are called *lateral moraine*. Material frozen in the ice is *englacial moraine*. Rocks in the bottom of the glacier are called *sub-glacial moraine* and rocks on the valley floor beneath the glacier are called *ground moraine*. At the snout of the glacier, worn material is dumped in ridges called *terminal moraine*.

Mountain A high land mass, whose summit covers a small area by comparison with its base.

Mud is a wet mass of clayey material. See CLAY.

Mudstone is a rock composed of compressed mud.

Nappe is a fold in rocks which has been pushed a great distance.

Native element An element, such as gold, which occurs by itself in rocks as a mineral.

Névé is the snow and ice at the head of a GLACIER. It is eventually compressed into glacier ice.

Nuée ardente means 'glowing cloud'. It is a feature of some volcanic eruptions when a burning-hot cloud of ash, gas, steam and rock emerges from a VOLCANO and rolls downhill, burning all in its path.

Nunatak is a mountain peak which juts through an ICE SHEET.

Oasis An area in a desert where there is water. Some oases are small SPRINGS. Others are long valleys, such as the Nile valley.

Obsidian is a glassy, extrusive igneous rock which is also called volcanic glass. Formed from fast-cooling lava, it is black or dark green in colour. Chemically, it is similar to granite.

Occlusion is a term used by meteorologists to describe the situation when a cold FRONT undercuts a warm front and the warm air is lifted above the cold air.

OCEANS		
	sq km	sq mi
Pacific	181,000,000	70,000,000
Atlantic	106,000,000	41,000,000
Indian	73,490,000	28,375,000
Arctic	14,350,000	5,541,000

Oil shale is a dark SEDIMENTARY ROCK which, when crushed, yields petroleum. The petroleum comes from a substance called kerogen. However, the yield of petroleum per metric tonne is low.

Oligocene epoch began about 38 million years ago and lasted 12 million years. It is part of the TERTIARY PERIOD and it was a time when many modern kinds of mammals were evolving.

Ooze is a deposit which accumulates on the sea-bed.

Ordovician period began about 530 million years ago and ended about 440 million years ago. There was no life on land during this period, but the first animals with backbones – armoured fish – evolved in the seas. The name Ordovician comes from Ordovices, a Stone Age tribe who lived in North Wales, where Ordovician rocks were first studied.

Organic rock is a rock, such as COAL and many LIMESTONES, which were formed mainly from the remains of once-living things – plants and animals.

Outwash plain An area covered by MORAINE, deposited by streams which flow from a melting glacier.

Ox-bow lakes form when a river cuts through the narrow neck of a large MEANDER. The meander is then abandoned, becoming a lake.

Oxygen is a gas which supports life. It forms 20.95 per cent of air and its presence in sea-water makes marine life possible. The Earth's early atmosphere probably contained little oxygen, but after the evolution of the first oxygen-producing plants, around 1900 million years ago, the proportion of oxygen in the air increased steadily. Oxygen is also a chemical element and is, by weight, the most abundant element in the Earth's crust.

Ozone is a form of OXYGEN. But, whereas oxygen molecules contain two oxygen atoms, ozone molecules have three atoms. Ozone is produced when electricity is discharged through oxygen or air. For example, it is formed when LIGHTNING flashes through a cloud. The ozone layer in the STRATO-SPHERE absorbs harmful ultraviolet radiation from the Sun.

Pack ice is sea-water frozen into thick blocks.

Pahoehoe is a Hawaiian word meaning 'satin-like'. It is used for LAVA which solidifies into ropy or corded shapes, but whose surface is smooth. See also AA.

Palaeocene epoch began about 63 to 64 million years ago. Pangaea started to break up and the first epoch of the TERTIARY PERIOD and was marked by an increase in the numbers and varieties of mammals, following the extinction of many large reptiles at the end of the preceding CRETACEOUS PERIOD.

Palaeontology is the study of FOSSILS.

Palaeozoic era began about 570 million years ago and ended 225 million years ago. Palaeozoic means 'ancient life'. When it began, life in the sea was abundant, but land areas were bare. The first fishes evolved in the ORDOVICIAN PERIOD, the earliest

land plants in the SILURIAN, the first amphibians crawled out of the seas in late DEVONIAN and the first reptiles emerged in the Upper CARBONIFEROUS.

Pangaea is the name for the ancient continent containing LAURASIA and GONDWANALAND which existed 200 million years ago. About 180 million years ago, Pangaea started to break up and the continents slowly drifted to their present positions.

Peneplain means 'almost a plain'. It is the end result of natural EROSION, when the land has been worn down to an almost level plain, although odd outcrops of resistant rock rise above the flat surface.

Peninsula is an area of land which is almost an island, because water surrounds nearly all of it.

Permafrost is a term used for layers of soil or rock that are permanently frozen.

Permeable rocks include such rocks as SANDSTONE, through which water can percolate.

Permian period began about 280 million years ago and ended 225 million years ago. The land at that time was dominated by small reptiles. The name Permian comes from Perm district in the Ural mountains of the USSR, where Permian rocks were studied.

Pillow lava is LAVA which has solidified underwater. It resembles heaps of pillows.

Plateau An upland whose surface is mostly level.

Pleistocene epoch began about two million years ago and ended between 10,000 and 25,000 years ago. It was marked by a great ICE AGE in the northern hemisphere.

Pliocene epoch began about seven million years ago and lasted for five million years. It was the last epoch of the TERTIARY PERIOD and, towards its close, man-apes were living in Africa.

Podzol is the name for leached, greyish-white soils, which occur widely in cool, moist climates where coniferous forests grow. Most podzols are poor soils for farming.

Poles The points at the ends of the Earth's axis are the geographical North and South poles. The MAGNETIC POLES are near the geographic poles.

Pot-hole is another name for a SWALLOW HOLE. Pot-holes are used by people called pot-holers who climb down them into LIMESTONE caves. Pot-hole can also mean a hole in a river bed which has been worn out by swirling stones and gravel.

Pre-Cambrian is a term used to describe nearly nine-tenths of the Earth's history – that is, the vast time span before the start of the CAMBRIAN PERIOD. The Pre-Cambrian is often divided into the AZOIC, ARCHAEOZOIC and PROTEROZOIC eras. There are few FOSSILS in Pre-Cambrian rocks, probably because living things were soft-bodied, lacking hard parts, and so rotted quickly after they died.

Precipitation includes any moisture caused by CONDENSATION of WATER VAPOUR from the air. Precipitation can also mean the separation of a solid from a liquid by chemical action.

Prevailing wind A wind which blows from a certain direction for most of the time. For example, the prevailing winds over north-western Europe are the WESTERLIES which blow from the south-west.

Prime meridian is longitude 0°. This line of longitude passes through Greenwich in London. The position of the prime meridian was fixed in 1884 at a conference in Washington DC.

Prismatic compass A magnetic COMPASS with a prism attached to it. As a result, by looking through the prism, you can sight any particular object and read the magnetic bearing at the same time.

Proterozoic era began about 1850 million years ago and ended 570 million years ago. Proterozoic rocks contain very few fossils, unlike the CAMBRIAN rocks which overlie them.

Pumice is a light grey, glassy volcanic rock. It contains masses of pores (holes) which are sealed off from each other. The pores were formed by gases in lava. Because of its pores, pumice is so light that it floats on water.

Pyroclasts are broken fragments of rock ejected from volcanoes during eruptions. Pyroclasts include LAPILLI, PUMICE, VOLCANIC ASH and VOLCANIC BOMBS.

Quartz is a common mineral, found in many rocks. In IGNEOUS ROCKS, the hard quartz crystals often resemble bits of glass and the purest form of quartz, rock crystal, is sometimes used in jewellery. Quartz also occurs in SEDIMENTARY ROCKS. For example, SANDSTONE consists mostly of quartz grains.

Quartzite is a hard metamorphic rock, derived from sandstones. The quartz grains have been recrystallized by great heat and pressure.

Quaternary period covers the last two million years of the Earth's history, including the PLEISTOCENE and HOLOCENE epochs.

Quicksand consists of fine sand which is saturated in water. People who accidentally walk on to quicksand sink into it, because quicksand has all the characteristics of a liquid. But they can float back to firm land if they remain calm.

Radiosonde is a device used in meteorology to obtain information about air conditions above ground-level. It consists of a hydrogen-filled balloon to which self-recording instruments are attached. These instruments measure temperature, pressure and humidity. After the balloon has been released, the readings are relayed to the ground by a small radio transmitter.

Radon is a radioactive gas which is produced by radium as it decays. This gas is normally trapped in underground rocks. But, when the rocks start to crack, the gas escapes and some of it is dissolved in GROUND WATER. Scientists think that if the amount of dissolved radon in well water increases, this means that the rocks nearby are under strain and an EARTHQUAKE may be imminent.

Rain is a form of PRECIPITATION. It is the end product of the CONDENSATION of WATER VAPOUR in the air. Convectional rain occurs when heated air rises and cools. Cyclonic rain occurs in DEPRESSIONS when warm air rises above cold air. Orographic rain results from air currents rising over high ground.

Rainbows are arcs of coloured light formed when the Sun's rays are reflected and refracted (bent) by drops of water in the air – falling rain or spray. The colours in rainbows are red, orange, yellow, green, blue, indigo and violet. A rainbow with red on the outside and violet on the inside is called a *primary bow*. Sometimes, the light is reflected twice and the colours are reversed in a *secondary bow*.

Rain   Rain shadow

Rain gauge is an instrument used at weather stations to measure PRECIPITATION. It consists of a funnel fitted in a glass collection vessel.

Rain shadow Moist winds which blow from a sea over a mountain range lose most of their moisture on the windward slopes. When the winds descend on the leeward side of the mountains, they are dry and gradually become warmer. The leeward side of the mountain is, therefore, dry and is called a rain shadow area.

Rapids form when the slope of a river increases and the river flows at a faster rate than before.

Reef A low ridge of rock in the sea, usually formed from CORAL.

Reg is a desert landscape where there is no sand. Instead, loose stones and gravel cover the land.

Relative humidity – see HUMIDITY

Relief is the general form of the land, including heights and depressions. On maps, CONTOURS, shading or coloured tints are used to depict relief.

Ria A narrow inlet of the sea. Rias are, in fact, flooded river estuaries. They may be caused by a rise in sea-level or because the coast has sunk downwards as a result of Earth movements.

Richter scale is used to measure the strength of EARTHQUAKES. It is a logarithmic scale – that is, each number on the scale represents 10 times the magnitude (strength) of the previous number. It also represents a 30-fold increase in the amount of energy released by the 'quake'. An earthquake with a 2-point magnitude is hardly noticeable, but a 7-point magnitude earthquake is severe, being 100,000 times as strong.

Rift valley A valley formed when a block of land sinks down between long FAULTS in the Earth's crust.

LONGEST RIVERS		
	km	mi
Nile (Africa)	6670	4145
Amazon (S. America)	6437	4000
Mississippi-Missouri-Red Rock		
(N. America)	6231	3872
Yangtze (China)	5470	3400
Ob-Irtysh (USSR)	5150	3200
Zaire* (Africa)	4828	3000
Lena (USSR)	4828	3000
Amur (Asia)	4506	2800
Yenisey (USSR)	4506	2800
Huang He (China)	4345	2700
Mekong (SE. Asia)	4184	2600
Niger (Africa)	4000	2486

*Formerly Congo River

River terraces are flat platforms of land which lie above the level of the valley floor. They are remnants of an earlier valley floor, higher than the present one. They are left behind when the river increases its erosive power, possibly because the land has been uplifted and the river's gradient increased.

Roche moutonée is an outcrop of bare, resistant rock over which glaciers have flowed. On the up-stream side, the slope is gentle and the surface is smooth, although it is scored by scratches caused by rocks that were frozen in the base of the ice. On the downstream side, the rock slopes more steeply and has a rough, jagged face.

Run-off is a term used to describe rain which, when it hits the ground, runs across the surface instead of seeping into the soil. On sloping land, run-off flows down into streams.

Salinity means saltiness. Sea-water contains an average of 35 parts of dissolved salts in every 1000 parts of water.

Salt dome A mass of underground salt which pushes through other rock layers. These structures are important because petroleum is often trapped around the top of the dome.

Sand consists of eroded fragments of rocks. It contains quartz grains, together with smaller amounts of other minerals. Geologists define sand by the size of the grains, which are between $\frac{1}{16}$ and 2 mm across. It is, therefore, coarser than SILT, but finer than gravel.

Sandstone is the second most common sedimentary rock (shale is the most common), forming about one-third of the sedimentary rocks exposed on the Earth's surface. It consists of grains of sand, mostly quartz, which have been compacted and cemented together. Its colour varies according to the minerals it contains and the cementing mineral.

Sandstorms occur in deserts, when strong winds blow sand across the surface. However, unlike DUSTSTORMS, the heavy sand particles are raised only about two m (6.5 ft) into the air.

Scale is a system by which large distances are represented by short distances. On some maps, you will find a *graphic scale*, which is a line divided into kilometres or miles. On other maps, you will see a *representative fraction*, such as 1 : 50,000. This means that 1 centimetre on the map represents 50,000 cm (0.5 km) on the ground. Sometimes, the scale is written in words and figures, such as 1 cm = 10 km.

Scarp, or escarpment, is a steep, inland slope. Fault scarps occur along the edges of blocks of land which have been raised or lowered, such as BLOCK MOUNTAINS or the walls of RIFT VALLEYS. Other scarps border layers of gently-tilted, resistant layers of rocks.

Schists are common metamorphic rocks. There are many kinds of schists but they all split along well-defined planes.

Scree, or talus, is a pile of loose rocks at the foot of mountains or cliffs. These rocks have been prised away from the upper slopes by WEATHERING.

Seasons are periods of the year, which have distinctive climates.

Sedimentary rocks are rocks formed from sediments, such as fragments of rocks worn from the land (CLASTIC ROCKS), the remains of once-living

Sextants are used in navigation to measure the altitude – the angle above the horizon – of heavenly bodies. These measurements are used to compute the position of the observer.

things (ORGANIC ROCKS) or from chemicals precipitated from water. Most sedimentary rocks accumulate, layer by layer, in water, but some accumulate on land. At first, sediments are loose, but they gradually become compressed and cemented together.

Seif dunes are long ridges of wind-blown sand.

Seismograph An instrument used to record Earth tremors and earthquakes. Seismographs are used by petroleum prospectors, who set off small explosions and record the passage of seismic waves through the ground. From the pattern of these waves, they can establish the nature of underground rock structures.

Sérac A jagged pinnacle of ice on a glacier. Séracs occur at places where the gradient (slope) increases and the surface of the glacier ice breaks up.

Serpentine is a colourful metamorphic rock. One variety, called *verde antique*, is dark green with white veins, while other varieties are black and red. Polished serpentine is often used for ornaments.

Sextant An instrument used in navigation to measure the vertical angles of heavenly bodies above the horizon. The mirror sextant has a small telescope, through which the navigator sights the horizon. At the same time, he can see the image of the Sun or a star, which is reflected by two mirrors. The navigator then moves a pivoted arm on the sextant until the Sun or star appears to be level with the horizon. He then reads the angle of the heavenly body above the horizon from a scale along the edge of the sextant, which is one-sixth of a circle (60°).

Shale is the most common sedimentary rock, forming nearly half of the sedimentary rocks exposed on the Earth's surface. Grey or black in colour, shale is formed from layers of fine silt and clay. Unlike mudstone, shale is *laminated* – that is, it is arranged in distinct layers.

41

In cross-section, shield volcanoes have gentle slopes, because the fluid lava from which they form flows great distances before solidifying.

Shield volcanoes are low volcanoes, shaped like an upturned saucer. Shield volcanoes, such as those in Hawaii, cover large areas and consist of layer upon layer of solid LAVA. They are caused by quiet eruptions, unlike steep volcanic cones which are formed by explosive volcanoes.

Sial Comparatively light rocks (mainly granite) of Earth's crust that lie underneath the continents; the term comes from *si*lica and *al*umina, which are the main components.

Silicon is the second most common element in the Earth's crust. It occurs as silica (the chemical silicon dioxide) in quartz and flint. It also occurs with other elements in many compounds called silicates, including CLAYS and feldspar.

Sill A deposit of MAGMA which is forced between layers of SEDIMENTARY ROCKS under the ground. When the magma hardens, it forms a nearly horizontal sheet of IGNEOUS ROCK.

Silt consists of eroded grains of rock which are transported by rivers. The size of silt grains ranges between $\frac{1}{256}$ and $\frac{1}{16}$ of a millimetre across. Silt is finer than SAND but coarser than CLAY particles. During floods, rivers spread silt over the valley floors. Silt deposits usually make fertile soils.

Silurian period began 440 million years ago and ended 410 million years ago. During this period, plants started to grow, for the first time, on the land areas. The name of the period comes from *Silures*, an ancient Welsh tribe who once lived in the area where Silurian rocks were first studied.

Sima Dense rocks that form most of the ocean beds and underly the lighter *sial* masses; named after their main components, *si*lica and *ma*gnesia.

Sirocco A dry, hot wind which blows from the Sahara to northern Africa and then across the Mediterranean Sea, where it picks up moisture, reaching Sicily and southern Italy as a hot and humid wind. Siroccos can be destructive because they wither plants.

Slate, derived from such rocks as mudstone and shale, is a metamorphic rock. Recrystallized by pressure and heat, slate splits easily into smooth, thin sheets. Most slate is grey or black, but other colours also occur.

Sleet is a form of PRECIPITATION, consisting of snow and rain.

Snow is a form of PRECIPITATION, consisting of delicate ice crystals. Snow falls only on about one-third of the Earth, because the tropics are too hot (except for high peaks). On average, 10 cm of snow is the equivalent of 1 cm of rain.

Snow-line is the level of the land above which snow remains all the year round. Near the poles, the snow-line is at sea-level but, around the equator, it is between 5200 and 5480 m (17,000 and 18,000 ft) above sea-level.

Soil erosion is the removal of the topsoil, which is caused by man's interference with nature. It differs from natural EROSION, which is much slower. The main agents of soil erosion are the rain, which removes exposed soils especially on slopes, and the wind.

Solfatara is a volcano which no longer erupts ash and LAVA, but steam and gases are ejected from small vents. The name comes from a dormant volcano, called Solfatara, which is near Naples, in Italy.

Solstices occur twice a year when the overhead Sun reaches its northernmost and southernmost points – the Tropic of Cancer (latitude 23° 27' North) and the Tropic of Capricorn (latitude 23° 27' South). At the Tropic of Cancer, the Sun is directly overhead about June 21 and this is called the summer solstice, which is midsummer in the northern hemisphere. At the Tropic of Capricorn, the Sun is directly overhead about December 22, which is midwinter in the northern hemisphere. In the southern hemisphere, June 21 is the winter solstice and December 22 is the summer solstice.

Spit A low mound of sand and gravel which projects from the land into the sea. It is built up by waves and currents from material which has been worn away from another part of the coast.

Spring A flow of water on to the surface, where a water-bearing rock meets the surface. In volcanic regions, spring water is often warmed by underground pockets of MAGMA to form hot springs.

Stack An isolated pillar of rock in the sea, near a coastline. It represents part of a former HEADLAND which has been partly worn away.

Stalactite An icicle-like growth of calcium carbonate, hanging from the roof of a limestone cave.

Stalagmite A column of calcium carbonate which grows upwards from the floor of a limestone cave.

Standard time is the internationally-agreed time used within TIME ZONES. It differs from local time which constantly changes as one travels east or west.

Stratigraphy, a branch of geology, is concerned with the study of the succession of rock layers.

Stratosphere Part of the atmosphere, extending from the TROPOPAUSE to about 80 km (50 mi) above the ground. It contains an important layer of OZONE.

Striations are scratches on rocks, made by other rocks frozen in the bottoms of moving glaciers.

Sunshine recorders are instruments used at weather stations to record the number of hours of sunshine that occur every day.

Swallow hole A hole in the surface of a LIMESTONE area which leads down to an underground network of passages and CAVES.

Syncline A downfold in layers of rocks. A complicated downfold, containing many small folds, is called a synclinorium.

Synoptic chart A weather map which gives a synopsis (or summary) of weather conditions over a large area at a certain time. Synoptic charts are used in weather forecasting.

Tertiary period began about 63 to 64 million years ago and ended two million years ago. It is divided into five epochs: the PALAEOCENE, EOCENE, OLIGOCENE, MIOCENE and PLIOCENE. The Tertiary period was marked by the development of mammals and is often called the 'age of mammals'. The variety of mammal species reached its peak in the Miocene epoch, and the number of species has decreased since then.

Thunder is the sound caused when the air in the path of a stroke of lightning is suddenly and violently expanded by heat from lightning which reaches 15,000°C. To discover how far you are away from the centre of a thunderstorm, you should count the number of seconds between a flash of lightning and the sound of thunder. Three seconds is roughly the equivalent of one kilometre (0.6 mi).

Thunderstorms are usually associated with towering cumulonimbus clouds, which are often anvil-shaped, rain, hail, LIGHTNING and THUNDER. The most violent thunderstorms occur in tropical regions. They are caused by fast heating of the ground which creates strong up-currents of moist air.

Tides are rises and falls in the sea-level which occur about twice a day. They are caused by the gravitational pull of the Moon and Sun on the waters of the Earth.

Time zone The Earth rotates on its axis (360°) once every 24 hr. As a result, the local, or solar (Sun), time changes by 4 min for every 1° of longitude. It would be impossible to use local time. For example, the difference in longitude between Greenwich in London (longitude 0°) and Paris in France (latitude 2° 20′ East) is $2\frac{1}{3}°$. This represents a difference in local time of $9\frac{1}{3}$ min. In 1884, an international conference agreed to divide the world into time zones, which would generally represent 15° of longitude – the equivalent of one hour. Within a zone, the time is the same throughout. But, when you cross from one zone into another, you change your watch by one hour. The conference also agreed to position the zones so that they would follow the borders of countries. Then, it was possible to avoid having two or more different times in a fairly small

country. In large countries, such as the USA, there are several time zones. For example, when it is noon in San Francisco, it is 1 PM in Denver, 2 PM in Houston, and 3 PM in Washington DC. See also INTERNATIONAL DATE LINE.

Tombolo is an Italian word for a BAR which links the mainland to an island or which links two islands. It therefore forms a natural bridge.

Topography is a description of land features. A topographic map shows land features, natural and man-made, in some detail, at a scale of, say, 1 : 50,000.

Tor An isolated rocky hill. Because of WEATHERING, tors often have strange shapes.

Tornado A violent storm, including the destructive whirlwinds of the United States.

Trade winds are the PREVAILING WINDS which blow towards the low-air-pressure DOLDRUMS. In the northern hemisphere, the trade winds blow from the north-east and, in the southern hemisphere, they blow from the south-east.

Triassic period, the first period of the MESOZOIC ERA, began about 225 million years ago and ended about 190 to 195 million years ago. Reptiles, including the first dinosaurs, developed quickly during this period. The Triassic gets its name from the three-fold division of rocks of this period which were studied in Germany.

Tributary A small stream or river which joins a main river.

Tropics The area between the Tropic of Cancer (23° 27′ North) and the Tropic of Capricorn (23° 27′ South). The Sun's radiation is most concentrated in the tropics and so tropical lands are the warmest parts of the Earth.

Tropopause The upper boundary of the TROPO-SPHERE in the ATMOSPHERE. Temperatures fall as one rises upwards through the troposphere, but the tropopause marks the level at which temperatures cease to fall and become stable at about

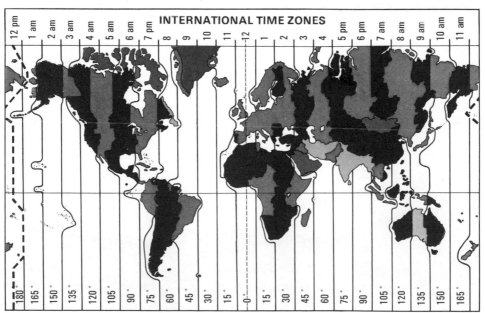

INTERNATIONAL TIME ZONES

—55°C. The height of the tropopause above ground-level varies between about 8 km (5 mi) over the poles to about 18 km (11 mi) over the equator.

Troposphere The lowest zone in the atmosphere, it contains about three-fourths of the mass of the atmosphere and nine-tenths of its moisture and dust. Most weather conditions felt on Earth originate in the troposphere. The upper boundary of the troposphere is the TROPOPAUSE.

Tsunami A destructive, fast-moving wave which is triggered off in the oceans by earthquakes or volcanic eruptions.

Tuff is a rock formed from compressed VOLCANIC ASH and VOLCANIC DUST.

Typhoon is a name used in eastern Asia for a tropical cyclone or HURRICANE.

Vent An opening in the top or side of a volcano through which MAGMA, gas or steam are erupted.

Volcanic ash is formed when explosive gases shatter MAGMA into small fine fragments, which form a dark cloud when erupted.

Volcanic bombs are chunks of MAGMA, erupted into the air by volcanoes. They consist of molten rock but, usually by the time they land, the outside of the bomb is hard. They vary in size and appearance, including bread-crust bombs which have a cracked, glassy crust, cow-dung bombs and spherical bombs.

Volcanic dust is extremely fine VOLCANIC ASH. Clouds of this light dust may be carried great distances by winds in the atmosphere.

Volcanic glass is the name for MAGMA which solidifies quickly on the surface, forming a glassy rock called obsidian.

Volcanic plug A mass of MAGMA which has solidified in the conduit, or pipe, which leads to the VENT. In extinct volcanoes, the land around the plug is often worn away until only the plug remains, forming a steep-sided rocky hill.

Volcanic steam Hot steam is released in many volcanic eruptions. It is also a feature of FUMAROLES and SOLFATARAS.

Volcano means either the vent in the ground through which MAGMA, gas and steam are ejected, or the mountains formed from magma.

V-shaped valley A valley which has been eroded downwards by a river, but whose valley slopes have been broadened into a V-shape by WEATHERING. This distinguishes V-shaped valleys from steep-sided canyons in arid regions where weathering is slight.

Wadi A dry watercourse in a desert. It contains water only after an occasional storm.

Water cycle The continuous movement of water from lakes and seas via the atmosphere to land areas, and back again.

Waterfall A vertical fall of river water, which usually occurs where hard, resistant rocks overlie softer rocks. The softer rocks are worn away quickly and the hard rocks remain, interrupting the smooth flow of the river.

MAJOR WATERFALLS		
Highest	m	ft
Angel Falls (Venezuela)	979	3,212
Tugela Falls (South Africa)	948	3,110
Yosemite Falls (California)	739	2,425
Greatest Volume	m³/sec	ft³/sec
Guaira (Brazil/Paraguay)	13,300	470,000
Niagara (N. America)	6,000	212,200

Watershed, or divide, is the boundary between the headstreams of two river basins.

Water spouts form when a funnel-shaped cloud sinks down from a storm cloud until it reaches a sea or lake. Particles of water are then sucked up by the whirling, rotating winds of this tornado-like feature.

Water table The surface of GROUND WATER which fills the zone of saturation beneath the Earth's surface.

Water vapour is invisible moisture in the atmosphere. It has the properties of a gas, until CONDENSATION changes it into tiny water droplets, which are visible in CLOUDS, FOGS and so on.

Weather is the day-to-day condition of the atmosphere. See also METEOROLOGY.

Weathering is the decay or breaking up of surface rocks. Chemical weathering includes chemical processes which change and decay rocks. Mechanical weathering includes the effects of heating by the Sun and the freezing of water.

Well A source of water which is obtained by

The top level of saturated porous rocks is called the water table. In the zone of aeration, air fills the pores in the rocks. The zone of saturation is underlain by compact rocks through which water cannot percolate. Lakes and swamps form where the water table reaches the surface.

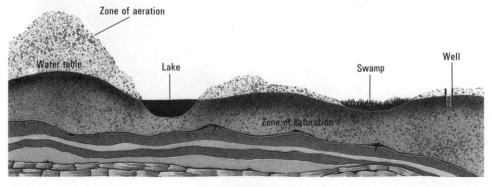

drilling or digging a hole down to the WATER TABLE. In ARTESIAN WELLS, water rises to the surface under pressure, but in most wells it is pumped to the surface.

Westerlies are belts of prevailing winds which blow north of the HORSE LATITUDES in the northern hemisphere and are called the south-westerlies and south of the horse latitudes in the southern hemisphere (the north-westerlies).

Whirlwind A narrow, rotating column of air, as in a TORNADO or in a DUST DEVIL.

Wind is a movement of air. We generally think of winds as currents of air which flow across the Earth's surface. But there are also upward and downward currents of air in the atmosphere and powerful JET STREAMS which blow in the upper TROPOSPHERE and lower STRATOSPHERE. Wind speeds are classified on the BEAUFORT SCALE.

Wind vane An instrument which is used to show the direction of winds.

Year The time taken for the Earth to complete one ORBIT around the Sun – that is, 365 days, 5 hr, 48 min and 46 sec. Calendar years consist of 365 days, or 366 in LEAP YEARS.

Zenith The point in the heavens which is directly above an observer.

THE CONTINENTS

AFRICA

Area: 30,319,000 km² (11,707,000 sq mi); **Population;** 624,000,000; **Independent countries** (1990): 52 (including island nations); **Highest Peak:** Mt Kilimanjaro, 5895 m (19,341 ft); **Lowest point:** Lake Assal (Djibouti), 155 m (509 ft) below sea level; **Largest lake:** Victoria, 69,484 km² (26,828 sq mi) in Kenya, Tanzania and Uganda; **Longest rivers:** Nile, Zaire, Niger, Zambezi; **Per capita GNP:** Oil-rich Libya has the highest per capita GNP, $8210, but South Africa ($1720) is the most developed nation. Chad ($110), Ethiopia ($130) and Somalia ($130) are among the poorest nations.

ASIA

Area: 44,387,000 km² (17,139,000 sq mi), including 75 per cent of the USSR (east of the Urals and Caspian Sea) and 97 per cent of Turkey; **Population:** 3,106,000,000; **Independent countries** (1990): 41; **Highest peak:** Mt Everest, 8848 m (29,028 ft); **Lowest point:** Shore of Dead Sea, 393 m (1289 ft) below sea level; **Largest lake:** Caspian Sea, 438,695 km² (169,390 sq mi); **Longest rivers:** Yangtze, Lena, Yenisey, Huang He, Ob, Mekong, Amur; **Per capita GNP:** The thinly populated, oil-rich nation of Kuwait has the highest per capita GNP, $17,270, but the most economically developed nation is Japan ($8800). Bhutan ($80) and Bangladesh ($100) have the lowest per capita GNPs.

NORTH AMERICA

Area: 24,249,000 km² (9,363,000 sq mi), including Mexico, Central America, the West Indies and Greenland, a self-governing county of Denmark; **Population:** 418,000,000; **Independent countries** (1990): 22; **Highest peak:** Mt McKinley (Alaska), 6194 m (20,322 ft); **Lowest point:** Death Valley (California), 86 m (282 ft) below sea level; **Largest lake:** Lake Superior, 82,409 km² (31,820 sq mi); **Longest rivers:** Mississippi-Missouri-Red Rock; **Per capita GNP:** The United States has the highest per capita GNP, $10,820, followed by Canada ($9650). Haiti ($260) has the lowest per capita GNP.

SOUTH AMERICA

Area: 17,832,000 km² (6,885,000 sq mi); **Population:** 290,000,000; **Independent countries** (1990): 12; **Highest peak:** Mt Aconcagua, 6960 m (22,835 ft); **Largest lake:** Maracaibo (Venezuela), 21,485 km² (8296 sq mi); **Longest river:** Amazon; **Highest waterfall:** Angel Falls in Venezuela (the world's highest), 979 m (3212 ft); **Per capita GNP:** Oil-rich Venezuela has the highest per capita GNP, $3130. Bolivia has the lowest, $550.

EUROPE

Area: 10,531,000 km² (4,066,000 sq mi), including 25 per cent of the USSR (west of the Urals and Caspian Sea) and 3 per cent of Turkey; **Population:** 693,000,000 – Europe is the most densely populated continent; **Independent countries** (1990): 31, besides the USSR and Turkey; **Highest point:** Mt Elbruz, 5633 m (18,481 ft); **Largest lake:** Caspian Sea on Europe-Asia border, 438,695 km² (169,390 sq mi); **Longest rivers:** Volga, Danube; **Per capita GNP:** Luxembourg ($12,820), Sweden ($11,920), Denmark ($11,900) and West Germany ($11,730) have the highest per capita GNPs. Albania ($840) has the lowest.

OCEANIA

Area: 8,510,000 km² (3,286,000 sq mi), of which Australia and New Zealand make up 93.5 per cent; **Population:** 28,300,000; **Independent countries:** 11; **Highest peak:** Mt Wilhelm (Papua New Guinea), 4694 m (15,400 ft); **Lowest point:** Lake Eyre (Australia), 12 m (39 ft) below sea level; **Longest rivers** (Australia): Murray, 2575 km (1600 mi) and its tributary, the Darling, 2740 km (1702 mi); **Per capita GNP:** Australia has the highest per capita GNP, $9100. Tonga ($460) has one of the lowest.

ANTARCTICA

Area: 13,209,000 km² (5,100,000 sq mi); **Population:** there is no permanent population; **Highest point:** 5139 m (16,860 ft) in the Vinson Massif; **Ice sheet:** Antarctica contains the world's largest ice sheet; the average thickness of the ice is 2000–3800 m (6560–12,470 ft).

Countries of the World

GAZETTEER

Note: In this Gazetteer, population figures for countries are recent estimates based on UN statistics except where otherwise stated. Populations of cities and towns are also the latest estimates or census figures. Adult literacy rates are generally for 1975, average life expectancies for 1978 and per capita GNPs (in US$) for 1979.

AFGHANISTAN, a landlocked republic in southeastern Asia. The land is mostly mountainous: major ranges include the Hindu Kush and the Pamirs. The north is arid. Rainfall generally averages 300 mm (12 in). Temperatures vary from 49°C (120°F) in the south in summer to −26°C (−15°F) in winter in the mountains. Some 79 per cent of the workforce are farmers, mainly in the subsistence sector. Only 10 per cent of the land is cultivable, mostly in irrigated valleys. Many people are nomads: sheep are the most numerous animals. Natural gas is exported, but mining and manufacturing are small-scale. Afghanistan, once part of the Persian Empire, was conquered by Alexander the Great in 331 BC. Islam was introduced in the 8th century. Modern Afghanistan was founded in 1747 by an Afghan chief, Ahmad Shah. His dynasty continued until 1973 when a republic was declared. In 1978 a Muslim rebellion against the pro-Soviet government led to civil war; Soviet forces moved in to back the government from 1979 to 1989.

Area: 647,497 km² (250,014 sq mi); **Population:** 18,136,000; **Capital:** Kabul (pop 1,036,000); **Other cities:** Kandahar (209,000), Herat (157,000); **Highest point:** 7620 m (25,000 ft) in the Hindu Kush; **Official languages:** Pushtu, Dari (Persian); **Religion:** Islam; **Adult literacy rate:** 12 per cent; **Average life expectancy at birth:** 42 years; **Unit of currency:** Afghani; **Main exports:** cotton, natural gas, fruit, karakul skins; **Per capital GNP:** US$170.

ALBANIA, the smallest European communist nation, borders the Adriatic Sea. The climate on the dry coast is Mediterranean in type. The land is mostly mountainous. Farmland covers 17 per cent of Albania, with fertile basins in the wetter uplands where the rainfall averages 1800 mm (71 in). Maquis and oak and pine forest cover 44 per cent of the land and pasture another 25 per cent. Farming is collectivized and 62 per cent of the workforce is employed on farms. But mining and manufacturing are the leading industries. Ottoman Turks introduced Islam in the 15th century. Albania became independent in 1912 and a kingdom in 1928. After

Left: Carpet-making and other handicraft industries are important activities in Algeria.

World War II a communist republic was set up. In 1961 Albania broke with the USSR and became allied to China, which helped it to industrialize. Albania officially became an 'atheist state' in 1967. The alliance with China ended in 1977. In 1990 Albania began slowly to relax its communism and to end its isolation from the West.

Area: 28,748 km² (11,100 sq mi); **Population:** 3,317,000; **Capital:** Tiranë (pop 22,000); **Other cities:** Shkodër (62,500), Durres (61,000); **Highest point:** Mt Korah, 2762 m (9063 ft); **Official language:** Albanian; **Religion:** formerly mainly Islam (all mosques and churches were closed in 1967); **Average life expectancy at birth:** 69 years; **Unit of currency:** Lek; **Main exports:** metal ores and metals (including chrome, copper, nickel), oil, bitumen, tobacco, fruit, vegetables; **Per capita GNP:** US$840.

ALGERIA, a large republic bordering the Mediterranean Sea in North Africa. The Sahara, which covers 85 per cent of the nation, yields oil and natural gas and oil accounts for 90 per cent of the exports. Between 1960 and 1980 the urban population increased from 30 per cent to 61 per cent. Of the workforce, agriculture now employs only 30 per cent, industry 25 per cent and services 45 per cent. Most people live in the northern Atlas mountain region and the fertile coastal plains. Barley, fruit, grapes, olives, vegetables and wheat are grown. Livestock are raised in the uplands. Islam and the Arabic language were introduced in the 7th century, but Berber languages survived in some areas. France ruled Algeria from 1848, but the Arab FLN (National Liberation Front) spear-headed a guerrilla war from 1954. In 1962 Algeria became independent: most of the 1 million French settlers left. Algeria became a one-party state, ruled by the FLN. An army junta took power in 1965, but the 1976 Constitution restored elections.

Area: 2,381,741 km² (919,646 sq mi); **Population:** 24,700,000; **Capital:** Algiers (pop 1,722,000); **Other cities:** Oran (485,000), Constantine (350,000), Annaba (313,000); **Highest point:** Mt Tahat, 2918 m (9573 ft); **Official language:** Arabic; **Religion:** Islam; **Adult literacy rate:** 37 per cent; **Average life expectancy at birth:** 56 years; **Unit of currency:** Dinar; **Main exports:** oil and oil products, natural gas, wine, fruit, vegetables; **Per capita GNP:** US$1580.

ANDORRA, a tiny, mountainous co-principality in the Pyrenees between France and Spain. Sovereignty is technically exercised by the 'co-princes', the Spanish Bishop of Urgel and the French President, but an elected, 28-member General Council

47

effectively rules the state. Tourism is the main industry: over 6 million people visited Andorra in 1978. Tobacco is the chief cash crop.

Area: 453 km² (175 sq mi); **Population:** 51,000 (1989); **Capital:** Andorra la Vella (pop 16,000); **Official language:** Catalan; **Units of currency:** French franc, Spanish peseta.

ANGOLA, a republic in west-central Africa, including the small enclave of Cabinda. The altitude affects the climate which is generally warmest and wettest in the north. Savanna covers much of the country, with forests in the south and north-east. Most people speak Bantu languages. The main groups are the Ovimbundu, the Mbundu and the Kongo. Tribalism has divided the nationalist movement in Angola. About 60 per cent of the people are farmers, mostly at subsistence level. The main food crops are cassava and maize. Mining is becoming increasingly important. The Portuguese explored Angola's coasts in the 1480s and later engaged in the slave trade there. In 1961 nationalists began a war against the Portuguese. Angola achieved independence in 1975. In the power struggle at the time of independence, the socialist MPLA, supported by Cuban troops, emerged triumphant. But the southern Ovimbundu UNITA resisted, and were backed by South Africa. Following a cease-fire in 1988 Cubans and South Africans agreed to withdraw.

Area: 1,246,700 km² (481,380 sq mi); **Population:** 9,733,000; **Capital:** Luanda (pop 600,000); **Other towns:** Huambo (62,000), Lobito (59,000); **Highest point:** Mt Moco, 2620 m (8596 ft); **Official language:** Portuguese; **Religion:** traditional religions, Christianity; **Adult literacy rate:** 20 per cent; **Average life expectancy at birth:** 41 years; **Unit of currency:** Kwanza; **Main exports:** oil, coffee, diamonds, iron ore, cotton, fish meal, sisal; **Per capita GNP:** US$440.

ANGUILLA, a low-lying coral island, about 110 km (68 mi) north-west of St Kitts, in the Leeward Islands. Its main products are lobsters and salt, but light industry and tourism have been developing recently. Anguilla has superb beaches and temperatures range between 24°C and 29°C (75°–84°F) all the year round. Anguilla became part of St Kitts-Nevis-Anguilla, a British Associated State, in 1967. But the Anguillans objected to rule from St Kitts and Britain appointed a Commissioner to handle the island's affairs. In 1976 Anguilla was granted a separate Constitution and formal separation from St Kitts-Nevis was achieved in 1980.

Area: 90 km³ (35 sq mi); **Population:** 8,000 (1990); **Status:** British dependency.

ANTIGUA, including the smaller and also low-lying islands of Barbuda and the uninhabited Redonda in the Leeward Islands, became an independent nation in the Commonwealth in 1981. The British monarch is its Head of State. Antigua exports cotton and rum, but tourism is the most important industry in this dry, sunny country. Discovered by Christopher Columbus in 1493,

Antigua was named after a church in Seville, Spain. British settlers colonized the islands in 1632 and they were declared a British possession in 1667. Antigua became a British Associated State in 1967. Most Antiguans are descendants of African slaves, but some are of European or Middle Eastern origin.

Area: 442 km² (171 sq mi); **Population:** 83,000; **Capital:** St John's (pop 24,000).

ARGENTINA, South America's second largest nation after Brazil, extends north-south through more than 32° of latitude. As a result the climate varies considerably. There are four main regions. The tropical, largely forested north is comparatively little developed. The west is arid, except around 'oases' where such towns as Mendoza and Tucumán have grown up, rising in the far west to the Andes Mountains. Here, on the border with Chile is Mt Aconcagua, the highest mountain in the western hemisphere. Southern Argentina, called Patagonia, consists of sparsely populated, wind-swept and semi-arid plateaus. In the far south is half of the barren and cold archipelago, Tierra del Fuego, whose southern tip is only about 960 km (600 mi) from Antarctica. The fourth and most densely populated region is the central *pampas* (or plains) which cover nearly 25 per cent of the country. The soils of the pampas are fertile and the climate is mild, with an average annual temperature range of 9°–23°C (48°–73°F) and an average annual rainfall of 510–760 mm (20–30 in). The *pampas* lie to the north-west and south of Buenos Aires, the elegant capital city. About 90 per cent of the population is of European descent, another 8 per cent being *mestizos* of mixed white and Indian origin, and 2 per cent pure Indians. Argentina is one of the world's leading food producers. Dairy products, hides, maize, meat, oats, vegetable oils, wheat and wool are major products. About 11 per cent of the country is cultivated and pastureland

Argentinian cowboys who work on the pampas (grasslands) are called gauchos. Pasture covers more than two-fifths of Argentina and supports vast herds of cattle and sheep.

covers another 41 per cent. In 1979 Argentina had 60 million cattle and 35 million sheep. In recent years, mining (for coal and oil) and manufacturing have become important. In the late 1970s, they accounted for 45 per cent of the GDP (manufacturing making up 37 per cent), while agriculture contributed only 13 per cent. The other 42 per cent came from service industries. The cities are growing quickly. The proportion of people in urban areas increased from 74 per cent in 1960 to 82 per cent in 1980. The Spanish explorer Juan de Solás was the first European to see the Rio de la Plata estuary, into which the Paraguay and Uruguay rivers flow, in 1516. The first permanent Spanish settlers arrived in 1535 and the city of Buenos Aires was founded one year later, although it was not permanently settled until 1580. Spanish rule continued until Buenos Aires declared itself independent in May 1810, followed by the provinces in 1816. Civil disorder ensued until a federal Constitution was adopted in 1853. In recent years Argentina has been disturbed by political and economic turmoil. Between 1946 and 1981, the Republic of Argentina had 14 presidents, seven of whom were deposed. The military government which had ruled Argentina since 1976 was dissolved in 1983 following the Falkland Islands defeat by Britain. President Bignone announced free elections.

Area: 2.766.889 km² (1.068.360 sq mi): **Population:** 32,425,000; **Capital:** Buenos Aires (pop with suburbs, 9,927,000); **Other cities:** Rosario (798,000), Cordoba (798,000), La Plata (408,000); **Highest point:** Mt Aconcagua, 6960 m (22,835 ft); **Official language:** Spanish; **Religion:** mainly Roman Catholicism, **Adult literacy rate:** 94 per cent; **Average life expectancy at birth:** 71 years; **Unit of currency:** Peso; **Main exports:** vegetable products, food, drink and tobacco, animals and animal products, textiles and leather, machinery and transport equipment; **Per capita GNP:** US$2280.

AUSTRALIA, the world's sixth largest country, has a low average population density of 2 people per sq km (5 per sq mi), because large tracts are desert or semi-desert. Some 89 per cent of the population is urban (1980), with more than 50 per cent of the people concentrated in the four largest cities. The western part of Australia is a vast plateau, averaging 300 m (984 ft) above sea level, although occasional mountain ranges rise above this level. The central plains extend from the Gulf of Carpentaria in the north to the Great Australian Bight in the south. These plains include the Great Artesian Basin, comprising western Queensland, the south-east of the Northern Territory, the north-east of South Australia and the northern part of New South Wales. Here artesian wells tap ground water that originally fell as rain on the Great Dividing Range in the east, and which has seeped through aquifers beneath the plains. The Lake Eyre basin in the south-west of the Great Artesian Basin, is usually dry and covered by salt. It is an internal drainage basin. The highest peak in the Great Dividing Range, an uplifted block of land, is Mt Kosciusko, in that part of the Range called the Australian Alps. The Range continues in the island state of Tasmania in the south-east, which is separated from the mainland by the shallow Bass Strait. In the north-east is the Great Barrier Reef, the world's longest reef, 2027 km (1260 mi) long. Australia's chief rivers are the Murray, 2575 km (1600 mi) long, and its tributaries, including the Darling, 2740 km (1703 mi) long, in the south-east. The climate varies according to the latitude. The north is tropical with summer monsoon rains. In the south, winters are cooler and rains are

Sydney is Australia's largest conurbation and chief seaport. This view looking south shows the expressway leading to Harbour Bridge from North Sydney.

brought by the prevailing westerlies. However, about two-thirds of Australia is too dry for farming. The tropical region in the north contains tropical forest and savanna and tropical crops, such as sugar-cane, flourish in Queensland. Deserts cover most of Western Australia, the southern part of Northern Territory, much of South Australia and the eastern parts of New South Wales. The mid-latitude grasslands are west of the Great Dividing Range in south-central Queensland and central New South Wales. The coastlands of New South Wales and south-eastern Victoria form a warm temperate zone, where eucalypt forests grow. The south-western part of Western Australia and parts of South Australia and western Victoria have a Mediterranean climate, with much scrub woodland vegetation. The cool temperate climate of Tasmania supports forests of beech and eucalypts. Australia has a wide range of animals, including kangaroos, koalas, platypuses and wallabies. Birds include the flightless emu and cassowary and the lyre bird. The first people in Australia were probably the Tasmanian Aborigines who were driven into Tasmania by the Australian Aborigines who arrived from Asia about 16,000 years ago. The Tasmanian Aborigines became extinct in 1876 and contact with Europeans caused the Australian Aborigines to decline in numbers. Today there are about 100,000 Australian Aborigines, but many are of mixed ancestry. Most Australians are of British origin, although the proportion of citizens of British origin has decreased to about 80 per cent. This is because many recent settlers have come from other parts of Europe. In 1978 industry accounted for 32 per cent of the GDP (manufacturing alone made up 19 per cent), agriculture for 5 per cent and services for 63 per cent. Australia has vast mineral reserves and is a major world producer of bauxite, iron ore and lead. Other metal ores, coal and oil are also mined, together with thorium and uranium. The Eastern Highlands contain many minerals, but the most spectacular finds since 1950 have been in Western Australia. The main product of the country is wool; Australia had 136 million sheep in 1980. New South Wales is the chief wool state, followed by Western Australia. There are also 26 million cattle and beef and dairy products are of great importance. Queensland is the chief cattle state. Only about 2 per cent of the land is cultivated, but yields are high and crops are varied because of the wide climatic range. But despite its importance, only 6 per cent of the workforce is employed in agriculture. Manufacturing industries are mostly in the towns and cities. The main steel centres are Newcastle, Wollongong and Whyalla. Dutch navigators landed in northern and eastern Australia in the early 17th century and in 1642 the Dutch explorer Abel Tasman discovered Tasmania without ever sighting the mainland. But the Dutch were not attracted by the arid coasts and their hostile inhabitants, the Aborigines. In 1770, however, the British Captain James Cook explored the fertile eastern coast and, in 1788, a British convict settlement was established on the present site of Sydney. In 1793 the first free settlers arrived. Gold rushes in the 1850s and 1890s accelerated immigration. In 1901 the Australian states united to form the Commonwealth of Australia and Parliament was moved to Canberra in Australian Capital Territory in 1927. Since 1945 immigrants to Australia have included people from central Europe, Greece, Italy, the Netherlands, Poland, Turkey and Yugoslavia, as well as Britons. In recent years, Australia's ties with Britain have been weakened by Britain's membership of the EEC and also by a new orientation of Australian foreign policy towards south-eastern Asia and the United States. But Australia, now one of the world's most prosperous nations, remains a member of the Commonwealth and the British monarch, represented by a Governor-General, is Head of State.

Area: 7.686.849 km^2 (2.968.071 sq mi): **Population:** 16,315,000(1989); **Capital:** Canberra (pop 248,441); **Other cities:** Sydney (3,193,000), Melbourne (2,740,000), Brisbane (1,015,000), Adelaide (933,000), Perth (884,000), Newcastle (380,000), Wollongong (224,000), Hobart (168,000), Gold Coast (143,000), Geelong (141,000); **Highest point:** Mt Kosciusko, 2228 m (7310 ft), in the Australian Alps; **Official language:** English; **Religion:** mainly Anglicanism and Roman Catholicism; **Adult literacy rate:** 100 per cent; **Average life expectancy at birth:** 73 years; **Unit of currency:** Dollar; **Main exports:** metals and metal ores; cereals, meat, coal and coke, textiles, sugar and honey, iron and steel, **Per capita GNP:** US$9100.

AUSTRIA, a federal republic in central Europe. The Alps cover about 75 per cent of the land and tourism is a major industry, especially winter sports. The Danube river valley in the north is the chief farming region. Livestock are also important: the uplands contain much summer pasture. Forests occupy about 40 per cent of the land. Industry

STATES AND TERRITORIES OF AUSTRALIA

State or territory	Area (sq km)	Area (sq mi)	Population (1989 est)	Capital
Australian Capital Territory	2,432	939	249,207	Canberra
New South Wales	801,428	309,450	5,402,000	Sydney
Northern Territory	1,347,519	520,308	155,000	Darwin
Queensland	1,727,522	667,036	2,587,000	Brisbane
South Australia	984,377	380,091	1,346,000	Adelaide
Tasmania	68,322	26,385	436,000	Hobart
Victoria	227,618	87,889	4,019,000	Melbourne
Western Australia	2,527,621	975,973	1,407,000	Perth

accounted for 42 per cent of the GDP in 1978 (agriculture supplied 5 per cent). Iron ore and lignite are mined, forming the basis of the iron and steel industry. Vienna is the main manufacturing and cultural centre; 54 per cent of the people lived in urban areas in 1980. Austria, part of the Holy Roman Empire, became a possession of the Hapsburg family in 1282. From 1438 this family supplied all but one of the Holy Roman Emperors. After the Empire ended (1806), the Hapsburg ruler became Emperor of Austria. From 1867 Austria became part of the dual monarchy of Austria-Hungary, which collapsed in 1918 ending Hapsburg power. In 1938 Germany annexed Austria. In 1945 Austria was partitioned between the Allies, but it became a neutral federal republic in 1955.

Area: 83,849 km² (32,376 sq mi); **Population:** 7,526,000; **Capital:** Vienna (pop 1,615,000); **Other cities:** Graz (248,000), Linz (203,000), Salzburg (129,000), Innsbruck (115,000); **Highest point:** Gross Glockner, 3797 m (12,457 ft); **Official language:** German; **Religion:** Roman Catholicism (88 per cent); **Adult literacy rate:** 99 per cent; **Average life expectancy at birth:** 72 years; **Unit of currency:** Schilling; **Main exports:** iron and steel, machinery, timber and wood products, chemicals, textiles and craft items; **Per capita GNP:** US$8620.

BAHAMAS, a group of 14 large and about 700 small islands with a mild climate, to the south-east of Florida. Tourism is the main industry and 1.8 million tourists, many from the USA, visited the islands in 1979. Christopher Columbus discovered the islands in 1492: the island of San Salvador was probably his first landing place. The Bahamas became a British colony in 1717. Full independence within the Commonwealth was achieved in 1973. About 85 per cent of the people are descendants of African Negroes (former slaves).

Area: 13,935 km² (5381 sq mi); **Population:** 257,000; **Capital:** Nassau (pop 130,000); **Official language:** English; **Unit of currency:** Bahamian dollar; **Per capita GNP:** US$2780.

BAHRAIN, a densely populated island nation in the Persian Gulf. The capital Manama is on the largest island, also called Bahrain. This hot, arid country is an important oil producer and revenue from oil sales has been used to provide free education, health and other services. The Arabs occupied Bahrain in the 7th century. British influence began in the early 19th century and, in 1861, it became a British protectorate. It became a fully independent sheikhdom in 1971.

Area: 622 km² (240 sq mi); **Population:** 483,000; **Capital:** Manama (pop 114,000); **Official language:** Arabic; **Unit of currency:** Dinar; **Per capita GNP:** US$5640.

The BALTIC STATES, Estonia, Latvia and Lithuania, are situated north of Poland, on the Baltic Sea. Formerly part of the Russian Empire, they became independent countries in 1918. In 1940 during World War II, they were seized by the Soviet Union and became Soviet republics. German troops invaded and controlled the Baltic States until they were driven out by the Soviet army at the end of the war. In 1991 while the Soviet Union was in a state of turmoil, Estonia, Latvia and Lithuania declared their independence. These three States are once more free of Soviet control. The Baltic States have kept their own languages, literature and traditions. Estonia has textile, shipbuilding and mining equipment industries. Latvia is an important producer of railway passenger coaches and telephone exchanges. Lithuania produces cattle, pigs and electrical appliances.

Estonia
Area: 45,100 km² (17,414 sq mi); **Population:** 1,600,000; **Capital:** Tallinn; **Language:** Estonian, Russian; **Industries:** Agricultural machinery, electric motors.
Latvia
Area: 63,700 km² (24,900 sq mi); **Population:** 3,340,000; **Capital:** Riga; **Language:** Latvian, Russian; **Religion:** mostly evangelical Lutheran; **Industries:** vehicles, paper.
Lithuania
Area: 65,000 km² (25,170 sq mi); **Population:** 3,700,000; **Capital:** Vilnius; **Language:** Lithuanian, Russian; **Religion:** mostly Roman Catholic; **Unit of currency:** rouble; **Industries:** engineering, shipbuilding.

BANGLADESH, a densely populated country in Asia, is one of the world's poorest. It has a tropical monsoon climate, with hot, dry winters and hot, wet summers. It is mostly flat, largely occupying the fertile deltas of the Ganges, Brahmaputra and other rivers. The rivers are the main transport arteries but they often flood causing disease and starvation. Coastal floods are also caused when cyclones in the Bay of Bengal drive the sea inland. About 71 per cent of the mainly Muslim Bengali population is engaged in agriculture, which accounts for 57 per cent of the GDP (13 per cent comes from industry). In 1980 only 11 per cent of the population was urban. Formerly part of British India, Bangladesh became the province of East Pakistan in 1947. A bitter, 9-month war between East and West Pakistan in 1971 ended with the secession of East Pakistan which became the People's Republic of Bangladesh.

Area: 143,998 km² (55,601 sq mi); **Population:** 112,335,000; **Capital:** Dhaka (pop 2,366,000); **Other cities:** Khulna (437,000), Chittagong (417,000); **Highest point:** Mt Keokradong, 1230 m (4035 ft); **Official language:** Bengali; **Religion:** Islam (80 per cent), Hinduism (10 per cent), Buddhism, Christianity; **Adult literacy rate:** 26 per cent; **Average life expectancy at birth:** 47 years; **Unit of currency:** Taka; **Main exports:** jute, hides and skins, leather, tea; **Per capita GNP:** US$100.

BARBADOS, the most easterly island in the West Indies. It is mostly flat, with a mild climate: annual temperatures average 25°–28°C (77°–82°F). More than 90 per cent of the people are descendants of African slaves, the rest being white or of mixed origin. Sugar and sugar products (molasses and rum) are the main products but tourism is now the

51

chief industry; there were 371,000 visitors in 1979. British colonization dates back to 1628. Full independence within the Commonwealth was achieved in 1966.

Area: 431 km² (166 sq mi); **Population:** 257,000; **Capital:** Bridgetown (pop with suburbs 88,000); **Official language:** English; **Unit of currency:** Dollar; **Per capita GNP:** US$2400.

BELGIUM, a densely populated, prosperous industrial nation in western Europe. Two-thirds of the land is flat, but the largely forested Ardennes rise in the south-east. The navigable Meuse and Scheldt rivers drain the fertile central plains. Antwerp, near the mouth of the Scheldt, is the main port. The 66-km (41-mi) coastline contains several resorts and fishing ports. The climate is mild and average temperatures in Brussels range between 3°C (37°F) and 17°C (63°F). The rainfall averages 720 mm (28 in) on the coast and 1200 mm (47 in) in the Ardennes. Three languages are spoken: Flemish (a Dutch dialect) in the north; French by the Walloons in the south; and German by a small group in the south-east. Conflict between Flemish- and French-speakers has led to rioting and complaints about discrimination. The population is highly urbanized: 72 per cent lived in urban areas in 1980. The lowlands are intensely cultivated. Most farms are small and only 3 per cent of the workforce is engaged solely in agriculture (which accounts for 2 per cent of the GDP): many farmers have jobs in industry, which employs 43 per cent of the workforce and contributes 37 per cent of the GDP. The main crops are cereals, notably wheat, flax, potatoes and sugar beet. There are 2.9 million cattle and 5 million pigs. Coal is mined in the north-eastern Campine (Kempen) region, which has become a major industrial area. The older industrial areas are in the south, in the Sambre-Meuse valley. This zone is based on coalfields which extend from Mons to Liège, but extraction of the coal has become expensive and the region has declined in consequence. Antwerp is a major industrial centre, some industries being based on imported oil, as is Brussels whose varied industries produce luxury goods and many other items. Textiles are important, particularly in Flanders; the main centre is Ghent. Belgium was divided into small counties in the Middle Ages. It came under the Austrian Hapsburgs in 1477 and the Spanish Hapsburgs in 1506. After a spell of independence (1598–1621), it came successively under Spain, Austria, France and the Netherlands. It declared its independence from the Netherlands in 1830. Germany occupied Belgium in both World Wars. After World War II, Belgium recovered quickly through economic co-operation with the Netherlands and Luxembourg in the Benelux customs union. It joined the European Coal and Steel Community in 1953 and was a founder-member of the EC in 1957. Brussels is the headquarters of the EC Commission and Council of Ministers. The Kingdom of Belgium is a constitutional, representative and hereditary monarchy, with an elected Senate and Chamber of Deputies.

Area: 30,513 km² (11,782 sq mi); **Population:** 9,941,000; **Capital:** Brussels (pop 1,009,000);

Other cities: Ghent (242,000), Charleroi (222,000), Liège (220,000), Antwerp (194,000), Bruges (118,000), Namur (101,000); **Highest point:** Botrange Mt, 694 m (2277 ft); **Official languages:** Dutch, French, German; **Religions:** Roman Catholicism, Protestantism; **Adult literacy rate:** 99 per cent; **Average life expectancy at birth:** 72 years; **Unit of currency:** Belgian franc; **Main exports:** engineering products. textiles. chemicals, glass, food, diamonds;

BELIZE, which faces the Caribbean Sea in Central America, is flat in the north, with uplands in the south. Forests flourish and sugar-cane is the chief cash crop in this hot, wet nation. More than 50 per cent of the people are Creoles; most of the others are of Mayan Indian, black Carib or European descent. Britain's contacts with Belize date back to the early 17th century. Belize was first declared a British colony in 1862, although neighbouring Guatemala has claimed it since 1821. The continuing dispute with Guatemala delayed full independence for Belize until 1981.

Area: 22,965 km² (8867 sq mi); **Population:** 179,000; **Capital:** Belmopan (pop 4000); **Official language:** English; **Unit of currency:** Dollar; **Per capita GNP:** US$1030.

BENIN, a People's Republic on the Gulf of Guinea in West Africa. Behind the sandy coast are low plateaux, with the highest land in the north-west. The formerly forested south has an equatorial climate but winters are dry in the tropical northern savanna. The black African population is divided into 50 groups, the largest being the Fon, Adja, Bariba and Yoruba. Agriculture employs 46 per cent of the workforce and accounts for 31 per cent of the GDP (13 per cent comes from industry). The chief food crops are maize and millet and the chief cash crop is palm kernels and oil. Oil was discovered offshore in the late 1970s. Benin (known as Dahomey until 1975) was ruled by France from the 1890s to 1960. Between 1960 and 1972 there were 6 coups. In 1977 there was an unsuccessful attempt by mercenaries to overthrow the government.

Area: 112,622 km² (43,486 sq mi); **Population:** 4,585,000; **Capital:** Porto Novo (pop 104,000); **Other cities:** Cotonou (178,000); **Official language:** French; **Religions:** traditional religions (65 per cent), Christianity (17 per cent), Islam (15 per cent); **Adult literacy rate:** 11 per cent; **Average life expectancy at birth:** 46 years; **Unit of currency:** Franc CFA; **Main exports:** palm kernels and oil, cotton, groundnuts; **Per capita GNP:** US$250.

BERMUDA, a British island colony in the North Atlantic, about 920 km (572 miles) from Cape Hatteras in the USA. Of the 150 islands, 20 are uninhabited. The climate is mild: annual temperatures average 21°C (70°F). About 60 per cent of the people are black. Tourism accounts for 41 per cent of the GDP: many of the 600,000 tourists come from the USA. Farming and fishing are important locally. Bermuda was named after its discoverer, the Spaniard Juan Bermúdez, in 1503. Britain took the islands in 1684 and internal self-government was granted in 1968.

Area: 53 km² (20 sq mi); **Population:** 72,000; **Capital:** Hamilton (pop 3000); **Per capita GNP:** US$9260 (1978).

BHUTAN, a mountainous landlocked kingdom between China and India. Most people, who are of Tibetan or Hindu Nepalese origin, live in fertile valleys where the climate is warm and wet. Agriculture, mostly at subsistence level, employed 93 per cent of the workforce in 1978; only 4 per cent lived in towns. Some rice, fruit and timber are exported. Most manufactures and fuels must be imported. Contact with the West began in 1774. The present ruling dynasty was founded in 1907, but an elected National Assembly can now dismiss the king. India assumed responsibility for Bhutan's foreign affairs in 1949.

Area: 47,000 km² (18,148 sq mi); **Population:** 1,538,000; **Capital:** Thimphu; **Official language:** Dzongkha; **Religion:** Buddhism; **Adult literacy rate:** 5 per cent; **Average life expectancy at birth:** 41 years; **Unit of currency:** Ngultrum; **Per capita GNP:** US$80.

BOLIVIA, a landlocked republic in South America. The Andes mountains in the south-west contain a central plateau, the Altiplano, where most Bolivians live. It has a cool climate, contrasting with the hot Amazon rain forests in the north-east. Lake Titicaca, the world's highest navigable lake, is on the border with Peru. More than 50 per cent of the people are American Indians, a third are *mestizos* and the rest of European origin. Agriculture employs 51 per cent of the people, but mining is the most valuable industry. Bolivia is the world's 2nd largest tin producer and antimony, copper, lead, oil and natural gas, silver and wolfram are also mined. Spain ruled Bolivia from 1532 to 1825 when Simón Bolívar's army liberated the country (then Upper Peru). Oil discoveries have recently offered hope for Bolivia, South America's poorest nation.

Area: 1,098,581 km² (424,188 sq mi); **Population:** 7,014,000; **Capital:** La Paz (seat of government, pop 881,000), Sucre (legal capital, 80,000); **Other cities:** Santa Cruz (256,000), Cochabamba (204,000); **Highest point:** Mt Tocopuri, 6755 m (22,162 ft); **Official language:** Spanish; **Religion:** Roman Catholicism; **Adult literacy rate:** 63 per cent; **Average life expectancy at birth:** 52 years; **Unit of currency:** Peso; **Main exports:** tin, oil, natural gas, cotton; **Per capita GNP:** US$550.

BOTSWANA, a thinly populated, landlocked republic in southern Africa. Most of the country is a plateau between 600 and 1200 m (1969–3937 ft) high. Average temperatures range between 27°C (81°F) and 32°C (90°F). The rainfall is less than 250 mm (10 in) in the south-west, but 760 mm (30 in) in the north. The Kalahari, a semi-desert, covers 84 per cent of the country and only a few nomadic Bushmen live there. Most people belong

American Indians hunt fish in the Xingu River in the Amazon basin of Brazil. Economic development is now threatening the survival of the Indians.

to the Bantu-speaking Tswana group, including the Bamangwato and Bangwaketse. They live mostly in the east around the Botswanan section of the Cape Town-Bulawayo railway. Minerals now dominate the economy: diamonds and copper-nickel matte made up 57 per cent of the exports in 1978. Most people work in agriculture. Arable land covers only 2 per cent of the country, but cattle farming is important – there were 3.3 million cattle in 1979. Botswana (formerly called Bechuanaland) became a British protectorate in 1885. It became fully independent within the Commonwealth in 1966.

Area: 600,372 km² (231,818 sq mi); **Population:** 1,284,000; **Capital:** Gaborone (pop 54,000); **Official language:** English; **Religions:** Christianity, traditional beliefs; **Adult literacy rate:** 20 per cent; **Average life expectancy at birth:** 46 years; **Unit of currency:** Pula; **Main exports:** diamonds, meat and meat products, copper, nickel; **Per capita GNP:** US$720.

BRAZIL, the world's 5th largest nation, occupies nearly half of South America. In the north, the equatorial Amazon basin covers more than 5.3 million km² (2 million sq mi). It contains the world's largest rain forest (*selvas*), which are now being reduced as economic development proceeds. The Amazon river, 6437 km (4000 mi) long, is the world's second longest, with a greater volume than any other. It is navigable into Peru. South of the *selvas* is a huge tropical grassland, plateau region, the *campos*. This region is still little developed despite the inauguration in its heart of the new capital of Brasilia in 1960. The north-east around Recife and Salvador has a forested coastal plain, but the inland plateaux are dry: long droughts cause much hardship to an already impoverished population. The central coastal region is the most densely populated and includes the great industrial cities of São Paulo and Rio de Janeiro. Inland are fertile plateaux and pleasant, mineral-rich highlands. The plateaux near São Paulo are Brazil's main coffee-producing region. The southern region around Porto Alegre has a temperate climate: pastoral farming is important. About 75 per cent of Brazil's population is of Portuguese or other

European origin. There are many people of mixed European/Indian/Negro descent, perhaps 200,000 pure Indians and some blacks: colour prejudice is almost absent. The population is increasing quickly (2.9 per cent per year in 1970–78). There is also a rapid shift of population from rural to urban areas. The urban population increased from 46 per cent in 1960 to 65 per cent in 1980 and slums now surround many cities. Agriculture still provides work for two-fifths of the people, although its contribution to the GDP is only 11 per cent. Brazil leads the world in producing bananas and coffee, and it is among the top world producers of beef, veal, cocoa, cotton, maize, sugar-cane, soya beans and tobacco. Industry accounts for 37 per cent of the GDP. Brazil is the leading producer in Latin America of cars, merchant ships, steel and cement. It has huge reserves of minerals, many of which are unexploited. Such minerals as asbestos, chrome ore, industrial diamonds, iron ore, quartz crystal and manganese are exported. In 1500 the Portuguese explorer Pedro Alvares Cabral claimed Brazil for Portugal. At that time an estimated 1.3 million Indians lived in the country. However, many were killed by Europeans and others died (and are still dying in the *selvas*) of European disease to which they lack resistance. African slaves were introduced to work European estates. Brazil declared itself an independent empire in 1822 but it became a republic in 1889, one year after slavery was abolished. From 1964 to 1985 Brazil was under military rule. In 1989 Brazil had its first direct presidential election since 1960, and Fernando Collor de Mello of the Workers' Party became president.

Area: 8,511,965 km² (3,286,668 sq mi); **Population:** 147,399,000; **Capital:** Brasilia (pop 1,177,000); **Other cities:** São Paulo (8,408,000), Rio de Janeiro (5,395,000), Belo Horizonte (1,857,000), Salvador (1,446,000), Recife (1,184,000), Fortaleza (1,256,000), Pôrto Alegre (1,184,000), Nova Iguacu (1,130,000); **Highest point:** Pico da Bandeira, 2890 m (9482 ft); **Official language:** Portuguese **Religion:** Roman Catholicism (91 per cent); **Adult literacy rate:** 76 per cent; **Average life expectancy at birth:** 62 years; **Unit of currency:** Cruzeiro; **Main exports:** coffee, machinery, soya beans, vehicles, cocoa; **Per capita GNP:** US$1690.

BRITAIN See United Kingdom.

BRUNEI, a small Sultanate in north-western Borneo. Behind the narrow coastal plain, the interior is rugged and forested. The climate is tropical. Some 68 per cent of the people are of Malay origin and 25 per cent are Chinese. Oil is the main product. Brunei ruled all of Borneo and nearby islands in the early 16th century, after which it gradually declined. It was a British protectorate between 1888 and 1971. It became independent in 1984.

Area: 5765 km² (2226 sq mi); **Population:** 267,000; **Capital:** Bandar Seri Begawan (pop 58,000); **Official language:** Malay; **Unit of currency:** Brunei dollar; **Per capita GNP:** US$10,680.

BULGARIA is an independent republic in south-eastern Europe, facing the Black Sea. The climate is transitional between Mediterranean and continental. The mountains include the Balkans in the north and the higher Rhodope Mts in the south. The capital Sofia is in a fertile mountain basin. The River Danube plain is in the north, but the central plains are the main farming region, producing fruit, mulberry leaves, attar of rose, sugar beet, tobacco and wine. Lignite, copper, iron ore and oil are mined and manufactures include cement, iron and steel goods and textiles. COMECON countries account for 80 per cent of Bulgaria's trade. Tourism is increasing. The Turks ruled Bulgaria from 1396. Bulgaria became an independent principality in 1878, East Rumelia (southern Bulgaria) being added in 1885. Bulgaria became an independent kingdom in 1908. From 1947 to 1989 Bulgaria had a Communist government, but became a Socialist republic after the Communists were overthrown.

Area: 110,912 km² (42,826 sq mi); **Population:** 8,999,000; **Capital:** Sofia (pop 1,032,000); **Other cities:** Plovdiv (333,000), Varna (279,000); **Highest point:** Musalla Mt, 2925 m (9596 ft); **Official language:** Bulgarian; **Religion:** Eastern Orthodox Church (27 per cent), Islam (7 per cent); **Average life expectancy at birth:** 72 years; **Unit of currency:** Lev; **Main exports:** machinery, metals and metal ores, food, tobacco, textiles; **Per capita GNP:** US$3690.

BURMA See Myanmar.

BURKINA FASO, known as Upper Volta until 1984, is a West African republic. Low plateaux cover most of the country. The east is in the River Niger basin; the centre and west are drained by the Black, Red and White Volta rivers. Burkina Faso has a hot, tropical climate. The main rainy season is July–October, and the average annual rainfall varies between 500 mm (20 in) in the north to 1140 mm (45 in) in the south-west. But droughts are common. Most people are Negroes: the Mossi (48 per cent) are the largest single group. There are few minerals. Food, textiles and metal products are the main manufactures. Remittances from migrant workers and revenue from transit trade play a major part in the economy. France subdued the country by 1896. Full independence was achieved in 1960. Since 1966 there have been a series of military coups. The name Burkina Faso, adopted in 1984, means "Land of the Honest People".

Area: 274,200 km² (105,875 sq mi); **Population:** 8,894,000; **Capital:** Ouagadougou (pop 375,000); **Official language:** French; **Religions:** Traditional beliefs, Islam (30 per cent), Roman Catholicism (9 per cent); **Adult literacy rate:** 5 per cent; **Average life expectancy at birth:** 42 years; **Unit of currency:** Franc CFA; **Main exports:** cotton, livestock, karité nuts and oil, groundnuts; **Per capital GNP:** US$180.

BURUNDI, a small, densely populated, landlocked republic in east-central Africa. Part of Lake Tanganyika is in the Rift Valley in the west, with highlands and high plateaux in the east. The altitude moderates the equatorial climate. The highlands are grassy, but woodlands flourish on the warmer plateaux. The main ethnic groups are the Bantu-speaking Hutu (85 per cent) and the Hamitic Tutsi (13 per cent). Agriculture employs 85 per cent of the people, accounting for 56 per cent of the GDP. The pastoralist Tutsi entered the area from the north in the 17th century. They founded a feudal society under their *mwami* (king), making the Hutu serfs. Germany occupied Burundi and Rwanda (then Ruanda-Urundi) in 1890, but Belgium took the area in World War I. Burundi became an independent monarchy in 1962, but a republic was set up in 1966.

Area: 27,834 km² (10,747 sq mi); **Population:** 5,290,000; **Capital:** Bujumbura (pop 157,000); **Official languages:** French, Kirundi; **Religions:** Roman Catholicism (60 per cent), Protestantism (7 per cent), traditional beliefs; **Adult literacy rate:** 25 per cent; **Average life expectancy at birth:** 45 years; **Unit of currency:** Burundi franc; **Main exports:** coffee; **Per capita GNP:** US$180.

CAMBODIA, a South-East Asian nation, briefly known as the Khmer Republic and later as Kampuchea. It reverted to Cambodia in 1990. Cambodia has a tropical monsoon climate and dense forests. Khmers make up 90 per cent of the population. There are Chinese and Vietnamese minorities. The economy is based on agriculture. The powerful Khmer empire flourished in the area between 800 and 1450, and a weaker Khmer kingdom survived until 1863, when the French took control. Cambodia became independent again in 1953. In the 1970s the country became involved in the Vietnamese War when the North Vietnamese took supplies through Cambodia. The Communist Khmer Rouge took control of the country in 1975 and began a reign of terror. Vietnam invaded in 1978 to suppress the Khmer Rouge, and withdrew in 1989. Civil war broke out again.

Area: 181,035 km² (69,902 sq mi); **Population:** 6,855,000 (1989 est); **Capital:** Phnom Penh (1983 est 500,000); **Official language:** Khmer; **Religion:** Buddhism; **Unit of currency:** Riel; **Main exports:** formerly rice and rubber.

CAMEROON, a republic in west-central Africa, bordering the Gulf of Guinea. The main uplands are on the western border. Most people are black, speaking one of about 200 Bantu or Sudanic languages. Agriculture employs 82 per cent of the people. Germany made Cameroon a colony in 1884 but, after World War I, it was partitioned between Britain and France. French Cameroon became independent in 1960 and was joined in a federal republic in 1961 by part of British Cameroon – the other part joined Nigeria. A unitary state was established in 1972.

Area: 475,442 km² (183,579 sq mi); **Population:** 10,874,000; **Capital:** Yaoundé (pop 314,000); **Other cities:** Douala (458,000); **Highest point:** Mt Cameroon, 4070 m (13,353 ft); **Official languages:** English, French; **Religions:** Christianity (52 per cent), Islam (18 per cent), traditional beliefs; **Adult literacy rate:** 19 per cent; **Average life expectancy at birth:** 46 years; **Unit of currency:** Franc CFA; **Main exports:** coffee, cocoa, timber; **Per capita GNP:** US$560.

CANADA, the world's 2nd largest nation after the USSR, but it has only 2.5 persons per sq km (6 per sq mi). There are 7 main regions: The *Appalachian region* in the north-east. The *St Lawrence and Lower Great Lakes* region, Canada's most densely populated. The *Canadian Shield*, a vast region of ancient rocks, mineral deposits, innumerable lakes and rivers. The *Hudson Bay* Lowland, a plain between the Canadian Shield and Hudson Bay. The *Western Interior Plains*, between the Canadian Shield and the *Western Mountains*. In the far north are the bleak *Arctic Islands*. Canada has extremely cold winters, especially north of the Arctic Circle. Southern Canada has warm, moist summers. Rainfall varies from 2500 mm (98 in) per year in the west to 300–500 mm (12–20 in) on the central prairies. Forests cover 35 per cent of Canada. The origins of the people are as follows: British (45 per cent), French (29 per cent), German (6 per cent), Italian (3 per cent) and Ukrainian (3 per cent). Most of the rest come from other parts of Europe. American Indians and Eskimos number 289,000 and 17,500 respectively. Canada has two official languages, English and French. Quebec is the main French-speaking province. In the 1980 referendum, 40.5 per cent.

The Niagara Falls are on the border between Canada and the United States between Lake Erie and Lake Ontario. The Falls are one of North America's finest natural wonders.

PROVINCES AND TERRITORIES OF CANADA

Province or territory	Area (sq km)	Area (sq mi)	Population (1986)	Capital
Alberta	661,187	255,300	2,375,000	Edmondon
British Columbia	948,599	366,276	2,889,000	Victoria
Manitoba	650,089	251,014	1,071,000	Winnipeg
New Brunswick	73,437	28,356	710,000	Fredericton
Newfoundland	404.518	156,194	568,000	St. John's
Northwest Territory	3,379,693	1,304,978	52,000	Yellowknife
Nova Scotia	55,491	21,426	873,000	Halifax
Ontario	1,068,586	412,606	9,114,000	Toronto
Prince Edward Is.	5,657	2,184	127,000	Charlottetown
Quebec	1,540,685	594,894	6,540,000	Quebec
Saskatchewan	651,902	251,795	1,010,000	Regina
Yukon Territory	536,326	207,088	24,000	Whitehorse

of the people voted for and 59.5 per cent against 'separatism'. Canada is a prosperous country. Only 7.2 per cent of the land is cultivated, but Canada is one of the world's leading producers of barley, fruits, oats, wheat, rye and timber. Livestock ranching and dairy farming are also important. But agriculture contributes only 4 per cent of the GDP as opposed to 31 per cent from industry. Canada is among the top six world producers of asbestos, copper, gold, iron ore, lead, molybdenum, natural gas, nickel, potash, silver, uranium and zinc. But more important than mining is manufacturing. The chief industrial area is the St Lawrence and Lower Great Lakes region. Much traffic is carried along the St Lawrence Seaway, the world's longest artificial seaway at 304 km (189 mi). Canada's first people, the Indians, entered North America from Asia around 20,000 years ago. The Eskimos were later arrivals. Vikings sailed down Canada's coasts in about AD 1000, but the first definite European landfall was made in 1497. Quebec was founded by Samuel de Champlain in 1604, but intense rivalry soon developed between the French and British. Between 1689 and 1763, the British conquered the French settlements. In 1867 the Dominion of Canada, comprising Quebec, Ontario, Nova Scotia and New Brunswick, was established. Canada is now a federation of 10 self-governing provinces and 2 territories. The federal parliament consists of a Senate and a House of Commons.

Area: 9.976.139 km² (3.852.019 sq mi); **Population:** 25,890,000; **Capital:** Ottawa (pop with suburbs 819,000); **Other cities:** Toronto (2,803,000), Montreal (2,802,000), Vancouver (1,166,000), Winnipeg (578,000), Edmonton (554,000), Quebec (542,000), Hamilton (529,000), Calgary (470,000); **Highest point:** Mt Logan, 6050 m (19,849 ft); **Official languages:** English, French; **Religions:** Roman Catholicism (46 per cent), Protestantism (42 per cent); **Adult literacy rate:** 98 per cent; **Average life expectancy at birth:** 74 years; **Unit of currency:** Dollar; **Main exports:** motor cars and vehicle parts, newsprint and wood pulp, oil and natural gas, wheat, industrial machinery, iron ore; **Per capita GNP:** US$9650.

CAPE VERDE, an island republic about 500 km (311 mi) west of Senegal in West Africa. The 10 large islands and 5 islets are of volcanic origin. The climate is tropical, but the rainfall is very

unreliable. Most people are of mixed Portuguese and African origin; 28 per cent are classed as 'pure' Africans. Most people are subsistence farmers, but severe droughts in the 1970s forced many people to emigrate and the government has had to provide work for destitute farmers. Portugal claimed the islands in 1460. From 1836 to 1879, Cape Verde was ruled with Portuguese Guinea (now Guinea-Bissau) and close ties between the two territories continued. In 1963–74, Cape Verdeans fought alongside Guineans against the Portuguese in Portuguese Guinea. Independence for Cape Verde was achieved in 1975.

Area: 4033 km² (1557 sq mi); **Population:** 358,000 **Capital:** Praia (pop 21,000); **Highest point:** Pico do Cano, 2829 m (9281 ft); **Official language:** Portuguese; **Religions:** Roman Catholicism (97 per cent), Protestantism (3 per cent), a few animists; **Adult literacy rate:** 28 per cent; **Average life expectancy at birth:** 50 years; **Unit of currency:** Escudo; **Main exports:** fish and lobsters, salt, sugar, bananas; **Per capita GNP:** US$270.

CAYMAN ISLANDS, a British island group in the West Indies. These tropical islands export turtle shells, turtle meat and fish, but tourism is more important. The people are of European, African or mixed origin. Columbus discovered in the islands in 1503. Britons settled there in the 17th century.

Area: 259 km² (100 sq mi); **Population:** 19,000; **Capital:** George Town (pop 4000).

CENTRAL AFRICAN REPUBLIC, a landlocked nation, consists largely of plateaux between 600 and 900 m (1969–2953 ft). Temperatures average 26°C (79°F) all the year. The south has an average annual rainfall of 2030 mm (80 in); the far north gets 510 mm (20 in). The south is forested, but wooded savanna covers most of the land. Wildlife is abundant. Most people speak Sudanese languages. Agriculture employs 89 per cent of the workforce, contributing 36 per cent of the GDP. Diamonds are mined and large uranium deposits have been found, but manufacturing is on a small scale. The country became part of French Equatorial Africa in the 1880s. It became independent in 1960. From 1965 it was ruled by Jean-Bédel Bokassa who, in 1977, made himself 'emperor'. The country was then named the Central African Empire. Bokassa was overthrown in 1979 and the nation again became a republic.

Area: 622,984 km² (240,549 sq mi); **Population:** 2,836,000; **Capital:** Bangui (pop 474,000); **Official language:** French; **Religions:** Roman Catholicism (46 per cent), Protestantism (36 per cent), traditional beliefs; **Adult literacy rate:** 8 per cent (1973); **Average life expectancy at birth:** 46 years; **Unit of currency:** Franc CFA; **Main exports:** coffee, diamonds, timber, cotton; **Per capita GNP:** US$290.

CHAD, a landlocked nation in north-central Africa. Southern Chad is savanna-covered, but sandy deserts and bare rocky uplands, notably the high Tibesti massif, are in the north. About 100 languages are spoken in Chad. In the south, where most of the population lives, most people are Negroid. Muslim Arabs and Berbers live in the north. Cultural divisions have caused much civil conflict and periodic war since the mid-1960s. In 1980 Libyan troops intervened in Chad but they were replaced in 1981 by an OAU force. Agriculture employs 86 per cent of the workers in this poor nation. Cotton is the chief crop. Chad became a French colony in 1897 and an independent republic in 1960. Civil war broke out a few years later and has continued ever since.

Area: 1,284,000 km² (495,782 sq mi); **Population:** 5,529,000; **Capital:** N'Djamena (pop 402,000); **Highest point:** Emi Koussi, 3415 m (11,204 ft); **Official language:** French; **Religions:** Islam (45 per cent), Christianity (5 per cent); traditional beliefs (50 per cent); **Adult literacy rate:** 15 per cent; **Average life expectancy at birth:** 43 years; **Unit of currency:** Franc CFA; **Main exports:** cotton (66 per cent), meat and cattle, fish; **Per capita GNP:** US$110.

CHILE, a narrow country stretching through 38° of latitude in South America. Its greatest width is about 400 km (249 miles). From west to east, there are generally three regions; coastal uplands, central lowland basins and valleys, and the high Andes. In the glaciated south, the coastal uplands are islands, the central lowlands becoming arms of the sea. Chile's climate changes north-south. The north is hot and arid, including the rainless Atacama Desert with its large mineral reserves. Central Chile, where most Chileans live, has hot summers and mild moist winters. The forested south with its beautiful fiords is cool: heavy rain falls in all seasons. Cape Horn, South America's stormy tip, is in the far south. People of mixed European and Indian origin make up 68 per cent of the population, Europeans 30 per cent, and Araucanian Indians 2 per cent. Agriculture provides work for 20 per cent of the people, accounting for 18 per cent of the GDP. Farmland covers 15 per cent of Chile, pasture 27 per cent and forests 29 per cent. The main farm products are barley, fruit, maize, wheat and wine. Industry accounts for 29 per cent of the GDP (with 20 per cent from manufacturing). Minerals include copper, which makes up 48 per cent of the exports, iron ore, nitrates and oil. Manufacturing industries are powered mainly by hydro-electricity.

Chile was a Spanish colony for about 300 years before becoming independent in 1818. It gained its mineral-rich northern provinces in a war with Peru and Bolivia in 1879–83. In 1970 a Marxist government led by Salvador Allende was elected to office, but it was overthrown in 1973 by the armed forces. After years of military government the country held a free presidential election in 1989, voting in 71-year-old Patricio Alwin Azócar.

Area: 756,945 km² (292,274 sq mi); **Population:** 12,796,000; **Capital:** Santiago (pop with suburbs 4,225,000); **Other cities:** Valparaiso (611,000), Concepción (513,000); **Highest point:** Ojos de Salado, 6885 m (22,590 ft); **Official language:** Spanish; **Religion:** Roman Catholicism (90 per cent), **Adult literacy rate:** 88 per cent; **Average life expectancy at birth:** 67 years; **Unit of currency:** Peso; **Main exports:** copper, paper and wood pulp, timber, iron ore, nitrates; **Per capita GNP:** US$1690.

CHINA, the world's 3rd largest country, contains about 20 per cent of the world's population. The land is extremely varied. In the north-east is the basin of the Huang He, one of the world's longest rivers at 4345 km (2700 mi) long. It cuts through a loess plateau which has coloured its waters yellow. The lower course of the Huang He crosses the North China Plain. To the north lie the central plain and eastern highlands of Manchuria. To the south, beyond the Qin Ling Mountains, lies the Yangtze Kiang basin of Central China. The Yangtze is Asia's longest river, 5470 km (3400 mi) in length. China's third important river basin is that of the Xi Jiang in the south-east, south of the South China Highlands. Outer or Western China contains the high and vast Tibetan plateau which rises in the south to the Himalayan range, crowned by Mt Everest. In the far west are other ranges including the lofty Pamirs and Tien Shan. North-eastern China contains some large deserts, including the vast Tarim and Dzungaria basins. The Gobi desert straddles the frontier between Inner Mongolia (in China) and Mongolia. The climate varies from north to south. North-eastern China has bitterly cold winters and warm summers. The average annual rainfall is between 635 and 760 mm (25–30 in). Central China has milder winters and more rainfall – about 1000–1500 mm (39–59 in) per year, while south-eastern China has a sub-tropical monsoon climate and many places get more than 2030 mm (80 in) of rain per year. The north-eastern deserts have less than 100 mm (4 in). About 94 per cent of the population are Han, or true, Chinese. But there are also large national minorities, including Manchus, Mongols, Tibetans and Uighurs, who maintain their own cultures. The population is densest in the fertile river basins and along the coasts of eastern China. Some 25 per cent of the population lives in urban areas. The rural population has been encouraged to live in communes, which are groups of villages where up to 20,000 people work together, share the produce and get wages that are geared to production. Some 62 per cent of the workforce is engaged in agriculture. China leads the world in millet, rice and tobacco production. It is among the top three

Left and below: A vase of the Chinese Ch'ing dynasty (1644–1911) and a ginger jar of the Ming dynasty (1368–1644). Right: A jade Han-dynasty monster (206 BC–AD 220).

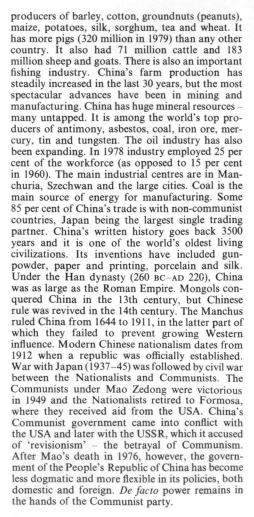

The family remains the most important social unit in China, despite Communist rule. China is a poor country in world terms, a consequence of its mainly peasant farming economy. But it has great resources and considerable economic potential.

producers of barley, cotton, groundnuts (peanuts), maize, potatoes, silk, sorghum, tea and wheat. It has more pigs (320 million in 1979) than any other country. It also had 71 million cattle and 183 million sheep and goats. There is also an important fishing industry. China's farm production has steadily increased in the last 30 years, but the most spectacular advances have been in mining and manufacturing. China has huge mineral resources – many untapped. It is among the world's top producers of antimony, asbestos, coal, iron ore, mercury, tin and tungsten. The oil industry has also been expanding. In 1978 industry employed 25 per cent of the workforce (as opposed to 15 per cent in 1960). The main industrial centres are in Manchuria, Szechwan and the large cities. Coal is the main source of energy for manufacturing. Some 85 per cent of China's trade is with non-communist countries, Japan being the largest single trading partner. China's written history goes back 3500 years and it is one of the world's oldest living civilizations. Its inventions have included gunpowder, paper and printing, porcelain and silk. Under the Han dynasty (260 BC–AD 220), China was as large as the Roman Empire. Mongols conquered China in the 13th century, but Chinese rule was revived in the 14th century. The Manchus ruled China from 1644 to 1911, in the latter part of which they failed to prevent growing Western influence. Modern Chinese nationalism dates from 1912 when a republic was officially established. War with Japan (1937–45) was followed by civil war between the Nationalists and Communists. The Communists under Mao Zedong were victorious in 1949 and the Nationalists retired to Formosa, where they received aid from the USA. China's Communist government came into conflict with the USA and later with the USSR, which it accused of 'revisionism' – the betrayal of Communism. After Mao's death in 1976, however, the government of the People's Republic of China has become less dogmatic and more flexible in its policies, both domestic and foreign. *De facto* power remains in the hands of the Communist party.

Area: 9,596,961 km² (3,705,610 sq km); **Population:** 1,097,432,000; **Capital:** Beijing (Peking, pop 9,330,000), Shanghai (11,940,000), Tianjin (Tientsin, 7,850,000), Shenyang (4,080,000), Wuhan (3,280,000), Guangzhou (Canton, 3,160,000), Chongqing (Chungking, 2,690,000), Harbin (2,560,000), Chengdu (Chengtu, 2,510,000), Nanjing (Nanking, 2,170,000); **Highest point:** Mt Everest, 8848 m (29,028 ft); **Official language:** Chinese; **Religions:** Confucianism, Taoism, Buddhism, Islam, Christianity; **Average life expenctancy at birth:** 70 years; **Unit of currency;** Yuan; **Main exports:** industrial products (including petroleum, chemicals, machinery, equipment), agricultural products; **Per capita GNP:** US$230 (1978).

CHRISTMAS ISLAND, an Australian territory in the Indian Ocean populated by Chinese, Malays and Europeans. The only industry is phosphate mining. It came under the Governor of the Straits Settlement in 1889 and was incorporated with Singapore in 1900. Australia took over in 1958.

Area: 135 km² (52 sq mi); **Population:** 3200; **Status:** Australian external territory.

COCOS (KEELING) ISLANDS, an Australian territory in the Indian Ocean comprising 27 coral islands that export copra. Britain annexed them in 1857 and they came under the Governor of the Straits Settlement in 1886. They were placed under Australian rule in 1955.

Area: 14 km² (5½ sq mi); **Population:** 500; **Status:** Australian external territory.

COLOMBIA, a republic in north-eastern South America, contains three ranges of the Andes whose high, fertile valleys contain most of the people. In eastern Colombia, *llanos* grasslands merge into the forests of the upper Amazon and Orinoco basins. The coastal lowlands are hot and wet, with average temperatures of 26°–28°C (79°–82°F) and about 2540 mm (100 in) of rain. The highlands are cooler and less rainy. The *llanos* have dry winters but wet summers. More than two-thirds of the people are of mixed Indian and European origin; Agriculture accounts for 31 per cent of the GDP. The chief export, coffee, is grown in the highlands. Industry accounts for 27 per cent of the GDP and 70 per cent of the people now live in urban areas. Spaniards opened up the region in the early 16th century. Spanish rule was overthrown in 1819. Greater Colombia then included Venezuela, Ecuador and parts of Panama. Venezuela and Ecuador soon split off and Panama broke away in 1903. A civil war in 1948–53 led to a military seizure of power but, after 1957, democracy was restored. In the 1980s, the government declared an all-out war on drug dealers.

Area: 1,138,914 km² (439,761 sq mi); **Population:** 30,164,000; **Capital:** Bogotá (pop 3,983,000); **Other cities:** Medellín (1,442,000), Cali (1,255,000); **Highest point:** Pico Cristobal Colón, 5775 m (18,947 ft); **Official language:** Spanish; **Religion:** Roman Catholicism; **Adult literacy rate:** 81 per cent; **Average life expectancy at birth:** 62 years; **Unit of currency:** Peso; **Main exports:** coffee, emeralds, meat, sugar, petroleum, fuel oils, hides and skins; **Per capita GNP:** US$1010.

COMOROS, an island Federal and Islamic Republic at the northern end of the Mozambique Channel. Geographically, there are 4 islands: Njazidja, Nzwani, Mahoré (or Mayotte) and Mwali. The republic contains three of them, but Mayotte is a French territory. The islands are mountainous: Mt Kartala, 2361 m (7746 ft), is an active volcano. The population is mixed, including elements from Africa, Asia and Europe. These tropical islands have few resources and most people are subsistence farmers. They came under French protection in 1886–1909 and became a colony in 1912. In 1946 they became a French overseas department. The people voted for independence in 1974, except in Mayotte where a majority opposed it. In 1975 the Chamber of Deputies voted for immediate independence, which France recognized on January 1, 1976. But Mayotte (a French colony since 1843) became a *collectivité particuliére*, a status part-way between a French Overseas Territory and an Overseas Department.

Area: 2171 km² (838 sq mi); **Population:** 502,000; **Capital:** Moroni; **Official languages:** Arabic, French; **Religions:** mainly Islam, Roman Catholicism (4 per cent); **Average life expectancy at birth:** 42; **Unit of currency:** Franc CFA; **Main exports:** vanilla, vegetable oils, cloves, copra, coffee, cocoa; **Per capita GNP:** US$210.

CONGO, a People's Republic in equatorial Africa. Behind a narrow coastal plain is an upland region; the north is a swampy plain drained by the Congo (Zaire) and Oubangui rivers. High temperatures and heavy rainfall, except on the coast, have encouraged the growth of rain forests and woodland savanna. Most people speak Bantu languages (including Kongo, Téké, Mbochi), but 12,000 pygmies live in central Congo. Less than 2 per cent of Congo is cultivated, but agriculture employs 35 per cent of the workforce, accounting for 13 per cent of the GDP. Industry accounts for 33 per cent; oil extraction and processing industries are especially important. 37 per cent of the population lives in urban areas. Discovered in 1482, Congo later became a slave trade centre. French rule was established in the 1880s; Congo later became part of French Equatorial Africa. Full independence was achieved in 1960. Military governments have ruled the country since 1968.

Area: 342.000 km² (132.054 sq mi): **Population:** 2,466,000; **Capital:** Brazzaville (pop 311,000); **Other towns:** Pointe-Noire (147,000); **Official language:** French; **Religions:** traditional beliefs (50 per cent); Christianity (48 per cent), Islam (2 per cent); **Adult literacy rate:** 50 per cent; **Average life expectancy at birth:** 46 years; **Unit of currency:** Franc CFA; **Main exports:** oil, timber, potash, fertilizers, coffee, cocoa; **Per capita GNP:** US$630.

COOK ISLANDS, a self-governing territory of New Zealand in the South Pacific. Of the 15 islands, 9 are atolls and 6 volcanic. Most people are Polynesians. Exports include fruits and copra. The islands became a British protectorate in 1888 and part of New Zealand in 1901.

Area: 234 km² (90 sq mi); **Population:** 18,000; **Capital:** Avarua; **Official language:** English.

COSTA RICA, a Central American republic with coastlines on the Caribbean Sea and the Pacific Ocean. Inland it is mountainous with volcanic peaks. Fertile plateaux lie between the mountains. About 70 per cent of the people live in the largest of these, the Central Plateau. The tropical climate is modified by the relief. More than 80 per cent of the population is of European origin. There are 1200 Indians and a few thousand blacks, but most non-whites are of mixed European and Indian origin. Agriculture employs 29 per cent of the people, accounting for 22 per cent of the GDP; industry accounts for 27 per cent and services 51 per cent. The main cash crop is coffee. Costa Rica is one of the more prosperous nations of Central America. Spain ruled the country from around 1530 to 1821. Dictatorships and revolutions marred its early years of independence, but it has enjoyed democracy since 1919.

Area: 50.700 km² (19,576 sq miles): **Population:** 2,721,000; **Capital:** San José (pop 560,000; **Highest point:** Chirripo, 3820 m (12,861 ft); **Official language:** Spanish; **Religion:** Roman Catholicism; **Adult literacy rate:** 90 per cent; **Average life expectancy at birth:** 70 years; **Unit of currency:** Colón; **Main exports:** manufactures, coffee, bananas; **Per capita GNP:** US$1810.

CUBA, the largest nation in the West Indies. Small islands, reefs and mangrove swamps skirt much of the coast. More than half of the land is flat and fertile. Forested mountain ranges occupy about 25 per cent of the land, the rest being gently undulating country. The climate is tropical, with average temperatures of 22°–28°C (72°–82°F). The rainfall averages 1270 mm (50 in) per year. About 75 per cent of the people are descendants of Spaniards, the rest being blacks or mulattos. Some 65 per cent of the population lives in urban areas. Agriculture employs 25 per cent of the workforce, industry 31 per cent and service industries 44 per cent. About 34 per cent of Cuba is cultivated, most being government-owned. Sugar and its by-products, molasses and rum, are the main products. Minerals, tobacco, bananas and fish are also exported. Columbus discovered Cuba in 1492 and Spain ruled it between 1511 and 1898 (except when Britain occupied it in 1762-63). US influence was strong in the 20th century until Communist guerrillas led by Dr Fidel Castro seized power in 1959. Cuba became an ally of the USSR and, in the late 1970s and early 1980s, Cuban troops aided left-wing regimes in Africa.

Area: 114,524 km² (44,220 sq mi); **Population:** 10,346,000; **Capital:** Havana (pop 1,735,000); **Official language:** Spanish; **Religions:** Roman Catholicism, Protestantism; **Adult literacy rate:** 96 per cent; **Average life expectancy at birth:** 72 years; **Unit of currency:** Peso; **Main exports:** sugar (80 per cent); **Per capita GNP:** US$1410.

CYPRUS, an island republic in the north-eastern Mediterranean Sea. There are fertile coastal plains and a broad central plain (the Mesaoria). The Kyrenia and Karpass mountains are in the north and the Troödos mountains in the south. The climate is typically Mediterranean. Greek Cypriots form 80 per cent of the population, Turkish Cypriots 18 per cent and Armenian, Maronite and other minorities also live there. Communal conflict characterizes social life; most people feel themselves to be Greeks or Turks rather than Cypriots. About 60 per cent of the land is cultivated; one-third of the work-force is employed in farming. Agriculture supplies about half of the exports and minerals (notably copper) about 30 per cent. Britain rented Cyprus from the Ottoman Empire in 1878 but it annexed it in 1914 and proclaimed it a colony in 1927. A fierce guerrilla war preceded independence in 1960. The independence Constitution, providing for power-sharing between the communities, proved unworkable. In 1974 Turkish forces occupied the north. The island was partitioned, the northern 40 per cent being proclaimed the 'Turkish Cypriot Federated State'.

Area: 9251 km² (3572 sq mi); **Population:** 665,000; **Capital:** Nicosia (pop 121,000); **Other cities:** Limassol (102,000); **Highest point:** Mt Olympus, 1951 m (6401 ft); **Official languages:** Greek, Turkish; **Religions:** Eastern Orthodox Christianity, Islam; **Average life expectancy at birth:** 71 years; **Unit of currency:** Pound; **Main exports:** fruit and vegetables, manufactures (including wine), minerals; **Per capita GNP:** US$2940.

CZECHOSLOVAKIA, A landlocked Socialist republic in eastern Europe. The saucer-shaped Bohemian plateau, bounded by mountains, is in the east. It is drained by the upper Elbe (the Vltava) on which Prague stands. Moravia, in the centre, is largely lowland, with rivers draining to the Danube. Slovakia, in the east, is mainly upland,

with some plains in the south. The climate is continental. The people include the Czechs (65 per cent of the population), in Bohemia and Moravia, the Slovaks (30 per cent) and various minorities. Industry, which is nationalized, accounts for 72 per cent of the GDP: 63 per cent of the population lives in urban areas. The country is rich in coal and lignite and has many metal ores, although metals are imported. Farmland covers 55 per cent of the country. Crops include barley, hops, rye, sugar beet and wheat. The republic was created in 1918. Germany occupied Czechoslovakia in 1939. After World War II, Communists ruled the country until 1989, when they were overthrown and Václav Havel became president. Free elections were held in 1990. In 1992 it was announced that the country would split into two parts, the Czech Republic and Slovakia.

Area: 127,869 km² (49,373 sq mi); **Population:** 15,556,000; **Capital:** Prague (pop 1,189,000); **Other cities:** Brno (369,000); Bratislava (368,000); **Highest point:** 2655 m (8737 ft); **Official languages:** Czech, Slovak; **Religions:** Roman Catholicism, Protestantism; **Average life expectancy at birth:** 70 years; **Unit of currency:** Koruna; **Main exports:** machinery, industrial consumer goods, raw materials and fuels; **Per capita GNP:** US$5290.

DENMARK, the smallest but most densely populated nation in northern Europe. It consists of the low-lying Jutland peninsula and about 500 islands, the largest of which, Sjaelland, contains Copenhagen. Moraine covers much of the land, but two-thirds is fertile farmland or pasture. Animal products (bacon, butter, cheese, eggs) are particularly important as is sea fishing. But only 8 per cent of the workforce is engaged in agriculture, forestry and fishing. The leading sector of the economy is manufacturing. Products include superb silverware, furniture, processed food, chemicals, engineering goods, machinery and ships. Denmark formed a union with Norway and Sweden in the late 14th century. Sweden became independent in 1523 and Denmark ceded Norway to Sweden in 1814. Neutral in World War I, Denmark was occupied by Germany in World War II. After the war, it helped to set up the Nordic Council. It joined the EC in 1973. The Faeroe Islands and Greenland are parts of Denmark.

Area: 43,069 km² (16,630 sq mi), not including Greenland; **Population:** 5,175,000; **Capital:** Copenhagen (pop 654,000); **Other cities:** Aarhus (245,000), Odense (169,000), Aalborg (154,000); **Highest point:** 173 m (568 ft); **Official language:** Danish; **Religion:** Lutheran Church; **Adult literacy rate:** 99 per cent; **Average life expectancy at birth:** 74 years; **Unit of currency:** Krone; **Main exports:** machinery and equipment, live animals and meat, dairy products and eggs, metals and metal manufactures; **Per capita GNP:** US$11,900.

DJIBOUTI, a small republic on the Red Sea in north-eastern Africa. The land is mostly hot desert. The people include the Somali-speaking Issas (40 per cent), the nomadic Afars (or Danakils, 33 per cent), both of whom are Muslims, and some

Europeans, Arabs and other foreigners. Stock raising is the main occupation. It became a French colony in 1881, called French Somaliland. In 1967 it was renamed the Territory of the Afars and Issas. It became independent as Djibouti in 1977.

Area: 22,000 km² (8495 sq mi); **Population:** 371,000; **Capital:** Djibouti (pop 150,000); **Official language:** French; **Main exports:** hides and skins, cattle; **Per capita GNP:** US$420.

DOMINICA, a volcanic island in the Windward Islands in the eastern Caribbean Sea. Its wet tropical climate supports dense forests. Most people are blacks or of mixed origin. There is a small Carib community, mostly of mixed origin. Agriculture and tourism are the main industries. Columbus discovered Dominica in 1493. It became a British colony in 1805 and a British Associated State in 1967. The Commonwealth of Dominica became an independent republic in 1978.

Area: 751 km² (290 sq mi); **Population:** 82,000; **Capital:** Roseau (pop 17,000); **Main exports:** bananas, citrus fruits; **Per capita GNP:** US$410.

DOMINICAN REPUBLIC, a nation occupying the eastern half of Hispaniola, an island in the West Indies. The land is mountainous and the climate tropical, with average temperatures of more than 20°C (68°F) and an average annual rainfall of 1000 mm (39 in). Rain forests are widespread, but the valleys are fertile. More than 70 per cent of the population is of mixed black and white descent, 15 per cent are white and 10 per cent are black. Agriculture employs 57 per cent of the workforce, contributing 21 per cent of the GDP (1978). Sugar is the chief export. Industry accounts for 35 per cent of the GDP: some bauxite, nickel, gold and silver are mined and there is some light industry. Tourism is increasingly important. Columbus discovered Hispaniola in 1492. Spain sold the area to France in 1795 but ruled it again in 1809–21. From 1822 to 1844 Haitians occupied the area. The Dominican Republic was founded in 1844, but its history has been marred by violence. From 1930–61 the country was a dictatorship. Elections were held in 1962, but a military coup in 1963 led to civil war in 1965 when US forces intervened. Since then the country has had elected governments.

Area: 48,734 km² (18,817 sq mi); **Population:** 6,824,000; **Capital:** Santo Domingo (pop 1,313,000); **Highest point:** Pico Duarte, 3124 m (10,249 ft); **Official language:** Spanish; **Religion:** Roman Catholicism; **Adult literacy rate:** 67 per cent; **Average life expectancy at birth:** 60 years; **Unit of currency:** Peso; **Main exports:** sugar, coffee; **Per capita GNP:** US$990.

ECUADOR, a republic on the Equator in north-western South America. It includes the 15 Galápagos Islands, about 970 km (603 mi) to the west. The Pacific coastlands have an average annual temperature of 27°C (81°F). The Andes ranges are much cooler; Quito at 2850 m (9350 ft) has an average temperature of 13°C (55°F). The hot Amazon basin occupies eastern Ecuador. The an-

nual rainfall varies between 1020 and 1520 mm (40–60 in). More than half the people are Indians. There are also people of European, African and mixed descent. Agriculture employs 46 per cent of the people, contributing 21 per cent of the GDP. Industry accounts for 35 per cent, oil being the leading product. The Incas ruled the area from about 1470 until Spaniards conquered it in 1533. Independence was achieved in 1822 and Ecuador became a separate republic in 1830. Weak governments, armed rebellions and military coups have marred much of Ecuador's recent history. In 1979, however, elections were held and civilian rule was restored.

Area: 283,561 km² (109,489 sq mi); not including land disputed with Peru; **Population:** 10,490,000; **Capital:** Quito (pop 866,000); **Other cities:** Guayaquil (823,000); **Highest point:** Mt Chimborazo, 6272 m (20,577 ft); **Official language:** Spanish; **Religion:** Roman Catholicism; **Adult literacy rate:** 74 per cent; **Average life expectancy at birth:** 60 years; **Unit of currency:** Sucre; **Main exports:** oil, bananas, cocoa, coffee; **Per capita GNP:** US$1050.

EGYPT, an Arab Republic in north-eastern Africa. The fertile, irrigated Nile valley contains 99 per cent of the population, although it covers less than 4 per cent of the country. The Nile flows about 1200 km (746 mi) through Egypt. Near the Mediterranean Sea it divides into two branches, the Dumyat (Damietta) and Rashid (Rosetta), which enclose the triangular delta. The rest of Egypt is desert. The western (Libyan) desert contains several large oases and depressions, notably the Qattara depression, which is 133 m (436 ft) below sea level. The eastern, or Arabian, desert rises to highlands that border the Red Sea. But the highest peak, Jabal Katrinah, is in the Sinai peninsula, east of the Suez Canal. This international waterway, opened in 1869, is 173 km (107 mi) long, linking the Mediterranean and Red seas. Average temperatures in Egypt vary between 27°C and 32°C (81°–90°F) in summer and 13°–21°C (55°–70°F) in winter. The average annual rainfall is about 200 mm (8 in) in the far north and barely 25 mm (1 in) in the south. Most Egyptians are Arabs, but there are Berber, Nubian and Sudanese minorities. Egypt is a poor country, although it is the 2nd most industrialized in Africa. About 45 per cent of the population lives in urban areas and industry contributes 30 per cent of the GDP. Energy comes mainly from hydro-electric stations, especially at the Aswan High Dam. Manufactures include cement, chemicals, plastics, steel, sugar and textiles. Some phosphates, iron ore and oil are mined. Agriculture accounts for 29 per cent of the GDP, employing 51 per cent of the workforce. The chief export is cotton, but most farmers are peasants (*fellahin*) who practise subsistence farming. Tourism is important: over 1 million foreigners visited Egypt in 1979. Ancient Egypt's pyramids and other monuments are special attractions. Ancient Egypt's history is divided into 30 dynasties. The first began in 3100 BC, when Upper and Lower Egypt were united. It reached its peak under King Thutmose III (1490–36 BC). From 525 BC Egypt was mostly under foreign rule. In 30 BC it became part of the Roman empire and, in AD 395, it was the centre of

The pyramids of Egypt testify to the glories of one of the world's most important early civilizations. Today more than a million people visit Egypt every year to see the pyramids and other magnificent remains of ancient Egypt. The money they spend is a major source of foreign exchange. The camel of North Africa and South-West Asia is a leading work animal and a means of transport across the burning hot, arid wastes that fully justifies the animal's popular name, 'the ship of the desert'.

the Coptic Christian Church. Arabs occupied Egypt in 639–642, introducing Islam and Arabic. In 1517 Egypt became part of the Ottoman empire, but it came under French rule in 1798–1801. In 1881 Britain occupied Egypt and made it a protectorate in 1914. In 1922 Egypt gained a degree of independence, becoming a monarchy. In 1948–49 Egypt fought alongside other Arabs against the creation of the state of Israel. Egypt became a republic in 1953 and, in 1956, nationalized the Suez Canal. Anglo-French and Israeli forces invaded Egypt, but they withdrew under UN and US pressure. Short Egyptian-Israeli wars occurred in 1967 and 1973. President Anwar as-Sadat initiated peace talks with Israel in 1977 and a Peace Treaty (opposed by most Arab nations) was signed in 1979. Sadat was assassinated in 1981.

Area: 1,001,449 km^2 (386,683 sq mi); **Population:** 51,405,000; **Capital:** Cairo (pop 5,875,000); **Other cities:** Alexandria (2,259,000), Giza (854,000); **Highest point:** Jabal Katrinah, 2637 m (8652 ft); **Official language:** Arabic; **Religions:** Islam (91 per cent), Coptic Christianity; **Adult literacy rate:** 44 per cent; **Average life expectancy at birth:** 54 years; **Unit of currency:** Egyptian pound; **Main exports:** cotton and cotton textiles, rice, fruit, vegetables; **Per capita GNP:** US$460.

EL SALVADOR, a densely populated republic in Central America, with a 270 km (168 mi) long coastline on the Pacific Ocean. The country is mountainous and the altitude modifies the tropical climate. San Salvador has an average temperature range of 24°–26°C (75°–79°F) and about 1800 mm (71 in) of rain per year. About 90 per cent of the population is of mixed European and Indian descent. Agriculture employs 52 per cent of the workforce, accounting for 29 per cent of the GDP; the main crops being coffee and cotton. Industry (mostly manufacturing) contributes 21 per cent of the GDP. Spain conquered the area in 1526. Independence from Spain was achieved in 1821 and El Salvador became an independent republic in 1841. The country has suffered from political instability. A military coup occurred in 1979 and a bitter war began between the US-backed government and left-wing guerrillas.

Area: 21,041 km^2 (8124 sq mi); **Population:** 5,900,000; **Capital:** San Salvador (pop 884,000); **Highest point:** Mt Santa Ana, 2385 m (7825 ft); **Official language:** Spanish; **Religion:** Roman Catholicism; **Adult literacy rate:** 62 per cent; **Average life expectancy at birth:** 63 years; **Unit of currency:** Colón; **Main exports:** coffee, cotton; **Per capita GNP:** US$670.

EQUATORIAL GUINEA, a republic in west-central Africa, comprises Río Muni on the mainland and the islands of Bioko (formerly Fernando Póo) and Pagalu. The islands are volcanic; Río Muni contains hills and plateaux. The climate is equatorial. The Bantu Fang form the majority in Río Muni. Fang, Bubi (the original inhabitants) and Fernandinos (descendants of liberated slaves) live on the islands. Most people are farmers: coffee is the main crop. Spain took the territory in the 1840s. Independence was achieved in 1968. The first President Francisco Macías Nguema ruled with much brutality until he was deposed in 1979.

Area: 28,051 km^2 (10,831 sq mi); **Population:** 378,000; **Capital:** Malabo (pop 37,000); **Highest point:** Pico de Santa Isabel, 3007 m (9865 ft); **Official language:** Spanish; **Religions:** Roman Catholicism (88 per cent), traditional religions (8 per cent); **Average life expectancy at birth:** 43 years; **Unit of currency:** Ekuele; **Main exports:** cocoa, coffee, timber; **Per capita GNP:** US$330 (1976).

ETHIOPIA, a republic in north-eastern Africa. The highlands are divided into two blocks by the deep Rift Valley. Lowlands occur in the east near the Red Sea coast. The main river, the Blue Nile, flows from Lake Tana in the north. The lowlands are hot and arid, contrasting with the cooler, moister uplands. About 100 languages are spoken: most belong to the Cushitic, Semitic or Nilotic families. Cushites include the nomadic Galla, the largest single ethnic group. The Amhara, who form the ruling class, speak a Semitic language while Nilotic languages are spoken by Negroid people in the east. Agriculture employs 81 per cent of the population. It accounts for 54 per cent of the GDP. Coffee makes up about 75 per cent of the exports.

Finland is a tranquil, beautiful land of forests and lakes. The lakes occupy ice-scoured rock basins or depressions dammed by moraine deposited during the Pleistocene Ice Age. Forestry is a major industry. Paper, pulp and other timber products account for 40 per cent of Finland's export earnings. But heavy industry has increased greatly in recent years and, in consequence, the proportion of Finns who live in urban areas increased from 38 per cent in 1960 to 62 per cent in 1980.

Ethiopia is the home of an ancient monarchy which embraced Christianity in the 4th century AD. It never became a colony, although it was occupied by Italy in 1935–41. The monarchy was abolished in 1974 and the country was ruled by a left-wing military group. Aided by the USSR, government forces fought against secessionist forces in Eritrea in the east and against Somali-speaking people in the Ogaden in the south-east.

Area: 1,221,900 km² (471,804 sq mi); **Population:** 47,709,000; **Capital:** Addis Ababa (pop 1,413,000; **Other cities:** Asmara (353,000) **Highest point:** Ras Dashan, 4620 m (15,157 ft); **Official language:** Amharic; **Religions:** Orthodox (Coptic) Christianity (46 per cent), Islam (34 per cent), traditional beliefs (14 per cent); **Adult literacy rate:** 10 per cent; **Average life expectancy at birth:** 39 years; **Unit of currency:** Ethiopian dollar; **Main exports:** coffee, hides and skins, pulses; **Per capita GNP:** US$130.

FALKLAND ISLANDS, a British colony in the South Atlantic, about 480 km (298 mi) east of the Strait of Magellan. There are 200 islands but only two are sizeable. Sheep farming is the main occupation. France founded a settlement in 1764 followed by Britain in 1765. Spain took over in 1770. From the early 19th century, independent Argentina claimed the islands which became a British Crown Colony in 1832. In 1982 Argentine forces occupied the islands and Britain sent a task force to recover the territory.

Area: 12,173 km² (4700 sq mi); **Population:** 1916 (1986).

FIJI, a nation in the south-central Pacific. Two mountainous, volcanic islands, Viti Levu and Vanua Levu, make up 87 per cent of the total area. About 48 per cent of the people are Indians (mainly Hindus); 44 per cent are Melanesians. Agriculture is the main activity and tourism is important. Discovered in 1643, the islands became a British colony in 1874 and an independent nation within the Commonwealth in 1970. Following a coup in 1987 Fiji became a republic and left the Commonwealth.

Area: 18,274 km² (7056 sq mi); **Population:** 758,000; **Capital:** Suva (pop 64,000); **Main exports:** sugar, coconut oil; **Per capita GNP:** US$1690.

FINLAND, a republic in north-eastern Europe. It contains 55,000 or so lakes that fill hollows created during the Ice Age; water covers 9 per cent of the country. Much of Lapland in the north is within the Arctic Circle. Winters are long and severe, but the short summers are warm. Forests cover more than four-fifths of the country and timber has been the mainstay of the economy. About 62 per cent of the people live in urban areas and industry contributes 35 per cent of the GDP, as opposed to 8 per cent from agriculture, which is mostly confined to the far south. In the past Sweden and Russia have struggled for control of the Baltic Sea region. Russia occupied Finland in 1809 but Finland declared itself independent in 1917, becoming a republic in 1919. In 1939 the USSR declared war on Finland and Finland lost one-third of its territory. It allied itself to Germany but lost more land to the USSR after World War II. Finland signed peace treaties with the USSR in 1948, 1955 and 1970.

Area: 337,009 km² (130,127 sq mi); **Population:** 4,829,000; **Capital:** Helsinki (pop with suburbs, 893,000); **Other cities:** Tampere (243,000), Turku (240,000); **Highest point:** 1328 m (4357 ft); **Official languages:** Finnish, Swedish, **Religion:** Lutheran National Church (90 per cent); **Adult literacy rate:** 100 per cent; **Average life expectancy at birth:** 72 years; **Unit of currency:** Markka; **Main exports:** paper and paperboard, machinery and transport equipment, wood and wood pulp; **Per capita GNP:** US$8260.

FRANCE, the 2nd largest nation in Europe after the USSR. Mountain ranges (the French Alps which contain France's highest peak, Mont Blanc, and the lower Jura Mts) form the south-eastern border. The Vosges Mts are in the north-east, overlooking the Rhine rift valley and the scenic Massif Central, which rises to 1886 m (6188 ft), is in south-central France. This latter region contains the headwaters of the Dordogne, Garonne,

Top left: France contains many magnificent medieval churches, including the 12th-13th-century cathedral at Chartres. Top right: Vineyards are a common sight in France, which leads the world in producing top-quality wine. Above: Superb châteaux adorn many rural areas in France.

Loire and Seine rivers. The north-west peninsula, including Brittany, is lower but also scenic, with a superb indented coastline. The Paris basin is a saucer-shaped depression enclosed by rings of hills with outward facing scarps. The Aquitaine basin in the south-west is a low plain, partly fringed by coastal sand dunes. It extends to the high Pyrenees along the border with Spain. The Rhône-Saône valley, in the south-east between the Massif Central and the south-eastern mountains, ends in the marshy Camargue. The climate varies from the moist, temperate north to the Mediterranean coastlands, with their hot, dry summers and mild, moist winters. The climate also changes from west to east. The west has a maritime temperate climate moderated by the North Atlantic Drift, but to the east it becomes increasingly continental, with colder winters especially in upland regions. Rain falls all the year round except for the Mediterranean region. Several minority languages are spoken: Breton, a Celtic tongue, in Brittany; Basque in the western Pyrenees; Catalan in the eastern Pyrenees; Provençal in the south-east; and German in the north-east. Foreign-born people, including Portuguese, Algerians, Spaniards and Italians, make up about 6½ per cent of the population. Some 78 per cent of the population lives in urban areas; industry and services accounted for 37 per cent and 51 per cent of the GDP respectively in 1978. The chief mineral resource is iron ore, notably in

Lorraine. Some coal, oil and natural gas are mined, but France imports much coal from West Germany. Energy also comes from hydro-electric stations and the River Rance tidal power station in Brittany. There is a wide range of manufacturing industries. Paris is known especially for its luxury and fashion products; Lyons is known for textiles; Marseilles and Bordeaux are major industrial ports; and Lille, on the north-western coalfield, is centre of a large industrial region. Farming is also important. In 1978 it contributed 5 per cent of the GDP (as against 10 per cent in 1960), employing 9 per cent of the workforce (22 per cent in 1960). Despite this trend away from the land, the proportion of farm workers in France is three times that in West Germany and the UK. The leading farming regions are the Paris basin, the Loire valley, the Aquitaine basin and the Rhône-Saône valley. Arable land covers 32 per cent of the country, pasture 24 per cent, vineyards 2 per cent, and forests 26 per cent. Agricultural yields per hectare tend to be low, because a high proportion of the farms are small and unmechanized, but France is a leading producer of wheat, barley, oats, flax and sugar beet. Livestock, including dairy cattle, are extremely important; in 1979 there were 23.5 million cattle, 11.5 million sheep and 11.7 million pigs. France is famous for its quality wines and cheeses, which are associated with particular regions. The fishing industry employs 28,000 fishermen. The tourist

64

industry, a major source of foreign earnings, employs about half a million people. West Germany is France's leading trading partner; the EEC as a whole accounts for more than half of France's trade. The Romans conquered France (then called Gaul) in the 50s BC and imposed on it a common language and government. Roman rule declined because of attacks by Germanic tribes. In AD 486 the Frankish realm (as France was called) became independent under a Christian king, Clovis. Charlemagne, who became king in 768, extended the Frankish realm and, in 800, he was crowned Emperor of the West by the Pope. In 843, however, his empire was divided into three, with France coming under Charles the Bald. France contracted in size and, after the Norman invasion of Britain

Boules, *or bowls, is a popular game in France. It can be played on any piece of land and does not require carefully prepared lawns.*

in 1066, large areas came under English rule. Following the French victory by Joan of Arc at Orléans in 1429, English rule in France was finally ended in 1453. A powerful monarchy was established, but in 1792 the 1st Republic was set up, a consequence of the French Revolution of 1789. In 1799 Napoleon Bonaparte took power. After a period of brilliant military exploits, which took him as far as Moscow, he was finally defeated in 1815. The monarchy was restored until 1848 when the short-lived 2nd Republic was established by a revolution. In 1852 Napoleon's nephew Napoleon III became monarch. The 3rd Republic began in 1875. In the 20th century France suffered greatly during World Wars I and II. In 1946 a new Constitution established the 4th Republic. But economic recovery was delayed by costly colonial wars and political instability, although France sponsored the successful European Coal and Steel Community (founded in 1952) and was a founder member of the EC in 1957. In 1958 Charles de Gaulle was elected President. He introduced a new Constitution, extending the President's powers and establishing the 5th Republic. Under stable right-wing governments, France made rapid economic progress. In 1981 the French socialist leader François Mitterrand was elected President and his Socialist Party gained majorities in parliament, which consists of two houses: the 305-member Senate and the 491-member National Assembly.

Area: 547,026 km² (211,219 sq mi); **Population:** 54,414,000; **Capital:** Paris (pop with suburbs, 8,550,000); **Other cities:** Lyons (1,171,000), Marseilles (1,071,000), Lille (936,000), Bordeaux (612,000), Toulouse (510,000), Nantes (454,000), Nice (438,000); **Highest point:** Mt Blanc, 4810 m (15,781 ft); **Official language:** French; **Religions:** Roman Catholicism, Islam (about 2 million people in 1978); Protestantism (about 750,000 people); **Adult literacy rate:** 99 per cent; **Average life expectancy at birth:** 73 years; **Unit of currency:** Franc; **Main exports:** cars, chemical products, iron and steel, textiles and leather goods, electrical equipment, wine, cereals; **Per capita GNP:** US$9940.

FRENCH GUIANA, a French Overseas Department on the Atlantic Ocean in north-eastern South America. Most of the land is low-lying with uplands in the south. Average temperatures are between 29°C and 32°C (84°–90°F) all the year round. Cayenne has an average annual rainfall of 3560 mm (140 in); parts of the interior are even rainier. Dense forest covers 88 per cent of the land. Most people are Creoles; pure Indians make up 11 per cent of the population. Cultivated land covers only 6000 ha. Bananas, maize, manioc and rice are the main crops. Shrimp fishing is important, but the main prospect is the bauxite deposits that have been discovered recently. The territory came under French control by the mid-17th century. The French set up convict settlements – Devil's Island was the best known. These were all closed by 1945 and Guiana became a department of France in 1946.

Area: 91,000 km² (35,137 sq mi); **Population:** 76,000; **Capital:** Cayenne (pop 36,000); **Per capita GNP:** US$2580.

FRENCH POLYNESIA, a French Overseas Territory in the eastern Pacific Ocean. There are about 130 tropical islands scattered across 4 million km² (1.5 million sq mi). The island groups are: the *Windward Islands*, including Tahiti and Moorea, capital Papeete; the *Leeward Islands* which, with the Windward Is, are often called the Society Islands, main town Uturoa; the *Tuamotu Archipelago*, comprising 78 atolls; the *Gambier Islands*, chief town Rikitea; the *Austral (Tubuai) Islands*, chief town Mataura; and the *Marquesas Islands*. Tourism is the main industry and copra the leading product. The islands have been French protectorates since 1843. They were given the status of an Overseas Territory in 1958.

Area 4000 km² (1544 sq mi); **Population:** 166,000; **Capital:** Papeete; **Per capita GNP:** US$6350.

GABON, a republic on the equator in west-central Africa. Behind the coastal plain are plateaux and mountains. Most of Gabon is in the River Ogooué drainage basin. Average annual temperatures are between 26°C and 28°C (79°–82°F). The average annual rainfall varies from 1500 mm (59 in) in the south-west to 4000 mm (157 in) in the north-west. Rain forests cover 75 per cent of the land. About 40 languages are spoken: the Bantu-speaking Fang form the largest ethnic group; a few pygmies form the smallest. About 70 per cent of the population is engaged in agriculture, the chief cash crops being cocoa, coffee, palm oil and bananas. But the main wealth of Gabon, which has the 2nd highest per capita GNP in Africa, comes from oil and natural gas, manganese and uranium. France established a settlement on the coast in 1843 and founded Libreville for free slaves in 1849. Gabon became a French colony in the 1880s and an independent republic in 1980. Many people visit Gabon to see the Nobel prize winner Dr Schweitzer's mission hospital at Lambaréné, which was founded in 1910.

Area: 267,667 km² (103,352 sq mi); **Population:** 1,245,000; **Capital:** Libreville (pop 350,000); **Highest point:** Mt Iboundji, 1580 m (5184 ft); **Official language:** French; **Religions:** Roman Catholicism (60 per cent), Protestantism and local Christian sects (29 per cent), traditional beliefs (10 per cent), Islam (1 per cent); **Adult literacy rate:** 30 per cent; **Unit of currency:** Franc CFA; **Main exports:** oil, manganese, uranium and thorium, timber; **Per capita GNP:** US$3280.

GAMBIA, THE, in West Africa, is the smallest nation in mainland Africa, only 24–48 km (15–30 miles) wide. It is a narrow strip of land bordering the Gambia River, being entirely enclosed by Senegal except along its short Atlantic coast. The climate is tropical, with an average annual temperature of 20°C (81°F) and an average annual rainfall of 750–1140 mm (30–45 in). The landscape is flat, with mangrove and low-lying forests covering the coastal areas, while the rest of the country is relatively dry and sandy. The largest of the 5 main ethnic groups are the Mandingo and the Fulbe (or Fulani). About 85 per cent of the population is engaged in agriculture, which accounts for 60 per cent of the GDP. The only major cash crop is groundnuts; they usually make up over 90 per cent of the exports. Other crops include cotton, fruit and vegetables. Manufactured products include soft drinks, clothing and brewing. Tourism is expanding rapidly. The majority of new hotels and tourist complexes are spread out along the south side of the River Gambia. The variety of birds found in the Gambia have meant that bird watching holidays have become increasingly popular. The Gambia became a British colony in 1888. Full independence was achieved in 1965 and the Gambia became a republic in 1970. Attempts to merge the Gambia and Senegal failed until 1981 when Senegalese troops helped to put down a coup in the Gambia. Following the coup, the Gambia and Senegal set up a confederation called Senegambia, which came into effect in 1982, although both countries retained their sovereignty.

Area: 11,295 km² (4361 sq mi); **Population:** 789,000; **Capital:** Banjul (pop 44,000); **Official language:** English; **Religions:** Islam (80 per cent), Christianity, traditional beliefs; **Adult literacy rate:** 35 per cent; **Average life expectancy at birth:** 41 years; **Unit of currency:** Dalasi; **Main exports:** groundnuts, groundnut products; **Per capita GNP:** US$260.

GERMANY, one of the largest and most important

The ancient city of Leipzig is a major industrial, commercial and cultural centre in eastern Germany. It is about 150 km (93 miles) south-south-west of Berlin. Leipzig is also known for its industrial fairs, and its old buildings and cultural life have recently been attracting many tourists.

countries in Europe. It was split into two countries, East and West Germany, from 1949 until 1990. Its Baltic sea coast is fringed by sand bars and lagoons, and the North Sea coast has sandy islands and dunes. The north is part of the North European Plain, which is largely covered by moraine deposited during the last Ice Age. In the east there are hills of boulder clay, between which there are many lakes and marshes, and vast areas of glacial sands. The natural vegetation over much of this area is moorland and heath, notably Luneburg Heath in the west. Although in the north the soil is generally not highly fertile, large areas have been cleared for farming. The southern part of the plain contains good soil, and is one of the most densely populated areas. The plain is drained by the Elbe, Weser and Ems rivers, and by the Oder-Neisse river system which forms the frontier with Poland. Most river valleys in this region run from south-east to north-west. They are wide and shallow, having been formed by melt waters from receding glaciers at the end of the Ice Age. They contain soft, fertile soil. Central Germany contains hills, plateaux and low block mountains, including the Harz Mountains and the Thüringerwald in the centre, and the Erzgibirge in the east. The northern foothills are a fertile loess belt. The leading region is the industrial Ruhr valley, with its rich coalfield. South-western Germany is the country's most important farming region. It includes block mountains, known as *horsts*, that border the valley of the River Rhine, which extends more than 300 km (186 mi) from Basle to Bingen. These mountainous regions include the Black Forest and the Odenwald. The Rhine is the most important river of western Europe. Rising in Switzerland, it forms part of Germany's borders

Above: Berliners congregate at the Brandenburg Gate along the wall that divided their city until Germany was reunified in 1990. Above right: The Rhine River Valley is a vital artery of German trade. Much of the valley is adorned by castles and pretty villages.

with Switzerland and France before it crosses the frontier with the Netherlands to flow into the North Sea. In its upper reaches it flows through spectacular gorges. The south-east is an upland zone which includes the scenic Bavarian Alps in the far south, where the highest peak, the Zugspitze, 2968 m (9738 ft), is situated. The Danube, which rises in the Black Forest, is Europe's second longest river after the Volga in the USSR. It flows eastward to the Black Sea, and drains much of south-eastern Germany. The climate of Germany is continental, with slightly warmer summers and colder winters in the north than in the south. Average annual temperatures range from −1°C in winter to 21°C in summer (30°F to 70°F). Rainfall is moderate, varying between 510 and 1020 mm (20–40 in) a year. About three-quarters of the people live in urban areas, working in industry and services. Germany is one of the most highly industrialized countries in Europe, though the eastern part lags behind the west as a result of years of communist rule. Manufacturing is more important in the east than the west in terms of contributions to the national economy. The main industrial regions are the Ruhr valley in the west, and the Dresden, Erfurt, Gera, Halle, Leipzig and Karl-Marx-Stadt (Chemnitz) districts in the east. Chemical and iron and steel industries underpin the economy. Other major industries include heavy engineering, electrical engineering, machinery, textiles, optical goods, plastics and vehicles. Germany is the world's fourth largest producer of coal, including lignite (soft coal) and has large deposits of potash. Lignite is used in the chemical industry, as is imported petroleum which has enabled industrial development in such cities as Munich and Nuremburg, far from any coalfield.

The main coalfields are the Ruhr, Aachen and Saar. Other mining outputs include copper, iron ore, nickel, petroleum, salt, tin and uranium. Many foreign or 'guests' workers are employed in the industries of the west, coming from Italy, Turkey, and countries of eastern Europe. The largest and most important cities include Berlin, formerly divided between East and West Germany, Bonn, Hamburg and Munich. The leading sea ports are Bremen and Hamburg, but the river port of Duisburg, at the meeting place of the Ruhr and Rhine rivers, handles a greater annual tonnage of shipping than Hamburg. From there ships ply to Europoort (Rotterdam) in the Netherlands, which handles a substantial part of German trade. Germany has a first-class transportation system. Rivers are linked by a network of canals, and carry a large part of Germany's heavy industrial traffic. Railroads link all the major cities. Germany has a fine system of highways called *Autobahns*. They were begun in the 1930s and have been greatly expanded since the end of World War II. Farms in the west are mostly small and are independently owned. Most of the eastern part of the country had large state-run collective farms, but the agricultural economy of the east is being brought into line with that of the west. The most fertile land is in the centre and the south. The main crops in the far north are potatoes and rye. The leading crops in the northern and central regions include barley, oats, potatoes, rye, sugar beet and wheat. In the south the people grow fruit, grapes for making wine, hops and tobacco. The south-east is mainly pastoral. Dairy products are especially important. Since the amalgamation of West and East Germany in 1990, it is difficult to estimate the proportion of workers employed in different industries, or the GDP, until the combined economy has settled down. Between the 4th and 6th centuries AD, German tribes conquered the western provinces of the Roman Empire. The Frankish ruler Charlemagne, who became Emperor of the West in 800, united German tribes into a *Reich* (empire), but it soon split again into a loose federation of principalities in the 9th century. In 962 King Otto I of Germany was crowned as emperor. From the 11th century to the 19th century this federation was known as the Holy Roman Empire. It was dominated by emperors from the House (family) of Habsburg. The Holy Roman Empire had a troubled history, with its boundaries constantly shifting. In the 12th century, German territory extended as far

67

as Prussia, but by the 15th century it was breaking up. During the reign of Charles V (1519–58) the empire had gained some cohesion but this was based more on dynastic principles than ecclesiastic ones. In 1555 the Protestant Reformation weakened the superficial unity of the empire irrecoverably when the Religious Peace of Augsburg permitted free cities and states to choose between Lutheranism and Catholicism. By 1600 the tension between the Catholic and Lutheran factions was great and in 1618 a Protestant revolt in Bohemia started the Thirty Years' War. The war weakened Germany physically and economically. At the end of the war though the combined electorate of Brandenburg and the Duchy of Prussia emerged as a strong Protestant state: its ruler Frederick took the title 'King of Prussia' in 1701. Prussia became a major European state. The Holy Roman Empire was finished, and in 1806, after Napoleon I of France conquered the country, the empire was declared abolished. It continued to be a loose federation of small states, known after 1815 as the German Conferation. It was finally united in 1871 following the Franco-Prussian War, in which Prussia, the most powerful state, defeated France. Prussia's king became *Kaiser* (emperor) of a new *Reich*. After World War I the Kaiser abdicated, and a republic was set up. In 1933 Adolf Hitler, leader of the National Socialist (Nazi) Party, became Chancellor, and proclaimed the Third *Reich*. Hitler's ambition for expansion led to World War II, in which Germany was defeated. After that war the country was split in two, the east dominated by the USSR, and the west by Britain, France and the USA. In 1949, West Germany became a federal republic, allied to western Europe and the USA, while east Germany became a Communist state, allied to the USSR. A treaty between the two Germanies in 1972 lessened tension and paved the way for their entry into the UN. In 1989 the Communist régime in East Germany collapsed and in October 1990 the two Germanies became one country again. West Germany was a founder member of the EC, to which the united Germany now belongs.

Area: 356,829 km² (137,773 sq mi); **Population:** 77,157,000; **Capital:** Berlin (pop 3,063,000); **Other cities:** Hamburg (1,653,000), Munich (1,300,000), Cologne (976,000), Essen (653,000) Frankfurt-am-Main (628,000), Dortmund (610,000), Düsseldorf (595,000), Stuttgart (582,000), Leipzig (564,000), Duisburg (559,000), Bremen (556,000), Hanover (536,000), Dresden (515,000), Karl-Marx-Stadt (Chemnitz, 315,000), Bonn (286,000), Magdeburg (284,000); **Highest point:** Zugspitze, 2968 m (9738 ft); **Official language:** German; **Religions:** Protestantism, Roman Catholicism; **Average life expectancy at birth:** 72; **Unit of currency:** Deutsche mark; **Main exports:** Engineering goods, precision instruments, optical equipment, chemicals, coke, consumer products and other manufactured goods.

GHANA, a republic in West Africa. It is mostly low-lying and contains the man-made Lake Volta, area, 8482 km² (3275 sq mi). The most fertile region is in the hilly south-west. The only highlands are in the south-east. The average annual tempera-

ture is 26°C (79°F) in the south and 28°C (82°F) in the north. The south-west has more than 2000 mm (79 in) of rain per year, the south-east has 730 mm (29 in), and the north 1080 mm (43 in). The people are Negroid: about 100 languages and dialects are spoken. Agriculture employs 54 per cent of the workforce, contributing 38 per cent of the GDP. The main crop and export is cocoa. Bauxite, diamonds, gold and manganese are mined, but manufacturing is small-scale. Portuguese mariners reached Ghana in 1471. The coast became a British colony in 1875 but the Ashanti prevented colonization of the interior until 1901. Independence was achieved in 1957 and Ghana became a republic in 1960. From 1966 to 1979 military and civilian regimes alternated. A new Constitution in 1979 led to the election of a civilian government, but this was overthrown in December 1981.

Area: 238,537 km² (92,105 sq mi); **Population:** 12,413,000; **Capital:** Accra (pop with suburbs, 738,000); **Highest point:** Mt Afadjato, 885 m (2904 ft); **Official language:** English; **Religions:** Christianity, traditional beliefs, Islam; **Adult literacy rate:** 30 per cent; **Average life expectancy at birth:** 48 years; **Unit of currency:** Cedi; **Main exports:** cocoa, timber, gold; **Per capita GNP:** US$400.

GIBRALTAR, A rocky limestone peninsula which rises sharply from the flat coast of south-west Spain at the eastern end of the narrow Strait of Gibraltar. It has always been very important strategically because of its position at the entrance to the Mediterranean. It has been a British dependency since 1713. A referendum was held in 1967 in an attempt to end British rule but nearly all Gibraltarians voted to retain the British connection. Spain continues to claim sovereignty. Britain has an important military base there which came into its own during both World Wars. The climate is Mediterranean in type, with temperatures that range from 13°–29°C (55°–85°F). Most people are of British, Genoese, Portuguese, Maltese or Spanish descent. English and Spanish are spoken, but English is the official language. British currency and local banknotes are used. There is no agriculture or mining. All food has to be imported. The dockyards, the government, the military base and tourism are the main sources of employment and fuel for the economy. Gibraltar's extensive limestone caves provide a natural habitat for the Barbary apes, the only native monkeys in Europe.

Area: 6.5 km² (2½ sq mi); **Population:** 35,000; **GNP per capita:** US$4320.

GREECE, a republic in south-eastern Europe. It contains the southern part of the mountainous and deeply indented Balkan peninsula and many islands. The southern Peloponnesus is linked to the north by the narrow Isthmus of Corinth. The 6.4 km (4 mi) long Corinth Canal cuts through the Isthmus, connecting the Gulf of Corinth to the Saronic Gulf. The northern part of the peninsula contains the Pindus Mts and Greece's highest peak, Mt Olympus. It also includes the Plain of Thessaly, the largest lowland apart from the coastal plains of Macedonia and Thrace in the north-east. Islands make up 20 per cent of the area of Greece. The Cyclades are 220 islands east of the Peloponnesus in the Aegean Sea. The South Sporades (or Dodecanese), including Rhodes, are Aegean islands nearer to Turkey than Greece. The North Sporades are north-east of Euboea. The Ionian Islands, including Corfu, lie off the west coast. In the south, the largest island, Crete, covers 8331 km² (3217 sq mi). The climate is Mediterranean, with hot, arid summers and mild, moist winters, but winters are severe in the mountains. Until recently most Greeks lived in tiny farming communities. But today 62 per cent of the population lives in urban areas, as opposed to 43 per cent in 1960. Industry now accounts for 31 per cent of the GDP compared with 17 per cent from agriculture. Mining is not important but Greece has many processing industries and manufactures are now the leading exports. Only one-third of the land is cultivable. Citrus fruits, grapes, olives, tobacco and wheat are major crops. In 1979 there were 8 million sheep, 4 million goats and nearly 1 million cattle. In 1978 5 million tourists visited Greece, providing much foreign exchange. The merchant navy, one of the world's largest, is another money-earner. Thousands of Greeks emigrate every year, finding work especially in Australia, West Germany and the US. Crete was the centre of the first Greek civilization (the Minoan) between about 3000 and 1400 BC. On the mainland, the Mycenean period (1580–1100 BC) ended when Dorians invaded the peninsula from the north. In about 750 BC the Greeks began to colonize the Mediterranean and trade brought wealth to Greece. Athens reached its peak in 461–431 BC but, in 338 BC, Macedonia became the dominant power. In 334–331 BC Alexander the Great conquered South-west Asia. In 146 BC Greece became a Roman province and, in AD 365, it became part of the East Roman (Byzantine) Empire, which collapsed when the Turks took Constantinople (Istanbul) in 1453. The Greeks rebelled against Turkey in the 1820s and became an independent monarchy in 1830. After World War II, when Greece was occupied by Germany, a civil war raged between communist and nationalist forces until 1949. From 1967 Greece was a military dictatorship. This regime collapsed in 1974 when it failed to stop the Turkish invasion of northern Cyprus. Democracy was restored and Greece became a republic. Greece joined the EC in 1981.

Area: 131,944 km² (50,947 sq mi); **Population:** 10,044,000; **Capital:** Athens (pop with suburbs, 3,027,000; **Others cities:** Salonika (346,000); **Highest point:** Mt Olympus, 2917 m (9570 ft); **Official language:** Greek; **Religion:** Eastern Orthodox Christianity (98 per cent). **Adult literacy rate:** 88 per cent (1972 est); **Average life expectancy at birth:** 73 years, **Unit of currency:** Drachma; **Main exports:** manufactured goods, food and live animals, raw materials, beverages and tobacco, chemicals; **Per capita GNP:** US$3890.

GREENLAND, a self-governing Danish county. It is the world's largest island and contains the world's 2nd largest ice sheet: only 341,700 km² (131,938 sq mi), or 16 per cent of the land, is ice-free. The main industry is fishing. Vikings founded a colony in Greenland in about AD 960 but it disappeared about 500 years later. Greenland became a Danish colony in 1721 and a Danish county in 1953. A 21-member parliament was elected in 1979.

Area: 2,175,600 km² (840,050 sq mi); **Population:** 50,000; **Capital:** Godthaab (pop 9000); **Per capita GNP:** US$7990.

GRENADA, a West Indian nation, the southernmost in the Windward Islands. The land is mountainous and largely forested. Temperatures remain around 27 °C (81 °F) throughout the year. Descendants of African slaves form the largest ethnic group. Most of the rest are of mixed black and European descent. The main exports are cocoa, nutmegs and bananas. Tourism is becoming important. Columbus discovered the island in 1498. In 1674–1763 it was a French colony. Thereafter, except for a period of French rule in 1779–83, it was ruled by Britain. It became a British Associated State in 1967 and a fully independent monarchy in the Commonwealth in 1974.

The skyline of Athens, capital of Greece, is dominated by the Acropolis, a rocky hill on which the ruins of the Parthenon and other ancient temples testify to 'the glory that was Greece'.

Greenland is thinly populated and ice sheets cover more than four-fifths of its area. Fishing is the leading industry and tiny fishing villages are scattered along its fiord-strewn coasts.

Area: 344 km² (133 sq mi); **Population:** 113,000; **Capital:** St George's (pop 30,000); **Official language:** English; **Per capita GNP:** US$630.

GUADELOUPE, a French Overseas Department in the Lesser Antilles. There are two main islands, Basse-Terre (or Guadeloupe) and Grande-Terre, and five small ones. Mt Soufriére, a volcano on Basse-Terre, is 1467 m (4813 ft) high. Temperatures exceed 24°C (75°F) for most of the time and the rainfall is more than 2000 mm (79 in) per year. Most people are of mixed African, Asian and French descent. Bananas and sugar are the main crops. Columbus discovered the islands in 1493. France colonized them in 1635 but had to fight off British attacks and put down a slave revolt in 1703. Slavery was abolished in 1848. Guadeloupe became a French Overseas Department in 1946.

Area: 1779 km² (687 sq mi); **Population:** 332,000; **Capital:** Basse-Terre (pop 15,000); **Per capita GNP:** US$3260.

GUAM, an 'unincorporated territory' of the United States in the Marianas Archipelago in the North Pacific Ocean. There are volcanic mountains in the south of the island and coral reefs in the north. The climate is tropical and crops include bananas, cassava, citrus fruits, coconuts, maize, sugar-cane, sweet potatoes and taro. Fishing is important and tourism is developing. Many people are Chamorros, of mixed Indonesian and Spanish descent. Spain ceded Guam to the US in 1898. The island was occupied by Japan in 1941–44. Full US citizenship for Guam's people was conferred in 1950.

Area: 549 km² (212 sq mi); **Population:** 120,000; **Capital:** Agaña; **Per capita GNP:** US$7830.

GUATEMALA, a Central American republic. Coastal lowlands face the Pacific Ocean in the south-west; a central highland region with 27 volcanoes, some active, is in the earthquake-prone centre; a low forested plain covers the north; and there is a short Caribbean coastline. The altitude modifies the climate. The capital, at about 1500 m (4291 ft), has average temperatures between 16°C and 20°C (61°–68°F) and 1320 mm (52 in) of rain per year. The lowlands are hotter and generally wetter. More than 50 per cent of the people are Indians; most of the rest are mixed European and Indian origin. In 1978 57 per cent of the people were farmers, mainly in the highlands. Coffee is the main crop. Mining is becoming important, especially for nickel. Spain conquered the area in the 1520s. Guatemala became independent in 1821 but attempts to form a Central American Federation failed and Guatemala became an independent republic in 1839. Dictatorships and violence have marred its modern history. In the 1970s Guatemala came into conflict with Britain over its claims on Belize, which was a British territory until 1981.

Area: 108,889 km² (42,045 sq mi); **Population:** 8,935,000; **Capital:** Guatemala City (pop 1,500,000); **Highest point:** Tajumulco, 4220 m (13,845 ft); **Official language:** Spanish; **Religion:** Roman Catholicism; **Adult literacy rate:** 47 per cent; **Average life expectancy at birth:** 57 years; **Unit of currency:** Quetzal; **Main exports:** coffee, cotton, bananas, beef; **Per capita GNP:** US$1020.

GUINEA, a West African republic. Behind the Atlantic coastal plain is the Fouta Djallon plateau, where the Gambia, Niger and Senegal rivers rise. The north-east contains the Upper Niger plains, while the south-east is mountainous, rising to Mt Nimba on the border. Guinea has a tropical monsoon climate and savanna covers most areas. Most people are Negroes and a large number of tribal languages are spoken. In 1978 82 per cent of the population was engaged in agriculture, which accounted for 32 per cent of the GDP. Industry accounted for 41 per cent of the GDP in 1978. The leading industry is bauxite mining: Guinea is the world's 2nd largest producer. France annexed part of Guinea in 1849 and gradually extended its rule. In 1958 the people of Guinea voted for independence. France withdrew its personnel and equipment rapidly and chaos was prevented only with Ghanaian and Soviet aid. Guinea adopted socialist policies and a one-party system of government. Despite attempted coups, Guinea's first president, Sékou Touré, survived until 1984. A military government took over. Most people remained poor.

Area: 245,957 km² (94,970 sq mi); **Population:** 6,706,000; **Capital:** Conakry (pop 736,000); **Highest point:** Mt Nimba, 1752 m (5748 ft); **Official language:** French; **Religions:** Islam (70 per cent), traditional beliefs, Christianity; **Adult literacy rate:** 10 per cent (1970); **Average life expectancy at birth:** 43 years; **Unit of currency:** Syli; **Main exports:** bauxite and aluminium, palm kernels, pineapples, coffee; **Per capita GNP:** US$270.

GUINEA-BISSAU, a West African republic. The land is mostly low-lying, with a broad coastal plain and flat offshore islands. It has a tropical monsoon climate. Most people are Negroes belonging to various tribal groups. There is a small mestiço (mulatto) community of Guinean and Cape Verdean descent. It has played an important part in the government. Most people are subsistence farmers, although arable land covers only 12 per cent of the country. The main food crop is rice; the main cash crop is groundnuts. There is no mining and little manufacturing. Portuguese explorers first sighted the coast in 1446. In 1836–79 Portugal ruled the country jointly with the Cape Verde Islands, establishing close ties that were to continue. A long guerrilla war began in 1963, led by Guineans and Cape Verdeans. Guinea-Bissau became independent in 1974, followed by Cape Verde in 1975, although no fighting had occurred on the islands. Guinea-Bissau became a one-party socialist state. A military coup in 1980 caused a deterioration in relations with Cape Verde. A new constitution was adopted in 1984.

Area: 36,125 km² (13,949 sq mi); **Population:** 929,000; **Capital:** Bissau (pop 109,000); **Official language:** Portuguese; **Religious:** Islam, traditional beliefs, Christianity; **Adult literacy rate:** 25 per cent; **Average life expectancy at birth:** 39

years; **Unit of currency:** Escudo; **Main exports:** groundnuts, fish; **Per capita GNP:** US$170.

GUYANA, a republic in north-eastern South America. Behind the flat, cultivated coastal zone, which is about 48 km (30 mi) wide, the land rises to a hilly upland and then to the Guiana Highlands in the east and south. Forest covers 83 per cent of the land with grassland in the highest mountain areas. The main river is the Essequibo. The climate is tropical and the rainfall varies between 2290 mm (90 in) on the coast to 1470 mm (58 in) inland. Most people live in the coastal zone: 51 per cent are of Asian origin; 33 per cent are descendants of African slaves; about 10 per cent are of mixed origin; and 5 per cent are Indians who live mostly in the forested interior. Antagonism between the two main groups has been reflected in political life. Bauxite is the main resource. The chief cash crop is sugar and the main food crop is rice. The Dutch and British struggled for ascendancy in the 17th and 18th centuries. The territory was finally ceded to Britain in 1814. Independence was achieved in 1966. The 1980 Constitution provided for a 53-member National Assembly.

Area: 214,969 km² (83,005 sq mi); **Population:** 887,000; **Capital:** Georgetown (pop with suburbs, 183,000); **Highest point:** Mt Roraima, 2810 m (9219 ft); **Official language:** English; **Religions:** Christianity (over 50 per cent), Hinduism (33 per cent), Islam (10 per cent); **Unit of currency:** Guyanese dollar; **Main exports:** bauxite and alumina, sugar and byproducts, rice, timber; **Per capita GNP:** US$570.

HAITI, a republic in the western part of the West Indian island of Hispaniola. The interior consists of wooded mountains: the Massif du Nord, the Massif de la Selle (in the south-east), and the Massif de la Hotte (in the south-west), Most people live on the fertile plains which make up about one-fifth of the country. About 95 per cent of the population is of black African descent. The mulattoes who form 5 per cent make up a social elite. Most people are subsistence farmers. The chief cash crops are coffee and sugar. Haiti is the poorest nation in Latin America. Columbus discovered Hispaniola in 1492 and Spain became established in the east (now the Dominican Republic), while France took the west in 1697. Independence was proclaimed in 1804 after a successful slave revolt in the 1790s. Haiti had a disturbed history in 1843–1915 when 16 of its 20 rulers were either deposed or assassinated. The US occupied Haiti from 1915 to 1934. In 1957 François Duvalier became president, assuming dictatorial powers and maintaining his power through voodoo and secret police. He died in 1971 and his son, Jean-Claude Duvalier, succeeded him. Jean-Claude was overthrown in 1986. A succession of military and civilian governments followed.

Area: 27,750 km² (10,715 sq mi); **Population:** 6,216,000; **Capital:** Port-au-Prince (pop 719,000); **Highest point:** Pic La Selle, 2680 m (8793 ft); **Official language:** French; **Religions:** Roman Catholicism, Protestantism; **Adult literacy rate:**

23 per cent; **Average life expectancy at birth:** 51 years; **Unit of currency:** Gourde; **Main exports:** coffee, manufactures; **Per capita GNP:** US$260.

HONDURAS, a wedge-shaped Central American republic. It has a 720 km (447 mi) coastline on the Caribbean Sea and an outlet to the Pacific Ocean through the Gulf of Fonseca. Behind the hot and humid Caribbean coastal plain, there are mountains and high plateaux with a healthy climate. Most Hondurans are of mixed European and Indian origin. About 8 per cent are pure Indians and 2 per cent are Negroes. Honduras is Central America's poorest nation. In 1978 64 per cent of the people were engaged in agriculture, which accounted for 32 per cent of the GDP. Bananas and coffee are the main cash crops. Forests cover 45 per cent of the country and timber is exported. Some lead, zinc and silver are also exported and there are many, mostly small, manufacturing and processing industries. Spain ruled Honduras between 1525 and 1821. It became part of a Central American Federation but it withdrew in 1838. Independent Honduras suffered from dictatorships and frequent revolutions. In the 1980s Nicaraguan rebels set up bases in Honduras for raids on Nicaragua. Free presidential elections took place in 1989.

Area: 112,088 km² (43,280 sq mi); **Population:** 4,952,000; **Capital:** Tegucigalpa (pop 571,000); **Highest point:** Cerros de Celaque, 2865 m (9400 ft); **Official language:** Spanish; **Religion:** Roman Catholicism; **Adult literacy rate:** 57 per cent; **Average life expectancy at birth:** 57 years; **Unit of currency:** Lempira; **Main exports:** bananas, coffee, meat, timber; **Per capita GNP:** US$530.

HONG KONG, a British colony on the south-eastern coast of China, consisting of 236 islands and an area on the mainland. Most of the land is rocky and hilly. The climate is tropical with heavy monsoon rains in May–September. Most people are Chinese; some are refugees from Communist China. There is little farmland in this densely populated colony (90 per cent of the population lives in urban areas) and much food is imported although every possible piece of land is farmed. Fishing is also important (many people live on boats), but the economy is based on manufacturing and entrepôt trade. A great variety of light manufactures are exported to Western nations, bringing much wealth to Hong Kong. Hong Kong Island was ceded to Britain in 1842. Kowloon peninsula was added in 1860, and the New Territories, on the mainland, were leased from China in 1898. In 1984 Britain agreed to transfer Hong Kong to Chinese rule in 1997.

Area: 1045 km² (403 sq mi); **Population:** 5,659,000; **Capital:** Victoria (pop 767,000); **Adult literacy rate:** 90 per cent; **Average life expectancy at birth:** 72 years; **Unit of currency:** Hong Kong dollar; **Main exports:** a wide range of light manufactures; **Per capita GNP:** US$4000.

HUNGARY, a landlocked socialist republic in eastern Europe. It is mostly low-lying and drained by the Danube and the Tisza, its tributary. The

Iceland is dotted with volcanoes, geysers and hot springs, barren lava fields, ice caps and valley glaciers. There are more than 100 volcanoes, including clusters of craters like those in the picture, and about one out of every four volcanoes has erupted in historic times. The reason for all this volcanic activity is that Iceland straddles the northern part of the mid-Atlantic ridge, along which new coastal rock is being formed. This addition of this rock is slowly widening the Atlantic Ocean and Iceland itself.

fertile, hilly Little Alföld is in the north-west. It is separated from the Great Alföld, or Hungarian Plain (56 per cent of the country), by a limestone ridge, the Bakony Forest. Low mountains northeast of Budapest are renowned for their wine. Winters are cold and summers hot. The rainfall averages 635 mm (25 in) on the plains, and 790 mm (31 in) on the uplands. Hungarians, or Magyars, are of Finno-Ugric and Turkic descent, mixed with local peoples. In 1980 64 per cent of the population lived in urban areas. Industry, which has developed rapidly in the last 30 years, accounted for 59 per cent of the GDP in 1978. Bauxite, coal and some other minerals are produced, but many raw materials must be imported. More than 50 per cent of the factories, all of which are nationalized, are in or around Budapest. Farming employs 18 per cent of the workforce and accounts for 15 per cent of the GDP. Arable land, orchards and vineyards cover 53 per cent of the land, pasture 14 per cent and forests 17 per cent. Maize and wheat are the main crops. There are about 2 million cattle, 2.8 million sheep, 8 million pigs and 63 million poultry. Hungary and Austria jointly controlled the Austro-Hungarian Empire from 1867 until it broke up in 1918. In World War II Hungary supported Germany but when it tried to negotiate a separate armistice, it was invaded by German troops. Soviet forces occupied Hungary in 1945 and a communist government was in power by 1948. In 1956 Russian troops put down a revolt. In 1989 the Communists were overthrown and free elections were held in 1990.

Area: 93,030 km² (35,921 sq mi); **Population:** 10,850,000; **Capital:** Budapest (pop 2,093,000); **Highest point:** Mt Kékes, 1015 m (3330 ft); **Official language:** Magyar (Hungarian); **Religions:** Roman Catholicism (50 per cent), Protestantism; **Adult literacy rate:** 98 per cent; **Average life expectancy at birth:** 70 years; **Unit of currency:** Forint; **Main exports:** transport equipment, electrical goods, bauxite and aluminium, food, pharmaceuticals, wine; **Per capita GNP:** US$3850.

ICELAND, an island republic in the North Atlantic Ocean. Large snowfields, glaciers, volcanoes, hot springs (which are used to heat homes in Reykjavik) and a deeply indented coastline are features of this rugged island. The warm North Atlantic Drift keeps the southern coats ice-free in winter. Summers are cool. Less than 1 per cent of the land is cultivated; the main crops are hay, potatoes and turnips. Iceland has about 57,000 cattle and 797,000 sheep, but fishing is the main industry. Norewegian Vikings colonized Iceland in AD 874. In 1262 it was united with Norway and, in 1380, it came under Denmark. Independence was achieved in 1918 although it stayed under the nominal rule of the Danish monarch. It became a republic in 1944. Between 1958 and 1976 it was involved in various fishing disputes. In 1963 it acquired a new volcanic island, Surtsey, which appeared from the sea near Iceland.

Area: 103,000 km² (39,771 sq mi); **Population:** 254,000; **Capital:** Reykjavik (pop 96,000); **Highest point:** Oraefajökull, 2119 m (6952 ft); **Official language:** Icelandic; **Religion:** Evangelical Lutheran; **Unit of currency:** Krona; **Main exports:** fish and whale products; **Per capita GNP:** US$10,490.

INDIA, the world's 7th largest nation, but the 2nd largest in terms of population. The Himalayan mountains in the north include India's highest peak, Nanda Devi. In the north-west Kashmir contains parts of the Karakoram and Hindu Kush ranges. The Indus, Ganges and Brahmaputra rivers rise in the Himalayas and reach the sea via broad alluvial plains. The fertile northern plains of India are densely populated. To the south, the Vindhya range borders the Deccan, a huge, triangular-shaped plateau. It is bounded by two other ranges: the Western Ghats and the lower Eastern Ghats. The main rivers, the Cauvery, Krishna and Godavari, flow from west to east into the Bay of Bengal. The climate and vegetation vary greatly. The highest mountains have an Arctic climate; the Thar desert borders Pakistan; Cherrapunji in the north-east holds the world rainfall record for one year – 26,461 mm (1041.7 in) were recorded in 1860–61; and the Deccan lies in the tropics. Most of India has three seasons: winter in October-February when it is cool and dry; the hot season in March–June when temperatures reach 49°C (120°F) in the northern plains; and the rainy season, June–September, when monsoon winds are drawn into

The river Ganges which drains the northern alluvial plains of India is regarded as sacred by Hindus, who make up just over four-fifths of India's population. Pilgrims visit the holy city of Varanasi on the Ganges to bathe in the water, regarding this as a form of spiritual cleansing. Religion plays a vital part in Indian life, as shown by the Hindu prohibition on the slaughter of cattle. Non-violence, as advocated by Mahatma Gandhi in the struggle for independence, and respect for life, are basic Hindu principles.

eastern India from the south-west. Hundreds of languages are spoken in India, but the government recognizes only 15 national languages: Assamese, Bengali, Gujerati, Hindi, Kannada, Kashmiri, Malayalam, Marathi, Oriya, Punjabi, Sanskrit, Sindhi, Tamil, Telegu and Urdu. India is a mainly poor agricultural nation; only $22\frac{1}{2}$ per cent of the population lived in urban areas in 1980. In 1978 agriculture employed 74 per cent of the workforce and accounted for 40 per cent of the GDP (industry for 26 per cent and services 34 per cent). India is the world's top producer of groundnuts, hemp (fibre), sugar-cane and tea; the 2nd leading producer of millet, rice and sorghum; the 3rd largest producer of coconuts, copra and tobacco; and the 4th producer of cotton and wheat. It has more cattle (182 million) than any other nation, but Hinduism forbids their slaughter. India has various minerals, including bauxite, coal, iron ore and manganese. Manufacturing has expanded greatly since 1947; the chief products are textiles, but there is also much heavy industry. Most Indians are descendants of the original Dravidians and the Aryans who invaded India in about 1500 BC. India gave birth to several religions, including Hinduism, Buddhism, Jainism and Sikhism. The Muslim Mughal Empire was founded in 1526, but it declined in the 17th century. The British East India Company became the dominant European trading group in India in 1757 and, in 1858, Britain took over the rule of India. Independence was achieved in 1947 when British India was partitioned into the mainly Hindu India and the Muslim Pakistan. India became a republic in 1950. It was controlled by the Congress Party from 1952 to 1977, and from 1980 to 1989. In the late 1980s there was ethnic violence in Assam State between Hindus and Muslim immigrants.

Area: 3,287,590 km² (1,269,415 sq mi); **Population:** 813,445,000; **Capital:** Delhi (pop 5,729,000); **Other cities:** Calcutta (9,194,000), Bombay (8,227,000), Madras (4,289,000), Bangalore (2,921,000), Hyderabad (2,187,000), Ahmadabad (2,059,000), Kanpur (1,482,000), Nagpur (1,215,000), Pune (1,203,000); **Highest point:** Nanda Devi, 7817 m (25,646 ft); **Official languages:** Hindi, English; **Religions:** Hinduism (82.7 per cent), Islam (11.2 per cent), Christianity (2.6 per cent), Sikhism (1.9 per cent), Buddhism (0.7 per cent), Jainism (0.5 per cent); **Adult literacy rate:** 36 per cent; **Average life expectancy at birth:** 51 years; **Unit of currency:** Rupee; **Main exports:** textiles, jute, tea; **Per capita GNP:** US$190.

INDONESIA, an island republic in South-East Asia. The largest regions are Kalimantan (part of Borneo), Sumatra, West Irian (part of New Guinea), Sulawesi (Celebes) and Java, the most densely populated island. There are many mountain ranges and more active volcanoes than in any other country: 77 have erupted in recent times. The climate is equatorial, hot and wet all the year round. Rain forests cover large areas. Most people are of Malay origin, mixed with Melanesians and Australasians, and at least 70 languages are spoken: In 1980 20 per cent of the population lived in urban areas. Agriculture employs 60 per cent of the workforce, accounting for 31 per cent of the GDP (33 per cent came from industry and 36 per cent from services). Rice is the main food. Coffee, copra, palm oil and kernels, rubber, tea and tobacco are major cash crops. Forestry is important. Indonesia is the leading oil producer in the Far East. Manufacturing is important, including shipbuilding, textiles, cement and chemicals. Indonesian princes adopted Islam in the 16th century as a political weapon against the Portuguese traders. It gradually replaced Hinduism. Dutch influence began in the late 16th century and the territory became Dutch in 1799. The Republic of Indonesia was formed in 1949. In 1957 army officers revolted because of communist influence in the government: a civil war continued until 1961. The formation of Malaysia in 1963 led to fighting between the two nations in 1964. A communist attempt to overthrow the government failed in 1965. Military leaders seized power in 1966, outlawing the Communist Party and ending confrontation with Malaysia. East (formerly Portuguese) Timor was incorporated into Indonesia in 1976.

Area: 2,027,087 km² (782,705 sq mi); **Population:** 178,505,000; **Capital:** Djakarta (pop 6,506,000); **Other cities:** Surabaya (1,762,000), Bandung (1,265,000), Semarang (916,000); **Highest point:** Djaja Peak (Mt Carstensz), 5030 m (16,503 ft); **Official language:** Bahasa Indonesian; **Religions:**

Islam (80 per cent), Christianity, Hinduism, Buddhism; **Adult literacy rate:** 62 per cent; **Average life expectancy at birth:** 47 years; **Unit of currency:** Rupiah; **Main exports:** oil (73 per cent), coffee, rubber, palm products, tin, tea, tobacco; **Per capita GNP:** US$380.

IRAN, a republic in south-western Asia. Around a barren plateau, which contains the Dasht e Kavir (Great Salt Desert) and the Dasht e Lut (Great Sand Desert), are mountains: the highest are the northern Elburz Mts; the Zagros Mts in the west and south; and several ranges in the east. The only fertile areas are near the Caspian Sea and in mountain foothills. The central plateau is arid and hot, but the Zagros Mts can be bitterly cold. Rainfall in the Caspian Sea region is about 2000 mm (79 in) per year; the south-east is arid. About 90 per cent of the people are Shia Muslims. Ethnically, two-thirds of the people are Persian in type and one-fourth are Turki. There are some Arabs and Sunni Muslim Kurds live in the north. In 1980 50 per cent of the population lived in urban areas. Industry, mainly oil and gas production, accounted for 54 per cent of the GDP in 1978, as opposed to 9 per cent from agriculture, although 40 per cent of the people were farmers. Cereals, fruit, cotton and tobacco are grown. Income from oil has been used to develop heavy industries and improve social services. Ancient Persia was a powerful empire between 550 and 330 BC. The country was Islamized in AD 641. Later it was invaded by Turks and Mongols. In the 19th century Britain and France competed for influence. In 1925 the Pahlavi family took power. In 1979 the Shah, Mohammad Reza Pahlavi, left Iran after much rioting. A religious leader, Ayatollah Khomeini, exiled since 1964, returned and Iran became an Islamic Republic. War broke out between Iran and Iraq in 1980, continuing until 1988.

Area: 1,648,000 km² (636,331 sq mi); **Population:** 53,141,000; **Capital:** Tehran (pop 5,734,000); **Other cities:** Esfahan (672,000), Mashhad (670,000), Tabriz (599,000); **Highest point:** Mt Damavand, 5604 m (18,386 ft); **Official language:** Persian (Farsi); **Religion:** Islam; **Adult literacy rate:** 50 per cent; **Average life expectancy at birth:** 52 years; **Unit of currency:** Rial; **Main exports:** oil, natural gas, cotton; **Per capita GNP:** US$2160 (1977).

IRAQ, a republic in south-western Asia. It contains Mesopotamia, the valleys of the Tigris and Euphrates rivers where the ancient civilizations of Babylonia and Assyria arose. There are swamps in the south where the two rivers join, deserts in the west and mountains in the north-east. Summers are hot and winters cool. The rainfall is generally 250 mm (10 in), but more falls on the uplands. More than half of the people are Shia Muslims. In 1978 72 per cent of the people lived in urban areas, as compared with 43 per cent in 1960. Oil production dominates the economy. The main crops are dates, cereals, pulses and cotton. Iraq was Islamized in AD 637 and, in 1638, it became part of the Ottoman Empire. British forces occupied Iraq in World War I and stayed until it became an independent mon-

archy in 1932. Since the 1950s oil production has provided income for developing social services. In 1958, however, the monarchy was overthrown and the army established a republic. Fighting with the Sunni Muslim Kurds in the north broke out 1960s, and continued on and off into the 1980s. In 1979 Saddam Hussein became president, and led his country into an abortive, eight-year war with Iran. In 1990 Iraq invaded neighbouring Kuwait and declared the state annexed. The United Nations ordered Iraq to withdraw, and when it refused a military campaing to liberate Kuwait, code named *Operation Desert Storm*, began early in 1991. Iraq withdrew several weeks later.

Area: 434,924 km² (167,934 sq mi); **Population:** 17,610,000; **Capital:** Baghdad (pop 3,206,000). **Other cities:** Basrah (334,000), Mosul (293,000); **Official language:** Arabic; **Religion:** Islam; **Average life expectancy at birth:** 55 years; **Unit of currency:** Iraqui dinar; **Main exports:** oil, iron ore, copper; **Per capita GNP:** US$2410.

IRELAND, REPUBLIC OF, occupies 80 per cent of the island of Ireland. It contains 26 counties, divided into 4 provinces: Connacht, Leinster, Munster and Ulster. But the 6 north-eastern counties of Ulster constitute Northern Ireland, which is part of the United Kingdom. Central Ireland is a moraine-covered lowland, containing areas of peat bog and some rich farmland. A broken rim of uplands surrounds the plain. The highest peak, Carrantuohill, is in scenic County Kerry in the south-west. The River Shannon, 386 km (240 mi) long, is the longest river in the British Isles. Along its course are several lakes, including Lough Ree and Lough Derg. Ireland has mild, wet winters and cool, wet summers. The average annual temperature range is around 5°–15°C (41°–59°F). The uplands have an average annual rainfall of 1020 to 1520 mm (40–60 in) and the lowlands about 760 mm (30 in). Most people are of Celtic or mixed Celtic and English descent. About 20 per cent speak Irish, but English is used in daily life. In 1980 58 per cent of the population lived in urban areas. In 1978 20 per cent were employed in agriculture, 37 per cent in industry and 43 per cent in services. But farming forms the basis of the economy. Arable land and pasture cover two-thirds of the land. Major crops are barley, hay, oats, potatoes, sugar beet and wheat. In 1979 there were 7.1 million cattle, 3.4 million sheep and 1.1 million pigs. There are many processing industries. The only large-scale manufacturing industries are in Dublin and Cork: most of the minerals and raw materials needed are imported. Fishing employs about 9000 men. Tourism is important: nearly 10 million people visited Ireland in 1979. Celts from France and Spain settled in Ireland in the early 4th century BC. Christianity was introduced by St Patrick in AD 432. Vikings arrived in about 795, but most of them were driven out in the 11th century. The Normans invaded Ireland in the 12th century and the island came under English rule. Much of Ireland's subsequent history was concerned with a struggle against English rule and, from the 1530s, the preservation of Roman Catholicism. In 1801 the Act of Union created the

Top left: Iran is an Islamic nation as exemplified by this mosque at Isfahan. Top right: Rural Ireland *has great charm. Above: The Dome of the Rock in Jerusalem contains a rock on which Abraham supposedly prepared to sacrifice Isaac.*

United Kingdom of Great Britain and Ireland. A potato famine in the 1840s, caused by a blight, led to the deaths of more than a million Irish people; another million emigrated. In 1916 there was an uprising in Dublin (the Easter Rebellion) which was put down. In 1919–21 the Irish fought for independence, finally achieving dominion status as the Irish Free State. Northern Ireland remained part of the UK. Ireland became a republic in 1949 and it joined the EC in 1973. In 1990 it elected its first woman president, Mary Robinson.

Area: 70,283 km² (27,138 sq mi); **Population:** 3,601,000; **Capital:** Dublin (pop 545,000); **Other cities:** Cork (139,000), Limerick (61,000); **Highest point:** Carrantuohill, 1042 m (3419 ft); **Official languages:** Irish, English; **Religion:** mainly Roman Catholicism; **Adult literacy rate:** 98 per cent; **Average life expectancy at birth:** 73 years; **Unit of currency:** Pound; **Main exports:** dairy products, meat and meat products, beer, whiskey; **Per capita GNP:** US$4230.

ISRAEL, a Middle Eastern republic created in 1948. The Galilee highlands containing Mt Meron are in the north. To the east is an extension of the East African Rift Valley, enclosing the Sea of Galilee (Lake Tiberias), the River Jordan and, in the south, the Dead Sea whose shoreline is 393 m (1289 ft) below sea level, the world's lowest point

on land. South of the Galilee Highlands are fertile plains and hilly regions. The Negev in the far south is desert. The coast has a Mediterranean climate; the rainfall decreases inland and to the south. More than 80 per cent of the people are Jews: the rest are Arabs. In 1980 89 per cent of the population lived in urban areas. In 1978 agriculture accounted for 7 per cent of the GDP, industry 37 per cent and services 57 per cent. Israel makes most industrial products and diamond finishing is the most valuable industry. Farming is efficient because of extensive irrigation and co-operative and collective farming methods. Cereals, citrus fruits, cotton, olives, tobacco and vegetables are important. About 1.1 million tourists visited Israel in 1979. Israel did not exist as a state for about 2500 years before 1948. Some Jews have always lived in Palestine, but most Israelis are descendants of settlers since the 1880s or recent immigrants. Britain ruled Palestine from 1917 but withdrew in 1948 when Israelis fought against their Arab neighbours, holding most of Palestine. In short Arab-Israeli wars in 1956, 1967 and 1973, Israel gained Arab territory. Though it returned Sinai to Egypt, it held on to land seized from Jordan and Syria.

Area: 20,770 km² (8020 sq mi); **Population:** 4,447,000; **Capital:** Jerusalem (pop 424,000); **Other cities:** Tel-Aviv/Jaffa (336,000), Haifa (229,000); **Highest point:** Mt Meron, 1208 m (3963 ft); **Official languages:** Hebrew, Arabic; **Religions:** Judaism, Islam; **Adult literacy rate:** 88 per cent; **Average life expectancy at birth:** 72 years; **Unit of currency:** Shekel; **Main exports:** cut diamonds, chemical and oil products, beverages and tobacco, citrus fruits; **Per capita GNP:** US$4170.

75

ITALY, a republic in southern Europe. It consists largely of a 1220 km (758 mi) long peninsula projecting like a boot between the Adriatic Sea to the east and the Ligurian and Tyrrhenian seas to the west. The scenic Alps, Italy's highest region, form a broad arc in the north. They overlook the North Italian plain which consists mainly of the River Po drainage basin. This is Italy's most densely populated region. The Po is Italy's longest river – it is about 650 km (404 mi) long. The Apennine Mts occupy much of peninsular Italy. Their highest point is Monte Corno, 2914 m (9560 ft) high, north-east of Rome. Within the Apennines are many fertile valleys and basins, and there are some rich coastal plains. Most rivers are short. The most important are the Arno on which Florence stands and the Tiber which flows through Rome. In the south-west are a series of volcanoes: Vesuvius, 1277 m (4190 ft) is near the port of Naples; Stromboli and Vulcano in the Lipari Islands; and Etna, Europe's highest volcano, reaches 3363 m (11,033 ft) in Sicily. Sicily is the largest of Italy's 70 or so islands, covering 25,708 km² (9926 sq mi). Southern Italy is subject to earthquakes: it lies near a subduction zone in the Earth's crust. Italy's second largest island is Sardinia to the west. This rugged island covers 24,090 km² (9302 sq mi). Southern Italy has hot, dry summers and mild winters. Winter rainfall is highest in the mountains and it increases northwards. Winters are colder in the more continental North Italian plain, where temperatures in January average between 1°C and 3°C (34°–37°F). The Alps are cold and snowy. In 1980 69 per cent of the population lived in urban areas. In 1978 industry accounted for 42 per cent of the GDP, agriculture for 7 per cent and services for 51 per cent. Oil and natural gas are extracted in the North Italian plain and in Sicily, but oil and coal have to be imported. Hydro-electric projects are numerous and 32 per cent of Italy's total electricity supply came from hydro-electric plants in 1977. Generally, Italy lacks minerals and metal ores are major imports. Leading industrial products include

Many of Italy's cities are museums of history and architecture. Left: The Forum at Rome recalls the days when the city was the capital of the western world. Above: Superb medieval buildings in Venice can be viewed from gondolas. Right: Exquisite churches, palaces and magnificent art galleries are among the many attractions of Florence.

textiles, especially silk, engineering goods, including transport equipment and motor vehicles (Alfa-Romeo, Fiat and Maserati are internationally known names), office and household equipment, chemicals and iron and steel. There are also many craft industries. The chief industrial region is the triangular area formed by Turin, Milan and Genoa. Farmland covers about two-thirds of the land, but agriculture now employs only 13 per cent of the workforce, as opposed to 31 per cent in 1960. Forests cover 21 per cent of the land, but timber is imported. Major crops include barley, citrus and other fruits, grapes (for wine-making), maize, olives, sugar beet, tobacco, vegetables and wheat. In 1979 there were 8.6 million cattle, 9.8 million pigs and 10 million sheep and goats. Italy is a major milk producer and its cheeses, such as Gorgonzola, are famous. In the 1970s Italy's main trading partners were West Germany, France, the United States and the UK. Adverse trade balances were partly covered by income from the huge tourist industry: Italy received 48.7 million foreign visitors in 1979. Tourist attractions include sunny beaches, historic sites, like the Forum in Rome and the lost city of Pompeii, the Vatican City State, and magnificent medieval cities, such as Florence and Venice, with their superb art galleries and churches. The most prosperous parts of Italy are in the north; this is reflected in the migration of poor farmers from the south to the north or abroad. The Roman empire developed around 500 BC and lasted until the 5th century AD. In the Middle Ages, Italy was divided into small rival states, although these made an enormous contribution to the Renaissance in

Mt Nimba, is on the Ivory Coast-Liberia-Guinea border. The south has an equatorial climate. The north is often scorched by the north-easterly Harmattan, a wind from the Sahara that may raise temperatures to 38°C (100°F). There is some forest in the south but savanna is the main type of vegetation. About 60 languages and dialects are spoken by the Negroid peoples. Ivory Coast is prosperous by African standards, but prosperity is confined mostly to the south-east. In 1978 agriculture employed 81 per cent of the workforce and accounted for 21 per cent of the GDP: 23 per cent came from industry and 56 per cent from services. Ivory Coast leads the world in cocoa production and is the 4th largest coffee producer. There is some mining, but the processing and consumer goods industries in Abidjan make a larger contribution to the economy. Ivory Coast became a French colony in 1893, although French influence dates back to the 17th century. Independence was achieved in 1960, since when Ivory Coast has pursued private enterprise economic policies, proving to be one of the most stable nations in Africa.

Area: 322,463 km² (124,510 sq mi); **Population:** 11,277,000; **Capital:** Abidjan (pop 3,500,000); **Highest point:** Mt Nimba, 1752 m (5748 ft); **Official language:** French; **Religions:** traditional beliefs (56 per cent), Islam (24 per cent), Roman Catholicism (20 per cent); **Adult literacy rate:** 20 per cent; **Average life expectancy at birth:** 46 years; **Unit of currency:** Franc CFA; **Main exports:** coffee, cocoa, timber, petroleum products; **Per capita GNP:** US$1060.

the 14th–16th centuries. After a long struggle for unity which began in 1848, Italy became a united kingdom in 1861 under King Victor Emmanuel II of Sardinia, although the Papal territories were not added until 1870. Italy entered World War I on the side of the Allies. In 1922 Benito Mussolini and his Fascist party took power. In 1935 Italian forces invaded Ethiopia and Italy entered World War II in 1940 on Germany's side. Italy surrendered in 1943 and declared war on Germany. In 1946 the monarchy was abolished and Italy became a republic. It was a founder member of NATO in 1949 and of the EC in 1958. The economy expanded rapidly and attempts were made through the EC to increase job opportunities for people in the relatively impoverished south. However, a succession of weak coalition governments, unemployment, high inflation (averaging 14 per cent per year in 1970–78), strikes and terrorist violence and assassinations have marred progress in recent years. Italy has a bicameral parliament, with an elected, 600-member Chamber of Deputies and a Senate elected on a regional basis. Members of both houses serve 5-year terms.

Area: 301,225 km² (116,310 sq mi); **Population:** 58,085,000; **Capital:** Rome (pop 3,700,000); **Other cities:** Milan (4,000,000), Naples (1,250,000), Turin (1,000,000), Genoa (850,000), Palermo (694,000), Bologna (487,000), Florence (465,000); **Highest point:** Mt Rosa, 4634 m (15,203 ft); **Official language:** Italian; **Religion:** Roman Catholicism; **Adult literacy rate:** 98 per cent; **Average life expectancy at birth:** 73 years; **Unit of currency:** Lira; **Main exports:** machinery, motor vehicles, iron and steel, textiles, footwear, plastics, fruit and vegetables; **Per capita GNP:** US$5240.

IVORY COAST, a republic in West Africa with a 550 km (342 mi) coastline on the Gulf of Guinea. Behind the broad coastal lowlands are high plains between 150 and 450 m (492–1476 ft). The main highlands are in the north-west: the highest peak,

JAMAICA, a West Indian island nation. The land is mainly mountainous, with spectacular scenery. The coast has a tropical climate, with average temperatures of 27°–30°C (81°–86°F), although there are pleasant ocean breezes. The altitude lowers temperatures inland. The Blue Mountains have an average annual rainfall of 5000 mm (197 in). The coasts are drier: Kingston has about 760 mm (30 in) per year. More than 75 per cent of the people are black, 14 per cent are of mixed black and white origin, and there are minorities of Asians, Afro-Asians and whites. In 1980 50 per cent of the population lived in urban areas where manufacturing is growing. Jamaica is the world's 3rd largest producer of bauxite, the main export. Agriculture employs 28 per cent of the people: bananas and sugar are the main products. Tourism is a major industry and more than 500,000 visitors went to Jamaica in 1978. Discovered by Columbus in 1494, Jamaica was ruled by Spain until 1655 when the English captured it. Full independence in the Commonwealth was achieved in 1962. The Head of State is the British monarch who is represented by a Governor-General.

Area: 10,991 km² (4244 sq mi); **Population:** 2,297,000; **Capital:** Kingston (pop 635,000); **Highest point:** Blue Mt Peak, 2256 m (7402 ft); **Official language:** English; **Religion:** Christianity, (Rastafarian minority); **Adult literacy rate:** 86 per cent; **Average life expectancy at birth:** 70 years; **Unit of currency:** Dollar; **Main exports:** alumina and bauxite, sugar; **Per capita GNP:** US$1240.

JAPAN, an island nation in the Far East that is separated from the Asian mainland by the Sea of Japan. There are 4 large islands (Honshu, Hokkaido, Kyushu and Shikoku) and about 3000 small ones, including the Ryukyu island chain that stretches towards Taiwan. The islands are largely mountainous, the most rugged region being the Japanese Alps on Honshu, including the highest peak Fujiyama, a dormant volcano south-west of Tokyo which last erupted in 1707. Japan contains more than 160 volcanoes; 54 are active. Earthquakes are common; about 1500 occur every year, but most cause little damage. The world's most destructive earthquake occurred in the Kwanto plain in 1923 when 575,000 buildings in Tokyo and Yokohama were destroyed and 143,000 lives were lost. Volcanic and seismic activity are caused because Japan lies above a subduction zone where the Pacific plate is being forced beneath the Eurasian plate. Earthquakes originating offshore trigger off tsunamis, destructive waves that strike the coasts with great force. Along the deeply indented coasts are some small coastal plains that are alluvial deltas formed by the short rivers that cascade from the mountains. The longest river, the Shinano on Honshu, is only 480 km (298 mi) long. Japan has a monsoon climate, with plentiful rain. The heaviest rains fall in June–July and September– October and typhoons are common. Temperatures are affected by the warm Kuro Siwa ocean current which comes from the south and the cold Oyashio current that chills the coasts of western Hokkaido and northern Honshu. Average January temperatures are −6°C (21°F) in Hokkaido and 7°C (45°F) in southern Kyushu. Average July temperatures are 20°C (68°F) in the north and 28°C (82°F) in the south. Most people are Mongoloid descendants of people who came from mainland Asia and Pacific islands. But one of the earliest peoples is Caucasoid. These are the bushy-haired Ainu, 15,000 of whom live in Hokkaido. Japan is Asia's most prosperous and industrialized nation. In 1980 78 per cent of the population lived in urban areas, compared with 62 per cent in 1960. In 1978 industry employed 39 per cent of the workforce, services 48 per cent and agriculture 13 per cent. Contributions to the GDP were industry 40 per cent, services 55 per cent and agriculture 5 per cent. Some minerals, including coal and copper, are mined, but the amounts are generally too small for the needs of manufacturers. Hence, many materials, including iron ore and oil, must be imported. Japan has a wide range of light and heavy industry.

Left: Express trains reflect Japan's outstanding technological progress in recent times, while the volcano Mount Fuji reminds us that Japan lies on a particularly unstable part of the Earth's crust. Religion plays a major part in life in Japan and Mount Fuji is a sacred mountain. Above: The Kinkakuji Temple is in Tokyo. Shintoism and Buddhism are Japan's chief religions. Right: This mosque is in Nairobi, capital of Kenya.

It is the world's 3rd largest producer of electrical energy, after the US and the USSR. In 1977 hydroelectricity made up 14 per cent of the total and nuclear power 6 per cent. Japan leads the world in producing many items, including motor cycles, merchant ships and television sets. Only the US makes more motor vehicles and Hong Kong more radios. Japan's main industrial regions are in the coastal lowlands between Tokyo and northern Kyushu. Most of Japan is too mountainous for farming; forests cover nearly 70 per cent of the land. Arable land makes up less than 15 per cent of Japan, but yields are high and farming intensive. Rice is the chief food and is grown on nearly 50 per cent of the farmland. Other major crops are barley, fruits, soya beans and wheat. Cattle number about 4.1 million and pigs 9.5 million: goats and sheep are unimportant because of the lack of pasture. About 50 per cent of Japan's protein comes from its large fishing and whaling industry. Seaweed is also harvested for food. But food is imported: it made up 13 per cent of the imports in 1979. According to tradition, Japan's monarchy dates back to 660 BC. Buddhism was introduced in AD 552. Emperors ruled Japan until a new warrior class, the *shoguns* ('great generals'), emerged in the 12th century. In 1192 the first shogun took power, ruling in the name of the emperor. Shogun rule continued until Emperor Meiji regained power in 1868. European contacts began when Portuguese navigators reached Japan in 1542. But in 1637 Japan expelled all Europeans, except for the Dutch, from Japan and outlawed Christianity. Isolationism continued until, in 1854, the American Commander Perry, with a fleet of warships, forced Japan to

agree a treaty with the US. This was followed by treaties with other western powers. Japan's imperialist ambitions began in the 1880s. In 1894–95 it fought a war with China and in 1904–05 it defeated Russia in a dispute over Russia's claims on Korea. In 1931 it occupied Manchuria and, in 1937, started a war with China. In 1941 Japan attacked US bases at Pearl Harbor, but defeat in World War II came when the US dropped atomic bombs on Hiroshima and Nagasaki in 1945. The US occupied Japan until 1952. In the 1960s and 1970s Japan became one of the world's great industrial powers. The 1947 Constitution made Japan a constitutional monarchy. The Emperor is Head of State but his duties are entirely ceremonial. Power is vested in the Diet, which consists of an elected 511-member House of Representatives and a 252-member House of Chancellors. The prime minister is chosen by the Diet and is usually the leader of the political party which holds most seats in the Diet.

Area: 372,313 km² (143,759 sq mi); **Population:** 123,980,000; **Capital:** Tokyo (pop 11,695,00); **Other cities:** Yokohama (2,786,000), Osaka (2,682,000), Nagoya (2,079,000), Kyoto (1,468,000), Sapporo (1,397,000), Kobe (1,372,000), Kitakyushu (1,068,000), Kawasaki (1,050,000); **Highest point:** Fujiyama, 3776 m (12,388 ft); **Official language:** Japanese; **Religions:** mainly Shintoism and Buddhism; **Adult literacy rate:** 99 per cent; **Average life expectancy at birth:** 76 years; **Unit of currency:** Yen; **Main exports:** chemicals, electronic goods, machinery and transport equipment, optical equipment, ships, textiles; **Per capita GNP:** US$8800.

JORDAN, a kingdom in south-western Asia. The fertile western uplands (the West Bank, occupied by Israel) overlook the rift valley which contains the River Jordan and the Dead Sea whose shoreline is 393 m (1289 ft) below sea level, the world's lowest point on land. The valley continues south to the Gulf of Aqabah, Jordan's only outlet to the sea. The east consists mainly of barren uplands: the highest point is Jebel Ram, 1754 m (5755 ft) high in the south. About 87 per cent of Jordan is desert. Some highland regions are cooler and have an average annual rainfall of 520 mm (20 in). Most people are Arabs and 56 per cent lived in urban areas in 1980. In 1978 agriculture employed 27 per cent of the population, industry 39 per cent and services 34 per

cent; they contributed 11 per cent, 29 per cent and 60 per cent respectively to the GDP. Fruit and vegetables are grown and there are about 1.25 million sheep and goats. The main export is phosphates. Jordan was home to some of the earliest settlements and political groups known to historians and archaeologists. Rocks carvings at Jabal have been attributed to people of the Paleolithic-Mesolithic era. There are vast numbers of biblical references to the region, some of which date back as far as the Bronze Age (3000–1000 BC). Four small states, – Amman, Edom, Gilead, and Moab – developed on the east side of the River Jordan. The Hebrew states of Judah and Israel developed on the West Bank. These areas all fell in time to the Assyrians, Egyptians, Babylonians and Persians. Jordan was further troubled by the Crusades, which lasted from 1095 to the middle of the 15th century. For some of this time parts of Jordan were governed by Christians. Once the Crusades were over Jordan was ruled by the Ottoman Turks until 1918. British forces occupied what is now Israel and Jordan in World War I. Transjordan became a separate country in 1923 and full independence was achieved in 1946. In 1948 Jordan was involved in the Arab-Israeli war and, in 1949, it adopted its present name, the Hashemite Kingdom of Jordan. In 1967 Israel occupied West Bank, Jordan's most fertile region. In 1970–71 civil war broke out when Jordan tried to expel militant refugees belonging to the Palestinian Liberation Organization. In 1975, however, King Hussein gave up his claim to the West Bank and passed responsibility for it, including financial support, to the PLO.

Area: 97,740 km² (37,740 sq mi); **Population:** 3,967,000; **Capital:** Amman (pop 1,100,000); **Official language:** Arabic; **Religion:** Islam; **Adult literacy rate:** 70 per cent; **Average life expectancy at birth:** 56 years; **Unit of currency:** Jordanian dinar; **Main exports:** phosphates, fruit and vegetables; **Per capita GNP:** US$1180.

KAMPUCHEA See Cambodia.

KENYA, an East African republic. Behind the narrow coastal plain is a large grassy or savanna-covered plateau broken by volcanic mountains, including the highest peak, Mt Kenya. Mt Kenya rises to 5200 m (17,058 ft), so high that although it is close to the equator it has a permanent covering of ice and snow. The East African Rift Valley in Kenya contains lakes Nakuru, Naivasha and Turkana. Part of Lake Victoria is in the south-east. The altitude moderates the equatorial climate, but only 15 per cent of Kenya has a reliable 760 mm (30 in) of rain per year, but high temperatures mean that what rainfall there is evaporates quickly, which enhances the aridity. There are about 40 language groups: the largest are the Kikuyu and Luo. In 1978 agriculture employed 79 per cent of the workforce, industry 8 per cent and services 13 per cent: their contributions to the GDP were 41 per cent, 19 per cent and 40 per cent respectively. The chief cash crops are coffee and tea. In 1979 there were 10.5 million cattle, 4 million sheep and 4.5 million goats. Mining

Beirut, capital of Lebanon, is the country's chief seaport and educational centre. It was devastated by fighting in summer 1982 between Israeli forces and the Palestinian Liberation Movement.

is not important but manufacturing is growing rapidly. In 1979 350,000 tourists visited Kenya enjoying the wildlife, scenery and beaches. Kenya's coast became a British protectorate in 1895 and Kenya was declared a British colony in 1920. Independence was achieved in 1963 and republican status was adopted in 1964. Since then Kenya has enjoyed stable government.

Area: 582,646 km² (224,973 sq mi); **Population:** 23,727,000; **Capital:** Nairobi (pop 828,000); **Other cities:** Mombasa (340,000); **Highest point:** Mt Kenya, 5199 m (17,057 ft); **Official languages:** English, Swahili; **Religions:** traditional beliefs, Islam, Christianity (25 per cent); **Adult literacy rate:** 40 per cent; **Average life expectancy at birth:** 53 years; **Unit of currency:** Kenya shilling; **Main exports:** coffee, petroleum products, tea, cement, hides, meat; **Per capita GNP:** US$380.

KIRIBATI, an island republic in the Central Pacific. It includes Ocean (Banaba) Island, the 16 Gilbert Islands, 8 of the 11 Line Islands (the rest are uninhabited US dependencies), and the 8 Phoenix Islands. The climate is hot and generally wet. Most people are Micronesians. Copra is the only export. The Gilbert and Ellice Islands became a British protectorate in 1892. Banaba was added in 1900, the Line Islands in 1919, and the Phoenix Islands in 1937. The Ellice Islands became a separate country, Tuvalu, in 1975. Kiribati (pronounced *Kiribas*) became fully independent in 1979.

Area: 684 km² (264 sq mi); **Population:** 69,000; **Capital:** Tarawa; **Per capita GNP:** US$670.

KOREA, NORTH, officially the Democratic People's Republic of Korea. The northern part of a peninsula, North Korea is mostly mountainous, the population being concentrated in coastal plains in the east. The average annual temperature range is between −7°C (19°F) and 21°C (70°F) and the annual rainfall is between 580 and 1140 mm (23–45 in). The people are Mongoloid. Only 16 per cent of the land is cultivable, but in 1978 agriculture employed 49 per cent of the workforce, industry 32 per cent and services 19 per cent. Rice is the main crop in irrigated areas: maize, millet and wheat grow in drier places. There are many minerals – coal, copper, iron ore, lead, manganese, nickel, tungsten and zinc. There are many light and heavy industries. Korea was partitioned in 1945. The USSR occupied the north above latitude 38°N;

the US controlled the south. The occupying powers withdrew in 1949. War between North and South (aided by other powers) raged between 1950–53, the cease-fire line being the present border. Talks on reunification in 1980 failed. See **Korea, South** for earlier history.

Area: 120,538 km² (46,543 sq mi); **Population:** 22,420,000; **Capital:** Pyongyang (pop 2,639,000); **Highest point:** Paektu-San, 2744 m (9003 ft); **Official language:** Korean; **Religion:** Buddhism; **Average life expectancy at birth:** 63 years; **Unit of currency:** Won; **Main exports:** iron ore, pig iron, other metal ores; **Per capital GNP:** US$1130.

KOREA, SOUTH, a republic in the Far East. The land is mostly mountainous with many islands in the west. Average annual temperatures vary from −3°C (27°F) to 24°C (75°F), although winters are warmer in the far south. Winters are dry. The average annual rainfall is between 1140 and 1400 mm (45–55 in). Forests cover 70 per cent of the land. Since partition, industry has overtaken agriculture in importance in South Korea. It accounted for 36 per cent of the GDP in 1978 (as opposed to 19 per cent in 1960). Agriculture accounted for 24 per cent (40 per cent in 1960) and services 40 per cent. Tungsten is the chief mineral; small deposits of many other minerals occur. The chief manufactures are light consumer goods, but chemical and heavy industries are growing. The chief crops are rice and other grains and tobacco. Livestock raising and fishing are also important. Korea became a united kingdom in the 7th century AD. It was occupied by Mongols between the 13th and 14th centuries and it was conquered by China in 1627. It became isolated until Japan forced it to open some ports to trade in 1876. In 1895 Japan defeated China in Korea and in 1905 it prevented Russia from taking it. Korea became a Japanese colony in 1910. In 1945 it was divided between the USSR and the US but their forces withdrew in 1949. In the Korean War (1950–53) the UN supported the South and Communist China the North. In the 1960s and 1970s the army has played an important part in the government of South Korea and attempts at reunification have failed.

Area: 98,484 km² (38,027 sq mi); **Population:** 43,068,000; **Capital:** Seoul (pop 9,646,000); **Other cities:** Pusan (3,160,000), Taegu (1,607,000), Inchon (1,084,000); **Highest point:** Halla-San, 1950 m (6398 ft); **Official language:** Korean; **Religions:** Buddhism, Confucianism, Christianity; **Adult literacy rate:** 93 per cent; **Average life expectancy at birth:** 63 years; **Unit of currency:** Won; **Main exports:** textiles, manufactures, chemicals; **Per capita GNP:** US$1500.

KUWAIT, a small Emirate at the head of the Persian Gulf. This low-lying, desert nation has erratic rainfall between 10 mm (0.4 in) per year and 380 mm (15 in). The average summer temperature is 24°C (75°F) but it occasionally soars to 52°C (126°F). Winters are cooler. Most people are Arabs. Kuwait has the world's highest per capita GNP, because of its oil production, which began in 1946. It is now one of the world's 10 top producers and revenue from oil sales finances one of the world's most elaborate welfare states. In 1899 Kuwait accepted British protection for certain rights. Kuwait became independent in 1914, but Britain remained responsible for Kuwait's foreign policy until 1961, when Kuwait became fully independent. In 1990, following a dispute over oil production, Iraq invaded Kuwait and declared it an Iraqi province. The United Nations ordered Iraq to withdraw, and began a military operation to liberate Kuwait early in 1991. As a result of the conflict, reliable statistics are hard to come by.

Area: 17,818 km² (6880 sq mi); **Population:** 1,697,000 (before the invasion); **Capital:** Kuwait City (pop 400,000); **Official languages:** Arabic; **Religions:** Islam; **Adult literacy rate:** 60 per cent; **Average life expectancy at birth:** 69 years; **Unit of currency:** Kuwait dinar; **Main export:** Oil; **Per capita GNP:** US$17,270 (before the invasion).

LAOS, a poor, landlocked People's Democratic Republic in South-East Asia. Forested mountains and plateaux cover much of the country: most people live in the Mekong River plains. Laos has a tropical monsoon climate. The average annual rainfall is 1020–2030 mm (40–80 in) in the north and 3800 mm (150 in) in southern uplands. The Lao-Lum (or Valley Lao), a Thai people, make up 56 per cent of the population. In 1978 75 per cent of the people were employed in agriculture, which accounted for 60 per cent of the GDP, as opposed to 14 per cent from industry and 26 per cent from services. Rice is the main food crop; timber and coffee are the main exports. A united kingdom was established in what is now Laos and northern Thailand in the 14th century. But Thailand and Laos were often in conflict. Laos became a French protectorate in 1893. Full independence as a kingdom was achieved in 1954. From 1953 there was a long struggle between the Royal Lao government and the pro-communist Pathet Lao (The Lao Patriotic Front's armed force). A coalition government was established in 1973, but the Pathet Lao took over in 1975. The King abdicated.

Area: 236,800 km² (91,434 sq mi); **Population:** 3,923,00; **Capital:** Vientiane (pop 120,000); **High-

est point:** Phu Bia, 2820 m (9252 ft); **Official language:** Lao; **Religions:** Buddhism, animism; **Average life expectancy at birth:** 42 years; **Unit of currency:** Kip; **Main exports:** timber, coffee; **Per capita GNP:** US$90 (1978).

LEBANON, a Middle Eastern republic. Behind the narrow coastal plain are the western Lebanon Mts, an interior plateau containing the fertile Bekaa valley, and the Anti-Lebanon Mts in the east. The climate is Mediterranean in type. Most people are Arabs but only 60 per cent of the population is Muslim: the rest are Christians. Lebanon has long been a financial and commercial centre and, in normal times, it has a major tourist industry. Hence, services are the leading sector of the economy, followed by industry and agriculture. Consumer goods are manufactured and cereals and fruit are the main farm products; 38 per cent of the land is cultivated. Lebanon was the centre of the ancient Phoenician empire. It came under the Romans in 64 BC and under Ottoman rule from 1517. France became involved from the 1860s in order to protect the Maronite (Christian) community which was under attack from the Druses, a sect founded in the 11th century AD. France ruled Lebanon from 1918 to 1946 when it became a fully independent republic. Lebanon was involved in the Arab-Israeli War in 1948; in 1969 and 1973 Lebanese forces clashed with Palestinian refugees; and in 1975–76 civil war broke out between Muslim and Christian forces. In 1978 Israel invaded southern Lebanon to destroy Palestinian bases and has kept a force in that area ever since. The civil war raged all through the 1980s, with fearful destruction in Beirut. Christian forces withdrew from Beirut in 1990.

Area: 10,400 km² (4016 sq mi); **Population:** 2,898,000; **Capital:** Beirut (pop 702,000); **Highest point:** Qurnet es Sauda, 3083 m (10,115 ft); **Official language:** Arabic; **Religions:** Islam, Christianity; **Average life expectancy at birth:** 65 years; **Unit of currency:** Lebanese pound; **Main exports:** jewellery, precious metals/stones, textiles; **Per capita GNP:** US$1070 (1974).

LESOTHO, a landlocked kingdom enclosed by South Africa. It was formerly called Basutoland. Mostly mountainous, it includes the high Drakensberg range, but most people live in the western lowlands and the southern Orange River valley. The climate is continental, with warm, moist summers and cold, dry winters. The people, called Basotho, speak Sesotho and English. In 1978 agriculture employed 87 per cent of the people. It accounted for 36 per cent of the GDP, with 15 per cent from industry and 49 per cent from services. Arable land covers 12 per cent of the land and pasture 82 per cent. The chief food crops are cereals and vegetables. The main exports are wool, mohair and alluvial diamonds. In 1979 there were 1.3 million sheep, 730,000 goats and 550,000 cattle. Tourism is increasing, mainly from South Africa. The nation was founded in the 1820s by Moshoeshoe I who united refugees from tribal wars in South Africa. The country became a British protectorate in 1884 and an independent kingdom in 1966, although it remained heavily dependent economically on South Africa. In the early 1980s a clandestine Lesotho Liberation Movement carried out a number of bombings in Maseru and other places.

Area: 30,355 km² (11,721 sq mi); **Population:** 1,686,000; **Capital:** Maseru (pop 289,000; **Highest point:** Thabana Ntlenyana, 3482 m (11,424 ft); **Official languages:** English, Sesotho; **Religion:** Christianity (80 per cent); **Adult literacy rate:** 55 per cent; **Average life expectancy at birth:** 50 years; **Unit of currency:** Loti; **Main exports:** wool, mohair, diamonds; **Per capita GNP:** US$340.

LIBERIA, a republic in West Africa. Behind the coastal plain, with its mangrove swamps and savanna country, are forested plateaux and grassy highlands. Average annual temperatures are between 21°C (70°F) and 26°C (79°F). The average rainfall on the coast is about 2540–4060 mm (100–160 in) per year; inland areas have 1780 mm (70 in). There are 16 main language groups. The 50,000 or so Americo-Liberians, descendants of freed slaves, have been important in ruling Liberia. In 1978 71 per cent of the workforce was employed in agriculture, which accounted for 35 per cent of the GDP. Industry accounted for 28 per cent and services for 37 per cent. Since 1973 iron ore has been the main product, having overtaken rubber. The main food crops are cassava and rice. Liberia has a large merchant navy: many foreign ships register in Liberia because of the low fees. In 1822 the American Colonization Society founded Monrovia for freed slaves. In 1847 Liberia became an independent republic, with a Constitution much like that of the US. In 1980 Master Sergeant Samuel Doe staged a military coup and became president. Civil war broke out in 1989, and in 1990 Doe was killed.

Area: 111,369 km² (43,002 sq mi); **Population:** 2,494,000; **Capital:** Monrovia (pop 425,000); **Highest point:** Mt Nimba, 1752 m (5748 ft); **Official language:** English; **Religion:** mainly Christianity; **Adult literacy rate:** 30 per cent; **Average life expectancy at birth:** 48 years; **Unit of currency:** Liberian dollar; **Main exports:** iron ore and concentrates, timber, rubber; **Per capita GNP:** US$490.

LIBYA, officially the Socialist People's Libyan Arab Jamahiriyah. (*Jamahiriyah* means 'state of the masses'.) About 95 per cent of Libya is desert or semidesert. The land rises towards the south. Most people live in the north-eastern and north-western coastal plains. Average annual temperatures on the coast range between 12°C–27°C (54°F–81°F). The world's highest shade temperature, 57.7°C (136.4°F) was recorded in 1922 at Al'Aziziyah, south of Tripoli. The rainfall averages 200–610 mm (8–24 in) per year in the north-east and 330 mm (13 in) in the north-west. Most people are of Arab or Berber origin. Industry, mainly oil production, dominates the economy, providing 71 per cent of the GDP in 1978, compared with 2 per cent from agriculture and 27 per cent from services. The main food crops are cereals, dates, olives and vegetables.

There were 4.8 million sheep and 2.1 million goats in 1979. The Turks controlled Libya from 1551 to 1911, when Italy occupied Tripoli. Italy lost Libya in World War II. Libya was divided between Britain and France until it became an independent kingdom in 1951. Col Mu'ammar Gaddafi led a military coup in 1969, deposing the king and setting up a republic. In 1977 Libya became a Jamahiriyah, which was a form of direct democracy. With its great wealth, Libya has become involved in the affairs of many other countries. For example, it has opposed Egypt's peace initiative with Israel and it intervened in the Chad civil war. It signed a treaty with Chad in 1989.

Area: 1,759,540 km² (679,399 sq mi); **Population:** 4,271,000; **Capital:** Tripoli (pop 1,000,000); **Other cities:** Benghazi (372,000); **Highest point:** Mt Bette, 2286 m (7500 ft); **Official language:** Arabic; **Religion:** Islam; **Adult literacy rate:** 50 per cent; **Average life expectancy at birth:** 55 years; **Unit of currency:** Libyan dinar; **Main export:** oil; **Per capita GNP:** US$8210 (the highest in Africa).

LIECHTENSTEIN, a small principality between Austria and Switzerland, with which it has close links. For example, it uses Swiss currency and is united with Switzerland in a customs union. The Rhine and Ill river plains are in the north, with mountains in the south. Most people are Roman Catholic. Farming, including the cultivation of cereals, fruits and vines and cattle rearing, was the most valuable activity, when light industry overtook it. The sale of postage stamps and tourism are also important. Liechtenstein was founded in 1719. It was part of the German Confederation from 1815, but it has been independent since 1866 and neutral since 1868. It is a constitutional monarchy with a unicameral parliament of 15 elected members.

Area: 157 km² (61 sq mi); **Population:** 29,000; **Capital:** Vaduz (pop 5000); **Official language:** German; **Per capita GNP:** US$8000 (1974).

LUXEMBOURG, a Grand Duchy between Belgium, France and West Germany. The north is part of the Ardennes plateau, with fertile lowlands in the south. The climate is mild and moist. Most people are Roman Catholics. Iron ore is the chief resource and there are large iron and steel works. About 52 per cent of the land is farmed: barley, oats, potatoes, sugar beet and wheat are major crops. Luxembourg became a Grand Duchy in 1354. The Spanish and then the Austrian Hapsburgs ruled it from 1482 to 1795, when France annexed it. In 1815 it became part of the Netherlands. In 1830 much of the Grand Duchy went to Belgium, but in 1839 the remaining eastern part (modern Luxembourg) achieved autonomy, although it was ruled by Dutch kings until 1890 when it broke away from the Netherlands. Germany occupied the country in World Wars I and II. In 1944 Belgium, the Netherlands and Luxembourg formed the Benelux Customs Union. Luxembourg was a founder member of NATO in 1949 and of the EC in 1957. It is a constitutional monarchy with an elected Chamber of Deputies.

Area: 2586 km² (999 sq mi); **Population:** 369,000; **Capital:** Luxembourg (pop 80,000); **Official languages:** French, Luxemburgish; **Unit of currency:** Franc; **Per capita GNP:** US$12,280.

MACAO, or Macau, a small Portuguese territory on the south-eastern coast of China. It is densely populated. Most people are Chinese: less than 3 per cent are Portuguese. Little land is available for farming. There is a small fishing industry and manufacturing is important, especially textiles. Transit trade with China and tourism are other sources of income. Macao has been Portuguese since 1557. Formerly a trading centre, it relies mainly on tourism and light industry. It is to be handed back to China in 1997.

Area: 16 km² (6 sq mi); **Population:** 330,000; **Capital:** Macao (pop 157,000); **Unit of currency:** Pataca; **Per capita GNP:** US$1750.

MADAGASCAR, an island republic separated from the African mainland by the 400 km (249 mi) wide Mozambique Channel. It was called the Malagasy Republic in 1960–75. A plateau 900–1500 m (2953–4921 ft) high covers about 66 per cent of the country; volcanic peaks, such as the Massif du Tsaratanana, rise above it. The coastal plain in the east is narrow, with broader lowlands in the west. The forested east coast is hot and humid. The grassy and savanna-covered plateau is cool, with an average annual temperature range of 14°–21°C (57°–70°F): the rainfall is between 1010 and 2030 mm (40–80 in) per year. The north-west is wet but the south-western lowlands are semi-desert. The people are of Indonesian and African origin: the largest of the main 18 groups is the Merina. In 1978 agriculture employed 86 per cent of the workforce, contributing 38 per cent of the GDP; industry accounted for 19 per cent and services 43 per cent. Only 5 per cent of the land is arable, 60 per cent is pasture and 21 per cent forest. Rice is the main food and coffee, cloves and vanilla are the main cash crops. There is little mining but there are many small processing industries and oil refining is important. Portuguese mariners discovered the island in 1500. France made it a protectorate in 1885. By 1896 the French had annexed the entire island and abolished the Merina monarchy. Independence was achieved in 1960. From 1972 the army has played a major part in government.

Area: 587,041 km² (226,670 sq mi); **Population:** 11,240,000; **Capital:** Antananarivo (pop 663,000); **Highest point:** Massif du Tsaratanana, 2876 m (9436 ft); **Official languages:** French, Malagasy; **Religions:** traditional beliefs (57 per cent), Christianity (40 per cent), Islam (3 per cent); **Adult literacy rate:** 50 per cent; **Average life expectancy at birth:** 46 years; **Unit of currency:** Franc Malgache; **Main exports:** coffee, cloves, vanilla; **Per capita GNP:** US$290.

MALAWI, a landlocked republic in southern Africa. It includes part of Lake Malawi (Nyasa) in the East African Rift Valley. The River Shire flows from the lake into the Zambezi in Mozambique. There are scenic highlands west of Lake Malawi, but the highest peak Mt Mlanje is east of the River Shire. An inland drainage basin around Lake Chilwa is in the south-east. The lowlands are hot and humid. The rainfall averages 760–1020 mm (30–40 in) per year. The highlands are wetter and cool. The people speak a number of Bantu languages. Agriculture employed 43 per cent of the workforce in 1978, accounting for 43 per cent of the GDP; industry contributed 19 per cent and services 38 per cent. Maize is the chief food crop. Tobacco accounted for 49 per cent of the exports and tea for 24 per cent in 1977. Arable land covers 19 per cent of the country, pasture 16 per cent, forests 20 per cent and water 21 per cent. The territory became the British Central African Protectorate in 1891: it was renamed Nyasaland in 1907. It became independent as Malawi in 1964 and adopted republican status in 1966. A one-party state, it has enjoyed stable government, though its people are poor.

Area: 118,484 km² (45,749 sq mi); **Population:** 7,928,000; **Capital:** Lilongwe (pop 103,000); **Other cities:** Blantyre-Limbe (229,000); **Highest point:** Mt Mlanje, 3000 m (9843 ft); **Official languages:** English, Chichewa; **Religions:** traditional beliefs, Christianity (20 per cent); **Adult literacy rate:** 25 per cent; **Average life expectancy at birth:** 46 years; **Unit of currency:** Kwacha; **Main exports:** tobacco, tea, sugar, groundnuts; **Per capita GNP:** US$200.

MALAYSIA, a South-East Asian monarchy. It contains the southern Malay peninsula and Sabah and Sarawak in northern Borneo. Forested mountains cover large areas. The most important lowlands are in the Malay peninsula. The climate is tropical, with average annual temperatures of 21°–32°C (70°–90°F) and the average rainfall is about 2500 mm (98 in). The Malay peninsula contains 84 per cent of the population. In the country as a whole, 47 per cent are Malays, 34 per cent are Chinese, 9 per cent are Indians and Pakistanis, 5 per cent are Dayaks, 5 per cent belong to other tribes in Borneo, and 2 per cent belong to other groups. In 1978 agriculture employed 50 per cent of the workforce, but industry accounted for 32 per cent of the GDP, as opposed to 25 per cent from agriculture and 43 per cent from services. Tin is the main mineral. Some oil is also produced and manufacturing is increasing. The main cash crops are rubber and palm oil; rice is the main food crop. Timber is also important. Portuguese traders reached Malacca in 1509 but the Dutch took over in 1641. The British East India Company became established in Penang in 1786 and, in 1826, Penang, Malacca and Singapore became the British Straits Settlement. Britain took over its government in 1867. In 1888 North Borneo (Sabah) and Sarawak became British protectorates. Malaysia was created in 1963 when Malaya, Singapore, Sabah and Sarawak joined a federation, although this led to fighting with Indonesia. However, Singapore seconded from the federation in 1965. Malaysia's Constitution provides that the 9 Rulers of the Malay states elect one of their number every 5 years to be *Yang di-Pertuan Agong* (Supreme Head of the Federation).

Area: 329,749 km² (127,324 sq mi); **Population:** 16,954,000; **Capital:** Kuala Lumpur (pop 938,000); **Highest point:** Mt Kinabalu, 4102 m (13,458 ft); **Official language:** Malay; **Religions:** mainly Islam, also Buddhism, Hinduism, Christianity; **Adult literacy rate:** 60 per cent; **Average life expectancy at birth:** 67 years; **Unit of currency:** Malaysian dollar; **Main exports:** rubber, tin, timber, palm oil; **Per capita GNP:** US$1320.

MALDIVES, an island republic about 650 km (404 mi) south-west of Sri Lanka. It includes about 2000 coral islands. Fishing is the main industry. Coconuts, millet and fruits are grown. The Maldives came under British protection in 1887. Full independence was achieved in 1965. The Maldives became a republic in 1968.

Area: 298 km² (115 sq mi); **Population:** 207,000; **Capital:** Malé (pop 30,000); **Official language:** Divehi; **Religion:** Islam; **Unit of currency:** Rupee; **Per capita GNP:** US$200.

MALI, a landlocked republic in north-western Africa. Plains cover most of Mali, with uplands in the north-east and south. The River Niger flows in a broad arc through southern Mali. Two-fifths of the river's total length of 4000 km (2486 mi) is in Mali. Average annual temperatures are 24°–35°C (75°–95°F). Bamako has about 1120 mm (44 in) of rain per year: the north is desert. There are people of Arab and Berber origin, such as Tuaregs, and some of mixed Caucasoid/Negroid origin, such as the Fulbe (Fulani). But more than 80 per cent of the population is Negroid. Agriculture employed 88 per cent of the workforce in 1978, accounting for 37 per cent of the GDP, as opposed to industry 18 per cent and services 45 per cent. Cultivated land covers only 8 per cent of this poor country. The chief cash crop is cotton. In 1979 Mali had 4.5 million cattle, 6.1 million sheep and 5.8 million goats. Mali was part of several medieval empires: Ancient Ghana, Mali and Songhai. In 1880 France made the area (then called French Sudan) a protectorate. Full independence was achieved in 1960. The army ruled from 1968 but elections were held again from 1979. Mali is a one-party state.

Area: 1,240,000 km² (478,793 sq mi); **Population:** 9,088,000; **Capital:** Bamako (pop 600,000); **Official language:** French; **Religions:** Islam (65 per cent), traditional beliefs (30 per cent), Christianity (5 per cent); **Adult literacy rate:** 10 per cent; **Average life expectancy at birth:** 42 years; **Unit of currency:** Mali franc; **Main exports:** cotton and cotton products, groundnuts, live animals; **Per capita GNP:** US$140.

MALTA, a Mediterranean island republic, south of Sicily. It includes Malta, 246 km² (95 sq mi), Gozo, 67 km² (26 sq mi), Comino, 3 km² (1 sq mi) and two islets. The climate is Mediterranean in type. Most people are of Arab, Italian and English descent. Cultivable land covers 39 per cent of the country but only 6 per cent of the workforce is engaged in agriculture and fishing, as opposed to 28 per cent in manufacturing. In 1979 Malta received 618,000 tourists. Malta was held by the

Phoenicians, Greeks, Carthaginians, Romans, Byzantines and Arabs until 1091 when it was joined to Sicily. From 1530 it was ruled by the Knights of St John. Napoleon's forces took it in 1798 but Britain aided the Maltese to drive out the French. In 1814 Malta became a British colony. It became fully independent in 1964 and a republic in 1974.

Area: 316 km² (122 sq mi); **Population:** 354,000; **Capital:** Valletta (pop 14,000); **Official languages:** Maltese, English; **Religion:** Roman Catholicism; **Unit of currency:** Maltese pound; **Main exports:** manufactures, machinery and transport equipment, food; **Per capita GNP:** US$2640.

MARTINIQUE, a French Overseas Department in the Lesser Antilles, between Dominica and St Lucia. It is a mountainous, volcanic island, with a warm, humid climate. The people are of African, Asian and French origin. The main activity is farming, but light manufacturing is developing. Discovered by Columbus in 1493, the island has been French for most of the time since 1635. It became a French Overseas Department in 1946.

Area: 1102 km² (426 sq mi); **Population:** 326,000; **Capital:** Fort-de-France (pop 99,000); **Highest point:** Mt Pelée, 1463 m (4800 ft); **Exports:** sugar, bananas, rum; **Per capita GNP:** US$4680.

MAURITANIA, an Islamic Republic in north-western Africa. Low plateaux cover most of the country which lies largely in the Sahara. But the fertile River Senegal plains are in the south-west. Average annual temperatures are between 25°C and 32°C (77°–90°F) and there are large diurnal variations in the Sahara. The average rainfall is 660 mm (26 inches) per year in the savanna-covered south. The north has little rainfall. About 80 per cent of the population is of Arab and Berber origin. The others are Negroid. Agriculture, particularly livestock rearing, employed 86 per cent of the workforce in 1978, accounting for 26 per cent of the GDP, as opposed to industry and services 37 per cent each. In 1979 Mauritania had 8.4 million sheep and goats and 1.6 million cattle. Sea fishing is important but the chief resource is iron ore: Mauritania is Africa's 3rd largest producer. Copper is also mined. France ruled Mauritania from 1903 to 1960. In 1976 Mauritania acquired one-third of neighbouring Western (formerly Spanish) Sahara. After prolonged resistance by Saharan guerrillas and an internal military coup in 1978, Mauritania withdrew from Western Sahara in 1979.

Area: 1,030,700 km² (397.977 sq mi); **Population:** 1,973,000; **Capital:** Nouakchott (pop 350,000); **Official language:** Arabic, French; **Religion:** Islam; **Adult literacy rate:** 17 per cent; **Average life expectancy at birth:** 42 years; **Unit of currency:** Ouguiya; **Main exports:** iron ore, fish, copper; **Per capita GNP:** US$320.

MAURITIUS, an island nation east of Madagascar in the Indian Ocean. It includes the mountainous, volcanic island of Mauritius and Rodrigues, 104 km² (40 sq mi) in area, which is about 560 km (348 mi) to the east. The climate is warm and humid, but it is modified by the altitude. The people are of Asian Hindu descent (53 per cent), Asian Muslim descent (17 per cent), and European, mixed and African descent (28 per cent). Sugar and its by-products form the basis of the economy. Tourism is increasing: foreign visitors numbered 128,000 in 1979. Britain captured Mauritius from France in 1810. It achieved independence in the Commonwealth in 1968 as a constitutional monarchy: the British monarch, represented by a Governor-General, is Head of State.

Area: 2045 km² (790 sq mi); **Population:** 1,123,000; **Capital:** Port Louis (pop 146,000); **Official language:** English; **Religions:** Hinduism, Christianity, Islam, Buddhism; **Unit of currency:** Rupee; **Main exports:** sugar, clothing; **Per capita GNP:** US$1040.

MEXICO, a republic in North America. It is largely mountainous, with high plateaux and volcanic peaks. The lowlands are in the Yucatán peninsula and along the Pacific and Gulf of Mexico coasts. The chief mountain ranges are the Sierra Madre Occidental and the Sierra Madre Oriental which enclose the central plateaux. These are dotted with lakes and volcanoes: one, Citlaltépetl, is Mexico's highest peak. The 760 km (472 mile) long peninsula, Lower or Baja California, is mostly separated from the rest of Mexico by the Gulf of California. It is a rugged, arid region. Mexico straddles the Tropic of Cancer, but there are 3 main climatic regions determined by the altitude: the tropical *tierra caliente*, below 1000 m (3281 ft); the mild *tierra templada*, between 1000 and 2500 m (3281–8202 ft), in which Mexico City is situated; and the *tierra fria* above 2500 m (8202 ft) with its cold winters. Rainfall in central Mexico averages 400–800 mm (16–31 in), but the north-west is arid. People of mixed European and Indian origin form 55 per cent of the population; Indians 29 per cent and Europeans 15 per cent. In 1978 agriculture

employed '39 per cent of the people, industry 26 per cent and services 35 per cent. Contributions to the GDP were agriculture 11 per cent, industry 37 per cent and services 52 per cent. Crops vary according to the altitude. They include coffee, cotton, maize, sisal and sugar. In 1979 Mexico had 29.9 million cattle, 7.8 million sheep, 8.1 million goats and 12.6 million pigs. Mining is important. Mexico is a major oil producer. Coal, copper, gold, iron ore, lead, manganese, mercury, silver, zinc and other minerals are mined. Manufacturing includes light and heavy industry: textiles and steel are leading manufactures. Aztec and other Indian ruins are tourist attractions: 3.7 million tourists visited Mexico in 1978. Spain ruled Mexico from 1521 to 1821. The country became a republic in 1824. Instability, wars and dictatorships marred Mexico's progress. From 1917, however, Mexico has made social and economic progress. Membership of the Latin American Free Trade Association since 1961 has helped to reduce Mexico's dependency on the United States.

Area: 1,972,547 km² (761,646 sq mi); **Population:** 86,988,000; **Capital:** Mexico City (pop 15,505,000); **Other cities:** Guadalajara (1,725,000), Monterrey (1,132,000); **Highest point:** Citlaltépetl, 5760 m (18,898 ft); **Official language:** Spanish; **Religion:** mainly Roman Catholicism; **Adult literacy rate:** 76 per cent; **Average life expectancy at birth:** 65 years; **Unit of currency:** Peso; **Main exports:** manufactures, oil, coffee, sugar, cotton; **Per capita GNP:** US$1590.

MONACO, a tiny principality on the Mediterranean Sea in south-eastern France. There are 4 districts: Monaco-Ville, the capital; la Condamine, a resort area; Monte-Carlo, a luxury resort with a famous casino; and Fontvieille. French currency is used. From 1297 Monaco belonged to the Genoese Grimaldi family. It became fully independent in 1861 and joined a customs union with France in 1865. In 1963 it ceased to be a tax haven for French citizens. Monaco is a constitutional monarchy with an elected National Council and Communal Council.

Area: 190 ha (467 acres); **Population:** 25,000; **Capital:** Monaco; **Official language:** French.

Below: An Aztec mask. The Aztecs ruled Mexico from the 13th to the early 16th centuries, but they were crushed by Spanish conquistadores. Below right: Acapulco, a major resort on the Pacific coast of Mexico, attracts many foreign tourists.

MONGOLIA, a landlocked People's Republic in northern Asia. A featureless plateau covers much of Mongolia, with mountains in the west and the Gobi desert, which covers one-third of the country, in the south. The main rivers are the Selenga, which flows into Lake Baykal, and the Kerulen, a tributary of the Amur River. The climate is severe. Temperatures average about 15°C (59°F) in July, but they plummet to −34°C (−29°F) in January. The average annual rainfall ranges from 500 mm (20 in) in the north to 130 mm (5 in) in the Gobi desert. The land is thinly populated. In 1978 agriculture employed 56 per cent of the people, industry 21 per cent and services 23 per cent. Most people were formerly nomadic herdsmen and in 1979 there were 14 million sheep, 4.7 million goats, 2.5 million cattle and 2 million horses. But all farmland is now organized in large state or collective farms: these farms own 80 per cent of the animals. Some oil, coal and other minerals are produced, but manufacturing is small-scale. The Mongol Empire became important in the 13th century under Genghis Khan. Mongolia became a Chinese province in 1691 but it became an independent Buddhist kingdom in 1912. In 1924 the communist Mongolian People's Republic was set up. But in 1990 multi-party elections took place, and Communist rule slackened.

Mongolia's economy was traditionally based on nomadic herding and most people lived in tents called ger *or yurts. These portable homes were made of felt which was stretched over a wooden frame. In recent years, an increasing number of Mongolians have adopted a more settled life.*

Area: 1,565,000 km² (604,283 sq mi); **Population:** 2,093,000; **Capital:** Ulan Bator (pop 400,000); **Official language:** Mongol; **Religion:** formerly Tibetan Buddhist Lamaism; **Average life expectancy at birth:** 63 years; **Unit of currency:** Tugrik; **Main exports:** cattle and horses, wool and hair, grains, hides, furs; **Per capita GNP:** US$780.

MONTSERRAT, a British colony in the Leeward Islands of the West Indies. It is volcanic and largely mountainous: earthquakes are common. Agriculture is the main industry: hot peppers, tomatoes and manufactures are exported. In 1979 14,400 tourists visited Montserrat. Columbus discovered the island in 1493. Irish settlers colonized it in 1632. It came under the British Crown in 1783.

Area: 98 km² (38 sq mi); **Population:** 12,000; **Chief town:** Plymouth (pop 3000); **Per capita GNP:** US$920 (1978).

MOROCCO, a monarchy in north-eastern Africa. The folded Atlas ranges cover much of the country: the highest point is Djebel Toubkal in the High Atlas range. The Anti-Atlas in the south is an uplifted rim of the African plateau. The fertile Rharb-Sebou lowlands and the Moulouya valley are in the north. Low plateaux border the narrow coastal plain in central Morocco. Tangier has an average annual temperature range of 11°–29°C (52°–84°F), but the south is cooler because of the cold Canaries current offshore. The average annual rainfall is about 760 mm (30 in) in some uplands, but the south and east merge into the Sahara. Most people are Arabs. About 30 per cent are Berbers and there is a small European minority. In 1978 agriculture employed 53 per cent of the workforce, but contributed only 14 per cent to the GDP, as opposed to 36 per cent from industry. Barley, citrus fruits, grapes and wheat are important crops. There are 13 million sheep, 3.6 million cattle and 5.6 million goats. Forestry and fishing are also important, but the main resource is phosphates. Iron ore, lead, manganese, oil, zinc and other minerals are mined. France ruled most of Morocco from 1912, although Spain held the north. Morocco became an independent kingdom in 1956, but Spain retained garrisons at Ceuta and Melilla. In 1976 Morocco and Mauritania partitioned the barren but phosphate-rich Western (formerly Spanish) Sahara. But guerrilla forces resisted the Moroccan and Mauritanian troops. In 1979 Mauritania withdrew and Morocco took the entire territory. The war continued into the 1980s.

Area: 446,550 km² (172,423 sq mi), not including Western Sahara; **Population:** 24,290,000; **Capital:** Rabat (pop 368,000); **Other cities:** Casablanca (1,506,000), Marrakesh (333,000), Fès (325,000); **Highest point:** Mt Toubkal, 4165 m (13,665 ft); **Official language:** Arabic; **Religion:** Islam; **Adult literacy rate:** 28 per cent; **Average life expectancy at birth:** 55 years; **Unit of currency:** Dirham; **Main exports:** phosphates, citrus fruits, fish; **Per capita GNP:** US$740.

MOZAMBIQUE, a People's Republic in south-eastern Africa. Coastal plains cover 44 per cent of the land, plateaux and hills 43 per cent and uplands 13 per cent. The main rivers are the Rovuma, Zambezi and Limpopo. Lake Nyasa (Malawi) is shared with Malawi and Tanzania. There is also a man-made lake behind the Cabora Bassa Dam on the Zambezi. The centre and north have a tropical climate. The far south is subtropical. The rainfall is generally low: Maputo has 760 mm (30 in) per year. There are 12 major Bantu-speaking tribes and more than 30 minor ones. Agriculture employed 67 per cent of the people in this poor nation in 1978, accounting for 45 per cent of the GDP; industry contributed 16 per cent. Arable land covers 4 per cent of the land and pasture 56 per cent. Leading crops are cashew nuts, copra, cotton,

This Berber family lives north of the Atlas mountains in Morocco. Berbers were the original inhabitants of north-western Africa, but they rapidly embraced Islam during the Arab conquest of North Africa between the 7th and the 12th centuries, although they retained their own language. Today some Berbers are nomadic herdsmen; others are sedentary farmers or skilled craftsmen. About three out of every ten Moroccans are Berbers.

groundnuts, maize, rice, sisal, sugar-cane and to-bacco. Disease-carrying tsetse flies restrict live-stock-rearing. Some coal is mined and the towns contain some industries. Portugal became established in Mozambique in the early 16th century. A guerrilla war (1964–74) preceded independence in 1975. FRELIMO, a Communist party, took power, but faced a 14-year civil war against Renamo, a guerrilla movement. Free multi-party elections were announced in 1990.

Area: 783,030 km² (302,346 sq mi); **Population:** 15,542,000; **Capital:** Maputo (pop 1,000,000); **Official language:** Portuguese; **Religions:** mainly traditional beliefs, Christianity (21 per cent), Islam (12 per cent); **Adult literacy rate:** 15 per cent; **Average life expectancy at birth:** 46 years; **Unit of currency:** Metical; **Main exports:** cashew nuts, textiles, tea, cotton; **Per capita GNP:** US$250.

MYANMAR, formerly known as Burma, a socialist republic in south-eastern Asia. The north, east and west are mountainous, but the southern valleys of the Irrawaddy and Sittang rivers are fertile. The Irrawaddy delta is one of the world's great rice-growing areas. The climate is tropical. The average temperature in the delta is 27°C (81°F) and the average annual rainfall is 2500 mm (98 in). Two-thirds of the people are Tibeto-Burmese. About 75 per cent of the people work in agriculture. Forests cover half the country, and teak is a major product. Myanmar produces oil and hopes to develop its natural gas reserves. It has many other mineral deposits. Manufacturing is mostly urban and publicly run. Britain made Burma a province of India in 1855. It became independent in 1948. A series of revolutions led to the establishment of a military government in 1962, and a one-party state. Multi-party elections were held in 1990. Burma was renamed the Union of Myanmar in 1989.

Area: 676,552 km² (261,232 sq mi); **Population:** 40,090,000 (1989 est); **Capital:** Yangon (pop 3,973,872; **Other cities:** Mandalay (532,985); **Official language:** Burmese; **Religion:** Buddhism; **Adult literacy rate:** 67 per cent; **Average life expectancy at birth:** 53 years; **Unit of currency:** Kyat; **Main exports:** teak, rice, oilcake, jute, rubber, minerals; **Per capita GNP:** US$160.

NAMIBIA, a South African-ruled country whose status is disputed. It is called South West Africa by South Africa. Behind the coastal plain (the Namib desert) is the central plateau. The Kalahari, a semi-desert, is in the east. The north is tropical and the south sub-tropical. More than 66 per cent of Namibia has less than 400 mm (16 in) of rain per year. The Namib is almost rainless: the northern interior is the wettest place. The people include Europeans (12 per cent), people of mixed origin (6 per cent), Khoisan and related peoples, including Nama (Hottentots) and Bushmen (16 per cent) and Bantu-speaking people who make up the rest of the population. Mining contributes 33 per cent of the GDP. Diamonds, lead, tin, zinc and uranium are exported. Agriculture contributes 13 per cent: the main activity is pastoralism. Fishing contributes 3 per cent and manufacturing 7 per cent. Britain annexed Walvis Bay in 1878 and later transferred it to South Africa. Germany took the rest of the country in 1884. South Africa occupied it in World War I. In 1920 the League of Nations mandated South Africa to rule the country. But in 1946 it refused to accept the trusteeship status that replaced the old mandate. A long-running dispute between South Africa and the UN was complicated by a guerrilla war beginning in 1966. Namibia achieved independence in 1990, and joined the Commonwealth.

Area: 824,292 km² (318,278 sq mi); **Population:** 1,319,000; **Capital:** Windhoek (pop 110,000); **Highest point:** 2483 m (8146 ft); **Official languages:** Afrikaans, English; **Religions:** Christianity, traditional beliefs (17 per cent); **Adult literacy rate:** 12 per cent (1971); **Unit of currency:** Rand; **Main exports:** diamonds and other minerals, fish products, livestock, karakul pelts; **Per capital GNP:** US$1220.

NAURU, an island republic close to the equator in the western Pacific Ocean. A raised atoll, it contains rich phosphate deposits on which the economy is based. 50 per cent of the people are Polynesians, 27 per cent are other Pacific islanders, 16 per cent are Chinese and 7 per cent are Europeans. Discovered in 1798, Nauru was annexed by Germany in 1888. Australia occupied it in 1914 and the League of Nations mandated Britain to rule it in 1920. Full independence, with a special relationship with the Commonwealth, was achieved in 1968.

Area: 21 km² (8 sq mi); **Population:** 9000; **Capital:** Nauru; **Main export:** phosphates.

87

Amsterdam, capital of the Netherlands, is built around a network of concentric and radial canals. The city contains about 400 bridges.

NEPAL, a landlocked monarchy between China and India. It includes some of the world's highest peaks in the Himalayas, including Mt Everest on the Chinese border. Two-thirds of Nepal is mountainous. There are temperate valleys and warm plains near the Indian border. The people are of Tibetan or Indian descent, including the warlike Gurkhas. In 1978 93 per cent of the people worked in agriculture, which accounted for 62 per cent of the GDP. Hydro-electricity and manufacturing are developing. The monarchs were figureheads between 1846 and 1951, but their power was restored in 1951. The monarch assumed absolute power in 1960, but protests led to political reform in 1990.

Area: 140,797 km² (54,365 sq mi); **Population:** 18,054,000; **Capital:** Katmandu (pop 235,000); **Highest point:** Mt Everest, 8848 m (29,028 ft); **Official language:** Nepáli; **Religion:** Hinduism (90 per cent); **Adult literacy rate:** 19 per cent; **Life expectancy at birth:** 43 years; **Unit of currency:** Rupee; **Main exports:** grains, timber, cattle, hides, resins, medicinal herbs; **Per capita GNP:** US$130.

NETHERLANDS, a prosperous monarchy, is one of the Low Countries. It is at the western edge of the North European Plain. About 40 per cent of the country is below sea-level at high tide: the sea is held back by dykes which enclose polders (reclaimed areas). The most recent polders are in the IJsselmeer (Zuider Zee) and the Delta region in the south-west. Polders make up more than 25 per cent of the land. The centre of the country consists of the flood plains of the Rhine and Maas (Meuse) rivers, and their branches (the IJssel, Lek and Waal). The Schelde river enters the sea in the south-west. The coastal region contains many islands, deep estuaries, marshes, sand dunes and polders. The highest land is in the south-east (Limburg). The annual temperature range is 2°–20°C (36°–68°F) and the average annual rainfall is about 760 mm (30 in). With about 350 people per sq km (908 per sq mi), the Netherlands is one of the world's most densely populated nations: 76 per cent lived in urban areas in 1980. In 1978 agriculture employed 6 per cent of the workforce, industry 45 per cent and services 49 per cent; they accounted for 4 per cent, 34 per cent and 62 per cent respectively of the GDP. Nearly 70 per cent of the land is farmed. Most farms are small but the yields are among the world's highest. Livestock are important: in 1980 there were 5.2 million cattle, 10.1 million pigs and 81.2 million poultry. Butter, cheese and eggs are major products. Leading crops include flowers and bulbs, potatoes, sugar beet and wheat. There is little mining apart from the extraction of natural gas and oil: in 1979 the Netherlands was the world's 4th largest natural gas producer and Western Europe's 5th oil producer. The chief manufacturing region is the Randstadt, a ring of cities around the polders of the west-centre: Rotterdam with its port Europoort, The Hague, Haarlem, Amsterdam and Utrecht. Eindhoven is another industrial centre. Petroleum products, ships, radio and television sets, textiles, and china and earthenware goods are major products. The country has been largely independent since the late 16th century. In the 17th century it built up a large overseas empire. France invaded the Netherlands in 1795 but it became a constitutional monarchy in 1815. In 1830 Belgium broke away followed by Luxembourg in 1890. Neutral in World War I, the Netherlands was occupied by Germany in 1940. After the war its economy thrived within the Benelux Customs Union. It joined NATO in 1949, the European Coal and Steel Community in 1953, and the EC in 1957. Its last two monarchs, Queen Wilhelmina and Queen Juliana, both abdicated in favour of their daughters. Queen Beatrix became Head of State in 1980. Parliament consists of a First, or Upper, Chamber with 75 members elected by the provincial legislatures, and a Second Chamber of 150 directly elected deputies.

Area: 40,844 km² (15,771 sq mi); **Population:** 14,324,000; **Capital:** Amsterdam (pop with suburbs, 1,015,000); **Other cities:** Rotterdam (1,018,000), The Hague (675,000), Utrecht (482,000), Eindhoven (369,000); **Highest point:** 332 m (1056 ft); **Official language:** Dutch; **Religions:** Roman Catholicism, Protestantism; **Adult literacy rate:** 99 per cent; **Average life expectancy at birth:** 74 years; **Unit of currency:** Florin (Guilder); **Main exports:** chemicals, petroleum products, machinery and engineering products, food, textiles; **Per capital GNP:** US$10,240.

NETHERLANDS ANTILLES, two groups of Dutch islands in the Caribbean Sea. Curaçao, Aruba and Bonaire are near the Venezuelan coast. St Maarten, St Eustatius and Saba are in the northern Leeward Islands, east of Puerto Rico. The refining of oil from Venezuela is the main industry. The islands became Dutch in the 17th century and were called Curaçao until 1949. They achieved full autonomy in internal affairs in 1954.

Sheep graze on Braemar Station at the foot of the Southern Alps on South Island, New Zealand. Lamb and wool are among the chief products.

Area: 961 km² (371 sq mi); **Population:** 273,000; **Capital:** Willemstad on Curaçao (pop 155,000); **Per capita GNP:** US$3540.

NEW CALEDONIA, a French Overseas Territory in the south-western Pacific, including New Caledonia and various small island dependencies, such as the Loyalty Islands. This tropical, mountainous country has a mainly Melanesian and European population. It possesses large reserves of nickel, chrome ore, iron ore and manganese, together with deposits of many other minerals. Only 6 per cent of the land is cultivable. Coffee, coconuts and meat are the main products. New Caledonia was discovered by Captain James Cook in 1774. It became a French colony in 1853 and an Overseas Territory in 1958.

Area: 19,058 km² (7359 sq mi); **Population:** 171,000; **Capital:** Nouméa (pop 74,000); **Per capita GNP:** US$5620.

NEW ZEALAND, a member nation of the Commonwealth in the south-western Pacific Ocean. It contains North Island, 114,681 km² (44,281 sq mi), South Island, 150,452 km² (58,093 sq mi), Stewart Island, 1735 km² (670 sq mi), the Chatham Islands, 963 km² (372 sq mi) and some smaller islands. North Island, where most people live, contains fertile plains, a volcanic central plateau, and fold mountain ranges in the east. Active volcanoes include Ngauruhoe, 2291 m (7516 ft), Ruapehu, 2796 m (9173 ft) and Tongariro, 1968 m (6457 ft). Lake Taupo in the centre is in a crater of an extinct volcano. North of the lake, hot springs are utilized to produce electricity. The eastern fold mountains continue in South Island as the Southern Alps, which reach their highest point in Mt Cook.

Glaciers flow down high valleys and the south-western coast is glaciated with scenic fiords. Important lowlands include the Canterbury Plains in the east and the Otago plateau in the south-east. New Zealand has a cool, temperate climate. The average annual temperature range at Dunedin is 6°–14°C (43°–57°F), while at Auckland it is 11°–19°C (52°–66°F). Heavy rain falls in the Southern Alps but the Canterbury plains get only about 600 mm (24 in). North Island has between 1000–2000 mm (39–79 in) per year. About 91 per cent of the population is of European, mostly British, origin; 8 per cent are Maoris and 1 per cent other Pacific peoples. In 1978 agriculture employed 10 per cent of the workforce, accounting for 10 per cent of the GDP; industry employed 35 per cent and contributed 31 per cent of the GDP. Farming is efficient and yields high. In 1979 there were 8.5 million cattle and 78 million sheep. Wool, beef, lamb, mutton and dairy products are the leading exports. Arable farming is less important than pastoralism, but cereals, fruits, tobacco and vegetables are all important. New Zealand has a few minerals, including some coal and ironsands. Nearly 70 per cent of the electricity, however, is generated by hydro-electric stations. Most older manufacturing industries process farm products, but New Zealand now has a variety of light and heavy industry. Tourism is growing: there were 339,000 tourists in 1979–80. Maoris probably settled in New Zealand in the 14th century. The Dutch navigator Abel Tasman reached New Zealand in 1642 but his discovery was kept a secret. Captain James Cook rediscovered it in 1769. Wars between early British settlers and the Maoris occurred between 1845 and 1870, reducing the Maori population to 42,000: they numbered 270,000 in 1976. New Zealand became an independent dominion in 1907. Its parliament consists of a House of Representatives which, in 1978, had 92 members elected for 3-year terms. The British monarch, represented by a Governor-General, is Head of State.

Area: 268,676 km² (103,742 sq mi); **Population:** 3,400,000; **Capital:** Wellington (pop 350,000); **Other cities:** Auckland (806,000), Christchurch (327,000), Hamilton (158,000), Dunedin (120,000); **Highest point:** Mt Cook, 3764 m (12,349 ft); **Official language:** English; **Religion:** Christianity; **Adult literacy rate:** 99 per cent; **Average life expectancy at birth:** 73 years; **Unit of currency:** New Zealand dollar; **Main exports:** meat, wool, dairy products, hides, aluminium; **Per capita GNP:** US$5940.

NICARAGUA, a Central American republic. Forested plains border the Caribbean Sea. In the centre is a highland region with some active volcanoes. It is broadest and highest in the north. The Pacific coastlands contain two huge lakes, Managua and Nicaragua. The country has a hot and humid climate. About 80 per cent of the people are of mixed white and Indian origin, 10 per cent are blacks and 4 per cent are pure Indians. Agriculture employed 44 per cent of the workforce in 1978, contributing 23 per cent of the GDP (26 per cent came from industry). Coffee, cotton and meat are major products. Gold, silver and copper are mined and manufacturing is expanding rapidly. Spain conquered Nicaragua in the early 16th century. Independence was achieved in 1821, but the country came under Mexico in 1822 and in 1823–38 it was part of the Central American Federation. A new Constitution was adopted in 1974, providing for a bicameral parliament. But in 1979 the left-wing Sandinista National Liberation Front overthrew the government. The Sandinistas lost power in 1990 and a coalition took over.

Area: 130,000 km² (50,196 sq mi); **Population:** 3,745,000; **Capital:** Managua (pop 668,000); **Highest point:** Cordillera Isabella, 2438 m (7999 ft); **Official language:** Spanish; **Religion:** Roman Catholicism; **Adult literacy rate:** 57 per cent; **Average life expectancy at birth:** 55 years; **Unit of currency:** Córdoba; **Main exports:** coffee, cotton, meat, chemical products; **Per capita GNP:** US$660.

NIGER, a poor landlocked republic in north-central Africa. The highest peaks are in the Aïr massif in the north; plateaux and plains cover most of Niger. The only river is the Niger in the southwest. The north is mostly in the hot Sahara, although there is some pasture in the Aïr massif. The far south has about 560 mm (22 in) of rain per year. Nomadic Tuaregs live in the Sahara, but most of the people are black Africans who live in the south. In 1978 agriculture employed 91 per cent of the workforce, accounting for 43 per cent of the GDP. Live animals, animal products, groundnuts and vegetables are important products. Niger also has large uranium deposits. France occupied Niger in 1897–1900. Full independence was achieved in 1960. In 1974 a military group seized power and a Supreme Military Council ruled the country. A new constitution was adopted in 1989.

Area: 1,267,000 km² (489,218 sq mi); **Population:** 6,894,000; **Capital:** Niamey (pop 410,000); **Official language:** French; **Religions:** Islam (85 per cent), traditional beliefs (14.5 per cent), Christianity; **Adult literacy rate:** 8 per cent; **Average life expectancy at birth:** 42 years; **Unit of currency:** Franc CFA; **Main exports:** uranium concentrates, live animals, vegetables, groundnuts; **Per capita GNP:** US$240.

NIGERIA, a Federal Republic in West Africa. Most of the country is drained by the Niger and Benue rivers. North of these rivers are the high plains of Hausaland and higher plateaux. The land descends to the Sokoto plains in the north-west and the Lake Chad internal drainage basin in the north-east. South and west of the Niger River are hilly uplands bordered by a broad coastal plain which extends to the huge, swampy Niger delta. In the south-east the land rises to mountains on the Cameroon border. The climate is equatorial. Temperatures average 27°C (81°F) throughout the year. In the south Lagos has an average annual rainfall of 1780 mm (70 in) while the north has 250–1000 mm (10–39 in). Forest is the typical vegetation in the south with savanna in the north and semi-desert in the Chad basin. About 250

languages and dialects are spoken in Nigeria, Africa's most populous nation. The largest groups are the Muslim Hausa and Fulani in the north, the Ibo in the south-east and the Yoruba in the south-west. Agriculture employed 56 per cent of the population in 1978 but accounted for only 34 per cent of the GDP, as opposed to 43 per cent from industry. Tropical crops remain important, but oil has dominated the economy in recent years, accounting for more than 90 per cent of the exports. Revenue from oil sales is being used to diversify the economy and to improve the infrastructure, including the building of a new federal capital at Abuja in central Nigeria, which is due to be completed in the mid-1980s. Southern Nigeria was a centre of the slave trade from the 15th century. Britain abolished the slave trade in 1807 and, in 1861, annexed Lagos to stop the slave trade there. Between 1885 and 1903 Britain extended its control over Nigeria. Full independence was achieved in 1960 and Nigeria became a republic in 1963. From 1966–79 military regimes ruled Nigeria. In 1967–70 a civil war occurred when the people of the south-east tried to secede and set up a new nation, Biafra. Nigeria has sought to reduce tensions caused by cultural diversity by extending powers to the states, which number 19. Civilian rule was restored in 1979 under a Constitution that provides for a federal parliament consisting of a Senate and a House of Representatives. In 1983 a military government took over, but a return to civilian rule was planned for 1992.

Area: 923,768 km² (356,688 sq mi); **Population:** 109,408,000; **Capital:** Lagos (pop 1,477,000), but a new capital at Ajuba is being constructed to take over; **Other cities:** Ibadan (885,000), Ogbomosho (432,000), Kano (399,000), Oshogbo (282,000), Ilorin (282,000); **Highest point:** about 2130 m (6988 ft) on Cameroon border; **Official language:** English; **Religions:** Islam, Christianity, traditional beliefs; **Average life expectancy at birth:** 48 years; **Unit of currency:** Naira; **Main exports:** oil, cocoa, palm kernels, tin, rubber; **Per capita GNP:** US$670.

NIUE ISLAND, a self-governing territory of New Zealand in the Cook Is in the South Pacific. These coral islands export copra and fruit. Britain annexed the island in 1899; New Zealand took over in 1901. It has been self-governing since 1974.

Opposite: Most people in northern Nigeria, including the Hausa and Fulani, are Muslims and mosques are common sights. Christianity and traditional religions are more important in southern Nigeria. Above: Norway's many fiords provide shelter for small fishing villages.

Area: 259 km² (100 sq mi); **Population:** 3954 (1976); **Chief town:** Alofi.

NORFOLK ISLAND, an Australian territory in the south-western Pacific. The climate of this volcanic island is pleasant: tourism is important. The island was an Australian penal colony in the 19th century. Most of the islanders are descendants of the *Bounty* mutineers.

Area: 36 km² (14 sq mi); **Population:** 2180 (1979); **Chief town:** Kingstown.

NORWAY, a monarchy in the western part of the mountainous Scandinavian peninsula. The Kjölen mountains form much of the border with Sweden. In the south there is an extensive region of high plateaux and mountains, including the highest peak, Galdhöppigen. The only large lowlands are in the south-east. The climate is mild, especially in winter, when the western coasts are warmed by the North Atlantic Drift. Even at North Cape, Norway's and Europe's most northerly point, the sea never freezes. Norway is thinly populated. In 1978 agriculture, forestry and fishing employed 8 per cent of the workforce and contributed 5 per cent of the GDP as opposed to 36 per cent from industry. Only 2 per cent of the land is cultivated and food must be imported. Coniferous forests cover 26 per cent of the land and the pulp and paper industry is important. Fishing is an important activity for people who live in the fiords or on the 50,000 or so islands. Bergen is the chief fishing port. Norway has rich oil reserves in the North Sea: it is Western Europe's 2nd largest oil producer. Iron ore, copper, lead and zinc are also mined and a high proportion of Norway's exports come from the electro-metallurgical, electro-chemical and paper industries. Hydro-electric power stations provide electricity for most purposes. Norway's large merchant shipping fleet is another major source of income. Between 1380 and 1814 Norway was united with Denmark under Danish rule. After a brief period of independence, Norway entered into a union with Sweden. This union was dissolved in 1905 and the Norwegians elected their own monarch, Haakon VII. After World War II, when it was occupied by Germany, Norway has made much economic progress and it now enjoys one of the world's highest standards of living. It rejected EC membership in 1971. Norway is a constitutional monarchy with an elected *Storting* (parliament).

Area: 324,219 km² (125,188 sq mi); **Population:** 4,138,000; **Capital:** Oslo (pop 455,000); **Other cities:** Bergen (209,000), Trondheim (135,000); **Highest point:** Galdhöppigen, 2472 m (8110 ft); **Official language:** Norwegian; **Religion:** Evangelical Lutheran Church; **Adult literacy rate:** 99 per cent; **Average life expectancy at birth:** 75 years; **Unit of currency:** Krone; **Main exports:** machinery and transport equipment, metals and metal products, oil, animal products, paper; **Per capita GNP:** US$10,710.

OMAN, a Sultanate in the south-eastern corner of the Arabian peninsula. Behind the fertile northern coast (the Batinah north-west of Muscat) is a barren upland that merges into an arid interior plateau. The only other fertile region is in the far south (Dhufar). Temperatures at Muscat vary between 21°C and 43°C (70°–109°F). The average annual rainfall is only 10 mm (0.4 inches). Arabs make up 90 per cent of the population. There are also some Indians, Iranians, Negroes and Pakistanis. Most people are farmers or fishermen, but the oil industry dominates the economy. Oil production began in 1967 and it is now the leading export, although dates, dried fish, limes and other fruits, tobacco and vegetables are also exported. Muscat was a major Indian Ocean trading centre from early times. Portugal controlled it in 1508–1648. The present royal family was founded in 1741. Britain established a special relationship with the area in 1891. Oman is now an independent, absolute monarchy, but it retains ties with Britain, which helped to suppress left-wing guerrilla activity in the south in 1964–75.

Area: 212,457 km² (82,035 sq mi); **Population:** 1,413,000; **Capital:** Muscat (pop 400,000); **Highest point:** Jabal Akhdar, 3047 m (9997 ft); **Official language:** Arabic; **Religion:** Islam; **Adult literacy rate:** 20 per cent; **Unit of currency:** Rial Omani; **Main exports:** oil, dates, limes, tobacco, frankincense; **Per capita GNP:** US$2970.

PACIFIC ISLANDS, TRUST TERRITORY OF, Micronesian islands governed by the United States since 1946. It includes the Mariana Is (excluding Guam), the Caroline Is and the Marshall Is. Tourism, fishing and farming are the main activities. From the late 1970s the US established Constitutions and set up local governments with the aim of creating a new status, either full independence or a continuing free association.

Area: 1779 km² (687 sq mi); **Population:** 149,000; **Capital:** Saipan; **Official language:** English; **Per capita GNP:** US$1340.

PAKISTAN, an Islamic Republic in southern Asia. The land is mountainous in the north where the Hindu Kush and Himalayas rise. Central and southern Pakistan contain fertile plains drained and irrigated by the River Indus and its tributaries (the Beas, Chenab, Jhelum, Ravi and Sutlej). The south-west includes the arid Baluchistan plateau and the Thar desert is in the south-east. Winters are cold in the mountainous north and cold north-easterly winds chill the northern plains in November–February. For example, the average January temperature in Lahore is 12°C (54°F) as compared with 18°C (64°F) in Karachi. In the hot season, March–May, the average temperature in Karachi rises to 29°C (84°F) but the northern plains are even hotter. It is cooler in the monsoon season, June–October, but the rainfall brought by the south-westerly winds is generally low. Karachi has an average annual rainfall of only 130 mm (5 in) although the north-east has 630–760 mm (25–30 in). Modern Pakistanis are descendants of the many peoples who have invaded the area. Several languages are spoken, including Urdu, Punjabi, Sindhi, Pashto and Baluchi. In 1980 72 per cent of the population of this extremely poor country lived in rural areas. Agriculture is the main activity, accounting for 32 per cent of the GDP as opposed to 24 per cent from industry in 1978. Leading crops are rice, winter wheat, cotton, maize and sugarcane. Hydro-electricity is important and Pakistan has large reserves of natural gas. Textiles, cement, sugar and fertilizers are leading manufactures. The Indus valley was the home of early civilizations dating back to 2500 BC. Islam was introduced in the 8th century AD. From 1526 the area came under the Mughal Empire, but this began to decline in the 17th century. By the 19th century, Britain was the dominant power and Pakistan became part of British India. At independence in 1947, however, the predominantly Muslim Pakistan broke away from India, although fighting for the disputed province of Kashmir continued until 1949. Newly-independent Pakistan consisted of two parts: West Pakistan, now Pakistan itself, and East Pakistan which became Bangladesh after a civil war in 1971. Pakistan withdrew from the Commonwealth in 1972, but was re-admitted as a member in 1989. A military government ruled from 1977 to 1985.

Area: 803,943 km² (310,421 sq mi); **Population:** 109,741,000; **Capital:** Islamabad (pop 250,000); **Other cities:** Karachi (3,499,000), Lahore (2,165,000), Faisalbad (822,000), Rawalpindi (615,000); **Official language:** Urdu; **Religions:** Islam (88 per cent), Hinduism (11 per cent), Christianity, Buddhism; **Adult literacy rate:** 21 per cent; **Average life expectancy at birth:** 52 years; **Unit of currency:** Rupee; **Main exports:** cotton and cotton goods, rice, carpets and rugs, leather; **Per capita GNP:** US$270.

PANAMA, a narrow Central American republic linking North and South America. Behind the Pacific and Caribbean coastal plains the interior is mountainous, the highest peak being Mt Chiriqui in the west. Panama's greatest width is only about 190 km (118 mi). It is at its narrowest at the point where the 81.6 km (50.7 mi) long Panama Canal is situated. The United States governed the Panama Canal Zone, a strip of land along the Canal, until 1979 when it reverted to Panama, although the US retained control over the Canal itself until 1999. Panama has a tropical climate, with an average annual rainfall of 3300 mm (130 in) on the Caribbean coast and 1500 mm (59 in) on the Pacific coast. More than 75 per cent of the people are of mixed white and Indian descent and in 1980 54 per cent of the population lived in urban areas. Only 18.5

per cent of the land is cultivated, although agriculture employed 35 per cent of the workforce in 1978, compared with 18 per cent in industry and 47 per cent in services. Bananas, rice and sugar-cane are major crops and there are copper reserves. But Panama's chief resource is the Canal. Panama became independent from Spain in 1819 as part of Colombia. It became a separate nation in 1914.

Area: 75,650 km² (29,210 sq mi); **Population:** 2,370,000; **Capital:** Panamá (pop 1,064,000); **Highest point:** Mt Chiriqui, 3374 m (11,070 ft); **Official language:** Spanish; **Religions:** Roman Catholicism (95 per cent); **Adult literacy rate:** 78 per cent; **Average life expectancy at birth:** 70 years; **Unit of currency:** Balboa; **Main exports:** petroleum products, bananas, sugar, shrimps; **Per capita GNP:** US$1350.

PAPUA NEW GUINEA, a nation in the south-western Pacific Ocean. It consists of the eastern part of New Guinea, the Bismarck Archipelago, including Manus Is, New Britain and New Ireland; Bougainville and Buka in the northern Solomon Is; the D'Entrecasteaux Is; the Louisiade Archipelago and the Trobriand Is; and about 600 smaller islands. New Guinea contains forested mountain ranges and broad, swampy river valleys. There are 40 active volcanoes in the north: this volcanic zone extends eastwards through the islands. The climate is hot and humid, but the uplands are cooler, Port Moresby has an average annual rainfall of 1200 mm (47 in). About 700 languages are spoken by the various tribal groups, a few of which have never come into contact with Western civilization. Tribal warfare still occurs. Agriculture employed 82 per cent of the people in 1978, accounting for 33 per cent of the GDP as opposed to 26 per cent from industry. The main resource, copper, is mined on Bougainville. Coffee, cocoa, copra, timber and fish are other major products. The Dutch took western New Guinea in 1828. Germany took the north-east in 1884 and Britain took the south-east, transferring it to Australia in 1906. Australia occupied German New Guinea in 1914 and ruled it with the south-east, called Papua. The combined territory was named Papua New Guinea in 1971 and it achieved full independence as a monarchy in the Commonwealth in 1975.

Area: 461,691 km² (178,270 sq mi); **Population:** 3,738,000; **Capital:** Port Moresby (pop 139,000); **Highest point:** Mt Wilhelm, 4694 m (15,400 ft); **Official language:** English; **Religions:** Protestantism (61 per cent), Roman Catholicism (31 per cent), tribal beliefs; **Adult literacy rate:** 32 per cent; **Average life expectancy at birth:** 50 years; **Unit of currency:** Kina; **Main exports:** copper ore and concentrates, coffee, cocoa, copra; **Per capita GNP:** US$650.

PARAGUAY, a landlocked republic in South America. Its main river, the Paraguay, divides it into the Chaco, a thinly populated, flat region of marsh and scrubland in the west, and a fertile plain and hills, rising to the Parana plateau, in the east. The climate is subtropical. About 75 per cent of the people are of mixed Indian and white descent, 21 per cent are of European origin, and 3 per cent are pure Indians. Agriculture employed 50 per cent of the workforce in 1978 and accounted for 32 per cent of the GDP, as compared with 24 per cent from industry. Cotton and soya beans are major crops. Forestry is also important: the bark of the quebracho tree is used to make tannin. Yerba maté, the plant from which a green tea is made, grows wild. In 1979 Paraguay had 5.2 million cattle. Mining is unimportant and most manufacturing is involved in processing farm products. Paraguay declared its independence in 1811. Wars against its neighbours in 1865–70 and in 1932–35 have marred its progress. A military coup in 1954 brought Gen Alfredo Stroessner to power. He introduced the 1967 Constitution which provides for a bicameral parliament (a Senate and Chamber of Deputies).

Area: 406,752 km² (157,056 sq mi); **Population:** 4,118,000; **Capital:** Asunción (pop 729,000); **Offi-**

Opposite: Rawalpindi is Pakistan's fourth largest city. It is a commercial and industrial centre. Above left: Asunción, Paraguay's capital, was founded on the Paraguay River by Spanish pioneers in 1537. Above: Inca ruins in the Peruvian Andes. The Incas were conquered by Spanish conquistadores in the early 16th century.

cial language: Spanish; **Religion:** mainly Roman Catholicism; **Adult literacy rate:** 81 per cent; **Average life expectancy at birth:** 63 years; **Unit of currency:** Guarani; **Main exports:** cotton, soya beans, timber; **Per capita GNP:** US$1060.

PERU, a republic in western South America. Behind the narrow, arid coastal plain are high Andean ranges. These mountains, which reach their highest peak at Mt Huascarán, contain the headwaters of the Amazon River, notably the Maranon and Ucayali. Lake Titicaca, the world's highest navigable lake, straddles the border with Bolivia. It has a total area of 8290 km² (3201 sq mi) Eastern Peru is in the low Amazon basin. The climate is tropical, but the highlands are cooler. People of mixed Indian and white origin and a roughly equal number of pure Indians make up the bulk of the population. There are also some people of European and Negroid origin. In 1978 39 per cent of the people worked in agriculture, which accounted for 21 per cent of the GDP (23 per cent came from industry). Sugar, cotton, coffee and wool are important: in 1979 there were 14.5 million sheep and 4.2 million cattle. Fishing is usually a major industry but catches in the late 1970s were reduced because of overfishing and abnormal conditions. Peru produces oil and a variety of minerals, which provide its main wealth. These include copper, lead, zinc, silver and iron ore. Manufacturing industries are mostly based in Lima. Spain conquered the Incas in 1531–33 and ruled Peru until it declared its independence in 1821. Military governments have governed for long periods, but democratic rule was restored in 1980. The 1980 Constitution provided for a bicameral parliament, with a Senate and a Chamber of Deputies.

Area: 1.285.216 km² (496.252 sq mi); **Population:** 21,790,000; **Capital:** Lima (pop 4,608,000); **Other cities:** Arequipa (305,000); **Highest point:** Mt Huascarán, 6768 m (22,205 ft); **Official languages:** Spanish, Quechua; **Religion:** Roman Catholicism; **Adult literacy rate:** 72 per cent; **Average life expectancy at birth:** 56 years; **Unit of currency:** Gold sol; **Main exports:** minerals and metals, fish and fish-meal, oil; **Per capita GNP:** US$730.

PHILIPPINES, a South-East Asian republic consisting of more than 7000 islands. The largest, Luzon, 104,682 km² (40,420 sq mi), and Mindanao, 94,625 km² (36,537 sq mi), together make up two-thirds of the land area. The large islands are volcanic and mountainous, but many islands are small coral outcrops. The country has a tropical monsoon climate. The plains are hot and humid: the uplands are cooler. Manila has an average annual rainfall of 2080 mm (82 in). Most Filipinos are of Malay-Polynesian origin. There are also some people of Pygmy, European and mixed descent. The Philippines is Asia's only predominantly Christian country. Agriculture employed 48 per cent of the workforce in 1978, but it accounted for only 27 per cent of the GDP, as opposed to industry 35 per cent and services 38 per cent. Rice and maize are the main food crops. Coconut products and sugar-cane are major cash crops. Copper is the leading mineral. Textiles, footwear, chemicals, beverages and food are leading manufactures. Nearly a million tourists visited the country in 1979. Spain ruled the Philippines from 1565 to 1898, when the archipelago was ceded to the United States. Independence was achieved in 1946. Ferdinand Marcos became president in 1965, but was voted out of power in 1986 and went into exile.

Area: 300,000 km² (115,837 sq mi); **Population:** 60,000,000; **Capital:** Manila (pop 1,630,000); **Other cities:** Quezon City (1,166,000), Davao (611,000); **Highest point:** Mt Apo, 2954 m (9692 ft); **Official language:** Philipino; **Religions:** Roman Catholicism (85 per cent), Islam (4 per cent); **Adult literacy rate:** 87 per cent; **Average life expectancy at birth:** 60 years; **Unit of currency:** Peso; **Main exports:** coconut oil, copper concentrates, timber; **Per capita GNP:** US$600.

PITCAIRN ISLAND, a British possession in the South Pacific Ocean (latitude 25°05′S, 130°05′W). Fruit and vegetables are grown, but postage stamps are the island's main source of revenue. Discovered in 1767, it received its first inhabitants, 9 *Bounty* mutineers and 18 Tahitians, in 1790. In 1856 the entire population (then 194) moved to Norfolk Island, but 43 returned in 1859–64. Britain took responsibility for the island in 1898.

Area: 5 km²; **population:** 65 (1990).

POLAND, a large republic in eastern Europe. Behind the lagoon-fringed Baltic coast is a broad plain, the northern part of which is mostly covered by infertile glacial deposits and forest. The central lowlands, in which Warsaw, Poznan and Łódź are situated, are more fertile. A low plateau in the south rises to the Sudeten Mts in the south-west and the Carpathians in the south-east. The plateau contains much fertile land and the major industrial region built around the Upper Silesian coalfield, major industrial centres being Katowice, Krakow and Wroclaw. The south is drained by the Oder and Vistula river systems. The climate becomes more continental from west to east, where the average annual temperature range is −5°–18°C (23°–64°F). Summers become warmer from north to south. Warsaw has an average annual rainfall of 560 mm (22 in): the south is wetter. In 1978 33 per cent of the population was employed in agriculture and 39 per cent in industry, as compared with 48 per cent and 29 per cent respectively in 1960. Farmland covers 60 per cent of Poland: unusually for a Communist country, 75 per cent is privately owned. Cereals, potatoes and sugar beet are major crops. In 1979 Poland had 13 million cattle, 21 million pigs, 85 million poultry and 4.2 million sheep. Poland is the world's 4th largest coal producer and it has large reserves of copper, lignite, lead, nickel, salt, sulphur and zinc. But much iron ore for the large steel industry is imported. With its massive, government-owned light and heavy industries, Poland is now one of the world's 15 top industrial nations. Poland's frontiers have changed several times in the last 200 years. In the late 18th century it disappeared from the map. Nominal independence was restored in 1807, but it was partitioned between Austria, Prussia and Russia in 1815. Poland was proclaimed an independent republic in 1918 but, in 1939, it was divided between Germany and the USSR. It again became independent in 1945, losing land to the USSR but gaining some from Germany. A Communist government was set up, but its attempts to nationalize farmland and discourage religious worship failed. Dissatisfaction with the government led to riots and strikes in 1970, 1976 and 1980, and a coalition of trade unions, Solidarity, was formed, led by Lech Walesa. Martial law drove Solidarity underground, but new strikes in 1988 led to the introduction of political freedom, and the fall of the Communists in 1989. Walesa later became president.

94

Area: 312,677 km² (120,732 sq mi); **Population:** 38,269,000; **Capital:** Warsaw (pop 1,659,000); **Other cities:** Łódź (832,000), Krakow (705,000), Wroclaw (608,000), Poznan (544,000); **Highest point:** Rysy Peak in the High Tatra, 2503 m (8212 ft); **Official language:** Polish; **Religion:** Roman Catholicism (93 per cent); **Adult literacy rate:** 98 per cent; **Average life expectancy at birth:** 71 years; **Unit of currency:** Zloty; **Main exports:** coal, lignite, coke, iron and steel goods, ships, transport equipment, textiles, food; **Per capita GNP:** US$3830.

PORTUGAL, a republic in the Iberian peninsula. Much of the land is an extension of the Spanish meseta: there are plateaux and continuations of the central Sierras of Spain. Lowlands border the coast. Portugal has hot, dry summers and mild, moist winters, but the rainfall decreases and temperatures increase from north to south. Lisbon has an average annual temperature range of 10°–21°C (50°–70°F) and 760 mm (30 in) of rain per year. Portugal has a lower per capita GNP than any other country in Western Europe. In 1978 agriculture, forestry and fishing employed 27 per cent of the workforce. It accounted for 13 per cent of the GDP, as opposed to 46 per cent from industry and 41 per cent from services. Cereals are the main crops. About 12 per cent of the land is devoted to vineyards and olive groves. Forests cover one-third of Portugal, which leads the world in cork production. About 37,000 people worked in fishing in 1979: sardines and cod form the bulk of the catch. Portugal produces some minerals, including coal, copper and some iron ore. Manufacturing, including iron and steel, chemicals and textiles, has increased rapidly in recent years. About 3 million tourists visited Portugal in 1977. Portugal's modern frontiers were established in the 13th century and Spain recognized Portugal as an independent kingdom in 1385. In the 15th century Portugal initiated the Age of Exploration

Below left: Gdansk, formerly Danzig, is a Baltic seaport and industrial centre in Poland. Strikes and riots in the city in the 1970s and 1980s were linked with a workers' movement to establish free trade unions in Communist Poland. Below: The Madeira Islands are a volcanic archipelago in the Atlantic Ocean west of Morocco. These Portuguese islands produce wine and attract many tourists.

and built up a large overseas empire. Portuguese power began to decline in the 16th century. Brazil was lost in 1822. In 1910 the monarchy was abolished and a republic proclaimed. Between the 1930s and early 1970s Portugal had an autocratic government. A coup in 1974 led to the restoration of democracy and to independence to Angola, Cape Verde, Guinea-Bissau and Mozambique in Africa. It joined the European Community in 1976.

Area: 92,082 km² (35,555 sq mi); **Population:** 10,390,000; **Capital:** Lisbon (pop with suburbs, 1,034,000); **Other cities:** Porto (693,000); **Highest point:** Malhao, 1991 m (6532 ft); **Official language:** Portuguese; **Religion:** Roman Catholicism; **Adult literacy rate:** 70 per cent; **Average life expectancy at birth:** 69 years; **Unit of currency:** Escudo; **Main exports:** timber and wood products, textiles, machinery, wine, chemicals, sardines; **Per capita GNP:** US$2160.

PUERTO RICO, a United States self-governing Commonwealth in the Caribbean Sea. The land is mostly rugged and scenic. The climate is tropical. Most people are of African and European descent. Over-population has caused substantial emigration to the US. Sugar cane is the chief product, but light industry and tourism are important. Columbus discovered the island in 1493 and it became a Spanish possession. It was ceded to the US in 1898. It has most of the powers of an American state, but its citizens cannot vote in US elections.

Area: 8897 km² (3435 sq mi); **Population:** 3,666,000; **Capital:** San Juan (pop 433,000); **Official languages:** Spanish, English; **Main exports:** sugar, rum, tobacco; **Per capita GNP:** US$2970.

QATAR, an Arab Emirate occupying a peninsula in the Persian Gulf. This hot, arid and mostly desert nation has little agriculture, although fruits and vegetables are grown. Oil, which was discovered in the 1930s, dominates the economy. Much oil revenue has been used to finance an elaborate welfare state. Qatar signed a treaty of friendship with Britain in 1916, but it became fully independent in 1971 when Britain withdrew from the Gulf.

Area: 11,000 km² (4247 sq mi); **Population:** 342,000; **Capital:** Doha (pop 220,000); **Official language:** Arabic; **Religion:** Islam; **Unit of currency:** Qatar Riyal; **Main export:** oil; **Per capita GNP:** US$16,590.

RÉUNION, a French Overseas Department about 780 km (485 mi) east of Madagascar. It contains 9 dormant and 1 active volcanoes. The island has a tropical climate and sugar cane is the chief product. The people are descendants of African slaves, French settlers, Malays, Indians and other South-East Asians. France annexed Réunion in the 1640s. It became an Overseas Department in 1946.

Area: 2510 km² (969 sq mi); **Population:** 546,000; **Capital:** St Denis (pop 104,000); **Highest point:** 3069 m (10,069 ft); **Religion:** Roman Catholicism; **Main exports:** sugar, molasses and rum; **Per capita GNP:** US$4180.

Attractive villages are a feature of the Romanian countryside. In 1980, 52 per cent of the population of Romania lived in rural areas, as compared with 66 per cent in 1960. Although the rural population has declined, it is still substantially greater than in most eastern European countries. Industry is currently expanding and so the population drift from the countryside to the cities will probably continue.

ROMANIA, a Socialist Republic on the Black Sea. Transylvania forms the heart of Romania. It includes a central plateau surrounded by the Bihor Mts to the west, the Carpathians to the east and the Transylvanian Alps to the south, where the country's highest peak is situated. In the far west are fertile plains. Other plains lie in the east and south. They are drained by the River Danube and its tributaries. A limestone plateau (Dobrogea) borders the Black Sea coast. The climate is continental. The average rainfall varies from 400 mm (16 in) in the east to 1400 mm (55 in) in the mountains. The people are descendants of several peoples, including the Romanized Dacian tribes of the Danube valley and Slavs. The Romanian language is based on Latin and contains many Slav words. In 1978 agriculture employed 50 per cent of the workforce, industry 31 per cent and services 19 per cent. Farmland covers 63 per cent of the country; most is government-owned. Cereals, potatoes, oilseeds and sugar beet are major crops and, in 1979, Romania had 6.5 million cattle, 10.9 million pigs and 15.8 million sheep. There are rich mineral resources, including oil and natural gas, coal, lignite, copper, chromite, gold, iron ore, manganese and zinc. The manufacturing sector has expanded greatly since the 1960s. In 1861 Moldavia and Walachia united to form the monarchy of Romania, which gradually extended its frontiers. In World War II it supported Germany at first but joined the Allies in 1944. In 1947 King Michael abdicated and a Communist government took control. In 1989 a revolution overthrew the dictatorial government of Nicolai Ceausescu, and ended Communist rule. But unrest continued.

Area: 237,500 km² (91,704 sq mi); **Population:** 23,155,000; **Capital:** Bucharest (pop with suburbs, 1,960,000); **Highest point:** Moldoreanu, 2543 m (8343 ft); **Official language:** Romanian; **Religion:** Romanian Orthodox Church (80 per cent); **Adult literacy rate:** 98 per cent; **Average life expectancy at birth:** 70 years; **Unit of currency:** Leu; **Main exports:** machinery, ores and metals, oil and natural gas, food, chemicals; **Per capita GNP:** US$1900.

RWANDA, a small, poor, landlocked republic in east-central Africa. The East African Rift Valley in the west contains part of Lake Kivu. It is bordered by highlands that descend in a series of plateaus to the River Kagera in the east. The equatorial climate is modified by the altitude. Bantu-speaking Hutu form 90 per cent of the population. There are also Nilo-Hamitic Tutsi and Pygmy, European and Asian minorities. Agriculture employed 91 per cent of the workforce in 1978, accounting for 46 per cent of the GDP (22 per cent came from industry and 32 per cent from services). The main cash crop is coffee. Cassiterite is mined and there are various small-scale manufacturing industries. Rwanda and Burundi were once part of German East Africa, but Belgium occupied them in 1916 and ruled them as Ruanda-Urundi. A Hutu peasants' revolt in 1959 caused the deaths of many Tutsi, who formed the ruling class. The Tutsi monarchy was abolished and Rwanda became an independent republic controlled by the Hutu in 1962. Communal conflict has caused instability since the 1960s.

Area: 26,338 km² (10,170 sq mi); **Population:** 6,939,000; **Capital:** Kigali (pop 156,000); **Highest point:** 4507 m (14,787 ft); **Official languages:** Kinyarwanda, French; **Religions:** traditional beliefs (about 50 per cent), Christianity; **Adult literacy rate:** 23 per cent; **Average life expectancy at birth:** 46 years; **Unit of currency:** Rwanda franc; **Main exports:** coffee, tin, tea; **Per capita GNP:** US$210.

ST HELENA, a British island territory in the South Atlantic, about 1930 km (1199 mi) west of Angola. It is a mountainous, volcanic island. There is some farming and fishing, but no mining or industry. St Helena became a British colony in 1833. In 1922 the volcanic island of Ascension, 1130 km (702 mi) to the north-west, was made a dependency of St Helena, as were the 4 islands of Tristan da Cunha in 1938. Ascension Island covers 88 km² (34 sq mi) and has a population of 991 (1979). Tristan da Cunha has an area of 98 km² (38 sq miles) and 320 people (1979).

Area: 122 km² (47 sq mi); **Population:** 5500 (1987); **Chief town:** Jamestown (pop 1500).

ST KITTS-NEVIS, an independent island country in the Leeward Is in the West Indies. The islands are of volcanic origin and export sugar and molasses. From 1623 they came under alternate French and British rule, but they were ceded to Britain in 1783. In 1967 St Kitts (or Christopher)-Nevis-

Anguilla became an Associated State in the Commonwealth. Because Anguilla objected to rule from St Kitts, Britain appointed a Commissioner to handle its affairs. St Kitts-Nevis became an independent country in 1983.

Area: 262 km² (101 sq mi); **Population:** 51,000; **Chief town:** Basseterre (pop 14,700); **Per capita GNP:** US$780.

ST LUCIA, a picturesque island nation in the Windward Is in the West Indies. Volcanic in origin, it has a tropical climate and bananas, cocoa, coconut oil and copra, and textiles are exported. Tourism is developing; there were 107,000 visitors in 1978. The island was contested between Britain and France from 1605, but it was ceded to Britain in 1814. Self-government was achieved in 1967 and full independence within the Commonwealth was gained in 1979.

Area: 616 km² (238 sq mi); **Population:** 151,000; **Capital:** Castries (pop 55,000).

ST PIERRE AND MIQUELON, a French Overseas Department consisting of 8 islands off the southern coast of Newfoundland, Canada. These rocky islands have a temperate, moist climate. The people are descendants of French immigrants, who have maintained their French culture. Fishing and fish processing are the main activities. The islands have been French almost continuously since 1660.

Area: 242 km² (93 sq mi); **Population:** 6000; **Capital:** St Pierre.

ST VINCENT AND THE GRENADINES, a West Indian nation in the Windward Is, consisting of the island of St Vincent, 345 km² (133 sq mi), and the small islands that make up the Northern Grenadines. St Vincent is a volcanic island with a tropical climate. Most people are blacks or of mixed origin. Farming is the main activity, but tourism is expanding. France and Britain alternately held St Vincent until it finally became British in 1805. It became a British Associated State in 1969 and a fully independent member of the Commonwealth in 1979.

Area: 388 km² (150 sq mi); **Population:** 113,000; **Capital:** Kingstown (pop 23,000); **Main export:** bananas; **Per capita GNP:** US$490.

SAMOA, AMERICAN, a group of 8 islands in the South Pacific, about 1050 km (652 mi) north-east of Fiji. The largest island, Tutuila, contains the capital Pago Pago. This mountainous island has heavy rainfall: the climate throughout is tropical. Most people are Polynesians. The chief exports are fish products, copra and handicrafts. The first recorded European landfall was in 1722. In 1899 a treaty between the US, Britain and Germany assigned the eastern Samoan islands to the US and the western islands (now Western Samoa) to Germany. A popularly elected Samoan Governor was inaugurated in 1978.

Area: 197 km² (76 sq mi); **Population:** 35,000; **Capital:** Pago Pago; **Per capita GNP:** US$8030.

SAMOA, WESTERN, a Pacific island nation about 720 km (447 mi) north-east of Fiji. The largest islands are Savai'i, 1714 km² (662 sq mi), and Upolu, 1118 km² (432 sq mi), where the capital Apia is situated. There are also two small islands, Manono and Apolima, and several uninhabited islets. The islands are volcanic in origin and have a tropical climate. The people are Polynesians and Christianity is the main religion. The chief products are bananas, cocoa and coconuts. Germany ruled the islands before World War I and New Zealand was in control in 1920–61. Western Samoa became a fully independent monarchy on January 1, 1962. HH Malietoa Tanumafili II became Head of State in 1963 and Western Samoa became a member of the Commonwealth in 1970.

Area: 2842 km² (1097 sq mi); **Population:** 164,000; **Capital:** Apia (pop 32,000).

SAN MARINO, the world's smallest independent republic. It is landlocked and situated in central Italy, south of Rimini. Its capital is on the slopes of Mt Titano, a 743 m (2438 ft) high spur of the Apennines. Most people are farmers, but tourism is the main industry. Building stone, textiles and wine are exported. Founded in the 4th century AD, San Marino joined a customs union with Italy in 1862.

Area: 61 km² (24 sq mi); **Population:** 21,000; **Capital:** San Marino (pop 4000).

SÃO TOMÉ AND PRINCIPE, an island republic in the Gulf of Guinea. It includes the volcanic island of São Tomé, 854 km² (330 sq mi) in area, Principe to the north, and some smaller islands. The people are descendants of slaves from the mainland and Europeans. Agriculture is the main activity. Portuguese mariners discovered the then uninhabited islands in 1471. From 1522 they were governed as a province of Portugal until full independence was achieved in 1975.

Area: 964 km² (372 sq mi); **Population:** 110,000; **Capital:** São Tomé (pop 17,000); **Highest point:**

2024 m (6640 ft); **Official language:** Portuguese; **Religion:** Roman Catholicism; **Unit of currency:** Dobra; **Main exports:** cocoa, copra, palm kernels; **Per capita GNP:** US$450.

SAUDI ARABIA, a kingdom occupying much of the Arabian peninsula. Behind the narrow, Red Sea coastal plain is a highland zone, including the Hejaz in the north and the Asir highlands in the south. East of these highlands are plateaux that slope gently towards the Persian Gulf coastal plain. The plateaux, which cover 90 per cent of the country, include the Nafud Desert in the north and the Rub'al-Khali (the 'Empty Quarter') in the south. The lowlands are hot, but the altitude modifies temperatures. The rainfall varies between 380 mm (15 in) in the Asir highlands to 80 mm (3 in) at Riyadh: virtually no rain falls in the Rub'al-Khali. Most Saudis are Muslim Arabs and Mecca, the birthplace of the Prophet Muhammad, and Medina are the two holiest places of Islam. In 1978 agriculture employed 62 per cent of the workforce, but it accounted for only 1 per cent of the GDP, while industry accounted for 76 per cent (of which only 5 per cent came from manufacturing). The economy is dominated by oil which was discovered in 1938. In 1980 only the USSR and US produced more oil than Saudi Arabia. The country was under the nominal rule of the Ottoman Turks in 1517–1916, when they were driven out. In 1927 the Sultan of Nejd, Abd Al-Aziz Ibn Saud, founded modern Saudi Arabia and became its king. The king now rules with a cabinet, but remains the focus of power. In recent years revenue from oil has been used to develop welfare services, industries, transport facilities and water conservation and land reclamation projects.

Area: 2,149,690 km² (830,045 sq mi); **Population:** 13,474,000; **Capital:** Riyadh (pop 1,380,000); **Other cities:** Jidda (561,000); Mecca (367,000), Medina (198,000); **Highest point:** around 3048 m (10,000 ft) in the Asir range; **Official language:** Arabic; **Religion:** Islam; **Average life expectancy at birth:** 53 years; **Unit of currency:** Riyal; **Main export:** oil; **Per capita GNP:** US$7370.

SENEGAL, a West African republic. It is mostly low-lying and covered by savanna. There is a low plateau in the south-east. Senegal is drained by the Senegal, Saloum, Gambia and Casamance rivers. The climate on the coast is pleasant but the interior is hot. The rainfall increases from the arid north to the south. Dakar has an average annual rainfall of 580 mm (23 in) while the far south-west has 1630 mm (64 in). Most people are Negroid. Agriculture employed 77 per cent of the workforce in 1978 but accounted for only 26 per cent of the GDP as opposed to 25 per cent from industry. Groundnuts and groundnut products dominate the economy. There were 2.8 million cattle and 2.9 million sheep and goats in 1979. Dakar is West Africa's most industrialized city. Tourism is growing: there were 198,000 tourists in 1979. French contacts date back to the early 17th century, but France did not colonize all of Senegal until 1887. In 1959 Senegal became part of the Federation of Mali, but it became a separate, fully independent

republic in 1960. In 1981 Senegalese troops helped to put down an uprising in Gambia, which is an enclave within Senegal. Soon afterwards Senegal and Gambia set up a confederation called Senegambia. This came into being in February 1982, although both nations retained their sovereignty.

Area: 196,192 km² (75,754 sq mi); **Population:** 7,177,000; **Capital:** Dakar (pop 1,000,000); **Official language:** French; **Religions:** Islam (90 per cent), traditional beliefs (5 per cent), Christianity (5 per cent); **Adult literacy rate:** 10 per cent; **Average life expectancy at birth:** 42 years; **Unit of currency:** Franc CFA; **Main exports:** groundnuts and groundnut products, fish, phosphate of lime; **Per capita GNP:** US$430.

SEYCHELLES, an Indian Ocean island republic north-east of Madagascar. There are about 90 islands. The rugged Mahé, or Granitic, islands make up 80 per cent of the area: the rest are flat coral islands. The largest island, Mahé, 144 km² (56 sq mi), contains the capital Victoria. The climate is tropical. Most people are Creoles, of mixed French and African origin. There are also some Chinese, Europeans and Indians. Tourism and agriculture are the main activities. French settlers arrived in the 1770s. Britain ruled the islands from 1810 until independence in the Commonwealth was achieved in 1976. A successful coup took place in 1977, but a mercenary invasion in 1981 was defeated.

Area: 280 km² (108 sq mi); **Population:** 70,000; **Capital:** Victoria (pop 23,000); **Official languages:** English, French; **Religion:** Roman Catholicism (90 per cent); **Unit of currency:** Rupee; **Main exports:** copra, cinnamon, fish; **Per capita GNP:** US$1400.

SIERRA LEONE, a West African republic. Behind the broad coastal plain are interior plateaux and mountains. The climate is tropical. Freetown has an average annual rainfall of 3360 mm (132 in): the wettest months are July–September. Most people are black Africans: there are 18 main groups. A Creole minority is composed of descendants of freed slaves brought to Freetown 200 years ago. In 1978 agriculture employed 67 per cent of the workforce and accounted for 39 per cent of the GDP, as compared with industry 22 per cent. Rice is the main food crop and coffee, cocoa and palm kernels are the chief cash crops. But diamonds and bauxite made up 67 per cent of the exports in 1978. Forestry and fishing are expanding, as is manufacturing, and tourism is being developed. In 1787 Britain founded Freetown as a settlement for freed slaves. In 1808 the Sierra Leone peninsula was made a colony and the interior was declared a protectorate in 1898. Full independence was achieved in 1961. Sierra Leone became a republic in 1971: it is now a one-party state with an elected House of Representatives.

Area: 71,740 km² (27,700 sq mi); **Population:** 4,021,000; **Capital:** Freetown (pop 470,000); **Highest point:** 1948 m (6391 ft); **Official language:** English; **Religions:** mainly traditional beliefs,

Islam (20 per cent), Christianity; **Adult literacy rate:** 15 per cent; **Average life expectancy at birth:** 46 years; **Unit of currency:** Leone; **Main exports:** diamonds, coffee, cocoa, bauxite; **Per capita GNP:** US$250.

SINGAPORE, a prosperous island republic off the southern tip of the Malay peninsula. A causeway links Singapore Island to the mainland. There are also many islets that make up 8 per cent of the country. The climate is hot and humid. Temperatures stay around 25°–27°C (77°–81°F) throughout the year and the average annual rainfall is 2440 mm (96 in). The main groups of people are Chinese (76 per cent), Malays (15 per cent) and Indians (7 per cent). Agriculture employed only 2 per cent of the people in 1978 and accounted for 2 per cent of the GDP. Industry contributed 35 per cent and services 63 per cent. Manufacturing is extremely important. The many products include ships, petrochemicals, steel and textiles. The port of Singapore is one of the world's largest and Singapore is a major financial centre. Britain took over the island in 1824. It was part of Malaysia from 1963 but it became a separate republic in 1965.

Area: 581 km² (224 sq mi); **Population:** 2,704,000; **Capital:** Singapore; **Highest point:** 177 m (581 ft); **Official languages:** Malay, Chinese, Tamil, English; **Religions:** Buddhism, Confucianism and Taoism (among the Chinese), Islam (the Malays), Hinduism (Indians), Christianity; **Adult literacy rate:** 75 per cent; **Average life expectancy at birth:** 70 years; **Unit of currency:** Singapore dollar; **Main exports:** petroleum products, electronic products, rubber, machinery; **Per capita GNP:** US$3820.

SOLOMON ISLANDS, an island nation in the Commonwealth in the south-western Pacific. It lies to the east of New Guinea and Papua New Guinea includes the two most northern islands, Bougainville and Buka. The largest of the Solomon Islands is Guadalcanal which, like the other large islands in the group, is volcanic and mountainous. The climate is equatorial. Most people are Melanesians. Agriculture, forestry and fishing are the main activities: copra, timber and palm-oil are major exports. The Solomons became a British protectorate in 1893–99. Full independence was achieved in 1978. The British monarch, represented by a Governor-General, is the official Head of State.

Area: 28,446 km² (10,984 sq mi); **Population:** 314,000; **Capital:** Honiara on Guadalcanal (pop 15,000); **Unit of currency:** Solomon Islands dollar; **Per capita GNP:** US$430 (1978).

SOMALI REPUBLIC, in the Horn of Africa, faces the Gulf of Aden in the north and the Indian Ocean to the east. Behind the narrow northern coastal plain are highlands containing Somalia's highest peaks. The south consists of plateaus and plains. It contains the only permanent rivers: the Wabi Shebele and the Juba. Rainfall increases from the north, where less than 250 mm (10 in) falls per year, to the south. Mogadishu has 400 mm (16 in). Temperatures are high throughout the year. The main types of vegetation are semi-desert and savanna. Most people speak a Cushitic language, Somali, which is also used in parts of Djibouti, Ethiopia and Kenya. In 1978 agriculture employed 82 per cent of the people and accounted for 60 per cent of the GDP (industry contributed 11 per cent). Most people are nomadic pastoralists: there were 16 million goats, 10 million sheep, 5.4 million camels and 3.8 million cattle in 1979. Animals, meat and hides and skins account for about 70 per cent of the exports. The main arable areas are in the southern river valleys. The north became a British protectorate in 1884, while Italy took the south in 1905. The two territories merged and became an independent republic in 1960. The army took control in 1969. In the 1970s Somalia was ravaged by drought. In 1977 the government supported Somali-speaking rebels in Ethiopia. Ethiopian refugees fled to Somalia, and war between the two countries lasted until 1988. Soon after the ceasefire, civil war broke out in Somalia, and thousands of Somali refugees fled to Ethiopia.

Area: 637,657 km² (246,214 sq mi); **Population:** 6,535,000; **Capital:** Mogadishu (pop 1,000,000); **Highest point:** Erigavo, 2406 m (7894 ft); **Official language:** Somali; **Religion:** Islam; **Adult literacy rate:** 60 per cent; **Average life expectancy at birth:** 43 years; **Unit of currency:** Somali shilling; **Main exports:** live animals, fruit, hides and skins; **Per capita GNP:** US$130 (1978).

SOUTH AFRICA, a republic since 1961. The interior is a vast, saucer-shaped plateau, with an uptilted rim, the highest section being the Drakensberg range in the south-east. The Orange and Limpopo rivers drain much of the plateau. Around the plateau, the land descends in steps to the sea. In southern Cape province two such steps are the Great and Little Karoo; these are plateaux bounded by mountain ranges. Most of South Africa has a subtropical climate, modified by the altitude. About 90 per cent of the land has an average annual rainfall of less than 760 mm (30 in) and about 50 per cent is arid. The population includes black Africans (70.2 per cent), people of European origin (17.5 per cent), Coloureds of mixed descent (9.4 per cent) and Asians (2.9 per cent). The whites, who are mostly Afrikaans or English speakers, control the country. From 1948, a policy of separate development was pursued, whereby each ethnic group was supposed to develop separately. For this reason, 10 African tribal Homelands have been set up for the main black groups, including the Zulu, Xhosa, Tswana, Sepedi (North Sotho) and Seshoeshoe (South Sotho). Agriculture employed 30 per cent of the workforce in 1978, industry 29 per cent and services 41 per cent. Their respective contributions to the GDP were 8 per cent, 45 per cent and 47 per cent. Manufacturing is especially important in the southern Transvaal and around the main ports: Cape Town, Durban and Port Elizabeth. South Africa produces most of the non-Communist world's gold and many other minerals, including asbestos, coal, diamonds, copper, iron ore, manganese, tin, uranium and zinc. Arable land covers 5 per cent of the country and pasture about 80 per cent: there were 13.2 million cattle and 31.5

PROVINCES OF SOUTH AFRICA

Province	Area sq km	Area sq mi	Population 1970	Seat of government
Cape of Good Hope	721,001	278,395	6,732,000	Cape Town
Natal	86,967	33,580	4,237,000	Pietermaritzburg
Transvaal	283,917	109,627	8,718,000	Pretoria
Orange Free State	129,152	49,869	1,716,000	Bloemfontein

million sheep in 1979. The chief food crop is maize, but a wide variety of cash crops is produced. Forestry, fishing and tourism are also important. The Portuguese Bartholomeu Dias rounded the Cape in 1488. The Dutch made the first settlement at the Cape in 1652. Gradually, European farmers spread inland where they clashed with Bantu-speaking peoples. In 1795–1803 and again in 1806, Britain occupied the Cape which became a British colony in 1814. The Dutch (called the Boers or Afrikaaners) resented British rule and many moved eastwards and north-eastwards to escape it. Anglo-Dutch rivalry finally led to wars in 1880–81 and 1899–1902. In 1910 the country was united in the Union of South Africa. In World War I, South Africa occupied Namibia (see Namibia). In 1961 South Africa became a republic and left the Commonwealth. Its racial policies made it increasingly isolated from the rest of the world, but in 1989 and 1990 the government, under President F. W. De Klerk, began to lift restrictions on the Black population, including legalizing Black political organizations. Apartheid appeared to be ending, but strife between rival Black groups flared up in 1990.

Area: 1,221,037 km² (471,471 sq mi); **Population:** 35,839,000; **Capitals:** Cape Town (seat of legislature, pop 1,097,000), Pretoria (seat of government, 562,000); **Other cities:** Johannesburg (1,433,000), Durban (843,000), Port Elizabeth (469,000); **Highest point:** Mont aux Sources, 3299 m (10,823 ft); **Official languages:** Afrikaans, English; **Religion:** mainly Christianity; **Average life expectancy at birth:** 60 years; **Unit of currency:** Rand; **Main exports:** minerals (including gold and diamonds), mineral products, metals and metal products, food, vegetable products, textiles, machinery, wool; **Per capita GNP:** US$1720.

SPAIN, a kingdom in the Iberian peninsula. Most of Spain is a plateau, or *Meseta*, between 610 and 910 m (2001–2986 ft) which is broken by several mountain ranges, including the Sierra de Gredos and the Sierra de Guadarrama near the capital Madrid, which itself is about 655 m (2149 ft) above sea level. The fold ranges of the Pyrenees and the Cantabrian Mts are in the north, while the Sierra Nevada in the south contains Muhacen, Spain's highest peak. The coastal plains vary in width. Some, like those around Alicante and Valencia, are fertile. Four major rivers. the Duero, Tagus, Guadiana and Guadalquivir, rise in the Meseta and discharge into the Atlantic. The Ebro River rises in the Cantabrian Mts and flows into the Mediterranean. The Balearic Islands (notably Majorca, Minorca and Ibiza) form a province in the Mediterranean. The volcanic Canary Islands, about 100 km (62 mi) off southern Morocco, consists of 2 provinces: Las Palmas de Gran Canaria and Santa

HOMELANDS OF SOUTH AFRICA

The Homelands, with the main peoples in them, are as follows: Basotho-Qwaqwa (South Sotho); Bophuthatswana (Tswana, independent 1977); Ciskei (Xhosa, independent 1981); Gazankulu (Shangaan); Kwazulu (Zulu); Lebowa (Pedi); Ndebele (Ndebele); Swazi (Swazi); Transkei (Xhosa, independent 1976); Venda (Venda, independent 1979).

Cruz de Tenerife. The northern Atlantic coast region has mild wet winters and cool summers, with an average annual temperature range of 9°–21°C (48°–70°F), as compared with 5°–26°C (41°–79°F) on the Meseta and 10°–27°C (50–81°F) on the southern and eastern Mediterranean coasts. The average annual rainfall varies from 1230 mm (48 in) at Bilbao in the north to 440 mm (17 in) at Madrid and 600 mm (24 in) at Málaga in the south. The Spanish language is Castilian. Basque is spoken in the north in the provinces bordering the Bay of Biscay and also in south-western France. Catalan is spoken in the north-east and Galician in the north-west. Separatist movements have developed in these regions and, in 1980, regional governments were established for the Basques and Catalans. In 1981 a similar government was set up in Galicia. In 1980 74 per cent of Spain's people lived in urban areas, as compared with 57 per cent in 1960. This change reflected a fall in the relative importance of agriculture in the economy. In 1978 industry employed 43 per cent of the population, services 39 per cent and agriculture 18 per cent; their respective contributions to the GDP were 38 per cent, 53 per cent and 9 per cent. Important minerals include coal, iron ore, copper, lead and zinc. In 1978 hydro-electric and nuclear power stations supplied 43 per cent and 7 per cent respectively of Spain's electrical energy. The leading manufacturing centres are Madrid and the Mediterranean port of Barcelona. Textiles are the leading manufactures, but Spain has a wide range of light and heavy industry. In 1979 38.9 million tourists visited Spain; tourism is a major source of foreign exchange. Crops vary according to the climate; irrigation is practised in many arid areas. Barley, citrus fruits, grapes (for wine), olives, potatoes, wheat and vegetables are leading crops. Spain is Europe's 3rd largest wine producer. Spain had 4.65 million cattle (mostly in the wetter north), 14.5 million sheep, 2.3 million goats and 9.9 million pigs in 1979. The fishing fleet contained more than 17,000 vessels in 1978. The Phoenicians, Carthaginians and Romans colonized Spain in early times. From about AD 400, Germanic tribes, first Vandals and later Visigoths, occupied Spain. The Moorish invasion began in 711. A Christian revival was mounted in the 11th century and, by 1276, the

Cape Peninsula extends south of Cape Town in South Africa. It was at Cape Town that the first European settlement in southern Africa was founded in 1652, as a provisioning centre for Dutch ships plying between Europe and Asia.

Moors had been driven back to the southern state of Granada, where the superb Alhambra testifies to their architectural genius. Granada finally fell to Christian armies in 1492. In the early 15th century, Castile had become the dominant kingdom in Spain and its union with Aragon in 1479 began the process that finally united the entire country. From the late 15th century, Spain became a world power, colonizing most of South America, parts of North America and Africa, and the Philippines in Asia. However, a gradual decline began in the late 16th century. The great Spanish Armada was destroyed in 1588 and Spanish sea power was finally crushed in the Battle of Trafalgar in 1805. France occupied Spain in 1808–13 and in the 1810s and 1820s most Spanish American colonies declared their independence. By the early 20th century, Spain was a poor agricultural nation. In 1931 Spain was declared a republic but a civil war in 1936–39 ended in defeat for the republicans. General Francisco Franco became dictator and Head of State, although Spain was technically a monarchy. When Franco died in 1975, Prince Don Juan Carlos de Borbón became king. Democracy was restored and a new Constitution was promulgated in 1978. Spain joined the European Community in 1986. Spain has a bicameral *Cortes* (parliament), which consists of a 350-member Chamber of Deputies and a 248-member Senate.

Area: 504,782 km² (194,908 sq mi); **Population:** 39,499,000; **Capital:** Madrid (pop 4,731,000); **Other cities:** Barcelona (1,750,000), Valencia (648,000), Seville (546,000), Zaragoza (470,000); **Highest point:** Mulhacén, 3478 m (11,411 ft); **Official language:** Spanish; **Religion:** Roman Catholicism; **Average life expectancy at birth:** 73 years; **Unit of currency:** Peseta; **Main exports:** manufactures, textiles, chemical products, footwear and leather goods, food, wine, fruit, fish, olive oil, vegetables; **Per capita GNP:** US$4340.

SRI LANKA, called Ceylon until 1972, is a South Asian republic and member of the Commonwealth. It is mostly low-lying; the central highlands which cover less than 20 per cent of the land reach their highest peak in Pidurutalagala. The climate is tropical and the capital Colombo has an average annual temperature of 27°C (81°F) throughout the year. The average annual rainfall varies from 1000 mm (39 in) in the north and east to 2000 mm (79 in) or more in the south and west. In 1981 74 per cent of the people were Sinhalese, 18 per cent were Tamils and 7 per cent were Moors. There are Burgher (European) and Malay minorities. In 1978 agriculture employed 54 per cent of the people, industry 15 per cent and services 31 per cent. About 36 per cent of Sri Lanka is cultivated. Rice is the main food. Tea, rubber and coconuts are the main cash crops. There were 1.6 million cattle in 1979. Gemstones and graphite are mined and there is a variety of manufacturing industries. The Sinhalese, from northern India, conquered the island in the 6th century BC, pushing the Veddas into the interior. Tamils arrived in the 11th century AD and Arabs (Moors) in the 12th and 13th centuries. Portugal ruled the island in 1505–1655, being replaced by the Dutch. Britain took over in 1796. Full independence was achieved in 1948. In 1960 Mrs Sirimavo Bandaranaike became prime minister, the first woman ever to hold this rank. Sri Lanka became a republic in 1972. Since 1983 guerrillas of the Tamil minority have been waging civil war.

Area: 65,610 km² (25,334 sq mi); **Population:** 17,215,000; **Capital:** Colombo (pop 624,000); **Highest point:** Pidurutalagala, 2527 m (8291 ft); **Official language:** Sinhala; **Religions:** Buddhism (67 per cent), Hinduism (18 per cent), Christianity (8 per cent), Islam (7 per cent); **Adult literacy rate:** 78 per cent; **Average life expectancy at birth:** 69 years; **Unit of currency:** Rupee; **Main exports:** tea, rubber, industrial products, coconut products; **Per capita GNP:** US$230.

SUDAN, Africa's largest nation. The land is mostly flat. It includes much of the Upper Nile basin. Highlands border the Red Sea plains in the northeast, the Darfur highlands are in the west, but the highest peak, Kinyeti, is in the far south. The

101

average annual temperature is about 21°C (70°F) but the central lowlands are hotter and the uplands cooler. The average annual rainfall varies from 50 mm (2 in) in the north to 1520 mm (60 in) in the far south. Much of Sudan is desert but large areas of *sudd* (masses of floating plants) occur in the Nile region south of latitude 10°N. In the north most people are Muslim Arabs, Hamites and Negroes. Negroid peoples predominate in the south: there is a cultural rift between the northerners and the animist and Christian southerners. In 1978 agriculture employed 79 per cent of the people, accounting for 43 per cent of the GDP, as opposed to industry 12 per cent and services 45 per cent. Cotton and cotton goods dominate the exports. Pastoral farming is also important: there were 17.3 million cattle, 17.2 million sheep and 12.2 million goats in 1979. Britain and Egypt ruled Sudan jointly as a condominium from 1899. Full independence was achieved in 1956. A North-South civil war (1964–72) ended when the government granted regional autonomy to the southern provinces, but fighting in the south broke out again in 1983. The country has also been severely affected by drought, famine and floods.

Area: 2,505,813 km² (967,553 sq mi); **Population:** 24,188,000; **Capital:** Khartoum (pop 1,000,000); **Other cities:** Omdurman (299,000); **Highest point:** Mt Kinyeti, 3187 m (10,456 ft); **Official language:** Arabic; **Religions:** Islam, traditional beliefs, Christianity; **Adult literacy rate:** 20 per cent; **Average life expectancy at birth:** 46 years; **Unit of currency:** Sudanese pound; **Main exports:** cotton, groundnuts, sesame, gum arabic; **Per capita GNP:** US$370.

SURINAM, a republic in north-eastern South America, formerly called Dutch Guiana. Behind the 25–80 km (16–50 mi) wide marshy coastal plain are savanna-covered hills that rise to forested highlands. The climate is tropical and the rainfall plentiful. About 35 per cent of the people are Creoles of mixed African and European origin, 35 per cent are Indians, 15 per cent are Javanese, 9 per cent are 'Bush Negroes' (descendants of runaway slaves), 2 per cent are Chinese and 2 per cent are pure Indians. Farming is confined to the coastal plain. Fruit, rice and sugar cane are major crops. Forestry is also important, but the most valuable resource is bauxite. Britain founded a colony in Surinam in 1650 but ceded the territory to the Dutch in 1667. The Dutch ruled it for most of the time until full independence was achieved in 1975.

Area: 163,265 km² (63,040 sq mi); **Population:** 404,000; **Capital:** Paramaribo (pop 152,000); **Official languages:** Dutch, English; **Religions:** Hinduism (29 per cent), Islam (19 per cent), Roman Catholicism (18 per cent), other Christians (14 per cent); **Unit of currency:** Guilder; **Main exports:** bauxite and aluminium, rice, citrus fruits; **Per capita GNP:** US$2360.

SWAZILAND, a landlocked kingdom in southern Africa between South Africa and Mozambique. There are 4 regions aligned north-south. The western High Veld, between 900 and 1830 m (2953–6004 ft), covers 30 per cent of Swaziland. The Middle Veld, mostly 400–850 m (1312–2789 ft) high, covers 28 per cent, and the Low Veld, 150–300 m (492–984 ft) above sea level, covers another 33 per cent. The fourth region, the Lebombo plateau in the east, reaches about 820 m (2690 ft). The average annual rainfall decreases from 1900 mm (75 in) in parts of the High Veld to 500 mm (20 in) in the east. Temperatures are modified by the altitude. Most Swazis live in rural areas. The main crops are citrus fruits, cotton, maize, pineapples, rice, sorghum, sugar cane and tobacco. In 1979 there were 650,000 cattle, 265,000 goats and 33,000 sheep. Asbestos and coal are mined and there are various factories in the towns. Tourism and remittances from Swazis working abroad are sources of foreign exchange. Swaziland came under the Transvaal Republic in 1894 but Britain ruled it after the Anglo-Boer War (1899–1902). Full independence in the Commonwealth was achieved in 1968. In 1973 the king (or Ngwenyama) took supreme power. Elections were held in 1978 but the king retained many powers.

Area: 17,363 km² (6704 sq mi); **Population:** 736,000; **Capital:** Mbabane (pop 30,000); **Official language:** English; **Religions:** Christianity (60 per cent), traditional beliefs (40 per cent); **Unit of currency:** Lilangeni; **Main exports:** sugar, wood pulp, asbestos, fruit; **Per capita GNP:** US$650.

SWEDEN, a Scandinavian monarchy. Norrland, north of latitude 61° North, contains vast coniferous forests and many streams and lakes in the glaciated valleys. Mountains run along the border with Norway; the highest peak Kebnekaise is in the north-west. But a plateau covers most of Norrland. In the far north of this thinly-populated region is part of Lapland, where some Lapps still follow their traditional nomadic way of life. South of Norrland, between Göteborg and Stockholm, is the Central Lake region, where lakes Vänern and Vättern are situated. This region has a milder climate than Norrland. South of the Lake region are the infertile southern uplands, but Scania in the far south is the most fertile region. Most of Sweden has long, cold winters and short, warm summers. Rainfall averages 500 mm (20 in) per year in the east and south-east. More than 2000 mm (79 in) falls on the western mountains. In 1980 87 per cent of the population lived in urban areas and Sweden is one of the world's most prosperous nations. In 1978 industry employed 37 per cent of the workforce, services 58 per cent and agriculture 5 per cent, their contributions to the GDP being 33 per cent, 63 per cent and 4 per cent. Sweden has little coal but hydro-electric and nuclear power stations produce 59 per cent and 22 per cent respectively of Sweden's electric energy. There are major reserves of metal ores, notably iron ore at Kiruna, Gällivare and Grängesberg. Steel and steel products are the chief manufactures. Forests cover 57 per cent of Sweden and timber and wood pulp are major exports. Only 8 per cent of the land is cultivated: cereals, potatoes, sugar beet and cattle fodder are grown. In 1979 Sweden had 1.9 million cattle and 2.7 million pigs. In the 9th–11th centuries. Swedish Vikings went eastwards and south-wards, plundering, trading and colonizing. Sweden was united with Denmark and Norway in 1397. It broke away in 1523, becoming a major power in the 17th century. In 1809 Sweden lost Finland to Russia but, after Napoleon's defeat in 1814, it gained Norway, which became independent in 1905. Sweden was neutral in World Wars I and II. It is a constitutional monarchy, with a unicameral parliament (*Riksdag*) with 349 members elected to 3-year terms.

Area: 449,964 km² (173,742 sq mi); **Population:** 8,462,000; **Capital:** Stockholm (pop 654,000); **Other cities:** Göteborg (437,000), Malmö (237,000); **Highest point:** Mt Kebnekaise, 2117 m (6946 ft); **Official language:** Swedish; **Religion:** Evangelical Lutheran Church; **Adult literacy rate:** 99 per cent; **Average life expectancy at birth:** 75 years; **Unit of currency:** Krona; **Main exports:** machinery and transport equipment, metals and metal goods, timber and timber products; **Per capita GNP:** US$11,920.

but chemicals, processed foods, glassware, machinery, metal products and textiles are all important today. Tourism is a major source of foreign exchange. In 1291 the people of Schwyz, Unterwalden and Uri formed a league to win their independence from Hapsburg rule. This league gradually grew into a loose alliance of independent cantons, whose existence was recognized formally in 1648. France conquered the area in 1798 but, in 1815, the Congress of Vienna guaranteed Switzerland neutrality. In 1848 a new Constitution was adopted by the 22 cantons; it was revised in 1874 to give more power to the federal government. In 1979 a 23rd canton, Jura, was created. Each canton has its own government. There is a bicameral federal parliament, comprising a 46-member *Ständerat* (Council of States) and a 200-member *Nationalrat* (National Council).

Area: 41,288 km² (15,942 sq mi); **Population:** 6,484,000; **Capital:** Bern (pop with suburbs, 282,000); **Other cities:** Zürich (707,000), Basle (364,000); **Highest point:** Mt Rosa, 4634 m

Stockholm, Sweden's capital, is a pleasant, largely modern city. It is called the 'Venice of the North', because part of the city stands on a group of islands in the Baltic Sea.

The canton of Valais in southern Switzerland contains fertile valleys and pleasant villages, overlooked by Alpine mountains that rise in altitude towards the Italian border.

SWITZERLAND, a landlocked federal republic. The Jura Mts run from the north-east to south-west along the border with France. These mountains are separated from the spectacularly scenic Alps, which make up 60 per cent of Switzerland, by the central plateau (*Mittelland*). This plateau contains 75 per cent of the population. It has many lakes between Lake Geneva in the south-west and Lake Constance in the north-east. Switzerland contains the head-waters of the Inn, Rhine, Rhône and Ticino rivers. The average annual temperature range on the plateau is 0°–19°C (32°–66°F). Basle has an average annual rainfall of 840 mm (33 in). The mountains are colder and wetter, although much of the precipitation falls as snow. Switzerland is a multilingual nation. In 1970 65 per cent of the population spoke German, 18 per cent French, 12 per cent Italian and 1 per cent Romansch (which is related to Latin). In 1978 agriculture employed 6 per cent of the workforce and industry and services 47 per cent each. Dairy farming is the main agricultural activity: there were 2 million cattle in 1979. Cereals, potatoes, sugar beet and fruits are grown and wine is produced. Switzerland is highly industrialized. Its superb precision instruments made it famous,

(15,203 ft); **Official languages:** French, German, Italian; **Religions:** Roman Catholicism (49 per cent), Protestantism (48 per cent); **Adult literacy rate:** 99 per cent; **Average life expectancy at birth:** 74 years: **Unit of currency:** Franc; **Main exports:** machinery, pharmaceutical goods, watches, processed foods; **Per capita GNP:** US$14,240.

SYRIA, an Arab republic in south-western Asia. Behind the coastal plain, with its Mediterranean climate, is a low mountain range that overlooks the fertile River Orontes valley. The River Euphrates drains the inland plains in the north. The highest peaks are in the Anti-Lebanon range in the south-west. To the east, the land slopes down to the hot Syrian desert. The rainfall decreases from west to east: about 60 per cent of Syria has less than 250 mm (10 in) of rain a year. About 90 per cent of the people are Arabs, 6 per cent are Kurds and there is a Palestinian minority. In 1978 agriculture employed 49 per cent of the people, industry 22 per cent and services 29 per cent. But their respective contributions to the GDP were 20 per cent, 28 per cent and 52 per cent. Cotton is the leading crop. Oil is produced and manufacturing is increasing. Tourism is important in peaceful times. The Euphrates valley was the home of early civilizations and the Syrian coast was part of Phoenicia. But, for most of its history, Syria has been under foreign rule. Islam was introduced in AD 636. After World War I, France ruled the area, but Syria was fully independent by 1946. Syria has participated in the Arab-Israeli wars which have sapped its resources. Power is concentrated in the army, although the 1973 Constitution declares Syria to be 'a democratic, popular Socialist state'.

Area: 185,180 km² (71,502 sq mi); **Population:** 12,177,000; **Capital:** Damascus (pop 1,200,000); **Other cities:** Halab (1,523,000), Homs (629,000); **Highest point:** Jabal ash Sheikh (Mt Hermon), 2814 m (9232 ft); **Official language:** Arabic; **Religion:** Islam; **Adult literacy rate:** 53 per cent; **Average life expectancy at birth:** 57 years; **Unit of currency:** Syrian pound; **Main exports:** cotton, oil, cereals, live animals; **Per capita GNP:** US$1070.

TAIWAN, an island republic (formerly called Formosa) off the coast of China. It is largely mountainous, with fertile plains in the west. The climate is tropical. Nearly all the people are Chinese. Rice, sugar cane, sweet potatoes and tea are major crops, but agriculture accounts for only 10 per cent of the GDP as compared with industry 48 per cent. Taiwan produces coal, some oil and natural gas, and various metals. But manufactures dominate the exports. Taiwan became Chinese in the 1680s. Japan ruled it between 1895–1945. When the Communists took over China in 1949, their Nationalist opponents led by Gen Chiang Kai-shek, set up a government on Taiwan. The economy expanded rapidly with US aid. Taiwan represented China in the UN until 1971, when Communist China was admitted.

Area: 35.961 km² (13,885 sq mi); **Population:** 20,289,000 (1989); **Capital:** Taipei (pop 3,050,000); **Other cities:** Kaohsiung (1,115,000); **Highest point:** Yu Shan, 3997 m (13,114 ft); **Official language:** Chinese; **Religions:** Confucianism, Buddhism, Taoism, Christianity; **Adult literacy rate:** 82 per cent; **Average life expectancy at birth:** 72 years; **Unit of currency:** Dollar; **Main exports:** textiles, electrical machinery, food, other machinery, plastics; **Per capita GNP:** US$1400 (1978).

TANZANIA, a United Republic in East Africa, consisting of mainland Tanganyika and the coral islands of Zanzibar and Pemba. Most of Tanganyika is a plateau between 900 and 1500 m (2953–4921 ft) high. The plateau is broken by arms of the East African Rift Valley: the western arm encloses lakes Nyasa (Malawi) and Tanganyika; the eastern arm contains smaller salt lakes. Lake Victoria in the north-west occupies a shallow depression and is not in the Rift Valley. There are mountains in the north and south. Mt Kilimanjaro is Africa's highest peak. The climate is equatorial, but modified by the altitude. The rainfall around Lake Victoria averages 1100 mm (43 in) a year; the

central plateau is drier and droughts are common. Savanna vegetation is the most common. The wildlife is rich and national parks cover 3 per cent of the land: tourism is expanding. The people are divided into 120 tribal groups. About 94 per cent of the people speak Bantu languages. Others speak Cushitic and Khoisan tongues. In 1978 agriculture employed 83 per cent of the people and accounted for 51 per cent of the GDP, as opposed to 13 per cent from industry. Major crops are coffee, cotton, cashew nuts and sisal. Diamonds are mined, but manufacturing is small-scale. In 1890 Tanganyika became a German territory, while Zanzibar (including Pemba) became a British protectorate. Britain occupied Tanganyika in World War I and ruled it until 1961 when it became an independent member of the Commonwealth. It became a republic in 1962. Zanzibar became independent in 1963 but, following a coup, it joined with Tanganyika in 1964, adopting the official title of the United Republic of Tanzania in October. But by 1981, Zanzibar was still not fully integrated into the union. Tanzania is a one-party state and it pursues socialist policies, concentrating on rural development.

Area: 945,087 km² (364,920 sq mi); **Population:** 25,079,000; **Capital:** Dar es Salaam (pop 1,096,000); Dodoma (44,000) will become the capital in the mid 1990s; **Highest point:** Mt Kilimanjaro, 5895 m (19,341 ft); **Official languages:** English, Swahili; **Religions:** Christianity (40 per cent), Islam (30 per cent), traditional beliefs (30 per cent); **Adult literacy rate:** 66 per cent; **Average life expectancy at birth:** 51 years; **Unit of currency:** Tanzanian shilling; **Main exports:** coffee, cloves, sisal, cotton, diamonds, cashew nuts; **Per capita GNP:** US$270.

THAILAND, a South-East Asian kingdom, called Siam until 1939. The fertile Chao Phraya river basin, the main farming region, is bordered by mountains in the east, west and north, where the highest peak, Inthanon, is situated. North-eastern Thailand, a plateau drained by the Mekong River, is infertile. The climate is tropical. Much of Thailand has an average annual rainfall of 1500 mm (59 in), but the north-eastern plateau has less than 250 mm (10 in). About 85 per cent of the people are Thais. There is a sizeable Chinese community, tribesmen in remote areas (Karen, Khmu, Mao and Yao), Malays and Indians. In 1978 agriculture employed 77 per cent of the people. It accounted for 27 per cent of the GDP, the same as industry. The main products are rice, rubber and tin. Manufacturing is increasing. The Thai state was founded in the 14th century. Its area was reduced in the 19th century but it remained independent. It was an absolute monarchy until 1932. In World War II it supported Japan. A military dictatorship ruled in 1947–51 and later it suffered from instability and frequent coups. A new democratic constitution was introduced in 1978. A major problem is a flood of refugees from Cambodia and Vietnam.

Area: 514,000 km² (198,467 sq mi); **Population:** 54,835,000; **Capital:** Bangkok (pop 5,154,000); **Highest point:** Inthanon Peak, 2595 m (8514 ft); **Official language:** Thai; **Religions:** Buddhism (94 per cent), Islam (4 per cent); **Adult literacy rate:** 84 per cent; **Average life expectancy at birth:** 61 years; **Unit of currency:** Baht; **Main exports:** rice, rubber, tapioca products, tin, maize; **Per capita GNP:** US$590.

TOGO, a West African republic. The Togo-Atacora Mts in the centre separate a low plateau in the north from the fertile southern plains. The climate is tropical, with an average temperature of 27°C (81°F) throughout the year. Lomé has an average annual rainfall of 740 mm (29 in). The rainfall increases inland to 1780 mm (70 in) in the mountains. There are about 30 tribal groups among the Negroid population. Farming is the main activity: cocoa and coffee are the leading crops. Phosphates made up 39 per cent of the exports in 1978, but manufacturing is small-scale. Togo was a German protectorate from 1884. It was invaded by British and French troops in World War I and partitioned between them. In 1957 the western (British) section joined Ghana. French Togo became a fully independent republic in 1960. Col Etienne Eyadéma took power in a coup in 1967. He was the sole candidate in an election in 1979 and remained the effective ruler of Togo.

Area: 56,000 km² (21,623 sq mi); **Population:** 3,345,000; **Capital:** Lomé (pop 366,000); **Highest point:** 1026 m (3366 ft); **Official language:** French; **Religions:** traditional beliefs (60 per cent), Christianity (25 per cent), Islam (7 per cent); **Adult literacy rate:** 18 per cent; **Average life expectancy at birth:** 46 years; **Unit of currency:** Franc CFA; **Main exports:** phosphates, cocoa, coffee; **Per capita GNP:** US$340.

TONGA, or the Friendly Islands, an island kingdom in the South Pacific. The 169 islands and islets are divided into 3 groups: Vava'u in the north; Ha'apai in the centre; and Tongatapu in the south, where Nuku'alofa is situated. There are both coral and volcanic islands. The climate is pleasant. Most people are Polynesians. Coconuts and bananas are leading products. Tonga was united under King George Tupou I in 1845. The islands were a British protectorate from 1900. Full independence within the Commonwealth was achieved in 1970.

Area: 699 km² (270 sq mi); **Population:** 108,000; **Capital:** Nuku'alofa (pop 30,000); **Unit of currency:** Pa'anga; **Per capita GNP:** US$460.

TRINIDAD AND TOBAGO, a West Indian republic close to South America. Trinidad covers 94 per cent of the country. Both islands are hilly and have a tropical climate. The people include Negroes (45 per cent), East Indians (35 per cent), people of mixed origin (17 per cent), Europeans (2 per cent) and Chinese (1 per cent). Oil is the main product. Citrus fruits, cocoa, coffee and sugar cane are grown. Columbus discovered the islands in 1498. They were both British by 1802. Full independence within the Commonwealth was achieved in 1962 and republican status was adopted in 1976.

Area: 5130 km² (1981 sq mi); **Population:** 1,193,000; **Capital:** Port-of-Spain (pop 63,000); **Official language:** English; **Unit of currency:** Dollar; **Main exports:** petroleum products, chemicals, food; **Per capita GNP:** US$3390.

TUNISIA, a North African republic. An extension of the Atlas Mts is in the north, surrounded by plains. A depression containing salt lakes, the Chott el-Djerid, is in the centre. Saharan plateaux are in the south. Tunis has an average annual temperature range of 10°–27°C (50°–81°F) and 460 mm (18 in) of rain a year. It becomes drier from north to south. Most people are Arabs or Berbers. In 1978 agriculture employed 45 per cent of the workforce, accounting for 18 per cent of the GDP as compared with 30 per cent from industry. Major crops are cereals, olives, grapes (for wine), fruit and vegetables. Fishing is important. Mining for oil, phosphates and metal ores has increased in recent years; manufacturing is also growing. Tourism is important: there were a million tourists in 1977. Carthage was founded (near present-day Tunis) in 814 BC, but Rome destroyed it in 146 BC. The Arabs conquered Tunisia in AD 647. France made Tunisia a protectorate in 1883. Full independence as a monarchy was achieved in 1956 and a republic was proclaimed in 1957. The first President, Habib Bourguiba, was elected President-for-life in 1974, but was deposed in 1987.

Area: 163,610 km² (63,174 sq mi); **Population:** 7,729,000; **Capital:** Tunis (pop 1,395,000); **Highest point:** Djebel Chambi, 1544 m (5066 ft); **Official language:** Arabic; **Religion:** Islam; **Adult literacy rate:** 55 per cent; **Average life expectancy at birth:** 57 years; **Unit of currency:** Dinar; **Main exports:** oil, olive oil, phosphates; **Per capita GNP:** US$1120.

TURKEY, a republic partly in Europe and partly in Asia. European Turkey, area 23,623 km² (9121 sq mi), lies west of the Dardanelles, the Sea of Marmara and the Bosporus. These waterways link the Mediterranean and Black seas. European Turkey is a fertile, low-lying region. Asian Turkey (Anatolia) has fertile coastal plains, with a Mediterranean climate. Central Anatolia, a mainly flat plateau, is arid with less than 250 mm (10 in) of rain per year. About 90 per cent of the people speak Turkish; Kurds make up 7 per cent of the population. In 1978 agriculture employed 60 per cent of the people and industry 14 per cent; their respective contributions to the GDP were 27 per cent and 28 per cent. Nearly 31 per cent of Turkey is cultivated. Major crops include barley, cotton, grapes (for wine), fruits, nuts, raisins, sugar beet and wheat. In 1979 Turkey had 14.9 million cattle, 43.9 million sheep (only the USSR, Australia, China and New Zealand had more), and 18.4 million goats. Turkey produces coal and lignite, chromium and some iron ore, copper and oil. Manufactures include iron and steel, petroleum products, paper, cement, chemicals, textiles and machinery. Tourism is important: there were more than 1.75 million tourists in 1978. From AD 330 Istanbul (then Constantinople) was capital of the Byzantine Empire. The Seljuk Turks invaded the area in the 11th century. The Ottoman Turks arrived in the late 13th century and, in 1453, they took Constantinople.

105

Right: Vast tracts of fertile land, particularly in the south-west, have made the USSR one of the world's great farming nations. This collective farm in the Caucasus region produces tobacco.

The Ottoman Empire gradually spread through south-eastern Europe, south-western Asia and northern Africa. It began its slow decline in the late 16th century and collapsed in World War I. In 1923 Mustafa Kemal (called Atatürk) made Turkey a republic and began to modernize it. Conflict with Greece continues and, in 1974, Turkey occupied northern Cyprus.

Area: 780,576 km² (301,399 sq mi); **Population:** 55,377,000; **Capital:** Ankara (pop 3,196,000); **Other cities:** Istanbul (2,132,000), Izmir (521,000); **Highest point:** Mt Ararat, 5165 m (16,946 ft); **Official language:** Turkish; **Religion:** Islam (98 per cent); **Adult literacy rate:** 60 per cent; **Average life expectancy at birth:** 61 years; **Unit of currency:** Turkish lira; **Main exports:** cotton, nuts, fruit, tobacco; **Per capita GNP:** US$1330.

TURKS AND CAICOS ISLANDS, a British colony in the' south-eastern Bahamas. Only 6 of the 30 or so small islands are inhabited. The largest is Grand Caicos, but the seat of government is on Grand Turk. Most people are descendants of African slaves. Fishing is the main industry. The islands became British in 1670 and from 1848 to 1962 they were dependencies of Jamaica.

Area: 430 km² (166 sq mi); **Population:** 14,000; **Seat of government:** Cockburn Town.

TUVALU, an independent member of the Commonwealth (formerly the Ellice Is) north of Fiji in the South Pacific. The islands are coral atolls. The people are Polynesians. Coconuts and copra are major products. The Gilbert and Ellice Is became a British protectorate in 1892. The Ellice Is broke away from the Micronesian Gilbert Is (now Kiribati) in 1975 to become Tovalu. Full independence was achieved in 1978.

Area: 8 km² (3 sq mi); **Population:** 7349; **Capital:** Funafuti (pop 2000).

UGANDA, a landlocked republic in equatorial Africa. Part of Africa's largest lake, Victoria, is in the south-east; the marshy Lake Kyoga is in the centre; and lakes Edward and Mobutu Sese Seko are in the Rift Valley in the west. The high Ruwenzori borders the Rift Valley. Most of Uganda is a plateau between 1100–1400 m (3609–4593 ft). Temperatures in the south-east are around 21°– 24°C (70°–75°F) throughout the year. The average annual rainfall is between 760 and 1520 mm (30–60 in). Uganda has about 40 tribal groups. Two-thirds of the people, including the largest single group, the Baganda, speak Bantu languages. Some Nilotic languages are also spoken. In 1978 agriculture employed 83 per cent of the workforce, accounting for 57 per cent of the GDP. Coffee, cotton, tea and hides and skins are important and copper is mined. Manufacturing is developing.

Britain took over Uganda between 1894 and 1914. Full independence was achieved in 1962 and Uganda became a republic in 1967. Gen Idi Amin ruled as a military dictator in 1971–79. After his overthrow by Ugandan and Tanzanian forces, the country has been struggling to overcome economic problems caused by his rule.

Area: 236,036 km² (91,139 sq mi) ; **Population:** 16,811,000; **Capital:** Kampala (pop 750,000); **Highest point:** Ruwenzori range on Zaire border, 5119 m (16,795 ft); **Official language:** English; **Religions:** Roman Catholicism (33 per cent), Protestantism (30 per cent), Islam (6 per cent), traditional beliefs; **Average life expectancy at birth:** 53 years; **Unit of currency:** Ugandan shilling; **Main exports:** coffee, cotton, tea, copper; **Per capita GNP:** US$290.

UNION OF SOVIET SOCIALIST REPUBLICS (former). This entry covers the 12 countries that, apart from the three Baltic states formerly made up the Union of Soviet Socialist Republics. The region spans both Europe and Asia. The European part, west of the Ural Mts. covers 5,571,000 km² (2,151,092 sq mi) – 25 per cent of the region – but it contains 75 per cent of the population. Much of the land is flat, including the fertile Ukraine, but there are many hilly areas. Major rivers are the Dnepr and Don which flow into the Black Sea, and the Volga which empties into the Caspian Sea. The Caspian Sea, at 438,695 km² (169,390 sq mi) is the world's largest lake, while the Volga, at 3690 km (2293 mi), is Europe's longest river. The highest point in the Urals is only 1894 m (6214 ft) but the Caucasus in

The Trans-Siberian Railway links Moscow to Vladivostok on the Pacific.

the south contain Mt Elbruz, which, at 5633 m (18,481 ft), is Europe's highest. East of the Urals is the West Siberian Plain, drained by the River Ob. Between the Yenisey and Lena rivers is the Central Siberian plateau, which is mostly between 500 and 1500 m (1640–4921 ft). In the far east are a series of mountain ranges. The south-east, which is drained by the Amur River, contains Lake Baykal, the world's deepest lake. South of the West Siberian plain is the Kazakh plateau, several mountain ranges, including the Pamir, Altai and Tien Shan, and in the west the plains around the Aral Sea. The climate varies from the Arctic north to the warm Mediterranean climates along the Black and Caspian sea coasts. Inland areas have a continental climate. Moscow's average July temperature of 21°C (70°F) is nearly 30°C (54°F) higher than the average January temperature. The north-west and the Caucasus region are the wettest places. There are deserts east of the Caspian Sea (the Kara Kum and the Kyzyl Kum). About 60 languages are spoken in the USSR. In the 10th–12th centuries, Kiev was the capital of the Russians but Kiev fell to Mongol invaders in the 13th century. Moscow then became the chief principality and by 1480 it had ended Mongol domination. In 1613 the Romanov dynasty was established. It lasted until 1917. Peter the Great westernized Russia in the early 18th century and extended its boundaries. By 1812, when Napoleon was defeated on Russian soil, Russia was a great European power. It was allied with Britain and France in World War I but Nicholas II, the last of the Romanovs, was forced to abdicate in 1917. The November 1917 Revolution led by Vladimir Lenin ousted a moderate government. The Bolsheviks took over and successfully overcame their enemies in 1918–22. From 1924, under Joseph Stalin, all opposition was ruthlessly suppressed. The economy was rebuilt with special emphasis on industrialization. The German invasion of 1941 caused much devastation and an estimated 20 million deaths. After the war, the USSR brought eastern Europe under its control and a Cold War with the West began. In 1989, under President Mikhail Gorbachev, the Cold War came to an end, but the USSR faced severe economic problems, weakening its position as a super-power. In 1990 most of its republics voted to move towards independence. At the end of 1991 the USSR broke up as Gorbachev resigned. The vast area that was the Soviet Union in 1990 became a complex of independent states, each trying to come to terms with its freedom from Kremlin control. Latvia, Lithuania and Estonia, the three Baltic States, declared their independence from the USSR at the end of 1991. By 1992, eleven of the republics that had formerly made up the USSR had become members of the Commonwealth of Independent States (CIS). They were: Armenia, Azerbaijan, Belorussia, Kazakhstan, Kyrgyzstan, Moldavia, the Russian Federation (Russia), Tajikistan, Turkmenistan, Ukraine, and Uzbekistan. Georgia, the fifteenth former Soviet republic, refused to join. However, each country eventually became fully independent. The CIS has been dominated economically and militarily by the power of Russia under the leadership of Boris Yeltsin. In 1991 the Communist Party was disbanded.

Armenia
Area: 29,800 km² (11,300 sq mi); **Population:** 3,376,000; **Capital:** Yerevan; **Language:** Armenian; **Religion:** mostly Christian; **Industries:** mining, chemical.

Azerbaijan
Area: 86,600 km² (33,400 sq mi); **Population:** 7,137,000; **Capital:** Baku; **Language:** Azer, Turkish, Russian; **Religion:** mostly Islam; **Industries:** oil refining.

Belorussia (or Belarus)
Area: 207,600 km² (80,150 sq mi); **Population:** 10,260,000; **Capital:** Minsk; **Language:** Belorussian, Russian; **Unit of currency:** rouble; **Industries:** food processing, chemicals, machine tools.

Georgia
Area: 69,700 km² (26,910 sq mi); **Population:** 5,500,000; **Capital:** Tbilisi; **Language:** Georgian, Russian; **Unit of currency:** rouble; **Industries:** manganese mining.

Kazakhstan
Area: 2,717,300 km² (1,049,200 sq mi); **Population:** 16,793,000; **Capital:** Alma-Ata; **Language:** Kazakh, Russian, German; **Unit of currency:** rouble; **Industries:** steel, cement, textiles.

Kyrgyzstan
Area: 198,500 km² (76,640 sq mi); **Population:** 4,291,000; **Capital:** Bishkek; **Unit of currency:** rouble; **Industries:** tanning, tobacco, mining.

Moldavia
Area: 33,700 km² (13,010 sq mi); **Population:** 4,400,000; **Capital:** Kishinev; **Language:** Romanian, Ukrainian; **Unit of currency:** rouble; **Industries:** canning, wine, textiles.

UNITED KINGDOM AND ISLANDS

	Area sq km	Area sq mi	Population (1981)	Capital	Population of capital
England	130,363	50,336	46,221,000	London	6,696,008
Wales	20,763	8,017	2,790,000	Cardiff	273,856
Scotland	78,772	30,416	5,116,000	Edinburgh	436,271
Northern Ireland	14,148	5,463	1,543,000[a]	Belfast	362,000[d]
Isle of Man	588	227	62,000[b]	Douglas	20,000
Channel Islands	195	75	131,000[c]	—	—

a 1979 est; b 1976 est; c estimates vary between islands; d 1971

Russian Federation (Russia)
Area: 17,075,000 km² (6,593,173 sq mi); **Population:** 148,000,000; **Capital:** Moscow; **Other cities:** St Petersburg, Samara; **Language:** Russian, Ukrainian, Byelorussian (and others); **Religion:** Russian Orthodox; **Unit of currency:** rouble; **Industries:** steel, machinery, vehicles, cement, textiles.

Tajikistan
Area: 143,100 km² (54,017 sq mi); **Population:** 5,358,000; **Capital:** Dushanbe; **Language:** Tadzhik, Russian; **Religion:** mostly Sunni Islam; **Unit of currency:** rouble; **Industries:** cement, knitwear, footwear.

Turkmenistan
Area: 488,100 km² (188,415 sq mi); **Population:** 3,622,000; **Capital:** Ashkhabad; **Language:** Turkmen, Russian; **Unit of currency:** rouble.

Ukraine
Area: 603,700 km² (233,100 sq mi); **Population:** 51,800,000; **Capital:** Kiev; **Other cities:** Kharkiv, Odessa, Lviv; **Language:** Ukrainian; **Religion:** Orthodox, Ukrainian Catholic, Islam; **Unit of currency:** Hryvnia; **Industries:** steel, chemicals, vehicles.

Uzbekistan
Area: 447,400 km² (172,700 sq mi); **Population:** 20,708,000; **Capital:** Tashkent; **Religion:** mostly Sunni Moslem; **Unit of currency:** rouble; **Industries:** steel, tractors, cars.

UNITED ARAB EMIRATES, an oil-rich federation of 7 Emirates (formerly the Trucial States), with coastlines on the Persian Gulf and the Gulf of Oman. The Emirates are Abu Dhabi, Ajman, Dubai, Fujairah, Ras al Khaimah, Sharjah and Umm al Qaiwain. The main resource of this flat, hot, desert nation is oil. About 70 per cent of the people are Arabs. The rest are Iranians or other Asians. The states entered into treaties with Britain from 1820. Britain withdrew in 1971 and ended its responsibility for the states' defence and foreign relations. The states then joined in an independent federation. The 7 rulers form a Supreme Council, which appoints the Council of Ministers.

Area: 83,600 km² (32,280 sq mi); **Population:** 1,534,000; **Capital:** Abu Dhabi; **Unit of currency:** Dirham; **Main exports:** oil and natural gas; **Per capita GNP:** US$15,590.

UNITED KINGDOM OF GREAT BRITAIN AND NORTHERN IRELAND (Great Britain consists of England, Scotland and Wales.) The Channel Islands (Jersey, Guernsey and Guernsey's dependencies: Alderney, Brechou, Great Sark, Herm, Jethou, Lihou and Little Sark) and the Isle of Man in the Irish Sea are dependencies of the British Crown, but they are largely self-governing. *Scotland* has 3 main land regions. The highlands are divided by Glen More into the rugged north-western highlands and the Grampians, which include Ben Nevis. The main island groups are the Orkney and Shetland Islands to the north and the Hebrides to the west. The central lowlands are the most densely populated region, with coalfields, the leading cities and much farmland. Scotland's southern uplands are a mainly farming region. Northern *England* contains the Cumbrian Mts (or the Lake District), where England's highest peak, Scafell Pike, 978 m (3209 ft), is situated, and the Pennines which run north-south. Coalfields near the edge of the Pennines have stimulated the growth of major industrial regions. England's other highland region includes Exmoor and Dartmoor in the south-west. Lowland England contains many fertile plains crossed by ranges of low hills, such as the Cotswolds, Chilterns and the North and South Downs in the south-east. *Wales* is a mainly highland country, rising to Snowdon, 1085 m (3560 ft). South Wales contains a large coalfield on which a major industrial region has been built. *Northern Ireland* contains uplands and plains. In the east Lough Neagh, the UK's largest lake, covers 396 km² (153 sq mi). The UK's longest rivers are the Severn and the Thames, on which the capital London stands. The UK has a moist, temperate climate, moderated by the warm North Atlantic Drift (Gulf Stream). Average temperatures seldom exceed 18°C (64°F) in summer or fall below 3°C (37°F) in winter. The highlands are wet, with about 2030 mm (80 in) of rain a year in places. The rainfall decreases to the east, where it averages 760 mm (30 in) per year. The UK is highly urbanized: 92 per cent of the population lived in urban areas in 1990. In 1978 agriculture employed only 2 per cent of the population, industry 43 per cent and services 55 per cent; their respective contributions to the GDP were 2 per cent, 36 per cent and 62 per cent. Farming is highly efficient but food is imported. Generally, livestock farming is most important in the wetter west. In 1979 there were 13.5 million cattle, 29.9 million sheep and 7.8 million pigs. Arable farming is most important in the drier east. Major crops are cereals, potatoes, sugar beet and vegetables. Fishing is

This aerial view of London shows that this great city, the capital of the UK, is a mixture of the old and new. One of its principal landmarks is Big Ben which is part of the Houses of Parliament in Westminster. Winding through the city is the river Thames, London's outlet to the sea.

ENGLISH COUNTIES

Metropolitan counties	Population 1981 census	Administrative HQ
Greater London	6,696,008	—
Greater Manchester	2,594,778	—
Merseyside	1,513,070	—
South Yorkshire	1,301,813	—
Tyne and Wear	1,143,245	—
West Midlands	2,644,634	—
West Yorkshire	2,037,510	—

Other counties		
Avon	909,408	Bristol
Bedfordshire	504,986	Bedford
Berkshire	675,153	Reading
Buckinghamshire	565,992	Aylesbury
Cambridgeshire	575,177	Cambridge
Cheshire	926,293	Chester
Cleveland	565,775	Middlesborough
Cornwall and the Isles of Scilly	430,506	Truro
Cumbria	483,427	Carlisle
Derbyshire	906,929	Matlock
Devon	952,000	Exeter
Dorset	591,990	Dorchester
Durham	604,728	Durham
East Sussex	652,568	Lewes
Essex	1,469,065	Chelmsford
Gloucestershire	499,351	Gloucester
Hampshire	1,456,367	Winchester
Hereford & Worcester	630,218	Worcester
Hertfordshire	954,535	Hertford
Humberside	847,666	Kingston upon Hull
Isle of Wight	118,192	Newport
Kent	1,463,055	Maidstone
Lancashire	1,372,118	Preston
Leicestershire	842,577	Leicester
Lincolnshire	547,560	Lincoln
Norfolk	693,490	Norwich
Northamptonshire	527,532	Northampton
Northumberland	299,905	Newcastle upon Tyne
North Yorkshire	666,610	Northallerton
Nottinghamshire	982,631	Nottingham
Oxfordshire	515,079	Oxford
Shropshire	375,610	Shrewsbury
Somerset	424,988	Taunton
Staffordshire	1,012,320	Stafford
Suffolk	596,354	Ipswich
Surrey	999,393	Kingston upon Thames
Warwickshire	473,620	Warwick
West Sussex	658,562	Chichester
Wiltshire	518,167	Trowbridge

WELSH COUNTIES

	Population 1981 census	Administrative HQ
Clwyd	390,173	Mold
Dyfed	329,977	Carmarthen
Gwent	439,684	Cwmbran
Gwynedd	230,468	Caernarfon
Mid-Glamorgan	537,866	Cardiff
Powys	110,467	Llandrindod
South Glamorgan	384,633	Cardiff
West Glamorgan	367,194	Swansea

SCOTTISH REGIONS

	Population 1981 census	Administrative HQ
Borders	99,248	Newton St Boswalls
Central	273,078	Stirling
Dumfries & Galloway	145,078	Dumfries
Fife	326,489	Glenrothes
Grampian	470,596	Aberdeen
Highland	200,030	Inverness
Lothian	735,892	Edinburgh
Strathclyde	2,397,827	Glasgow
Tayside	391,529	Dundee
Island Authorities		
Orkney	18,906	Kirkwall
Shetland	27,716	Lerwick
Western Isles	31,766	Stornaway

COUNTIES OF NORTHERN IRELAND

	Population 1971 census	Administrative HQ
Antrim	356,000	Belfast
Armagh	134,000	Armagh
Belfast CB	362,000	—
Down	312,000	Downpatrick
Fermanagh	50,000	Enniskillen
Londonderry	131,000	Londonderry
Londonderry CB	52,000	—
Tyrone	139,00	Omagh

important: there were nearly 7000 fishing vessels in 1979. The UK's industrial economy was originally based on its abundant coal and iron ore resources. Coal-mining, however, has declined, although the economy has recently been boosted by the discovery of oil and natural gas in the North Sea. Manufactures are extremely varied. Invisible earnings from banking, insurance, tourism and other services make a vital contribution to the economy. The UK's early history is one of successive invasions by various peoples, including Iberians, Celts, Romans, Angles, Saxons, Jutes, Norsemen, Danes and Normans (1066). Resistance to Norman rule continued in Wales, which was conquered in 1282 and united with England. In 1603 James VI of Scotland became James I of England. But the Act of Union giving England and Scotland a common parliament was not passed until 1707. In 1801 Ireland became part of the United Kingdom of Great Britain and Ireland. In the 18th century the UK began to build a great empire, although it lost its 13 American colonies in 1783. In the late 18th century, the UK was the first nation to change from an agricultural to an industrial society. Wealth from trade and industry made the UK one of the world's greatest nations in the 19th century. It played a major role in World War I, but this sapped its resources. After the war, southern Ireland broke away to become the Irish Free State (see Ireland). World War II proved an even greater drain on the UK's economy than World War I, and financial problems have marked its post-war history. However, the UK transformed its empire into the Commonwealth, which has given it a voice in world affairs. Many people from the non-white Commonwealth have settled in the UK, making up an estimated 3 per cent of the population in 1975. The UK joined the EEC in 1973, but it suffered from the world recession in the early 1980s. Its many problems included high inflation, increasing competition for its manufactures in world markets, and violent conflict in Northern Ireland.

Area: 244,046 km² (94,232 sq mi), not including the Isle of Man and the Channel Islands; **Population:** 56,658,000 (1989); **Capital:** London (met. pop 6,696,000); **Other cities** (prelim 1981 census): Birmingham (920,389), Glasgow (763,162), Liver-

pool (510,306), Sheffield (477,142), Manchester (449,168), Leeds (448,528), Edinburgh (436,271), Bristol (387,977), Belfast (362,000 in 1971), Coventry (314,124), Bradford (280,691), Leicester (279,791), Cardiff (273,856), Nottingham (271,080), Kingston upon Hull (268,302), Wolverhampton (252,447), Stoke-on-Trent (252,351); **Highest point:** Ben Nevis, 1347 m (4419 ft); **Official language:** English; **Religion:** mainly Christianity; **Adult literacy rate:** 99 per cent; **Average life expectancy at birth:** 73 years; **Unit of currency:** Pound sterling; **Main exports:** electrical and engineering products, transport equipment, textiles, chemicals and plastics, ceramics; **Per capita GNP:** US$6340 (Channel Is, US$5240 and Is of Man US$3890).

UNITED STATES OF AMERICA, a federal republic and the world's 4th largest nation. The bulk of the US lies between Canada and Mexico. The 49th state, Alaska, is in north-western North America, while the 50th state, Hawaii, is in North Pacific Ocean, about 3870 km (2404 mi) south-west of San Francisco. (Both Alaska and Hawaii became states in 1959.) The main part of the US contains 5 land regions. The *eastern coastal plains* are broadest around the Gulf of Mexico. The Atlantic coastal plains are broadest in the south and narrowest in New England. The Atlantic coast is deeply indented and contains several natural harbours. West of the Atlantic seaboard are the *Appalachian Mts*. This complex region which runs roughly from Newfoundland (Canada) in the north-east to Alabama in the south-west contains many ridges, plateaux and deep valleys. The *central (interior) lowlands* stretch westwards from the Appalachians. In the north are the five Great Lakes: Lake Superior, which covers 82,409 km² (31,820 sq mi), is the world's largest freshwater lake. To the south, the central plains are drained by the Mississippi River and its tributaries, notably the Missouri and Ohio. To the west are the higher Great Plains, mostly between 450 and 1800 m (1476–5906 ft). Beyond these plains the land rises to the *western highlands*, which include the folded Rocky Mountains, the Sierra Nevada range and the Cascade range, which includes the volcano Mt St Helens which erupted in 1980. The Colorado

San Francisco, California's third largest city after Los Angeles and San Diego, is a largely modern city. It was rebuilt after it was devastated by the 1906 earthquake and the ensuing fires. A seaport with a fine harbour, San Francisco is a colourful, cosmopolitan city; its Chinatown district is the largest Chinese settlement outside Asia. California has a larger population than any other state in the United States and its thriving mixed economy is more substantial than those of many nations that are members of the United Nations.

US STATES

State	Capital	Area sq km	Area sq mi	Population (1980)	State Bird/State Flower
Alabama	Montgomery	133,667	51,612	3,890,061	Yellowhammer/Camellia
Alaska	Juneau	1,518,800	586,444	400,481	Willow ptarmigan/Forget-me-not
Arizona	Phoenix	295,023	113,915	2,717,866	Cactus wren/Saguaro
Arkansas	Little Rock	137,539	53,107	2,285,513	Mockingbird/Apple blossom
California	Sacramento	411,013	158,702	23,668,562	California valley quail/Golden poppy
Colorado	Denver	269,998	104,253	2,888,834	Lark bunting/Rocky Mountain columbine
Connecticut	Hartford	12,973	5,009	3,107,576	Robin/Mountain laurel
Delaware	Dover	5,328	2,057	595,225	Blue hen chicken/Peach blossom
Florida	Tallahassee	151,670	58,563	9,739,992	Mockingbird/Orange blossom
Georgia	Atlanta	152,488	58,879	5,464,265	Brown thrasher/Cherokee rose
Hawaii	Honolulu	16,705	6,450	965,000	Hawaiian goose/Hibiscus
Idaho	Boise	216,412	83,562	943,935	Mountain bluebird/Syringa
Illinois	Springfield	146,075	56,403	11,418,461	Cardinal/Native violet
Indiana	Indianapolis	93,993	36,293	5,490,179	Cardinal/Peony
Iowa	Des Moines	145,790	56,293	2,913,387	Eastern goldfinch/Wild rose
Kansas	Topeka	213,063	82,269	2,363,208	Western meadow lark/Sunflower
Kentucky	Frankfort	104,623	40,397	3,661,433	Kentucky cardinal/Goldenrod
Louisiana	Baton Rouge	125,674	48,526	4,203,972	Brown pelican/Magnolia
Maine	Augusta	86,026	33,217	1,124,660	Chickadee/White pine cone and tassel
Maryland	Annapolis	27,394	10,577	4,216,446	Baltimore oriole/Black-eyed Susan
Massachusetts	Boston	21,386	8,258	5,737,037	Chickadee/Mayflower
Michigan	Lansing	150,779	58,219	9,258,344	Robin/Apple blossom
Minnesota	St Paul	217,735	84,073	4,077,148	Common loon/Pink and white lady's-slipper
Mississippi	Jackson	123,584	47,719	2,520,638	Mockingbird/Magnolia
Missouri	Jefferson City	180,486	69,690	4,917,444	Bluebird/Hawthorn
Montana	Helena	381,086	147,146	786,690	Western meadow lark/Bitterroot
Nebraska	Lincoln	200,017	77,231	1,570,006	Western meadow lark/Goldenrod
Nevada	Carson City	286,297	110,546	799,184	Mountain bluebird/Sagebrush
New Hampshire	Concord	24,097	9,304	920,610	Purple finch/Purple lilac
New Jersey	Trenton	20,295	7,836	7,364,158	Eastern goldfinch/Purple violet
New Mexico	Santa Fe	315,113	121,672	1,299,968	Roadrunner/Yucca
New York	Albany	128,401	49,579	17,557,288	Bluebird/Rose
North Carolina	Raleigh	136,197	52,589	5,874,429	Cardinal/Flowering dogwood
North Dakota	Bismarck	183,022	70,669	652,695	Western meadow lark/Wild prairie rose
Ohio	Columbus	106,765	41,224	10,797,419	Cardinal/Scarlet carnation
Oklahoma	Oklahoma City	181,089	69,923	3,025,266	Scissor-tailed flycatcher/Mistletoe
Oregon	Salem	251,180	96,986	2,632,663	Western meadow lark/Oregon grape
Pennsylvania	Harrisburg	117,412	45,336	11,866,728	Ruffed grouse/Mountain laurel
Rhode Island	Providence	3,144	1,214	947,154	Rhode Island Red/Violet
South Carolina	Columbia	80,432	31,057	3,119,208	Carolina wren/Carolina jessamine
South Dakota	Pierre	199,551	77,051	690,178	Ring-necked pheasant/Pasqueflower
Tennessee	Nashville	109,411	42,246	4,590,750	Mockingbird/Iris
Texas	Austin	692,402	267,353	14,228,383	Mockingbird/Bluebonnet
Utah	Salt Lake City	219,931	84,920	1,461,037	Sea gull/Sego lily
Vermont	Montpelier	24,887	9,609	511,456	Hermit thrush/Red clover
Virginia	Richmond	105,716	40,819	5,346,279	Cardinal/Flowering dogwood
Washington	Olympia	176,617	68,196	4,130,163	Willow goldfinch/Coast rhododendron
West Virginia	Charlestown	62,629	24,183	1,949,644	Cardinal/Rhododendron
Wisconsin	Madison	145,438	56,157	4,705,335	Robin/Wood violet
Wyoming	Cheyenne	253,596	97,919	470,816	Meadow lark/Indian paintbrush

Much of Pennsylvania, a state in the north-eastern United States, lies in the Appalachian mountain region. The Appalachians, which extend from Newfoundland to Alabama, are a far older and more eroded range than the Rockies in the west. Hence, they have much gentler slopes and contain extensive farming regions. However, because of the slopes, soil erosion is always a danger in this moist region and contour ploughing is one of the ways of combatting this threat. Pennsylvania was one of the original 13 states of the USA.

111

River in the south-west has carved the Grand Canyon, which is more than 349 km (217 mi) long and 1675 m (5495 ft) deep in places. The *Pacific slope* contains fertile valleys and coastal ranges. One feature is the 960 km (597 mi) long San Andreas Fault in California. Movements along the fault cause earthquakes. In 1906 San Francisco was devastated by an earthquake and again, in 1989, the city suffered some serious damage as a result of another movement. Alaska also has much earthquake and volcanic activity and the Alaska range contains North America's highest peak, Mt McKinley. Hawaii consists of a string of volcanic and coral islands. The climate varies greatly from Arctic conditions in Alaska to deserts in the south-west, including Death Valley, the US's lowest point at 86 m (282 ft) below sea level, and a humid, subtropical climate in the south-east. California has a pleasant Mediterranean climate, but much of the interior has a continental climate, with hot summers, cold winters and a relatively low annual rainfall. The first inhabitants, American Indians, entered North America about 20,000 years ago, via the Bering Strait. When Christopher Columbus arrived at the end of the 15th century there were about 1,500,000 Indians. In 1970 they numbered 790,000. In 1980 about 86 per cent of the population was of European descent and 11 per cent were blacks, the descendants of slaves. Other races, including American Indians, Chinese, Japanese and Filipinos made up the other 3 per cent. Nearly 47 per cent of the land is farmed but only 2 per cent of the workforce was engaged in agriculture in 1978, as opposed to 33 per cent in industry and 65 per cent in services. Farming is highly efficient and the US is among the world's top producers of cotton, fruits, maize, oats, soya beans, sugar beet, tobacco, timber, wheat and livestock. About half the land area of the US is farmland. Wheat production centres on the Great Plains. Texas produces the most beef cattle. In 1979 there were 110.9 million cattle, 59.9 million pigs and 12.2 million sheep. In 1979 agriculture accounted for 3 per cent of the GDP, industry 34 per cent and services 63 per cent. The US is one of the world's top producers of copper, iron ore, oil and natural gas, lead, phosphates, sulphur and uranium. The US is the world's most industrialized nation, accounting for about half of the world's industrial goods. Its technology was exemplified by its feat of landing men on the Moon in 1969. The first European to land in North America was probably Leif Ericsson, a Viking, in about AD 986. The continent was rediscovered in 1497 by John Cabot. The first Europeans to settle in large numbers were the English, who founded a settlement in Virginia in 1607. By 1760 there were 13 colonies between Georgia and Massachusetts. The American War of Independence (1775–83) ended British rule. The Declaration of Independence was signed on July 4th, 1776, and the Revolutionary War continued until 1783, when the British and the Americans signed the Treaty of Paris, which officially ended the War and the British surrendered their claim. Under the 1787 Constitution, George Washington was elected the first President in 1789. In 1800, Washington, D.C. became the national capital. In 1803 Louisiana was purchased from France, which almost doubled the

Spanish cultural influences are evident throughout Uruguay where more than 90 per cent of the people are of European descent. This Roman Catholic church is in Soriano, in south-western Uruguay.

size of the United States. Florida was bought from Spain in 1809. The US-Mexican War of 1846–48 ended with the acquisition of much of the south-west: the US-Mexico border was fixed in 1853–54. As the pioneers moved westward they infringed on many of the Indian territories. US soldiers were sent to protect the pioneers and by the 1840s most of the Indians had been driven west of the Mississippi River. Many died on the way, the tragic journey becoming known as the 'Trail of Tears'. The Civil War (1861–65) ended the threat of the secession of the South and slavery was abolished. The Civil War took more American lives than any other battle in history. About 620,000 troops died altogether. Industrialization and the opening up of the West caused the economy to expand in the late 19th century. The development of the automobile had the greatest single impact on the US economy. Other new products included the electric light, typewriters and the telephone. Abundant water supplies powered the industrial machinery. The nation's coal and iron ore resources were converted into steel, which was then used in the construction and manufacturing industries. Petroleum resources became especially important with the rise of the automobile. The US intervened in World War I in 1917. This was the first war that the US got involved in on foreign territory. Between the wars there was a severe economic depression, but the New Deal policy of the 32nd President Franklin D. Roosevelt helped it to recover. Roosevelt led the US into World War II in 1941 after the Japanese attack on Pearl Harbor in Hawaii. After World War II, the US accepted its role as a super-power, becoming involved in wars in Korea (1950–53) and Vietnam (1964–1973) aimed at halting the spread of communism in Asia. Internally, the US has been troubled by ethnic conflict and assassinations of leading figures.

Area: 9,363,123 km² (3,615,319 sq mi); **Population:** 249,632,692 (1989 est); **Capital:** Washington DC (pop of District of Columbia, 637,651, pop of

Caracas, capital and by far the largest city of Venezuela, has grown rapidly in recent years, much of the development having been financed by revenue from the country's massive oil sales.

city, 635,185); **Other cities:** New York City (7,322,564), Los Angeles (3,485,398), Chicago (2,783,726), Houston (1,630,553), Philadelphia (1,585,577), San Diego (1,110,549), Detroit (1,027,974), Dallas (1,006,877), Phoenix (983,403), San Antonio (935,933), San Jose (782,248), Indianapolis (741,952), Baltimore (736,014), San Francisco (723,959), Jacksonville (672,971), Columbus (632,910), Milwaukee (628,088), Memphis (610,337), Boston (574,283), Seattle (516,259), El Paso (515,342), Nashville (510,784); **Highest point:** Mt McKinley (Alaska), 6194 m (20,322 ft); **Official language:** English; **Religions:** in 1978, 54.7 per cent of church members were Protestants, 37.2 per cent were Roman Catholics, and 4.3 per cent were Jews; **Adult literacy rate:** 99 per cent; **Average life expectancy at birth:** 73 years; **Unit of currency:** Dollar; **Main exports:** machinery, vehicles, grains, aircraft and parts, chemicals, coal, soya beans, textiles, cotton, iron and steel goods; **Per capita GNP:** US$10,820.

UPPER VOLTA See Burkina Faso.

URUGUAY, a South American republic facing the Atlantic Ocean. It is mostly low-lying, with hills in the north. The River Negro, a tributary of the Uruguay on the western border, drains the central region. The average annual temperature range is 10°–23°C (50°–73°F), while the annual rainfall averages 1000 mm (39 in) in the south and 1260 (50 in) in the north. More than 90 per cent of the population are of European descent. Most others are of mixed European and Indian descent. In 1979 agriculture employed 12 per cent of the workforce, industry 33 per cent and services 55 per cent. About 89 per cent of the land is farmed; 90 per cent of this is pasture. In 1979 Uruguay had 10 million cattle and 18.7 million sheep; livestock products are the chief exports. Crops include fruits, maize, rice, sugar and wheat. There are processing, oil refining, light engineering, transport, chemical and textile industries. Europeans first landed in Uruguay in 1515. Spain founded Montevideo in 1726 to stem

Portugese influence in the area. The Portuguese were driven out in the late 18th century. Brazil annexed Uruguay in 1820, but Uruguay joined with Argentina in 1825 to fight Brazil. Uruguay finally became an independent nation in 1828. In 1903 José Batlle y Ordóñez became president and introduced many reforms, including extensive welfare services. Economic problems and the activities of the Tupamaros (an urban guerrilla movement) have caused political instability and army intervention in government in recent years.

Area: 176,215 km² (68,041 sq mi); **Population:** 2,934,000; **Capital:** Montevideo (pop 1,230,000); **Official language:** Spanish; **Religion:** Roman Catholicism; **Adult literacy rate:** 94 per cent; **Average life expectancy at birth:** 71 years; **Unit of currency:** Peso; **Main exports:** meat, wool, hides and skins; **Per capita GNP:** US$2090.

VANUATU, an island republic in the south-western Pacific Ocean, formerly called the New Hebrides. There are about 80 islands, which are mountainous and volcanic. The climate is tropical and the rainfall is generally abundant. Most people are Melanesians. Copra and fish are exported. Tourism is growing: there were 30,450 tourists in 1979. A Spanish explorer discovered the islands in 1606. Britain and France jointly ruled the islands as a condominium from 1906 until independence in 1980.

Area: 14,763 km² (5700 sq mi); **Population:** 150,000; **Capital:** Port-Vila (pop 25,000); **Per capita GNP:** US$590.

VATICAN CITY STATE, the world's smallest independent state. It is in north-western Rome, on a hill on the right bank of the River Tiber. It contains the government of the Roman Catholic Church, headed by the Pope, and the magnificent St Peter's Basilica. It has been the residence of the Pope since the 5th century and was formerly centre of the Papal States in central Italy. In 1870 Victor Emmanuel II took Rome, making it capital of the newly united kingdom which included the Papal States. The Pope refused to recognize the new government. But, in 1929, the Italian government and Pope Pius IX signed the Lateran Treaty, which officially recognized the independence of the Vatican City State.

Area: 44 ha (108.7 acres); **Population:** 1000.

VENEZUELA, an oil-rich republic in northern South America. The hot Maracaibo lowlands surround Lake Maracaibo, a freshwater lake open to the sea, beneath which are large oil deposits. Overlooking the lowlands are the Venezuelan highlands, extensions of the Andes. The central plain is drained by the River Orinoco, one of the world's longest at 2560 km (1591 mi). This plain is covered by *llanos* (savanna). The south-eastern Guiana Highlands are thinly populated. They contain the world's highest waterfall, Angel Falls, with a drop of 979 m (3212 ft). The equatorial climate is modified by the altitude. About 70 per cent of the people are *mestizos* (of mixed white and Indian origin), 18 per cent are mulattos or blacks, 10 per cent are whites and 2 per cent are Indians. In 1978 agriculture employed 20 per cent of the people, industry 27 per cent and services 53 per cent. Their respective contributions to the GDP were 6 per cent, 46 per cent and 48 per cent. The chief resource is oil: Venezuela was the world's 5th largest producer in 1980. Other minerals, including bauxite, gold and iron ore, are now being exploited and manufacturing has been expanding quickly. Coffee, cocoa, maize and sugar cane are major crops; livestock are reared in the central plains. Spain ruled the area from the 16th century. Simón Bolívar liberated Venezuela from Spain in 1821, but it became part of Grand Colombia until 1830. Violence and dictatorships have marked much of its history. But democratic governments have ruled since 1958. The elected National Congress consists of a Senate and a Chamber of Deputies.

Area: 912,050 km² (352,164 sq mi); **Population:** 19,244,000; **Capital:** Caracas (pop 3,508,000); **Other cities:** Maracaibo (652,000); **Highest point:** Pico Bolívar, in Sierra Nevada de Mérida, 5007 m (16,427 ft); **Official language:** Spanish; **Religion:** Roman Catholicism; **Adult literacy rate:** 82 per cent; **Average life expectancy at birth:** 66 years; **Unit of currency:** Bolívar; **Main exports:** oil, iron ore, coffee, cocoa; **Per capita GNP:** US$3130.

VIETNAM, a Socialist Republic in South-East Asia. The northern Red River delta is ringed by hills and mountains, including Fan Si Pan, the nation's highest peak. In central Vietnam, a narrow coastal plain is backed by the Annamite range. In the far south is the huge delta of the Mekong River, one of the world's longest at 4184 km (2600 mi). Temperatures are around 26°C (79°F) throughout the year in the south, but temperatures average 17°C (63°F) in January–February in the north. The rainfall is generally abundant. About 84 per cent of the people are Vietnamese (Kinh). There are also Khmers, Thais and various remote tribal groups. In 1978 agriculture employed 73 per cent of the population, industry 8 per cent and services 19 per cent. Rice, maize, sugar cane, sweet potatoes and cotton are major crops. In 1979 there were 1.6 million cattle and 9.3 million pigs. Fishing is also important. The north is rich in minerals, including coal, lignite, bauxite, chromite, iron ore, manganese and titanium. Manufacturing has been steadily increasing. In the past the north was often under Chinese rule, while the south came under the Khmers. By 1802, Vietnam was united and independent. Between the 1860s and 1880s, France took over Vietnam which, with Laos and Cambodia (Kampuchea), became French Indochina. Japan occupied the area in World War II. In 1946 war began between the French and the nationalist Viet Minh. France withdrew in 1954 and Vietnam was partitioned into the Communist North and the non-Communist South. From 1959 Communist Viet Cong guerrillas fought against the government of South Vietnam, which was aided by the US. American forces withdrew in 1973 and South Vietnam fell to the North in 1975. Vietnam was united as a Socialist Republic with close relations with the USSR in 1976. Vietnamese troops attacked Kampuchea in December 1978 in support of a group friendly to the USSR. This group formed a government in 1979 although resistance to it continued into the 1980s. China attacked North Vietnam in 1979 but soon withdrew its forces.

Area: 329,556 km² (127,249 sq mi); **Population:** 64,807,000; **Capital:** Hanoi (pop 2,000,000); **Other cities:** Ho Chi Minh City (3,500,000); **Highest point:** Fan Si Pan, 3143 m (10,312 ft); **Official language:** Vietnamese; **Religions:** Buddhism, Taoism, Christianity; **Adult literacy rate:** 87 per cent; **Average life expectancy at birth:** 62 years; **Unit of currency:** Dong; **Main exports:** coal, farm produce, fish; **Per capita GNP:** US$170 (1978).

VIRGIN ISLANDS (British), a territory in the West Indies east of Puerto Rico. There are 36 main islands: 16 are inhabited. The climate is tropical. Most people are Negroes. The chief products are fish, fruit, livestock and vegetables, but tourism is the basis of the economy. British settlers became established on the islands in 1666.

Areas: 153 km² (59 sq mi); **Population:** 11,500; **Capital:** Road Town (pop 3500).

VIRGIN ISLANDS (US), an archipelago east of Puerto Rico. It includes three sizeable islands, St Thomas, St Croix and St John, and about 50 islets. The climate is tropical. Prevailing winds serve to moderate the temperature, which averages about 26.7°C (80°F). There is lush, tropical vegetation. The land is generally hilly to mountainous. The highest peak is Crown Mt on St Thomas, standing at 474 m (1556 ft). About 90 per cent of the people are descendants of African slaves. Most others are Europeans. Tourism is the main industry: there were 1.2 million visitors in 1979. Pharmaceuticals, textiles, watches and rum are manufactured in the islands. The US bought the islands from Denmark in 1917. The islanders were made US citizens in 1927, but the islands remain an 'unincorporated territory'.

Area: 344 km² (133 sq mi); **Population:** 119,000; **Capital:** Charlotte Amalie (pop 15,000); **Per capita GNP:** US$5580.

WALLIS AND FUTUNA ISLANDS, a French Overseas Territory in the south-western Pacific, about 400 km (249 mi) west of Samoa. The Wallis group contains Uvea on which the capital Mata-Mata is situated. The people are Polynesians. Bananas, copra, taro roots and yams are grown. The Wallis Islands became French in 1842 and the entire group became a French protectorate in 1887. The islands became an Overseas Territory of France in 1961.

Area: 200 km² (77 sq mi); **Population:** 9000; **Capital:** Mata-Utu (pop 6000).

WESTERN SAHARA, a North African territory facing the Atlantic Ocean, lying between Morocco, Algeria and Mauritania. It was called Spanish Sahara until 1976. Behind the coastal plains are low

Beef Island and Guana Island are in the British Virgin Islands, the easternmost group in the Greater Antilles. Beef Island contains the chief airport. A bridge links Beef Island to Tortola, the largest of the islands where more than four-fifths of the territory's population lives.

plateaux dissected by watercourses formed when the region had a moist climate. Today, however, the climate is hot and arid, with generally less than 50 mm (2 in) of rain per year. The soil is both rocky and sandy. There is little farming: most people are nomadic herders, raising sheep, goats and camels. The population comprises mainly Berbers and Arabs. Fishing is important, but the chief resource is a huge deposit of phosphates at Bu Craa in the north, discovered in 1963. Exploitation of the deposits began in the 1970s. Spain ruled Western Sahara in the early 1500s and again from 1884. In the 1970s the nationalist Popular Front for the liberation of Saharan Territories (Polisario) demanded independence. In 1975, after consultation with community leaders and local chiefs, Spain agreed to withdraw and divide the territory between Morocco and Mauritania. In early 1976 Morocco took the northern two-thirds and Mauritania occupied the south. However, Polisario, with support from Algeria, proclaimed their country independent as the Sahrawi Arab Democratic Republic and launched a guerrilla war. Mauritania withdrew from the south in 1979 and Morocco moved in. Polisario's guerilla war continued until 1988 when a UN peace plan was accepted. This provided for a referendum on the land's future.

Area: 266,000 km² (102,709 sq mi); **Population:** 76,000 (1970); **Capital:** formerly El Aiun.

YEMEN, REPUBLIC OF, is in the south-western corner of the Arabian peninsula. The Red Sea coastal plain, called the *Tihama*, is 30–80 km (19–50 mi) wide. Behind it the land is mountainous, rising to 3760 m (12,336 ft), Arabia's highest point, west of San'a. The coastal plain on the Gulf of Aden is narrow, and also has mountains behind it. Inland from the gulf is a fertile valley (the Hadhramaut), and to the east is a barren stony desert, the Rub al

Khali (the Empty Quarter). The coastal plains and the desert are very hot, and their rainfall averages only 130 mm (5 in) a year. The highlands have around 510 mm (20 in) of rain, and contain Arabia's best farmland. Parts of the Hadhramaut have as much as 760 mm (30 in) of rainfall. The average annual temperature range in Aden, a major port of the Gulf of Aden is 24°–32°C (75°–90°F). Nearly all Yemenis are Arabs who follow the Muslim religion. Most of the people live in the cooler regions of Yemen, the majority in rural areas, where they work in agriculture. They grow cereals, coffee, cotton, fruit and vegetables, and tend herds of goats and sheep. In recent years the Yemenis have reclaimed parts of the desert for farmland by means of dams and irrigation schemes. Along the coasts many of the people live by fishing. More people work in industry and services in the southern part of the country than in the north. Some salt is mined, and manufacturing is increasing. Oil production is an important industry. At Aden oil is refined and exported. Yemen was a properous land 3000 years ago, and was known as Sheba. It lay on important trading routes linking Europe, Africa and Asia. Its prosperity lasted only about 1000 years. For centuries until 1962 Yemen was ruled by an *imam*, a religious and political leader. From 1849 to 1918 most of Yemen was part of the Ottoman Empire. The British annexed Aden in 1839 and made it into an important port. After the opening of the Suez Canal in 1869 Aden became a staging post and coaling station for ships voyaging between Europe and India. Britain later took over the rest of the southern part of the country. Northern Yemen became a republic in 1962. Southern Yemen, with Aden as its capital, became independent under a Marxist government as a Democratic People's Republic in 1967. The two Yemens merged in 1990 to become the Republic of Yemen.

Area: 527,970 km² (203,850 sq mi); **Population:** 8,600,000; **Capital:** San'a (pop 449,000); **Highest point:** Hadur Shu'ayb, 3760 m (12,336 ft); **Official language:** Arabic; **Religion:** Islam; **Adult literacy rate:** 13 per cent in the north, 27 per cent in the south; **Average life expectancy at birth:** 39 years in the north, 44 years in the south; **Units of currency:** Dinar and Riyal (1 Dinar = 26 Riyals).

115

YUGOSLAVIA (former), a Socialist Federal Republic on the Adriatic Sea. Large areas are mountainous; the mountains are extensions of the Alpine system. They are narrowest in the north, but the entire south is mountainous. The limestone Dinaric Alps display typical karst scenery. The mountains on the coast have been submerged, such that former ridges now form long, narrow islands parallel to the coast and former valleys are harbours. To the north and east is hill country descending to the interior plains drained by the Danube river system. The coastal climate is typically Mediterranean, but the interior plains, the main farming region, have a continental climate. Belgrade has an average annual temperature range of − 2°C to 22°C (28°F–72°F). Its average annual rainfall is 610 mm (24 in).

Until 1991, Yugoslavia was a federation of six republics: Bosnia-Herzegovina, Croatia, Macedonia, Montenegro, Serbia and Slovenia. Its 24 million (estimated) people spoke many different languages and followed different religions – Roman Catholic, Muslim and Greek Orthodox – and included Serbs, Croats, Slovenes, Albanians and Macedonians as well as other minority groups. Most people are South Slavs: the Serbs and Croats are the two largest groups; the Slovenes live in the north; and the Montenegrins and Macedonians live in the south. Various non-Slav minorities live mainly in the east and south. Between 1459 and the mid-19th century, Turkey ruled most of the area, but before World War I, some parts, including Serbia, were independent, while other parts were in Austria-Hungary. The murder of Archduke Franz Ferdinand of Austria-Hungary by a Bosnian-Serb sparked off World War I. Yugoslavia was founded as a union of South Slavs in 1918, although the name Yugoslavia was not adopted until 1929. Germany invaded Yugoslavia in World War II. After the war, the monarchy was abolished and a socialist republic was established by the partisan Communist leader Tito (Josip Broz), as a federation of socialist republics. In 1991, growing tensions between the republics led to Croatia and Slovenia declaring their independence from Yugoslavia. Bosnia-Herzegovina also declared independence in 1992. Fierce fighting followed these declarations, first of all, briefly, between Serbia and Slovenia, then between Serbia and Croatia and Serbia and Bosnia-Herzegovina. By 1993, the Federal Republic of Yugoslavia was made up only of Serbia and Montenegro, but Serbia was still trying to regain control of Bosnia-Herzegovina.

Bosnia-Herzegovina
Area: 51,125 km² (19,740 sq mi); **Population:** 4,173,000; **Capital:** Sarajevo; **Language:** Serbo-Croat; **Religion:** Eastern Orthodox, Catholic, Islam; **Unit of currency:** dinar; **Industries:** textiles, timber.

Croatia
Area: 56,533 km² (21,830 sq mi); **Population:** 4,567,000; **Capital:** Zagreb; **Language:** Croatian; **Religion:** Roman Catholic; **Unit of currency:** Croatian crown; **Industries:** textiles, chemicals.

Macedonia
Area: 25,711 km² (9,928 sq mi); **Population:** 1,925,000; **Capital:** Skopie

Serbia and Montenegro
(Federal Republic of Yugoslavia)
Area: 101,690 km² (39,265 sq mi); **Population:** 10,337,000; **Capital:** Belgrade; **Language:** Serbo-Croat, Albanian (and others); **Religion:** Eastern Orthodox, Roman Catholic, Islam; **Unit of currency:** dinar; **Industries:** steel, wood products.
Slovenia
Area: 20,249 km² (7,819 sq mi); **Population:** 1,884,000; **Capital:** Ljubljana; **Language:** Slovenian; **Religion:** Roman Catholic; **Unit of currency:** tolar; **Industries:** steel, textiles, printing.

ZAIRE, a republic in west-central Africa, is the continent's 2nd largest nation. Most of the country lies in the drainage basin of the River Zaire (formerly Congo), which is one of the world's longest at 4828 km (3000 mi). There are highlands and plateaux in the south and east along the Rift Valley where Zaire's border passes through lakes Tanganyika, Kivu, Edward and Mobutu Sese Seko (formerly Albert). The climate is equatorial with an average annual rainfall of 1250–2030 mm (49–80 in). There is rain forest in the centre and savanna in the north and south. About 200 language and ethnic groups live in Zaire. About two-thirds of the people speak Bantu languages: Hamitic, Nilotic, Sudanic and pygmy languages are also spoken. In 1978 agriculture employed 76 per cent of the people, accounting for 27 per cent of the GDP; 20 per cent came from industry and 53 per cent from services. The chief cash crops are coffee, cotton, palm products and rubber. Fishing is important but livestock can be reared only in areas free from the disease-carrying tsetse fly. Minerals made up 74 per cent of the exports in 1976–78. The main mining region is Shaba, where copper (the most valuable export), cobalt, manganese, silver, uranium and zinc are mined. Some oil is produced and diamonds are mined in the Kasai provinces. Hydro-electricity is being developed and manufacturing is growing especially around Kinshasa and Lubumbashi. The Portuguese reached the area in 1482 and slavery was practised along the coast. Henry Morton Stanley explored the Zaire River in 1874–77 and the country became the personal property of King Leopold of Belgium in 1884. Because of ill-treatment of local people by concessionaires, Belgium took over the country in 1908 as the Belgian Congo. Full independence in 1960 was followed by civil war, including a secessionist struggle in Shaba.

Area: 2,345,409 km² (905,617 sq mi); **Population:** 33,797,000; **Capital:** Kinshasa (pop 2,444,000); **Other cities:** Kananga (704,000), Lubumbashi (451,000); **Highest point:** Ruwenzori range on the Ugandan border, 5119 m (16,795 ft); **Official language:** French; **Religions:** traditional beliefs (59 per cent), Roman Catholicism (36 per cent), Protestantism (4 per cent), Islam (0.5 per cent); **Adult literacy rate:** 15 per cent; **Average life expectancy at birth:** 46 years; **Unit of currency:** Zaire; **Main exports:** copper, cobalt, coffee, diamonds, oil, cassiterite; **Per capita GNP:** US$260.

ZAMBIA, a landlocked republic in south-central Africa, called Northern Rhodesia until 1964. It consists mostly of a plateau, 900–1520 m (2953–

4987 ft). In the south and east, the Zambezi and Luangwa rivers occupy downfaulted troughs that are part of the East African Rift Valley system. The Zambezi has been dammed to form Lake Kariba, which Zambia shares with Zimbabwe. Kariba's hydro-electric plants have given Zambia an abundance of electrical energy. Parts of lakes Mweru and Tanganyika are in Zambia, as is the entire Lake Bangweulu. The main upland region is the Muchinga Mts in the north-east; they rise to more than 2100 m (6890 ft). The tropical climate is modified by the altitude. The rainfall varies between 1300 mm (51 in) in the north to 500 mm (20 in) in the south. Wildlife is abundant in the savanna, which covers most of Zambia. Six major Bantu languages and 66 dialects are spoken. In 1978 agriculture employed 68 per cent of the workforce (mostly at subsistence level), but it accounted for only 17 per cent of the GDP, compared with 39 per cent from industry and 44 per cent from services. The chief resource is copper, which accounts for 90 per cent of the exports. Cobalt, lead and zinc are also exported as are maize and tobacco, the main cash crop. There are processing and metal industries in the towns. The British

hotter. The high veld has an average annual rainfall of 700–900 mm (28–35 in), the eastern highlands getting 1520 mm (60 in). But the low veld is arid with 410 mm (16 in) per year. About 96 per cent of the people are black Africans who speak Bantu languages. The largest groups are the Ndebele in the south and the Shona in the north. Most other people are of European descent. There were 244,000 Europeans in mid-1979, but some emigration has occurred since then. Asians and Coloureds numbered 35,000 in 1979. In 1978 agriculture employed 60 per cent of the workforce. In 1977 it accounted for 20 per cent of the GDP, compared with 35 per cent from industry and 45 per cent from services. European farming is efficient but African farming is mostly at subsistence level. Tobacco, sugar cane, tea and fruits are the leading cash crops. In 1979 there were 5 million cattle. Asbestos, chrome, coal and gold are mined. Manufacturing is important in the towns. Political conditions have retarded the development of Zimbabwe's great tourist potential. Cecil Rhodes obtained mining rights in the area in the 1880s. Between 1898 and 1923, Southern Rhodesia (as Zimbabwe was then called) was ruled by a British High Commissioner

The man-made Lake Kariba is on the Zimbabwe-Zambia border. These countries share the electricity generated at the Kariba Dam.

South Africa Company entered the area in 1889 and, in 1911, it became the British protectorate of Northern Rhodesia. Full independence as the Republic of Zambia was achieved in 1964. Zambia became a one-party state in 1972.

Area: 752,614 km² (290,602 sq mi); **Population:** 7,643,000; **Capital:** Lusaka (pop 1,000,000; **Official language:** English; **Religions:** mostly Christianity; **Adult literacy rate:** 39 per cent; **Average life expectancy at birth:** 48 years; **Unit of currency:** Kwacha, **Main exports:** copper, zinc, cobalt, lead, tobacco; **Per capita GNP:** US$510.

ZIMBABWE, a landlocked republic in southern Africa, formerly called Rhodesia. The north is in a deep trough through which the River Zambezi flows. Lake Kariba, a man-made lake on the Zambezi, is shared with Zambia, as is the electricity produced at Kariba dam. Central Zimbabwe (the high veld) is between 1220 and 1530 m (4003–5020 ft), but the land rises to 2595 m (8514 ft) on the Mozambique border. The southern low veld is drained by the River Limpopo. These lowlands are less than 910 m (2986 ft) in height. The high veld has a pleasant climate with an average annual temperature of 20°C (68°F). The lowlands are much

based in South Africa. In 1923 it became a self-governing British colony. Its white government passed a law in 1930 reserving 47.6 per cent of the land for European settlement. This created long-term resentment among black Africans. In 1963 the white leaders asked for independence, which Britain did not grant because the whites were not prepared to give up their dominant status, a condition demanded by African nationalists. In 1965 Rhodesia declared its independence unilaterally. Britain declared this act illegal and imposed economic sanctions through the UN. A guerrilla war began in the early 1970s. Britain negotiated an independence Constitution in 1979 and independence, with a majority black government led by Prime Minister Robert Mugabe, was achieved in 1980.

Area: 390,580 km² (150,812 sq mi); **Population:** 10,137,000; **Capital:** Harare (pop 658,000); **Other cities:** Bulawayo (357,000); **Highest point:** Mt Inyangani, 2595 m (8514 ft); **Official language:** English; **Religions:** traditional beliefs, Christianity; **Average life expectancy at birth:** 54 years; **Unit of currency:** Dollar; **Main exports:** tobacco, asbestos, gold, cotton, steel, meat, ferrochrome, copper, maize; **Per capita GNP:** US$470.

117

'LAWS OF ECONOMICS'

Diminishing Returns Hypothesis that if one factor of production is increased while the others stay constant, a point is reached when the addition of one more unit of the variable quantity adds less to output than the previous unit.

Engel's Law The greater the income of a household, the lower the proportion spent on food (Ernst Engel, 1821–96).

Gresham's Law Bad money drives out good; i.e. the public tend to hoard (or even melt down) coins with greater bullion content, such as new coins (Sir Thomas Gresham, 1519–79).

Malthusian Theory Population tends to increase by geometric progression, natural resources by (slower) arithmetic progression; thus unrestricted population growth would eventually lead to universal hardship (Thomas Robert Malthus, 1766–1834).

Pareto's Law Whatever the political or tax system in a country, the distribution of income is more or less the same (Vilfredo Pareto, 1848–1923).

Parkinson's Law Work expands to fill the time available for its completion (C. Northcote Parkinson, in 1955).

Peter Principle, The In an organization every employee tends to rise to his level of incompetence, so that all important work is done by those who have not reached that level (L. J. Peter, in 1969).

Say's Law Supply creates its own demand (Jean-Baptiste Say, 1767–1832; several interpretations, but taken literally it has proved to be not strictly true).

Supply and Demand, Law of Increase in supply tends to lead to a lower price for any particular product unless there is an increase in demand, and vice versa.

Economics

GLOSSARY OF ECONOMICS

Account Credit allowed on commercial dealings, and on stock exchanges. See also CURRENT ACCOUNT; DEPOSIT ACCOUNT.

Actuary Person who calculates risks and probabilities, especially in life assurance.

Adjuster Person who settles insurance claims.

Annuity Payment of a certain sum of money each year to a person.

Assets The entire property of an individual or organization.

Assurance Insurance, usually life or endowment, which is not dependent on a possibility; with life assurance, payment due on death of person assured. See also ENDOWMENT; INSURANCE; TERM INSURANCE; WHOLE LIFE.

Audit Examination of a firm's books to confirm their accuracy.

Average In marine insurance, loss or damage; in fire and accident insurance, a condition under which insurers pay less for a loss if property is insured for less than its true value.

Backwardation On a stock exchange, a fine imposed by a buyer on a seller who seeks to postpone delivery of stock sold ahead.

Balance of payments Difference between country's payments to and receipts from other countries; includes BALANCE OF TRADE and 'invisible' trade such as insurance and tourism.

Balance of trade Difference between value of country's exports and imports.

Balance sheet Statement showing the financial condition of a company.

Banker's order Same as STANDING ORDER.

Bankruptcy Inability of a person or business to pay its debts.

Bargain Transaction on stock exchange; any agreement settling terms between buyer and seller.

Bear On a stock exchange, a person who sells what he does not possess, hoping to buy it cheaply before SETTLING DAY.

Bill of exchange Written order to second person to pay sum of money to third party.

Bill of sale Document transferring ownership of goods, in return for a loan.

Blue chip The most reliable industrial shares on a stock exchange.

Left: The New York Stock Exchange on Wall Street, the city's financial centre. Economics has been defined as the study of how goods and services are produced and distributed, goods and services meaning anything that is bought and sold. Economics is a notoriously difficult field and no economic 'laws' have been found infallible. Nations struggle to control their economies but with uncertain results.

Bond Written evidence of debt.

Boom Period of increased business activity, rising stock market prices, and prosperity.

Budget Financial statement showing future expenditure and income.

Building society See FINANCE COMPANY.

Bull On a stock exchange, a person who buys shares hoping to sell them at a higher price.

Bullion Gold or silver, except in current coins, usually in bars of specific purity.

Capital Unused wealth resulting from LABOUR working on LAND; one of the FACTORS OF PRODUCTION.

Capital gains Profit from sale of capital assets.

Capitalism Economic system based on private ownership of production, etc.

Cash card Coded card enabling holder to draw specific sum from dispenser located on outside of bank.

Cash flow Regular cash supply for meeting current financial obligations of company.

Cheque Written order to a bank to pay a sum of money.

Closed economy Term used in economics for hypothetical economy that does not participate in international trade.

Collateral Security for a bank loan.

Commodity Any tangible object satisfying human needs and limited in supply; raw materials, such as coffee, tin, and wheat, that may be graded to international standards.

Common market Group of countries in economic alliance.

Company Collection of people who have subscribed the CAPITAL (money) to run a business. See also LIMITED COMPANY.

Competition Condition in which large number of producers are able to supply consumers with similar products.

Consumption Use of wealth produced; total expenditure of economy on goods and services.

Controlled economy System in which government exercises extensive control. See also PLANNED ECONOMY.

Corporate personality A company is said to be incorporated – it has a legal existence or corporate personality apart from those of its owners.

Corporation tax Percentage levy on profits of company.

Costing Estimating the outlay needed for a particular business enterprise.

Cost of living Amount of money needed to support certain standards of life.

Crawling peg Term for devaluation or revaluation effected in small, regular steps.

Credit Allowing the purchaser of a commodity or service to pay at a later date; in book-keeping, an entry made for payment received.

Credit card Document that allows its holder to buy goods on credit; it may be issued by a company or a bank.

Creditor Party to whom money is owed.

Credit rating Assessed creditworthiness of prospective customer.

Currency Coins and bank or treasury notes.

Current account At a bank, an account on which the depositor can draw at will and make payments by cheque.

Customs duty Tax paid on imports or exports.

Customs union Alliance of two or more countries with no customs barriers between them.

Days of grace In insurance, period after premium due in which it may be paid without loss of cover.

Death duty See INHERITANCE TAX.

Debenture Document indicating that a company has borrowed money from a person; debenture holders receive interest before shareholders.

Debit An entry in book-keeping for payment made or owed.

Debt Money owed to a person or company.

Debtor Party that owes money.

Deed Written contract signed under legal seal.

CURRENCIES AROUND THE WORLD

Country	Currency	Country	Currency
Afghanistan	afghani (100 puls)	Gibraltar	pound (100 pence)
Albania	lek (100 qindarka)	Greece	drachma (100 lepta)
Algeria	dina (100 centimes)	Grenada	dollar (100 cents)
Andorra	franc (Fr) & peseta (SP)	Guatemala	quetzal (100 centavos)
Angola	kwanza (100 lweis)	Guinea	syli
Antigua	dollar (100 cents)	Guyana	dollar (100 cents)
Argentina	peso (100 centavos)	Haiti	gourde (100 centimes
Australia	dollar (100 cents)	Honduras	lempira (100 centavos)
Austria	schilling (100 groschen)	Hungary	forint (100 fillér)
Bahamas	dollar (100 cents)	Iceland	krona (100 aurar)
Bahrain	dinar (1,000 fils)	India	rupee (100 paise)
Bangladesh	taka (100 paise)	Indonesia	rupiah (100 sen)
Barbados	dollar (100 cents)	Iran	rial (100 dinars)
Belgium	franc (100 centimes)	Iraq	dinar (1,000 fils)
Belize	dollar (100 cents)	Ireland, Repub. of	pound (100 pence)
Benin	franc	Israel	pound (100 agorot)
Bermuda	dollar (100 cents)	Italy	lira
Bhutan	ngultrum	Ivory Coast	franc
Bolivia	peso (100 centavos)	Jamaica	dollar (100 cents)
Botswana	pula (100 thebe)	Japan	yen
Brazil	cruzeiro (100 centavos)	Jordan	dinar (1,000 fils)
Brunei	dollar (100 sen)	Kenya	shilling (100 cents)
Bulgaria	lev (100 stotinki)	Korea, North	won (100 jun)
Burkina Faso	franc	Korea, South	won (100 jun)
Burundi	franc	Kuwait	dinar (1,000 fils)
Cambodia	riel (100 sen)	Laos	kip (100 ats)
Cameroon	franc	Lebanon	pound (100 piastres)
Canada	dollar (100 cents)	Lesotho	rand (100 cents) (SA)
Central African		Liberia	dollar (100 cents)
Republic	franc	Libya	dinar (1,000 dirhams)
Chad	france	Liechtenstein	franc (Swiss)
Chile	new peso (100 old escudos)	Luxembourg	franc (100 centimes)
		Macau (Port.)	pataca (100 avos)
China: People's		Madagascar	franc
Republic	yuan (10 chiao; 100 fen)	Malawi	kwacha (100 tambala)
Colombia	peso (100 centavos)	Malaysia	dollar (100 cents)
Congo	franc	Maldives, Rep of	rupee (100 laris)
Costa Rice	colón (100 centimos)	Mali	franc
Cuba	peso (100 centavos)	Malta	pound (100 cents; 1,000 mils)
Cyprus	pound (1,000 mils)		
Czechoslovakia	koruna (100 haleru)	Mauritania	ouguiya (5 khoums)
Denmark	krone (100 öre)	Mauritius	rupee (100 cents)
Dominica	dollar (100 cents)	Mexico	peso (100 centavos)
Dominican Republic	peso (100 centavos	Monaco	franc (French)
Ecuador	sucre (100 centavos)	Mongolian People's	
Egypt	pound (100 piastres; 1,000 millèmes)	Republic	turgrik (100 möngö)
		Morocco	dirham (100 centimes)
El Salvador	colón (100 centavos)	Myanmar	kyat (100 pyas)
Equatorial Guinea	ekuele	Namibia	rand (100 cents)
Ethiopia	dollar (100 cents)	Nauru	dollar (100 cents (SA)
Fiji	dollar (100 cents)	Nepal	rupee (100 pice)
Finland	markka (100 penniä)	Netherlands	guilder (100 cents)
France	franc (100 centimes)	New Zealand	dollar (100 cents)
Gabon	franc	Nicaragua	códoba (100 centavos)
Gambia	dalasi (100 bututs)	Niger	franc
Germany	mark (100 pfennings)	Nigeria	naira ((100 kobo)
Ghana	cedi (100 paesewas)	Norway	krone (100 öre)

Deed of covenant Agreement under which party undertakes to pay set sum to organization (such as charity) for fixed period.

Deflation Reduction in business activity in economy, resulting in lower level of employment and imports, and slowing down of wage and price increases.

Demand Quantity of goods or services people are prepared to pay for at given price and specific time.

Deposit account At a bank, an account on which depositor may be required to give notice before making withdrawal; interest is paid on it.

Country	Currency
Oman	rial (1,000 baiza)
Pakistan	rupee (100 paisas)
Panama	balboa (100 cents)
Paraguay	guarani (100 céntimos)
Peru	sol (100 centavos)
Philippines	peso (100 centavos)
Poland	zloty (100 groszy)
Portugal	escudo (100 centavos)
Qatar	riyal (100 dirhams)
Romania	leu (100 bani)
Rwanda	franc
St Kitts-Nevis	dollar (100 cents)
St Lucia	dollar (100 cents)
St Vincent	dollar (100 cents)
San Marino	lira (Italian)
Saudia Arabia	riyal (20 qursh)
Senegal	franc
Sierra Leone	leone (100 cents)
Singapore	dollar (100 cents)
Somali Republic	shilling (100 cents)
South Africa	rand (100 cents)
South-West Africa	rand (100 cents) (SA)
Spain	peseta (100 céntimos)
Sri Lanka	rupee (100 cents)
Sudan	pound (100 piastres; 1,000 milliemes)
Surinam	guilder (100 cents)
Swaziland	lilangeni (pl. emalangeni) (100 cents)
Sweden	krona (100 öre)
Switzerland	franc (100 centimes)
Syria	pound (100 piastres)
Taiwan	do'llar (100 cents)
Tanzania	shilling (100 cents)
Thailand	baht (100 satangs)
Togo	franc
Tonga	pa'anga (100 seniti)
Trinidad & Tobago	dollar (100 cents)
Tunisia	dinar (1,000 millimes)
Turkey	lira (100 kurus)
Uganda	shilling(100 cents)
United Arab Emirates	dirham (100 fils)
United Kingdom	pound (100 pence)
United States	dollar (100 cents)
Uruguay	peso (100 centésimos)
USSR	rouble (100 copecks)
Vatican City State	lira
Venezuela	bolivar (100 céntimos)
Vietnam	dong (100 zu)
Western Samoa	tala (100 sene)
Yemen	riyal (100 fils) and dinar (100 fils)
Yugoslavia	dinar (100 paras)
Zaire	zaire (100 makuta [sing. likuta]; 1,000 sengi)
Zimbabwe	dollar (100 cents)

Depreciation Fall in value of asset.

Depression Same as SLUMP.

Devaluation Lowering of currency values against currency of other countries.

Direct taxation Taxes levied on wealth or income.

Discount Sum deducted from face value of bill of exchange in consideration of early payment; any deduction from price; difference between par value of shares and lower buying price.

Distribution Economic theory concerned with determination of prices of FACTORS OF PRODUCTION and resultant incomes; movement of goods from producer to consumer.

Draft Written order to transfer money from one person to another.

Endorsement Signature on back of bill of exchange, transferring it to third party; in insurance, note added to policy to modify or change certain terms.

Endowment Money given for a specific purpose; in insurance, fixed sum to be paid at end of certain period.

Entrepreneur Person who undertakes business risks and provides jobs for others.

Estate duty See INHERITANCE TAX.

Excess insurance Cover only for losses exceeding specific limit.

Exchange rate Value of one country's currency in terms of another.

Excise duty Tax on goods produced inside country.

Ex dividend Of shares sold without right to dividend due.

Exports Goods or services sold to other countries.

Factors of production LABOUR, LAND, and CAPITAL, the factors needed to make a commodity.

Finance company Firm that lends money to be repaid with interest over fixed period; building society is form of finance company in some countries.

Free (enterprise) economy System relying on supply and demand to regulate economy with minimum government intervention. See also LAISSEZ-FAIRE.

Galloping inflation See INFLATION.

Gilt-edged security Safest share, usually government stock.

'Gnomes of Zurich' Popular name for group of bankers thought to influence world finance.

Gold standard Relating the buying power of currency to a definite value of gold.

Gross national product (GNP) Total market value of goods and services produced by country over specific period, normally a year.

Hire purchase British form of INSTALMENT PLAN, in which goods do not become property of buyer until final instalment is paid.

Imports Goods or services bought from other countries.

Income Money and benefits accruing to individual, firm, or economy in specific period.

Income tax Tax levied on income, including wages, interest, capital gains, etc.

Indemnity In insurance, compensation paid for loss or injury.

Indirect taxation Taxes levied on expenditure rather than wealth or income, as purchase tax or value added tax.

Inflation Economic situation in which speedily rising prices bring about decrease in purchasing power of money; galloping inflation is rapid inflation that threatens breakdown of monetary system.

Inheritance tax Tax levied on estate of deceased person before heirs can inherit; also called death duty.

Instalment plan Selling goods on fixed sum down, and rest of price in regular equal instalments that include interest; goods become property of buyer on payment of first instalment.

Insurance Plan whereby person or company indemnifies others against loss in return for small regular payments (premiums).

Interest Price paid for use of somebody else's money.

CALCULATING INTEREST

Simple interest $I = Prn$
Compound interest $I = P(1+r)^n - P$

I stands for *interest*. P for *principal* (starting amount), r for *rate* (e.g. for 6% interest, $r = 6/100$ or 0.06), and n for *time* (number of years or months or whatever the unit period is).

International Monetary Fund IMF Organization set up by Bretton Woods Agreement (1944), organized to promote international co-operation and remove foreign exchange restrictions (came into operation 1947).

In the red In debt; of an account, overdrawn.

Investment Use of money to provide income or profit.

Invisible imports and exports Generally, interest on overseas investments, commission on financial transactions, payment for services, expenditure by tourists, government grants overseas, cost of membership of international bodies, etc.

IOU ('I owe you') Informal written promise to pay.

Labour Work of men applied to natural resources; one of the FACTORS OF PRODUCTION.

Laissez-faire Economic system in which there is minimum of government intervention.

Land All natural resources; one of the FACTORS OF PRODUCTION.

In the early 1920s the German mark became almost worthless. In October 1923 the city of Cologne issued this billion-mark note; elsewhere people were bartering possessions like silver for sacks of flour and other foodstuffs.

Letter of credit Document allowing traveller (especially overseas) to draw money from banks other than his own.

Limited company Company in which owners' responsibility limited to nominal value of shares held; strictly, limited liability company.

Liquidation Winding up of company by selling assets and paying liabilities; any remaining money goes to owners.

Mercantilism A 16th–17th-century theory that a country should export more than it imports, and store its wealth in gold or other valuable metals.

Middleman Man who brings buyers and sellers together, taking percentage of price for services.

Money A means of exchange; any medium men agree to use to pay for goods or services.

Monometallism System of currency in which one metal (usually gold) is used as standard.

Monopoly When one person or group controls sufficient of the supply of a commodity or service to control its price.

Mortgage Document giving title to property as security for loan. Mortgagor always has right to redeem.

National debt Money borrowed by a government from individuals and institutions to pay for expenditure that cannot be covered by ordinary revenue.

Nationalization The transformation from private to public (state) ownership of an industry or service.

Oncosts See OVERHEADS.

Operational research Study, using scientific principles, designed to find procedures for solving management problems.

Ordinary shares Shares in company which do not carry fixed rate of interest.

Organization and methods Application of work study to systems to achieve maximum efficiency of organization.

Overdraft Type of bank loan in which account shows customer owes bank money; interest is charged on amount outstanding.

Overheads Ordinary running costs of business, such as administrative or selling costs, not directly identified with product; also called oncosts.

Paid-up policy Whole life or endowment insurance on which holder stops paying premiums, the sum insured being reduced accordingly.

Partnership Simple form of business, in which each partner (two or more people) is liable for all debts of business.

Planned economy System of state control over allocation of resources rather than price controls.

Portfolio Various shares, etc., held by institution or individual.

Preference shares Shares of company on which interest is paid before any others, and owners have prior right to repayment of capital if company is wound up.

Price Amount in money that seller requests or obtains for goods or services.

Price-earnings ratio Ratio of market value of share capital to profit for year, used as guide to rating of stock.

Production Means by which commodities are made and wealth is created. See FACTORS OF PRODUCTION.

Productivity Amount produced by FACTORS OF PRODUCTION in given time.

Profit Reward of enterprise; increase in wealth resulting from operating a business or other enterprise.

Profit sharing System in which employees receive share of company's profits in addition to wages.

Profits tax Tax levied on total annual profits of company (superseded in Britain by CORPORATION TAX).

Promissory note Unconditional promise in writing to pay certain sum of money; can be negotiable.

Protection Customs duties designed to protect home manufacturers from competition from imports.

Public liability insurance Policy covering businessman against claims resulting from accidents on his premises or defective products.

Recession Condition of economy in which decline in business activity is accompanied by short-term unemployment of men and machinery. See also SLUMP.

Reflation Deliberate inflation to counter serious deflation.

Rent Price for use of land or goods.

Reserves Profits of a business set aside for policy reasons.

Revaluation Upward change in value of country's currency compared with other currencies; opposite of DEVALUATION.

Sanctions Withholding of goods or services as punishment or to enforce certain actions.

Saving Postponement of consumption; accumulation of wealth not being immediately used.

Scrip issue Free shares issued to shareholders by capitalization of reserves; if dividend is maintained, shareholders are better off in that they do not have extra tax on profits they would have made with higher dividends.

Security Anything used by borrower as safeguard for loan or debt.

Services Non-material goods produced by service industries such as transport, teaching, catering, etc.

Settling day On stock exchange, day when all bargains are completed.

Share capital Money raised by issuing shares.

Share index Statistical indicator of overall share values, based on selected group.

Shares Equal portions of the capital of a limited company.

Slump Period, also called depression, when workers and machines are persistently unemployed; the opposite of BOOM.

Specie Minted coins as opposed to notes, bills, etc.

Standard of living Degree to which people's needs and wants are satisfied.

Standing order Instruction to bank to make payments at regular intervals to third party.

Statement Report of condition of business, debt, or credit balance.

Stock Total capital of public company; differs from shares in that it can be sold in any amount instead of in fixed units.

Stock exchange Market for sale of stocks and shares.

Stopped cheque Cheque on which bank has instructions not to pay.

Subsidy Money or other aid given, usually by government, to industry, usually to prevent rise in prices.

Superannuation Retirement pension.

Supply Quantity of goods or services offered at given price.

Surrender value Value of life insurance policy at any time before full term.

Surtax Additional tax levied on income over certain amount.

Takeover bid Offer to take over any or all of company's shares in order to acquire control.

Taxation Compulsory contribution by individuals, groups, etc., to government funds.

Term insurance Policy covering insured (or property) for specific period.

Third party insurance Cover against claims involving damage or loss suffered by someone not involved in contract.

Traveller's cheques Cheques for specific amounts issued for convenience abroad (or at home); may be cashed by bank's agents and are usually accepted at hotels, shops, etc.

Trust Legal transfer of property from one person to a second, to hold and use on behalf of third party; in business, a trade combination of companies to secure monopoly.

Underwriter Person or company who guarantees, in return for commission, to take up certain proportion of shares if these are not subscribed to by public; in insurance, one who guarantees cover.

Unearned income Income received from investment and not as wages or profit.

Unearned increment Increase in property value, especially land, through no effort of owner.

Unemployment Shortage of work for labour available.

Unit trust Organization that invests money widely in stocks and shares on behalf of subscribers.

Upmarket Of goods aimed at 'high quality' end of market.

Utilitarianism Philosophy of government aimed at 'greatest happiness of the greatest number'.

Utility Power of commodity or service to satisfy human wants.

Value Exchange power of commodity or service in terms of other commodities or services.

Value added tax Form of sales tax levied at each point at which value is added to commodity or service.

Wages Reward for labour.

Wealth Possessions that have a market value, either tangible (such as money, shares, property, goods) or intangible (such as good-will, connections, skills).

Wealth tax Levy on capital or property.

Whole life Insurance that matures only on death.

Wildcat strike Strike organized without support of union.

Without profits policy Insurance in which person is insured for fixed sum.

With profits policy Insurance in which person insured is entitled to share in profits of insurance company in form of bonuses.

Work study Management technique to improve production efficiency of labour.

Yield Net interest on a share or stock relative to the price at which it is bought.

Government, Politics and Law

GOVERNMENT AND POLITICAL TERMS

Absolutism Government by one person or body having complete power.

Activist Person favouring vigorous action and carrying it out.

Agent provocateur Government agent who incites others to break law.

Ambassador Diplomatic envoy regarded as the personal representative of a country's head of state.

Amnesty Universal pardon for people who have broken law.

Anarchism Opposition to all government or rule of law.

Apartheid In South Africa, a policy of segregation for whites and non-whites.

Asylum Refusal to deliver up a convicted or suspected person who has taken refuge in another state or in premises enjoying diplomatic immunity.

Authoritarianism Government carried on by rulers without the people's consent.

Autonomy Self-government.

Brinkmanship Art, or folly, of pursuing policy to edge of, but not into, war, etc.

Buffer state Neutral country between two others which might go to war.

Caucus Pressure group within a political party, or meeting of such a group.

Cession Transfer of territory by mutual agreement.

Civil rights Freedoms that members of community ought to enjoy, such as right to own property, freedom from being imprisoned without cause. Civil Rights bill, passed by US Senate in 1964, aimed to end segregation.

Codification Restatement or reform of law in written form.

Collective security System of mutual assistance with a defensive purpose.

Collectivism Theory of collective ownership of land and capital.

Common market An economic union based on the concepts of free trade amongst member states, the adoption of common or harmonized policies and customs union.

Communism In theory, society in which the people own all property in common, except for personal possessions.

Condominium Joint control of a territory by two or more countries.

Confederation Close alliance of several countries for a particular purpose.

Congress An assembly of people; in some countries, the legislature.

Conservatism Resistance to change.

Consul Representative of a state whose main responsibilities are the furtherance of trade relations and assisting visiting nationals from the home state.

Corporatism Government based on system of corporations, representing workers and employers.

Coup d'état Sudden change of government by force, usually from within.

De facto recognition Acknowledgement that a government actually holds power.

De jure recognition Acknowledgement that a government holds power as of right.

Demagogy Government by 'oratory'.

Democracy Form of government organized by the people and in most cases run by representatives elected by popular vote.

Dependent state State which has consented to submit to foreign control.

Détente Easing of a political situation.

Dictatorship Form of ABSOLUTISM in which one man holds supreme power, and is answerable to no law or legislature.

Diplomatic immunity Exemption of accredited foreign diplomats, their staff and officers of international organizations from jurisdiction of local courts.

In September 1990, demonstrators in the Ukranian city of Lvov attach a bannner reading 'Lenin out of Lvov' to a monument. Similar anti-Russian demonstrations in other Soviet republics threatened to pull the country apart.

FORMS OF GOVERNMENT	
System	Rule by
anarchy	harmony, without law
aristocracy	a privileged order
autocracy	one man, absolutely
bureaucracy	officials
democracy	the people
despotocracy	a tyrant
diarchy	two rulers or authorities
ergatocracy	the workers
ethnocracy	race or ethnic group
gerontocracy	old men
gynocracy	women
hierocracy	priests
isocracy	all – with equal power
kakistocracy	the worst
matriarchy	a mother (or mothers)
meritocracy	those in power on ability
monarchy	hereditary head of state
monocracy	one person
ochlocracy	the mob
oligarchy	small exclusive class
patriarchy	male head of family
plutocracy	the wealthy
stratocracy	the military
technocracy	technical experts
theocracy	divine guidance

Disarmament Policy of reducing armed forces and weapons.

Embargo Stoppage of movement of people or property; used to exert economic pressure on another country.

Emerging country Country that is beginning to develop economically.

Escalation Step-by-step measure and counter-measure, usually towards, and sometimes into, war.

Expatriation Renunciation of nationality by an individual.

Extradition Handing an accused or convicted person over to another country for trial or imprisonment.

Fascism Form of ABSOLUTISM in which a country has only one political party, and is ruled by a dictator.

Federation Union of states that retain a large measure of self-government, but yield certain powers to a central or federal government.

Fellow traveller Term used in western countries to describe a Communist sympathizer who is not a party member.

Franchise Right to vote.

Free-trade area Agreement between states to remove tariffs and other trade barriers.

Geneva Protocol An international agreement made in 1925 designed to prohibit the use of poisonous gases, chemical weapons and bacteriological methods of warfare.

Genocide Acts intended to destroy a nation.

Geopolitics Science of politics in terms of land and geographical space.

Gerrymander To manipulate voting districts, facts, or arguments in favour of a particular political party.

Hague and Geneva Conventions Collection of rules concerning the conduct of land warfare, the protection of non-combatants and the treatment of wounded and prisoners of war.

Hawks and doves Hawks are politicians who favour military action; doves favour any moves to preserve peace.

Hegemony Attempt by one state to attain a position of pre-eminence in its relations with other states.

Home rule Self-government by the people of a country, particularly one that has been the colony of another.

Imperialism Control by one country of other countries or territories, which are ruled as colonies.

Insurgency Internal insurrection or revolution falling short of actual civil war.

Intervention Interference in affairs which fall within the jurisdiction of another state.

Isolationism Policy that a country should keep itself to itself.

Junta Council of state, or group holding power in country.

Left wing Political group or party holding radical views; from position of radicals in French Revolutionary assembly.

Liberalism Policy favouring change to suit existing conditions.

Lobbying Attempting to influence members of a legislature; from the lobby or anteroom of a legislative chamber.

Mandated territory Territory put under control of another country by League of Nations.

Martial law Administration of law and order in state by armed forces.

Mediation Reconciliation of conflicting claims by some third party.

Monroe Doctrine United States guarantee to all independent countries in Americas against European interference (President James Monroe, 1823).

Municipal law The law operating within a particular country, as opposed to international law.

Nationalism Desire for independence and statehood by people with same language and culture; exalting one's country above all others.

Nationalization State ownership of industry or business.

Neutrality Status of a country when not at war involving a duty of impartiality in relation to the belligerents.

New Deal Reform programme introduced in United States in 1930s to combat Great Depression.

Nihilism Denial of all accepted ideas.

Ombudsman Independent investigator who protects citizens against maladministration by civil servants.

Political science Study of government.

Power politics System of international relations governed by the use or threatened use of force or reprisal.

Proletariat Body of people, with little or no property, who live by their own work, especially manual workers.

Proportional representation Voting system designed to give political parties seats in proportion to total votes cast for them.

Protectorate Country under control of another country.

Racialism Dislike and persecution of people on account of race.

Radicalism Belief in political and social change and reform.

Rapprochement Reconciliation.

Recognition Formal acknowledgement of the existence of a nation state and a fundamental principle of international law.

Referendum National vote on a particular issue.

Reparation Redress, usually by forcible means, of an illegal act.

Revisionism An attempt to introduce socialist ideas by reform rather than by revolution.

Right wing Conservative, traditionalist political group. From position of conservatives in French Revolutionary assembly.

Sanctions Measures which can be taken to enforce legal obligations.

Secession Withdrawal of state, party, or any large group from country or federation.

Segregation Separation of people according to race.

Separation of powers Division of government among executive, legislative, and judicial branches; applies especially to United States.

Socialism Belief that country's people should own means of production; less extreme form of communism.

Soviet Legislature in Russia.

Suffragism Belief in right to vote.

Syndicalism System in which means of production are controlled by workers.

Third World Name given to countries that do not support either of the blocs led by United States and Soviet Union.

Totalitarianism System in which central government controls all aspects of people's lives and work.

Treaty An agreement, subject to ratification, between one or more states which may deal with political, defence, economic, legal, social or cultural matters.

Trust territory Land administered by country on behalf of United Nations.

Utilitarianism Belief that only useful actions are those that promote greatest happiness of greatest number.

Zionism Movement to set up Jewish state in Palestine (accomplished in 1948), and belief in protection of that state.

INTERNATIONAL ORGANIZATIONS

ASEAN	Association of South-Eastern Asian Nations
COMECON	Council for Mutual Economic Aid
ECSC	European Coal and Steel Community
EC	European Community
EFTA	European Free Trade Association
EURATOM	European Atomic Energy Community
NATO	North Atlantic Treaty Organization
OAS	Organization of American States
OAU	Organization of African Unity
OECD	Organization for Economic Development and Co-operation
OPEC	Organization of Petroleum-Exporting Countries
UN	United Nations

MEMBERS OF INTERNATIONAL ORGANIZATIONS

COMECON Bulgaria, Cuba, Czechoslovakia, Hungary, Mongolia, Poland, Romania, USSR, Vietnam (as at January 1, 1991).

Commonwealth: Antigua and Barbuda; Australia; Bahamas; Bangladesh; Barbados; Belize; Botswana; Brunei; Canada; Cyprus; Dominica; Gambia; Ghana; Grenada; Guyana; India; Jamaica; Kenya; Kiribati; Lesotho; Malawi; Malaysia; Maldives; Malta; Mauritius; Namibia; Nauru; New Zealand; Nigeria; Pakistan (left 1972, rejoined 1989); Papua-New Guinea; St Kitts-Nevis; St Lucia; St Vincent and the Grenadines; Seychelles; Sierra Leone; Singapore; Solomon Islands; Sri Lanka; Swaziland; Tanzania; Tonga; Trinidad and Tobago; Tuvalu; Uganda; United Kingdom; Vanuatu; Western Samoa; Zambia; Zimbabwe.

European Community: Belgium, Denmark, France, Germany, Greece, Ireland, Italy, Luxembourg, Netherlands, Portugal, Spain, United Kingdom.

NATA (North Atlantic Treaty Organization): Belgium, Canada, Denmark, France, Germany, Greece, Iceland, Italy, Luxembourg, Netherlands, Norway, Portugal, Spain, Turkey, United Kingdom, United States.

Warsaw Pact: Bulgaria, Czechoslovakia, Hungary, Poland, Romania, USSR (as at January 1, 1991).

A team from the World Health Organization enters a village in the Himalayas. The WHO, as it is known, is one of the most successful of the specialized agencies of the United Nations Organization. It works to prevent the spread of diseases such as malaria and tuberculosis, and to help developing countries to improve their public health services.

UNITED NATIONS: MEMBER COUNTRIES

Country	Joined*	Country	Joined	Country	Joined
Afghanistan	1946	Ghana	1957	Paraguay	1945
Albania	1955	Greece	1945	Peru	1945
Algeria	1962	Grenada	1974	Philippines	1945
Angola	1976	Guatemala	1945	Poland	1945
Antigua and Barbuda	1981	Guinea	1958	Portugal	1955
Argentina	1981	Guinea-Bissau	1974	Qatar	1971
Australia	1945	Guyana	1966	Romania	1955
Austria	1955	Haiti	1945	Rwanda	1962
Bahamas	1973	Honduras	1945	St Kitts-Nevis	1983
Bahrain	1971	Hungary	1955	St Lucia	1979
Bangladesh	1974	Iceland	1946	St Vincent &	
Barbados	1966	India	1945	the Grenadines	1980
Belgium	1945	Indonesia	1950	São Tome e Principe	1975
Belize	1981	Iran	1945	Saudi Arabia	1945
Benin	1960	Iraq	1945	Senegal	1960
Bhutan	1971	Ireland, Rep. of	1955	Seychelles	1976
Bolivia	1945	Israel	1949	Sierra Leone	1961
Botswana	1966	Italy	1955	Singapore	1965
Brazil	1945	Ivory Coast	1960	Solomon Islands	1978
Brunei	1984	Jamaica	1962	Somali Republic	1960
Bulgaria	1955	Japan	1956	South Africa	1945
Burkina Faso	1960	Jordan	1955	Spain	1955
Burundi	1962	Kenya	1963	Sri Lanka	1955
Byelorussian SSR	1945	Kuwait	1963	Sudan	1956
Cambodia	1955	Laos	1955	Surinam	1975
Cameroon	1960	Lebanon	1945	Swaziland	1968
Canada	1945	Lesotho	1966	Sweden	1946
Cape Verde	1975	Liberia	1945	Syria	1945
Central African		Libya	1955	Tanzania	1961
Republic	1960	Luxembourg	1945	Thailand	1946
Chad	1960	Madagascar	1960	Togo	1960
Chile	1945	Malawi	1964	Trinidad & Tobago	1962
China†	1945	Malaysia	1957	Tunisia	1956
Colombia	1945	Maldives, Rep. of	1965	Turkey	1945
Comoros	1975	Mali	1960	Uganda	1962
Congo	1960	Malta	1964	Ukrainian SSR	1945
Costa Rica	1945	Mauritania	1961	USSR	1945
Cuba	1945	Mauritius	1968	United Arab Emirates	1971
Cyprus	1960	Mexico	1945	United Kingdom	1945
Czechoslovakia	1945	Mongolia PR	1961	United States	1945
Denmark	1945	Morocco	1956	Uruguay	1945
Djibouti	1977	Mozambique	1975	Vanuatu	1981
Dominica	1978	Myanmar	1948	Venezuela	1945
Dominican Republic	1945	Namibia	1990	Vietnam	1976
Ecuador	1945	Nepal	1955	Western Samoa	1976
Egypt	1945	Netherlands	1945	Yemen, Republic of	1967
El Salvador	1945	New Zealand	1945	Yugoslavia	1945
Equatorial Guinea	1968	Nicaragua	1945	Zaire	1960
Ethiopia	1945	Niger	1960	Zambia	1964
Fiji	1970	Nigeria	1960	Zimbabwe	1980
Finland	1955	Norway	1945		
France	1945	Oman	1971		
Gabon	1960	Pakistan	1947		
Gambia	1965	Panama	1945		
Germany	1973	Papua New Guinea	1975		

*The UN came into existence in 1945.
†In 1971 the UN voted for the expulsion of Nationalist China and the admittance of Communist China in its place.

UN: PRINCIPAL ORGANS	UNITED NATIONS AGENCIES	
General Assembly Consists of all members, each having one vote. Most of work done in committees: (1) Political Security. (2) Economic & Financial, (3) Social, Humanitarian & Cultural, (4) Decolonization (including Non-Self Governing Territories), (5) Administrative & Budgetary, (6) Legal. **Security Council** consists of 15 members, each with 1 vote. There are 5 permanent members — China, France, UK, USA, and USSR — the others being elected for two-year terms. Main object: maintenance of peace and security. **Economic and Social Council** is responsible under General Assembly for carrying out functions of the UN with regard to international economic, social, cultural, educational, health, and related matters. **Trusteeship Council** administers Trust Territories. **International Court of Justice** is composed of 15 judges (all different nationalities) elected by UN. Meets at The Hague. **The Secretariat** is composed of the Secretary-General, who is chief administrative officer of the UN and is appointed by the General Assembly, and an international staff appointed by him. Secretary-Generals of the UN:	FAO	Food and Agriculture Organization
	GATT	General Agreement on Tariffs and Trade
	IAEA	International Atomic Energy Authority
	IBRD	International Bank for Reconstruction and Development (World Bank)
	ICF	International Court of Justice
	ICAO	International Civil Aviation Organization
	IDA	International Development Association
	IFC	International Finance Corporation
	ILO	International Labour Organization
	IMCO	Inter-Governmental Maritime Consultative Organization
	IMF	International Monetary Fund
	ITU	International Telecommunications Union
	UNCLOS	United Nations Conference on the Law of the Sea
	UNCTAD	United Nations Conference on Trade and Development
	UNEF	United Nations Emergency Fund
	UNESCO	United Nations Educational, Scientific and Cultural Organization
	UNICEF	United Nations Children's Emergency Fund
	UNIDO	United Nations Industrial Development Organization
	UNRRA	United Nations Relief and Rehabilitation Administration
	UPU	Universal Postal Union
	WHO	World Health Organization
	WMO	World Meteorological Organization

Secretary-Generals of the UN:

Trygve Lie (Norway)	1.2.46	to 10.4.53
Dag Hammarskjöld (Sweden)	10.4.53	to 17.9.61
U Thant (Burma)	3.11.61	to 31.12.71
Kurt Waldheim (Austria)	1.1.72	to 31.12.81
Javier Pérez de Cuellar	1.1.82	to

GLOSSARY OF LEGAL TERMS

Administrator Person appointed to manage the property of another — normally by way of a formal grant of administration (administratrix — female).

Adoption Order Court order which vests the parental rights and duties relating to a child in the persons making the adoption and extinguishes those rights of its natural parents.

Adverse Possession The uncontested occupation of land contrary to another's rights of actual ownership and which may in course of time enable the person in occupation to gain ownership.

Affidavit A written voluntary statement given under oath.

Alibi Defence available to an accused person who claims to have been elsewhere at the time the offence of which he is charged was committed.

Apostille Document, usually provided by a government authority for use abroad, certifying the authenticity of the notary's seal as affixed to a document.

Arbitration An informal procedure, usually by prior agreement, whereby disputes are resolved by one or more persons acting as arbitrators. A valid arbitration award can be enforced through a court of law but can only be appealed against on the ground of a mistake in law.

Arrest The seizure and detention of persons or objects (such as ships). An unlawful arrest of a person may give rise to a claim for false imprisonment.

Attorney A person appointed by another to represent or look after their interests, normally by the grant of a power of attorney.

Bail The conditional release from custody of an accused person upon the surety of others, who are liable to forfeit the sums of money specified when bail is granted, should the accused fail to attend at the future appointed time and place.

Bailee A person to whom the possession of goods is entrusted by another (the bailor) usually the owner. No transfer of ownership is involved and the bailee is bound to take care of the goods and deliver them up when requested.

Bailiff An officer of the Court, subordinate to the Sheriff, who normally undertakes such duties as the serving of writs, seizure of goods, eviction and carrying out other court orders.

Bankruptcy Arises from an act of insolvency by an individual whereby a petition is made to the court for a receiving order to be granted. Thereafter all the property and assets of the debtor pass to an Official Receiver.

Barrister A person who, unlike a solicitor, has an

exclusive right of audience in the English High Court and higher courts to represent his clients' interests. He may only be approached through a solicitor.

Beneficiary A person to whom property is due to pass under a will or trust.

Bona Fide Acting in good faith without dishonest intent.

Breach of Contract The breaking of an obligation under a contract which thereby confers a right of action upon the injured party. He may be entitled to treat the contract as at an end or alternatively seek its proper performance and in any event claim damages.

Cartel An agreement, often unlawful, between two or more producers to maintain artificially high prices for their products.

Caveat Emptor 'Let the buyer beware' but nowadays the purchaser of goods is protected in the event of their proving defective or not conforming to their intended specification.

Charge A form of security for the repayment of a debt which may be 'fixed' to specific property or 'floating' over the assets of a concern by way of a legal mortgage or debenture.

Chattels Movable articles of personal property.

Chose in Action A right of action in a court of law normally arising out of the non-payment of a sum of money.

Codicil A document under seal whereby a testator can amend, alter or amplify a will previously made.

Common Law The historical source of much modern law, it is essentially judge-made and has given rise particularly to the law of CONTRACT and TORT.

Condition Fundamental term of a contract breach of which entitles the injured party to repudiate the contract and claim damages. The condition may be expressed or implied by law.

Conspiracy The agreement of two or more persons to commit an unlawful act.

Consumer Protection Collection of laws designed to protect the interests of consumers as regards such things as the supply of goods and services and the provision of credit or hire purchase facilities.

Contempt of Court Conduct which is calculated to prejudice or interfere with the due process of law and operation of the courts.

Contract An agreement, whether oral or in writing, which creates obligations enforceable by law. There must be an intention to create legal relations and valuable consideration. Various statutary provisions also provide that certain contracts be recorded in writing, e.g. transfers of land.

Conversion The misappropriation and use of goods inconsistent with the rights of the lawful owner who is entitled to claim for their return or their value.

Conveyance Formal transfer of property or an interest in land by way of deed or other instrument.

Copyright Exclusive rights attaching to an original literary or artistic work which normally last for the lifetime of the author and 50 years after his death.

Coroner Person appointed principally to preside over inquests into suspicious, violent or unnatural deaths within the coroner's jurisdiction.

Court The forum within which justice is administered. Comprises the integral part of a judicial system with separate courts to adjudicate on different legal aspects as between criminal and civil matters. A formal procedure exists to enable a person to appeal to higher judicial authorities where for instance the verdict of a jury is considered unsafe or unsatisfactory, that the judgment was wrong in law or that there was a material irregularity during the conduct of the trial.

Covenant An agreement contained in a deed creating an obligation which may be positive, negative or restrictive in effect.

Damages The form or measure of compensation due to a person who has suffered loss or injury as the result of some breach of contract, tort or the negligence of some other person. Exemplary damages are awarded as a punishment to the offender.

Decree An order of court.

Decree Nisi A decree granted for the dissolution of a marriage, which usually becomes final (absolute) after a period of 3 months.

Deed A written document which is signed and given under seal.

Defamation The making of a false or derogatory statement concerning another person either in writing or other published form (libel) or by spoken word (slander) and without lawful justification.

Defendant The person against whom a court action is brought or who is charged with a criminal offence.

Discharge To release a person from some obligation or prison. A convicted person may be given an absolute or conditional discharge.

Disclaimer A form of words in a contract document which attempts to exclude or restrict another's rights in the event of a breach or non-performance of that contract.

Discontinuance The voluntary ending of an action by the PLAINTIFF.

Discovery The mutual disclosure of documents which are intended to be used in evidence by the parties to an action.

Distrain The lawful seizure of goods either for disposal or to be held pending payment of compensation.

Divorce The legal dissolution of a marriage which has broken down irretrievably.

Easement A right which exists over the land of another – such as right of way, right of light or right to a flow of water.

Endowment The donation or making of a permanent provision for some charitable or other purpose.

Engrossment A deed prior to its execution.

Equity A body of rules which run parallel to the other rules of law and which are primarily based upon the concepts of fairness and natural justice. In the event of conflict between them, equity will prevail.

Estate An interest in land.

Estoppel Legal doctrine whereby a person is prohibited or 'estopped' from denying the truth of some statement or representation previously made by him.

Evidence Those facts or statements, as opposed to legal arguments, which when presented to the court tend to prove or disprove the matter under scrutiny, but the truth of which is subject to judicial investigation.

Execution The act of signing, sealing and delivering a deed in the presence of witnesses.

Executor The person responsible for putting into effect the provisions of a will (executrix – female).

Extradition The delivery up by government authorities of a person seeking refuge to the authorities of another state where he is alleged to have committed a crime. An extradition treaty is required between the respective states which normally excludes 'political' or minor offences.

Ex Gratia 'As a favour', not intended to create any legally binding obligation.

Ex Parte An application for a judicial remedy made on behalf of some other person.

Fairtrading Collective title to a body of rules designed to protect the interests of consumers generally in such areas as monopolistic practices, credit services and the like.

False imprisonment The unlawful confinement and restraint of a person.

Fiduciary A relationship between one person and another where the former is bound to act in good faith and for the benefit of the other.

Firm An individual or group of persons (partnership) who carry on a business, trade or profession and who remain personally liable for its debts.

Fixtures Articles of private property which become attached to land or houses which are removable by the tenant.

Foreclosure The process by which a mortgagor, having defaulted in repaying the loan and interest, is compelled to forfeit his right to redeem the property secured.

Forfeiture The removal or loss of a person's property by way of a penalty for some act or omission. A forfeiture clause in a lease provides that in the event of breach of certain covenants the lease shall automatically end and the lessor may re-enter to take possession.

Freehold An interest in land which arose from the feudal system and the privileges granted to a free man. It is an estate of uncertain duration without specific time limit.

Frustration Occurs where intervening factors or circumstances beyond the control of the parties to a contract render its performance impossible.

Goodwill The difference between the amount of the purchase price and the actual value of the assets acquired. In a business transfer it normally represents the value which the business has in connection with its customers and reputation.

Guarantee A form of undertaking given by one person (the guarantor) to another.

Guardian A person who has the right and the duty to protect the interests or rights of another who is incapable of managing his own affairs (e.g. a minor).

Habeas Corpus A writ demanding the release of a person detained in custody which requires that person to be brought before the court.

Harassment The use of unlawful means to recover a debt.

Hearsay What someone else has been heard to say.

In criminal proceedings hearsay evidence is generally excluded whilst in civil proceedings the rules are less strict.

In Camera The hearing of a case where the public are specifically excluded.

Incitement In general a person who incites another to commit a crime is equally guilty in the eyes of the law as the person who commits the crime.

Incorporation The conferring of legal personality upon a body of persons, company or association.

Indemnify To make good a loss which one person has incurred as the result of an act or omission on the part of another.

Indictment The written accusation of a crime which sets out a statement of and particulars concerning the alleged offence.

Informations The normal procedure whereby criminal proceedings are instituted before a lower court.

Injunction An order or decree of the court requiring a person to refrain from (preventive) or to do (compulsive) a particular thing. An injunction may be granted as an interim measure or be perpetual but failure to comply constitutes contempt of court.

Inquest An inquiry conducted by a coroner before a jury into the death of a person who has been killed, died suddenly, or in prison or under suspicious circumstances.

Interlocutory Proceedings taken during the course of a court action but incidental to it.

Interpleader Procedure whereby person in possession of property to which two or more persons lay claim can apply to the court to determine who is entitled to it.

Inter vivos During the lifetime of a person.

Intestate Dying without leaving a valid will. Partial intestacy arises where an otherwise valid will does not cover all the property of a person.

Intra vires Within the law, legally permissible.

Joint Tenancy The ownership of land by two or more persons with a right of survivorship, so that on the death of one joint owner the land automatically vests in the others.

Judgment The decision of a court in a legal proceeding. Often used to mean the reasoning of the judge which leads to his verdict.

Jurisdiction The authority which a court has to decide matters that are litigated before it.

Jury A body of twelve persons sworn to give a verdict upon such evidence as is before them. Usually the jury decides facts while the judge decides questions of law.

Landlord The owner or holder of land which has been leased to another, a tenant being the person actually occupying the land.

Lease A document creating an interest in land for a fixed period of certain duration, usually in consideration of the payment of rent.

Legacy A bequest or gift of personal property left to a person (a legatee) by a will. A legacy is categorized as either specific, demonstrative or general.

1) A specific legacy is a gift of a specified item e.g. 'My gold earrings'.

2) A demonstrative legacy is a gift of a certain sum directed to be paid out of a specified fund, e.g. '£100 out of my Post Office account'.

3) A general legacy is a gift payable out of the assets of the estate.

Lessor The granter of a LEASE is known as the lessor. The person to whom a lease is granted is known as the lessee.

Licence An authority to do something which would otherwise be wrongful or unlawful e.g. permission to enter onto land which would otherwise constitute to trespass.

Lien A lien is the right to retain possession of the property of another as security for the performance of an obligation, e.g. a repairer may retain possession until his account is paid.

Limitation, Statutes of Proceedings must normally be brought within a specified time from the date upon which the matters of complaint arose.

Limited Company Name given to a legal entity where the liability of the shareholders' investment in the business is limited in the event of it going into liquidation.

Liquidator A person appointed to carry out the winding-up of a company. His task is to conduct the affairs of the company so that it may be wound up as quickly as possible.

Locus Standi The right to be heard in court or other judicial proceeding, or the legal capacity to challenge a decision.

Minor (Infant) A person who has not attained majority, often 21 or 18. A minor can neither bring proceedings nor defend save through an adult acting on his behalf.

Misrepresentation An incorrect statement which induces a person to enter into a contract and thereby entitles them to discharge the contract and/or claim damages for any loss caused as a result.

Mitigation A plea in mitigation occurs where a prisoner or defendant seeks to introduce facts tending to reduce the punishment or damages to be imposed against him.

Mortgage A CONVEYANCE of a legal estate or interest in land for the purpose of securing the repayment of a debt. The mortgage document will contain a provision for redemption, i.e. that upon repayment of the loan the conveyance shall become void or the interest shall be reconveyed.

The borrower is known as the 'mortgagor', the lender as the 'mortgagee'.

Murder Unlawful homicide committed with malice aforethought. Death must normally result within a year and a day after the cause of death has been administered.

Natural Justice The rules of natural justice are minimum standards of fair decision-making imposed upon persons and bodies who have the duty of adjudicating upon disputes of others. The two basic rules of natural justice are: audi alteram partem (hear the other side) and neamo judex in causa sua (nobody is to be a judge in his own cause).

Negligence A TORT consisting of an unintentional breach of a legal duty to take care which results in damage or injury to another.

Next Friend A MINOR or mental patient may only bring an action through the agency of an adult called a 'next friend'. An action is defended through an adult called a 'guardian ad litem'.

Next of Kin A person's nearest blood relations.

Notary Public A person who attests (witnesses) deeds or writings to make them authentic particularly for use in another country.

Nuisance A TORT arising from an unlawful interference with another's use or enjoyment of or right over land. Nuisance is of two kinds, public and private. A public nuisance (e.g. obstruction of a highway) can also be a crime. A private nuisance is one which materially impairs the use or enjoyment by another of a person's property.

Oath An appeal (usually to God) to witness the truth of a statement. All evidence is usually given under oath as follows: 'I swear by Almighty God that the evidence which I shall give shall be the truth, the whole truth, and nothing but the truth'.

Option A right to accept.or reject a present offer within a stated period of time. See PRE-EMPTION.

Pardon The release of a person from punishment following conviction for an offence.

Passing-Off Carrying on a business or selling goods in a manner designed to mislead the public into believing that business or goods are those of another. Remedy lies in an action for DAMAGES or an INJUNCTION may be sought.

Patent A privilege granted by letters patent and registered for the exclusive use and benefit to the inventor or discoverer of some new process or invention. A patent usually lasts 20 years although it can be extended.

A Patent Agent is one who practises in the registration of patents.

Perjury An offence committed by a person who, sworn as a witness in a judicial proceeding, wilfully makes a statement in a matter material to the issue which he knows to be false or does not believe to be true.

Personal Representative An executor or administrator whose duty it is to settle the affairs and dispose of the property of a deceased person.

Plaintiff A person who brings an action into a court of law.

Pleadings Formal written statements in a civil action exchanged between the parties whereby the issues in dispute between them are identified.

Power of Attorney Formal authority given by one person to another to act for that person in his absence.

Precedent A judgment or decision of a court cited as an authority for deciding a later case which has a similar set of facts.

Pre-emption A right to purchase before others or a right of first refusal. See OPTION.

Prima Facie On the face of it, or on first impressions. Thus a prima facie case is one where the evidence is sufficient to cast the burden of disproving it on the defence.

Privilege A special immunity or exemption conferred on some person or body by virtue of his office or status.

Probate A document issued under seal of the court giving evidence of the authority of the EXECUTOR. The original is deposited in the registry of the court, and a sealed copy, called the 'probate copy', is delivered to the executor.

Property Defined as that which can be owned i.e. is capable of ownership.

Property is often classified as either real property (realty) or personal property (personalty). Real property is limited to FREEHOLD estates in land. Personal property is property which is not real property, e.g. LEASES, CHATTELS and other moveable goods.

Proxy A person appointed to vote with the authority or power of another.

Purchaser One who acquires PROPERTY in exchange for money.

Quantum Meruit (As much as he has earned). Where one person renders a service at another's request without specifying the payment in advance there is an implied promise to pay quantum meruit.

Ratio Decidendi The reason or grounds of a judicial decision.

Redemption The buying back of a mortgaged property by payment of the sum due on the mortgage.

Registered Office The official address of a company to which notices, WRITS and other communications may be addressed or sent.

Rescission Remedy for breach of contract so that the parties are restored to their original position.

Res Ipsa Loquitor The thing speaks for itself. A phrase used in actions for injury caused by negligence where the mere fact of the accident occurring raises the inference of the defendant's negligence.

Restitutio in Integrum Restoration to the original position, e.g. by RESCISSION.

Reversion The right of the owner of an estate to have the estate restored to him when an estate existing for a shorter period has expired.

Revocation An act by which a person annuls something he has already done.

Seal Wax impressed with a device to a document so as to authenticate it.

Service Service of process is the delivery of a WRIT or summons by personal service on the defendant named therein or on his legal representative if he is so authorized.
Service on a limited company may be effected by posting the writ or summons by first class post to its REGISTERED OFFICE.

Solicitor An English lawyer of the Supreme Court employed to conduct legal proceedings and advise on legal matters.

Specific Performance A discretionary remedy whereby the court can order a party in default of an agreement to carry out the promise he has made. Granted only where the appropriate remedy at law is inadequate but is never available to compel the performance of a contract for personal services.

Stamp Duty Taxes levied on certain types of instruments, e.g. Ad valorem (according to value). Stamp duty is payable on a CONVEYANCE over a certain value.

Statements of Claim A written or printed statement by the PLAINTIFF of the material facts on which he relies, showing the ground of the complaint and the relief or remedy he seeks. A defence is the statement delivered by a defendant in answer to the statement of claim.

Strict Liability Liability without fault. The intention of the offender is not important, the mere fact that the particular act has resulted is sufficient to make the offender liable (e.g. speeding offences).

Subject to Contract A phrase used to prevent a document from becoming a concluded bargain, the intention being to defer this until a final contract is agreed and signed.

Subpoena A WRIT directed to an individual requiring him to attend and give evidence.

Sue To bring an action or other civil proceeding against some person(s).

Summons Generally a court document requiring the person cited to appear before the court.

Surety A person who gives security to satisfy the obligation of another.

Testate Having made and left a will. A Testator is the person who makes a will.

Test Case An action, the outcome of which determines the legal position affecting other similar cases which are not litigated.

Testimony Proof of a witness by oral evidence.

Title The right of ownership of land or goods or the evidence of such right.
Title-deeds are those documents comprising evidence of legal ownership of land.

Tort A civil wrong, independent of contract, for which there lies a remedy for damages. Examples include negligence, nuisance, defamation, tresspass, etc. Tortfeasor is one who commits a tort.

Tresspass Any wrong or TORT involving an unjustifiable interference with another's possession of land or other property – usually the unauthorized walking on it.

Trial The conclusion, by a competent court or tribunal, of questions in issue in legal proceedings, whether civil or criminal.

Tribunal A body outside the court system with administrative or judicial functions.

Trust The obligations and duties imposed on one person (the trustee) by virtue of his holding property on behalf of another.

Ultra Vires A thing done outside the scope of the authority conferred by law.

Vendor A seller, usually of land. See PURCHASER.

Verdict The answer given to the court by the jury to a question of fact in civil or criminal proceedings.

Vest To give legal rights to a person.

Void (voidable) A void act is one which is devoid of legal consequences. A voidable act is one which is capable of being set aside but has legal effect until this happens.

Waiver Occurs when a person freely relinquishes or renounces a benefit, right or remedy he otherwise would have.

Ward of Court A person brought under the authority and protection of the court.

Warrant 1) A document issued for the apprehension of an accused person in order to compel him to hear and answer a charge brought against him. 2) A document authorizing something to be done.

Warranty A statement (express or implied) of something which a party undertakes shall be part of a contract. In consumer law a breach of warranty only gives rise to an action for damages for the innocent party. See CONDITION.

Will A revocable disposition or declaration in the prescribed form providing for the distribution of property after death.

Winding-up The process that brings to an end the carrying on of the business of a company. It may be done compulsorily by the court or voluntarily by the shareholders or the creditors.

Ideas and Beliefs

GLOSSARY OF RELIGION

Absolution Remission of a penitent's sins, performed officially by a priest.

Adventists Protestant sects that sprang from the teachings of William Miller in mid-1800; they believe in the 2nd and premillennial advent of Christ. *Seventh-day Adventists* (founded 1960) form largest group.

Agapemonites Members of English sect that lived in 'abode of love' (founded 1859); practised 'spiritual wedlock'.

Agnosticism (from the Greek, meaning 'not knowing'). Belief that man cannot know whether or not God exists.

Allah Arabic name for supreme being of Muslims.

Anabaptists See BAPTISTS

Ancestor Worship Veneration of the dead, particularly important in Asia (China for example) and common in primitive societies.

Anglicans Members of churches that agree with Church of England.

Anglo-Catholics Those who hold to the catholicity of the Church of England.

Animism Belief that inanimate objects (rocks, trees, rivers) and natural phenomena (wind, rain, sun) have living souls.

Apocrypha Biblical books of the Old Testament excluded from the canon at the Reformation because of doubts about their authenticity.

Apostles' Creed Statement of the principal Christian beliefs; the oldest of such creeds, possibly used by Christ's apostles.

Armageddon Symbolical battlefield of final struggle between good and evil.

Assemblies of God Largest of the Pentecostal sects, which lay stress on 'speaking with other tongues'.

Atheism Intellectual refutation of the existence of God.

Atonement An act of repentance or sacrifice that will bring person back to God. Most Christians believe that death of Jesus atoned for sins of all. See YOM KIPPUR.

Ayatollah An Iranian Shi'ite Islamic religious leader.

Bahá'í Persian religion founded in 1800s; members believe in unity of mankind and peace through religion and science.

Baptism Christian rite of plunging person into, or sprinkling him with, water as sign of purification.

Baptists Differ from most other Nonconformist churches in that they limit total immersion to adults and oppose the baptism of infants. Anabaptist movements in Europe – mainly in Germany, Switzerland and the Netherlands – also confined baptism to adults but turned political, advocating a primitive form of communism.

Bar Mitzvah Confirmation ceremony for Jewish boys at age of 13.

Bhagavad-Gita Long philosophical poem forming part of the Hindu scriptures.

Bible Collection of many holy books that forms the scriptures of Christians and Jews.

Brahma One of chief gods (creator of world) in Hindu religion.

British Israelites Religious group who believe that white English-speaking peoples are descendants of the lost 10 Tribes of Israel; hence that Anglo-Saxons are God's chosen people.

Buddha (circa 567–487 BC) Title meaning the 'Enlightened One' bestowed on Siddhartha Gautama, Indian prince, spiritual teacher, and founder of Buddhism.

Buddhism Major oriental religion founded by Buddha that teaches way of salvation through ethics and discipline. Buddha's eight-fold path to Nirvana – the goal of the Buddhist way of life – was: right intention; right conduct; right means of livelihood; right effort; right knowledge; right speech; right mindfulness; and right concentration. He enunciated four great truths: 1. Suffering is universal: 2. The cause of suffering is craving or selfish desire: 3. The cure is the elimination of selfish craving: 4. Take the Middle Way between extreme asceticism and self-indulgence. Right conduct, according to the Buddhists, includes abstinence, not only from immorality, but also from taking life, human or animal. A universal god plays no part in Buddhist thought.

Caliph Title of Muhammad's successors as civil and spiritual leaders.

Calvinists Followers of teachings of John Calvin (1509–64), who accept absolute sovereignty of God and supremacy of Bible.

Chauvinism was in no way associated with Calvin (Chauvin) but was derived from Nicolas Chauvin, whose excessive devotion to the Emperor Napoleon made him a figure of ridicule, so chauvinism came to mean absurd devotion to a cause.

Christadelphians Members of a religious sect founded in the US in the late 1840s by John Thomas. They believe Christ will return soon to set up the Kingdom of God with Jerusalem as its capital. They believe, too, in the prophecies of the Bible.

Christianity Religion founded on life and teachings of JESUS Christ which are recorded in the four gospels of the New Testament. There are many different sects and churches of Christianity.

Left: This gigantic statue of the Buddha is in Sri Lanka (formerly Ceylon). The Buddhist way of life advocates moderation in all things, respect for all people, compassion and respect for even the lowest forms of life, and above all tolerance. The Buddha, the former prince Siddhartha Gautama, laid down the guidelines for this way of life in the 500s BC.

Christian Scientists Followers of religious movement founded in late 1800s by Mary Baker Eddy; stress present perfectibility of God and man, and practise spiritual healing.

Church of England The established church in England, springing mainly from fusion of the Celtic Church with that of St. Augustine; during Reformation, royal supremacy was substituted for that of pope.

Church of Scotland National church of Scotland much influenced by Calvin and John Knox.

Confession Statement of religious belief; in the Roman Catholic Church, the acknowledgment of sins, to priest.

Confirmation Ceremony associated with baptism in many Christian churches; called *bar mitzvah* in Judaism.

Confucius (Kung Fu-tzu) Chinese philosopher of the non-super-natural (551–479 BC), who advocated a life based on humanity, moral self-cultivation and social order; Confucianism became the dominant philosophical/religious influence in China (mingled with TAOISM).

Congregationalists Nonconformist Christians who believe that each local congregation is responsible only to God and that all Christians are equal.

Copts Members of an Egyptian Christian church, branch of EASTERN ORTHODOX CHURCH; have dietary laws and practise circumcision.

Determinism The philosophy usually credited to Descartes (1596–1650), a Frenchman who believed that mind and body must be separated by philosophers – the mind is free but the body is determined in every aspect. But he had to accept that the mind can influence the body.

Dialectical Materialism Philosophical basis of MARXISM. According to the German thinker, Hegel, the universal reason behind events works through the ideas held by a particular society until they are challenged by ideas which replace them and, in their turn, are challenged, usually by war. So war, reasoned Hegel, is an instrument of progress.

Druidism The religion of Celtic Britain and of Gaul. Stonehenge and Avebury were believed to hold its temples. Little is known of the religion.

Dukhobors Members of Russian sect, many of whom have settled in Canada since 1899; opposed to military service, they trust to 'inner light' for guidance.

Eastern Orthodox Church Federation of Christian churches (Russian Orthodox, Greek Orthodox, etc.) found in eastern Europe and Egypt; faith is expressed in Creed of Constantinople. Split from the Western Church in the 11th century.

Ecumenical Movement Among Christians of different denominations, the desire to increase interchurch co-operation and recreate unity.

Episcopalians Members of church governed by bishops.

Eucharist Christian sacrament that celebrates the Lord's Supper.

Existentialism A philosophical, literary and theological movement often connected with the French aesthetes Jean-Paul Sartre and Albert Camus, poses the questions What is man? and, more subjectively, Who am I? It seeks to distinguish between essence and existence. Answers to the questions are many and even conclude with the short commands 'Become committed to something, even yourself'.

Fetishism In primitive religion, the attribution to objects (charms) of magical powers.

Friends, Society of Christian group founded by George Fox in 1640s; it rejects creeds, rites, and organized religion in favour of spontaneous worship; members popularly known as Quakers.

Fundamentalists Protestant Christians who believe that Bible is literally true, without error, and wholly inspired by God.

Gnostics Members of early Christian sect who claimed to possess secret knowledge *(gnosis)* based on spiritual insight.

Hedonism Was founded by the Greek Epicurus, born in Samos in 342 BC, who taught that pleasure is the chief aim of a happy life. But he also urged moderation in all things.

Hegira Flight of Muhammad from Mecca to Medina in AD 622.

Hinayana Austere form of Buddhism, found in Sri Lanka, Burma, Thailand and Vietnam

Hinduism One of the great eastern religions; the main religion of India. Hindu thought is expressed in a series of writings known as the Upanishads. In these writings the twin doctrines of *samsara* (rebirth) and *karma* (action) are propounded. The individual, by active participation in life, so implicates himself in this world that, after death, he returns to it again in some other form. The belief in reincarnation was born. Karma causes the individual to cling to existence in this world of time and space and determines the form of his next existence. The Veda, or Sacred Lore, has been passed down in the form of mantras. The deity takes three forms: represented by the divine trinity of BRAHMA, VISHNU and SIVA. There are also lesser gods, demi-gods and supernatural beings and members of the divine trinity may even become incarnate – for example, Vishnu became identified with a legendary hero Krishna.

Imam Islamic official who conducts prayers of mosque.

Islam Major eastern religion founded by Muhammad in AD 600s. Muhammad taught that there was one God (ALLAH) and that he was his prophet. Each MUSLIM has five duties (the name of his religion means 'submission to the will of Allah'): 1. Once in his lifetime he must say wth utter conviction 'There is no God but Allah and Muhammad is His Prophet'. 2. He must wash and pray at least fives times daily: on rising, at noon, in mid-afternoon, after sunset, before retiring. 3. He must give alms generously, especially offering provisions to the poor. 4. He must observe the fast of the holy month, Ramadan. 5. Once in his life he must, if he can, make pilgrimage to Mecca. Has many followers (called Muslims) in Africa and Asia.

Jainism Small Indian sect, offshoot of Hinduism in the 6th century BC; teaches that salvation depends on rigid self-effort and non-violence towards all creatures.

Jehovah Name used by Christians for the Hebrew God.

Jehovah's Witnesses Adherents of a religious movement founded by the American C. T. Russell in late

Left: Muhammad taming the lion – one of several legends told about the Prophet. Islam forbids the portrayal of Muhammad's face, so it is shown veiled.

MAJOR RELIGIONS: ESTIMATED WORLD MEMBERSHIP (millions)

Christians 1000
  Roman Catholics 585
  Eastern Orthodox 90
  Protestants 325
Jews 15
Muslims 500
Shintoists 60
Taoists 30
Confucians 300
Buddhists 200
Hindus 500

1800s, they believe that Christ returned invisibly in 1914, and that Armageddon is near.

Jesus Founder of Christianity: his followers believe him to be the Christ or Messiah.

Judaism Religion of the Jews, based on Old Testament and TALMUD. It is the only truly monotheistic religion.

Karma Law that says a man's deeds determine his destiny; subscribed to by Buddhists and Hindus.

Koran The sacred book of ISLAM.

Kosher Term that means 'fit to be eaten according to Jewish ritual'; Jewish law prohibits eating of certain animals, and states that those that are eaten must be slaughtered and prepared in certain ways.

Lama Buddhist priest in Tibet and Mongolia.

Latter-day Saints See MORMONS.

Liturgy Regular form of service at church.

Lutherans Members of oldest and largest Protestant church, founded by Martin Luther in 1500s; Bible is only authority.

Mahayana Ritualistic, less austere form of Buddhism, followed in Nepal, China, Mongolia, Korea and Japan.

Manichaeism Doctrine preached by the Babylonian prophet Mani in the 3rd century AD that Good and Evil exist as separate and opposed principles. Persecuted as heretical teaching by Christians and Muslims, and died out in the Middle Ages.

Maoism The Chinese interpretation of communism according to the Thoughts of Chairman Mao Tsetung (1893–1976). He interpreted the theories of Karl Marx in a manner peculiar to China and fitted them into the Chinese way of life.

Marxism Karl Marx and Friederich Engels provided the inspiration for modern communism and cooperated in 1848 in writing the Communist Manifesto. But it was Marx's great work, Das Capital, which became the 'Bible' of most communist parties. He worked out a new theory of society, postulating that all social systems are economically motivated. He interpreted history in terms of economics and explained the evolution of society through the class struggle. He visualised his theories as revolutionising the more advanced countries but it was the backward ones like Russia and China which adopted them.

Mennonites Branch of Anabaptists organized in 1525 at Zurich; several groups now in US, some opposing all ritualism.

Methodists Members of Protestant movement founded by John Wesley (1703–91) and his brother, Charles. They stress evangelical Christianity and religious experience.

Metropolitan Archbishop of the Eastern Orthodox Church; occasionally, a Roman Catholic archbishop.

Mohammed See MUHAMMAD.

Mohammedanism See ISLAM.

Monotheism Belief in one god.

Moral Rearmament International movement for character reformation on Christian principles; founded by American educationist Frank Buchman in 1920s; formerly called *Oxford Group*.

Moravians Members of Protestant church founded in Bohemia and Moravia in 1457, based on teachings of John Huss.

Mormons Members of American religious sect founded by Joseph Smith (1830), officially, Church of Jesus Christ of Latter-day Saints.

Moslem See MUSLIM.

Mosque Muslim place of worship.

Muezzin Muslim official who calls to prayer.

Muhammad (570–632) The prophet and founder of ISLAM.

Muslim (Moslem) A follower of ISLAM.

Mysticism Common to several great religions, the experience of direct contact and unity with ultimate reality through prayer, meditation, trance or other means.

Nonconformists Protestants who do not follow the practises of the Church of England; term was first used after the Restoration (1660). Also known as Free Church members.

Oneida Community Spiritually communistic experiment run by J. H. Noyes from 1848 to 1880 at Oneida Creek, New York; based on perfectionism and community sharing.

Pantheism Identification of God with the Universe.

Passion Sufferings and death of Jesus.

Passover Jewish festival, celebrates exodus from Egypt; lasts 8 days and starts in March or April.

Pentecostal sects Group of fundamentalist sects distinguished mainly by 'speaking with tongues', also called 'Holy Rollers' because some devotees fall to ground in trance.

Platonism The early Greek philosopher, Plato, held that mankind often defeats the purpose of the Universe and its Creator – it is man's duty to live a good life but he may well choose to live a wicked one.

Plymouth Brethren Members of a sect founded in ·1827 by J. N. Darby and E. Cronin; they believe that Christianity has fallen from New Testament ideals and this corruption can be remedied only by direct approach to God.

Polytheism Belief in more than one god.

Pope Title of head of Roman Catholic Church; recognized by Catholics as lawful successor to St. Peter.

Positivism Philosophy founded last century by a Frenchman August Comte (1798–1857). He put forward the thesis that mankind had lived through three major stages in thought: 1. the theological; 2. the metaphysical and 3. the final positive and scientific phase when he proceeds by experimental and objective observation eventually to reach 'positive truth'. He tried unsuccessfully to found a religion for the worship of humanity instead of a deity and declared himself High Priest.

Presbyterians Members of Protestant churches that follow system of government established by John Calvin during Reformation.

Protestant Any Christian outside Roman Catholic and Eastern Orthodox churches.

Purgatory In Roman Catholic theology, a 'cleansing place' where souls of the departed wait for atonement of sins before being able to enter heaven.

Puritans General term applied to various English Protestants who broke away from the Anglican Church in the 16th and 17th centuries.

Quakers See FRIENDS, SOCIETY OF.

Rabbi Teacher and expounder of Jewish law, and spiritual leader of synagogue.

Ramadan In Islam, the 9th month of the year, when strict fasting is observed during daylight hours.

Rastafarians A Jamaican sect practising a religion of nature which requires members to wear their hair in long 'dreadlocks', to smoke marijuana as a 'wisdom herb' (which they call ganja) and to work out their beliefs for themselves. Followers have no central organisation or leadership – they look to Ethiopia as their spiritual and racial home and regard the late Haile Selassie I, former Emperor of Ethiopia, as divine, the king of kings and lord of lords.

Resurrection Belief held by Jews, Christians, and Muslims that the dead will eventually return to life in bodily form; specifically, the return to life of Jesus Christ.

Roman Catholics Christians who accept the pope as spiritual leader on earth; they claim to belong to the one Holy and Apostolic Church.

Rosh Hashanah Festival of Jewish New Year.

Sabbath Day of week set aside for rest and religious observances; for Jews it is Saturday, for most Christians, Sunday.

This fresco by the artist Giotto shows St Francis preaching to the birds. In 1210 St Francis founded the first order of friars, known as the Franciscans. They lived lives of poverty and simplicity, earning a living by working as they preached and taught.

PATRON SAINTS

St Agatha	Nurses
St Andrew	Scotland (November 30)
St Anthony	Gravediggers
St Augustine of Hippo	Brewers
St Benedict	Speleologists
St Cecilia	Musicians
St Christopher	Sailors
St Crispin	Shoemakers
St David	Wales (March 1)
St Dunstan	Goldsmiths and silversmiths
St George	England (April 23)
St Hubert	Hunters
St Jerome	Librarians
St John of God	Booksellers
St Joseph	Carpenters
St Lawrence	Cooks
St Luke	Physicians
St Martha	Dieticians
St Matthew	Tax-collectors
St Michael	Policemen
St Nicholas	The original Santa Claus
St Patrick	Ireland (March 17)
St Paul	Carpet-weavers and tent-makers
St Peter	Blacksmiths and fishermen
St Valentine	Sweethearts
St Vincent	Wine-growers
St Vitus	Dancers and comedians
St William	Hatters
St Winifred	Bakers

Saint Person venerated for special merit or religious martyrdom. In the Roman Catholic Church, beatification (blessedness) can lead to canonization (sainthood). Anglican Christians may venerate saints for their example, but do not worship them or invoke them through prayer. The idea of patron saints (for countries, cities, trades, etc.) arose in the Middle Ages.

Salvation Army Religious movement founded by William Booth (about 1865); aims to preach evangelical Christianity to the masses normally untouched by religion.

Scientology An intellectual system launched by an American science-fiction writer, 'Dr.' Ron Hubbard, aimed at improving the physical and mental well-being of its adherents.

Seventh-day Adventists See ADVENTISTS.

Shakers Members of small American sect, United Society of Believers; originally offshoot of Quakers in 1700; devotees shake with religious fervour.

Shamanism Tribal mysticism prevalent in primitive societies of Siberia, eastern Asia, also among Eskimoes and North American Indians; founded on the shaman or medicine man, leader, healer and mystic able to leave body at will during ritualistic ecstacy.

Shi'ism Branch of ISLAM, originally founded by supporters of Ali, son-in-law of prophet Muhammad. Dominant in Iran.

Shintoism Peculiarly Japanese version of Buddhism, with a strong emphasis on ancestor worship. Its influence is now petering out but its 1,500-year existence has given Japan many thousands of magnificent shrines. The religion was disestablished in 1945 when the Emperor Hirohito renounced his 'divine' powers.

Sikhism India's fourth largest religion, located mainly in the Punjab. Nanak (1469–1538), the founder of Sikhism, sought to harmonize Islam and Hinduism. To this end he organized his disciples, called Sikhs, into a closed community with himself as the first guru, or teacher. He preached universal toleration. The guru tradition ended with Govind Singh who was responsible for the abolition of caste distinctions; the wearing of long hair; and the addition of the word Singh (lion) to the original name. Sikhism is the only devotional sect to separate itself from the fold of Hinduism.

Siva One of three main Hindu deities; destroyer and reproducer; also called Shiva.

Spiritualism Nowadays Spiritualists are defined as 'those who believe in life after death, the possibility of communication with the spirits of the dead, and the essential goodness of this activity'.

Stoics The followers of Zeno, Greek philosopher of the 4th century BC. He maintained that man should guide his life by reason and not by passion. Thus virtue, according to the Stoics, was the greatest good. They also made a fundamental distinction between goals which are under human control and those which are not. In the second case, man must endure what cannot be altered while he cultivates the self-sufficient life of reason.

Sunnism Majority branch of ISLAM; name refers to the *sunna* or way of the prophet Muhammad.

Swedenborgians Followers of the teachings of Emanuel Swedenborg (1688–1722); founded Church of the New Jerusalem, claiming that teachings were new dispensation of Christianity.

Synagogue Jewish house of worship.

Talmud Encyclopedia of Jewish laws and tradition supplementing first five books of Old Testament, called the Pentateuch.

Taoism Major Chinese religion founded by Lao Tzu in 500s BC; believers yield to *Tao*, 'the way', in order to restore human harmony.

Theosophy An occult philosophy sympathetic to Hinduism and opposed to orthodox Christianity – its path to wisdom or self-knowledge is through the practice of Yoga. The modern Theosophical Society was founded by Madame H. P. Blavatsky and Col. Olcott in 1875. In India Mrs. Annie Besant, an ardent believer in theosophy, outdid even Hindu reformers in her zeal and, more than any other foreigner, helped the movement of Hindu renaissance.

Torah The Mosaic law; the Pentateuch or first five books of the Bible.

Transmigration of souls Belief that after death the soul enters the body of another living creature; held by ancient Greeks, certain Hindus, Buddhists, and others.

Transubstantiation Belief that bread and wine used in EUCHARIST are mystically changed into body and blood of Christ; held by Roman Catholics and members of Eastern Orthodox Church.

Trinity Christian belief that there are three divine persons in God: Father, Son, and Holy Ghost.

Unitarianism Christian doctrine stressing tolerance and reason; opposes the orthodox doctrine of the Trinity. First Unitarian chapel in London, 1774.

United Reform Church Nonconformist union (1972) of the Congregationalist and Presbyterian Churches in England and Wales.

Utilitarianism That the greatest good of the greatest number is the criterion of morality was the philosophy propounded by Jeremy Bentham (1748–1832) and improved by John Stuart Mill (1806–73) who insisted that the real test of goodness was the social consequence.

Utopia The Greek word for Nowhere; it came to mean the perfect society and was used by Sir Thomas More (1478–1535) as the title of his book describing a mythical paradise in the South Pacific. In modern journalism it is often used to ridicule a fanciful idea of a better society.

Vedas Four holy books of the Hindus.

Vishnu One of the Hindu trinity of deities; preserver of man in various incarnations.

Voodoo Represents a sinister merger of African beliefs and French Catholicism. Prevalent in Haiti. Through voodoo, the spirits of the dead may be called on for advice and help when human resources prove inadequate. Death is a great occasion – the spirit of the dead one is ceremonially removed by the houngan (priest) and allowed to lodge in a surviving member of the family or in a close friend. There is a real terror of the zombie – a person buried and raised from the dead by a mystical formula which makes him a total slave to the sorcerer. There is also a fear of black magic e.g. ouangas, or symbols which can cause harm, sickness, even death.

World Council of Churches Set up in 1948; aims include improving inter-church relations, ecumenical work, aid and welfare. The Roman Catholic

Church is not a member but most other Christian churches are.

Yoga System of Hindu philosophy involving union with the Absolute Being; includes progressive stages of physical and mental exercises.

Yom Kippur Jewish fast day, Day of Atonement.

Zen A Buddhist sect introduced to Japan from 6th century China where it was founded by a half-legendary teacher called Bodidharma. The word means a technique of meditation and the sect has recently been revived in the Western world due to the writings of Dr. D. T. Suzuki and Christmas Humphreys.

Zoroastrians Believers in teachings of Persian prophet Zoroaster (600s BC); morality is greatest virtue in battle between good and evil.

BIBLICAL CHARACTERS

OLD TESTAMENT

Aaron Elder brother of Moses and Miriam; interpreter of Moses and 1st High Priest of Hebrew nation (*Exodus, Leviticus, Numbers*).

Abel Second son of Adam and Eve; shepherd who became the first murder victim when killed by his brother Cain (*Genesis*).

Abraham (Abram) Father of Hebrew nation and traditionally head of Judaism, Christianity, and Islam; journeyed from Ur to Canaan with his family, where he received God's promises. Symbolizes fidelity (*Genesis*).

Absalom David's 3rd son; handsome and spoilt, he plotted against his father but was defeated and killed (*2 Samuel*).

Adam The first man, who, with his wife Eve, was expelled from Garden of Eden for disobeying God's laws (*Genesis*).

Baal Supreme god of Canaanites and Phoenicians, and a temptation to Israelites at various times (*Judges, 1 Kings*).

Bathsheba Wife and widow of Uriah the Hittite; later married David and became mother of Solomon (*2 Samuel*).

Belshazzar Last Babylonian king who, during a feast, saw handwriting miraculously appear on a wall; Daniel interpreted message to mean overthrow of the kingdom (*Daniel*).

Benjamin Youngest son of Jacob and Rachel and young brother of Joseph; held as hostage by Joseph to guarantee return of his brothers when they went to buy food at Pharaoh's court (*Genesis*).

Cain Eldest son of Adam and Eve; world's first farmer, and murderer – killed his brother Abel out of jealousy (*Genesis*).

Daniel Jewish prophet at the court of Babylon, where he had been taken by Nebuchadnezzar; had a gift for interpreting dreams; miraculously protected when thrown into den of lions (*Daniel, Ezekiel*).

David Shepherd boy of Bethlehem who succeeded Saul as King of Israel, ruling for 40 years. Was skilled swordsman and harpist, and as a boy killed the giant Goliath. Grieved at death of his friend Jonathan and son Absalom; repented his betrayal and murder of Uriah, husband of Bathsheba (*1 Samuel, 2 Samuel, 1 Kings*).

Delilah Philistine woman who seduced Samson and betrayed him to foes (*Judges*).

Elijah Fearless Hebrew prophet (flourished about 850 BC) who denounced idolatry uncompromisingly and performed many miracles; carried into heaven by fiery chariot and horses (*1 Kings, 2 Kings*).

Elisha Elijah's disciple and successor as prophet of Israel; author of many miracles (*2 Kings*).

Enoch Father of Methuselah; did not see death 'for he walked with God . . . and he was not' (*Genesis*).

Ephraim Son of Joseph and grandson of Jacob; Jacob on his deathbed gave him the greater blessing over his elder brother (*Genesis*).

Esau Elder of Isaac's twin sons and his favourite; tricked out of birthright by his brother Jacob with mother's connivance (*Genesis*).

Esther Beautiful Jewess brought up as orphan ward of her cousin Mordecai in Persia; devoted to her people, risked her life to protect them (*Esther*).

Eve The first woman; with Adam she was expelled from the Garden of Eden after being tempted by serpent to eat forbidden fruit (*Genesis*).

Ezekiel A major prophet of Israel; captured by Babylonians in 597 BC; his cryptic utterances were highly regarded by fellow prisoners (*Ezekiel*).

Gideon Hero and judge of Israel; led famous and successful night attack on Midianite camp with only 300 men (*Judges*).

Goliath Philistine giant killed by David (*1 Samuel*).

Hezekiah 13th king of Judah, one of the greatest; restored temple worship (*2 Kings*).

Isaac Son of Abraham and Sarah, conceived in their old age; 'heir of promise' and father of Jacob and Esau (*Genesis*).

Isaiah Greatest of Old Testament prophets, who ministered to Jerusalem and Judah in 700s BC; emphasized God's holiness and greatness of House of David (*Isaiah*).

Ishmael Son of Abraham and Hagar, handmaiden to Sarah, Abraham's wife; became rival to Isaac, was expelled into desert, and became ancestor of 12 famous clans (*Genesis*).

THE PROPHETS

Traditional classification according to their writings:

Major Prophets – Isaiah, Jeremiah, Ezekiel, and (except in Hebrew scriptures) Daniel

Minor Prophets – Hosea, Joel, Amos, Obadiah, Jonah, Micah, Nahum, Habakkuk, Zephaniah, Haggai, Zechariah, and Malachi

---

Israel Jacob's new name, given to him after reunion with Esau (*Genesis*).

Jacob Second son of Isaac and Rebekah, and younger twin brother of Esau; tricked Esau out of inheritance and fled from his wrath, but was later reunited with him and changed his name to Israel. The 12 tribes of Israel were named after his 12 sons (*Genesis*).

Jeremiah One of the major prophets; foretold destruction of Jerusalem (*Jeremiah*).

Jew Member of the Hebrew race; originally member of the tribe of Judah (*2 Kings*).

Jezebel Wife of Ahab, King of Israel, and worshipper of Baal. Cruel, murderous, and lustful, she was in constant conflict with Elijah (*1 and 2 Kings*).

Job Pious but suffering man who lived in Uz; his drama posed the question: 'Why does God allow suffering?' (*Job*).

Jonah Minor prophet of Israel; after ignoring God's commands was thrown into sea, but rescued by big fish that swallowed him and then cast him ashore (*Jonah*).

Jonathan Saul's eldest son and renowned friend of David; brave warrior, he was killed in battle. David's lament for him is famous in literature (*1 and 2 Samuel*).

Joseph Favourite son of Jacob and Rachel, had 'coat of many colours'. Sold into slavery by 10 jealous brothers; eventually became prime minister of Egypt and reunited with family (*Genesis*).

Joshua Successor to Moses and leader of Israelites in conquest of Canaan; in his defeat of Jericho, the walls fell down (*Exodus, Numbers, Joshua, Judges*).

Judah Fourth son of Jacob and Leah; founder of tribe of Judah (*Genesis*).

Lot Abraham's nephew; accompanied his uncle from Ur to Harran and thence to Canaan; chose fertile Jordan basin for his home; rescued from destruction of Sodom, he eventually became ancestor of Moabites and Ammonites (*Genesis*).

Methuselah Son of Enoch and, reputedly 969 years, the oldest person who ever lived (*Genesis*).

Miriam Sister of Moses and Aaron; nursemaid to infant Moses, and later leader of Israelites and a prophetess. Finally stricken with leprosy for rebelling against Moses (*Exodus, Numbers*).

Moses Israel's great leader, lawgiver, prophet, and priest, and founder of Israel's religious and national life. Rescued from Egyptian murder of male babies, he was brought up in Egyptian court; eventually led Israelites out of Egyptian captivity to promised land of Canaan, receiving Ten Commandments on the way (*Exodus, Deuteronomy*).

Nathan Hebrew prophet at courts of David and Solomon, courageously denounced David for his adultery with Bathsheba and his arranged murder of Uriah (*1 Chronicles, 2 Samuel*).

Nebuchadnezzar Powerful Babylonian king who reigned in 500s BC; captured Jerusalem twice and deported Jews to Babylon (*2 Chronicles, Jeremiah, Daniel*).

Nehemiah Jewish exile who became cupbearer to King Artaxerxes in Persia; twice returned to Jerusalem to help re-establish the city (*Nehemiah*).

Noah Grandson of Methuselah; had 3 sons (Shem, Ham, Japheth) at age of 500. Built ark to save his family, himself, and a male and female of every living thing from great flood (*Genesis*).

Rebekah Wife of Isaac and mother of Jacob and Esau; brought to Isaac from Mesopotamia by Abraham's servant (*Genesis*).

Ruth Moabite widow who accompanied her widowed mother-in-law, Naomi, to Bethlehem, where she married Boaz. She is symbol of devotion and loyalty (*Ruth*).

Samson Judge of Israel, of enormous physical strength; harassed the Philistines until seduced and betrayed by Delilah (*Judges*).

Samuel Prophet of Israel and last of the judges; anointed Israel's first two kings (*1 Samuel*).

Sarah Wife of Abraham and, at an advanced age, mother of Isaac (*Genesis*).

Saul First king of Israel; given to fits of madness, and jealous of his lieutenant David; eventually killed in battle with the Philistines (*1 Samuel*).

Solomon Son of David and Bathsheba; wisest and wealthiest of Israel's kings; built great temple in Jerusalem (*2 Samuel, 1 Kings*).

The birth of Jesus in a stable in Bethlehem, shown here in a 15th-century stained glass window from Ulm in Germany. Such windows helped to tell the Bible story to people who could not read or write.

NEW TESTAMENT

Andrew Peter's brother, one of the 12 apostles; he was a fisherman (*Matthew, Mark, Luke, John, Acts*).

Barabbas Robber and murderer who was freed instead of Jesus (*Matthew, Mark*).

Barnabas Cypriot who introduced Paul to the Church and was commissioned with him for missionary work; sometimes classed as apostle (*Acts*).

Bartholomew One of the 12 apostles; possibly identical with Nathanael.

The New Testament stories have always provided artists with inspiration. Top: A 6th-century mosaic from Ravenna showing Christ calling St Peter and St Andrew. Centre: The Annunciation of the Virgin Mary, painted by the 16th-century Italian Lorenzo di Credi. Bottom: The Shipwreck of St Paul, by the 19th-century Frenchman Gustave Doré.

Caiaphas High priest of Jews to whom Jesus was first taken after his arrest (*Matthew, Luke, John*).

Elisabeth Wife of Zechariah and mother of John the Baptist, as well as cousin of Mary the mother of Jesus (*Luke*).

Gabriel Angel who announced to Zechariah birth of John the Baptist, and to Mary birth of Jesus (*Luke*).

Herod (1) Herod the Great, ruled when Jesus was born (*Matthew*); (2) Herod Antipas, his son, ruled when John the Baptist was murdered (*Matthew, Mark, Luke*); (3) Herod Agrippa, who killed James the brother of John (*Acts*); (4) Herod Agrippa II, before whom Paul was tried (*Acts*).

James (1) James the Greater, one of the 12 apostles, son of Zebedee, brother of John (*Matthew, Mark, Acts*); (2) James the Less, one of the 12 apostles, son of Alphaeus; (3) James, 'brother' of Jesus, leader of the Jerusalem Church and author of *The Epistle of James* (*Matthew, Acts, 1 Corinthians, James*).

Jesus Founder of Christianity and central figure of New Testament.

John Youngest of the 12 apostles, 'the disciple whom Jesus loved' (*Matthew, Mark, Luke, John, Acts, Epistles of John, Revelation*).

John the Baptist Forerunner of Jesus whom he baptized (*Mark, Luke*).

Joseph (1) Husband of Mary the mother of Jesus (*Luke*); (2) Joseph of Arimathaea, secret disciple in whose tomb Jesus was lain (*Matthew*).

Judas Iscariot The disciple who betrayed Jesus; committed suicide (*Matthew, Luke, John*).

Lazarus Brother of Martha and Mary; raised from the dead by Jesus (*John*).

Luke Christian physician and Paul's travelling companion; author of *Luke* and *Acts* (*Colossians, 2 Timothy, Philemon*).

Mark Author of the 2nd gospel; accompanied Paul and Barnabas and also Peter (*Acts, Colossians, 2 Timothy, Philemon, 1 Peter*).

Martha Close friend of Jesus and sister of Mary and Lazarus of Bethany (*Luke*).

Mary (1) Mother of Jesus; (2) Mary of Bethany, sister of Martha and Lazarus, who anointed Jesus (*Luke, John*); (3) Mary Magdalene, out of whom Jesus cast 7 devils, and who was first to see him after his resurrection (*Matthew, Mark, Luke, John*).

Matthew One of the 12 apostles, author of the 1st gospel, and a tax-collector (*Mark Luke*).

Matthias Apostle chosen by lot to replace Judas Iscariot (*Acts*).

Michael One of chief archangels (*Revelation*).

Nathanael See BARTHOLOMEW.

Nicodemus A Pharisee who came to talk to Jesus secretly by night (*John*).

Paul Apostle to the Gentiles who, before his conversion, was called Saul, and persecuted Christians; author of 13 epistles (*Acts*).

Peter (Simon) Apostle and leader of the early Church; denied Jesus before the crucifixion but later became 'the rock' on which Church was founded (*Matthew, Mark, Luke, John, Acts*).

Philip One of the 12 apostles (*Matthew, John, Acts*).

Pilate Roman procurator of Judea who allowed Jesus to be crucified (*Matthew, Mark, Luke, John*).

Prodigal Son Main character of one of Jesus's

parables; errant younger son who squandered his money before returning to a forgiving father (*Luke*).

Sadducees Jewish religious group made up of a few influential people opposed to Pharisees (*Matthew, Mark, Luke, John*).

Salome (1) Wife of Zebedee, mother of James and John, present at crucifixion (*Mark*); (2) daughter of Herodias who danced before Herod and was rewarded with John the Baptist's head (*Matthew*).

Saul of Tarsus See PAUL.

Silas Paul's companion on his 2nd and 3rd missionary journeys (*Acts*).

Simon (1) Simon Peter (see PETER); (2) Simon the Canaanite, one of the 12 apostles (*Matthew*); (3) one of Jesus's four 'brothers' (*Matthew*); (4)

Simon the Leper, in whose house Jesus was anointed (*Matthew, Mark*); (5) Simon of Cyrene, who carried Jesus's cross (*Matthew*); (6) Simon the Tanner, in whose house Peter had his vision (*Acts*).

Stephen The first Christian martyr, who was stoned to death (*Acts*).

Thomas One of the 12 apostles; known as 'doubting Thomas' because he at first doubted resurrection (*Matthew, John, Acts*).

Timothy Paul's young helper and fellow-missionary; there are two letters to him from Paul (*Acts, 1 Corinthians, 1 and 2 Timothy*).

Titus Convert of Paul's and his travelling companion; Paul sent him one letter (*2 Corinthians, Galatians, 2 Timothy, Titus*).

MYTHOLOGY

GREEK MYTHOLOGY

When there is a Latin equivalent of a Greek name, the character is listed under the Greek version, with the Latin in parentheses. A separate table in this section lists the Roman deities alphabetically and gives their Greek equivalents.

Achilles Greek hero of Trojan War; died when Paris wounded vulnerable heel.

Adonis Beautiful youth loved by Aphrodite; killed by boar.

Aeneas A Trojan, son of Venus, carried his father to safety out of Troy; married and deserted Dido, queen of Carthage.

Agamemnon King of Mycenae, Greek leader against Troy; murdered by wife Clytemnestra, avenged by son Orestes.

Ajax Greek warrior; killed himself when Achilles' arms awarded to Odysseus.

Amazons Female warriors from Asia.

Andromeda Chained to rock as prey for monster, rescued by Perseus.

Aphrodite (Venus) Goddess of beauty and love; sprang from foam in sea, but also said to be daughter of Zeus; mother of Eros.

Apollo Son of Zeus and Leto; god of poetry, music, and prophecy; ideal of manly beauty; sometimes known as *Phoebus*.

Ares (Mars) God of war, son of Zeus and Hera; Roman god *Mars*, father of Romulus and Remus, identified with Ares.

Argonauts Jason and 50 heroes who sailed on *Argo* in search of Golden Fleece.

Artemis (Diana) Twin sister of Apollo; goddess of moon and famous huntress.

Asclepius (Aesculapius) Mortal son of Apollo, later deified as god of medical art; killed by Zeus for raising dead.

Athene (Minerva) Goddess of wisdom and war, daughter of Zeus and Metis; sprang fully grown and armed from father's head.

Atlas A Titan, made war on Zeus, condemned by him to bear heavens on shoulders; later turned into mountain.

A bronze head of Apollo, the Greek god of poetry, the arts, and prophecy; he was also the healer and sender of plagues. The Greeks thought of their gods and goddesses as living in a large, often quarrelsome family in a land beyond the clouds that gather over Mount Olympus in northern Greece. Their human faults and virtues are described in many legends. Apollo was also important to the Romans, who had equivalents to many Greek deities, though usually under different names.

ROMAN-GREEK EQUIVALENTS			
Roman	Greek	Roman	Greek
Aesculapius	Asclepius	Luna	Selene
Apollo	Apollo	Mars	Ares
Aurora	Eos	Mercury	Hermes
Bacchus	Dionysus	Minerva	Athene
Ceres	Demeter	Mors	Thanatos
Cupid	Eros	Neptune	Poseidon
Cybele	Rhea	Ops	Rhea
Diana	Artemis	Pluto	Pluto
Dis	Hades	Proserpine	Persephone
Faunus	Pan	Saturn	Cronos
Hecate	Hecate	Sol	Helios
Hercules	Heracles	Somnus	Hypnos
Juno	Hera	Ulysses	Odysseus
Jupiter	Zeus	Venus	Aphrodite
Juventas	Hebe	Vesta	Hestia
Latona	Leto	Vulcan	Hephaestus

Bellerophon Corinthian hero, rode winged horse Pegasus; fell to death trying to reach Olympus.

Centaurs Race of half-horses half-men.

Cerberus Three-headed dog, guarded Hades.

Cronos (Saturn) A Titan, god of agriculture and harvests; father of Zeus.

Cyclopes Race of one-eyed giants led by Polyphemus; (singular, *Cyclops*).

Daedalus Athenian craftsman, builder of Labyrinth in Crete; imprisoned there with son Icarus, escaped with home-made wings.

Demeter (Ceres) Goddess of agriculture.

Dionysus (Bacchus) God of wine and fertile crops; son of Zeus and Semele.

Elysium Paradise of Greek mythology to which heroes passed without dying.

Eos (Aurora) Goddess of dawn.

Eros (Cupid) God of love, son of Aphrodite.

Fates Three sisters, goddessess who determined destiny of man.

Graces Three beautiful goddesses, daughters of Zeus, personifying brilliance (Aglaia), joy (Euphrosyne), and bloom (Thalia).

Hades (Dis) Abode of dead, ruled by Pluto; name sometimes used for Pluto.

Hebe (Juventas) Goddess of youth, cupbearer of gods; daughter of Zeus and Hera; wife of Heracles.

Hecate Goddess of witchcraft and ghosts.

Hector Eldest son of Priam; chief hero of Trojans; slain by Achilles.

Helen of Troy Fairest woman in world; daughter of Zeus and Leda; cause of Trojan War.

Hephaestus (Vulcan) God of destructive fire, heavenly blacksmith; husband of Aphrodite; son of Zeus and Hera or just Hera.

Hera (Juno) Queen of heaven, daughter of Cronos and Rhea, wife and sister of Zeus; guardian spirit of women and marriage.

Heracles (Hercules) Famous strong man and greatest of deified heroes, performed 12 labours to be free from bondage; son of Zeus and Alcmene.

Hermes (Mercury) Messenger of gods, son of Zeus and Maia; god of physicians, traders, and thieves.

Hestia (Vesta) Goddess of the hearth, sister of Zeus; her temple held Sacred Fire guarded by Vestal Virgins.

TWELVE LABOURS OF HERCULES
1 Killing Nemean lion
2 Killing Hydra (many-headed snake)
3 Capturing hind of Artemis
4 Capturing Erymanthian boar
5 Cleansing Augean stables in a day
6 Killing man-eating Stymphalian birds
7 Capturing Cretan wild bull
8 Capturing man-eating mares of Diomedes
9 Procuring girdle of Amazon Hippolyta
10 Killing the monster Geryon
11 Stealing apples from garden of Hesperides
12 Bringing Cerberus up from Hades

Hypnos (Somnus) God of sleep.

Janus Roman god of doors and gates, represented by two faces facing opposite ways.

Jason Son of Aeson; see ARGONAUTS.

Laocoön Priest of Apollo at Troy; he and two sons killed by serpents sent by Athene.

Midas King of Phrygia; touch turned everything to gold.

Muses Nine lesser divinities who presided over arts and sciences; daughters of Zeus and Mnemosyne.

Narcissus Beautiful youth beloved by Echo; fell in love with own image in pool.

Odysseus (Ulysses) Greek hero of Trojan War; king of Ithaca, husband of Penelope, he roamed ten years after fall of Troy.

Oedipus King of Thebes, unwittingly murdered father (Laius) and married mother (Jocasta); tore out own eyes.

Olympus Mountain in north of Greece, abode of gods.

Orpheus Skilled musician; son of Calliope and Apollo, who gave him his famed lyre.

Pan (Faunus) God of woods and fields, flocks and shepherds; part man, part goat.

Pandora First woman on earth; opened box containing all human ills.

Persephone (Proserpine) Daughter of Zeus and Demeter; wife of Pluto and queen of infernal regions.

Perseus Son of Zeus and Danaë; killed Medusa; married Andromeda.

Phoebus see APOLLO.

Pluto God of Hades, brother of Zeus.

Plutus Greek god of wealth.

Poseidon (Neptune) Chief god of sea, brother of Zeus.

THE NINE MUSES		
Name	Art	Symbol
Calliope	Epic poetry	Tablet & stylus
Clio	History	Scroll
Erato	Love poetry	Lyre
Euterpe	Lyric poetry	Flute
Melpomene	Tragedy	Tragic mask, sword
Polyhymnia	Sacred song	none
Terpsichore	Dancing	Lyre
Thalia	Comedy; pastoral poetry	Comic mask, shepherd's staff
Urania	Astronomy	Globe

The pre-Christian people of Scandinavia thought of their gods as fearless warriors and seafarers, like themselves. This Viking stone from Sweden depicts a world of heroes, battles, and adventure, where those who died bravely in battle would sit and feast in the great hall of Valhalla.

Prometheus A Titan; stole fire from heaven; punished by being chained to mountain while vultures ate his liver.

Psyche Princess loved by Eros but punished by jealous Aphrodite; became immortal and united with Eros.

Rhea Greek nature-goddess, wife and sister of Cronos; mother of Zeus, Poseidon, Pluto, Demeter, Hera; later identified with Roman goddesses Ops and Cybele.

Romulus Founder of Rome; suckled with twin brother Remus by she-wolf; killed Remus.

Satyrs Hoofed demigods of forests, fields, and streams.

Selene (Luna) Goddess of the moon.

Thanatos (Mors) God of death.

Titans Offspring of Uranus and Ge; one, Cronos, dethroned Uranus, but his son Zeus in turn hurled Titans from heaven.

Uranus Oldest of Greek gods, personification of heaven, father of Titans.

Zeus (Jupiter) Chief of the Olympian gods, son of Cronos and Rhea; god of thunder and lightning.

NORSE MYTHOLOGY

Aesir Collectively, the chief Norse gods.

Asgard Home of the gods.

Balder God of summer sun; son of Odin and Frigga; killed by mistletoe twig.

Bragi God of poetry; son of Odin.

Frey God of fertility and crops.

Freya (Freyja) Beautiful goddess of love and night; sister of Frey; sometimes confused with *Frigga*.

Frigga Goddess of married love; wife of Odin.

Heimdal Guardian of Asgard; he and Loki slew one another.

Hel Goddess of the dead, queen of the underworld; daughter of Loki.

Hödur (Hoth) Blind god of night; unwitting killer of twin brother Balder.

Loki God of evil; contrives Balder's death.

Odin Supreme god, head of Aesir; god of wisdom and of the atmosphere.

Thor God of thunder; eldest son of Odin.

Valhalla Hall in Asgard where Odin welcomed souls of heroes killed in battle.

Valkyries Nine handmaidens of Odin who chose warriors to die in battle and conducted them to Valhalla.

EGYPTIAN MYTHOLOGY

Amon (Ammon, Amen) A god of Thebes, united with Ra as Amon-Ra, supreme king of the gods.

Anubis Jackel-headed son of Osiris; guided souls of the dead.

Apis Sacred bull of Memphis.

Hathor Cow-headed sky goddess of love.

Horus Hawk-headed god of light, son of Osiris and Isis.

Isis Goddess of motherhood and fertility; chief goddess of Ancient Egypt.

Osiris Supreme god, ruler of the afterlife; husband of Isis.

Ptah The creator, chief god of Memphis.

Ra Sun god; ancestor of the pharaohs.

Serapis God combining attributes of Osiris and Apis.

Set God of evil; jealous brother-son of Osiris, whom he slew and cut into pieces.

Thoth Ibis-headed god of wisdom.

The Arts

ARCHITECTURAL TERMS

Abacus Slab forming the upper part of a CAPITAL.
Acanthus Plant with scalloped leaves, which are reproduced in carving on the CAPITALS of CORINTHIAN and other columns.
Acropolis The upper part of a Greek city.
Adam style A form of NEO-CLASSICISM devised by the Scottish architect Robert Adam (1728–1792).
Adobe Sun-dried brick, especially that used in Spain and Latin America.
Agora The Greek market place or meeting-place, equivalent to the Roman FORUM.
Aisle Section of a church or basilica parallel to the nave, from which it is usually divided by a COLONNADE.
Ambulatory A semi-circular aisle.
Amphitheatre In Roman times, an ARENA surrounded by tiers of seats, used for sporting events.
Apse A semi-circular or multi-angled end to a church or basilica.
Arabesque Fanciful decoration of flowing lines, flowers, leaves and abstract patterns, first used in Arabian architecture.
Arcade A row of arches supported by columns or piers, sometimes attached to a wall (blind arcade).
Arch Curved structure spanning an opening.
Architrave The lowest section of an ENTABLATURE.

Left: Castle Drogo in Devon was the last large building to be constructed of granite in England. Built by Sir Edwin Lutyens between 1910 and 1930, it is reminiscent of a medieval castle.

Arena An open space, generally circular or elliptical, used for Roman sporting or gladiatorial events.
Art Nouveau A style flourishing from 1890 to 1910, characterized by the use of coloured materials, moulded stonework, writhing floral motifs, tapered wrought-iron brackets and other sinuous ornament: it was a reaction against both the technological revolution and imitations of past styles.
Ashlar Masonry constructed of smooth, squared stones (hewn stone in North America).
Bailey The open area of a castle.
Balusters A series of uprights, often short pillars, supporting a coping or rail.
Bargeboard A board fixed to the edge of a sloping roof, often fancifully decorated.
Baroque A heavily-decorated European style from about 1600 to 1750, involving a flamboyant use of RENAISSANCE forms.
Barrel vault An arched ceiling semi-circular in shape, like half a barrel.
Basilica In Roman times, an oblong building with a nave and side aisles, ending in an apse, used as a justice court or civic hall. Basilicas were converted into Christian churches, which have retained the same basic shape.
Battered Term applied to a wall that slopes in towards the top.
Battlement A parapet having a series of indentations, called embrasures, behind the uprights of which soldiers could shelter from missiles.

ARCHITECTS
Aalto, Alvar (1897–1976), Finnish
Adam, Robert (1728–92), Scottish
Alberti, Leone Battista (1404–72), Italian
Bernini, Gianlorenzo (1598–1680), Italian
Bramante, Donato (1444–1514), Italian
Brunelleschi, Filippo (1377–1446), Italian
Cortona, Pietro da (1596–1669), Italian
Fischer von Erlach, Johann (1656–1723), Austrian
Gaudi, Antonio (1852–1926), Spanish
Gropius, Walter (1883–1969), German
Jefferson, Thomas (1743–1826), American
Jones, Inigo (1573–1652), English
Le Corbusier (1887–1965), French–Swiss
Mansart, François (1598–1666), French
Michelangelo, Buonarroti (1475–1546), Italian
Mies van der Rohe, Ludwig (1886–1969), Ger./US
Nash, John (1752–1835), English
Nervi, Pier Luigi (1891–1979), Italian
Niemeyer, Oscar (1907–   ), Brazilian
Palladio, Andrea (1518–80), Italian
Saarinen, Eero (1910–1960), Finnish-American
Vitruvius Pollo, Marcus (1st Cent. BC), Roman
Wren, Sir Christopher (1632–1723), English
Wright, Frank Lloyd (1868–1959), American

PERIODS OF ARCHITECTURE	
Greek	600s–100s BC
Roman	100s BC–AD 400s
Byzantine	AD 400s–1453
Romanesque (N Europe)	mid-900s–late 1100s
Norman (England)	late 1000s–1100s
Gothic	mid-1100s–1400s
Renaissance (Italy)	1400s–1500s
French Renaissance	1500s
Baroque (Italy)	1600–1750
Georgian (England)	1725–1800
Rococo	mid-1700s
Regency (England)	1800–1825
Art Nouveau (Europe)	1890–1910
Expressionism (Germany)	1910–1930s
Functionalism	1920s–
International Style	1920s–
Brutalism	1950s–

Bauhaus A school of arts and crafts in Germany, run by the architect Walter Gropius (1883–1969) from 1919. Its simple styles had great influence until it was closed in the early 1930s by the Nazis.

Bays Sections into which the interior of a building is divided, generally only by divisions marked on the walls or ceiling.

Bond The regular pattern in which brickwork is laid. Bonds include Flemish, in which the headers (ends) and stretchers (sides) of bricks appear alternately in each row, and English, in which there are alternate courses of headers and stretchers.

Boss A projecting ornament at a point where ribs of a vault or ceiling meet.

Brutalism A movement in modern architecture starting in the 1950s aimed at the straightforward, often rough, use of materials, based on the uncompromising ruthlessness of the architects Le Corbusier and Mies van der Rohe.

Buttress A mass of stone or brick built against a wall to give added strength; in a flying-buttress, the masonry is freestanding with a half arch transferring the thrust from the wall.

Byzantine Style that flourished in the East Roman or Byzantine Empire from the 400s to the 1400s, characterized by ornately domed churches.

Campanile Italian term for a bell-tower.

Cantilever A horizontal beam supported in the middle and weighted at one end, allowing it to support an equal weight at the other.

Capital The broad top part of a COLUMN, supporting the ENTABLATURE.

Cartouche An ornamental panel shaped like a sheet of paper, with the ends curling; in ancient Egypt, an oval panel bearing a royal name.

Caryatid A draped female figure, used as a pillar in classical architecture.

Centring A temporary wooden frame used to support an arch or vault under construction.

Chancel The eastern-end of a church, reserved for the clergy and choir.

Choir Another term for a CHANCEL.

Circus In Roman times, a long amphitheatre; in modern towns, a circular street intersection.

Classical The style of ancient Greece or Rome, or any later style based on these.

Clerestory, or **clearstory** The upper part of the nave of a church, pierced by windows.

Cloisters Covered ways around a quadrangle or open space, on to which they generally open through an ARCADE.

Cob A mixture of mud and chopped straw, used for walling.

Colonnade A range of columns.

Column A vertical support, consisting of a base, a circular shaft, and a CAPITAL.

Columnar and trabeate Using columns and beams (posts and lintels) for support rather than arches: a feature of Egyptian and Greek buildings.

Coping The cap or covering topping a wall.

Corbel A block of stone projecting from a wall, supporting a beam.

Corbel arch An arch made by overlapping blocks on either side until the gap can be bridged at the top by a single slab.

Corinthian See ORDERS.

Cornice The top, projecting section of an ENTABLATURE, supporting a roof.

Crenellation An opening in the upper part of a parapet, as in BATTLEMENTS.

Crossing The space where the CHANCEL, NAVE and TRANSEPTS of a church meet.

Crucks Pairs of curved timbers used as the main supports of a FRAME BUILDING.

Cupola A cup-shaped roof, or a small DOME.

Dado Part of a pedestal between its base and its cornice; also, the lower part of a wall when decorated differently from the rest.

Decorated See GOTHIC.

Dome A vault shaped like half a sphere; a cupola. The name comes from DUOMO, Italian for cathedral, because it was a common form of roofing for such buildings.

Doric See ORDERS.

Dormer A small gabled window, projecting from a sloping roof.

Elizabethan English style of the late 1500s, marking the change from Gothic to Renaissance styles and featuring sturdy, squared buildings with large windows.

Embrasure A CRENELLATION in a parapet, or a small opening in a wall, splayed on the inside.

Engaged column A column partly attached to a wall or other structure.

Entablature Part of a classical building between the top of a colonnade and the roof, consisting of ARCHITRAVE, FRIEZE and CORNICE.

Entasis The slight outward curving of the shaft of a column, to counter the optical illusion that a straight-sided shaft appears concave.

Expressionism Style that flourished in Germany from about 1910 to the 1930s, in which reality was distorted to express the artist's inner feelings.

Façade The main face of a building.

Fanlight A semi-circular window over a door, with glazing bars radiating like a fan.

Fan vault A vault in which fan-like ribs meet at the apex.

Fenestration The arrangement of windows in a building.

Finial Ornament at the top of a gable, a pinnacle, or similar feature.

Fluting Longitudinal grooves in a column.

Folly A useless structure built to satisfy a whim, often a mock ruin.

Forum The Roman equivalent of the AGORA.

Frame building A structure where the load is carried by a frame instead of by load-bearing walls. The frame may be of timber or steel.

Frieze The middle section of an entablature.

Functionalism Modern principle that the form of a building should follow from its proposed function and that of its parts.

Gable The triangular upper part of wall at the end of a roof which has two sloping sides.

Galilee A church porch or chapel, intended for the use of penitents in medieval times.

Garderobe A wardrobe, or in medieval times, especially in castles, a privy.

Gargoyle A projecting stone spout, often grotesquely carved, to take water from a roof.

Gazebo A summerhouse placed so as to obtain a fine view.

Geodesic dome A light, strong dome constructed on a framework of triangular or other straightline elements.

Georgian An English style of the 1700s, based on the late RENAISSANCE style and classical models.

Gothic Style developed in France in the 1100s, lasting until the RENAISSANCE. It was characterized by pointed arches, elaborate vaulting, slender pillars, large windows and intricate tracery, clerestories and flying buttresses. English Gothic is divided into three styles: Early English (late 1100s to 1200s); decorated (late 1200s to 1300s) and perpendicular (mid-1300s to 1500s). The term Gothic was originally one of contempt for anything not CLASSICAL.

Gothic revival A recreation of the Gothic style in the late 1700s and the 1800s, lasting into the early 1900s.

Greek A beautifully proportioned CLASSICAL style lasting from about 700 BC until the Roman conquest of Greece in the mid-100s BC. Its graceful buildings were constructed on the post and lintel pattern, copying in stone the main features of wooden buildings. See also ORDERS.

Groin vault Vault produced by the intersection of two BARREL VAULTS.

Hall church A church (common in medieval Germany) in which nave and aisles are of about the same height, with no CLERESTORY.

Hammerbeam roof Roof in which wooden brackets spring from the walls, carrying arched braces and struts, and allowing shorter main beams to be used.

Helm roof A pointed roof with four diamond-shaped sides.

Herm A bust on a square PEDESTAL instead of a human body, used in classical times to mark boundaries (from Hermes, a Greek god).

Hood mould A projecting moulding above a door or arch to throw off the rain.

Hypocaust The system of underground ducting in Roman central heating systems, through which hot air was conducted.

Hypogeum An underground chamber.

Hypostyle A hall in which the roof is supported on rows of columns.

Iconostasis The screen between the nave and chancel of a Byzantine church; often covered with icons, religious portraits.

International style The term given to a modern style of architecture that evolved in western Europe in the 1920s, and became popular in the United States. Its basic concepts are generally cubic shapes, often asymmetrical, and a great deal of window space – principles employed in buildings ranging from houses to skyscrapers.

Ionic See ORDERS.

Jamb The side of a door or window.

Joists Horizontal timbers in a building, forming the floors.

Keep The main tower of a castle, and its principal strongpoint; also called a donjon.

Keystone Locking stone at the top of an arch.

King post Part of a roof: a vertical post between the ridge and a TIE-BEAM.

Kremlin In Russia, a citadel or fortified part of a town.

Lancet A slender, sharply pointed arch or window.

Lantern A small decorative turret or tower at the top of a dome or other roof, with windows to admit light.

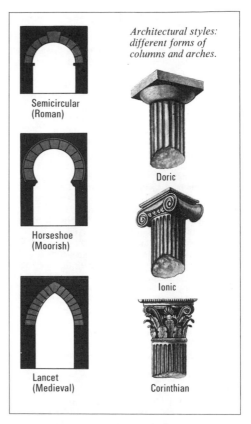

Architectural styles: different forms of columns and arches.

Semicircular (Roman)

Horseshoe (Moorish)

Lancet (Medieval)

Doric

Ionic

Corinthian

Lattice A window with leaded lights or a network of glazing bars.

Leaded lights Small panes of glass set between thin bars of lead to form a window.

Linenfold Panelling carved to resemble linen folded vertically, popular in the 1500s.

Lintel A horizontal beam of wood or stone supported on posts or columns.

Machicolation A projecting parapet on a fortification with openings through which boiling oil and other substances could be dropped.

Mannerism A later RENAISSANCE style in which the strictest rules of CLASSICISM were relaxed.

Mansard roof Roof with a flatter upper part and steeper lower slopes.

Mausoleum A grand tomb; named after the tomb of Mausolus at Halicarnassus, in Asia Minor – one of the Seven Wonders of the World.

Mews A row of stables with living quarters above them, built in cities.

Mezzanine A floor intermediate between two others.

Minaret The usually slender tower of a mosque, with a gallery from which a muezzin calls the faithful to prayer.

Monolith A single, often very large, stone.

Mosaic A decoration for floors, walls and roofs made of small cubes of stone or glass.

Motte A steep artificial mound within a BAILEY, the strongpoint of early medieval castles.

Moulding Decorative edging.

Mullion A vertical bar dividing a window.

Narthex A porch leading to the nave of a Christian BASILICA, where penitents gathered.

Nave The main body of a church, flanked by AISLES.

Neo-classical A style of the 1700s and later, which aimed at the simplicity of classicism, by contrast to BAROQUE and ROCOCO.

Norman The ROMANESQUE style in England.

Obelisk A tall, tapering pillar of square section.

Orders The various styles of columns in CLASSICAL architecture, with base, shaft, capital and entablature. There were five orders: Doric, Tuscan, Ionic, Corinthian and Composite.

Organic architecture The complete harmony of the parts of a building with the whole, and with its surroundings.

Oriel Window projecting from the face of a wall.

Pagoda Tower, of Chinese origin, partitioned horizontally with balconies or cornices.

Palladian A NEO-CLASSICAL style based on the designs of the Italian architect Andrea Palladio (1508–1580), popular in the 1600s.

Pantile A roofing tile in section like a flattened S.

Parapet A low wall, sometimes with BATTLEMENTS, often found at the top of a building.

Pedestal Block used to support a column.

Pediment Triangular end of a sloping roof in classical architecture, often decorated.

Penditive Curved triangular support to enable a dome to be fitted to a square building.

Peristyle A row of columns around a courtyard.

Piazza A public open space surrounded by buildings.

Pier A free-standing vertical support for an arch or beam, such as for a bridge.

Pilaster A flat pillar attached to a wall.

Pillar An upright support which, unlike a *column*, need not be round in section.

Plateresque An elaborate Spanish style of the late 1400s and early 1500s, named because it resembled the work of silversmiths.

Plinth The lowest square part of the base of a column.

Portico A roofed entrance way to a building, with columns on at least one side.

Post and lintel Form of construction using vertical posts with horizontal beams.

Postern A small entrance to a fortified place.

Prefabrication The manufacture of complete buildings or sections thereof in a factory for assembly on site.

Pre-stressed concrete Concrete in which wire cables are put under tension and concrete is cast around them. It gives greater load-bearing strength.

Pylons In Egyptian architecture, OBELISK-like towers flanking a gateway.

Quadrangle Square or rectangular courtyard surrounded by buildings.

Quoin Cornerstone at the angle of a building.

Rampart Defensive wall surrounding a castle or a city.

Regency English style of the early 1800s, mainly NEO-CLASSICAL, showing much Greek influence.

Renaissance The revival of classical architecture and styles in the 1400s, lasting until about 1600.

Reredos Wall or screen behind an altar.

Rococo A light, airy version of the BAROQUE style which emerged in France in the early 1700s.

Roman Style based on the wall rather than (as in Greece) the column; it made great use of concrete, especially for domes and barrel vaults.

Romanesque Style which immediately preceded GOTHIC. It is characterized by massive pillars and rounded arches; known as Norman in England.

Romanticism Style prevalent in England and France in the late 1700s, in which emphasis was on picturesque design.

Rotunda A circular building, usually domed.

Rustication Giving a rough appearance to the surface of building-blocks.

Sally-port A postern gate, sometimes an underground passage, from which the garrison of a castle could sally to launch an attack.

Screen A partition of stone or wood, often pierced and decorated; in churches, used to separate choir from nave.

Shaft The main cylindrical part of a column.

Shingle A wooden tile, used for roofing.

Solar In the Middle Ages, an upper room, often the private chamber of a lord.

Spandrel The roughly triangular space between arches, or an arch and a wall.

Squinches Diagonal arches or vaults across the corners of a square building to support a dome.

Squint or hagioscope An oblique opening in a wall to allow an altar to be seen from an angle.

Starling A pointed mass of masonry on a pier of a bridge to break the force of the water.

Steel-frame A skeleton of steel girders, forming the framework for a building.

Stoa A PORTICO in Greek architecture.

String-course Horizontal band of brick projecting across the face of a building.

Stucco Plasterwork, especially external plasterwork in which imitation carving can be moulded.

Stud An upright timber in a FRAME BUILDING.

Terrazo Flooring made of marble chips in mortar.

Tesserae The small cubes used in MOSAIC.

Tie-beam A horizontal beam in a roof, tying together the feet of the sloping rafters.

Trabeated See COLUMNAR AND TRABEATE.

Transept In a cruciform church, part running at right angles to the nave and choir.

Transom A horizontal bar dividing a window.

Triforium The middle storey of a medieval church.

Truss A number of timbers or steel girders fastened together in frames to bridge a gap.

Tudor English late Gothic period of the 1500s, exhibiting the effect of the RENAISSANCE on the English perpendicular style.

Tufa A form of limestone much used by the Romans.

Turret A small tower, often carrying a staircase.

Undercroft A vaulted room below a building such as a hall or church.

Vault A brick or stone ceiling built on the arch principle.

Volute The spiral scroll of an Ionic capital.

Voussoir Wedge-shaped block used in forming arches.

Wainscot Timber lining or panelling to walls.

Ward The BAILEY of a castle.

Weathering The slope given to a window-sill, or the top of a wall or buttress, to throw off rain.

Ziggurat Pyramid-shaped, tiered tower used in ancient Mesopotamia and Mexico to support a temple or an altar.

LITERARY FORMS

Allegory Story in which the characters and events have a secondary, symbolic meaning.

Alliteration Beginning two or more consecutive words with the same letter or sound.

Amphibrach A FOOT containing a long syllable between two short ones.

Anapest A FOOT composed of two short syllables followed by a long one.

Anthology A choice collection of works.

Aphorism A short, pithy statement.

Apologue A fable with a moral.

Arsis A strong syllable in English verse.

Assonance Correspondence of vowel sounds in poetry or prose (see also RHYME).

Autonomasia Use of name of person (fact or fiction) to represent type e.g. veritable Solomon.

Ballad Story in verse, often traditional.

Ballade Poetic form originating in France in the 1300s, with three stanzas of 8 or 10 lines and one of 4 or 5.

Bathos The descent from the sublime to the ridiculous.

Belles-lettres Term including all fine literature.

Blank verse Verse without RHYME; usually written in iambic pentameters.

Bound verse Verse based on a metrical pattern.

Cadence Rhythm and phrasing of language.

Caesura Pause in a line of verse.

Comedy Humorous dramatic piece: high comedy has well-drawn characterization and witty dialogue; low comedy, or slapstick, has absurd situations and boisterous action; farce is exaggerated comedy; tragi-comedy is a blend of the tragic and comic; satire uses sarcasm and wit to ridicule people's follies and vices.

Couplet Two successive lines of verse that rhyme with one another.

Dactyl A FOOT consisting of one long syllable followed by two short ones.

Dénouement Final unwinding of a complex plot.

Detective fiction Novels in which the detection of crime is the main theme.

Dimeter A line of verse of two feet.

Disyllable A word or FOOT of two syllables.

Dramatic irony Situation or remark that has a significance unperceived by the character involved.

Eclogue A short poem, particularly a pastoral dialogue between shepherds.

Elegy Mournful poem, often lamenting death.

Enjambment Carrying on the sense of one line of verse into the next.

Epic Long narrative poem, especially one about heroic characters and deeds.

Epigram Neat, brief, witty saying; e.g. The vain have only one to please.

Essay Short prose composition expressing the author's views on a particular subject.

Euphuism Affected and bombastic style of writing.

Fable Short tale, often with animals as the characters, illustrating a moral.

Faction Modern term for a work of fiction that is basically a retelling of fact.

Farce See COMEDY.

Fiction Any narrative which is not pure fact.

First person Style of writing in which the narrator is a character in the story.

Folk tale Story handed down by word of mouth from generation to generation.

Foot In poetry a rhythmic unit of two or three syllables (rarely one), in which some are long (stressed) and others short (unstressed).

Free verse (vers libre) Poetry free from mechanical restrictions such as METRE and RHYME, cadenced according to meaningful stress.

Haiku Japanese verse form composed of 17 syllables, arranged in lines 5, 7, 5.

Heroic couplet Rhymed COUPLET in heroic lines (that is, iambic pentameters).

Heroic verse That used in EPIC poetry.

Hexameter Line of verse containing six feet.

High comedy See COMEDY.

Homonym The same word used to denote different things.

Homophones Words sounding the same but with different meanings.

Hypallage Emphasizing of an adjective or adverb by using it to describe, by position, a word to which it does not belong.

Hyperbole Use of exaggerated terms to emphasize importance or meaning.

Iambus A FOOT of one short syllable followed by a long one; iambic pentameter, a line of five iambic feet.

Idyll Short pastoral poem conveying a mood of happy innocence.

Imagism School of poetry of the early 1900s, concerned with precise language, direct treatment, and freedom of form.

Limerick Humorous verse form of five lines rhyming a-a-b-b-a (a in TRIMETER, b in DIMETER).

Litotes Emphasis by use of negative with word of opposite meaning.

Low comedy See COMEDY.

Lyric poem A short, song-like poem in which the poet expresses personal feelings.

Malapropism Ludicrous misuse of words (from Mrs Malaprop, a character in Richard Brinsley Sheridan's play *The Rivals*).

Meiosis Expression by means of understatement.

Metaphysical poetry Poetry rich in far-fetched imagery, popular in the 1600s.

Metre The rhythm of a line of verse, as described in the number and kind of FEET.

Narrative poem Poem that tells a story.

Neo-classicism Movement of the 1600s and 1700s reviving classical values in English literature, emphasizing discipline, reason, and clarity.

New Wave (la Nouvelle vague) Term applied to movement in literature and cinema originating in France in the late 1950s that attempted to eschew fixed values, revealing a character by the way he experienced objects and events, which were often meticulously described.

Novel Long prose work of FICTION.

Novelette Long short-story of some 15,000 words.

Novella Short novel (about 30,000 words); originally, a short prose narrative in medieval and Renaissance Italy.

Octet The first eight lines of a SONNET.

Ode Lyric poem devoted to the exaltation of its subject. Pindaric ode (Ancient Greece) was written for choral recital in units of three stanzas called strophe, antistrophe and epode; Horatian ode (ancient Rome) consisted of a succession of stanzas of identical pattern.

Oxymoron Use of words of opposite meaning together to express an idea.

Paeon Metrical FOOT of four syllables, one long and three short, varying in order.

Parable Brief story that uses everyday events to illustrate a moral or doctrine.

Parody Comic imitation of a serious piece of writing, often satirical and exaggerated.

Pastoral Literature depicting idealized rural life.

Pentameter Verse line of five FEET.

Picaresque Literature chronicling the adventures of a rogue; it originated in Spain in the 1500s.

Prose Writings not in verse.

Prosody Study of the handling of language in poetry.

Pyrrhic A FOOT consisting of two short syllables.

Realism Literature that attempts to depict life objectively and faithfully.

Rhyme Agreement in sound of two syllables, but with differing preceding consonants.

Roman à clef Novel based upon actual people under disguised names.

Romance Originally, a tale of chivalry; now applied mainly to a love-story.

Romanticism Movement originating in late 1700s, emphasizing an imaginative style of writing.

Rondeau Short form of poem, derived from the French, consisting of either 13 or 11 lines with the first words of the first line used as a refrain.

Rondel Similar in form to the RONDEAU, but with whole lines repeated as a refrain.

Saga Prose story in the ancient literature of Iceland and Norway.

Satire See COMEDY.

Scansion Determination of the metrical pattern of a piece of poetry.

Science fiction Literature based on scientific fact or fantasy, often set in the distant future.

Sestet The second, six-line part of a SONNET.

Sestina Poem of six six-lined, unrhymed stanzas, plus one of three lines, the same final words being used in each stanza in a different order.

Short story Work of fiction, usually 3,000–5,000 words, based on a single event.

Slapstick See COMEDY.

Sonnet Poem of 14 lines and a set rhyme-scheme: Shakespearean sonnet, ababcdcdefefgg; Petrarchan sonnet, abbaabba cdecde (or cdcdcd).

Spenserian stanza Stanza invented by Edmund Spenser (1552–1599) consisting of five iambic pentameters and one iambic hexameter, rhymed ababbcbcc.

Spondee FOOT of two stressed syllables.

Stanza Group of lines of verse in a definite pattern; a poem may contain several stanzas.

Symbolism French poetic movement of the late 1800s that developed as a revolt against REALISM, concentrating on evoking emotions by the use of indirect suggestion (symbol and metaphor); it flourished in Russia at the turn of the century as a literary movement, and later appeared in British novels.

Synonym Word having the same general meaning as another, but often with subtle distinction.

Thesis Generally, a weak syllable in English verse; also, an ESSAY on a theme, especially scholastic.

Third person Style of writing in which the narrator is outside the action.

Tornada The final three-line stanza of a SESTINA, in which the six end-words are used at the midpoints and ends of the lines.

Tragedy Drama in which human conflict ends in calamity.

Tragi-comedy See COMEDY.

Trilogy A group of three, especially three novels, with a common theme.

Trimeter Line with three metrical feet.

Triolet Short form of verse of French origin, in which the first and second lines are repeated, and rhymed ABaAabAB (capitals denote repeated lines).

Trochee FOOT of two syllables, the first stressed.

Verse Originally a line of poetry; now generally a STANZA, or a complete poem.

Versification Study of how traditional forms of verse are constructed; the making of verse.

Vers libre See FREE VERSE.

Villanelle Form of verse, of French origin, of 19 lines on two rhymes, some of the lines being repeated (marked here by capitals): A1-b-A2; a-b-A1; abA2; abA1; abA2; abA1A2.

POETS LAUREATE

Ben Johnson	1619–1637
Sir William Davenant	1638–1668
John Dryden	1668–1688
Thomas Shadwell	1689–1692
Nahum Tate	1692–1715
Nicholas Rowe	1715–1718
Laurence Eusden	1718–1730
Colley Cibber	1730–1757
William Whitehead	1757–1785
Thomas Warton	1785–1790
Henry James Pye	1790–1813
Robert Southey	1813–1843
William Wordsworth	1843–1850
Lord Tennyson	1850–1892
Alfred Austin	1896–1913
Robert Bridges	1913–1930
John Masefield	1930–1967
Cecil Day Lewis	1968–1972
Sir John Betjeman	1972 –1984
Edward (Ted) Hughes	1984 –

William Wordsworth became Poet Laureate in 1843; his greatest work was done between 1796 and 1806.

THEATRE

Activism Theory that playwrights should look for realistic solutions to social problems.

Anti-masque Comic-grotesque prelude to MASQUE.

Apron-stage Stage projecting into auditorium.

Arena theatre THEATRE-IN-THE-ROUND.

Backdrop Painted cloth hung across rear of stage.

Ballad opera Popular drama with spoken dialogue; evolved from English opera of late 1600s.

Broadway Generic term for American professional theatre; from the New York street where many theatres are, compare WEST END.

Burlesque Play that mocks or parodies another; in America, vulgar kind of variety performance for male audiences.

Buskin High, thick-soled boot worn by Greek tragic actors; hence tragedy itself.

Business Player's minor actions on stage, performed when not centre of attraction.

Cabaret Intimate entertainment performed while audience wines and dines.

Cast The actors taking part in a play.

Catwalk Narrow platform above stage from which stagehands adjust scenery, etc.

Chorus In Greek drama, group of actors performing role of commentators; in modern theatre, singers and dancers in musicals, etc.

Closet drama Drama read rather than acted.

Commedia dell'arte Italian comedy (16th–18th century) performed by travelling group of actors who improvised play with stock plot and characters.

Cyclorama Curved wall at the back of a stage, on which light patterns or pictures can be thrown.

Deus ex machina (Latin, god from a machine) Character who appears at end of play to sort out difficulty in plot (from crane in Greek drama used to show actor flying).

Director US: Person who stages a play and instructs (PRODUCER in Britain until recent years).

Dry Forget one's words in performance.

Downstage Part of stage near audience.

Entr'acte Diversion between acts, usually musical.

Epilogue Speech delivered at end of play, usually in verse and by member of cast.

Expressionism German movement of the 1920s which concentrated on psychology rather than events.

Farce Extravagant comedy based on tortuous manipulation of situation rather than wit.

Feed line Part of dialogue designed to lead to a comical retort.

Flats Flat piece of scenery used to build up three-dimensional set.

Flies Space above PROSCENIUM, from which scenes are controlled.

Float FOOTLIGHTS.

Footlights Stage lights arranged across front of stage at stage level.

Forestage Part of stage in front of the PROSCENIUM arch.

Fourth wall Theory of drama that the audience is viewing the action through a wall which has been removed without the characters knowing it.

The Royal Shakespeare Company's stage adaptation of Charles Dickens's novel Nicholas Nickleby in 1980 won acclaim in London and later in New York. This company, most famous for its productions of Shakespeare's plays at Stratford-upon-Avon, also has a repertoire of later, and even modern, works, which are performed by members of the Company. In the past these have included most of Britain's most distinguished actors and actresses, among them Sir Ralph Richardson, Dame Peggy Ashcroft, Paul Schofield, Jeremy Irons, Diana Rigg, John Hurt and Glenda Jackson.

Gallery Uppermost tier of seats in a theatre, traditionally the cheapest; also called the Gods from their nearness to heaven.

Grand guignol Play built round sensational situation, with element of horror.

Groundlings In Elizabethan theatre, spectators who stood closest to the stage and paid least.

Harlequinade 18th-century play built round version

153

of Harlequin and Columbine story, with much use of machinery and magic.

Ingénue Stock character of an innocent young girl.

Joruri Major Japanese puppet-theatre in which puppet masters operate in full view of audience.

Kabuki Japanese theatre, popular version of Nō with far less stylization.

Kitchen-sink drama Term for realistic working-class drama originating in 1950s.

Legitimate theatre Straight drama, without music.

Manager UK: Person responsible for the business side of a production, as against the dramatic side; US PRODUCER.

Masque Spectacular entertainment (mid-1500s to 1600s) performed on special occasions, usually as tribute to a monarch in form of songs, dances, and recitation.

Matinee Daytime performance, especially one held in the afternoon.

Melodrama Play with conventional, sensational plot, with hero triumphing in the end over villain; audience's emotions artificially heightened by music, etc.

Method, the Acting based on living the part in which actor loses himself completely in role.

Mime Acting without speech, by exaggerated action and gesture; particularly popular in France.

Miracle play, miracle Medieval drama in verse, based on miracles of Virgin Mary or saints; in English drama, also includes MYSTERY PLAYS.

Morality play, morality Late medieval allegorical drama in verse, with personified characters used to present sermon.

Musical comedy Light-hearted entertainment with songs (and dances) held together by loose plot.

Music hall Entertainment popular in Britain (mid-1800s to early 1900s, latterly revived as old-time music hall) which includes variety of turns – singers, comic acts, acrobats, etc.

Mystery play, mystery Medieval religious drama based on scenes from Bible or, in England, on lives of saints (see MIRACLE PLAY).

Naturalism Movement of the late 1800s, aiming at a realistic picture of life.

Nō Traditional Japanese theatre in which stylized plays based on well-known historical themes are performed to music, with chanting and dancing.

O P side See PROMPT SIDE.

Open stage Stage jutting out into auditorium, with part of audience sitting round sides.

Pantomime US: Acting without words, *mime*; UK, an extravagant Christmas entertainment loosely based on a fairy tale, developed from the HARLE-QUINADE.

Pass door Door between the auditorium and the back of the stage.

Passion play Religious drama based on crucifixion of Christ (such as famous one at Oberammergau, in Bavaria, performed every 10 years by villagers).

Picture stage See PROSCENIUM THEATRE.

Pit The ground floor of the auditorium.

Playbill Theatre poster.

Producer In UK, the person who directs the action of a play, the US DIRECTOR; in US, the MANAGER.

Prologue Speech, like EPILOGUE, but delivered at beginning of play.

Prompter Person who holds a copy of the play and reminds actors if they forget their lines.

Prompt side Side of stage where prompter sits – to actors' left in UK, to right in US. OP (Opposite Prompt) the opposite side.

Properties, props Articles required on stage apart from costume. furniture, and scenery.

Proscenium theatre Usual western type of theatre in which wall divides auditorium from stage, the wall having large rectangular opening, the proscenium, top of which is called the proscenium arch; also known as picture-frame stage.

Rake Slope of a stage towards audience, designed to give a better view.

Realism Movement (late 1800s) towards natural style of acting, away from histrionics and contrived drama; pioneered by Ibsen, Shaw, etc.

Repertory theatre Theatre with repertoire of plays and permanent company of actors.

Revolve Rotating part of a stage, enabling quick changes of scenery and special effects.

Revue Entertainment comprising number of short items (sketches, songs, etc.), often topical or satirical.

Safety curtain Fireproof curtain which can be lowered in front of the TABS.

Scenery The setting for a play, which may be painted FLATS or three-dimensional constructions; scene-dock, room where scenery is stored.

Shadow play Theatre, popular particularly in Indonesia, in which flat leather puppets are manipulated in front of palm-oil lamp which throws shadows onto translucent screen; stories from Mahabharata and Ramayana (ancient epics of India) played out to music.

Showboat Floating theatre (1800s) on American rivers, presenting vaudeville, etc.

Son et lumière Open-air entertainment (in castle, cathedral, etc.) relating history of place, using special lighting and sound effects.

Soubrette Coquettish maidservant in comedy; female member of company specializing in such roles.

Stage door Side or rear door through which the actors and technicians enter a theatre.

Stock company US: A REPERTORY company, sometimes a travelling one.

Super, supernumerary Player without speaking part.

Tabs Front curtain; sometimes used for curtains on stage.

Theatre-in-the-round Theatre in which stage or acting area is surrounded by audience.

Theatre of the absurd Drama based on fantastic, unreal situations, abandoning all logical thought and processes; pioneered by Beckett, Ionesco, Pinter, etc.

Tormentors Sides of PROSCENIUM ARCH.

Toy theatre Miniature replicas in cardboard, popular in early 1800s, with cut-out actors in costume.

Trap Opening in floor of stage.

Upstage Back of stage, away from audience; to upstage another actor is to manoeuvre him into less favourable position.

Vaudeville American equivalent of British music hall, popular from late 1890s to advent of talking pictures.

West End In London, the area where most theatres are; by analogy, professional theatre (compare BROADWAY).

Wings Side scenery; sides of stage.

CINEMA

ACADEMY AWARDS 1927–49

YEAR	BEST PICTURE	BEST ACTOR	BEST ACTRESS	BEST DIRECTOR
27–28	Wings	Emil Jannings (The Way of All Flesh and The Last Command)	Janet Gaynor (Seventh Heaven; Street Angel; and Sunrise)	Frank Borzage (Seventh Heaven), Lewis Milestone (Two Arabian Knights)
28–29	The Broadway Melody	Warner Baxter (In Old Arizona)	Mary Pickford (Coquette)	Frank Lloyd (The Divine Lady)
29–30	All Quiet on the Western Front	George Arliss (Disraeli)	Norma Shearer (The Divorcee)	Lewis Milestone (All Quiet on the Western Front)
30–31	Cimarron	Lionel Barrymore (A Free Soul)	Marie Dressler (Min and Bull)	Norman Taurog (Skippy)
31–32	Grand Hotel	Frederic March (Dr Jekyll and Mr Hyde) Wallace Beery (The Champ)	Helen Hayes (The Sin of Madelon Claudet)	Frank Borzage (Bad Girl)
32–33	Cavalcade	Charles Laughton (The Private life of Henry VIII)	Katherine Hepburn (Morning Glory)	Frank Lloyd (Cavalcade)
34	It Happened One Night	Clarke Gable (It Happened One Night)	Claudette Colbert (It Happened One Night)	Frank Capra (It Happened One Night)
35	Mutiny on the Bounty	Victor McLaglan (The Informer)	Bette Davis (Dangerous)	John Ford (The Informer)
36	The Great Ziegfield	Paul Muni (The Story of Louis Pasteur)	Luise Rainer (The Great Ziegfield)	Frank Capra (Mr Deeds Goes to Town)
37	The Life of Emile Zola	Spencer Tracy (Captains Courageous)	Luise Rainer (The Good Earth)	Leo McCarey (The Awful Truth)
38	You Can't Take It With You	Spencer Tracy (Boy's Town)	Bette Davis (Jezebel)	Frank Capra (You Can't Take it with You)
39	Gone With The Wind	Robert Donat (Goodbye Mr Chips)	Vivien Leigh (Gone with the Wind)	Victor Fleming (Gone With the Wind)
40	Rebecca	James Stewart (The Philadelphia Story)	Ginger Rogers (Kitty Foyle)	John Ford (Grapes of Wrath)
41	How Green Was My Valley	Gary Cooper (Sergeant York)	Joan Fontaine (Suspicion)	John Ford (How Green Was My Valley)
42	Mrs Miniver	James Cagney (Yankee Doodle Dandy)	Greer Garson (Mrs Miniver)	William Wyler (Mrs Miniver)
43	Casablanca	Paul Lukas (Watch on the Rhine)	Jennifer Jones (The Song of Bernadette)	Michael Curtiz (Casablanca)
44	Going My Way	Bing Crosby (Going My Way)	Ingrid Bergman (Gaslight)	Leo McCarey (Going My Way)
45	The Lost Weekend	Ray Milland (The Lost Weekend)	Joan Crawford (Mildred Pierce)	Billy Wilder (The Lost Weekend)
46	The Best Years of Our Lives	Frederic March (The Best Years of Our Lives)	Olivia de Havilland (To Each His Own)	William Wyler (The Best Years of Our Lives)
47	Gentleman's Agreement	Ronald Colman (A Double Life)	Loretta Young (The Farmer's Daughter)	Elia Kazan (Gentleman's Agreement)
48	Hamlet	Laurence Olivier (Hamlet)	Jane Wyman (Johnny Belinda)	John Huston (The Treasure of Sierra Madre)
49	All the King's Men	Broderick Crawford (All the King's Men)	Olivia de Havilland (The Heiress)	Joseph L. Mankiewicz (A Letter to Three Wives)

ACADEMY AWARDS 1950–68

YEAR	BEST PICTURE	BEST ACTOR	BEST ACTRESS	BEST DIRECTOR
1950	*All About Eve*	Jose Ferrer *(Cyrano de Bergerac)*	Judy Holliday *(Born Yesterday)*	Joseph L. Mankiewicz *(All About Eve)*
1951	*An American in Paris*	Humphrey Bogart *(The African Queen)*	Vivien Leigh *(A Streetcar Named Desire)*	George Stevens *(A Place in the Sun)*
1952	*The Greatest Show on Earth*	Gary Cooper *(High Noon)*	Shirley Booth *(Come Back, Little Sheba)*	John Ford *(The Quiet Man)*
1953	*From Here to Eternity*	William Holden *(Stalag 17)*	Audrey Hepburn *(Roman Holiday)*	Fred Zimmerman *(From Here to Eternity)*
1954	*On the Waterfront*	Marlon Brando *(On the Waterfront)*	Grace Kelly *(The Country Girl)*	Elia Kazan *(On the Waterfront)*
1955	*Marty*	Ernest Borgnine *(Marty)*	Anna Magnani *(The Rose Tattoo)*	Delbert Mann *(Marty)*
1956	*Around the World in 80 Days*	Yul Brynner *(The King and I)*	Ingrid Bergman *(Anastasia)*	George Stevens *(Giant)*
1957	*The Bridge on the River Kwai*	Alec Guinness *(The Bridge on the River Kwai)*	Joanne Woodward *(The Three Faces of Eve)*	David Lean *(The Bridge on the River Kwai)*
1958	*Gigi*	David Niven *(Separate Tables)*	Susan Hayward *(I Want to Live)*	Vincente Minelli *(Gigi)*
1959	*Ben-Hur*	Charlton Heston *(Ben-Hur)*	Simone Signoret *(Room at the Top)*	William Wyler *(Ben-Hur)*
1960	*The Apartment*	Burt Lancaster *(Elmer Gantry)*	Elizabeth Taylor *(Butterfield 8)*	Billy Wilder *(The Apartment)*
1961	*West Side Story*	Maximilian Schell *(Judgment at Nuremberg)*	Sophia Loren *(Two Women)*	Robert Wise & Jerome Robbins *(West Side Story)*
1962	*Lawrence of Arabia*	Gregory Peck *(To Kill a Mockingbird)*	Anne Bancroft *(The Miracle Worker)*	David Lean *(Lawrence of Arabia)*
1963	*Tom Jones*	Sidney Poitier *(Lilies of the Field)*	Patricia Neal *(Hud)*	Tony Richardson *(Tom Jones)*
1964	*My Fair Lady*	Rex Harrison *(My Fair Lady)*	Julie Andrews *(Mary Poppins)*	George Cukor *(My Fair Lady)*
1965	*Sound of Music*	Lee Marvin *(Cat Ballou)*	Julie Christie *(Darling)*	Robert Wise *(The Sound of Music)*
1966	*A Man for All Seasons*	Paul Scofield *(A Man for All Seasons)*	Elizabeth Taylor *(Who's Afraid of Virginia Wolf?)*	Fred Zimmerman *(A Man for All Seasons)*
1967	*In the Heat of the Night*	Rod Steiger *(In the Heat of the Night)*	Katherine Hepburn *(Guess Who's Coming to Dinner)*	Mike Nichols *(The Graduate)*
1968	*Oliver*	Cliff Robertson *(Charity)*	Katherine Hepburn *(A Lion in Winter)*, Barbara Streisand *(Funny Girl)*	Sir Carol Reed *(Oliver)*

Right: A scene from William Wyler's Award-winning epic Ben Hur; *it won 'Oscars' (as Academy awards are nicknamed) for best picture, best actor (Charlton Heston as Ben Hur), and best director.*

ACADEMY AWARDS 1969–92

YEAR	BEST PICTURE	BEST ACTOR	BEST ACTRESS	BEST DIRECTOR
1969	Midnight Cowboy	John Wayne (True Grit)	Maggie Smith (The Prime of Miss Jean Brodie)	John Schlesinger (Midnight Cowboy)
1970	Patton	George C. Scott (Patton)	Glenda Jackson (Women in Love)	Franklin J. Schaffner (Patton)
1971	The French Connection	Gene Hackman (The French Connection)	Jane Fonda (Klute)	William Friedkin (The French Connection)
1972	The Godfather	Marlon Brando (The Godfather)	Liza Minnelli (Cabaret)	Robert Fosse (Cabaret)
1973	The Sting	Jack Lemon (Save the Tiger)	Glenda Jackson (A Touch of Class)	George Roy Hill (The Sting)
1974	The Godfather Part II	Art Carney (Harry and Tonto)	Ellen Burstyn (Alice Doesn't Live Here Any More)	Francis Ford Coppola (The Godfather Part II)
1975	One Flew Over the Cuckoo's Nest	Jack Nicholson (One Flew Over the Cuckoo's Nest)	Louise Fletcher (One Flew Over the Cuckoo's Nest)	Milos Forman (One Flew Over the Cuckoo's Nest)
1976	Rocky	Peter Finch (Network)	Faye Dunaway (Network)	John G. Avildsen (Rocky)
1977	Annie Hall	Richard Dreyfus (Goodbye Girl)	Diane Keaton (Annie Hall)	Woody Allen (Annie Hall)
1978	Deer Hunter	John Voight (Coming home)	Jane Fonda (Coming Home)	Michael Cimino (The Deerhunter)
1979	Kramer Vs Kramer	Dustin Hoffman (Kramer Vs Kramer)	Sally Field (Norma Rae)	Robert Benton (Kramer Vs Kramer)
1980	Ordinary People	Robert De Niro (Raging Bull)	Sissy Spacek (Coalminer's Daughter)	Robert Redford (Ordinary People)
1981	Chariots of Fire	Henry Fonda (On Golden Pond)	Katherine Hepburn (On Golden Pond)	Warren Beatty (Reds)
1982	Gandhi	Ben Kingsley (Gandhi)	Meryl Streep (Sophie's Choice)	Sir Richard Attenborough (Gandhi)
1983	Terms of Endearment	Robert Duval (Tender Mercies)	Shirley MacLaine Terms of Endearment	James L. Brooks (Terms of Endearment)
1984	Amadeus	F. Murray Abraham (Amadeus)	Sally Field (Places in the Heart)	Milos Forman (Amadeus)
1985	Out of Africa	William Hurt (Kiss of the Spider Woman)	Geraldine Page (The Trip to Bountiful)	Sydney Pollack (Out of Africa)
1986	Platoon	Paul Newman (The Color of Money)	Marlee Matlin (Children of a lesser God)	Oliver Stone (Platoon)
1987	The Last Emperor	Michael Douglas (Wall Street)	Cher (Moonstruck)	Bernardo Bertolucci (The Last Emperor)
1988	Rain Man	Dustin Hoffman (Rain Man)	Jodie Foster (The Accused)	Barry Levinson (Rain Man)
1989	Driving Miss Daisy	Daniel Day-Lewis (My Left Foot)	Jessica Tandy (Driving Miss Daisy)	Oliver Stone (Born on the Fourth of July)
1990	Dances with Wolves	Jeremy Irons (Reversal of Fortune)	Kathy Bates (Misery)	Kevin Costner (Dances with Wolves)
1991	The Silence of the Lambs	Antony Hopkins (The Silence of the Lambs)	Jodie Foster (The Silence of the Lambs)	Jonathan Demme (The Silence of the Lambs)
1992	The Unforgiven	Al Pacino (The Scent of a Woman)	Emma Thompson (Howard's End)	Clint Eastwood (The Unforgiven)

INSTRUMENTS OF THE ORCHESTRA

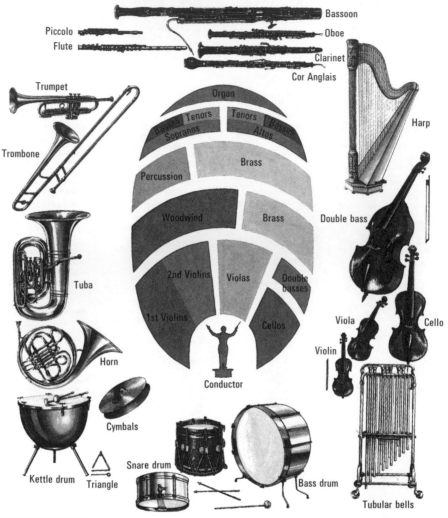

Bassoon
Piccolo
Oboe
Flute
Clarinet
Cor Anglais
Harp
Trumpet
Organ
Basses Tenors Tenors Basses
Sopranos Altos
Trombone
Brass
Percussion
Brass
Double bass
Woodwind
Tuba
2nd Violins Violas Double basses
1st Violins Cellos Viola Cello
Violin
Horn
Conductor
Cymbals
Kettle drum Triangle Snare drum Bass drum Tubular bells

MUSICAL TERMS

A cappella in church music style.

Accelerando Becoming gradually faster.

Accent Stress laid on certain BEATS, especially the first of a BAR.

Acciaccatura Small note with a stroke through its tail, played on the BEAT as quickly as possible before the following note.

Accidental Sign changing the PITCH of a written note by a TONE or SEMITONE.

Adagio At a slow pace.

Agitato Restless or agitated.

Allegretto At a fairly lively pace.

Allegro At a lively pace.

Alto Highest adult male voice; CONTRALTO, a low female voice.

Andante At a slowish, flowing pace.

Animato Quickening, in a spirited fashion.

Appogiatura Ornament written as a small note without a line through it; it takes part of the value of the note which follows.

Arpeggio Notes of a CHORD played in rapid succession, as on a harp.

Atonality Absence of a sense of KEY, used by some 20th-century composers who discard traditional MAJOR and MINOR scales.

Bar Group of notes bounded by vertical bar-lines indicating the principal BEAT.

Baritone Male voice higher than bass and lower than tenor.

Bass Lowest male voice; basso profundo, exceptionally deep bass; BASS also means the lowest part of HARMONY or COUNTERPOINT.

Beat Rhythmic pulse; beats are grouped into bars to make the music easier to read.

Brass instruments Metal instruments sounded by blowing through mouthpiece and altering tension of the lips; they include cornet, trumpet, horn, euphonium, trombone and tuba.

Cadenza Solo passage in a musical piece (written or improvised) for soloist to show off technique.

Cantabile Expressive or songlike.

Cantata Vocal work, typically for soloists, chorus and orchestra.

Cantus firmus Fixed part to which others are added.

Chamber music Music for a room or small hall, played by two or more solo instruments.

Chanting Unaccompanied singing in free rhythm, used in church services.

Choir A body of singers.

Chord Two or more notes sounded together.

Chorus Main body of singers in a CHOIR: words and music repeated after each stanza of a song.

Chromatic scale SCALE made up of SEMITONES.

Classical music Music that aims at perfection of structure and design (period of Bach to Brahms).

Clef Sign in musical notation that fixes the pitch of each note written on the STAVE; most music is written in the treble and bass clefs, but music for viola is written in the alto clef, and higher cello and double-bass music in the tenor clef.

Coda A rounding-off passage of music.

Concerto Substantial work for one or more solo instruments and orchestra.

Concerto grosso Work in which a small group of instruments (the concertino) is contrasted with the main body of instruments (the ripieno).

Contralto Lowest female voice.

Contrapuntal Adjective formed from COUNTERPOINT.

Counterpoint Two or more MELODIES combined to form a satisfying HARMONY.

Counter-tenor Another name for male ALTO.

Crescendo Increasing in loudness.

Da capo From the beginning.

Decrescendo Gradually decreasing in loudness.

Descant The addition of a second melody above a given melody; form of COUNTERPOINT.

Diminuendo Gradually softer.

Discord Combination of sounds not considered satisfactory in itself, needing RESOLUTION

Dissonance Another name for DISCORD.

Dominant The fifth note of a major or minor SCALE.

Equal temperament System of toning in which the OCTAVE is divided into 12 equal SEMITONES; used for keyboard instruments such as piano or organ.

Fine The end.

Flat Conventional sign showing that pitch of a certain note has been lowered by a semitone.

Forte Played or sung loudly.

Fortissimo Very loud (loudest).

Fugue Method of writing contrapuntal music for various parts or voices in which one or more subjects are treated imitatively.

Glissando Gliding; rapid scales, played with sliding movement.

Grace notes Ornaments – extra notes added to a melody.

Ground bass Repeated theme in the bass with varying melodies and harmonies above it.

Harmony Combining of chords to make musical sense.

Interval Distance in pitch between notes.

Intonation Correctness or otherwise of PITCH.

Inversion Turning upside down; an INTERVAL is inverted by reversing the upper and lower notes; a CHORD is inverted if the ROOT is not in the bass.

Key Classification of the notes of a scale.

Key-note Note on which a scale is based.

Key signature Indication of number of sharps or flats in piece of music; usually written at beginning of each line.

Largo At a slow, dignified pace.

Leading note The seventh note of a major or minor scale.

Ledger lines Short extra lines added above or below stave to accommodate very high or low notes.

Legato One note leading smoothly to next.

Lied German word for song (plural Lieder).

Major One of the two main scales, with semitones between 3rd and 4th and 7th and 8th notes.

Measure Bar (American).

Melody A tune; series of musical sounds following each other, as distinct from harmony.

Mezzo-soprano Female voice between contralto and soprano.

Microtone Interval smaller than a semitone; used in Asian music.

Minor One of the two main scales. Harmonic minor scales have a semitone between 2nd and 3rd, 5th and 6th, and 7th and 8th notes. In the melodic minor, there are semitones between 2nd and 3rd and 7th and 8th notes ascending, and between 6th and 5th and 3rd and 2nd descending.

Mode Form of scale used in Middle Ages. There were 12 modes, two of which, Ionian and Aeolian, are the modern major and minor scales.

Modulation Changing from one. key to another according to rules of harmony.

Movement Complete section of larger work (such as a symphony), played at a different speed from its predecessor.

Musique concrète Music based on pre-recorded sound patterns rearranged electronically.

Natural Conventional sign that restores note to its natural pitch after it has been previously sharpened or flattened.

Nocturne A night-piece, tuneful but sad.

Obbligato An optional part (in contrast to the word's original meaning of essential!).

Octave Interval made up of 8 successive notes of scale, from one note to note of same name, above or below.

Opus A work; when followed by a number indicates order of musician's published compositions.

Oratorio Religious musical composition for soloists, chorus, and orchestra, but without costume or scenery.

Ornament Decoration of the basic notes of a melody.

Pause Sign indication that a note is to be held on longer that its time value.

Pentatonic scale Scale of five notes only (the black keys of a piano produce one such scale).

Percussion instruments Instruments that are struck

(drums, tambourine, cymbals, bells, glockenspiel, xylophone, vibraphone, marimba, triangle, gong, castanets, etc.).

Pianissimo Very soft (softest).

Piano Played or sung softly; shortened to p.

Pitch Highness or lowness in sound of one note compared with another.

Pizzicato Playing strings by plucking.

Plainsong Unaccompanied vocal melody used in medieval church music.

Prestissimo Extremely fast.

Presto At a fast pace.

Programme music Music that tells a story.

Resolution A concord (a musically complete chord) following a DISCORD.

Rest Conventional sign denoting silence on performer's part.

Ritardando Slowing down; often abbreviated to rit.

Romantic music Music (mainly 19th century) that plays on the emotions, as distinct from classical music.

Root Note on which a CHORD is built up; see also INVERSION.

Scale Progression of successive notes ascending or descending.

Scherzo A jest; hence a lively, unsentimental piece of music.

Score Written music showing all parts (vocal and instrumental) of composition on separate staves.

Semitone A half-tone; smallest interval commonly used in Western music.

Shake or trill Ornament consisting of the rapid alternation of a note with the note above it.

Sharp Conventional sign indicating that note referred to has been raised in pitch by semitone.

Solo Piece for a solo performer.

Sonata Musical piece, usually for one or two players, consisting of three or four MOVEMENTS in contrasting rhythms and speeds.

Sonata form Way of writing a MOVEMENT consisting of exposition, in which the theme or themes are stated; development, in which the themes are elaborated and changed; and recapitulation, in which the original subject matter returns; there may be a CODA to end the movement.

Soprano Highest female voice; also the voice of boys before puberty.

Sostenuto Sustained.

Sotto voce Passage performed in undertone.

Staccato In short, detached fashion; notes to be

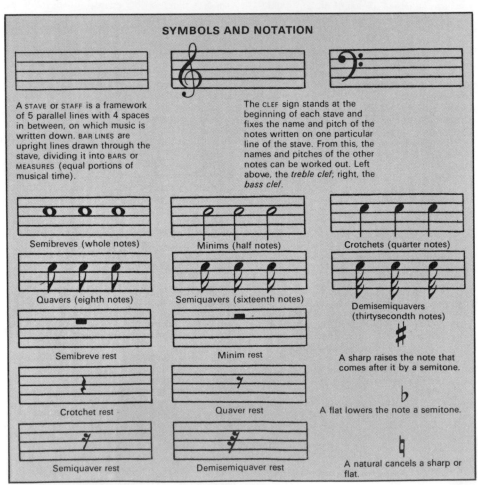

played thus have a dot over them.

Stave or staff Framework of lines and spaces on which music is usually written.

Stringed instruments Instruments that are played with a bow (violins, violas, cellos, double basses).

Suite Orchestral piece in several movements.

Symphony Large orchestral piece of music of a serious nature, usually in four movements; also a SONATA for orchestra.

Syncopation Shifting of accent onto beat not normally accented.

Tempo Pace or speed of piece of music.

Tenor High male voice; also the viola.

Time signature Figures written at beginning of piece to indicate kinds of BEATS in a BAR and their number.

Toccata Instrumental piece (usually for one performer) that requires a rapid and brilliant touch (e.g. for organ).

Tonality Another term for KEY.

Tone Quality of musical sound; an interval made up of two semitones.

Tonic First note of a musical SCALE.

Treble Upper part of a composition; a high voice, usually of children.

Tremolo Literally, trembling; on stringed instruments, a single note repeated extremely rapidly over and over again, with an alternation in volume.

Trill See SHAKE.

Tutti All performers (not soloists) together.

Twelve-note Method of composition in which all 12 notes in octave (on piano, 5 black and 7 white)

THE TONIC SOL-FA

The tonic sol-fa is a method of musical notation using letters and syllables instead of notes on a stave. It was devised by the English musician John Curwen (1816–1880), who based it on the system known as solmization used in the middle ages.

The eight notes of a major scale are denoted by the syllables doh, re, mi, fah, soh (or sol), lah, te, doh. It works for any scale by just changing the note which represents doh. Sharpened and flattened notes are indicated by changing the vowel sounds (for example, sol sharp is se, and te flat is taw).

---

have equal importance.

Unison United sounding of same note by two or more instruments or voices, sometimes by the same instrument on two strings or keyboards.

Vibrato Rapid regular fluctuation in pitch of note produced by string player or singer to increase emotional effect; sometimes called a close SHAKE.

Virtuoso Musician of outstanding technical skill.

Vivace Played in a lively manner.

Whole-tone scale Scale consisting only of whole tone. There are only two whole-tone scales.

Woodwind instruments that are blown and are traditionally, but not always, made of wood; they may be blown direct or by means of reed; they include clarinet. oboe, flute, recorder, saxophone and bassoon.

OPERATIC TERMS

Aria (Italian, air) A solo; a da capo aria is in three parts, with the third a repeat of the first.

Ballad opera Simple kind of opera, made up of popular tunes interspersed with spoken dialogue.

Bel canto (Italian, beautiful song) Style of singing favoured by great Italian opera singers of 1700s, in which tone was more important than emotion.

Bis See ENCORE.

Bleat (also Bockstrilles, goat's trill) Rapid repetition of a note.

Buffo Singer of comic rôles.

Burletta Opera midway between BALLAD OPERA and COMIC OPERA.

Cadenza Elaborate solo flourish.

Cantilena Smooth, melodious song.

Castrato Male soprano whose boyhood voice has been kept by means of surgery; no longer heard, but important in opera of the 1600s and 1700s.

Chorus Main body of singers.

Claque Group of concert-goers hired to applaud particular singer or opera.

Comic opera Opera with a farcical plot.

Diva Another name for PRIMA DONNA.

Encore (French, again) Demand by an audience for a repeat of a number (French audiences, like other Europeans, cry Bis).

Entr'acte Orchestral interlude between acts or scenes.

Finale Closing portion of act or opera; usually

Dame Kiri Te Kanawa, the great Maori soprano from New Zealand, in Mozart's opera The Marriage of Figaro.

whole company sings together.

Folk opera Opera based on folk music and folk tales.

Grand opera Opera with libretto entirely set to music.

Intermezzo Instrumental piece interposed between scenes or acts of opera; also called interlude.

Leitmotiv (German, leading motive) Short theme in opera that emphasizes by repetition an individual character, object, or idea.

Libretto Text of opera.

Light opera English term for OPERETTA.

Opera buffa Humorous opera, but not farcical as COMIC OPERA; typical is Rossini's *Barber of Seville*.

Opéra-comique Opera that includes spoken dialogue; not necessarily COMIC OPERA.

Opera seria Serious opera, as distinct from OPERA BUFFA.

Operetta Light opera based on amusing subjects and implying some spoken dialogue; nowadays often synonymous with musical comedy.

Orchestra pit Space below and in front of the stage for the orchestra.

Overture Instrumental prelude to an opera.

Patter song Comical song made up of string of words and sung at high speed; Gilbert and Sullivan operas include many such.

Prima donna (Italian, first lady) Principal female singer in cast; or, more often, most famous or most highly paid; also called diva.

Recitative Sung dialogue or narrative.

Repertory Roles an opera singer is able to perform; programme of operas put on by company during a season.

Singspiel (German, singplay) Opera that has spoken dialogue interspersed with songs; usually has humorous subject.

Soubrette Light soprano comedienne.

Stretta Passage in which the tempo is increased towards the end of an aria or act.

Travesti Male rôles sung by women; sometimes called breeches rôles.

THE BALLET

Adagio Opening section of a PAS DE DEUX; in class, a sequence of slow exercises.

Air, en 'l Steps in which the dancer has both feet off the ground.

Allegro Fast turning steps, usually following an ADAGIO.

Arabesque Position in which dancer stands on one leg with arms extended, body bent forward from hips, while other leg is stretched out backwards.

Attitude Position in which dancer stretches one leg backwards, bending it a little at knee so that lower part of leg is parallel to floor.

Ballerina Female ballet dancer.

Barre Exercise bar fixed to classroom wall at hip level; dancers grasp it when exercising.

Battement Beating movement made by raising and lowering leg, sideways, backwards, or forwards.

Batterie Any step in which the feet cross in the air or beat together.

Choreography Art of dance composition.

Coda Final section of a PAS DE DEUX.

Corps de Ballet Main body of ballet dancers, as distinct from soloists.

Coryphée Member of the CORPS DE BALLET promoted to dance a minor solo.

Divertissement A dance or dances that have no connection with the main plot of a ballet.

Elevation Jumping high in the air.

Entrechat Leap in which dancer rapidly strikes heels together in air.

Fouetté Turn in which dancer whips free leg round.

Glissade Gilding movement.

Jeté Leap from one foot to another.

Léotard One-piece garment covering the torso, worn for practise and sometimes on stage.

Pas Any dance step.

Pas de Chat A light jumping step in which the feet are in turn drawn up beneath the body.

Pas de Cheval Pawing the ground like a horse.

Pas de deux Dance for two.

Pas seule Solo dance.

Pirouette Movement in which dancer spins completely round on one foot.

Pliés Bending exercises to loosen up the muscles.

Pointes Tips of dancer's toes, on which many movements are executed.

Positions Five positions of feet on which ballet is based.

Prima Ballerina Principal female dancer.

Répétiteur Dancer who teaches new dancers their parts in a ballet.

Tutu Short, stiff, spreading skirt.

BASIC BALLET POSITIONS

First   Second   Third   Fourth   Fifth

POPULAR MUSIC

A cappella In the world of popular music, singing unaccompanied, especially in groups.

Acoustic Non-electric, with reference usually to guitars.

Backing group Group of singers who sing in support of a soloist.

Bebop, bop Intellectual type of jazz that started in 1940s in attempt to break monotonous rhythm of earlier jazz.

Big bands Dance bands of SWING era (late 1930s and early 1940s), featuring many musicians and one or more vocalists.

Bluegrass Folk music with overdrive; folk and country music played with a distinctive beat; line-up includes some or all of following: acoustic guitar, banjo, mandolin, fiddle, dobro, autoharp, string bass.

Blues Form of jazz using 12-bar melodic section; essentially vocal, the music is often slow and sad.

Boogie woogie A jazz barrelhouse style of piano playing, with repetitive bass in left hand and stylized melodic variations in right.

Calypso Folk music of West Indies, usually sung, in 4/4 time.

Combo Small group of musicians.

Country and western Topical and traditional rural music, mainly vocal and American, evolved from folk, blues, and hillbilly music; now known simply as country.

Cover version Re-issue of a number, often to compete with the original.

Crossover jazz Jazz mixed with rock elements.

Dixieland jazz Originally, early Negro jazz; later applied to music of white imitators.

Doo-wop Style of singing by backing groups to nonsense syllables such as doo-wop; popular from the 1930s to the 1960s.

Folk music, folk song Music and ballads of the people, usually handed down from one generation to another.

Gig One-night stand or engagement.

Gospel music Country version of the SPIRITUAL, heavily commercialized from the 1930s onwards.

Jitterbugging Improvised, all-in, athletic dancing, originating in late 1930s with development of boogie woogie.

Jive A later, slightly more sober and respectable form of jitterbugging.

Mainstream jazz Middle-of-the-road jazz that avoids extremes of TRAD or progressive jazz; expertly played by experienced professionals.

New wave Movement beginning in the 1970s which included PUNK ROCK and offbeat arrangements, and also heavy rock.

Pop Currently popular music or song, generally launched and performed with maximum publicity and an eye to record sales.

Progressive jazz Attempt to fuse jazz with other musical elements and thus break away from more traditional aspects.

Punk rock Rock music with outrageous, often obscene, words, accompanied by equally outrageous behaviour by its performers.

Ragtime Essentially Negro piano music based on

rigidly syncopated pattern; had some influence on jazz.

Reggae A gay West Indian type of rock jazz with simple 2-beat rhythm.

Rhythm and blues Urban blues performed mainly by black musicians; traditional blues were hotted up with infusions of rock and roll and later developments.

Riff Device used mainly in jazz, consisting of prolonged repetition of 2-bar or 4-bar phrase behind soloist.

Rock and roll, rock 'n roll, rock Rhythmic development of blues and skiffle, with undisguised emphasis on the beat, and body movements of dancers.

Skiffle Makeshift jazz music (in vogue mid-1950s) that included guitars, banjos, mandolins, and a number of home-made instruments such as washboard, tea-chest bass, and paper-and-comb; repertoire largely folk music with a beat.

Soul music Popular, often religious music written and performed by Negroes; used for dancing.

A member of the cast of One Mo' Time, a Black musical celebrating the jazz tradition of New Orleans and set during the Great Depression.

Spiritual Religious folk song, usually of Negro origin (also white spirituals); generally superseded by GOSPEL MUSIC.

Steel bands West Indian percussion bands, originating in Trinidad, that use as instruments the tops of oil drums, tuned to various pitches.

Swing Commercialized jazz featured by the BIG BANDS; period 1935–46 known as swing era.

Third stream music Combination of jazz and classical styles.

Tin Pan Alley Originally 28th Street in New York City, where most of commercial song hits were published; today, term describes any well-known area of the pop publishing business.

Traditional jazz, trad Jazz that adheres to old traditional New Orleans highly improvised, contrapuntal sounds.

Western swing Kind of hillbilly jazz, a cross between country music and jazz which lasted through the 1930s and 1940s.

Abstract art Art form that represents ideas (by means of geometric and other designs) instead of natural forms; pioneered by Kandinsky (early 1900s), and taken up by Miró and de Kooning.

Abstract expressionism A combination of abstract art and expressionism; consists mainly of dripping and smearing paint at random. It was pioneered in US by Jackson Pollock after World War II.

Acrylic paint Form of emulsion paint which can be used thick, like OIL PAINT, or as a thin wash like WATER-COLOUR.

Action painting Type of abstract expressionism.

Airbrush Device used by artist to spray paint, varnish, or fixative; worked by compressed air.

Aquarelle A water-colour painting.

Ashcan school Group of US painters of the late 1800s–early 1900s, interested in sordid views of city life.

Autograph Painting executed entirely by one artist.

Barbizon School Group of mid-19th-century French landscape painters (including Corot, Millet, and Rousseau) who worked in village of Barbizon (Forest of Fontainebleau). The tried to paint nature as it is.

Baroque Style that flourished from late 1500s to early 1700s. Characterized by exaggerated shapes, with rich, flowing curves (Tintoretto, El Greco, Rubens).

Biomorphic Art Kind of ABSTRACT ART based on living forms.

Bistre Brown pigment made from charred wood.

Blaue Reiter (blue rider) Group of Munich artists (1911) who highlighted various modern art forms; started by Kandinsky and Marc; joined later by Klee.

Body colour Water-colour mixed with white.

Bolus ground Canvas prepared with a dark brown pigment, which shows through the paint.

Brush work Way in which a painter applies paint with a brush, as personal as handwriting.

Byzantine Style practised in Eastern Roman Empire (400s–1453); figures are stiff and formal, with rich colours.

Camden Town Group Splinter group of English painters who came out of New English Art Club in early 1900s; possibly introduced post-impressionism into English art. Group led by Sickert and included Gilman.

Cartoon Full-sized drawing, often in colour, used as a basic for finished painting.

Cave paintings Pictures (mostly animals) painted by prehistoric artists on the walls of caves; best known are in Lascaux (France) and Altamira (Spain).

Chiaroscuro (light-dark) Balance of light and shade in a picture and the artist's skill in handling this.

Classicism Style based on the art of ancient Greece and Rome.

Collage Picture built up from pieces of fabric or paper stuck on to a ground, and possibly embellished with paint.

Composition Way in which the elements of a painting are grouped.

Concrete art Synonym for ABSTRACT ART.

Conversation piece Type of portrait painting that included two or more people (usually of the same family) informally or casually posed; popular in Netherlands (1600s) and England (1700s); often painted by Hogarth, Zoffany, Devis.

Craquelure Network of hair-line cracks on the surface of an old painting.

Cubism Important movement in modern French painting started by Picasso and Braque in 1907. Cubists aimed to reduce objects to basic shapes of cubes, spheres, cylinders, and cones.

Dadaism (derived from dada, French for hobbyhorse) Outrageous and nihilistic movement started in Zurich (1916) as protest against all artistic and civilized standards. Duchamp was a leading exponent; Modigliani and Kandinsky dabbled.

Diptych Picture painted on two panels, often hinged like pages of a book; popular in 15th-century Flanders.

Direct painting School of American landscape painters of late 1800s; characterized by extremely bold brushwork (Redfield, Symons, etc.).

Distemper Cheap and impermanent method of painting in which powdered colours are mixed with glue; often used for theatrical scenery.

Dutch School Art and artists of Netherlands in 1600s; typified by precise draughtsmanship, wonderful colour, and great attention to detail. Leading exponents were Rembrandt, Hals, Van der Velde, Maes, Metsun, Hobbema, Cuyp, Huysum.

Egg tempera A painting medium in which the colours are ground with pure egg yolk; one of the most permanent media available.

Encaustic painting Use of pigments mixed with hot wax, used in the ancient world up to the AD 800s.

Ethnic art Term used increasingly, particularly in America, when describing art produced by distinct groups – such as Puerto Ricans or Negroes – and reflecting the increased importance given to the rights of minority groups in society.

Expressionism Movement that aims at expressing the artist's inner feelings and experiences, rejecting reality and idealism even to point of distortion. Began in late 1800s; Van Gogh, Gauguin, Matisse, Picasso, and Rouault were adherents at various times.

Fauves (wild beasts) Group of Parisian painters of early 1900s (Dufy, Matisse, Rouault, Vlaminck, etc.) who shocked the critics by their brilliant use of colour.

Finger painting Chinese water-colour technique using finger instead of a brush.

French Romantic School Early 19th-century movement of French painters, led by Delacroix; artists mixed fantasy with realism and at the same time aimed at getting back to nature.

Fresco Method of great antiquity but perfected during Italian Renaissance; uses pigments ground in water applied to a freshly-plastered wall or ceiling; it has to be done in sections before the plaster dries.

Futurism Italian artistic movement (1905–15) that emphasized violence, machinery, and politics, and was anti-cultural and anti-romantic. Painters used cubist forms and strong colours.

Genre painting One that shows simple scenes from everyday life; some pictures tell a story. Dutch painters of 1500s and 1600s (De Hooch, Steen, Metsu, etc.) were experts.

Gesso Mixture of plaster and glue used to cover wooden panels before painting.

Glaze Transparent layer of paint applied over another to modify its colour.

Gouache Non-transparent water-colour paint that provides easy way of obtaining oil-painting effects. Turner and Girtin pioneered the method in England.

Grisaille Painting executed in a monochrome grey.

Ground Surface on which a painting is made, a form of undercoat. White oil paint or GESSO are often used.

Icon Religious picture (usually painted on wood or ivory) associated with Eastern Orthodox Church. Earliest surviving icons date from 500s.

Illusionism Use of painting techniques to give the impression of three dimensions, often used architecturally.

Impasto Thick laying on of paint on canvas or wood. Brush marks are clearly visible on oil paintings with heavy impasto.

Impressionism Important movement that developed among French painters just after mid-1800s. Impressionists were particularly concerned with light and its effects. They put down on canvas their immediate impressions of nature. Monet, Renoir, Pissaro, Sisley, Cézanne, and Degas were leading impressionists.

Intimisme Kind of impressionism technique applied to intimate and familiar interiors instead of landscape; adopted by small group of French painters led by Bonnard and Vuillard.

Kitcat Portrait 36 × 28 in (910 × 711 mm); so-called because members of the Kitcat Club, a 17th-century London dining club, had their portraits painted this size.

Kitchen Sink School Group of British painters who aimed at depicting REALISM of the 1950s; pioneered by David Bomberg and John Bratby.

Landscape painting Picture whose main subject is pure landscape without human figures; rare before 1600s. Dutch painters (van Ruisdael, Hobbema) and later British painters (Turner, Constable, Cox) made the form fashionable.

Lay figure Jointed wooden figure on which draperies can be arranged.

Limner Painter of illuminated manuscripts in medieval times; later, a painter of MINIATURES.

London Group Group (founded 1913) formed by union of Camden Town Group and Vorticists. Members included Gilman and Sickert. It still exhibits (including many avant-garde works).

Mahlstick Stick with one end padded, used to steady the painting hand in delicate work.

Mannerism Style of European art (1520–1600) that set out to break rules with strained, exaggerated figures in vivid colours. Vasari was prominent mannerist.

Mariola Painting of the Virgin Mary.

Medium Liquid in which colours are dissolved to make paint; most commonly linseed oil and turpentine.

Meldrum School Australian group of painters inspired by Max Meldrum; founded 1913.

Miniature Tiny painting (less than 6 in, or 15 cm, across), usually a portrait, most often in gouache or water-colour on card, parchment, ivory, or metal sheet. English artists of 1500s and 1600s (Hilliard, Oliver, Hopkins) excelled.

Monochrome Painting carried out in a single colour.

Montage Sticking one layer on top of another; it may be combined with painting to make a picture.

Mural Wall-painting, usually executed in FRESCO, OIL, or TEMPERA.

Nabis (Hebrew, prophet) Small group of French painters, founded in late 1890s, who tried to convey a depth of emotion and mysticism to everyday scenes. Inspired by Maurice Denis; led by Vuillard and Bonnard.

Narrative painting One that tells a story; popular in Victorian England and exploited by Landseer, Mulready, etc.

Naturalism Style that portrays objects with photographic detail. Compared with *realism* it is often stilted and monotonous.

Nature morte French term for STILL LIFE

Nazarenes Semi-religious group of artists founded in Vienna (1809) by Overbeck and Pforr. They held that art should be subject to religious ideas.

Neo-classicism Movement, started in Rome in mid-1700s, that imitated simple art of the Greeks and Romans. In painting, mythological and anatomical subjects were popular. David, Ingres, Alma-Tadema, Lord Leighton, and Allston were leading artists.

Neo-impressionism Type of painting that developed in France in late 1800s. Relied largely on formal composition and application of pure blobs of colour. Pioneered by Seurat and Signac. Also called POINTILLISM.

Neo-romanticism Romantic realism of the 1900s in England. Inspired by words of Blake and works of Palmer and Calvert; typified by paintings of Sutherland, Nash, Piper.

Nimbus Halo or disc surrounding head of religious figure.

Nocturne Night scene; musical term adopted by Whistler.

Norwich School Group of East Anglian painters of 1700s. Leading members included Crome and Cotman.

Oeuvre Total output of an artist.

Oil painting Technique of covering a slightly absorbent surface with pigment ground in oil; introduced in 1400s, perfected by Van Eyck brothers.

Op art (optical art) Modern technique with which painter creates optical illusions by means of dazzling patterns.

Orphism French abstract movement founded in 1912. Followers described it as 'art of painting new structures out of elements that have ... been created entirely by the artist himself'. Delaunay was one of founders. Later called SIMULTANEISM.

Palette Range of colours available to a painter; usually arranged on little board for easy mixing, with thumb-hole for holding.

Palette knife Flexible-bladed spatula used by painters to mix colour on the palette or remove paint from canvas; some painters use it instead of a brush to apply paint.

Pastel Painter's colouring medium consisting of crayon of pure pigment or pigment mixed with chalk and other materials. First used in 1500s; Chardin and Fantin La Tour became masters of pastel in 1700s.

Pastiche Painting made up of motives and fragments copied from another artist.

Perspective Method of representing in two dimensions the optical effect of distance in three dimensions, based on the assumption that receding parallel lines appear to meet; first used in the 1400s.

Pigments Dry paints or dyes that are mixed with oil, water, or other fluid and used to paint with.

Pochade Quick preliminary sketch for a larger painting.

Pointillism See NEO-IMPRESSIONISM.

Polyptych Series of painted doors, panels, etc., with more parts than TRIPTYCH, hinged or folded together.

Pop art Movement born independently in Britain and US in 1950s and 1960s. Uses photos, strip cartoons, adverts, etc., as sources, often enlarged and painted surrealistically in garish colours. Paolozzi, Johns, and Rauschenberg were among pioneers.

Portrait painting Representation in painting of a human being. First portraits were usually of kings and other leaders. Among self-portraits, those of Rembrandt are the most numerous and famous.

Post-impressionism Work of French painters that followed impressionism between 1885 and 1905. Artists experimented freely with expression, form, and design instead of representing nature realistically; typified by Cézanne, Gauguin, Van Gogh, Renoir, and Degas.

Pre-Raphaelite Brotherhood Group mainly of painters who advocated return to spirit and manner of art before time of Raphael (1483–1520). Founded in England (mid-1800s) by Rossetti, Holman Hunt, and Millais; members practised truthful adherence to natural forms and effects.

Primary colours In painting, red, yellow and blue, from which all other colours can be mixed; black and white do not rank as colours.

Priming Preliminary coat on which later coats are laid; see also GROUND.

Primitive Three meanings: 1, work of artist who has not received formal training; 2. work of pre-RENAISSANCE artists; 3. work of artists of simple civilizations, such as Pacific islanders.

Realism Approach to painting that began with Courbet in France in 1800s. Its adherents tried to portray an impression of everyday life.

Renaissance Rebirth in arts and learning that took place in Europe (especially Italy) from 1300s to 1500s. In painting it was typified by original styles, underived from antiquity. Among the masters of this period were Leonardo da Vinci, Michelangelo, Titian, and Raphael.

Replica Exact copy by artist of his own work.

Representational art Type of painting that shows objects as nearly as possible as they actually are; the opposite of ABSTRACT ART.

Rococo European art style (about 1735–1765) characterized in painting by lavish decoration and extravagant ornament.

Romanticism Works in which painter allows his emotions, personal feelings, and imagination free play; the opposite of CLASSICISM. Géricault, Delacroix, Turner, Constable, and Blake were romanticists.

Scumbling Putting an opaque layer of paint unevenly over a contrasting one.

Secco painting Method of wall-painting in which wall is first soaked with lime water. Pigments are mixed with solution of glue, casein, or egg yolk and applied to moist wall. Easier to use but less permanent than fresco.

Sepia Much-used brown pigment made from the inky fluid of cuttlefish.

Sfumato Gradual shading of tones from dark to light.

Simultaneism See ORPHISM.

Sinopia Red ochre used to make guide line drawings for FRESCO.

Stijl, de Dutch art magazine (1917–1932) and the group of artists associated with it.

Still life Art form in which subject of picture is

Below right: A detail of Pablo Picasso's painting of Guernica, produced after the bombing of this Basque town in 1937 during the Spanish Civil War. It is painted in shades of grey and black.

Below: A drawing by Leonardo da Vinci, one of the great artists of the Renaissance.

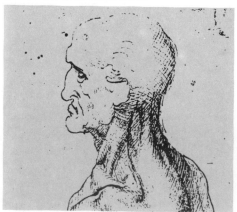

made up of inanimate objects; favourite form of Dutch School.

Stippling Type of water-colour painting in which artist applies colours in series of minute spots; Holman Hunt favoured this method.

Sung Period Painting executed during Sung Dynasty (960–1280), characterized by magical landscapes, paintings on silk, and huge temple frescoes.

Surrealism 20th-century art movement that aimed at escaping control of reason and tried to express subconscious mind pictorially. Ernst, Arp, and Dali have been leading exponents.

Symbolism See SYNTHETISM.

Synthetism A movement started by Gauguin in late 1800s as kind of post-impressionism involving the use of broad, flat tones of colour; also called SYMBOLISM.

Tachisme (from French for stain or blot) Freest form of action painting. Accidental patterns are produced by applying paint to any surface in any way at all. Dubuffet was a pioneer.

Tempera Binding medium for powder colours, made up of egg yolk, sometimes thinned with water. Tempera mixtures last longer than oil colours.

Tenebrists School of painters in 1500s who followed style of Caravaggio. Their pictures, often gloomy,

made great use of light and shade.

Tondo Circular painting.

Triptych Series of three painted panels or doors that are hinged or folded.

Trompe l'oeil Form of ILLUSIONISM, especially on a small scale with much detail.

Underpainting First thin layers of colour in oil painting.

Utrecht School Group of Dutch painters who worked in Utrecht in early 1600s. Among them were Terbrugghen, Honthurst, and Baburen.

Vehicle Liquid in which pigments are suspended, the medium or any substance used for dilution.

Venetian School Painters who worked in Venice during High Renaissance. They included Titian, Veronese, Tintoretto, and Giorgione; work marked by masterly use of chiaroscuro and rich colouring.

Vorticism English avant-garde art movement started by Wyndham Lewis in 1912. Adherents painted in an abstract style.

Water-colour Technique of painting with colours that have been mixed with water-soluble gum; paints are applied to paper with soft, moistened brush. English painters such as Cozens, Sandby, Cotman, Girtin, and Turner were supreme at the art.

GLOSSARY OF SCULPTURE

Alto rilievo High RELIEF, with the figures almost detached from the background.

Armature Wood or metal framework used to support sculptor's model.

Assemblage Building a sculpture from ready-made materials.

Bas relief Shallow RELIEF, in which the figures hardly stand out from their background.

Boucharde Stonemason's hammer with heavy steel

head with pyramidal points; used for initial blocking out of stone.

Bronze Alloy of copper and tin used by sculptors in Ancient Greece, Rome, China, and Africa; revived in modern times.

Bust Sculpture of the upper part of the human body.

Carving Cutting a sculpture out of a solid block of stone or wood.

Cast Figure made from mould of original model. See CIRE PERDUE, PLASTER CAST, SAND CAST.

Cavo rilievo Kind of relief in which the highest surface is level with the surface of the stone, which is left as a border.

Chisel See BOUCHARDE, PITCHER, POINT, CLAW CHISEL.

Ciment fondu Fine-grade black or white aluminous cement used for delicate modelling.

Cire perdue (French, lost wax) Traditional method for casting bronze sculptures: Model with wax surface is enclosed in mould; wax is melted and runs out through holes at bottom; molten metal poured through holes at top, filling up space left by wax.

Claw chisel Toothed chisel that gives furrow-like effect to stone; used prior to final defining of form with cutting chisel or by abrasion.

Direct metal sculpture Building up sculptures by welding metal sections together.

Drill Tool used for making holes and special effects when carving.

Figurine Miniature figure.

A sculptor at work; the utmost care and skill are needed as the artist carves away wood or stone to shape his image.

Found object Any object treated as a work of art as it is; if 'improved' it is a found object composed.

Free-stone An easily worked fine-grained limestone or sandstone.

Genre sculpture Style that reflects everyday or rustic life; hallmark of Etruscan art and of Biblical subjects in Middle Ages.

Glyptic Carved as opposed to modelled.

Heroic Any figure or group of figures carved larger than life.

Intaglio Hollow relief, in which the form is cut out of the surface.

Kinetic sculpture Sculpture that moves, either freely, as a MOBILE, or when driven by an electric motor.

Maquette (French, small model) Small wax or clay model made by sculptor in preparation for larger work.

Marble Popular stone for sculpture because of its extreme durability; found in all colours from nearly pure white to nearly pure black.

Mezzo rilievo Form of relief midway between ALTO RILIEVO and BAS RELIEF.

Mobile Movable sculpture of shapes cut out of wood or sheet metal, linked by wires or rods in order to revolve easily or move up and down; invented by American sculptor Alexander Calder (1932).

Modelling Building-up of forms in three dimensions by means of plastic material such as clay or wax.

Patina Greenish surface film on old bronze, generally enhancing appearance.

Pitcher Wide chisel, used after BOUCHARDE, for removing large quantities of material from flat surfaces.

Plaster cast Intermediate stage in bronze sculpture from which final mould is made.

Point Pointed chisel used for channelling surface to near required depth; used after PITCHER.

Pointing machine Device for reproducing a cast or statue in stone.

Polychromatic sculpture Sculpture painted in naturalistic colours to make it more lifelike; mostly pre-1500s.

Relief Sculpture not free-standing from background; various degrees, from BAS RELIEF (low relief) to ALTO RILIEVO (high relief).

Riffler Small, curved file for intricate work in wood, stone, or metal.

Sand cast Mould of special sand made from plaster model and from which bronze cast is made.

Sculpture-in-the-round Sculpture that can be seen from all sides.

Stabile Sculpture that does not move, as opposed to MOBILE.

Torso Trunk of human body, especially without head or limbs.

POTTERY TERMS

Agate Wares made of different coloured clays to imitate agate stone.

Art pottery Pottery made in individual studios.

Bellarmines Bulbous stoneware bottles with a bearded mask in relief, named after Cardinal Roberto Bellarmino (1542–1621).

Biscuit ware Pottery fired but not glazed.

Blanc de chine Chinese PORCELAIN made from about 1600 onwards, varying in colour from blue-white to deep ivory.

Blue-and-white Pottery and porcelain with a white base, decorated with blue designs under the glaze.

Body Term applied to a mixture of clays for making EARTHENWARE or STONEWARE.

Bone china The type of porcelain made in England since 1800, containing bone ash.

Celadon ware Chinese porcelain with a pale grey or bluish-green glaze.

Ceramics Term for anything made of baked clay; the potter's art.

China (originally Chinaware) At first, Chinese porcelain of the 1500s; now, any porcelain.

China clay Kaolin.

Chinese Lowestoft An incorrect name for Chinese export porcelain, that is porcelain made in China in the 1600s–1800s especially for Europe.

Chinoiserie Decoration on European porcelain from about 1600 to 1765 in imitation of the Chinese style.

Clay The basic material of the potter, formed by the decomposition of rock; kaolin, or china clay, is a pure white coarse clay; ball clay, a highly plastic, fine pure clay; fireclay, a dark clay that withstands high temperatures but is not plastic; buff or stoneware clay, a smooth plastic clay hardening at high temperatures.

Crackle A network of fine cracks (crazing) in the glaze, produced intentionally as a decorative effect. Crazing is due to uneven shrinkage of glaze and body.

Creamware A high-quality earthenware perfected by Josiah Wedgwood in Staffordshire in the 1700s, and widely imitated, particularly in North America.

CHINESE DYNASTIES

Chinese pottery and porcelain is dated by the dynasty (royal family) or individual emperor in whose time it was made. Some of the most important are:

Dynasty	Dates
Han	206 BC–AD 220
Three Kingdoms	220–265
Six Dynasties	265–588
Sui	589–618
T'ang	618–906
Five Dynasties	906–959
Sung	960–1279
Yüan (Mongol)	1280–1368
Ming	1368–1644
Ch'ing (Manchu)	1644–1912
(Emperor Chi'en Lung 1736–1795)	

Delftware Tin-glazed earthenware, named after Delft in the Netherlands which was a centre of its manufacture in the 1600s. Compare FAÏENCE; MAJOLICA.

Diapered Decorated with a scalloped border.

Earthenware Pottery fired to a relatively low temperature (about 1100°C), easy to work and having a dull finish.

Enamel colours Coloured glazes used to decorate pottery or porcelain already glazed.

Faïence French name for tin-glazed earthenware; originally from Faenza, in Italy.

Famille rose Enamelled porcelain made in China in the 1700s, distinguished by a deep rose-pink.

Famille verte Chinese enamelled porcelain made in the late 1600s and early 1700s, characterized by a brilliant green; famille noir is similar but with a black ground-colour.

Firing Process of hardening shaped clay; heat melts a substance (usually silica) in the clay, which binds the other constituents.

Glaze A glassy substance applied to pottery and porcelain which makes it smooth and waterproof. It is a liquid, clay-like mixture containing substances which produce the hard finish; these include lead and tin. The article is fired after glazing, usually having been fired once beforehand.

Hard-paste porcelain See PASTE.

Hausmaler German name for outside, independent decorators, who bought porcelain in the white and painted it in their own workshops.

Imari Japanese porcelain decorated in a rich pattern of blue, red and gold; named after the port from which it was mostly shipped.

Impasto Laying colour on so thickly that it stands out in relief.

Jasper Fine, unglazed Wedgwood stoneware adorned in white relief on delicate colours.

Kakiemon Japanese porcelain with delicate, asymmetrical decoration; named after a potter who first introduced the style about 1600.

Kaolin See CLAY.

Kiln Oven in which clay is fired.

Majolica (maiolica) White, tin-glazed earthenware, originally from Majorca; compare FAÏENCE.

Onion pattern A Meissen porcelain pattern originating in the 1700s and based on a Chinese design.

Lustre A pale, pearly pink; also gold and silver.

Parian ware A fine porcelain resembling white Parian marble, particularly used for portrait busts and statues.

Paste The mixture from which porcelain is made; hard-paste porcelain is made from kaolin and petuntse (a form of feldspar): this is the true porcelain made in China and rediscovered at Meissen in Europe; soft-paste porcelain was made from white clay and fusible silicate; it is more translucent than hard-paste porcelain but with a softer whiteness.

Porcelain The finest kind of pottery, white all through and translucent.

Pottery Strictly, all baked-clay ware except STONEWARE and PORCELAIN, but more widely the term includes them, too.

Redware Simple, lead-glazed wares with a soft, reddish clay body.

Refractory Able to withstand great heat.

Repairer A workman responsible for assembling a figure from various moulded parts (not one who mended broken articles).

Resist lustre Lustre ware in which a pattern is painted on with a resist (a protective coating) before the lustre is applied; after firing the resist is rubbed away to leave the pattern in the ground colour against the lustre.

Rice-grain A kind of decoration in which holes in the clay are filled with glaze, giving a translucent rice-grain pattern when the ware is held up to the light.

Sgraffiato Cutting through a coating of slip to reveal the underlying body, usually in a deeper colour.

Slip Clay in liquid form, used for casting in moulds; joining parts together; or for making decorations.

Soft-paste porcelain See PASTE.

Stoneware Hard, strong type of pottery fired at about 1250°C and able to hold liquid without glazing, made from clay and fusible stone such as feldspar.

Terracotta Brownish-red burnt-clay pottery, baked in moulds and used for architectural mouldings.

Throwing Shaping wet clay by hand on a potter's wheel.

Tin glaze Glaze containing tin ashes which make it opaque.

Transfer printing Transferring decorations from engraved copper plates to pottery by means of slabs of gelatine or sheets of tissue, and using enamel colours; invented in the 1750s.

Turning Trimming nearly dry pottery on a lathe or on a potter's wheel.

Tyg Beaker or vessel with several handles.

Vitrification The process by which the silica in clay turns to glass under heat, fusing the other constituents of the clay; porcelain is completely vitrified, earthenware only partially and so still porous.

Wedging Initial preparation of clay, cutting and banging it together to make it homogeneous and remove air bubbles.

SOME HISTORIC POTTERY AND PORCELAIN FACTORIES

Belleek (Ireland)	1857–
Bennington (US)	1793–1894
Bow (England)	1744–1776
Bristol (England)	1749–1781
Caughley (England)	1754–1814
Chantilly (France)	1725–1800
Chelsea (England)	1745–1784
Coalport (England)	1796
Copenhagen (Denmark)	1774–
Derby (England)	1750–1848
Derby, Royal Crown	1876–
Frankenthal (Germany)	1755–1799
Greenpoint (US)	1848–
Hoechst (Germany)	1750–1798
Limoges (France)	1771–
Liverpool (England)	1710–c.1800
Ludwigsburg (Germany)	1758–1824
Meissen (Germany)	1710–
Mennecy (France)	1735–1785
Nymphenburg (Germany)	1753–
Sèvres (France)	1756–
Spode (England)	1770–
Tucker (US)	1826–1838
Vincennes (France)	1738–1756
Wedgwood (England)	1759–
Worcester (England)	1751–

World History

CHRONOLOGY OF WORLD HISTORY

BC

40,000 Last Ice Age; Cro-Magnon Man begins to enter Europe from Near East.

30,000 Neanderthal Man dies out.

28,000 First people cross Bering Straits landbridge from Asia to Americas.

20,000 Cave art flourishes at Lascaux, Altamira, and other sites. Man living in Australia.

10,000 Man reaches the tip of South America.

8400 First domesticated dog found in Idaho, USA.

8000 Agriculture gradually develops in Near East; sheep and cattle domesticated.

7000 Walled settlement at Jericho. Pottery develops. Man begins to learn to use metals.

5000 Rising sea level severs last landbridge between Britain and mainland Europe. First settlements in fertile river valleys of Sumer, in lower Mesopotamia.

4236 First date in ancient Egyptian calendar.

4000 Yang-shao rice farming culture in China.

3760 First date in Jewish calendar.

3372 First date in Mayan calendar.

3100 Menes unites kingdoms of Upper and Lower Egypt, founding 1st Dynasty.

3000 Bricks first used in Egyptian and Assyrian cultures.

First cities in Sumer and Egypt. Windmill Hill culture in Britain. Phoenicians settle along eastern coast of Mediterranean. Invention of wheel.

2800 Foundation of the 'Old Kingdom' of Egypt, covering IIIrd to VIth Dynasties.

2780 Zoser becomes ruler of Egypt; his physician Imhotep designs the Step Pyramid at Saqqara, the first pyramid.

2700 Khufu (Cheops) rules Egypt and builds the Great Pyramid at Giza.

2697 Huang-ti, the 'Yellow Emperor', comes to the throne in China.

2500 Early Minoan civilization in Crete; foundation of Knossos. Indus Valley civilization of India founded.

2350 Yao Dynasty in China; Sargon the Great of Akkad begins the conquest of Sumeria, founding the first great empire.

2200 Hsia Dynasty of China founded.

2100 The Empire of Ur (to 2000).

Middle Kingdom of Egypt, beginning with the VIIth Dynasty. The patriarch Abraham migrates from Ur, in Mesopotamia and leads his people

to Canaan (Palestine). Aryans begin invasion of Indus Valley.

2000 Bronze Age under way in northern Europe.

1950 Sesostris I of Egypt invades Canaan. End of the Empire of Ur.

1925 The Hittites conquer Babylon.

1860 Construction of Stonehenge begins in Britain.

1760 Shang Dynasty founded in China.

1730 The Hyksos, a Semitic tribe, begin conquest of Egypt, founding XVth Dynasty.

1728 Accession of Hammurabi the Great of Babylon, author of great Code of Laws.

1570 Beginning of the New Kingdom in Egypt; Hyksos driven out; Temple of Amun at Karnak begun.

1500 Mohenjo-Daro, in Indus Valley, destroyed.

1420 Amenhotep III begins Golden Age in Egypt.

1400 Knossos, capital of Minoan civilization in Crete, is destroyed by fire. Temples at Luxor under construction. Iron Age under way in India and western Asia.

1379 Accession of Amenhotep IV in Egypt; he introduces Sun worship, abolishes all old gods, and takes name Akhenaton after Aton, the Sun-god.

1375 Suppiluliumas becomes king of the Hittites in Asia Minor and begins to make his kingdom into a powerful empire.

1366 Assuruballit I becomes ruler of Assyria and begins Assyrian rise to power.

1361 Boy-king Tutankhamun succeeds Akhenaton; his advisers restore the worship of the old Egyptian gods.

1319 Rameses I founds vigorous XIXth Dynasty in Egypt.

1304 Accession of Rameses II, the Great, of Egypt.

1300 Construction of great Egyptian rock temples of Abu Simbel begins; oppression of Israelite colony in Egypt. Sidon flourishes as great Phoenician port.

1275 Shalmaneser I becomes ruler of Assyria, and extends its conquests.

1250 The Exodus: the Israelites under Moses leave Egypt.

1232 Israelites in Canaan; Rameses II's son Merneptah defeats them in battle.

1200 Period of the Judges begins in Israel.

1193 City of Troy is destroyed by Greek armies after a prolonged siege.

1175 Invasion of Egypt by Confederation of Sea Peoples including Philistines, Greeks, Sardinians, and Sicilians; defeated by Rameses III.

1170 Growing power of newly independent Phoenician cities, especially Tyre.

1125 Nebuchadrezzar I, King of Babylon; he holds off renewed attacks by the Assyrians.

Left: This carving comes from ancient Mesopotamia, and dates from before 3000 BC. It shows people from the river areas of Sumer in the south of the region. The markings are in an early form of writing, which first developed in this area in the 3000s.

This bronze statue shows a wolf suckling Romulus and Remus, abandoned twin sons of the war-god Mars and a Vestal Virgin. According to legend they founded Rome in 753 BC and shortly afterwards Romulus killed his brother in a quarrel.

A stone head of the Buddha, who founded a new religion at the end of the 6th century BC.

1122 Emperor Wu Wang founds Chou Dynasty in China, and establishes feudal system.

1116 Tiglathpileser I becomes ruler of Assyria; he fights off invasions from the north and eventually conquers Babylon.

1065 New Kingdom in Egypt ends with death of Rameses XI; Smendes, a rich merchant, becomes Pharaoh and founds the XXIst Dynasty.

1050 Philistines conquer Israel.

1020 Samuel, last of the Israelite judges, anoints Saul as King of Israel; Saul leads successful rebellion against the Philistines.

1000 Saul is killed at battle of Gilboa; succeeded by David, first as King of Judah, later as King of Israel; after a campaign, David captures Jerusalem and makes it his capital.

961 Death of David; succeeded by his son Solomon.

953 Dedication of Temple at Jerusalem, built by Solomon with help and materials from Hiram of Tyre.

935 Revival of Assyria begins with the accession of Assurdan II; by 860 he and his successors have re-established Assyria's ancient boundaries.

922 Death of Solomon; succeeded by his son, Rehoboam; rebellion against Rehoboam's rule led by Jeroboam; kingdom split into Judah in the south, under Rehoboam, and Israel in the north under Jeroboam.

814 The Phoenicians found Carthage (literally 'new town') near their North African colony of Utica.

810 Sammuramat (the Semiramis of legend) rules Assyria as regent for her son Adad-Nirari III.

800 Traditional date for the composition of Homer's epic poems *The Iliad* and *The Odyssey*.

783 Jeroboam II, King of Israel (to 748); period of prosperity.

776 First definitely dated performance of the Olympic Games in Greece.

770 Eastern Chou Dynasty in China (to 256).

753 Traditional date of the foundation of Rome by Romulus and Remus.

743 Sparta begins the First Messenian War to conquer Messenia; ends 716.

722 Sargon II of Assyria captures Samaria and brings kingdom of Israel to an end.
Ethiopian kings rule over Egypt (to 682) – the XXVth Dynasty.

710 The Assyrians destroy the kingdom of Chaldea.

705 Sennacherib, King of Assyria (to 682).

701 Sennacherib establishes his capital at Nineveh.

689 Assyrians destroy Babylon and flood the site.

683 Athens ends rule of hereditary kings; replaces them with nine *archons* chosen each year from among the nobles.

682 Judah surrenders to Assyria.

669 Assurbanipal rules as King of Assyria (to 627).

663 Assurbanipal with an Assyrian army sacks Thebes in Egypt.

650 Sparta conquers rebellious subjects in the Second Messenian War (to 630).

621 Dracon introduces Athens' first written laws, noted for their severity.

612 Medes, Babylonians, and Scythians destroy Nineveh.

609 End of the Assyrian Empire.

608 Necho of Egypt defeats and kills Josiah, King of Judah, at the battle of Megiddo.

594 Solon becomes sole Archon of Athens; introduces new, milder laws to replace those of Dracon, creates court of citizens and reforms election of magistrates.

586 Nebuchadrezzar II of Babylon sacks Jerusalem and takes the people of Judah into capitivity in Babylon.

580 Nebuchadrezzar begins building the Hanging Gardens of Babylon, one of the Wonders of the World.

563 Birth of Prince Siddhartha Gautama, later the Buddah (Enlightened One) (to 483).

559 Cyrus the Great, ruler of Persia (to 530), founds the Persian Empire.

551 Birth of K'ung Fu-tzu (Confucius), Chinese philosopher (to 497).

546 Battle of Sardis: Croesus, last King of Lydia, defeated by Cyrus; Persians overrun Asia Minor.

539 Greeks defeat the Carthaginians in battle.
Cyrus conquers Babylonia, and makes Judah and Phoenicia into Persian provinces.
538 Edict of Cyrus allows some Jewish exiles to return to Judah.
530 Cambyses, ruler of Persia (to 521).
525 Cambyses conquers Egypt; Egypt under Persian kings until 404.
521 Darius I, ruler of Persia (to 486); Persian Empire divided into 20 satrapies (provinces), of which Egypt is one.
520 Work is resumed on the Temple in Jerusalem (completed 515).
510 Tarquinius Superbus, last King of Rome, overthrown by rebellion.
509 Traditional date for the foundation of the Roman Republic.
508 Cleisthenes reforms the constitution of Athens, and introduces democratic government. The Etruscan ruler Lars Porsena attacks Rome; heroic defence of the bridge over the river Tiber by Horatius Cocles.
Rome makes treaty with Carthage.
507 Spartans under Cleomenes try to restore the aristocracy in Athens; Athenians rise and put Cleisthenes back into power.
500 About this time Bantu-speaking peoples begin spreading in East Africa.
494 Plebeians in Rome revolt, and win political rights from patricians.
492 Mardonius leads first Persian expedition against Athens; his fleet is shattered by a storm.
490 Second Persian expedition: Athenians defeat the Persians at the battle of Marathon.
486 Xerxes I, the Great, ruler of Persia (to 465); he demands tribute from the Greek states, most of which is refused.
480 Third Persian expedition: Xerxes invades Greece with 180,000 men; Greek rearguard is wiped out defending Pass of Thermopylae; Greek fleet defeats Persians at battle of Salamis.
479 Battle of Plataea: Greek army defeats Persian army; Persian fleet is destroyed at Mycale. Athens and Piraeus fortified.
470 The Carthaginian leader Hanno sails down

Part of the great staircase at the magnificent Persian palace of Persepolis; carvings show subjects and tribute bearers. Inset: Darius III of Persia.

the African coast as far as Cameroon.
460 'Age of Pericles' in Athens (to 429).
First Peloponnesian War between Athens and Sparta (to 451).
450 Herodotus, first historian, visits Egypt.
Carthage begins to develop new trading centres along north and west African coasts.
449 Sacred War between Sparta and Athens over control of the oracle at Delphi (to 448).
447 Athenians begin building the Parthenon.
431 Second Peloponnesian War (to 421).
430 Epidemic of plague breaks out in Athens.
429 Pericles dies of the plague. The Acropolis is completed. Birth of philosopher Plato.
424 Xerxes II of Persia assassinated; Darius II, ruler of Persia (to 404).
415 War between Athens and Sparta breaks out again.
413 Athenian attack on Sicily fails.
411 Revolution in Athens: 'Government of the 5000' seizes power, but democracy is soon restored.
409 Carthage begins invasion of Sicily.
407 Alcibiades, Athenian general, quells revolt in subject states.
406 Athenian fleet defeats a Spartan fleet at the battle of Arginusae.
405 Lysander of Sparta defeats the Athenian fleet off Aegospotami.
404 Spartans capture Athens; Athenian hero Alcibiades is assassinated in exile.
Short-lived Government of the Thirty Tyrants in Athens.
403 Pausanius restores democracy in Athens.
400 Greek army under Xenophon is defeated at Cunaxa in revolt against Artaxerxes II of Persia: 'Retreat of the Ten Thousand'.
399 Greek philosopher Socrates is condemned to death for heretical teaching.

173

395 Athens, Thebes, Corinth, and Argos form coalition against Sparta; Lysander killed in battle.

394 Battle of Coronae: Sparta defeats the coalition.

391 Romans under the dictator Marcus Furius Camillus subjugate the Etruscans.

390 Gauls under Brennus sack Rome, but fail to capture the Capitol.

386 Spartan ruler Antalcidas negotiates peace with Persia, and forces other Greek states to agree to it.

371 The Athenian League and Sparta make peace.

370 Thebes forms the Arcadian League against Sparta (to 362).

366 First plebeian council elected in Rome.

359 Philip II, King of Macedonia (to 336).

355 Third Sacred War (to 346) begins when Phocians seize Delphi and use the oracle funds to raise an army; Macedonia fights against Athens. Alexander the Great born.

351 Persian invasion of Egypt fails.

350 Jewish revolt against the Persians fails.

346 Peace of Philocrates: Athenian statesman Philocrates leads a delegation to sue for peace from Macedonia.

343 Artaxerxes III of Persia leads an army into Egypt and conquers it.

339 The Fourth Sacred War (to 338): Philip of Macedonia conquers Greece.

336 Assassination of Philip of Macedonia.
Alexander III (the Great), son of Philip and Olympias, King of Macedonia (to 323).
Alexander crushes a revolt by Athens, Thebes, and other Greek cities.

334 Alexander begins campaign against Persia; defeats Darius III of Persia at the river Granicus in Asia Minor.

333 Alexander defeats Darius again at the battle of Issus, capturing the Persian queen and her children; Alexander refuses Darius's offer of ransom and part of his empire. Alexander captures Tyre; end of Phoenician Empire.

332 Alexander invades and conquers Egypt; foundation of Alexandria.

331 Renewal of the Persian campaign; Alexander defeats Darius at Arbela; end of the Persian Empire.

330 Darius is murdered; Alexander in complete control of Persia.

327 Alexander begins invasion of India.

326 Alexander wins battle of the Hydaspes, but his soldiers refuse to go any farther east, and he has to retreat.

323 Alexander dies at Babylon; his generals divide his empire among themselves.
Ptolemy satrap (governor) of Egypt.
Birth of Euclid.

321 Chandragupta founds the Maurya Dynasty in northern India; it lasts until 184.

320 Ptolemy captures Jerusalem; Libya becomes an Egyptian province.
Birth of Theocrites.

316 Olympias, mother of Alexander the Great, murdered in revenge for killings she had ordered.

312 Seleucus, one of Alexander's generals, begins to take control in Syria.

305 Ptolemy I takes the title of king in Egypt, and is soon proclaimed pharaoh; Seleucus I becomes king of Babylon, founding the Seleucid Dynasty.
Agathocles, tyrant of Syracuse in Sicily, makes

Alexander the Great became king of Macedon at the age of 20 and died only 12 years later. His vast empire (below) was divided by his generals.

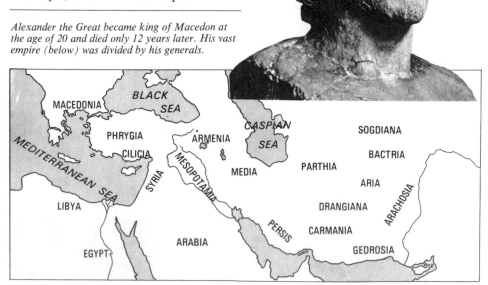

peace with Carthage after a heavy defeat and is allowed to take the title of king.

304 Seleucus cedes his claim on India to Chandragupta in exchange for 500 elephants.

Rome makes peace with the Samnites and its other enemies; gains area around Naples.

300 State of Choson is formed in northern Korea.
Treaty between Rome and Carthage.

298 Third Samnite War: ends in 290 in Roman victory in central Italy.

264 First Punic War between Rome and Carthage (ends 241).

254 Rome takes Panormus in Sicily from Carthage.

250 Hebrew scriptures translated into Greek.

247 Asoka rules the Maurya Empire in India (to 236), and becomes a Buddhist.

241 Peace between Rome and Carthage; Carthage surrenders Sicily, which becomes the first Roman province.

240 Revolt of Carthaginian mercenaries; crushed by Hamilcar Barca in 238.

238 Carthaginians begin conquest of Spain.

225 Romans defeat Celts at Telamon in Italy.

223 Antiochus III, the Great, ruler of Babylonian Empire (to 187).

221 Ch'in Dynasty in China (to 207), from which the country takes its name.

218 Second Punic War between Rome and Carthage (ends 201); Carthaginian general Hannibal leads army from Spain over the Alps to invade Italy, defeating Publius Cornelius Scipio at river Ticinus, and Sempronius Longus at river Trebia.

217 Hannibal annihilates a Roman army at Lake Trasimene.

216 Hannibal wins another great victory at Cannae.

215 First Macedonian War: Philip of Macedonia attacks Rome in support of Carthage; ends in Peace of Phoenice in 205.

Roman general Marcus Claudius Marcellus defeats Hannibal at Nola.

214 Construction of Great Wall of China begins.
Marcellus begins conquest of Sicily from the Carthaginians; completed 210.

206 Publius Cornelius Scipio the Younger defeats the Carthaginians in Spain.

202 Han Dynasty in China (to AD 9), founded by Liu Pang.

200 Second Macedonian War (ends 196): Greeks with Roman support rebel against Macedonian rule; Philip is forced to surrender Greece.

192 Syrian War (to 189): Antiochus III defeated in war with Rome.

184 Sunga Dynasty in India founded by Pushayanitra.

183 Hannibal commits suicide to avoid being handed over to the Romans.

179 Perseus, son of Philip V, King of Macedonia; continues the war with Rome until 167.

171 Third Macedonian War (to 167): Macedonians under Perseus again attack Rome.

168 Battle of Pydna: Romans defeat and capture Perseus.

160 Judas Maccabaeus killed in battle against the Seleucids. Jonathan Maccabaeus, younger brother of Judas, leader of the Jews (to 143).

157 Judaea becomes an independent principality.

149 Fourth Macedonian War (to 148): Macedonia becomes a Roman province.

Third Punic War (ends 146): Romans destroy Carthage.

143 Simon Maccabaeus, elder brother of Judas and Jonathan, leader of the Jews (to 134).

141 Jerusalem liberated by the Jews; Judaea is proclaimed an independent kingdom.

140 Wu Ti, 'Martial Emperor', of China (to 86).

135 First Servile War (to 132): revolt of Roman slaves in Sicily crushed.

116 Ptolemaic Empire is split up under will of Ptolemy VIII; years of strife follow.

111 War begins between Rome and Jugurtha, King of Numidia in northern Africa.

108 Emperor Wu Ti of China conquers Choson.
Celtic Cimbri ravages Gaul.

106 Gaius Marius elected consul; sent to Africa.

105 Marius and Lucius Cornelius Sulla defeat Jugurtha of Numidia, who is taken to Rome and killed.

103 Second Servile War in Rome (ends 99).

91 War between Rome and Italian cities; civil war in Rome; Sulla defeats Marius.

90 Revolt of Pharisees in Judaea.

89 Roman army under Sulla regains control of Italy; all Italians granted Roman citizenship.

88 First Mithridatic War (to 84): Rome against Mithridates IV Eupator, King of Pontus.
Civil war in Rome (to 82); Sulla victorious.

87 Sulla defeats Mithridates and takes Athens.
Death of Emperor Wu Ti leads to period of disorder in China.

83 Second Mithridatic War (to 81): the Romans successfully invade Pontus.

82 Sulla becomes dictator of Rome.

78 Death of Sulla; revolt of Marcus Aemilius Lepidus, who is defeated by Gnaeus Pompeius (Pompey the Great).

74 Third Mithridatic War (to 61): Mithridates annexes Bithynia, which Rome claims.

73 Lucius Licinius Lucullus with a Roman army defeats Mithridates and occupies Pontus.

Third Servile War (to 71): Spartacus leads a revolt of slaves and gladiators, which is crushed by the consuls Pompey and Marcus Licinius Crassus.

65 Pompey with a Roman army invades Syria and conquers Palestine.

63 Pompey captures Jerusalem and annexes Syria.
Death of Aristobulus II, King of Judaea; Pompey annexes Judaea.

61 Gaius Julius Caesar, nephew of Marius and governor of Spain, wins first major victories.

60 First Triumvirate formed to rule Rome: Pompey, Crassus, and Caesar.

58 Caesar appointed governor of Gaul.

55 Caesar conquers northern Gaul, and unsuccessfully attempts to invade Britain.

54 Second invasion of Britain by Romans under Caesar, Cassivellaunus, powerful British leader, agrees to pay tribute to Rome.

53 Battle of Carrhae: Crassus is killed fighting the Parthians.

52 Pompey appointed sole consul in Rome.
Vercingetorix leads the Gauls in revolt; is crushed by Caesar.

51 Cleopatra VII and her brother Ptolemy XIII become joint rulers of Egypt.
Caesar completes the conquest of Gaul, and writes *De Bello Gallico*.

50 Political manoeuvring between Caesar and Pompey; Pompey's supporters attempt to thwart Caesar's return to the consulship.

49 The Senate orders Caesar to give up his command in Gaul; Caesar crosses the river Rubicon into Italy, a gesture of defiance starting a civil war; Pompey flees to Greece.

48 Caesar defeats Pompey at Pharsalia in Greece.

47 Cleopatra orders Pompey to be murdered; Caesar conquers Cleopatra's enemies and makes her his mistress.
Antipater becomes procurator of Judaea, and his son Herod governor of Galilee.

46 Caesar returns to Rome with Cleopatra, and crushes a mutiny by the Tenth Legion; Caesar defeats Pompey's son Sextus in Africa, which becomes a Roman province.

45 Caesar becomes virtual dictator of Rome; introduces the Julian Calendar; again defeats Sextus, in Spain; adopts his nephew Gaius Octavius (Octavian) as his heir.

44 Caesar is assassinated by a group of conspirators headed by Junius Brutus and Cassius Longinus; Marcus Antonius (Mark Antony), Caesar's master of the horse, seizes power; rivalry between Antony and Octavian.

43 Second Triumvirate formed by Octavian, Antony, and Marcus Lepidus.
Birth of Ovid.
Antony orders murder of Cicero, the orator.

42 Caesar deified: temple to him is erected in the Forum, where he was murdered.
Battle of Philippi: the Triumvirate defeats Brutus and Cassius, who commit suicide.

40 Antony marries Octavian's sister Octavia.

37 Triumvirate is renewed for five years.
Herod the Great, King of Judaea (to 4).
Antony, still married to Octavia, marries Cleopatra in Egypt.

36 Octavian's fleet defeats Pompey's fleet; death of Pompey.

32 Antony formally divorces Octavia; Octavian declares war on Antony and Cleopatra.

31 Battle of Actium: Octavian's fleet defeats the combined fleets of Antony and Cleopatra.

30 Antony and Cleopatra commit suicide, Octavian declares Egypt a Roman province.

29 Octavian, back in Rome, holds three triumphs and proclaims peace.

27 Octavian is given supreme power by the Senate, with the title of Augustus; but the republic nominally continues.
Augustus begins two-year campaign in Spain to subdue rebellious tribes.

23 Augustus resigns the consulship but gains other privileges; adopts the unofficial title of *princeps* – chief of the republic.

15 Roman Empire extended to the upper Danube.

12 Revolt in Pannonia (now northern Yugoslavia); quelled after three years by Augustus's stepson, Tiberius Claudius Nero Caesar.

8 Death of the Roman poets Virgil and Horace.

5 Probable year of birth of Jesus of Nazareth at Bethlehem.

4 Death of Herod the Great: kingdom is partitioned among his sons: Herod Archaelaus, ethnarch of Samaria and Judaea; Herod Antipas, tetrarch of Galilee; Philip, tetrarch of Ituraea.

AD

5 Rome acknowledges Cymbeline, King of the Catuvellauni, as king of Britain.

6 Romans depose Herod Archaelaus and appoint procurators to govern Judaea.

9 Usurper Wang Mang becomes Emperor of China (to AD 23) – the Hsin Dynasty.

14 Death of Augustus.
Tiberius, Emperor of Rome (to 37).

18 Death of poet Ovid.
Caiaphas, high priest in Jerusalem (to 36).

25 Later Han Dynasty in China (to 220).

26 Tiberius retires to Capri; continues to govern in absence.
Pontius Pilate, procurator of Judaea (to 36).

27 Baptism of Jesus by John the Baptist.

28 John the Baptist is executed on Herod's orders.

30 Pilate orders the crucifixion of Jesus.

31 Martyrdom of Stephen.

32 Conversion to Christianity of Saul (Paul) of Tarsus.

34 Paul's first visit to Jerusalem.

37 Herod Agrippa, King of northern Palestine (to 44).
Gaius Claudius Caesar ('Caligula', meaning 'little boot'), Emperor of Rome (to 41).

41 Caligula's irrational conduct leads to his assassination.
Claudius Drusus, Roman Emperor (to 54).
Claudius makes Agrippa king of Judaea.

43 Romans under Aulus Plautius invade Britain; London is founded.

44 Judaea under procurators again.

45 Paul beings his missionary journeys.

48 Claudius's wife Messalina executed; he marries his niece Agrippina.

51 Caractacus, British general, is captured and taken to Rome.

54 Claudius is murdered, possibly by Agrippina.
Nero Drusus, Agrippina's son, Emperor (to 68).

58 Emperor Ming-Ti of China introduces Buddhism into his country.
Paul the Apostle is imprisoned in Caesarea.

59 Nero murders his mother, Agrippina.

60 Paul, brought to trial before Festus, procurator of Judaea, appeals to Rome.

61 Boudicca, Queen of the Iceni, leads a rebellion in Britain; defeated and killed by the Roman governor, Suetonius Paulinus.

62 Nero divorces and exiles his wife, Octavia, then has her murdered; he marries Poppaea Sabina, wife of his friend Otho.

64 Fire destroys most of Rome; Nero orders the persecution of Christians as scapegoats; probable date of Apostle Peter's martyrdom.

65 Philosopher Seneca commits suicide on Nero's orders.
The Gospel according to Mark is written about this time.

67 Roman general Vespasian is sent to Judaea to suppress revolt.
Probable date of the martyrdom of Paul.

THE EMPIRE OF TRAJAN

68 Rebellion against Nero, who commits suicide. Galba, legate of Hispania Tarraconensis, Emperor of Rome (to 69).

69 Otho has Galba murdered and becomes emperor; is defeated by Vitellius, who then becomes emperor; Vespasian, recalled from Judaea, defeats and kills Vitellius.

Vespasian, Emperor of Rome (to 79).

70 Vespasian's son Titus captures and destroys Jerusalem and suppresses the Jewish revolt.

The Gospel according to Matthew is written about this time.

73 Fall of Masada, last stronghold of the Jewish Zealots in Palestine.

Vespasian begins extending the Empire in Germany (until 74).

75 *The Gospel according to Luke* is written about this time.

77 The Roman conquest of Britain; Julius Agricola is imperial governor (to 84).

78 Kamishka rules as Great King in northern India (to 96), founding the Second Kushana Dynasty.

79 Titus, Emperor of Rome (to 81).

Vesuvius erupts, burying the cities of Pompeii, Herculaneum, and Stabiae.

80 Another fire in Rome; the Colosseum and the Baths of Titus are completed.

81 Domitian, younger brother of Titus, Roman Emperor (to 96).

Domitian begins building defence lines on German frontier of the Empire.

95 Probable time of the writing of *The Gospel according to John* and *The Book of Revelation.*

96 Assassination of Domitian; Nerva, Emperor of Rome (to 98).

98 Trajan, general commanding in lower Germany, Emperor of Rome (to 117).

101 The Dacian Wars (end 107): Trajan increases the Empire to its greatest extent; commemorated by Trajan's Column, in Rome.

115 The Jews in Egypt, North Africa, Palestine, and Cyprus rebel against Roman rule; repressed with great severity by Trajan.

116 Trajan makes the river Tigris the Empire's eastern boundary, forming new provinces in Mesopotamia and Assyria.

The Roman Empire at its greatest extent under Trajan. It proved too vast to be ruled over by one man, or ultimately to be defended against the invasions of barbarians.

117 Hadrian, legate of Syria and cousin of Trajan, Roman Emperor (to 138).

122 Hadrian visits Britain and begins construction of wall and fortifications between northern England and Scotland.

124 The Pantheon in Rome is completed.

130 Hadrian visits Egypt; new capital city is begun at Antinopolis.

132 Jews led by Shimeon Bar-Kokhba and Rabbi Akiba Ben-Joseph rebel against Roman rule; they capture Jerusalem and set up an independent state of Israel.

133 Julius Severus, governor of Britain, is sent to Palestine to crush the revolt.

135 End of the Jewish revolt; death of Bar-Kokhba and Akiba Ben-Joseph.

Final Diaspora (dispersion) of the Jews.

138 Antoninus Pius, Emperor of Rome (to 161).

150 Claudius Ptolemy completes his *Geographia.*

161 Marcus Aurelius, Roman Emperor (to 180).

166 The Emperor Huan Ti receives gifts from Marcus Aurelius.

Serious outbreak of plague in the Empire until 167.

180 First African Christians are martyred at Scillium. Commodus, son of Marcus Aurelius, Emperor of Rome (to 192).

189 Reign of Hsien-Ti, last of the Han emperors (to 220); government is in the hands of military dictators.

193 Pertinax chosen emperor, but is murdered by the Praetorian Guard, who choose Didius Julian instead.

Septimus Severus becomes emperor of Rome (to 211), seizes Rome, and ends Julian's reign after two months; Julian is executed.

197 Clodius Albinus, governor of Britain, another claimant to the imperial throne, is killed by Severus at the battle of Lyon.

208 Severus goes to defend Britain, and repairs Hadrian's Wall.

211 Caracalla, Severus's eldest son, Emperor of Rome (to 217).
212 Caracalla murders his brother and rival, Geta. Edict of Caracalla extends citizenship to almost all freemen in the Empire.
217 Macrinus, Emperor of Rome (to 218).
218 Elagabalus, Emperor of Rome (to 222); his mother, Julia Maesa, actually rules.
220 Period of the Three Kingdoms in China (until 265).
222 Alexander Severus, Emperor of Rome (to 235).
227 Ardashir founds new Persian Empire.
230 Emperor Sujin, first known ruler of Japan.
235 Maximinus, Emperor of Rome (to 238).
238 Gordian III, Emperor of Rome (to 244).
244 Philip the Arabian, Emperor of Rome (to 249).
249 Decius, Emperor of Rome (to 251).
250 Decius orders persecution of the Christians; emperor-worship is made compulsory.
251 Gallus, Emperor of Rome (to 253); following Decius's death in battle with the Goths.
253 Valerian, Emperor of Rome (to 259), with his son Gallienus as co-Emperor.
259 Shapur I of Persia captures Valerian in battle; Valerian dies in captivity.
Gallienus, Emperor of Rome (to 268); period of the Thirty Tyrants (pretenders to the throne).
265 China reunited under Western Chin Dynasty until 317.
268 Goths sack Athens, Corinth, and Sparta.
Claudius II, Emperor of Rome (to 270).
270 Aurelianus, Emperor of Rome (to 275).
275 Tacitus, Emperor of Rome; is killed by his troops in 276.
276 Probus, Emperor of Rome; is killed in 282 by soldiers who object to doing peaceful work.
282 Carus, Emperor of Rome; is killed in battle in 283 by his own troops.
284 Diocletian, Emperor of Rome (to 305).
286 Diocletian divides the Empire: he rules the East and Maximian the West.
287 Revolt by Carausius, commander of the Roman British fleet, who rules Britain as emperor until murdered by Allectus, a fellow rebel, in 293.
303 Diocletian orders a general persecution of the Christians.
305 Diocletian and Maximian abdicate; a power struggle follows.
306 Constantine I, the Great, Emperor in the East (to 337).
308 Maxentius, son of Maximian, Emperor in the West (to 312).
312 Constantine defeats and kills Maxentius at battle of Milvian Bridge; Constantine is converted to Christianity.
313 Edict of Toleration proclaimed at Milan; Constantine allows Christianity in the Empire.
320 Chandragupta I, ruler in northern India (to 330); foundation of the Gupta Dynasty.
324 Constantine reunites the Roman Empire.
330 Constantine inaugurates new city of Constantinople, on the site of Byzantium, as capital of the Roman Empire.
337 Constantine is baptized a Christian on his deathbed. Joint rule of Constantine's three sons:

Constantine II (to 340); Constans (to 350); Constantius (to 361).
350 Christianity reaches Ethiopia.
351 Constantius reunites the Roman Empire. Julian attempts to reintroduce paganism instead of Christianity.
363 Jovianus, Emperor of Rome (to 364); he surrenders Mesopotamia to the Persians.
364 Valentine, Emperor of Rome (to 375).
Valens, Emperor in the East (to 378).
369 Roman general Theodosius drives the Picts and Scots out of Roman Britain.
370 Huns from Asia invade Europe.
372 Buddhism is introduced into Korea.
375 Gratian, Emperor of Rome (to 383).
Chandragupta II, Emperor of the Gupta Empire in northern India (to 415).
378 Valens, Emperor in the East, is defeated and killed by the Goths at Adrianople.
379 Theodosius the Great, Roman Emperor in the East (to 395).
383 Magnus Maximus, Emperor in the West (to 388); he conquers Spain and Gaul.
Roman legions begin to leave Britain.
388 Theodosius captures Magnus Maximus and executes him.
394 Theodosius briefly reunites the Roman Empire.
395 Honorius, Emperor in the West (to 423); his brother Arcadius, Emperor in the East (to 408). Stilicho, Vandal leader of the Roman forces (to 397), drives the Visigoths out of Greece.
401 Innocent I, Pope (to 417); he claims universal jurisdiction over the Roman Church.
406 Vandals and other barbarians overrun Gaul.
407 The first Mongol Empire, founded by the Avars (until 553).
Last Roman troops withdraw from Britain; Romano-Britons are left to fend for themselves.
410 The Goths under Alaric sack Rome.
425 Valentinian III, Emperor in the West (to 455).
Raids by Angles, Saxons, and Jutes on Britain.
429 Vandal kingdom in northern Africa until 535.
432 St Patrick begins mission to Ireland.
433 Attila, ruler of the Huns (to 453).
439 Vandals under Gaiseric capture Carthage.
440 Leo the Great, Pope (to 461).
449 The Jutes under Hengest and Horsa conquer Kent, in southern Britain.
451 Attila invades Gaul; repulsed by Franks, Alemanni, and Romans at battle of Châlons.
452 Attila invades northern Italy.
455 Gaiseric and the Vandals sack Rome.
465 White Huns dominate northern India.
471 Theodoric the Great, King of the Ostrogoths (to 526).
475 Romulus Augustus, last Roman Emperor in the West (to 476).
476 Goths under Odovacar depose Romulus Augustus; end of the Western Empire.
477 Budhagupta, last important Gupta Emperor in northern India (to 495).
481 Clovis, King of the Franks (to 511).
493 Theodoric the Great, King of all Italy.
496 Clovis is converted to Christianity.
503 Britons under war leader Arthur defeat Saxons at Mount Badon.
War between Byzantine Empire and Persia.

507 Franks conquer the Visigoths in southern France.

511 Death of Clovis; the Frankish Empire is divided among his four sons.

524 War between Byzantine Empire and Persia (ends 531).

527 Justinian, Byzantine Emperor (to 565).

529 Justinian has all the Empire's laws codified in three volumes (finished in 565).

533 So-called 'Eternal Peace' is signed between Byzantine Empire and Persia.

534 The Byzantine general Belisarius conquers the Vandal kingdom of North Africa.
The Franks conquer Burgundy.

535 Byzantine forces begin to reconquer Italy, which takes until 554.

540 New war breaks out between the Byzantine Empire and Persia; lasts until 562.

542 Epidemic of plague in the Empire (ends 546).

550 St David takes Christianity to Wales.

552 Buddhism is introduced into Japan.

553 Justinian reforms the administration of Egypt.

554 Byzantine armies conquer south-eastern Spain.

562 End of effective Japanese power in Korea.

563 Irish monk St Columba founds a monastery on island of Iona and begins conversion of the Picts to Christianity.

565 Justin II, nephew of Justinian, Byzantine Emperor (to 578).

568 Lombards conquer northern Italy; kingdom is founded by Alcuin.

570 Muhammad, founder of Islam, born at Mecca.

572 Persians dominate Arabia (until 628).
War between Byzantium and Persia (ends 591).

581 Wen Ti, formerly chief minister of the Chou, founds the Sui Dynasty in China.

584 Foundation of the Anglo-Saxon kingdom of Mercia in England.

587 Visigoths in Spain are converted to Christianity.

589 Arabs, Khazars, and Turks invade Persia, but are defeated.
Wen Ti conquers the southern Ch'en and re-unites China.

590 Gregory I, the Great, Pope (to 604).

593 Suiko, Empress of Japan (to 628).

597 St Augustine lands in England and converts the kingdom of Kent to Christianity.

605 Grand Canal built in China (finished 610).

606 Harsha, Emperor in northern India (to 647).

610 Vision of Muhammad.

618 T'ang Dynasty in China (to 907), founded by T'ai Tsu; murder of Yang Ti 'The Shady', last of the Sui emperors.

620 Vikings begin invading Ireland.

622 The Hegira: Muhammad flees from Mecca to Yathrib (now Medina).

624 Muhammad marries Aisha.
Buddhism becomes the established religion of Japan.

625 Persian attack on Constantinople fails.
Muhammad begins dictating the *Koran*.

626 Emperor Heraclius I of Byzantium expels the Persians from Egypt.

627 Heraclius defeats the Persians at Nineveh.

T'ai Tsung, the Great, Emperor of China (to 649); period of military conquest and patronage of arts and letters.

630 Muhammad captures Mecca, and sets out the principles of Islam.

632 Death of Muhammad; is succeeded as leader of Islam by his father-in-law, Abu Bekr, first Caliph (to 634).

633 Mercians under Penda defeat Northumbrians.

634 Omar I, Caliph at Mecca (to 644): beginning of Islamic Holy War against Persians.

635 Muslims begin conquest of Syria (to 641) and Persia (to 642).

638 Muslims capture Jerusalem.

639 Muslims begin conquest of Egypt (to 642).

642 Mercians under Penda again defeat the Northumbrians.

645 Byzantine forces recapture Alexandria, whose people rise against the Arabs.
The Taikwa edict of reform nationalizes land in Japan and reorganizes the government; period of imitation of Chinese way of life.

646 The Arabs recapture Alexandria.

649 The Arabs conquer Cyprus.

655 Battle of the Masts: Arab fleet defeats Byzantine fleet off Alexandria – first major Arab naval victory.
Oswy, King of Northumbria, defeats and kills Penda of Mercia.

661 Omayyad Dynasty in Islam (lasts until 750) is founded by Muawiya, Caliph to 680.

663 Japanese finally withdraw from Korea.

664 Synod of Whitby: Oswy abandons the Celtic Christian Church and accepts the faith of Rome; decline of the Celtic Church.

668 Korea is reunited under the kingdom of Silla; the Silla Period (to 935).

669 The Greek monk Theodore of Tarsus is sent to England as Archbishop of Canterbury to reorganize the Church in England.

673 Arabs besiege Constantinople until 678 without success.

674 Arab eastward conquest reaches the river Indus, in modern Pakistan.

675 Bulgars begin settling south of the river Danube, founding their first empire.

687 Pepin the Younger, mayor of the palace, unites the Frankish kingdom by a victory at Tertry.
The Arabs destroy Carthage.

700 The Arabs capture Tunis; Christianity in North Africa is almost exterminated.
Thuringia becomes part of the Frankish kingdom.
The Psalms are translated into Anglo-Saxon; production of the Lindisfarne Gospels.

707 Muslims capture Tangier.

710 Justinian II confirms papal privileges.
Roderic, last Visigothic king in Spain (to 711).

711 The Moors (Arabs and Berbers from Morocco) invade Spain; Roderic is defeated and the Visigothic monarchy ends.

712 Muslims establish a state in Sind, now in Pakistan.

716 Second Arab siege of Constantinople (until 717); it fails.

718 Visigothic prince, Pelayo, founds kingdom of

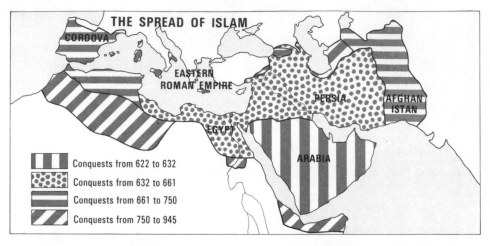

THE SPREAD OF ISLAM

CORDOVA

EASTERN ROMAN EMPIRE

PERSIA

AFGHAN ISTAN

EGYPT

ARABIA

	Conquests from 622 to 632
	Conquests from 632 to 661
	Conquests from 661 to 750
	Conquests from 750 to 945

Above: With astonishing speed the Muslim Arabs conquered a great empire and spread not only their religion but also their way of life.

Right: This map shows the extent of the Vikings' voyages during their great period of expansion from 790 to 1080.

the Asturias in Spanish mountains; the Moors now hold most of the rest of Spain and Portugal, and advance northwards.
Christians defeat Moors in Spain at battle of Covadonga.
726 King Ine of Wessex first levies 'Peter's Pence', tax to support a college in Rome.
731 Venerable Bede, British monk, completes his history of the Church in England.
732 Charles Martel, mayor of the palace and real ruler of the Franks, defeats the Moors at Tours, halting northward advance.
735 Death of the Venerable Bede.
737 Charles Martel again defeats the Moors at Narbonne.
741 Pepin the Short succeeds his father, Charles Martel, as mayor of the palace.
746 Greeks retake Cyprus from the Arabs.
751 Pepin the Short is crowned King of the Franks, founding the Carolingian Dynasty.
Arabs defeat the Chinese at Samarkand.
Lombards under Aistulf capture Ravenna from the Byzantine Empire.
756 Abd-al-Rahman ibn Mu' awiya establishes the Omayyad Dynasty at Córdoba, Spain.
Pepin leads an army to protect Pope Stephen III from the Lombards; formation of the Papal States in Italy.
757 Offa, King of Mercia (to 796); he builds Offa's Dyke to keep out the Welsh.
771 Charlemagne (Charles the Great), son of Pepin, sole King of the Franks (to 814).
772 Charlemagne subdues Saxony and converts it to Christianity.
773 Charlemagne annexes the Lombard kingdom.
778 Moors and Basques defeat the Franks at Roncesvalles, in the Pyrenees.
779 Offa, King of Mercia, becomes King of all England.
782 Charlemagne summons the monk and scholar Alcuin of York to head the palace school at Aachen; revival of learning in Europe.

786 Harun al-Raschid, Caliph at Baghdad (to 809).
787 Council of Nicaea orders resumed worship of images in the Church.
Danes invade Britain for the first time.
788 Charlemagne annexes Bavaria.
796 Death of Offa; end of Mercian supremacy in England.
800 Pope Leo III crowns Charlemagne in Rome as Holy Roman Emperor of the West.
Vikings invade Germany.
802 Egbert, King of Wessex (to 839).
814 Louis the Pious, son of Charlemagne, Emperor and King of the Franks (to 840).
The Arabs adopt Indian numerals (0–9).
828 Egbert of Wessex is recognized as overlord of other English kings.
838 Louis the Pious divides his empire among his sons Lothair, Louis the German, and Charles the Bald.
839 Ethelwulf, son of Egbert, King of Wessex (to 858).
840 Lothair I, Emperor of the Franks (to 855); his brothers are allied against him.
Mojmir forms a confederation of Slav tribes in Bohemia, Moravia, Slovakia, Hungary, and Transylvania.
843 Treaty of Verdun redivides the Frankish Empire; Louis the German rules east of the Rhine, Charles the Bald rules France, Lothair rules Italy, Provence, Burgundy, Lorraine.
844 Kenneth MacAlpine, King of the Scots, conquers the Picts; founds a unified Scotland.
850 Acropolis of Zimbabwe in Rhodesia is built.
855 Louis II, son of Lothair, Emperor (to 875); Lothair's lands are again divided.
856 Main tide of Viking assaults on England until 875.
858 Ethelbald, eldest son of Ethelwulf, King of Wessex (to 860).
860 Ethelbert, second son of Ethelwulf, King of Wessex (to 865).

Viking journeys
— — — **Eric the Red**
········· **Leif Ericsson?**

861 Vikings discover Iceland.
862 Rurik with the Viking tribe of Russ seizes power in northern Russia, founding Novgorod.
865 Ethelred I, third son of Ethelwulf, King of Wessex (to 871).
Russian Vikings attack Constantinople.
Major Viking force invades England, conquering Northumbria, East Anglia, and Mercia.
867 The Photian Schism: the Byzantine Church under Photius, Patriarch of Constantinople, challenges the authority of the Pope.
869 The Arabs capture Malta.
871 The Danes attack Wessex; are defeated by Ethelred at Ashdown.
Alfred the Great, last son of Ethelwulf, King of Wessex (to 891).
874 Vikings settle in Iceland.
875 Charles the Bald, Emperor (to 877); anarchy follows his death.
878 Alfred decisively defeats the Danes at Edington; by the Treaty of Wedmore England is divided between Wessex in the south and the Danes in the north – the Danelaw.
880 Byzantine Emperor Basil recovers Italy from the Arabs.
881 Charles III, the Fat, Emperor and King of Germany, becomes King of the Franks, reuniting Charlemagne's empire.
886 Alfred captures London from the Danes.
891 Alfred founds the Anglo-Saxon Chronicle, history of England.
893 Charles the Simple, King of France (to 929).
899 Edward the Elder, King of Wessex (to 924).
Magyars from the East invade Moravia.
900 Alfonso III, the Great, of Castile begins to reconquer Spain from the Moors.
Mayas emigrate to the Yucatán peninsula of Mexico.
Hausa kingdom of Daura founded in Nigeria.
Bulgars accept the Eastern Orthodox religion.
901 Edward the Elder takes the title 'King of the Angles and Saxons'.

906 Magyars begin invading Germany.
907 End of T'ang Dynasty in China is followed by civil war until 960.
Mongols begin their capture of Inner Mongolia and parts of northern China (completed 1123).
910 Abbey of Cluny founded in France.
911 Viking Rollo (Hrolf the Ganger) granted Normandy by the Franks, who are unable to dislodge him from France.
912 Rollo baptized a Christian as Robert.
913 Edward the Elder recaptures Essex from the Danes.
918 State of Korgo founded in Korea.
919 Henry I, the Fowler, King of Germany (to 936).
920 Golden Age of the Empire of Ghana begins.
922 Fatimid Dynasty seize Morocco.
924 Athelstan, son of Edward the Elder, becomes king of Wessex and effective ruler of most of England (to 939).
926 Athelstan annexes Northumbria, and forces the kings of Wales, Strathclyde, the Picts, and the Scots to submit to him.
929 Murder of King Wenceslas of Bohemia.
932 Wood-block printing adopted in China for mass-producing classical books.
935 Koryo Period in Korea (to 1392); country under the control of state of Koryo.
936 Otto I, the Great, son of Henry the Fowler, King of Germany (to 973).
937 Battle of Brunanburh: Athelstan defeats alliance of Scots, Celts, Danes, and Vikings, and takes the title of 'King of all Britain'.
939 Edmund, brother of Athelstan, King of England (to 946).
First of a series of civil wars breaks out in Japan.
942 Malcolm I, King of Scots (to 953).
945 Dunstan becomes abbot of Glastonbury.
The Scots annex Cumberland and Westmorland from the English.
946 Edred, younger brother of Edmund, King of England (to 955); Dunstan his chief minister.

950 Otto I conquers Bohemia.

Kupe, great Maori (Polynesian) navigator, discovers New Zealand on canoe voyage.

951 Otto campaigns in Italy.

955 Battle of the Lechfeld: Otto defeats the Magyars and ends their westward advance.

Edwy, son of Edmund, King of England (to 959).

956 Edwy sends Dunstan into exile.

957 Mercians and Northumbrians rebel against Edwy.

959 Edgar the Peaceful, younger brother of Edwy, King of England (to 975).

Dunstan recalled from exile; becomes Archbishop of Canterbury.

960 Sung Dynasty in China (to 1275).

Mieszko I, first ruler of Poland (to 992).

961 Otto I undertakes a second expedition to Italy to protect Pope John XII (ends 964).

962 Pope John XII crowns Otto as Emperor in Rome; revival of the Empire in the West.

St Bernard's Hospice founded in Switzerland.

966 Otto's third expedition to Italy (to 972): his son, Otto II, crowned as future emperor.

971 Kenneth II, King of Scots (to 995).

973 Otto II, King and Emperor (to 983).

975 Edward the Martyr, son of Edgar, King of England (to 978).

978 The Chinese begin compiling an encyclopedia of 1000 volumes.

Edward the Martyr murdered at Corfe Castle.

Ethelred II, the Redeless (ill-counselled), younger brother of Edward the Martyr, King of England (to 1016).

980 Arabs begin settling along the eastern coast of Africa.

The Danes renew their raids on England, attacking Chester and Southampton.

981 Viking explorer Eric the Red, exiled from Iceland, settles in a land he names Greenland to attract other colonists.

985 Sweyn Forkbeard, King of Denmark (to 1014).

987 Hugh Capet elected King of France (to 996); foundation of the Capetian Dynasty.

988 Vladimir of Kiev introduces Eastern Orthodox religion into his lands.

991 Battle of Maldon: Byrhtnoth of Essex defeated by Danish invaders.

Ethelred II buys off the Danes with 10,000 pounds of silver.

992 Ethelred makes a truce with Duke Richard I of Normandy.

Boleslaw the Brave, son of Mieszko, King of Poland (to 1025).

993 Olaf Skutkonung, first Christian King of Sweden (to 1024).

994 Danes under Sweyn and Norwegians under Olaf Trygvesson sail up river Thames and besiege London; bought off by Ethelred.

995 Japanese literary and artistic golden age under the rule of Fujiwara Michinaga (to 1028).

Olaf Trygvesson returns to Norway, deposes Haakon the Great, and makes himself king.

996 Richard II, Duke of Normandy (to 1027).

Robert II, the Pious, son of Hugh Capet, King of France (to 1031).

998 Stephen I (St Stephen), first King of Hungary (to 1038).

Mahmud, Turkish ruler of Ghazni (to 1030), founds empire in northern India and eastern Afghanistan.

999 Bagauda, first King of Kano, in northern Nigeria.

The Poles conquer Silesia.

1000 The Viking Biarni Heriulfsson, blown off course, sights coast of North America.

Battle of Svolder: Sweyn kills Olaf of Norway and annexes Norway to Denmark.

Ethelred II ravages Cumberland.

Gunpowder perfected by Chinese about now.

1002 Leif Ericsson, son of Eric the Red, leads an expedition to the West; journeys down coast of North America possibly as far as Maryland.

Ethelred marries Emma, sister of Duke Richard of Normandy.

Massacre of St Brice's Day: Ethelred orders the slaughter of all Danish settlers and mercenaries in southern England.

1003 Sweyn and an army of Norsemen land in England and wreak a terrible vengeance.

1007 Ethelred buys two years' peace from the Danes for 36,000 pounds of silver.

1012 The Danes sack Canterbury: bought off for 48,000 pounds of silver.

1013 Sweyn lands in England and is proclaimed king; Ethelred flees to Normandy.

1014 The English recall Ethelred II as king on the death of Sweyn; Canute retreats to Denmark.

1015 Canute again invades England; war between Danes and Saxons.

1016 Edmund Ironside, son of Ethelred II, King of England; he and Canute divide the kingdom, Canute holds the north and Edmund Wessex; Edmund is assassinated.

Canute, King of England (to 1035).

Olaf II, King of Norway (to 1028).

1017 Canute divides England into four earldoms.

1018 Mahmud of Ghazni pillages the sacred city of Muttra, in India.

1019 Canute marries Emma of Normandy, widow of Ethelred II.

1021 Caliph al-Hakim proclaims himself divine, and founds the Druse sect.

1024 Conrad II, German King and Holy Roman Emperor (to 1039).

1027 Robert le Diable, Duke of Normandy (to 1035).

1028 Zoë, Empress of Byzantine Empire (to 1050). Canute conquers Norway; his son Sweyn becomes king of that country.

1030 Olaf tries to regain throne of Norway; is killed at battle of Stiklestad.

1031 Henry I, King of France (to 1060).

1034 Duncan becomes King of Scots (to 1040).

1035 Death of Canute; his possessions are divided. William, bastard son of Robert, becomes Duke of Normandy (to 1087).

Harold I, Harefoot, King of England (to 1040).

Hardicanute, King of Denmark (to 1042).

1039 Henry III, the Black, Holy Roman Emperor (to 1056).

1040 Hardicanute, King of England (to 1042); he dies of drink.

Macbeth, Mormaer of Moray, kills Duncan in battle at Elgin. Macbeth, King of Scots (to 1057).

1042 Edward the Confessor, son of Ethelred II,

King of England (to 1066); power is in the hands of Earl Godwin and his sons.

Magnus the Good, son of Olaf II, King of Denmark (to 1047).

1046 Harald Haardraada, King of Norway (to 1066).

1047 Sweyn II, Canute's nephew, King of Denmark (to 1076).

1051 Earl Godwin exiled (until 1052).

1052 Godwin returns to England with a fleet and wins back his power.

Edward the Confessor founds Westminster Abbey, near London.

1053 Death of Godwin; his son Harold succeeds him as Earl of Wessex.

1054 Abdallah ben Yassim begins the Muslim conquest of West Africa.

Final break between the Byzantine Empire and the Roman Church; Eastern Church is now completely independent.

1055 Harold's brother Tostig becomes Earl of Northumbria.

1056 Henry IV, Holy Roman Emperor (to 1106); his mother, Agnes, acts as regent until 1065.

1057 Battle of Lumphanan: Malcolm Canmore ('Big head'), son of Duncan, defeats and kills Macbeth. Lulach, stepson of Macbeth, King of Scots (to 1058).

1058 Boleslav II, the Bold, King of Poland (to 1079); conqueror of Upper Slovakia.

Malcolm Canmore, King of Scots (to 1093), having killed Lulach in battle.

1060 Philip I, King of France (to 1108).

1061 Muslim Almoravid Dynasty in North Africa; later conquers Spain.

Malcolm Canmore invades Northumbria.

1062 Yusuf ben Tashfin founds Marrakesh, in Morocco.

1063 Harold and Tostig subdue Wales.

1064 Harold is shipwrecked in Normandy, and swears a solemn oath to support William of Normandy's claim to England.

1065 Northumbria rebels against Tostig, who is exiled.

1066 Harold II is crowned king the day after Edward the Confessor dies.

Tostig and Harold Haardraada of Norway invade England; Harold defeats them at the battle of Stamford Bridge, killing both.

Battle of Hastings, 19 days after battle of Stamford Bridge: William of Normandy with a motley invasion force defeats and kills Harold II.

William I, the Conqueror, first Norman King of England (to 1087).

1067 Work is begun on building the Tower of London.

1068 Shen Tsung, Emperor of China (to 1085); radical reforms are carried through by his minister Wang An-shih.

The Norman Conquest continues until 1069: William subdues the north of England (the 'Harrying of the North'): the region is laid waste.

1069 Famine in Egypt (until 1072).

1070 Hereward the Wake begins a Saxon revolt in the Fens of eastern England.

1071 Battle of Manzikert: the Seljuk leader Alp Arslan defeats the Byzantines and conquers most of Asia Minor.

1072 William invades Scotland, and also receives the submission of Hereward the Wake.

The Norman conquest of Sicily (ends 1091).

Alfonso VI, King of Castile (to 1109).

1073 Gregory VII (Hildebrand of Soana), Pope (to 1085).

1075 Seljuk leader Malik Shah conquers Syria and Palestine.

Dispute between Pope and Emperor over who should appoint bishops.

1076 Synod of Worms: bishops declare Pope Gregory deposed.

Gregory excommunicates Emperor Henry IV.

1077 Henry, fearful for his throne, does penance to Gregory at Canossa.

Civil war in the Holy Roman Empire (ends 1080)

Almoravid Dynasty in Ghana (until 1087).

1080 Canute IV, King of Denmark (to 1086).

Gregory again excommunicates Henry IV and declares him deposed.

1083 Henry IV storms Rome.

A detail from the Bayeux tapestry. It tells the story of the battle of Hastings at which William of Normandy defeated Harold Godwinsson who had been elected king of England. When the Normans landed Harold was in the north-east, fighting off an attack by his brother and King Harold Haardraada of Norway. He hastened south with only his bodyguard and raised fresh, inexperienced troops who proved unable to withstand the Normans. William was crowned king on Christmas Day 1066.

1084 Robert Guiscard, Duke of Paulia, forces Henry to retreat to Germany.

1085 Alfonso VI captures Toledo from the Moors.

1086 Canute IV of Denmark is assassinated; Danish threat to England is lifted.

Domesday Book is completed in England.

1087 William II, Rufus, King of England (to 1100); his elder brother Robert is Duke of Normandy.

1090 Hasan ibn al-Sabbah, first 'Old Man of the Mountain', founds the Assassin sect in Persia.

1093 Donald Bane, King of Scots (to 1097), following the death of his brother, Malcolm III, in battle against the English.

1096 First Crusade begins, following an appeal by Pope Urban II to free the Holy Places.

1097 Edgar, second son of Malcolm Canmore, King of Scotland (to 1107); he defeats Donald Bane with the assistance of William II of England.

1098 St Robert founds the first Cistercian monastery at Cîteaux, France.

Crusaders defeat the Saracens (Muslims) at Antioch.

1099 Crusaders capture Jerusalem; Godfrey of Bouillon is elected King of Jerusalem.

1100 Henry I, youngest son of William the Conqueror, King of England (to 1135), following assassination of William Rufus.

Colonization of Polynesian islands under way.

1104 Crusaders capture Acre.

1106 Henry V, Holy Roman Emperor (to 1125).

Henry I defeats his brother Robert, Duke of Normandy, at battle of Tinchebrai; Robert remains captive for life.

1107 Alexander I, younger brother of Edgar, King of Scotland (to 1124).

1108 Louis VI, King of France (to 1137).

1109 War between England and France (until 1113).

1111 Emperor Henry V forces Pope Paschal II to acknowledge power of the emperor.

1113 Founding of the Order of St John is formally acknowledged by the papacy.

1114 Matilda (Maud), daughter of Henry I of England, marries Emperor Henry V.

1115 Stephen II, King of Hungary (to 1131).

St Bernard founds the Abbey of Clairvaux, France, and becomes its first abbot.

1119 Hugues de Payens founds the Order of Knights Templars.

1120 William, heir of Henry I of England, is drowned in wreck of the 'White Ship'.

1122 Concordat of Worms: conference of German princes ends the dispute between pope and emperor over appointing bishops.

1123 Death of Omar Khayyám, Persian poet.

1124 David I, younger brother of Alexander I, King of Scotland (to 1153).

1125 Lothair of Saxony elected Holy Roman Emperor (to 1137).

1126 Alfonso VII, King of Castile, Spain (to 1157).

1128 Alfonso Henriques, Count of Portugal; makes Portugal independent of Spain by 1143.

1129 Empress Matilda, widow of Henry V, marries Geoffrey the Handsome, Count of Anjou, nicknamed 'Plantagenet'.

1130 Almohad Dynasty, founded by the preacher Ibn Tumart, comes to power in Morocco (until 1169).

1135 Stephen of Boulogne seizes the English crown on the death of his uncle, Henry I; civil war breaks out.

1137 Louis VII, King of France (to 1180).

1138 Conrad III, Holy Roman Emperor (to 1152).

Battle of the Standard: defeat of David I of Scotland, fighting on behalf of Matilda in English civil war.

1139 Matilda lands in England.

The Second Lateran Council ends a schism in the Church following the illegal election of Anacletus II as rival to Innocent II.

1141 Matilda captures Stephen at the battle of Lincoln, and reigns disastrously as queen; she is driven out by a popular rising, and Stephen restored.

1143 Alfonso becomes King of Portugal (to 1185).

1145 The Almohades begin conquest of Moorish Spain which continues until 1150.

1147 The Second Crusade, following an appeal by St Bernard of Clairvaux (ends 1149).

1148 The Crusaders fail to capture Damascus.

Matilda leaves England for the last time.

1151 Toltec Empire in Mexico comes to an end.

Death of Geoffrey of Anjou.

1152 Marriage of Louis VII of France and Eleanor of Aquitaine is annulled on grounds of blood relationship.

Eleanor marries Henry of Anjou, allying Aquitaine to his lands of Anjou and Normandy, two months after her divorce.

Frederick I Barbarossa, Holy Roman Emperor (to 1190).

1153 Malcolm IV, 'The Maiden', grandson of David I, King of Scotland (to 1165).

Henry of Anjou, son of Matilda, invades England and forces Stephen to make him heir to the English throne.

1154 Henry II, King of England (to 1189); he also rules more than half of France.

Pope Adrian IV (to 1159) (Nicholas Breakspear, the only English pope).

1155 Henry II appoints the Archdeacon of Canterbury, Thomas à Becket, as Chancellor.

Adrian IV grants Henry II the right to rule Ireland.

1156 Civil wars ravage Japan (until 1185).

1158 Alfonso VIII, King of Castile (to 1214).

1159 Alexander III, Pope (to 1181).

Henry II levies scutage – payment in cash instead of military service.

1161 Explosives are used in China at the battle of Ts'ai-shih.

1162 Becket is appointed Archbishop of Canterbury and at once quarrels with Henry II over the Church's rights.

1164 Constitutions of Clarendon: restatement of laws governing trial of ecclesiastics in England; Becket is forced to flee to France.

1165 William the Lion, younger brother of Malcolm IV, King of Scotland (to 1214).

1167 Amalric, King of Jerusalem, captures Cairo.

1168 Arabs recapture Cairo.

1169 Saladin (Salah-al-Din Yusuf ibn-Ayyub), vizier of Egypt (to 1193); sultan from 1174.

Right: The crusader stronghold Krak des Chevaliers in Syria.

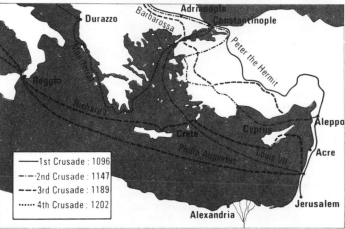

In 1095 Pope Urban called the first Crusade to free the Holy Land from Muslim control. It was successful but the Muslims soon regained the area and later crusades failed to drive them out. The map shows routes taken by crusaders like the knight above.

1170 Becket is reconciled with Henry II; returns to Canterbury; is murdered by four knights after Henry's hasty words against him.
1171 Henry II formally annexes Ireland.
1173 Rebellion of Henry's eldest sons, Henry, Richard, and Geoffrey, supported by their mother, Eleanor of Aquitaine.
Thomas à Becket canonized.
1174 Saladin conquers Syria.
1177 Baldwin IV of Jerusalem defeats Saladin at Montgisard.
1179 Grand Assize of Windsor; increasing power of royal courts in England.
Saladin besieges Tyre.
1180 Truce between Baldwin IV and Saladin.
Philip II, King of France (to 1223).
1182 Philip II banishes the Jews from France.
1185 Sancho I, King of Portugal (to 1211).
Kamakura period in Japan (until 1333).
1187 Saladin captures Jerusalem.
1189 Richard I, Coeur de Lion, eldest surviving son of Henry II, King of England (to 1199).

Last recorded Norse visit to North America.
Third Crusade (ends 1192): leaders are Frederick Barbarossa, Philip of France and Richard of England.
1190 Mongol leader Temujin begins to create an empire in eastern Asia.
Frederick Barbarossa is drowned on his way to Palestine.
Henry VI, Holy Roman Emperor (to 1197).
Lalibela, Emperor of Ethiopia (to 1225).
1191 Richard I conquers Cyprus and captures the city of Acre.
1192 Richard I captures Jaffa; makes peace with Saladin; on the way home he is captured by his enemy, Duke Leopold of Austria.
Minamoto Yoritomo, Shogun of Japan.
1193 Death of Saladin.
Leopold hands Richard over to Emperor Henry VI, who demands a ransom.
Muslims capture Bihar and Bengal.
Al-Aziz Imad al-Din, successor to Saladin (to 1198).
1194 Emperor Henry VI conquers Sicily.
Richard is ransomed and returned to England.
1196 Marimid Dynasty in Morocco (lasts until 1464); founded at Fez.
Pedro II, King of Aragon (to 1213).
1197 Ottakar I, King of Bohemia (to 1230).
Civil war follows the death of Henry VI in Germany.

1198 Otto IV, Holy Roman Emperor (to 1212).
Innocent III, Pope (to 1216).
1199 John Lackland, youngest son of Henry II,
King of England (to 1216).
1200 Hunac Ceel revolts against the Maya of
Chichén Itzá and sets up a new capital at
Mayapán.
Jews are given special privileges in Morocco.
1202 Famine in Egypt (until 1204).
Fourth Crusade (ends 1204): crusaders, unable
to pay Venice for transport, agree to conquer
on its behalf.
1203 John of England orders the murder of his
nephew Arthur, Duke of Brittany.
1204 Crusaders capture Constantinople and sack
it, installing a Latin ruler.
1206 Temujin is proclaimed Genghis Khan, 'Emperor within the Seas'.
Dynasty of slave kings in India (until 1290).
1207 Pope Innocent III appoints Stephen Langton
Archbishop of Canterbury; John refuses to let
him take office.
1208 Innocent III lays England under interdict.
Crusade against Albigensians, heretical sect in
France (until 1213).
1209 Cambridge University is founded.
Innocent excommunicates John for attacks on
Church property.
1210 Innocent excommunicates Emperor Otto IV.
Francis of Assisi founds the Franciscan Order.
Mongols led by Genghis Khan begin invasion
of China.
1211 Alfonso II, King of Portugal (to 1223).
1212 Frederick II, Holy Roman Emperor (to
1250). Children's Crusade: 30,000 children from
France and Germany set off for Palestine –
probable origin of 'Pied Piper' legend; thousands
are sold into slavery.
1213 Innocent declares John deposed; John hur-
riedly makes peace.
James I, the Conqueror, King of Aragon (to
1276).
1215 Magna Carta: English barons force John to
agree to a statement of their rights.
St Dominic founds the Dominican Order, a
body of preaching friars, at Toulouse.
1216 Henry III becomes king of England at age
nine (to 1272).
1217 Fifth Crusade (ends 1222): it fails to capture
Egypt.
1218 Genghis Khan conquers Persia.
1219 Mongols conquer Bokhara.
Hojo clan rules Japan (until 1333), following the
end of the Minamoto family.
1223 Louis VIII, King of France (to 1226).
Mongols invade Russia.
1224 War between France and England (ends
1227).
1226 Louis IX (St Louis), King of France (to
1270).
1227 Henry III begins personal rule in England.
Genghis Khan dies, and his empire is divided
among his sons.
1228 Sixth Crusade, led by Emperor Frederick II
(ends 1229); Crusaders recapture Jerusalem.
Teutonic Knights begin conquering Prussia.
1229 Ogadai, son of Genghis, is elected khan (to
1241).

1232 Earliest known use of rockets in war between
Mongols and Chinese.
1234 Mongols annex the Chin Empire.
1235 Sundiata Keita, King of Mali (to 1255).
1236 Alexander Nevski, Prince of Novgorod (to
1263).
1240 End of the Empire of Ghana; it is incorporated into the Kingdom of Mali.
Mongols capture Moscow.
Mongols destroy Kiev.
Battle of Neva: Alexander Nevski defeats the
Swedes.
1241 Mongols withdraw from Europe following
the death of Ogadai Khan.
1242 Batu establishes Mongol kingdom of 'The
Golden Horde' on lower Volga River.
1243 Egyptians capture Jerusalem from the
Christians.
1245 Pope Innocent IV calls the Synod of Lyon,
which declares Frederick II deposed.
1247 Bitter war in Italy between Frederick and
papal allies (ends 1250).
1248 Seventh Crusade, led by Louis IX of France
(ends 1270).
1250 Conrad IV, Holy Roman Emperor (to 1254).
Saracens capture Louis IX in Egypt; he is
ransomed.
1253 Ottokar II, the Great, King of Bohemia (to
1278).
1254 The Great Interregnum: bitter struggle for
the Imperial crown (to 1273).
1256 Pope Alexander IV founds the Augustinian
Order from several groups of hermits.
Prince Llewellyn sweeps English from Wales.
1260 Kublai, Mongol leader, is elected khan by
his army at Shan-tu, in China.
Yüan (Mongol) Dynasty in China (until 1368).
1263 Norway gives up the Hebrides to the Scots.
1264 Simon de Montfort and other English barons
defeat Henry III at battle of Lewes.
1265 De Montfort's Parliament: burgesses from
major towns summoned to Parliament for the
first time.
Henry III's son Edward defeats and kills Simon
de Montfort at battle of Evesham.
1268 Muslims from Egypt capture Antioch, held
by the Christians.
Papacy vacant until 1271.
1270 Death of Louis IX of France on Seventh
Crusade.
Philip III, the Bold, King of France (to 1285).
1271 Marco Polo, his father, and his uncle set off
to visit the court of Kublai Khan; return 1295.
1272 Edward I, King of England (to 1307).
1273 Rudolf I, Holy Roman Emperor (to 1291).
1274 Synod of Lyons, called by Pope Gregory X,
recommends that conclaves should be secret to
avoid corruption.
1274 First Mongol invasion of Japan at orders of
Kublai Khan; Mongols fail to gain a foothold.
1275 Marco Polo enters the service of Kublai
Khan.
1276 Innocent V, first Dominican to become pope,
dies five months after election.
Adrian V revokes conclave rules but then dies
five weeks after being elected pope.
1277 English Franciscan philosopher Roger
Bacon is exiled for heresy (until 1292).

1278 Rudolf I defeats and kills Ottokar of Bohemia at battle of the Marchfeld.

1279 Rudolf I surrenders claims to Sicily and the Papal States.

1280 Death of Albertus Magnus, German philosopher and scientist.

1281 Second Mongol invasion of Japan ends in disaster.

1283 Edward I defeats and kills Llewellyn, Prince of Wales, and executes Llewellyn's brother David; conquest of Wales complete.

1285 Philip IV, the Fair, King of France (to 1314).

1286 Margaret, the Maid of Norway, Child Queen of Scotland, in succession to her grandfather Alexander III (to 1290).

burgesses from English shires and towns summoned; first representative Parliament.

1296 Edward I of England deposes John Balliol from Scottish throne.

Interregnum in Scotland (until 1306).

Conflict between Philip IV of France and Pope Boniface VIII over papal powers in France (ends 1303).

1297 Battle of Cambuskenneth: Scottish patriot William Wallace defeats English army.

1298 Edward I defeats Wallace at battle of Falkirk and reconquers Scotland.

Albert I, Holy Roman Emperor (to 1308) following defeat and death of Adolf at battle of Göllheim.

Below: The caravan of the Venetian explorer Marco Polo, from a map based partly on his descriptions. Marco Polo set out for the court of Kublai Khan, Mongol emperor of China, with his father and uncle; they returned to Venice in 1295, laden with rubies and emeralds. Marco dictated the story of his travels and although at the time his tales were dismissed as imaginary, research has confirmed many of them.

Above: Kublai Khan ruled directly over China and was acknowledged Great Khan by other Mongol rulers. The grandson of Genghis Khan, he was a skilled soldier and administrator and his greatness was recognized by his Chinese, Islamic and European contemporaries.

1289 Friar John of Montecorvino becomes the first archbishop of Peking.

1290 Struggle for the succession in Scotland follows the death of Margaret, the Maid of Norway; 13 people claim the throne.

Turkish leader Firuz founds the Khalji Dynasty (until 1320) in Delhi.

Edward I expels all Jews from England.

1291 Saracens (Muslims) capture Acre, last Christian stronghold in Palestine. End of the Crusades. Scots acknowledge Edward I of England as suzerain.

1292 John Balliol, King of Scotland on the nomination of Edward I (to 1296).

Adolf, Count of Nassau, Holy Roman Emperor (to 1298).

1294 Death of Kublai Khan.

Celestine V (the hermit Peter of Morrone), Pope; he resigns after five months.

Boniface VIII, Pope, lawyer, diplomat, and practiser of magic arts (to 1303).

1295 Temur Oljaitu (Ch'eng Tsung), grandson of Kublai Khan, Emperor of China (to 1307).

Model Parliament of Edward I: knights and

1300 Wenceslas II, King of Poland.

1301 Edward I of England invests his baby son Edward as Prince of Wales.

Osman, founder of the Ottoman Turks, defeats the Byzantines.

1302 Battle of Courtrai: burghers of Flanders defeat the flower of French chivalry and save their country from French occupation.

Papal Bull *Unam Sanctam* declares papal authority to be supreme.

1303 Guillaume de Nogaret, emissary of Philip IV of France, captures Pope Boniface VIII at Anagni, Italy, and ill-treats him; the Pope is rescued by the citizens of Anagni, but dies soon after in Rome.

1304 Petrarch, Italian poet, born (dies 1374).

1305 Clement V, Pope (Bertrand de Got, Archbishop of Bordeaux) (to 1314).

The 'Babylonian Captivity': the papal see removed from Rome to Avignon, France (until 1377).

The English capture and execute William Wallace.

1306 Philip IV expels the Jews from France.

New Scottish rebellion against English rule led by Robert Bruce.

Robert I, the Bruce, crowned King of Scotland (to 1329) at Scone.

1307 Edward I dies on march north to crush Robert Bruce.

Edward II, King of England (to 1327).

1308 Henry VII, Holy Roman Emperor (to 1313).

1310 English barons appoint 21 peers – the Lords Ordainers – to manage Edward II's household.

1312 Order of Knights Templars abolished for malpractices.

1314 Battle of Bannockburn: Robert Bruce defeats Edward II and makes Scotland independent.

Louis X, the Quarrelsome, King of France (to 1316).

Louis IV, Holy Roman Emperor (to 1347); civil war with his rival, Frederick of Austria.

1315 Swiss defeat Leopold of Austria at battle of Morgarten.

1316 The papacy sends eight Dominican friars to Ethiopia in search of Prester John, a legendary Christian emperor.

Philip V, the Tall, King of France (to 1322).

1317 France adopts the Salic Law, excluding women from succession to the throne.

1318 Swiss make peace with the Habsburgs.

1320 Tughluk Dynasty in Delhi (until 1413), founded by the Turk Ghidyas-ud-din Tughluk.

1322 Charles IV, the Fair, King of France (to 1328).

1325 Traditional foundation date of Tenochtitlán (now Mexico City) by the Aztecs.

1326 First Polish War: the Teutonic Knights defeat the Poles in 1333.

Queen Isabella and Roger Mortimer sail from France with an army to rebel against Edward II of England.

1327 Parliament declares Edward II deposed, and his son accedes to the throne as Edward III. Edward II is murdered nine months later.

Holy Roman Emperor Louis IV invades Italy and declares Pope John XXII deposed.

1328 Philip VI, King of France (to 1350); first king of the House of Valois.

1329 David II, King of Scotland (to 1371), succeeding his father, Robert Bruce.

1332 Edward Balliol, son of John Balliol, attempts to seize the throne of Scotland, with the help of the English; he is driven back over the border.

1333 Edward III invades Scotland on Balliol's behalf and defeats the Scots at battle of Halidon Hill.

Emperor Daigo II of Japan overthrows the Hojo family of shoguns and sets up period of personal rule (to 1336).

1335 Pope Benedict XII issues reforms of the monastic orders.

1336 Revolution in Japan; Daigo II is exiled.

Ashikaga family rule Japan as shoguns (until 1568); period begins with civil war lasting until 1392.

1337 Edward III of England, provoked by French attacks on his territories in France, declares himself King of France. Beginning of 'The Hundred Years' War' between England and France (ends 1453).

1338 Declaration of Rense: Electors of the Holy Roman Empire declare the empire to be independent from the papacy.

Treaty of Coblenz: alliance between England and the Holy Roman Empire.

1340 Naval victory at Sluys gives England the command of the English Channel.

English Parliament passes four statutes providing that taxation shall be imposed only by Parliament.

1341 Sulaiman, King of Mali (to 1360).

Italian poet Petrarch (Francesco Petrarca) is crowned Poet Laureate at the Capitol in Rome.

1343 Peace of Kalisch gives the Teutonic Knights land, cutting off Poland from access to the Baltic Sea.

1344 First known use of the term Hanseatic League.

1346 Edward III of England invades France with a large army and defeats an even bigger army under Philip VI at the battle of Crécy.

Stephen Dushan, King of the Serbs, is crowned 'Emperor of the Serbs and Greeks'.

Battle of Neville's Cross: David II of Scotland defeated and captured by the English.

1347 The English capture Calais.

The Black Death (bubonic plague) reaches Cyprus from eastern Asia.

Charles IV, Holy Roman Emperor (to 1378).

Italian patriot Cola da Rienzi assumes power in Rome, taking the title of 'tribune'; but is soon driven from office.

1348 Edward III establishes the Order of the Garter.

The Black Death ravages Europe.

Black Death reaches England.

1349 Persecution of the Jews in Germany.

1350 John II, King of France (to 1364).

Pedro the Cruel, King of Castile (to 1369).

1351 The Black Death sweeps Russia.

The English remove the pope's power to give English benefices to foreigners.

1353 Statute of Praemunire: English Parliament forbids appeals to the pope.

1354 Rienzi returns to power in Rome and is killed by his opponents.

1356 The Golden Bull: new constitution for the Holy Roman Empire, providing for seven electors.

Edward the Black Prince, son of Edward III, defeats the French at the battle of Poitiers, capturing King John II.

1357 The French Estates-General, led by Etienne Marcel, attempts a series of reforms.

1358 The *Jacquerie*: revolt by French peasants; suppressed by the Regent Charles, son of John II.

1360 Treaty of Brétigny ends the first stage of the Hundred Years' War; Edward III gives up claim to French throne.

1363 Philip the Bold, son of John II, becomes Duke of Burgundy.

Mongol leader Tamerlane (Timur the Lame) begins the conquest of Asia.

1364 Charles V, the Wise, becomes King of France (to 1380), on the death in London of his father, John II, in captivity.

1367 Confederation of Cologne: 77 Hanse towns prepare for struggle with Denmark.

1368 Rebellion led by Chu Yüan-chang overthrows the Yüan (Mongol) Dynasty in China. Ming Dynasty in China (to 1644).

1369 Tamerlane (Timur the Lame) becomes king of Samarkand.

Second stage of war between England and France begins.

1370 Peace of Stralsund establishes the power of the Hanse towns, with the right to veto Danish kings.

Edward the Black Prince sacks Limoges.

1371 Robert II, King of Scotland (to 1390); the first Stuart monarch.

1372 French troops recapture Poitou and Brittany.

Naval battle of La Rochelle: French regain control of the English Channel.

1373 John of Gaunt, Duke of Lancaster, son of Edward III, leads new English invasion of France.

1374 John of Gaunt returns to England and takes charge of the government; Edward III in his dotage, the Black Prince ill.

1375 Truce of Bruges ends hostilities between England and France.

1376 The Good Parliament in England, called by Edward the Black Prince, introduces many reforms of government.

Death of Edward the Black Prince, aged 45.

The *Civil Dominion* of John Wyclif, an Oxford don, calling for Church reforms.

1377 Richard II, son of the Black Prince, King of England (to 1399).

Pope Gregory XI returns to Rome, ending the 'Babylonian Captivity' in Avignon.

1378 The Great Schism (ends 1417): rival popes elected.

Urban VI, Pope at Rome (to 1389).

Clement VII, antipope at Avignon (to 1394).

Wenceslas IV, Holy Roman Emperor (to 1400).

1380 Charles VI, King of France (to 1422).

1381 Peasants' Revolt in England.

1382 John Wyclif is expelled from Oxford because of his opposition to Church doctrines.

John I, King of Portugal (to 1433), founder of the Avis Dynasty.

The Scots, with a French army, attack England.

1386 Battle of Sempach: Swiss defeat and kill Leopold III of Austria.

John of Gaunt leads an expedition to Castile, which he claims in his wife's name (fails 1388).

1387 Poet Geoffrey Chaucer begins work on *The Canterbury Tales*.

1389 Truce halts fighting between England, and the French and Scots.

Richard II, aged 22, assumes power.

1390 Robert III, King of Scotland (to 1406).

Turks complete conquest of Asia Minor.

1392 The I Dynasty in Korea (to 1910).

Charles VI of France becomes insane.

1394 Prince Henry the Navigator, son of John I of Portugal, pioneer of exploration, born; founds naval institute at Sagres, 1439; dies 1460.

Richard II leads expedition to subdue Ireland; returns to England 1395.

1396 Richard II marries the seven-year-old Princess Isabella of France.

Ottoman Turks conquer Bulgaria.

1397 Union of Kalmar unites Norway, Denmark, and Sweden under one king, Eric of Pomerania.

1398 Tamerlane ravages kingdom of Delhi, 100,000 prisoners massacred; returns home 1399.

Absolute rule of Richard II.

1399 Death of John of Gaunt.

Gaunt's eldest son, Henry of Bolingbroke, lands in Yorkshire with 40 followers, and soon has 60,000 supporters; Richard II is deposed. Bolingbroke becomes Henry IV, King of England (to 1413).

1400 Richard II murdered at Pontefract Castle.

Owen Glendower proclaims himself Prince of Wales and begins rebellion.

Holy Roman Emperor Wenceslas IV is deposed for drunkenness.

1401 Tamerlane conquers Damascus and Baghdad.

1402 Henry IV enters Wales in pursuit of Glendower. Tamerlane overruns most of Ottoman Empire.

1403 Battle of Shrewsbury: rebellion by the Percy family; Henry IV defeats and kills Harry 'Hotspur' Percy.

1405 French soldiers land in Wales to support Glendower; initial successes.

Death of Tamerlane.

1406 Gregory XII, Pope at Rome (to 1415).

James I, King of Scotland (to 1437); captive in England from 1406 to 1423.

Henry, Prince of Wales, defeats Welsh.

1409 Council of Pisa, called to resolve the Great Schism, declares the rival popes deposed and elects a third.

1410 Sigismund, Holy Roman Emperor (to 1437).

Battle of Tannenberg: Ladislaus II of Poland defeats the Teutonic Knights.

John XXIII (Baldassare Cossa), antipope at Pisa (to 1415).

1412 Jeanne d'Arc (Joan of Arc) born; dies 1431.

1413 Henry V, King of England (to 1422).

1414 Council of Constance (until 1417) called by John XXIII, deposes John, persuades Gregory XII to resign, and isolates Benedict XIII.

1415 Henry V invades France, and defeats the French at Agincourt.

1416 Death of Owen Glendower.

1417 Martin V, Pope (to 1431); end of the Great Schism.

1420 Treaty of Troyes: Henry V, acknowledged as heir to the French throne, marries Charles VI's daughter Catherine.

1422 Deaths of Henry V of England and Charles VI of France.

Henry VI, King of England (to 1461).

Charles VII, King of France (to 1461); known as Dauphin until 1429.

1424 John, Duke of Bedford, regent for Henry VI of England, defeats the French at Cravant.

1428 English begin siege of Orléans.

1429 Jeanne d'Arc appointed military commander; raises siege of Orléans. Charles VII crowned King of France at Rheims.

1430 Burgundians capture Jeanne d'Arc and hand her over to the English.

1431 Khmer city of Angkor abandoned.

Jeanne d'Arc burned as a witch at Rouen.

Henry VI of England crowned King of France in Paris.
1434 Cosimo de Medici becomes ruler of Florence.
1437 James I of Scotland murdered at Perth.
James II, King of Scotland (to 1460).
1438 Albert II, Holy Roman Emperor (to 1439).
Inca Empire established in Peru.
1439 Council of Basle deposes Pope Eugene IV.
Felix V, antipope (to 1449).
1440 Frederick III, Holy Roman Emperor (to 1493).
Johannes Gutenberg invents printing from movable type.
1451 Mohammed II, Sultan of Turkey (to 1481).
Christopher Columbus born; dies 1506.
1453 Hundred Years' War ends; England's only French possession is Calais.
Henry VI becomes insane.
Ottoman Turks capture Constantinople; end of the Byzantine Empire and of the Middle Ages.
1454 Richard, Duke of York, is regent of England while Henry VI is insane.
Printing with movable type is perfected in Germany by Johannes Gutenberg.
1455 Henry VI recovers. Richard of York is replaced by Somerset and excluded from the Royal Council.
Wars of the Roses: civil wars in England between royal houses of York and Lancaster (until 1485).
Battle of St Albans: Somerset defeated and killed.
Cadamosto, Venetian sailor, explores the Senegal and Gambia rivers, and discovers Cape Verde Islands (1456).
1456 Turks capture Athens.

1458 Matthias Corvinus, King of Hungary (to 1490).
George Podiebrad, King of Bohemia (to 1471).
1459 Ottoman Turks conquer Serbia.
1460 Battle of Westfield: Richard of York is defeated and killed.
Earl of Warwick (the Kingmaker) captures London for the Yorkists.
Battle of Roxburgh: James II of Scotland is killed.
James III, King of Scotland (to 1488).
Battle of Northampton: Henry VI is captured by Yorkists.
1461 Battles of Mortimer's Cross and Towton: Richard's son, Edward of York, defeats Lancastrians and becomes king.
Edward IV, King of England (to 1483).
Louis XI, King of France (to 1483).
Turks conquer Trebizond, last surviving Greek state.
1462 Ivan III (the Great), Duke of Moscow (to 1505).
Castile captures Gibraltar from Arabs.
1463 Ottoman Turks and Venetians at war (until 1479).
1464 Edward IV marries Elizabeth Woodville.
1465 Henry VI imprisoned by Edward IV.
League of the Public Weal: Dukes of Alençon, Berri, Burgundy, Bourbon, and Lorraine conspire against Louis XI.
1466 Peace of Thorn: Poland gains much of Prussia from the Teutonic Knights.
Warwick's quarrels with Edward IV begin.
Warwick forms alliance with Louis XI.
1467 Charles the Bold becomes Duke of Burgundy, chief rival to Louis XI.

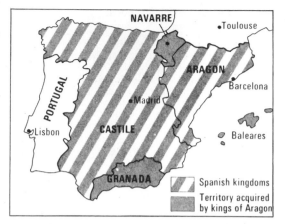

Opposite: Turkish forces storm the walls of Constantinople in 1453. The city fell after a six-week siege, and its capture saw the end of the Byzantine empire. Renamed Istanbul, it became the capital of the great Ottoman empire which stretched through North Africa and the Near East for the next four centuries.

Above left: As the Christians drove the Muslims from Spain a number of kingdoms were formed. By

the mid-15th century two of these, Castile and Aragon, ruled almost all the country and they were united by the marriage of Ferdinand of Aragon with Isabella of Castile. In 1492 they captured Granada, the last Moorish kingdom, and in 1512 Ferdinand annexed Navarre.

Above right: Ivan III of Moscow, known as the Great, laid the foundations of the Russian empire. He was the first to use the title tsar *(emperor).*

Period of civil war begins in Japan and lasts for more than 100 years.

1468 Margaret of York marries Charles the Bold.
Sonni Ali captures Timbuktu and founds the Songhai Empire in West Africa.

1469 Marriage of Ferdinand of Aragon and Isabella of Castile, uniting Spain.

1470 Warwick turns Lancastrian; he defeats Edward IV and restores Henry VI.

1471 Battle of Barnet: Edward IV defeats and kills Warwick.
Henry VI dies, probably murdered, in the Tower of London.
The Portuguese, under Alfonso V, take Tangier from the Muslims.
Vladislav of Poland elected King of Bohemia after the death of Podiebrad.

1472 Venetians destroy Smyrna.
Battle of Otluk-beli: Turks, under Mohammed II, defeat the Persian ruler, Uzun Hasan, chief ally of Venice.
Fernando Po discovered by the Portuguese.

1474 Louis XI goes to war against Charles the Bold. Alliance between Charles the Bold and Edward IV of England.
Triple alliance of Florence, Venice and Milan.
War between Charles the Bold and the Swiss Confederation (ends 1477).
Isabella succeeds to throne of Castile.

1475 Edward IV invades France.
Peace of Piéquigny between England and France.
Birth of Leonardo da Vinci.
Turks conquer the Crimea.

1476 William Caxton sets up printing press at Westminster.

1477 Maximilian, son of Frederick III, marries Mary, daughter of Charles the Bold.
Battle of Nancy: Charles the Bold is defeated and killed by the Swiss.

1478 Spanish Inquisition established by Ferdinand and Isabella with the consent of Sixtus IV; its main aim is to punish so-called 'converted' Jews who still practise their old faith in secret. Lorenzo de Medici, ruler of Florence (to 1492).
Pazzi Conspiracy against the Medicis.
Giuliano de Medici assassinated.
Ivan III conquers Novgorod and incorporates it into duchy of Moscow.
Hungary gains Moravia and Silesia.
Turks conquer Albania.

1479 Ferdinand succeeds to the throne of Aragon. Spain united by the formal union of Aragon and Castile.
Ferdinand V of Castile, King of Aragon (to 1516); known as the Catholic king.
Treaty of Constantinople: Venice agrees to pay tribute to the Ottoman Empire for trading rights in the Black Sea.

1480 Ivan III, known as 'the Great', ends allegiance to the Tatars.
Turks besiege Rhodes, held by the Knights of St John.

1481 Death of Mohammed II, founder of the Ottoman Empire.

1482 Portuguese navigator Diego Cao explores the Congo River (until 1484).
Portuguese establish settlements on the Gold Coast (Ghana).

1483 Death of Edward IV.
Edward V, King of England; he is deposed by

191

his uncle, Richard, Duke of Gloucester.
Richard III, King of England (to 1485).
Edward V and his brother are murdered in the Tower of London.
Charles VIII, King of France (to 1498).
1484 Caxton prints *Morte D'Arthur*, the poetic collection of legends about King Arthur compiled by Sir Thomas Malory.
1485 Battle of Bosworth Field: Henry Tudor, Earl of Richmond, defeats and kills Richard III. He becomes Henry VII, King of England (to 1509), and first of the Tudor monarchs.
Hungary captures Vienna and acquires lower Austria; Hungary becomes the most powerful state in central Europe.
1486 Maximilian of Habsburg, King of Germans.
Henry VII of England marries Elizabeth of York; unites the houses of York and Lancaster.
1488 Diaz rounds the Cape of Good Hope.
James IV, King of Scotland (to 1513).
1492 Ferdinand V of Castile conquers Granada and ends Muslim influence in Spain.
Alexander VI (Roderigo Borgia), Pope (to 1503).
Christopher Columbus crosses the Atlantic and discovers the West Indies.
1493 The Songhai Empire reaches its greatest heights under Askia Mohammed who takes over much of the Mandingo Empire.
Pope Alexander VI divides newly discovered lands between Spain and Portugal.
Maximilian I, Holy Roman Emperor (to 1519).
1494 Charles VIII invades Italy.
Treaty of Tordesillas: Spain and Portugal move pope's line of demarcation farther west.
1495 Charles VIII enters Naples. The Holy League – Milan, Venice, Maximilian, Pope Alexander VI, and Ferdinand V – forces him to withdraw.
1496 Henry VII of England joins the Holy League.
Commercial treaty between England and Netherlands.
1497 John Cabot discovers Newfoundland.
1498 Louis XII, King of France (to 1515).
Vasco da Gama of Portugal reaches India.
Columbus discovers Trinidad and South America.
Savonarola burned at the stake.
1499 Louis XII of France invades Italy.
1500 Louis XII conquers Milan. Treaty of Granada: Louis and Ferdinand V agree to divide Naples.
Pedro Cabral claims Brazil for Portugal.
1501 France and Spain occupy Naples.
Amerigo Vespucci explores the coast of Brazil (until 1502).
Russia and Poland at war. Russia gains Lithuania and border territories (1503).
1502 Margaret, daughter of Henry VII, marries James IV of Scotland.
War breaks out between France and Spain.
Columbus discovers Nicaragua.
Shah Ismail (dies 1524) founds the Safavid dynasty in Persia.
1503 Battles of Cerignola and Garigliano: France defeated.
1505 Treaty of Blois: France keeps Milan but cedes Naples to Spain; Spain now has control of southern Italy.

Portuguese trading posts established on the Malabar coast.
The Portuguese found Mozambique.
Basil III, ruler of Moscow (to 1533).
1506 Christopher Columbus dies in poverty.
1507 Martin Waldseemüller produces a world map; for the first time it shows South America as separate from Asia and uses the name *America* after Amerigo Vespucci.
1508 The League of Cambrai: Emperor Maximilian, Louis XII, and Ferdinand V ally against Venice.
1509 Henry VIII, King of England (to 1547).
Battle of Diu establishes Portuguese control of Indian seas.
1510 Pope Julius II and Venice form Holy League to drive Louis XII out of Italy.
1511 Ferdinand V and Henry VIII join Holy League.
1512 Swiss join the League and drive French out of Milan.
Selim I, Sultan of Turkey (to 1520).
Russia and Poland at war (until 1522).
1513 Battle of Novara: French driven out of Italy.
Leo X (Giovanni de Medici), Pope (to 1521).
The Portuguese reach Canton, China.
Vasco Núñez de Balboa discovers the Pacific.
Battle of Flodden Field. James IV of Scotland killed.
James V, King of Scotland (to 1542).
1514 Mary, sister of Henry VIII, marries Louis XII.
War breaks out between Turkey and Persia.
Battle of Chaldiran: Persians defeated.
1515 Thomas Wolsey, Archbishop of York, is made Lord Chancellor of England and Cardinal.
François I, King of France (to 1547).
Battle of Marignano: the French defeat the Swiss and regain Milan.
1516 Treaty of Noyon between France and Spain: French relinquish claims to Naples.
War between Ottoman Empire and Egypt (until 1517).
Battle of Marjdabik: Selim defeats Egyptians.
Charles I, King of Spain (to 1556).
1517 The Reformation begins; Martin Luther nails his 95 Theses, protesting against the sale of indulgences, on the church door at Wittenberg.
Ottoman Turks capture Cairo: end of Mameluke Empire; Syria and Egypt are added to the Ottoman Empire.
1519 Reformation begins in Switzerland, led by Ulrich Zwingli.
Charles V (Charles I of Spain), Holy Roman Emperor (to 1556), on the death of Maximilian I.
1520 Field of Cloth of Gold: François I of France meets Henry VIII of England but fails to gain his support against Holy Roman Emperor Charles V.
Secret treaty between Henry VIII and Charles V.
Suleiman I, Sultan of Turkey (to 1566). Turkish power at its height.
1521 Diet of Worms: Martin Luther is condemned as a heretic and is excommunicated.
Henry VIII receives the title 'Defender of the Faith' from Pope Leo X for his opposition to Luther.
France and Spain at war over rival claims to

Martin Luther (above left) began the Reformation in 1517 with criticisms of Catholic practices. His followers, known as Protestants, soon split from the Catholic Church; prominent among them was John Calvin (above right) who introduced the Reformation to Switzerland. Left: The title page of Luther's German translation of the Bible; he thought everyone should have the chance to read the Bible for himself. Right: Ignatius Loyola founded a new religious order, the Society of Jesus (the Jesuits), to spread the Catholic Counter-Reformation.

Italy (until 1529).
Belgrade is captured by the Turks.
Hernan Cortés conquers the Aztec capital, Tenochtitlán (Mexico City).
1522 Battle of Biocca: Charles V defeats the French, driving them out of Milan.
One ship from Magellan's expedition completes the first circumnavigation of the world.
1523 Gustavus Vasa of Sweden leads revolt against Danish rulers and is elected Gustavus I, King of Sweden.
1524 France invades Italy and recaptures Milan.
1525 Battle of Pavia: François I is captured.
1526 Treaty of Madrid: François I is to give up claims to Milan, Genoa, and Naples but fails to keep the Treaty.
League of Cognac: alliance between François I, Pope Clement VII, Francesco Sforza of Milan, Venice, and Florence against Charles V.
Battle of Mohacs: Turks defeat and kill Louis II of Bohemia and Hungary.
Ferdinand of Austria, brother of Charles V, succeeds to the Bohemian throne.
Dispute over Hungarian succession between Ottoman Empire and Ferdinand (until 1528).
Battle of Panipat: Babar defeats last Delhi Sultan and founds the Mughal (Mongol) Empire.
1527 Sack of Rome by Spanish and German troops; Pope Clement VII is captured.
1528 Ferdinand of Austria succeeds to the Hungarian throne.
1529 Henry VIII dismisses Lord Chancellor Thomas Wolsey for failing to obtain the Pope's consent to his divorce from Catherine of Aragon.
Sir Thomas More appointed Lord Chancellor.
Henry VII summons the 'Reformation Parlia-

ment' and begins to cut the ties with the Church of Rome.
Peace of Cambrai between France and Spain: France renounces claims to Italy.
Treaty of Barcelona between Pope Clement VII and Charles V.
The Turks unsuccessfully besiege Vienna.
1530 Knights of St John established at Malta by Charles V.
Thomas Wolsey dies.
Charles V crowned emperor by Pope Clement VII, the last Imperial coronation by a pope.
Civil war in Switzerland between Catholic and Protestant cantons: Protestants are defeated.
1532 Sir Thomas More resigns over the question of Henry VIII's divorce.
Religious Peace of Nuremberg: Protestants allowed to practise their religion freely.
Calvin starts Protestant movement in France.
Turks invade Hungary but are defeated.
1533 Henry VIII marries Anne Boleyn and is excommunicated by Pope Clement VII.
Thomas Cranmer, Archbishop of Canterbury.
Peace between Suleiman I and Ferdinand of Austria.
Francisco Pizarro captures the Inca capital, Cuzco, and conquers Peru.
Ivan IV, the Terrible, ruler of Russia, succeeds at the age of three (to 1584).
1534 Act of Supremacy: Henry VIII declared supreme head of the Church in England.
Ignatius Loyola founds the Society of Jesus (Jesuits).
The Turks capture Tunis, Baghdad, and Mesopotamia.
1535 Sir Thomas More is executed for failing to take the Oath of Supremacy.

Death of Francesco Sforza; Milan comes under direct Spanish control.

War between France and Spain (until 1538). Jacques Cartier navigates the St Lawrence River (and in 1536).

The Spaniards explore Chile (to 1537).

1536 Anne Boleyn is executed; Henry VIII marries Jane Seymour.

Suppression of monasteries in England under the direction of Thomas Cromwell, completed 1539. Pilgrimage of Grace – Catholic uprising in the north of England – suppressed.

Calvin leads Protestants in Geneva.

France invades Savoy and Piedmont.

France forms alliance with Turkey.

1537 Jane Seymour dies after the birth of a son, the future Edward VI.

1538 Truce of Nice between France and Spain.

1539 Truce of Frankfurt between Charles V and Protestant princes.

1540 Henry VIII marries Anne of Cleves following negotiations by Thomas Cromwell.

Henry VIII divorces Anne of Cleves and marries Catherine Howard.

Thomas Cromwell executed on charge of treason.

Philip, son of Charles V, made Duke of Milan.

Pope Paul III officially recognizes Society of Jesus.

1541 John Knox brings the Reformation to Scotland.

Hernando de Soto discovers the Mississippi.

Turks conquer Hungary.

1542 Catherine Howard is executed.

Battle of Solway Moss: James V, King of Scotland, is killed.

Mary Stuart, Queen of Scotland (to 1567).

1543 Henry VIII marries Catherine Parr.

Alliance between Henry VIII and Charles V against Scotland and France.

1544 Henry VIII and Charles V invade France.

Treaty of Crépy between Spain and France.

1545 Pope Paul III opens the Council of Trent which, under Jesuit guidance, is to reform the Roman Catholic Church.

1547 Edward VI, King of England (until 1553); Duke of Somerset acts as Protector.

Henri II, King of France (until 1559).

Battle of Mühlberg: Charles V defeats Schmalkaldic League.

Ivan IV crowned Tsar (Emperor) of Russia.

1548 Holy Roman Emperor Charles V annexes the Netherlands.

1549 Introduction of uniform Protestant service in England with Edward VI's *Book of Common Prayer*.

St Francis Xavier in Japan (until 1551), introduces Christianity.

1550 Fall of Duke of Somerset; Duke of Northumberland succeeds as Protector.

1551 Turkey and Hungary at war (until 1562).

Archbishop Cranmer publishes Forty-two Articles of religion.

Treaty of Friedewalde between Saxony and France.

1552 War between Charles V and Henri II of France (until 1556).

France seizes Toul, Metz and Verdun.

Peace of Passau between Saxony and Holy Roman Empire.

1553 On death of Edward VI Lady Jane Grey proclaimed queen of England by Duke of Northumberland; reign lasts nine days.

Mary I, daughter of Henry VIII and Catherine of Aragon, Queen of England (to 1558).

Restoration of Roman Catholic bishops in England.

1554 Execution of Lady Jane Grey.

Mary I marries Philip, heir to throne of Spain.

Turks conquer coast of North Africa (completed 1556).

1555 England returns to Roman Catholicism; Protestants are persecuted and about 300, including Cranmer, are burned at the stake.

Religious Peace of Augsburg: Protestant princes are granted freedom of worship and the right to introduce the Reformation into their territories.

1556 Abdication of Charles V (dies 1558); Spain and its colonies, the Netherlands, Naples, Milan, and Franche-Comté to go to his son Philip; the office of Emperor and the Habsburg lands to go to his brother, Ferdinand.

Philip II, King of Spain (to 1598).

Alliance between Pope Paul IV and Henri II.

Battle of Panipat: Akbar the Great defeats Hindus.

1557 Battle of St Quentin: France is defeated by Spain and England.

Portuguese settle at Macao, China.

Livonian War (until 1582) involves Poland, Russia, Sweden, and Denmark in a dispute over the succession to the Balkan territories. Russia invades Poland.

1558 England loses Calais, last English possession in France.

Death of Mary I; Elizabeth I, daughter of Henry VIII and Anne Boleyn, Queen of England (to 1603).

Repeal of Catholic legislation in England.

Mary Queen of Scots marries François, Dauphin (crown prince) of France.

Ferdinand I, Holy Roman Emperor (to 1564).

1559 François II, King of France (to 1560).

Treaty of Cateau-Cambrésis between Spain and France ends the Habsburg-Valois wars; France gives up all conquests except Toul, Metz, and Verdun; Spain now controls virtually all Italy.

1560 Treaty of Berwick between Elizabeth I and Scottish reformers.

Charles IX, King of France (to 1574).

Treaty of Edinburgh among England, France, and Scotland.

1561 Mary Queen of Scots, widowed, returns to Scotland.

1562 Religious wars in France between the Huguenots (French Protestants) and Roman Catholics (until 1598).

Truce between Ferdinand I and Turkey.

1563 The Thirty-nine Articles, which complete establishment of the Anglican Church.

Ivan the Terrible conquers part of Livonia.

1564 Peace of Troyes between England and France.

Maximilian II, Holy Roman Emperor (to 1576).

William Shakespeare and Galileo Galilei born.

'Reign of Terror' begins in Russia.

1565 Turks besiege Malta without success.
Portuguese attack French colony and found Rio de Janeiro (1567).
1566 Pope Pius V (later Saint), Pope (to 1572).
Selim II, Sultan of Turkey (to 1574).
1567 Murder of Lord Darnley, husband of Mary Queen of Scots, probably by Earl of Bothwell.
Mary Queen of Scots marries Bothwell, is imprisoned, and forced to abdicate.
James VI, King of Scotland (to 1625).
1568 Netherlands revolt against Spain (independence gained 1648).
Mary Queen of Scots escapes to England and is imprisoned by Elizabeth I.
1569 Union of Lublin merges Poland and Lithuania.
1570 Peace of St Germain: Huguenots given conditional freedom of worship.
Turks attack Cyprus.
Ivan IV ravages Novgorod.
1571 Battle of Lepanto: combined papal and Venetian fleet under Don John of Austria defeats the Turks under Ali Pasha.
Bornu Empire in the Sudan (until 1603) reaches its greatest height under Idris III.
1572 Gregory XIII, Pope (to 1585).
Massacre of St Bartholomew: mass murder of Protestants (Huguenots) in France on St Bartholomew's Day.
1573 Venice abandons Cyprus and makes peace with Turkey.
Don John recaptures Tunis.
1574 Henri III, King of France (to 1589).
Turkey regains Tunis from Spain.
1576 Rudolf II, Holy Roman Emperor (to 1612).
Pacification of Ghent: Netherlands provinces unite to drive out the Spaniards.
Protestantism forbidden in France.
1577 Alliance between England and Netherlands.
Akbar the Great completes the unification and annexation of northern India.
Francis Drake sails around world (to 1580).
1578 Duke of Parma subdues the southern provinces of the Netherlands.
Battle of Al Kasr Al-kabil: Portuguese defeated by the Muslims.
1579 Northern provinces of the Netherlands form Union of Utrecht.
1580 Spanish conquer Portugal.
1581 Union of Utrecht declares itself the Dutch Republic, independent of Spain, and elects William of Orange as its ruler.
Poland invades Russia.
1582 Gregorian calendar introduced into Roman Catholic countries.
Peace between Russia, and Poland and Sweden.
1584 William of Orange is murdered.
England sends aid to the Netherlands.
Alliance of Bern, Geneva, and Zurich against Roman Catholic cantons.
Fedor I, Tsar of Russia (to 1598).
1585 England sends troops to the Dutch Republic.
'War of the Three Henrys' – Henri III of France, Henri of Navarre and Henri of Guise.
1586 Expedition of Sir Francis Drake to the West Indies.
Conspiracy against Elizabeth I involves Mary Queen of Scots.

1587 Execution of Mary Queen of Scots.
England at war with Spain.
Sir Francis Drake destroys Spanish fleet at Cadiz.
Savoy and the Catholic cantons form an alliance with Spain.
1588 The Spanish Armada is defeated by the English fleet under Lord Howard of Effingham, Sir Francis Drake, and Sir John Hawkins; war between Spain and England continues until 1603.
Henri of Guise is murdered.
1589 Henri III of France is murdered and the Protestant leader Henri of Navarre succeeds to the throne as Henri IV (to 1610).
Antonio of Crato, with British support, lands in Portugal and marches on Lisbon to reconquer the throne; he is defeated by the Spaniards.
1590 Peace between Turkey and Persia.
Battle of Ivry: Henri IV victorious against the Roman Catholic party.
1591 Songhai Empire is destroyed by Spanish and Portuguese mercenaries in the service of Morocco.
1592 Hideyoshi invades Korea with plans to conquer China, but is forced to withdraw (1593).
Akbar the Great conquers Sind.
1593 Diet of Uppsala in Sweden upholds Martin Luther's doctrines.
War between Austria and Turkey (until 1606).
1595 Treaty of Teusina between Sweden and Russia: Sweden gains Estonia.
1596 Battle of Keresztes: Turkish victory in Hungary.
1597 Irish rebellion under Hugh O'Neill, Earl of Tyrone (put down 1601).
1598 Edict of Nantes ends civil wars in France by giving Protestant Huguenots equal political rights with Roman Catholics.
Philip III, King of Spain (to 1621).
Treaty of Vervins between France and Spain: all conquests restored to France.
Boris Godunov, Tsar of Russia (to 1605).
1599 Confederation of Vilna: alliance formed between Orthodox and Dissidents in Poland.
Irish rebels defeat the Earl of Essex; he returns to England in disgrace.
1600 Elizabeth I grants charter to English East India Company.
Battle of Sekigahara: Tokugawa Ieyasu defeats rivals to become ruler of Japan; he establishes a military and administrative headquarters at Edo (Tokyo).
1601 Elizabethan Poor Law charges the parishes with providing for the needy.
Essex attempts rebellion, and is executed.
1602 Savoy attacks Geneva; Protestant cantons ally with France.
Dutch East India Company formed.
Holy War between Persia, under Shah Abbas I and Turkey (until 1618).
1603 Ieyasu appointed shogun of Japan.
James VI, King of Scotland becomes James I of England (to 1625).
Samuel de Champlain explores the St Lawrence river.
1604 Time of Troubles in Russia (to 1613).
French East India Company founded.

Hampton Court Conference: no relaxation by the Church towards Puritans; James bans Jesuits.

England and Spain make peace.

Russians begin settlement of Siberia and found Tomsk.

1605 Gunpowder Plot to blow up English Parliament is discovered; Guy Fawkes and other conspirators arrested and tried.

Fedor II, Tsar of Russia, deposed and murdered.

1606 Laws passed in England against Roman Catholics.

Basil Shuisky, Tsar of Russia (to 1610).

Several attempts by pretenders to gain the Russian throne; Cossack and peasant uprisings (until 1608).

Treaty of Zsitva-Torok between Turks and Austrians: Austria abandons Transylvania but ceases to pay tribute to Turkey.

Willem Jansz sights Australia.

1607 English Parliament rejects proposals for union between England and Scotland.

English colony of Virginia is founded at Jamestown by John Smith.

Henry Hudson begins voyage of discovery to eastern Greenland and Hudson River.

1608 Protestant Union formed in Germany and led by Frederick IV.

French explorer Samuel de Champlain founds settlement of Quebec.

1609 Twelve Years Truce ends fighting between Spain and the United Provinces; it ensures the virtual independence of the Netherlands.

The Catholic League led by Maximilian of Bavaria is formed in opposition to the Protestant Union.

Poland intervenes in Russia during the Time of Troubles (until 1618).

Johannes Kepler publishes his first two laws of planetary motion.

1610 The Great Contract: James I to receive an annual income of £200,000.

Galileo Galilei reveals stellar observations, made for the first time with a telescope.

Henri IV assassinated; Louis XIII, King of France (to 1643).

Henry Hudson discovers Hudson Bay.

Tea introduced to Europe.

Basil Shruisky is deposed and the Russian throne offered to Wladyslaw, son of Sigismund, King of Poland.

1611 James I's authorized version of the Bible is completed.

Plantation of Ulster: English and Scottish Protestant colonists settle in Ulster.

1612 Matthias, Holy Roman Emperor (to 1619).

1613 Michael Romanov, Tsar of Russia (to 1645) founder of the Romanov Dynasty.

1614 James I dissolves the 'Addled Parliament' which has failed to pass any legislation.

Estates-general summoned in France to curb the nobility – last such meeting until 1789.

1615 Tribes in northern China begin to form military organizations; later called *Manchus*.

1616 Willem Schouten, Dutch navigator, rounds Cape Horn.

1617 Treaty of Stolbovo between Russia and Sweden.

A Danish guardsman of the Thirty Years' War which lasted from 1618 to 1648. It was really a series of wars between Protestants and Catholics, with Catholic France, from self-interest, backing the Protestants.

1618 'Defenestration of Prague' (incident when Bohemians claiming independence threw two Catholic governors from a window) sparks off Thirty Years' War; general conflict in Europe lasts until 1648.

Paul Imbert, French explorer, reaches Timbuktu.

1619 Ferdinand II, Holy Roman Emperor (to 1637).

Bohemians depose Ferdinand II and elect Frederick V ('the Winter King') as ruler.

First American parliament meets at Jamestown, Virginia.

First Negro slaves arrive in Virginia.

1620 Battle of the White Mountain: Frederick V is defeated by Maximilian of Bavaria.

Pilgrim Fathers reach Cape Cod, Massachusetts, in the *Mayflower* and found New Plymouth.

1621 Philip IV, King of Spain (to 1665).

Dutch West Indies Company is founded.

Nurhachi expels the Ming and sets up Manchu capital at Liaoyang.

1622 James I dissolves Parliament for asserting its right to debate foreign affairs.

Spain occupies Valtelline Pass; war with France follows.

Battles of Wimpfen and Rochst: Protestant forces defeated by Count Tilly.

Execution of Christian missionaries in Japan reaches its height (to 1624).

1623 Duke of Buckingham and Charles, Prince of Wales, visit Spain on unsuccessful attempt to negotiate a marriage treaty.

Gustavus Adolphus of Sweden won several victories for the Protestants in the Thirty Years' War. He introduced light guns which could be moved quickly round the battlefield, and revolutionized artillery warfare.

Massacre of English by the Dutch at Ambonia in the Moluccas Islands.

1624 Alliance between James I and France: Parliament votes supplies for war against Spain.

Cardinal Richelieu becomes Chief Minister in France (to 1642).

Virginia becomes a crown colony.

1625 Charles I, King of England (to 1649).

Charles I marries Henrietta Maria, sister of Louis XII of France; dissolves Parliament which fails to vote him money.

Christian IV, Protestant King of Denmark, enters the war against Ferdinand II.

1626 Battle of Dessau: Catholic forces under von Wallenstein defeat Protestants.

Battle of Lutter: Christian IV defeated.

Dutch found New Amsterdam (New York).

1627 Siege of La Rochelle: Huguenots at La Rochelle besieged by Richelieu.

Charles I raises forced loan to aid Huguenots.

A new constitution in Bohemia confirms hereditary rule of the Habsburgs.

Imperial forces under Counts Tilly and Wallenstein subdue most of Protestant Germany.

1628 Petition of Right: Charles I forced to accept Parliament's statement of civil rights in return for finances.

Duke of Buckingham assassinated.

Huguenots surrender to Richelieu, losing all political power.

William Harvey demonstrates circulation of the blood.

1629 Charles I dissolves Parliament and rules personally until 1640.

Treaty of Lübeck between Ferdinand II and Christian IV.

Edict of Restitution issued by Ferdinand II entitles Catholics to reclaim Protestant lands.

1630 England makes peace with France and Spain.

Gustavus Adolphus II, King of Sweden, enters war against Ferdinand II.

About 16,000 colonists from England begin to settle in Massachusetts, in a migration lasting till 1642.

Turks, under Murad IV, take Hamadan.

1631 City of Magdeburg sacked by Catholic forces under Tilly.

Battle of Leipzig (Brietenfeld): Swedish and Saxon forces defeat Tilly.

1632 Battle of Lützen: Swedish victory, but Gustavus Adolphus II is killed.

1634 Wallenstein dismissed; later murdered.

Battle of Nördlingen: Swedes defeated by imperial forces.

Treaty of Polianov between Russia and Poland.

1635 Treaty of Prague: Ferdinand II revokes Edict of Restitution and makes peace with Saxony.

Treaty is accepted by most Protestant princes.

France declares war on Spain.

1637 Ferdinand III, Holy Roman Emperor (to 1657).

Russian explorers reach the Pacific Ocean, having crossed Siberia.

1638 Scottish Presbyterians sign the Solemn League and Covenant.

Turks conquer Baghdad.

Shimbara uprising and slaughter of Japanese Christians virtually stamps out Christianity in Japan.

1639 First Bishops' War between Charles I and the Scottish Church; ends with Pacification of Dunse.

1640 Charles I summons the 'Short' Parliament;

The Great Fire of 1666 raged through London destroying about 14,000 buildings, most of them wooden. St Paul's Cathedral, over 80 churches, markets, wharves and even shipping were burned. Among the men chosen to supervise the rebuilding was Sir Christopher Wren, whose greatest achievement was the new St Paul's.

dissolved for refusal to grant money.

Second Bishops' War; ends with Treaty of Ripon.

The Long Parliament of Charles I (until 1660).

Revolution in Catalonia against Spain (until 1659).

Revolt of the Portuguese against Spain, led by João Ribeiro with French support.

1641 Triennial Act requires Parliament to be summoned every three years.

Star Chamber and High Commission abolished by Parliament.

Catholics in Ireland revolt; some 30,000 Protestants massacred.

Grand Remonstrance of Parliament to Charles I.

1642 Charles I attempts to arrest five members of Parliament but fails; he rejects Parliament's Nineteen Propositions.

Civil War in England between Cavaliers (Royalists) and Roundheads (Parliamentarians) (until 1646); opens with battle of Edgehill.

Second battle of Leipzig: Swedish victory.

Montreal founded by the French.

Abel Tasman sights Van Diemen's Land (Tasmania) and New Zealand.

1643 Solemn League and Covenant is signed by English Parliament.

Louis XIV, King of France at age of 5; Cardinal Mazarin chief minister. Louis reigns until 1715.

Battle of Rocroi: France defeats Spain.

Denmark and Sweden at war for Baltic supremacy (until 1645).

1644 Battle of Marston Moor: Oliver Cromwell defeats Prince Rupert.

Manchu (Ta Ch'ing) Dynasty begins; lasts until 1912.

1645 Formation of Cromwell's New Model Army.

Battle of Naseby: Charles I defeated.

Turkey and Venice at war (until 1664) over Turkish designs on Candia (Crete).

1646 Charles I surrenders to the Scots.

1647 Scots surrender Charles I to the English Parliament; he is captured in turn by the army but escapes to the Isle of Wight; makes secret treaty with Scots.

1648 Scots invade England; defeated by Cromwell at battle of Preston; Pride's Purge: Presbyterians expelled from English Parliament which is now known as the 'Rump'.

Treaty of Westphalia ends Thirty Years' War;

Dutch and Swiss republics recognized as independent.

Revolt of the Fronde or *parlement* faction in Paris against Louis XIV (suppressed 1649).

1649 Charles I is tried and executed.

The Commonwealth (until 1660) – England governed as a republic.

Cromwell harshly suppresses Catholic rebellions in Ireland.

Serfdom completely established in Russia.

1650 Second revolt of Fronde is suppressed.

Charles II lands in Scotland; proclaimed king.

1651 Charles II invades England; defeated in battle of Worcester and escapes to France.

First Navigation Act: England gains virtual monopoly of foreign trade.

1652 Anglo-Dutch war (until 1654).

Spain intervenes in Fronde revolt against Louis XIV (to 1653).

Barcelona surrenders to Philip IV; end of Catalan revolt.

Cape Town founded by the Dutch.

1653 Cromwell dissolves the 'Rump' and becomes Lord Protector of England.

1654 Treaty of Westminster between England and Dutch Republic.

Portuguese take Brazil from the Dutch.

1655 England divided into 12 military districts by Cromwell.

England seizes Jamaica from Spain.

Sweden declares war on Poland.

1656 First Villmergen War in Switzerland between Protestant and Catholic cantons.

England and Spain at war (until 1659).

Battle of Warsaw: Swedish victory; Russia, Denmark, and Holy Roman Empire declare war on Sweden.

Turks routed by Venetians off Dardanelles.

1657 Dutch Republic and Portugal at war (to 1661).

1658 Oliver Cromwell dies; succeeded as Lord Protector by son Richard.

Battle of the Dunes: England and France defeat Spain; England gains Dunkirk.

Leopold I, Holy Roman Emperor (to 1705).

1659 Richard Cromwell forced to resign by the army; 'Rump' Parliament restored.

Treaty of the Pyrenees between France and Spain: settles borders and confirms supremacy of France over Spain.

1660 Convention Parliament restores Charles II to the English throne.

Charles II, King of England and Scotland (to 1685).

Treaty of Oliva: Poland cedes Livonia to Sweden.

Treaty of Copenhagen: Denmark surrenders territory to Sweden.

1661 Treaty of Kardis: Russia and Sweden restore all conquests to each other.

Clarendon Code: 'Cavalier' Parliament of Charles II (to 1665) passes a series of repressive laws against Nonconformists.

Death of Cardinal Mazarin; Louis XIV of France becomes absolute monarch.

English acquire Bombay.

Chinese general Koxinga takes Formosa.

Turkey and Holy Roman Empire at war (until 1664).

1662 Act of Uniformity passed in England.

1664 England seizes New Amsterdam from the Dutch; its name changed to New York.

Battle of St Gotthard: Austrians under Count Raimund Montecucculi defeat Turks.

Treaty of Vasvar between Empire and Turkey.

1665 Great Plague in London.

Second Anglo-Dutch war (until 1667): English fleet defeats the Dutch off Lowestoft.

Newton discovers laws of gravitation.

1666 Great Fire of London.

1667 Dutch fleet defeats the English in the Medway river.

Treaties of Breda among Netherlands, England, France, and Denmark.

War of Devolution: France invades Spanish Netherlands.

Treaty of Andrussovo: Russia gains Smolensk and eastern Ukraine from Poland.

1668 Triple Alliance of England, Netherlands, and Sweden against France.

Treaty of Lisbon: Spain recognizes Portugal's independence.

Treaty of Aix-la-Chapelle ends War of Devolution; France keeps most conquests in Flanders.

1669 Venice surrenders Candia (Crete) to Turkey.

Hindu religion prohibited and Hindus persecuted by Aurangzeb, Emperor of India.

1670 Secret Treaty of Dover between Charles II of England and Louis XIV of France to restore Roman Catholicism to England.

Hudson's Bay Company founded.

Uprisings by peasants and Cossacks in Russia (to 1671).

1672 Third Anglo-Dutch war (until 1674).

France at war with Netherlands (until 1678): French troops invade southern Netherlands.

William III (of Orange) becomes hereditary *stadholder* (ruler) of Netherlands (until 1702).

Treaty of Stockholm between France and Sweden.

Poland and Turkey at war for control of the Ukraine (until 1676).

1673 Test Act aims to deprive English Roman Catholics and Nonconformists of public office.

1674 Holy Roman Empire declares war on France in defence of the Dutch.

Treaty of Westminster between England and the Netherlands.

1675 Battle of Fehrbellin: Swedish forces defeated by Frederick William (the Great Elector) of Brandenburg.

King Philip's War (to 1676): American Indians attack settlers in New England.

1676 Sikh uprisings in India (until 1678).

Treaty of Zuravno between Poland and Turkey; Turkey gains Polish Ukraine.

Fedor III, Tsar of Russia (to 1682).

1677 William III of the Netherlands marries Mary, daughter of James, Duke of York, heir to the English throne.

Russia and Turkey at war (until 1681).

1678 'Popish Plot' in England: Titus Oates falsely alleges a Catholic plot to murder Charles II.

Treaty of Nijmegen ends Franco-Dutch war.

1679 Act of Habeas Corpus passed in England, forbidding imprisonment without trial.

Parliament's Bill of Exclusion against the Roman Catholic Duke of York blocked by Charles II; Parliament dismissed.

Charles II rejects petitions (to 1680) calling for a new Parliament; petitioners become known as *Whigs*; their opponents (royalists) known as *Tories*.

1680 Chambers of Reunion established by Louis XIV of France to annex territory; France occupies Strasbourg, Luxemburg and Lorraine (1683).

1681 Whigs reintroduce Exclusion Bill; Charles II dissolves Parliament.

Treaty of Radzin: Russia gains most of Turkish Ukraine.

1682 Turkey and Austria at war (until 1699).

Ivan V, Tsar of Russia (to 1689).

1683 Siege of Vienna by Turkish forces; city is relieved by German and Polish troops.

Koxinga's grandson, Cheng Chin, surrenders Formosa to the Manchus.

1684 Holy League formed by Pope Innocent XI: Venice, Austria, and Poland united against Turkey.

France occupies Trier in the Rhineland.

1685 Louis XIV revokes Edict of Nantes; all religions except Roman Catholicism forbidden, more than 50,000 Protestant (Huguenot) families leave France.

James II, King of England (James VII of Scotland) (to 1688).

Rebellion by Charles II's illegitimate son, Duke of Monmouth, against James II put down.

1686 James II disregards Test Act; Roman Catholics appointed to public office.

League of Augsburg formed between Holy Roman Empire, Spain, Sweden, Saxony, Bavaria, and the Palatinate against France.

Austrians advance on Budapest.

Venetians take Morea.

1687 James II of England issues Declaration of Liberty of Conscience; extends toleration to all religions.

Battle of Mohács: Turks defeated; Habsburg succession to Hungarian throne confirmed.

1688 England's 'Glorious Revolution': William III of Orange is invited to save England from Roman Catholicism; he lands in England; James II flees to France.

Austrians capture Belgrade.

1689 War of the League of Augsburg (until 1697); France invades the Palatinate.
Convention Parliament issues the Bill of Rights; establishes a constitutional monarchy in Britain; bars Roman Catholics from the throne.
William III and Mary II, joint monarchs of England and Scotland (to 1694).
Toleration Act grants freedom of worship to dissenters in England.
Grand Alliance of the League of Augsburg, England, and the Netherlands.
Peter I, the Great, Tsar of Russia (to 1725).
1690 Battle of the Boyne: William III of Great Britain defeats exiled James II in Ireland.
Battle of Beachy Head: France defeats Anglo-Dutch fleet.
Turks retake Belgrade from Austrians.
1691 Pope Innocent XII, Pope (to 1700).
1692 Massacre of Glencoe: Campbells slaughter MacDonalds in Scotland on pretext of disloyalty to William III.
Battle of La Hogue: France defeated by Anglo-Dutch fleet.
Salem witchcraft trials in New England.
1694 Death of Mary II; William III, sole ruler of England and Scotland (to 1702).
1696 Peter the Great of Russia makes incognito visits to Western Europe (until 1697).
1697 Treaty of Ryswick among France, England, Spain, and the Netherlands.
Battle of Zenta: Eugène of Savoy defeats Turks.
1698 Charles II of Spain names Prince Elector of Bavaria as his heir.
1699 Treaty of Karlowitz: Austria receives Hungary from Turkey; Venice gains Morea and much of Dalmatia; Poland receives Podolia and Turkish Ukraine.
Death of Prince Elector of Bavaria.
1700 Charles II of Spain names Philip of Anjou, grandson of Louis XIV of France, as heir; he succeeds as Philip V (to 1746).
Great Northern War caused by rivalry between Russia and Sweden for supremacy in the Baltic (until 1721).
Battle of Narva: Russians defeated by Charles XII, King of Sweden.
Clement XI, Pope (to 1721).
1701 Act of Settlement establishes Protestant Hanoverian succession in Britain.
Death of exiled James II.
Grand Alliance formed among England, the Netherlands, Holy Roman Emperor Leopold I, and the German states against France.
War of the Spanish Succession (until 1713).
Frederick III, Elector of Brandenburg, is crowned Frederick I, King of Prussia.
Charles XII of Sweden invades Poland.
1702 Anne, Queen of England and Scotland (to 1714).
1703 Methuen Agreement trade treaty between England and Portugal.
Hungarian revolt begins against Austria; led by Francis II Rákóczi (until 1711).
1704 British fleet captures Gibraltar from Spain.
Battle of Blenheim: allies under Duke of Marlborough and Prince Eugène defeat French.
Isaac Newton publishes *Optics*.
1705 Joseph I, Holy Roman Emperor (to 1711).

1706 Battle of Ramillies: French forces defeated by Duke of Marlborough.
Battle of Turin: Prince Eugène defeats French in Italy.
Treaty of Altranstädt between Augustus II, King of Poland, and Charles XII of Sweden.
1707 Act of Union unites England and Scotland under the name of Great Britain.
Battle of Almanza: Allied forces defeated by Spain.
Death of Aurangzeb leads to disintegration of Mughal Empire.
1708 Battle of Oudenarde: French defeated by allied forces under Duke of Marlborough and Prince Eugène.
Charles XII of Sweden invades Russia.
1709 Battle of Malplaquet: French defeated but more than 20,000 Allied troops killed.
Battle of Poltava: Peter I of Russia defeats Charles XII of Sweden.
1711 Duke of Marlborough dismissed as Allied commander.
Charles VI, Holy Roman Emperor (to 1740).
Peace of Szatmar between Austria and Hungary.
1713 Pragmatic Sanction issued by Emperor Charles VI to guarantee the succession of his daughter, Maria Theresa.
Treaty of Utrecht ends War of Spanish Succession; France recognizes Protestant succession in Britain; cedes Newfoundland, Nova Scotia, and Hudson Bay territory; Spanish Netherlands ceded temporarily to the Netherlands; Britain gains the *asiento*, contract to supply slaves to Spanish America, and gains Gibraltar and Minorca.
Papal Bull *Unigenitus* condemns Jansenists.
Frederick William I, King of Prussia (to 1740) establishes a standing army of more than 80,000 men.
1714 George I, King of Great Britain and Ireland, first Hanoverian monarch (to 1727).
Treaty of Rastatt and Baden between Austria and France cedes Spanish Netherlands to Austria.
1715 Louis XV, King of France (to 1774); Duke of Orléans regent until 1723.
First Jacobite uprising in Scotland (until 1716) in support of James Edward (the Old Pretender).
1717 Spain seizes Sardinia from Austria.
1718 Spain seizes Sicily from Savoy.
Quadruple Alliance (until 1719) of Austria, Britain, France, and Netherlands against Spain.
Treaty of Passarowitz ends war between Turkey and Austria.
1720 Collapse of John Law's Mississippi Company in France.
'South Sea Bubble': South Sea Company fails in England, causing financial panic.
Treaty of the Hague between Quadruple Alliance and Spain.
Treaties of Stockholm among Sweden, Prussia, Hanover, Denmark, Savoy and Poland (to 1721).
1721 Administration of Sir Robert Walpole, Britain's first prime minister (to 1742).
Treaty of Nystadt between Russia and Sweden confirms Russia as a great power.

At the battle of Blenheim in 1704 the Duke of Marlborough and Prince Eugène of Savoy led the English and Austrian forces to defeat the French. It put an end to Louis XIV's hopes of defeating Austria and checked him from gaining greater power in Europe. The War of the Spanish Succession left France diplomatically isolated, militarily weakened, and impoverished.

1724 State of Hyderabad, India, achieves independence from Mughals.

1725 Treaty of Vienna between Spain and Austria.

Treaty of Hanover: alliance between Britain, France, Prussia, Sweden, Denmark, and the Netherlands.

Catherine I, widow of Peter the Great, succeeds to throne of Russia.

1726 Administration of Cardinal Fleury, chief minister in France (to 1743).

1727 George II, King of Great Britain (to 1760).

Spain at war with Britain and France (until 1729).

1730 Maratha government becomes pre-eminent in India (to 1735).

1733 First family pact between Bourbons of France and of Spain.

War of Polish Succession between France and Spain, and Austria and Russia (until 1735).

1734 France invades Lorraine.

1735 Preliminary Treaty of Vienna ends War of Polish Succession.

1736 Russia and Austria at war with Turkey (to 1739).

Nadir Shah, ruler of Persia (to 1747); conquers Afghanistan and invades northern India (1738).

Chi'en Lung, Emperor of China (to 1799).

1738 Treaty of Vienna formally resolves War of Polish Succession; Lorraine to be ceded to France on death of Stanislaus I, defeated claimant to Polish throne.

1739 War of Jenkins' Ear between Britain and Spain (until 1741).

British Admiral Edward Vernon captures Porto Bello in the West Indies from Spain.

Treaty of Belgrade ends Austro-Russian war against Turkey.

Nadir Shah sacks Delhi.

John Wesley founds Methodist movement.

1740 Frederick II, the Great, King of Prussia (to 1786).

Death of Charles VI ends male line of Habsburgs; Maria Theresa succeeds to thrones of Austria, Bohemia, and Hungary.

Frederick the Great of Prussia seizes Silesia.

War of Austrian Succession (until 1748): caused by rival claims of Bavaria, Spain, and Saxony to the Austrian throne.

1741 Alliance of Nymphenburg among France, Bavaria, Spain, Saxony, and Prussia.

Sweden and Russia at war (until 1743).

1742 Charles VII, Holy Roman Emperor (to 1745).

Treaty of Berlin between Prussia and Austria.

1743 Battle of Dettingen: French defeated by British army under George II.

Treaty of Abö between Sweden and Russia.

1744 Frederick the Great invades Bohemia; driven out by Austrian and Saxon forces.

King George's War between Britain and France in North America (until 1748).

1745 'The Forty-Five': Jacobite rebellion in England and Scotland led by Charles Edward Stuart ('the Young Pretender').

Alliance among Austria, Saxony, Britain, and the Netherlands against Prussia.

Bavaria, defeated, withdraws claims to Austrian throne.

Battle of Fontenoy: French defeat British forces in War of Austrian Succession.

Battles of Hohenfriedberg and Soor: Austrians defeated.

Francis I, Holy Roman Emperor (to 1765).

Treaty of Dresden between Prussia and Austria.

British capture Louisburg, French fortress in Canada.

1746 Battle of Culloden: Jacobites defeated.

1747 Nadir Shah assassinated; his general, Ahmad Shah, becomes ruler of Afghanistan.

1748 Treaty of Aix-la-Chapelle ends War of Austrian Succession; Prussia keeps Silesia.

1751 English soldier Robert Clive seizes Arcot; ends French plans for supremacy in southern India.

1752 Chinese invade and conquer Tibet.

Benjamin Franklin invents lightning conductor.

1755 Earthquake in Lisbon kills some 30,000 people.

The French and Indian War between Britain and France in North America (until 1763).

1756 Treaty of Westminster: alliance between Britain and Prussia.

Treaty of Versailles: alliance between France and Austria.

Start of Seven Years' War; caused by colonial rivalry between Britain and France, and by rivalry between Austria and Prussia.

'Black Hole of Calcutta': Siraj-ud-Daulah, Nawab of Bengal, captures Calcutta and imprisons 146 British in small room; most die.

1757 Russia joins alliance with France and Austria.

Battles of Rossbach and Leuthen: Prussia defeats French and Austrian armies.

Robert Clive captures Calcutta.

Battle of Plassey: Clive defeats Nawab of Bengal; establishes British rule in India.

1758 Battle of Zorndorf: Russians defeated by Prussians.

1759 Britain captures Quebec; French general Marquis de Montcalm and British general James Wolfe killed.

Battle of Quiberon Bay: French defeated.

Battle of Kunersdorf: Austrian victory.

1760 George III, grandson of George II, King of Great Britain and Ireland (to 1820).

1761 Battle of Panipat: Afghan forces defeat Marathas.

1762 Britain declares war on Spain.

Treaty of St Petersburg between Russia and Prussia.

Catherine II, the Great, Tsarina of Russia (to 1796).

French philosopher Jean-Jacques Rousseau

publishes *The Social Contract*.

1763 Peace of Paris among Britain, France and Spain ends Seven Years' War; Britain gains Canada and virtually all lands east of the Mississippi River.

Peace of Hubertsburg among Prussia, Saxony, and Austria.

North American Indian uprising against the British led by Ottawa chief, Pontiac.

1764 Spinning jenny invented by Englishman, James Hargreaves.

1765 Stamp Act passed by British Parliament imposes a tax in the American colonies on publications and legal documents.

Joseph II, Holy Roman Emperor (to 1790), co-regent until 1780 with his mother, Maria Theresa.

1766 British Parliament repeals Stamp Act.

1767 Townshend Acts: tax imposed on various imports into North America.

Mason-Dixon line established between Maryland and Pennsylvania; separates free states from slave states.

Confederation of Bar: anti-Russian association is formed in Poland.

Russia and Turkey at war (until 1774).

James Cook, English navigator on first voyage (to 1771), discovers and explores east coast of Australia, calling it New South Wales.

1770 Boston Massacre: British troops fire on mob in Boston; five citizens killed.

Townshend Acts repealed; tax on tea imported into North America is kept.

1771 Russia conquers the Crimea.

Carl Scheele discovers oxygen.

1772 First Partition of Poland among Russia, Prussia, and Austria.

1773 Boston Tea Party: citizens, disguised as North American Indians, dump tea into Boston Harbour.

Pope Clement XIV suppresses Society of Jesus (Jesuits).

Peasant uprising in Russia led by Cossack

Left: On April 19, 1775 American colonists met British troops at Lexington on their way to destroy an arms cache. The 'shot heard round the world' was fired and the War of Independence began. Its first battle was the British victory at Bunker Hill (above).

Pugachev (suppressed 1775).

1774 Louis XVI, King of France (to 1792).
Treaty of Kuchuk Kainarji between Russia and Turkey; Russia gains Black Sea ports and the right to represent Greek Orthodox Church in Turkey.
'Intolerable Acts': British Parliament passes series of repressive acts against North American colonies. First Continental Congress meets at Philadelphia to protest.
Warren Hastings, Governor of Bengal, is appointed first Governor-General of India.

1775 War of American Independence (until 1783); George Washington leads American troops.
Battles of Lexington and Concord: British troops retreat to Boston; battle of Bunker Hill: British victory.
Catherine the Great reorganizes local government in Russia.
War between British and Marathas in India (until 1782).
British engineers James Watt and Matthew Boulton form partnership to produce first commercial steam engines.

1776 British troops evacuate Boston.
Declaration of Independence drawn up by American colonies in Philadelphia adopted by Continental Congress.
Viceroyalty of Rio de la Plata formed by Argentina, Bolivia, Paraguay and Uruguay.
Wealth of Nations published by Scottish economist Adam Smith.

1777 Battle of Saratoga: British army under General John Burgoyne surrenders to American General Horatio Gates.

1778 France enters American War of Independence in support of the colonists.
War of Bavarian Succession (until 1779): bloodless war between Prussia and Austria.
Death of French philosopher Voltaire.

1779 Spain joins Americans against Britain.
France and Spain besiege Gibraltar without success (until 1783).

1780 Riots against Roman Catholics in London; led by Protestant Lord George Gordon.
British capture Charleston, South Carolina.
Armed Neutrality of the North formed by Russia, Denmark, Sweden and Netherlands, to protect neutral shipping from British.
Peruvian Indians, led by Inca Tupac Amarú, revolt against Spain; put down by 1783.

1781 British troops under General Charles Cornwallis besieged by French and American forces at Yorktown, Virginia; British surrender.
Joseph II introduces religious toleration in Austria and abolishes serfdom.
Austro-Russian alliance against Turkey.

1782 Treaty of Salbai ends war between British and Marathas.

1783 Treaty of Paris ends American War of Independence; Britain recognizes independence of American colonies.
Russia annexes Crimea.
French brothers Joseph and Jacques Montgolfier build first successful hot-air balloon.

1784 India Act: British Prime Minister William Pitt (the Younger) establishes government control of political affairs in India.

1785 League of German Princes formed by Frederick the Great against Joseph II of Austria.

1787 Assembly of Notables in France dismissed after refusing to introduce financial reforms.
Russia and Turkey at war (until 1792).
New Constitution of the United States drawn up and signed at Philadelphia.
Famine causes rice riots in Edo, Japan.

1788 First convicts transported from Britain to New South Wales, Australia.
Gustavus III of Sweden at war with Russia (until 1790) to consolidate his rule.

1789 Estates-General meets at Versailles, France.
French Revolution begins.
Third Estate (representatives of the middle class) forms National Assembly; as Constituent Assembly it governs France until 1791.
Storming of the Bastille in Paris.
George Washington, first President of the United States (to 1797).

1790 Treaty of Wereloe ends Russo-Swedish war.
Leopold II, Holy Roman Emperor (to 1792).

1791 Flight and capture of Louis XVI of France and family; Louis accepts new Constitution; Constituent Assembly replaced by Legislative Assembly.
Treaty of Sistova between Austria and Turkey.
Canada Act divides Canada into French- and English-speaking territories.
Bill of Rights: first 10 amendments to US Constitution.
Negro slave revolt against French in Haiti led by Toussaint l'Ouverture.

1792 Coalition of Austria and Prussia against France.
Francis II, Holy Roman Emperor (to 1806).
France declares war on Austria and Prussia; battle of Valmy: French defeat Prussians.
National Convention governs France (until 1795); France is declared a republic.
Treaty of Jassy between Russia and Turkey.
China invades Nepal after Gurkhas menace Tibetan borders.

1793 Louis XVI is executed; his wife, Marie Antoinette subsequently beheaded.

Revolutionary France declares war on Britain, the Netherlands, and Spain.

Royalist uprising in La Vendée, France.

Reign of Terror (to 1794); France ruled largely by Maximilien Robespierre and the Committee of Public Safety.

Conscription in France for revolutionary army.

Second partition of Poland between Russia and Prussia.

In India, Lord Cornwallis, Governor-General, stabilizes revenue system and reorganizes judicial system on British lines.

1794 Dutch republic invaded, and Dutch fleet captured by France (1795).

Execution of Georges Danton and, subsequently, of Robespierre; Reign of Terror draws to an end; Jacobins suppressed in France.

French occupy the Netherlands (until 1795).

Jay's Treaty: commercial and shipping treaty between Britain and United States.

Qajar (Kajar) Dynasty founded in Persia by Aga Mohammed; lasts until 1925.

1795 Batavian Republic set up by France in the Netherlands (until 1806).

Treaty of Basle between France and Prussia; Spain also makes peace with France.

The Directory, a five-man executive set up by the 1795 constitution, rules France.

Third partition: remainder of Poland divided among Russia, Prussia and Austria.

British take Cape of Good Hope from Dutch.

Mungo Park, a Scot, explores Gambia River; reaching Niger River.

Warren Hastings, former Governor-General of India, acquitted by British Parliament of corruption charges.

1796 The Corsican, Napoleon Bonaparte, leads French army and conquers most of Italy (to 1797).

Paul I, Tsar of Russia (to 1801).

British capture Ceylon from the Dutch.

1797 British navy mutinies at Spithead and Nore.

Battle of Cape St Vincent: British navy defeats Franco-Spanish fleet.

Treaty of Campo Formio:Austria makes peace with France.

Frederick William III, King of Prussia (to 1840).

American ships trade with Japan on behalf of Dutch (until 1809); end of Japanese isolation policy.

1798 Rebellion at Vinegar Hill, Ireland, by the United Irishmen wanting separation.

French occupy Rome; establish Roman Republic.

French invade Switzerland; Helvetic Republic set up.

Bonaparte leads French army on expedition into Egypt (lasts until 1799); battle of the Pyramids: Cairo taken by the French.

Battle of the Nile (Aboukir Bay): British fleet under Horatio Nelson defeats French.

1799 Bonaparte invades Syria.

Coalition of Britain, Austria, Russia, Portugal, Naples, and Ottoman Empire against France.

Battles of Zurich, Trebbia and Novi: French driven out of Italy.

Bonaparte returns to France; overthrows Directory and sets up a Consulate; headed by Bonaparte, it rules France until 1804.

Tippoo Sahib, last ruler of Mysore, killed in battle with British troops; British control extends over most of southern India.

Combination Laws prohibit trade unions in Britain (second series, 1800).

Discovery of Rosetta Stone enables Egyptian hieroglyphics to be understood.

1800 Battles of Marengo and Hohenlinden: French defeat Austrians.

Pius VII, Pope (to 1823).

Italian physicist Alessandro Volta produces first electric battery.

1801 Act of Union formally unites Great Britain and Ireland as the United Kingdom.

Treaty of Lunéville between France and Austria; leads to break-up of Holy Roman Empire;

France gains left bank of the Rhine and keeps most of Italy.

Concordat between Bonaparte and Pius VII.

Alexander I, Tsar of Russia (to 1825).

1802 Treaty of Amiens between Britain and France.

Bonaparate is created First Consul for life.

Portuguese explorers begin crossing of Africa from west (Angola) to east; reach Tete, on the Zambezi, in Mozambique in 1811.

1803 War breaks out again between Britain and France.

'Louisiana Purchase': France sells Louisiana to the United States; Ohio becomes 17th state of the Union.

1804 Bonaparte crowns himself Napoleon I, Emperor of the French.

The First Empire in France (until 1814).

Persia and Russia at war over annexation of Georgia.

Serbian nationalists revolt against Turks in modern Yugoslavia; suppressed 1813.

American explorers Meriwether Lewis and

William Clark set out to explore the north-western United States as far as the Pacific Ocean which they reach in November 1805.
Haiti achieves independence from France.
English inventor Richard Trevithick builds first successful steam locomotive.
Third Coalition formed by Britain, Russia, Austria, and Sweden against France.
1805 Battle of Ulm: French defeat Austrians.
Battle of Trafalgar: British navy under Horatio Nelson defeats Franco-Spanish fleet.
Battle of Austerlitz: French defeat Austro-Russian forces.
Mohammed Ali appointed *pasha* (governor) of Egypt by Selim III, Sultan of Turkey.
1806 Louis Bonaparte, brother of Napoleon, becomes King of Holland.
Napoleon I dissolves Holy Roman Empire; replaces it by Confederation of the Rhine.

1810 Louis, King of Holland abdicates; France annexes Holland.
British troops in Portugal hold lines of Torres Vedras against the French (until 1811).
1811 French driven out of Portugal.
Luddite riots in England against mechanization in textile industry; repressive legislation introduced (1812).
Mamelukes (ruling family) massacred in Cairo by Mohammed Ali.
Paraguay and Venezuela achieve independence.
George III of England declared insane; Prince of Wales rules as regent.
1812 Britain and United States at war over shipping and territory disputes (until 1814).
Battle of Salamanca: British victory in Spain.
Treaty of St Petersburg between Sweden and Russia.
Treaty of Bucharest ends Russo-Turkish war.

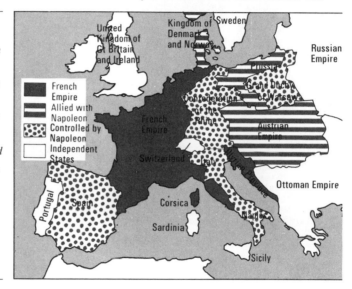

Left: The head of Louis XVI is displayed to cheering crowds after his guillotining in 1793. Later that year the French Revolution entered an appalling new phase known as the Reign of Terror, headed by Robespierre, when anyone suspected of opposing the new regime was executed. In 1794 Robespierre himself was guillotined and the Terror died away. Right: At its height Napoleon's empire dominated most of Europe. He had been given command of the French army in 1795 and in 1799 headed a Consulate which ruled France until 1804 when he became emperor. His downfall was his unsuccessful attempt to conquer Russia.

Emperor Francis II becomes Francis I of Austria (to 1835).
Battles of Jena and Auerstädt: Prussia defeated by French.
Berlin Decree issued by Napoleon to attempt economic blockade of Britain (the Continental System).
Turkey at war with Russia and Britain (until 1812).
1807 Slave trade abolished in British Empire.
Battle of Friedland: Russian defeat.
Treaties of Tilsit between Tsar Alexander I of Russia and Napoleon.
French invade Portugal; capture Lisbon.
1808 French occupy Spain; Joseph Bonaparte becomes King of Spain. Peninsular War (until 1814): France opposed by British forces and Spanish and Portuguese guerrillas.
Battle of Vimeiro: British victory.
Russia and Sweden at war (until 1809).
1809 Battle of Coruna: British defeated: death of Sir John Moore, commander-in-chief of the British troops.

Treaty of Örebro among Britain, Sweden, and Russia.
Napoleon invades Russia with Grand Army; battle of Borodino: French victory; French occupy Moscow but are forced to retreat; only 100,000 survive from army of 600,000.
1813 War of Liberation from France begins in Prussia, led by King Frederick William III.
Treaty of Kalisch between Russia and Prussia against France; coalition joined by Britain, Austria, and Sweden.
Battle of Dresden: French victory.
Battle of Leipzig (Battle of the Nations): French defeated by combined Austrian, Russian, and Prussian forces.
Battle of Vittoria: French entirely driven out of Spain by Wellington.
Allied forces invade France; enter Paris in March 1814.
1814 Napoleon abdicates and is exiled to Elba.
Louis XVIII, brother of Louis XVI, King of France (to 1824).
Treaty of Paris ends Napoleonic Wars.

Congress of Vienna (to 1815): heads of state discuss settlement of post-war Europe.

Treaty of Kiel: Sweden gains Norway.

Treaty of Ghent ends Anglo-American war.

1815 The Hundred Days: Napoleon escapes from Elba and marches on Paris.

Battle of Waterloo: Napoleon defeated and exiled to island of St Helena.

Final Act of Congress of Vienna: Austrian and Prussian monarchies restored; German Confederation replaces Confederation of the Rhine; Kingdom of Netherlands formally unites Belgium and Holland.

Holy Alliance of Russia, Austria, and Prussia.

Second Treaty of Paris: France's boundaries restored to those of 1790.

Quadruple Alliance of Britain, Austria, Prussia, and Russia to maintain Congress System.

British Corn Laws restrict corn imports.

Serbs revolt against Turkey in Balkans; Serb leader Milosh Obrenovich recognized by Turks as Prince of Serbia, 1817.

1818 Congress of Aix-la-Chapelle: France joins the four Great Powers (Quintuple Alliance).

Border between Canada and United States fixed along 49th parallel; both countries occupy Oregon.

Chile becomes independent from Spain.

Zulu Empire founded in southern Africa by Chaka, great military chieftain.

1819 Peterloo Massacre: soldiers fire on political meeting in Manchester, England; several people killed.

Carlsbad Decrees in Germany suppress political activity.

Zollverein (customs union) begins in Germany under influence of Prussia.

Spain cedes Florida to the United States.

Latin American revolutionary, Simón Bolivar, secures independence of Greater Colombia.

Kashmir conquered by Sikh leader, Ranjit Singh.

Singapore founded by British administrator, Sir Stamford Raffles.

1820 Cato Street conspiracy in England to assassinate cabinet ministers fails.

Liberal revolutions in Spain, Portugal, and Italy.

George IV, King of Britain (to 1830).

Congress of Troppau considers Naples revolt.

Missouri Compromise: admission of several states to the Union, including Missouri (1821) as a slave state.

Egyptian conquest of Sudan (completed 1822).

1821 Congress of Laibach authorizes Austria to put down Neapolitan revolt.

Greek War of Independence against Turkey; succeeds in 1829.

Peru and Mexico proclaim independence.

Persia and Turkey at war (until 1823).

1822 Congress of Verona; breaks down over Britain's refusal to intervene in Spain; ends Congress System.

Brazil achieves independence from Portugal.

Colombia and Ecuador liberated.

Liberia, West Africa, founded as colony for freed American slaves.

1823 Spanish revolution crushed.

United States' President, James Monroe, issues Monroe Doctrine warning European powers not to interfere in American politics.

1824 Combination Acts repealed in Britain, stimulating trade union movement.

Charles X, brother of Louis XVI and XVIII, King of France (to 1830).

War between British and Ashanti in Gold Coast (Ghana), West Africa (until 1827).

First Anglo-Burmese War (until 1826): Britain begins annexation of Burma.

Nicholas I, Tsar of Russia (to 1855).

1825 Decembrist rising in Russia against Tsar.

Egyptian forces under Ibrahim, son of Mohammed Ali, invade Greece.

New Republic of Bolivia independent.

1826 Russia and Persia at war (until 1828).

Turks capture Missolonghi from Greeks.

1827 Treaty of London: Britain, Russia and France to guarantee Greek independence.

Battle of Navarino: Egyptian fleet destroyed by French, Russian, and British.

1828 Miguelite Wars in Portugal: regent Dom Miguel overthrows government; finally defeated 1834.

War between Russia and Turkey (to 1829).

1829 Catholic Emancipation Act in Britain; Roman Catholics can hold public office.

Russo-Turkish Treaty of Adrianople.

Greater Colombia divided into Colombia, Venezuela, Ecuador and New Granada.

1830 William IV, King of Britain (to 1837).

July Revolution in Paris; Charles X overthrown.

First passenger steam railways open.

Louis Philippe, descendant of Louis XIII, King of France (the Citizen King) (to 1848).

Revolution in Belgium against Dutch rule.

Greece formally declared independent.

Revolution in Poland crushed by Russia (1831).

1831 Gregory XVI, Pope (to 1846).

Uprisings in Modena, Parma and Papal States; put down by Austria.

Italian revolutionary, Giuseppe Mazzini, forms *Young Italy* movement.

Britain and France guarantee Belgian independence; Leopold of Saxe-Coburg becomes Leopold I, King of the Belgians (to 1865).

1832 Reform Act passed in Britain: extends vote to middle class.

War between Egypt and Turkey (until 1833).

Battle of Koniah: Turks defeated.

1833 Factory Act in England forbids employment of children under nine in factories.

Act abolishing slavery in British colonies.

Convention of Kutahia: Mohammed Ali gains Syria.

Treaty of Unkiar Skelessi between Russia and Turkey.

Munchengratz Agreement between Russia and Austria.

1834 'Tolpuddle Martyrs': six Dorset labourers transported for attempt to form a trade union.

Carlist Wars in Spain (until 1839); Pretender Don Carlos attempts to gain Spanish throne.

Quadruple Alliance formed by Britain, France, Spain, and Portugal to safeguard governments in Spain and Portugal.

Beginning of foundation of South Australia (1836) and Victoria (1837).

Portuguese possessions
Spanish possessions

South America was ruled by Spain and Portugal from the early 16th century for 300 years. Then Napoleon's occupation of Spain and the Peninsular War encouraged the colonies to seek independence. By the mid-1820s, under leaders such as Bolívar and San Martín, they had achieved it.

1835 Ferdinand I, Emperor of Austria (to 1848).
Great Trek (to 1837): Boer (Dutch) settlers in southern Africa found Transvaal.
1836 Chartist movement begins in Britain; demands votes for all adult males; violent support eventually moderates.
Texas wins independence from Mexico; battles of the Alamo and San Jacinto.
1837 Victoria, Queen of Britain (to 1901).
1838 Battle of Blood River: Boers defeat Zulus in Natal, South Africa.
1839 British occupy Aden.
Commissioner Lin destroys foreign opium.
Opium war between Britain and China (to 1842).
Anti-Corn Law League formed in Britain.
Turks invade Syria.
Battle of Nesib: Turks defeated.
Rebellions in Upper and Lower Canada.
Britain and Afghanistan at war.
1840 Treaty of Waitangi: New Zealand becomes a British Crown Colony.
Treaty of London: Britain, Russia, Prussia, and Austria agree to limit Egyptian expansion.
British navy bombards Beirut.
Union Act unites Upper and Lower Canada.
Penny post introduced in Britain.
1841 Convention of Alexandria: Mohammed Ali to be hereditary ruler of Egypt.
Straits Convention among Britain, Austria, Russia, Prussia, and France; Dardanelles and Bosporus to be closed to foreign ships in peacetime.
1842 Webster-Ashburton Treaty settles boundary dispute between Canada and United States.
Boers and British at war; British victorious.
British withdraw from Kabul, Afghanistan.
Treaty of Nanking between Britain and China; Hong Kong ceded to Britain.
1843 Natal becomes a British colony.
1845 Anglo-Sikh Wars in India (to 1848); Britain annexes the Punjab, northwest India.
Texas joins the United States.
1846 Potato famine reaches height in Ireland; about one million die by 1851.
Corn Laws repealed in Britain.
Pius IX, Pope (to 1878).
United States and Mexico at war (until 1848).
War between *Kaffirs* (Bantu) and British in South Africa; Bantu defeated (1847).
First act of segregation in South Africa; Zulu reserves set up in Natal.
Growth of anti-British movement in Ireland.
1848 Year of revolutions in Europe.
Revolution in Paris; Louis Philippe abdicates; Second Republic with Louis Napoleon, nephew of Napoleon I, as president, set up in France.
Revolutions in Milan, Naples, Venice and Rome; most suppressed within a year.
Revolutions in Berlin, Vienna, Prague, and Budapest; initially successful.
Prince Metternich resigns; Emperor Ferdinand abdicates.
Franz Josef I, Emperor of Austria (to 1916).
Frankfurt National Assembly meets (to 1849) to discuss unification of Germany.
Uprising in Wallachia (Romania) is suppressed by Russia.
Switzerland introduces federal constitution.
Insurrection in Tipperary, Ireland, is put down.
Treaty of Guadalupe Hidalgo: United States gains California, New Mexico.
Californian gold rush begins.
First Convention of Womens' Rights, New York.
The Communist Manifesto written by German socialists, Karl Marx and Friedrich Engels.
1849 Revolutions in Italy and Hungary crushed.
Frankfurt Parliament collapses.
1850 Don Pacifico Affair: British foreign secretary, Lord Palmerston, defends rights of British citizens abroad.
Treaty of Olmütz: German Confederation restored under Austrian leadership.
T'ai P'ing rebellion: revolt in China against Manchu Dynasty (until 1864).
1851 Great Exhibition held in London.
1852 Louis Napoleon sets up Second Empire as Napoleon III, Emperor of the French (to 1870).
Sand River Convention: Britain recognizes independence of the Transvaal.
Second Burmese War (until 1853): British victory.
1853 Turkey declares war on Russia after Franco-Russian disputes over Holy Places in Palestine.
Scottish explorer David Livingstone begins crossing of Africa; discovers Victoria Falls (1855).
1854 The Crimean War (until 1856): Britain,

The Crimean War of 1854–1856 saw the defeat of Russia by an alliance of Britain, France, Turkey (the Ottoman Empire) and Sardinia. It began when Russia invaded Turkish European territory, claiming to protect Christians in Turkish lands and demanding free passage for its warships. Most of the 650,000 casualties died from bad leadership, disease or exhaustion in the terrible conditions like those shown above.

France, and Turkey against Russia.

Battles of Balaclava and Inkerman: Russians defeated.

Siege of Sevastopol: Russians besieged for nearly a year.

Liberal revolution in Spain overthrows government.

US naval officer Matthew Perry forces Japan to make commercial treaty with United States.

Orange Free State set up in South Africa.

1855 English nurse Florence Nightingale reforms nursing during Crimean War.

Alexander II, Tsar of Russia (to 1881).

1856 Treaty of Paris ends Crimean War.

Persia captures Herat, Afghanistan; act leads to war with Britain.

Anglo-Chinese war breaks out.

1857 Indian Mutiny (to 1858): rebellion of *sepoys* (native soldiers) in Bengal Army; eventually put down by Britain.

Sepoys take Cawnpore and besiege Lucknow.

Treaty of Paris between Britain and Persia.

1858 Lucknow relieved; Indian mutiny ends.

India Bill: government of India passes to British Crown from East India Company.

Italian nationalist, Felice Orsini, attempts to assassinate Napoleon III.

Secret alliance between Napoleon III and Count Cavour, Premier of Piedmont.

Fenian Society founded in United States by Irish emigrants.

Treaty of Aigun: Russia gains Amur region from China.

Treaties of Tientsin open 11 Chinese ports.

British explorers Sir Richard Burton and John Speke discover Lake Tanganyika.

1859 France and Piedmont at war with Austria.

Battles of Magenta and Solferino: Austria defeated.

Treaty of Zurich between France and Austria: Piedmont gains Lombardy.

1860 Italian states Parma, Modena, Tuscany, and Romagna unite with Piedmont.

Italian patriot Giuseppe Garibaldi and his 'Thousand Redshirts' conquer Naples and Sicily.

South Carolina withdraws from the Union.

British and French occupy Peking; end of Anglo-Chinese war.

1861 Italy, except for Rome and Venice, united as one kingdom under Victor Emmanuel, King of Piedmont.

William I, King of Prussia (to 1888).

Abraham Lincoln inaugurated president of the United States.

Confederate States of America formed by South Carolina and ten other southern states.

Civil War in America (until 1865) between Confederates and the Union (Federals); first battle at Bull Run: Confederate victory.

Serfs freed in Russia.

Prince Albert, husband of Queen Victoria, dies.

1862 Otto von Bismarck becomes Prime Minister of Prussia.

French establish protectorate over Cochin-China (western provinces fall in 1867).

1863 Lincoln proclaims abolition of slavery in United States.

Polish insurrection; fails (1864).

Battle of Gettysburg: Confederate defeat.

French occupy Mexico City.

French establish protectorate in Cambodia.

General Ulysses S. Grant, victorious commander of the Union forces in the American Civil War, with some of his staff. War broke out over the slavery issue; northern states did not wish to extend this to new states being settled and the slave-dependent southern states, afraid of being outnumbered by non-slave states, separated into a new nation. At first the South was victorious but after the Union victory at Gettysburg it suffered a series of defeats, finally surrendering in 1865.

1864 Austria and Prussia take Schleswig-Holstein from Denmark.
United States Union Army controls Georgia.
Expedition of British, Dutch, French and Americans, bombards Shimonoseki, Japan.
Karl Marx founds *First International* in London.
1865 Confederate General Lee surrenders to Union General Grant; American Civil War ends.
President Lincoln assassinated.
1866 Prussia forms alliance with Italy.
Austro-Prussian war over Schleswig-Holstein (Seven Weeks' War).
Battle of Sadowa: Prussian victory.
Battles of Custozza and Lissa: Italy defeated but gains Venice.
Treaty of Prague ends Austro-Prussian war; Austria to withdraw from German affairs.
1867 Second Reform Act passed in Britain.
North German Confederation formed under Prussian leadership.
Austro-Hungarian Monarchy: Franz Josef of Austria also King of Hungary.
Russia sells Alaska to United States.
Dominion of Canada established.
France forced to withdraw from Mexico.
1868 Uprising in Spain; Queen Isabella II forced to abdicate.
Ten Years' War (until 1878): Cuba, unsuccessfully, attempts to gain independence from Spain.
British expedition to Ethiopia forces release of British diplomats.
Meiji Period in Japan (until 1912).
1869 Disestablishment Act passed; Irish Church ceases to exist, 1871.
The Suez Canal is opened.
1870 Irish Land Act provides compensation for eviction; fails to ease Irish problem.
Franco-Prussian War (until 1871).
French defeated at Sedan; Napoleon III captured; Prussians besiege Paris.
Second French Empire ends.
Third French Republic (until 1914).
Kingdom of Italy annexes Papal States; Rome becomes capital of Italy.
1871 Trade unions legalized in Britain.
German Empire declared with King William I of Prussia as Emperor.

Paris surrenders after gruelling siege.
Paris Commune set up in opposition to national government and peace terms.
Treaty of Frankfurt ends Franco-Prussian war; Alsace-Lorraine ceded to Germany and France forced to pay heavy indemnity.
Government troops crush Paris Commune.
1872 League of the three emperors: William I, Franz Josef, Tsar Alexander II.
1873 First Republic in Spain (to 1874).
Second Ashanti War in West Africa (to 1874): Ashanti defeated by British.
1874 First Impressionist exhibition held in Paris.
Spanish monarchy restored.
1875 British Prime Minister Benjamin Disraeli buys shares in Suez Canal from Egypt.
Insurrection breaks out in Herzegovina and Bosnia (now in Yugoslavia) against Turkey.
1876 Anti-Turkish insurrection in Bulgaria is suppressed; thousands massacred.
Serbia and Montenegro (now in Yugoslavia) declare war on Turkey but are defeated.
Battle of Little Big Horn: Sioux Indians led by Chief Sitting Bull kill General George Custer and his men; last major North American Indian victory.
Britain and France assume joint control of Egypt's finances.
Porfirio Diaz becomes dictator of Mexico.
Korea opened to Japanese trade.
1877 Queen Victoria proclaimed Empress of India.
Russia and Turkey at war over the Balkans.
Transvaal annexed by Britain.
Satsuma rebellion in Japan is crushed.
1878 Treaty of San Stefano between Russia and Turkey: Montenegro, Serbia, Bulgaria, and Romania to be independent.
Berlin Congress: Great Powers discuss Balkan situation; revise Treaty of San Stefano.
Second Anglo-Afghan War (until 1880): Britain gains control of Afghan affairs.
1879 Britain and France control Egypt.
Irish Land League formed by Irish MP Charles Stewart Parnell.
Alliance between Germany and Austria.
Zulu War between British and Zulus; battle of Ulundi: Zulus defeated.

1880 Boer revolt against British in South Africa.
1881 Alexander III, Tsar of Russia (to 1894).
France establishes protectorate in Tunis.
US President James Garfield assassinated.
Battle of Majuba Hill: Boer victory; Treaty of Pretoria; South African Republic (Transvaal) gains virtual independence.
1882 Phoenix Park Murders: Lord Frederick Cavendish, Chief Secretary for Ireland, and Thomas Burke, Under-secretary, murdered in Dublin.
Triple Alliance formed by Germany, Austria, and Italy; lasts until 1914.
British bombard Alexandria and occupy Cairo to suppress nationalists; leads to French withdrawal from Egypt.
Anti-Egyptian revolt in Sudan (until 1885) led by Muslim leader, Mahdi Mohammed Ahmed.
1883 Sickness insurance introduced in Germany.
1884 Third Reform Act passed in Britain.
Berlin Conference: European powers decide on 'spheres of influence' in Africa; partition of Africa virtually complete by 1895.
Germany occupies Togoland, Cameroons, and South-West Africa.
British General Charles Gordon sent to the Sudan to rescue Egyptian garrisons; besieged at Khartoum.
1885 New Guinea annexed by Britain and Germany.
Khartoum taken and Gordon killed by Mahdi.
Congo Free State set up under Leopold II of Belgium.
French chemist Louis Pasteur gives first inoculation against rabies.
France gains protectorates over Annam and Tonkin (Indochina).
Britain establishes protectorates over southern Nigeria and Bechuanaland, south Africa.
German East Africa established.
Third Anglo-Burmese War (until 1886): Britain annexes Upper Burma.
1886 Irish Home Rule Bill, introduced by British Prime Minister William Gladstone, is defeated.
Gold discovered in South Africa.
1887 War between Italy and Ethiopia.
1888 William II, German Emperor (to 1918).
1889 Georges Boulanger, former French war minister, flees after plotting against Third Republic.
Treaty of Uccialli: Italy gains protectorate over Ethiopia.
Brazil becomes a republic.
Cecil Rhodes founds British South Africa Company.
Panama scandal: financial scandal in France caused by collapse of Panama Canal Company; de Lesseps and associates tried for corruption (1892–93); sentences set aside.
1890 German Chancellor Otto von Bismarck dismissed by William II.
Zanzibar Settlement: Britain receives Zanzibar, East Africa; Heligoland goes to Germany.
1893 Gladstone reintroduces Irish Home Rule Bill; defeated by House of Lords.
Independent Labour Party founded in Britain by socialist Keir Hardie.
General strike in Belgium.

French set up protectorate over Ivory Coast, West Africa.
1894 French officer Alfred Dreyfus convicted of treason and deported; becomes major political affair.
Nicholas II, last Tsar of Russia (until 1917).
War between China and Japan over Korea (until 1895).
In China, Sun Yat-sen founds first of several revolutionary societies.
1895 War between Italy and Ethiopia (until 1896).
Armenians massacred in Constantinople.
Revolutionary movement active in Cuba against Spain (to 1898).
Treaty of Shimonoseki: Japan gains Formosa; China recognizes Korea's independence.
Territory of South African Company named Rhodesia after Cecil Rhodes.
Jameson Raid: attack on Boer republic of Transvaal fails (1896).
1896 Anglo-Egyptian forces led by General Kitchener begin reconquest of Sudan.
Battle of Adua: Ethiopian victory.
Final Anglo-Ashanti War; Ashanti defeated.
Treaty of Addis Ababa: Italy recognizes independence of Ethiopia.
France annexes Madagascar.
Anglo-French agreement settles boundaries in Siam (Thailand).
British protectorates established in Sierra Leone and East Africa.
1897 Greek and Turkey at war over Crete.
Germans occupy Kiaochow, China.
1898 Battle of Omdurman: British defeat Sudan rebels.
Fashoda Incident: confrontation between Britain and France in the Sudan; France withdraws (1899).
Spain and United States at war over Cuba.
Treaty of Paris: Cuba gains independence; Spain cedes Puerto Rico, Guam, and Philippines to United States.
China cedes Port Arthur to Russia.
Social Democratic Party founded in Russia.
United States annexes Hawaii.
1899 First Hague Peace Conference held; aims to settle international disputes peacefully.
Boer War between British and Boers in South Africa (to 1902); Boers besiege Mafeking, Kimberley and Ladysmith.
1900 Boxer Rebellion: Nationalist forces (Boxers) in China rebel and besiege foreign legations; rebellion suppressed by international forces.
Labour Representation Committee founded in Britain.
Kimberley, Ladysmith and Mafeking relieved by British forces under Generals Roberts and Kitchener; Britain annexes Orange Free State and Transvaal.
British conquest of northern Nigeria begins; completed in 1903.
German Navy Law provides for massive increase in sea power; starts arms race with Britain.
1901 Edward VII, King of England (to 1910).
Terrorist activities increase in Russia.
Russia occupies Manchuria, north-eastern China.
1902 Treaty of Vereeninging ends Boer War.

Anglo-Japanese alliance formed.

British and German fleets seize Venezuelan navy to force payment of debts.

1903 Women's Social and Political Union formed in Britain by suffragette Mrs Emmeline Pankhurst.

General agitation about appalling labour conditions in Congo Free State; Belgian commission investigates, 1904.

Pius X, Pope (to 1914).

Panama achieves independence from Colombia.

Russian Social Democratic Party meets in London; split between moderate *Mensheviks* and extreme *Bolsheviks*.

1904 Russia and Japan at war (until 1905).

Entente cordiale (friendly understanding) reached between Britain and France.

British explorer Sir Francis Younghusband leads expedition to Tibet; treaty opens Tibet to western trade.

British troops during the South African War of 1899–1902. The Boer (Dutch) settlers of South Africa resented British annexation of their land, and denied civil rights to foreigners seeking gold. They declared war in 1899, finally surrendering only after prolonged guerilla warfare.

1905 Moroccan crisis between France and Germany.

Union of Sweden and Norway ends. Prince Carl of Denmark, chosen by independent Norway, becomes King Haakon VII (to 1957).

Reforming Liberal government in Britain.

Port Arthur falls to Japan.

Battle of Mukden: Russian defeat; battle of Tsushima: Russian fleet destroyed by Japanese.

Treaty of Portsmouth ends Russo-Japanese war.

'Bloody Sunday': troops fire on workers in St Petersburg, Russia – several killed; general strike and revolution; October Manifesto issued by Tsar Nicholas II grants limited reforms.

Bengal partitioned, arousing strong nationalist feelings in India.

1906 First Labour MPs returned in British general election; Labour Party formed.

French officer Alfred Dreyfus declared innocent of treason on retrial.

Algeciras conference: international meet , to discuss Morocco; French rights recognizea.

First Russian *Duma* (representative body) meets, but is dissolved.

Liberal revolution in Persia: Shah Nasir ud-Din grants constitution.

HMS *Dreadnought*, first modern battleship, launched in Britain.

Severe earthquake in San Francisco, USA.

1907 Second Hague Peace Conference: Germany opposes proposed arms limitation.

Second Duma dismissed in Russia; third, more conservative Duma lasts until 1912.

Entente cordiale between Russia and Britain.

Triple *entente* among Britain, France and Russia in opposition to Triple Alliance of Germany, Austria-Hungary and Italy.

1908 Belgium takes over Congo Free State; changes name to Belgian Congo.

Austria annexes Bosnia and Herzegovina.

Revolution in Turkey led by Young Turk movement.

Crete proclaims union with Greece.

Bulgaria declares independence from Turkey.

Successful counter-revolution in Persia, supported by Russia.

1909 Old age pensions introduced in Britain.

Sultan Abdul Hamid II of Turkey overthrown.

American manufacturer Henry Ford begins 'assembly line' production of cheap motorcars.

Indian Councils Act: increases elected members on Indian councils.

American explorer Robert Peary reaches North Pole, after seven visits to the Arctic.

1910 George V, King of England (to 1936).

Revolution in Portugal; republic declared.

Union of South Africa becomes independent dominion within British Empire.

Japan annexes Korea.

British suffragette movement becomes increasingly militant.

1911 Parliament Act reduces power of House of Lords in Britain.

British MPs receive salaries for first time.

Agadir Crisis between France and Germany: Germany sends gunboat to Morocco, but withdraws claims.

Italy occupies Tripoli, Libya; war with Turkey.

Revolution in Mexico overthrows President Diaz; period of disorder follows.

Norwegian explorer Roald Amundsen reaches South Pole.

Sun Yat-sen leads revolution in China and overthrows Manchu Dynasty; republic formed (1912).

1912 French protectorate established in Morocco; Spanish zone defined by agreement.

Treaty of Ouchy ends Italo-Turkish war; Tripoli ceded to Italy.

Fourth Russian Duma (to 1916).

Miners' strike in Britain.

British liner *Titanic* sinks with loss of 1513 lives.

First Balkan War: Bulgaria, Greece, Serbia, and Montenegro unite against Turkey.

1913 Third Irish Home Rule Bill passes House of Commons; rejected by House of Lords. Threat of civil war in Ireland; Ulster Volunteers (private Protestant army) formed in opposition to proposed Home Rule Bill.

Young Turks establish dictatorship in Turkey. Treaty of London ends First Balkan War; Balkan states victorious; new state of Albania created.

Greece officially takes over Crete.

Second Balkan War: Serbia, Greece, Romania, and Turkey unite against Bulgaria; war caused by Serbian claims to Macedonia.

Treaty of Bucharest ends Second Balkan War; Bulgaria defeated; Balkan states again partitioned.

Treaty of Constantinople between Turkey and Bulgaria.

1914 June 28 Archduke Franz Ferdinand of Austria assassinated at Sarajevo by a Bosnian student.

World War I (until 1918): major Allied Powers – Britain, France, Russia, Italy and the United States; Central Powers – Germany, Austria-Hungary and Turkey.

July 28 Austria invades Serbia.

July to November Declarations of war.

August 4 Germans attack Belgium.

August 26 Battle of Tannenburg: Russians defeated by German forces.

September 5 Battle of the Marne: lasts until September 9; Allies halt German advance on Paris.

September 6 Battle of the Masurian Lakes: lasts until September 15; Russians retreat from East Prussia.

October 30 Battle of Ypres: ends November 24; Germans fail to reach Channel ports.

Trench warfare on Western and Eastern Fronts, until end of World War I.

Irish Home Rule Act provides for separate Parliament in Ireland, with some MPs at Westminster. Position of Ulster (Northern Ireland) to be decided after the War.

Panama Canal opened.

1915 January 5 Britain announces naval blockade of Germany.

Gallipoli Campaign (until March 22, 1916): Allied forces land on Gallipoli Peninsula, Turkey, but fail to gain control of Dardanelles Straits.

February 18 Germany begins submarine blockade of Britain.

April 22 Second Battle of Ypres: ends May 25; poison gas used for first time by Germans.

May 7 German U-boat sinks British liner *Lusitania*; many civilians including Americans drowned.

May 22 Italy joins Allied Powers.

September Battles of Artois, Champagne and Loos: British and French offensive fails.

October 15 Bulgaria joins Central Powers.

Swiss physicist Albert Einstein publishes his *General Theory of Relativity*.

1916 February 21 Battle of Verdun: German offensive on Western Front, February to July; appalling losses; stalemate continues.

April 24 Easter rising in Ireland; suppressed after one week.

May 31 Battle of Jutland: only major naval battle between Britain and Germany.

June 4 Brusilov offensive: Russian attack led by General Alexei Brusilov fails.

July 1 Battle of the Somme: British offensive lasts until November 18; more than one million killed; tanks used for first time by Britain.

1917 March 11 British capture Baghdad from Turkey. Revolution in Russia: Nicholas II abdicates; replaced by provisional government.

April 6 United States declares war on Germany.

July 6 British soldier T E Lawrence ('Lawrence of Arabia') takes over command of Arab revolt against Turkey (until 1918).

July 31 Third battle of Ypres (Passchendaele): major British offensive on Western Front; initially successful but little gained after German counter-attack.

October 24 Battle of Caporetto: Italians defeated.

November 7 October Revolution: Bolsheviks

Left: German positions on the Western Front during World War I.

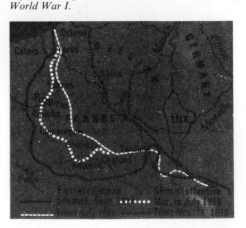

led by Vladimir Lenin seize power in Russia.
November 8 Balfour Declaration: Britain announces support for Jewish state in Palestine.
December 9 British capture Jerusalem.
1918 March 3 Treaty of Brest-Litovsk between Russia and Germany; Russia withdraws from war.
Women over 30 get vote in Britain.
July 15 Second battle of the Marne: last major German offensive fails on August 2.
July (?) Tsar Nicholas II and family murdered.
August 8 Allies' offensive on Western Front begins; Germans forced to retreat.
October 24 Battle of Vittorio Veneto: Italian victory; Austria-Hungary surrenders.
November 7 Revolution in Germany; William II abdicates; republic declared.
Nov 11 Germany signs Armistice; World War I ends.
Russia adopts Gregorian calendar.
1919 January Peace conference begins in Paris; founding of League of Nations.
June Treaty of Versailles signed by Germany; Germany to lose Alsace-Lorraine and colonies; also to pay *reparations* (compensation) to Allies.
September Treaty of Saint-Germain signed by Austria; ends Habsburg monarchy; Austria to recognize independence of Czechoslovakia, Poland, Yugoslavia, and Hungary.
Rebellion in Ireland led by Irish nationalist movement, the *Sinn Fein* party.
Weimar Constitution adopted in Germany.
Spartacist (Communist) rising in Berlin crushed; socialist leader Rosa Luxembourg murdered.
Italian nationalist Gabriel d'Annunzio seizes Fiume from Yugoslavia.
Fascist movement founded in Italy by Benito Mussolini.
Indian leader Mohandas Gandhi (Mahatma)

Members of the Bolshevik party in the 1917 Russian Revolution. When they came to power they centralized control of land and food production, confiscated property, and ruled dictatorially.

begins campaign of passive resistance to Britain.
Amritsar massacre: British troops fire on nationalist rioters in India.
1920 Civil war in Ireland; situation aggravated by British auxiliaries, the 'Black and Tans'.
Northern Ireland accepts Home Rule Act.
Treaty of Rapallo between Italy and Yugoslavia.
Russia and Poland at war.
League of Nations meets for first time.
Prohibition in United States (until 1933).
Treaty of Sèvres between Allies and Turkey opposed by Turkish nationalists led by Mustafa Kemal (later Ataturk).
Palestine established as Jewish state under British administration.
1921 Irish Free State established; Irish Republican Army (IRA) continues opposition.
Greece attacks Turkey but is finally defeated (1922).
Turkish nationalist government set up at Ankara.
Treaty of Riga ends Russo-Polish war.
Mutiny of Russian sailors at Kronstadt, Finland, is put down.
Washington Conference (to 1922) held to discuss naval armaments: four-power Pacific Treaty among Britain, France, Japan and the United States.
1922 Fascists march on Rome; King Victor Emmanuel III invites Benito Mussolini to be Prime Minister.
Egypt declared independent from British and French influence.
Pius XI, Pope (to 1939).
Union of Soviet Socialist Republics established.
Sultan of Turkey deposed by Mustafa Kemal.
1923 French and Belgian troops occupy Ruhr district, west Germany, after Germany fails to pay reparations.
Virtual dictatorship in Spain under Spanish General Primo de Rivera (until 1930).
Mussolini creates Fascist state in Italy.
Adolf Hitler, founder of the National Socialist (Nazi) Party in Germany, attempts to overthrow Bavarian government but is imprisoned.
Treaty of Lausanne between Greece and Turkey.
Turkey proclaimed a republic; first president, Mustafa Kemal.
1924 First Labour government in Britain.
Dawes Plan settles reparation payments to be made by Germany.
Italian socialist, Giacomo Matteotti, murdered by Fascists.
Death of Vladimir Lenin; Joseph Stalin succeeds him.
Chinese government set up at Canton under Sun Yat-sen; it includes Communist members.
1925 Locarno Conference: the great powers agree to put disputes to arbitration.
Arab uprising in Morocco led by Abd-el-Krim; crushed by France and Spain (1926).
1926 General strike in Britain.
Army in Portugal overthrows government.
Germany is admitted to League of Nations.
Canberra becomes the federal capital of Australia.
1927 Chiang Kai-shek, successor to Sun Yat-sen, purges Communists; sets up government at

Nanking; civil war begins between Communists and Nationalists.

American pilot Charles Lindbergh makes first solo transatlantic flight.

1928 Kellogg-Briand Pact signed in Paris; great powers denounce war.

Scottish scientist Alexander Fleming discovers penicillin.

1929 Young Plan reassesses German reparation payments; replaces Dawes Plan.

United States' stock market collapses, leading to worldwide economic depression.

First major conflict between Jews and Arabs in Palestine.

American explorer Richard Byrd flies over South Pole.

1930 London naval conference: great powers fail to agree on naval limitations.

Treaty of Ankara between Greece and Turkey.

1931 Statute of Westminster clarifies status of Britain and the dominions.

Britain abandons the gold standard.

King Alfonso XIII of Spain flees the country; republic is proclaimed.

Japanese occupy Manchuria; set up puppet state Manchukuo (1932).

1932 Disarmament conference meets at Geneva but achieves nothing.

Imperial conference at Ottawa; Britain gives limited trading preference to Commonwealth.

Portuguese finance minister, Antonio de Oliveira Salazar, becomes dictator of Portugal.

War between Paraguay and Bolivia (until 1935) over the Chaco region.

1933 Adolf Hitler is appointed chancellor by German President Paul von Hindenburg.

Burning of German *Reichstag* (parliament).

International economic conference in London.

Germany withdraws from League of Nations.

National Socialists begin to eliminate all opposition and gain control of Germany.

Communist Party in USSR purged by Stalin.

Anarchist uprisings in Barcelona put down by Spanish Government.

Prohibition ends in United States.

1934 Austrian chancellor Dollfuss killed by Nazis.

President Hindenburg dies; Hitler becomes *Führer* (leader) of Germany.

Balkan Pact formed among Turkey, Greece, Romania, and Yugoslavia.

Mao Tse-tung leads Chinese Communists northwards on the Long March from Kiangsi; reach Yenan in 1935.

1935 Hitler renounces Treaty of Versailles; announces policy of rearmament.

Italian forces invade Ethiopia (Abyssinia); League of Nations fails to intervene effectively.

Nuremberg Laws; persecution of Jews begins in Germany.

Monarchy restored in Greece.

Persia officially called Iran.

Government of India Act passed by British Parliament; sets up provincial councils.

1936 Edward VIII, King of Great Britain; abdicates after 325 days.

George VI, King of Great Britain (to 1952).

Italians take Addis Ababa; annex Ethiopia.

Germany reoccupies Rhineland.

Adolf Hitler, dictator of Nazi Germany from 1933 to 1945, at a mass rally of the Nazi party. His ambitions to establish a thousand-year German Reich (kingdom) led to World War II.

July 17 Military revolt led by General Francisco Franco against Spanish government begins Spanish Civil War (lasts until July 1939); Italy and Germany support rebels; Soviet Union sends aid to Republicans.

October 25 Agreement between Italy and Germany: Rome-Berlin Axis set up.

1937 April 26 German planes bomb Guernica, Spain.

May 28 Coalition government formed in Britain under Neville Chamberlain.

July 7 Japanese invade China; capture Shanghai and Peking.

September Britain adopts policy of appeasement.

1938 March 13 Germany invades and annexes Austria.

September 29 Munich Pact signed by Hitler, Mussolini, Chamberlain, and French premier, Edouard Daladier; Germany to gain Sudetenland in Czechoslovakia.

1939 January 26 Nationalists under General Franco capture Barcelona.

March 10 Germany annexes Czechoslovakia.

April 1 Madrid surrenders; ends Spanish Civil War.

April 7 Italy invades Albania.

September 1 Germany invades Poland; beginning of World War II (until 1945).

September 3 Britain and France declare war on Germany.

September 17 Russia invades Poland.

September 29 Nazi-Soviet pact: Poland partitioned between Russia and Germany.

Russo-Finnish war: Finland defeated November 1940.

1940 April 9 Germany invades Denmark and Norway; on May 10 invades Belgium, the Netherlands, and Luxembourg.

April 30 Japan joins Axis Powers.

May 17 Germany invades France.

May 27 British army evacuated from Dunkirk.

June 10 Italy declares war on Britain and France.

June 14 Germans occupy Paris, France surrenders.

War in the desert: Allied tanks and infantry advance to gain victory at El Alamein in 1942, a turning point in the war. Right: The 1945 Yalta Conference of the 'Big Three'.

July 10 Battle of Britain: British air victory prevents German invasion (to October 31).
October 28 Italy invades Greece.
1941 June 22 Germany invades Russia.
September 1 Italy and Germany invade Egypt.
Leningrad besieged by German forces; relieved January 1944.
December Russian counter-offensive in Ukraine.
December 7 Japan launches air attack on United States' Pacific Fleet in Pearl Harbor, Hawaii, and between then and May 1942 overran Hong Kong, Malaya, the Dutch East Indies, Burma, and the Philippines.
December 8 United States declares war on Axis.
1942 September 6 Battle of Stalingrad: Germans defeated.
October 23 Battle of El Alamein: Germans under General Rommel defeated by Allies.
Germans retreat from North Africa; Anglo-American forces take Tripoli and Tunis; end of Axis resistance in North Africa (May 1943).
1943 January 31 German forces at Stalingrad surrender.
July 1 United States begins recapture of Japanese-held islands in the Pacific.
September 3 Italian government surrenders.
1944 June 4 Allies enter Rome.
June 6 Allies land in Normandy, northern France; German forces begin retreat.
July 20 Bomb plot to assassinate Hitler fails.
September 2 Allies liberate Paris and Brussels.
September 8 First V-2 missile lands in England.
October 3 Warsaw resistance crushed by Germans.
October 25 Battle of Leyte Gulf: Japanese navy defeated.
1945 January 17 Warsaw captured by Russians.
February 7 Yalta Conference: meeting of Churchill, Roosevelt, and Stalin to discuss post-war settlements. March 7 Allies invade Germany: Dresden bombed.
April 28 Mussolini assassinated by Italian partisans.
April 30 Adolf Hitler commits suicide.
May 7 Germany surrenders.

San Francisco conference: United Nations charter signed.
August 5 and 9 First atomic bombs used against Japan; Hiroshima and Nagasaki devastated.
Japan surrenders; World War II ends.
Potsdam conference: main Allied powers meet to discuss peace terms and post-war settlements.
1946 League of Nations formally ended.
Norwegian statesman, Trygve Lie, elected Secretary General of United Nations.
Peace conference opens in Paris.
Nuremberg trials: Nazi leaders sentenced for war crimes by international court.
Republic of Hungary proclaimed.
Transjordan (Jordan) gains independence.
Britain and United States agree on economic fusion of their zones in Germany.
Civil war in Indochina (until 1954) between Vietnamese nationalists led by Ho Chi Minh, and the French.
1947 Allied peace treaties signed in Paris with Italy, Romania, Hungary, Bulgaria, and Finland.
Four-power conference of foreign ministers on Germany fails to reach agreement.
Marshall Aid: programme of aid for Europe introduced by United States' Secretary of State George Marshall.
Cominform (Communist Information Bureau) is set up with headquarters at Belgrade, Yugoslavia.
Cheribon Agreement between Dutch and Indonesians; United States of Indonesia established.
India gains independence; two dominions created – India (Hindu) and Pakistan (Muslim).
Dispute between India and Pakistan over Kashmir; state ceded to India.
Burma gains independence.
Partition of Palestine into Arab and Jewish states agreed by United Nations; Arabs reject proposals.
1948 Communist *coup* (takeover) in Czechoslovakia; People's Republic formed.
State of Israel declared.

215

War between Israel and Arab League (until 1949).

Indian statesman Mahatma Gandhi assassinated by Hindu extremist.

Soviet Union blockades West Berlin; zone supplied by airlift (until 1949).

Ceylon (now Sri Lanka) becomes a self-governing dominion.

China split by conflict between Communists and Nationalists.

Division of Korea into Republic of Korea (South Korea) and People's Republic (North Korea).

1949 South African government adopts *apartheid* (separation of black and white) as official policy.

North Atlantic Treaty Organization (NATO) formed as defensive alliance by Western nations.

Mao Tse-tung establishes Communist regime in China; Chinese Nationalist government escapes to Formosa (Taiwan).

Germany is divided into Federal Republic (West) and German Democratic Republic (East).

Comecon (Council for Mutual Economic Assistance) founded by Soviet Union and Communist states.

France recognizes independent Vietnam and Cambodia.

Russian blockade of Berlin ends.

Arab-Israeli armistice: Jerusalem partitioned.

Russia recognizes newly established People's Republic of China.

1950 Korean war (until 1953) between North Korea supported by China, and South Korea supported by United Nations forces.

Anglo-Egyptian dispute over the Sudan and Suez Canal.

American senator Joseph McCarthy heads inquiry into 'un-American (Communist) activities'.

Agreement between East Germany and Poland fixes Oder and Neisse Rivers as frontier.

1951 West Germany admitted to the Council of Europe.

Egypt withdraws from Anglo-Egyptian agreement on Suez Canal; British troops occupy Canal Zone.

Schuman Plan: France, West Germany, Italy, Belgium, Netherlands, and Luxemburg agree to set up market for coal and steel; becomes effective 1952.

Marshall Plan ends.

Peace treaty signed at San Francisco by Japan, and most of Japan's opponents during World War II.

Chinese Communist forces occupy Tibet.

Colombo Plan for economic development of south and south-east Asia comes into effect.

1952 Elizabeth II, Queen of Britain.

Bonn Convention: agreement among Britain, France, United States, and West Germany ends occupation of West Germany.

Greece and Turkey join NATO.

European Coal and Steel Community holds first meeting at Luxembourg.

China accuses United States of waging germ warfare in Korea.

Mau Mau (secret organization of Kikuyu tribesmen) begins terrorist activities against British in Kenya.

First national election in India; Jawaharlal Nehru elected prime minister.

1953 New Zealand mountaineer Edmund Hillary and Sherpa Tenzing first to climb highest mountain in the world, Mount Everest in the Himalayas.

Swedish statesman Dag Hammarskjöld replaces Trygve Lie as secretary-general of United Nations.

Stalin dies; Georgi Malenkov becomes Soviet premier.

Bermuda conference of British, American, and French statesmen.

Treaty of Panmunjon ends Korean War.

Military *coup* in Egypt, monarchy ends; republic established.

French forces occupy Dien Bien Phu, North Vietnam; Viet Minh forces invade Laos.

Kenyan politician Jomo Kenyatta imprisoned on charges of Mau Mau involvement.

Yugoslav Communist leader Marshal Tito becomes president of Yugoslavia.

1954 Disturbances in Cyprus and Greece over *enosis* (union of Cyprus and Greece).

French finally defeated by Viet Minh at Dien Bien Phu, North Vietnam.

Geneva conference: Vietnam divided; North Vietnam under Communist government of Ho Chi Minh, South Vietnam supported by Britain and United States; beginning of Communist attempts to take over country.

South-East Asia Treaty Organization (SEATO) formed to prevent spread of Communism in South-East Asia.

1955 Warsaw Pact: eastern European defence treaty signed by Communist nations.

EOKA, Greek Cypriot organization led by Grivas, begins terrorist activities in Cyprus.

Israel raids Egyptian and Syrian borders.

Baghdad Pact signed by Turkey, Iraq, Iran, Pakistan, and Britain.

Bandung Conference: first major meeting of 29 Asian and African nations.

West Germany admitted to NATO.

International conference at Geneva discusses peaceful uses of atomic energy.

Armed rebellion and general strike in Argentina: President Juan Peron goes into exile.

1956 Soviet Premier Nikita Khrushchev denounces former premier Joseph Stalin.

Anti-Russian uprising in Hungary crushed by Soviet troops.

Britain withdraws troops from Suez Canal Zone; Colonel Gamal Abdul Nasser elected president of Egypt.

Nasser nationalizes Suez Canal; Israeli forces invade Egypt; Anglo-French forces occupy Suez Canal zone; United Nations calls for cease-fire and sends in emergency forces to enforce it.

France recognizes independence of Morocco and Tunisia.

1957 Guerrilla activity in Cuba begins under leadership of Fidel Castro against dictatorship of Fulgencio Batista.

Treaty of Rome signed by Belgium, France, West Germany, Italy, Luxemburg and Nether-

Top: American troops in the Korean War. Centre: Hillary and Tenzing, first to climb Mount Everest in 1953. Bottom: 1960s Communist leaders Castro of Cuba and Khrushchev of the USSR.

lands establishes European Economic Community (the 'Common Market').

Suez Canal re-opened to all shipping.

Soviet Union launches *Sputnik I*, first artificial satellite.

1958 Egypt and Syria form United Arab Republic (UAR); Yemen joins to form United Arab States.

Military revolt in Iraq led by Abdul Kassem; King Faisal II assassinated; republic declared.

United States launches *Explorer I*, its first satellite; space race begins.

Charles de Gaulle elected first president of French Fifth Republic.

John XXIII, Pope (to 1963).

1959 Batista government in Cuba overthrown; Communist guerilla leader Fidel Castro becomes premier.

Uprising in Tibet against Chinese rule; Dalai Lama escapes to India; revolt crushed.

Anti-European riots in Léopoldville, capital of Belgian Congo.

1960 Seventeen colonies in Africa gain independence.

In newly independent Congo (Léopoldville) civil war breaks out as Katanga province, under Moise Tshombe, breaks away.

European Free Trade Association (EFTA) and Central American Common Market formed.

United States' reconnaissance aircraft shot down over Soviet territory.

Cyprus becomes independent republic under President Archbishop Makarios.

John Fitzgerald Kennedy becomes youngest, and first Roman Catholic, president of United States (to 1963).

International agreement to reserve Antarctica for scientific research; all territorial claims waived.

1961 East Germany tightens borders: Berlin Wall is built.

Latin American Free Trade Association is formed (LAFTA).

Britain begins application to join European Economic Community.

Death of Patrice Lumumba, president of Congo (Léopoldville).

Soviet cosmonaut Yuri Gagarin becomes first man in space.

Bay of Pigs: exiles' invasion of Cuba fails.

Dag Hammarskjöld, UN secretary-general, killed in air crash while travelling to talks in Congo; succeeded by Burmese U Thant.

South Africa becomes a republic and withdraws from the Commonwealth.

1962 Disarmament conference in Geneva.

Confrontation between United States and Soviet Union over Russian missiles and bombers based in Cuba; Soviet Union agrees to withdraw its Cuban bases.

Border clashes between China and India.

Telstar communications satellite launched: first

live TV broadcasts between United States and Europe.

Algeria gains independence from France.

1963 South Vietnamese government overthrown by military coup.

Organisation of African Unity formed by independent African states (OAU).

Paul VI Pope (until 1978).

Nuclear test ban treaty signed by Britain, Soviet Union, and United States.

President John F. Kennedy of United States assassinated; succeeded by Vice-President Lyndon B. Johnson.

1964 Fighting breaks out between Greeks and Turks in Cyprus; United Nations troops sent in to maintain peace.

United States' involvement in Vietnam war increases; support declared for South Vietnam against Communist Viet Cong.

Civil rights Act becomes law in United States.

Soviet premier Nikita Khruschev falls from power, succeeded by Aleksei Kosygin.

1965 United States undertakes regular bombing raids on North Vietnam.

India and Pakistan go to war over Kashmir; United Nations calls for ceasefire.

First American marines land in South Vietnam.

Death of Sir Winston Churchill.

White government of Rhodesia under premier Ian Smith makes unilateral declaration of independence (UDI) from Britain; British economic pressure fails to halt crisis.

Britain abolishes death penalty for murder.

1966 War between Indonesia and Malaysia ends.

South African Prime Minister Dr Verwoerd assassinated; succeeded by John Vorster.

'Cultural Revolution' in China (to 1968); Red Guards formed.

1967 Military a *coup* in Greece.

Six Day War (June 5–10) between Arabs and Israelis; Israel occupies Sinai Desert, Jerusalem and west bank of Jordan River; cease fire arranged by United Nations.

Civil war in Nigeria (to 1970): Biafra region breaks away from Nigeria Federation.

1968 Civil rights leader Martin Luther King assassinated in United States.

Assassination of presidential candidate Robert Kennedy.

Soviet troops invade Czechoslovakia to crush liberalism of Czechoslovakian secretary, Alexander Dubcek.

Crisis in Northern Ireland begins.

Tet Offensive: Viet Cong launch major offensive in Vietnam.

1969 Britain sends troops to Northern Ireland.

French President Charles de Gaulle resigns.

American astronauts land on the Moon.

1970 Biafra surrenders; ends Nigerian civil war.

United States President, Richard Nixon, announces invasion of Cambodia.

Civil war in Jordan between government troops and Palestinian guerilas.

1971 East Pakistan becomes independent as Bangladesh after civil war and intervention by India.

Communist China joins United Nations; Taiwan (Formosa) expelled.

1972 Ceylon becomes republic as Sri Lanka.

Britain takes over direct rule of Northern Ireland.

1973 Britain, Ireland and Denmark join EEC.

United States withdraws troops from Vietnam; peace settlement signed at Paris.

Military *coup* in Chile overthrows Marxist President, Salvadore Allende.

October War: Arab states attack Israel; ceasefire imposed after five weeks of fighting.

Arab oil-producing nations restrict oil supplies, resulting in world economic crisis.

1974 Greek-Turkish conflict in Cyprus; Greek military junta resigns; Turks occupy Nicosia.

President Richard Nixon forced to resign after Watergate scandal. Gerald Ford succeeds him.

Coup in Portugal ends dictatorship of President Caetano. Former Portuguese colonies Guinea, Bissau, Angola, and Mozambique gain independence.

1975 Communist victories in Cambodia; South Vietnam surrenders to North Vietnam; ends Vietnam War.

Spanish dictator Franco dies; his protégé Juan Carlos, grandson of last king of Spain becomes king.

1976 Race riots erupt in South Africa.

Rhodesian whites accept Kissinger plan for black majority rule; later rejected by blacks.

Death of Mao Tse-tung.

Jimmy Carter wins US presidential election.

1977 President Sadat of Egypt goes to Israel on a peace mission. Prime Minister Begin of Israel returns the visit. Negotiations on peace terms start.

1978 A UN force is sent to Lebanon, because of border troubles with Israel.

Pope Paul VI dies; Pope John Paul I is installed. He dies two months later. John Paul II is elected as the first non-Italian Pope for over 450 years.

USA agrees to diplomatic relations with China and ends those with Taiwan.

Vietnamese troops invade Cambodia to support the rebels.

1979 A peace Treaty between Israel and Egypt is signed in Washington.

Phnom Penh, capital of Cambodia (Kampuchea) captured by Vietnamese and rebel forces; serious famine develops in the country.

Conservatives win power in Britain; Margaret Thatcher becomes first woman prime minister.

Kampala captured by Tanzanian troops and Ugandan exiles; General Amin forced to flee.

Adolfo Suarz becomes Spain's first elected Prime Minister for more than 40 years.

Following riots and political pressure the Shah of Iran is deposed; exiled Muslim leader Ayatolah Khomeini returns to Iran which is declared an Islamic republic.

Russian forces move into Afghanistan.

1980 Robert Mugabe, leader of ZANU, wins election in Zimbabwe-Rhodesia; the country becomes independent as Zimbabwe with Mugabe its first president.

Polish Solidarity trade union, led by Lech Walesa, confronts Communist government.

War betwen Iran and Iraq.

1981 Ronald Reagan becomes 40th President of the United States. US hostages in Iran freed.

Greece becomes 10th member of Common

Market.

Francois Mitterand defeats Valéry Giscard d'Estaing for the French presidency.

First flight of US space shuttle.

President Sadat of Egypt assassinated; assassination attempts on President Reagan and Pope John Paul II fail.

1982 A new political party, the Social Democratic Party, is founded in Britain.

Argentina invades Falkland Islands and South Georgia; a British task force reoccupies the islands.

1983 Yuri Andropov becomes Soviet head of state.

Conservatives win British General Election.

1984 Yuri Andropov dies; Konstantin Chernenko succeeds him as Communist party leader.

American President Ronald Reagan wins landslide re-election victory.

1985 Konstantin Chernenko dies: Mikhail Gorbachev succeeds him.

Spain and Portugal join the Common Market.

English soccer fans riot at Heysel Stadium, Brussels, leading 38 dead.

Mexican earthquake kills 7,000 people.

1986 *Challenger* space shuttle explodes after take-off, killing all seven crew members.

Philippine President Ferdinand Marcos is overthrown; Mrs Corazon Acquino succeeds him.

Nuclear reactor at Russia's Chernobyl power station explodes, killing more than 30 people and spreading dangerous radioactivity across Europe.

1987 British car ferry capsizes at Zeebrugge; 188 people die.

Conservatives win third successive General Election.

Stock market crashes in New York, Tokyo and London wipe ten per cent off share values.

USA and USSR agree to cut their nuclear arsenals.

1988 In Britain Liberals and some Social Democrats vote to merge their parties.

Soviet troops begin to withdraw from Afghanistan.

Ceasefires halt the Gulf War and Angola bush war.

Earthquake kills 45,000 people in Soviet Armenia.

Kuwait soldiers received a hero's welcome when they returned to liberate their capital on 27 February 1991. Iraq had occupied Kuwait since 2 August 1990.

Sabotaged US jumbo jet crashes at Lockerbie, Scotland; 270 people killed.

Benazir Bhutto becomes prime minister of Pakistan.

1989 Emperor Hirohito of Japan dies.

George Bush takes office as 41st US president.

In Poland, Solidarity is declared legal again.

Kampuchea changes its name back to Cambodia.

A million Chinese students and workers demonstrate in Beijing, calling for greater democracy.

Death of Ayatollah Khomeini.

President P. W. Botha of South Africa resigns; succeeded by F. W. de Klerk.

Troops massacre student protesters in Beijing.

Communist rule ends in Poland, Hungary, Czechoslovakia, Bulgaria and East Germany; Berlin Wall goes.

In a coup, President Ceausescu of Romania is overthrown and shot.

1990 African National Congress leader Nelson Mandela is freed from prison after 27 years.

US ousts President Manuel Noriega of Panama.

Soviet republics led by Lithuania, Russia and Azerbaijan call for independence from the USSR.

North and South Yemen amalgamate.

South Africa begins to dismantle apartheid.

President Saddam Hussein of Iraq invades and annexes Kuwait; UN imposes sanctions.

East and West Germany amalgamate.

President Gorbachev is given sweeping powers to westernize the ailing Soviet economy.

Pakistan's PM Benazir Bhutto is removed from office.

Britain's Conservative MPs vote against Margaret Thatcher as party leader; she resigns.

John Major becomes Britain's PM.

UN gives Iraq until January 15, 1991, to leave Kuwait.

1991 Saddam Hussein defies UN deadline; military action forces the Iraqis out of Kuwait several weeks later.

Middle East peace conference opens in Madrid.

Baltic States of Estonia, Latvia and Lithuania become independent countries.

Civil war in Yugoslavia as Slovenia and Croatia pursue independence.

Rajiv Gandhi, former prime minister of India, is assassinated.

125,000 killed by cyclone in Bangladesh.

Boris Yeltsin elected president of Russia.

US and British hostages in Lebanon are freed.

Kiichi Miyazawa becomes premier of Japan.

1992 Bill Clinton elected 42nd President of the US.

Conservative party is re-elected in general election in Britain.

France's first woman premier, Edith Cresson, resigns.

Fighting continues among newly-formed nations of what was once Yugoslavia. United Nations imposes sanctions to stop the bloodshed.

Delegates from 178 countries attend Earth Summit in Rio de Janeiro.

Fidel Ramos becomes president of Philippines.

52 killed in riots in Los Angeles after 4 policemen are aquitted of beating a black man.

1993 Fighting continues in Bosnia-Herzegovina.

Macedonian independence recognized by UN.

Eritrea becomes independent.

MAJOR BATTLES

GREEKS AND ROMANS

Marathon 490 BC Force of 10,000 Athenians and allies defeated 50,000 Persian troops, crushing a Persian invasion attempt and boosting Greek morale.

Salamis 480 BC Greek fleet of 360 ships under Themistocles defeated Persian fleet of 1000 ships commanded by Xerxes, and Persians had to withdraw from Greece.

Siege of Syracuse 414–413 BC Athenians besieged city of Syracuse in the Peloponnesian War; siege ended when night attack led by Athenian general Demosthenes was decisively repulsed.

Aegospotami 405 BC Spartan fleet under Lysander defeated last Athenian fleet, and ended the Peloponnesian War.

Arbela 331 BC Alexander the Great's Greek army defeated a Persian force twice the size under Darius III, conquering Persia. The battle was fought at Gaugamela, 25 mi (40 km) from Arbela.

Zama 202 BC Romans under Scipio Africanus defeated the Carthaginians under Hannibal, winning Second Punic War.

Actium 31 BC Roman fleet of 400 ships under Octavian (later Emperor Augustus) defeated 500 ships, combined fleet of Mark Antony and Cleopatra. The victory made Octavian master of Rome and its empire.

Teutoberg Forest AD **9** German tribesmen under the chief Arminius destroyed three Roman legions, ending Roman plans to invade and conquer their lands.

Adrianople AD **378** Visigoths under Fridigern defeated and killed the Roman Emperor Valens at Adrianople (now Edirne, Turkey).

Châlons-sur-Marne AD **451** Romans led by Flavius Aetius and Visigoths led by Theodoric I defeated the Huns under Attila, curbing their threat to the West.

EARLY EUROPE

Tours 732 The Franks under Charles Martel defeated the Saracens (Muslims), halting their advance in western Europe.

Hastings 1066 About 8000 troops under Duke William of Normandy defeated an equal force under Saxon king Harold II. England thereafter came under Norman rule.

Crécy 1346 Invading army of 10,000 English under Edward III defeated 20,000 French men-at-arms. English archers won the day.

Poitiers 1356 Edward the Black Prince of England crushed a French army, capturing the French King John II.

Agincourt 1415 Henry V of England with 10,000 troops defeated 30,000 Frenchmen, and recaptured Normandy.

Siege of Orléans 1428–1429 English troops began siege in October 1428, but in April 1429 Joan of Arc came to the aid of city, and forced the besiegers to withdraw. Victory was a turning point in French campaign to drive the English out of France.

Siege of Constantinople 1453 Ottoman Turkish army of more than 100,000 under Mohammed the Conqueror captured the city, held by 10,000 men led by the last Byzantine emperor, Constantine Paleologus.

WARS OF FAITH & SUCCESSION

Lepanto 1571 Allied Christian fleet of 208 galleys under Don John of Austria defeated Ali Pasha's Turkish fleet of 230 galleys.

Invincible Armada 1588 Spanish invasion fleet led by Duke of Medina Sidonia was defeated by the English under Lord Howard of Effingham.

Naseby 1645 Sir Thomas Fairfax with 14,000

The 'Invincible Armada' of some 130 warships which Philip II of Spain sent to invade England in 1588 was out-manoeuvred and out-gunned by the faster English ships. At night the English caused panic among the anchored Spanish ships by sending fireships floating into them. They fled northwards, rounding Britain to head to Spain. Fewer than 60 returned home; the English lost not one ship.

MAJOR WARS

Name	Date	Won by	Against
Abyssinian War	1935–1936	Italy	Abyssinia (Ethiopia)
American War of Independence	1775–1783	Thirteen Colonies	Britain
Austrian Succession, War of the	1740–1748	Austria, Hungary, Britain, Holland	Bavaria, France, Poland, Prussia, Sardinia, Saxony, Spain
Boer (South African) War	1899–1902	Britain	Boer Republics
Chinese-Japanese Wars	1894–1895	Japan	China
	1931–1933	Japan	China
	1937–1945	China	Japan
Civil War, American	1861–1865	23 Northern States (The Union)	11 Southern States (the Confederacy)
Civil War, English	1642–1646	Parliament	Charles I
Civil War, Nigerian	1967–1970	Federal government	Biafra
Civil War, Pakistani	1971	East Pakistan (Bangladesh) and India	West Pakistan
Civil War, Spanish	1936–1939	Junta de Defensa Nacional (Fascists)	Republican government
Crimean War	1853–1856	Britain, France, Sardinia, Turkey	Russia
Franco-Prussian War	1870–1871	Prussia and other German states	France
Hundred Years War	1337–1453	France	England
Korean War	1950–1953	South Korea and United Nations forces	North Korea and Chinese forces
Mexican-American War	1846–1848	United States	Mexico
Napoleonic Wars	1792–1815	Austria, Britain, Prussia, Russia, Spain, Sweden	France
October War	1973	Ceasefire arranged by UN: fought by Israel Jordan, against Egypt, Syria, Iraq, Sudan, Saudi Arabia, Lebanon	
Peloponnesian War	431–404 BC	Peloponnesian League, led by Sparta, Corinth	Delian League, led by Athens
Punic Wars	264–146 BC	Rome	Carthage
Russo-Japanese War	1904–1905	Japan	Russia
Seven Years War	1756–1763	Britain, Prussia, Hanover	Austria, France, Russia, Sweden
Six-Day War	1967	Israel	Egypt, Syria, Jordan, Iraq
Spanish-American War	1898	United States	Spain
Spanish Succession, War of the	1701–1713	England, Austria, Prussia, the Netherlands	France, Bavaria, Cologne, Mantua, Savoy
Thirty Years War	1618–1648	France, Sweden, the German Protestant states	The Holy Roman Empire, Spain
Vietnam War	1957–1975	North Vietnam	South Vietnam, United States
War of 1812	1812–1814	United States	Britain
Wars of the Roses	1455–1485	House of Lancaster	House of York
World War I	1914–1918	Belgium, Britain and Empire, France, Italy, Japan, Russia, Serbia, United States	Austria-Hungary, Bulgaria, Germany, Ottoman Empire
World War II	1939–1945	Australia, Belgium, Britain, Canada, China, Denmark, France, Greece, Netherlands, New Zealand, Norway, Poland, Russia, South Africa, United States, Yugoslavia	Bulgaria, Finland, Germany, Hungary, Italy, Japan, Romania

Parliamentary troops defeated Prince Rupert with 10,000 Royalist soldiers, virtually ending Charles I's power.

Boyne 1690 William III of England with 35,000 mixed troops routed his rival, James II, with 21,000 men, ending Stuart hopes of regaining the throne.

Blenheim 1704 A British-Austrian army led by Duke of Marlborough and Prince Eugène defeated the French and Bavarians under Marshal Camille de Tallard during War of the Spanish Succession.

Poltava 1709 The Russians under Peter the Great routed an invading Swedish army led by Charles XII of Sweden, overturning Swedish power in the Baltic.

COLONIAL STRUGGLES

Plassey 1757 Robert Clive with an Anglo-Indian army of 3000 defeated the Nawab of Bengal's army of 60,000, conquering Bengal and setting Britain on the road to domination in India.

Quebec 1759 British troops under James Wolfe made a night attack up the St Lawrence River, climbing the cliffs to the Plains of Abraham overlooking the city. They defeated the French forces under the Marquis de Montcalm; he and Wolfe were killed.

Saratoga 1777 British troops under John Burgoyne surrendered to American colonial forces under Horatio Gates; defeat led France to declare war on Britain.

Yorktown 1781 Charles Cornwallis with 8000 British troops was bottled in, and surrendered to a larger force under George Washington, ending the American War of Independence.

AGE OF NAPOLEON
Valmy 1792 A French Revolutionary army defeated the Prussians in heavy fog. The victory gave new heart to the Revolutionary forces in France.

Nile 1798 Horatio Nelson commanding a British fleet of 15 ships destroyed a 16-ship French fleet under Francis Paul Brueys in Aboukir Bay, cutting off Napoleon Bonaparte's French army in Egypt.

Trafalgar 1805 British fleet of 27 ships under Horatio Nelson shattered Franco-Spanish fleet of 33 ships under Pierre de Villeneuve, ending Napoleon's hopes of invading England. Nelson was killed.

Austerlitz 1805 Emperor Napoleon I with 65,000 French troops defeated an 83,000-strong Austro-Russian army under the Austrian and Russian emperors. The Austrians sued for peace, and the Russians withdrew. Called *Battle of the Three Emperors*.

Jena and Auerstädt 1806 French forces routed the main Prussian armies on the same day (October 14), shattering Prussian power.

Leipzig 1813 Napoleon I with 190,000 French troops was surrounded and crushed by an allied force of 300,000 Austrian, Prussian, Russian, and Swedish troops. This *Battle of the Nations* ended Napoleon's domination of Europe.

Waterloo 1815 A British, Dutch, and Belgian force of 67,000 fought off 74,000 French troops under Napoleon I until the arrival of the Prussian army of Gebhard von Blücher. It ended Napoleon's final bid for power.

FIRST MODERN CONFLICTS
Gettysburg 1863 Federal forces under George Meade defeated Robert E. Lee's Confederate army, a turning point in the American Civil War.

Vicksburg 1863 Federal general Ulysses S. Grant captured Confederate army under John Pemberton, the day after Gettysburg.

Sedan 1870 French army of 100,000 men defeated and surrounded by German force of more than twice the size in decisive battle of Franco-Prussian War.

Tsushima 1905 Japanese fleet destroyed Russian fleet of equal size, bringing victory for Japan in Russo-Japanese War.

WORLD WAR I
Marne 1914 French and British armies halted German forces invading France. From then on war on the Western Front became a trench-based slogging match.

First battle of Ypres 1914 German forces trying to reach Calais lost 150,000 men; British and French armies thwarted attack, losing more than 100,000 men.

Verdun 1916 In a six-month struggle French forces held off a major attack by German armies commanded by Crown Prince William. French losses were 348,000 men, the German losses 328,000.

Jutland 1916 British Grand Fleet led by John Jellicoe fought German High Seas Fleet under Rheinhard Scheer. The Germans never again ventured out to sea.

Somme 1916 In a 141-day battle following Verdun British and French captured 125 sq mi (320 sq km) of ground, losing 600,000 men; German defenders lost almost 500,000.

Passchendaele 1917 (also known as third battle of Ypres). British forces launched eight attacks over 102 days in heavy rain and through thick mud, gaining five miles and losing 400,000 men.

St Mihiel Salient 1918 American victory in World War I: German line broken and Salient flattened out. In first major air battle 1480 Allied planes defeated German air force.

WORLD WAR II
Britain 1940 A German air force of 2500 planes launched an attack lasting 114 days to try to win air supremacy over Britain. The smaller Royal Air Force defeated the attack, preventing a German invasion.

Coral Sea 1942 American fleet drove back a Japanese invasion fleet bound for New Guinea in four-day battle in which all the fighting was done by aeroplanes.

Midway 1942 A 100-ship Japanese fleet led by Isoruko Yamamoto aiming to capture Midway Island was defeated by American fleet half the size, under Raymond Spruance.

El Alamein 1942 British Eighth Army under Bernard Montgomery drove back German Afrika Korps under Erwin Rommel, out of Egypt and deep into Libya.

Stalingrad 1942–1943 Twenty-one German divisions tried to capture Stalingrad (Now Volgograd), but siege was broken, and Friedrich von Paulus had to surrender with more than 100,000 German troops.

Normandy 1944 Allied forces under Dwight D. Eisenhower invaded German-held northern France in biggest-ever sea-borne attack; after a month of heavy fighting Normandy was cleared and Germans began to retreat.

Leyte Gulf 1944 US 3rd and 7th fleets defeated a Japanese force, ending Japanese naval power in World War II.

Ardennes Bulge 1944–1945 Last German counter-attack in west through Ardennes Forest failed; Germans lost 100,000 casualties and 110,000 prisoners.

POST-WAR
Inchon 1950 US forces made surprise landing behind North Korean lines in Korean War, leading to major victory over North Korea.

Dien Bien Phu 1954 French surrendered to Vietminh after 8-week siege; end of French influence in Indochina.

EXPLORATION AND DISCOVERY

Place	Achievement	Explorer or discoverer	Date
World	circumnavigated	Ferdinand Magellan (Port. for Sp.)	1519–21
Pacific Ocean	discovered	Vasco Núñez de Balboa (Sp.)	1513
Africa			
River Congo (mouth)	discovered	Diogo Cão (Port.)	c. 1483
Cape of Good Hope	sailed round	Bartolomeu Diaz (Port.)	1488
River Niger	explored	Mungo Park (Scot.)	1795
River Zambezi	discovered	David Livingstone (Scot.)	1851
Sudan	explored	Heinrich Barth (Germ. for GB)	1852–5
Victoria Falls	discovered	Livingstone	1855
Lake Tanganyika	discovered	Richard Burton & John Speke (GB)	1858
River Congo	traced	Sir Henry Stanley (GB)	1877
Asia			
China	visited	Marco Polo (Ital.)	c. 1272
India (Cape route)	visited	Vasco da Gama (Port.)	1498
Japan	visited	St Francis Xavier (Sp.)	1549
China	explored	Ferdinand Richthofen (Germ.)	1868
North America			
North America	discovered	Leif Ericson (Norse)	c. 1000
West Indies	discovered	Christopher Columbus (Ital. for Sp.)	1492
Newfoundland	discovered	John Cabot (Ital. for Eng.)	1497
Mexico	conquered	Hernando Cortés (Sp.)	1519–21
St Lawrence River	explored	Jacques Cartier (Fr.)	1534–6
Mississippi River	discovered	Hernando de Soto (Sp.)	1541
Canadian interior	explored	Samuel de Champlain (Fr.)	1603–9
Hudson Bay	discovered	Henry Hudson (Eng.)	1610
Alaska	discovered	Vitus Bering (Dan. for Russ.)	1728
Mackenzie River	discovered	Sir Alexander Mackenzie (Scot.)	1789
South America			
South America	visited	Columbus	1498
Venezuela	explored	Alonso de Ojeda (Sp.)	1499
Brazil	discovered	Pedro Alvares Cabral (Port.)	1500
Rio de la Plata	discovered	Juan de Solis (Sp.)	1516
Tierra del Fuego	discovered	Magellan	1520
Peru	explored	Francisco Pizarro (Sp.)	1530–8
River Amazon	explored	Francisco de Orellana (Sp.)	1541
Cape Horn	discovered	Willem Schouten (Dut.)	1616
Australasia, Polar regions, etc.			
Greenland	visited	Eric the Red (Norse)	c. 982
Australia	discovered	unknown	1500s
Spitsbergen	discovered	Willem Barents (Dut.)	1596
Australia	visited	Abel Tasman (Dut.)	1642
New Zealand	sighted	Tasman	1642
New Zealand	visited	James Cook (Eng.)	1769
Antarctic Circle	crossed	Cook	1773
Antarctica	sighted	Nathaniel Palmer (US)	1820
Antarctica	circumnavigated	Fabian von Bellingshausen (Russ.)	1819–21
Australian interior	explored	Charles Sturt (GB)	1828
Antarctica	explored	Charles Wilkes (US)	1838–42
Australia	crossed (S–N)	Robert Burke (Ir.) & William Wills (Eng.)	1860–1
Greenland	explored	Fridtjof Nansen (Nor.)	1888
Arctic	explored	Abruzzi, Duke of the (Ital.)	1900
North Pole	reached	Robert Peary (US)	1909
South Pole	reached	Roald Amundsen (Nor.)	1911
Antarctica	crossed	Sir Vivian Fuchs (Eng.)	1957–8

David Livingstone

Columbus's Santa Maria

Captain James Cook

Robert Peary

BRITISH RULERS

Rulers of England (to 1603)

Saxons

Egbert	827–839
Ethelwulf	839–858
Ethelbald	858–860
Ethelbert	860–865
Ethelred I	865–871
Alfred the Great	871–899
Edward the Elder	899–924
Athelstan	924–939
Edmund	939–946
Edred	946–955
Edwy	955–959
Edgar	959–975
Edward the Martyr	975–978
Ethelred II the Unready	978–1016
Edmund Ironside	1016

Danes

Canute	1016–1035
Harold I Harefoot	1035–1040
Hardicanute	1040–1042

Saxons

Edward the Confessor	1042–1066
Harold II	1066

House of Normandy

William I the Conqueror	1066–1087
William II	1087–1100
Henry I	1100–1135
Stephen	1135–1154

House of Plantagenet

Henry II	1154–1189
Richard I	1189–1199
John	1199–1216
Henry III	1216–1272
Edward I	1272–1307
Edward II	1307–1327
Edward III	1327–1377
Richard II	1377–1399

House of Lancaster

Henry IV	1399–1413
Henry V	1413–1422
Henry VI	1422–1461

House of York

Edward IV	1461–1483
Edward V	1483
Richard III	1483–1485

House of Tudor

Henry VII	1485–1509
Henry VIII	1509–1547
Edward VI	1547–1553
Mary I	1553–1558
Elizabeth I	1558–1603

Rulers of Scotland (to 1603)

Malcolm II	1005–1034
Duncan I	1034–1040
Macbeth	1040–1057
Malcolm III Canmore	1058–1093
Donald Bane	1093–1094
Duncan II	1094
Donald Bane (restored)	1094–1097
Edgar	1097–1107
Alexander I	1107–1124
David I	1124–1153
Malcolm IV	1153–1165
William the Lion	1165–1214
Alexander II	1214–1249
Alexander III	1249–1286
Margaret of Norway	1286–1290
Interregnum	1290–1292
John Balliol	1292–1296
Interregnum	1296–1306
Robert I (Bruce)	1306–1329
David II	1329–1371

House of Stuart

Robert II	1371–1390
Robert III	1390–1406
James I	1406–1437
James II	1437–1460
James III	1460–1488
James IV	1488–1513
James V	1513–1542
Mary	1542–1567
James VI	1567–1625

Became James 1 of England in 1603.

Rulers of Britain

House of Stuart

James I	1603–1625
Charles I	1625–1649
Commonwealth	1649–1660

House of Stuart (restored)

Charles II	1660–1685
James II	1685–1688
William III } jointly	1689–1702
Mary II }	1689–1694
Anne	1702–1714

House of Hanover

George I	1714–1727
George II	1727–1760
George III	1760–1820
George IV	1820–1830
William IV	1830–1837
Victoria	1837–1901

House of Saxe-Coburg

Edward VII	1901–1910

House of Windsor

George V	1910–1936
Edward VIII	1936
George VI	1936–1952
Elizabeth II	1952–

Henry VIII of England. He inherited a rich and stable country from his father Henry VII, the first Tudor king, and made England a major European power. When the Pope refused to annul his first marriage (to his brother's widow), so that he could remarry and produce a son, Henry broke with the Roman Church and made himself head of the Church of England.

BRITISH PRIME MINISTERS

W=Whig, T= Tory, Cin=Coalition, P=Peelite,
L=Liberal, C=Conservative, Lab=Labour

Sir Robert Walpole (W)	1721–42	Earl Russell (L)	1865–66
Earl of Wilmington (W)	1742–43	Earl of Derby (C)	1866–68
Henry Pelham (W)	1743–54	Benjamin Disraeli(C)	1868
Duke of Newcastle (W)	1754–56	William Gladstone (L)	1868–74
Duke of Devonshire (W)	1756–57	Benjamin Disraeli (C(	1874–80
Duke of Newcastle (W)	1757–62	William Gladstone (L)	1880–85
Earl of Bute (T)	1762–63	Marquess of Salisbury (C)	1885–86
George Grenville (W)	1763–65	William Gladstone (L)	1886
Marquess of Rockingham (W)	1765–66	Marquess of Salisbury (C)	1886–92
Earl of Chatham (W)	1766–67	William Gladstone (L)	1892–94
Duke of Grafton (W)	1767–70	Earl of Roseberry (L)	1894–95
Lord North (T)	1770–82	Marquess of Salisbury (C)	1895–1902
Marquess of Rockingham (W)	1782	Arthur Balfour (C)	1902–05
Earl of Shelburne (W)	1782–83	Sir Henry Campbell-Bannerman (L)	1905–08
Duke of Portland (Cin)	1783	Herbert Asquith (L)	1908–15
William Pitt (T)	1783–1801	Herbert Asquith (Cin)	1915–16
Henry Addington (T)	1801–04	David Lloyd-George(Cin)	1916–22
William Pitt (T)	1804–06	Andrew Bonar Law (C)	1922–23
Lord Grenville (W)	1806–07	Stanley Baldwin (C)	1923–24
Duke of Portland (T)	1807–09	James Ramsay MacDonald (Lab)	1924
Spencer Perceval (T)	1809–12	Stanley Baldwin (C)	1924–29
Earl of Liverpool (T)	1812–27	James Ramsay MacDonald (Lab)	1929–31
George Canning (T)	1827	James Ramsay MacDonald (Cin)	1931–35
Viscount Goderich (T)	1827–28	Stanley Baldwin (Cin)	1935–37
Duke of Wellington (T)	1828–30	Neville Chamberlain (Cin)	1937–40
Earl Grey (W)	1830–34	Winston Churchill (Cin)	1940–45
Viscount Melbourne (W)	1834	Winston Churchill (C)	1945
Sir Robert Peel (T)	1834–35	Clement Attlee (Lab)	1945–51
Viscount Melbourne (W)	1835–41	Sir Winston Churchill (C)	1951–55
Sir Robert Peel (T)	1841–46	Sir Anthony Eden (C)	1955–57
Lord John Russell (W)	1846–52	Harold Macmillan (C)	1957–63
Earl of Derby (T)	1852	Sir Alec Douglas-Home (C)	1963–64
Earl of Aberdeen (P)	1852–55	Harold Wilson (Lab)	1964–70
Viscount Palmerston (L)	1855–58	Edward Heath (C)	1970–74
Earl of Derby (C)	1858–59	Harold Wilson (Lab)	1974–76
Viscount Palmerston (L)	1859–65	James Callaghan (Lab)	1976–79
		Margaret Thatcher (C)	1979–1990
		John Major (C)	1990–

AMERICAN PRESIDENTS

F = Federalist; DR = Democratic-Republican;
D = Democratic; W = Whig; R = Republican;
U = Union *Died in office †Assassinated in office

	Term		
1 George Washington (F)	1789–1797	27 William H. Taft (R)	1909–1913
2 John Adams (F),	1797–1801	28 Woodrow Wilson (D)	1913–1921
3 Thomas Jefferson (DR)	1801–1809	29 Warren G. Harding* (R)	1921–1923
4 James Madison (DR)	1809–1817	30 Calvin Coolidge (R)	1923–1929
5 James Monroe (DR)	1817–1825	31 Herbert C. Hoover (R)	1929–1933
6 John Quincy Adams (DR)	1825–1829	32 Franklin D. Roosevelt* (D)	1933–1945
7 Andrew Jackson (D)	1829–1837	33 Harry S. Truman (D)	1945–1953
8 Martin Van Buren (D)	1837–1841	34 Dwight D. Eisenhower (R)	1953–1961
9 William H. Harrison* (W)	1841	35 John F. Kennedy† (D)	1961–1963
10 John Tyler (W)	1841–1845	38 Lyndon B. Johnson (D)	1963–1969
11 James K. Polk (D)	1845–1849	37 Richard M. Nixon (R)	1969–1974
12 Zachary Taylor* (W)	1849–1850	38 Gerald R. Ford (R)	1974–1977
13 Millard Fillmore (W)	1850–1853	39 Jimmy Carter (D)	1977–1981
14 Franklin Pierce (D)	1853–1857	40 Ronald Reagan (R)	1981–1989
15 James Buchanan (D)	1857–1861	41 George Bush (R)	1989–
16 Abraham Lincoln† (R)	1861–1865		
17 Andrew Johnson (U)	1865–1869		
18 Ulysses S. Grant (R)	1869–1877		
19 Rutherford B. Hayes (R)	1877–1881		
20 James A. Garfield† (R)	1881		
21 Chester A. Arthur (R)	1881–1885		
22 Grover Cleveland (D)	1885–1889		
23 Benjamin Harrison (R)	1889–1893		
24 Grover Cleveland (D)	1893–1897		
25 William McKinley† (R)	1897–1901		
26 Theodore Roosevelt (R)	1901–1909		

John F. Kennedy, assassinated in 1963.

POPES

List of popes and their dates of accession.   Antipopes and doubtful popes are not included.

St Peter	42	Honorius I	625	John XVII	1003
St Linus	67	Severinus	640	John XVIII	1004
St Anacletus (Cletus)	76	John IV	640	Sergius IV	1009
St Clement I	88	Theodore I	642	Benedict VIII	1012
St Evaristus	97	St Martin I	649	John XIX	1024
St Alexander I	105	St Eugene I	654	Benedict IX	1032
St Sixtus I	115	St Vitalian	657	Gregory VI	1045
St Telesphorus	125	Adeodatus II	672	Clement II	1046
St Hyginus	136	Donus	676	Benedict IX †	1047
St Pius I	140	St Agatho	678	Damasus II	1048
St Anicetus	155	St Leo II	682	St Leo IX	1049
St Soterus	166	St Benedict II	684	Victor II	1055
St Eleutherius	175	John V	685	Stephen IX (X)	1057
St Victor I	189	Conon	686	Nicholas II	1059
St Zephyrinus	199	St Sergius I	687	Alexander II	1061
St Callistus I	217	John VI	701	St Gregory VII	1073
St Urban I	222	John VII	705	Victor III	1086
St Pontian	230	Sisinnius	708	Urban II	1088
St Anterus	235	Constantine	708	Paschal II	1099
St Fabian	236	St Gregory II	715	Gelasius II	1118
St Cornelius	251	St Gregory III	731	Callistus II	1119
St Lucius I	253	St Zachary	741	Honorius II	1124
St Stephen I	254	Stephen II (III)*	752	Innocent II	1130
St Sixtus II	257	St Paul I	757	Celestine II	1143
St Dionysius	259	Stephen III (IV)	768	Lucius II	1144
St Felix I	269	Adrian I	772	Eugene III	1145
St Eutychian	275	St Leo III	795	Anastasius IV	1153
St Caius	283	Stephen IV (V)	816	Adrian IV	1154
St Marcellinus	296	St Paschal I	817	Alexander III	1159
St Marcellus I	308	Eugene II	824	Lucius III	1181
St Eusebius	309	Valentine	827	Urban III	1185
St Melchiades	311	Gregory IV	827	Gregory VIII	1187
St Sylvester I	314	Sergius II	844	Clement III	1187
St Marcus	336	St Leo IV	847	Celestine III	1191
St Julius I	337	Benedict III	855	Innocent III	1198
Liberius	352	St Nicholas I	858	Honorius III	1216
St Damasus I	366	Adrian II	867	Gregory IX	1227
St Siricius	384	John VIII	872	Celestine IV	1241
St Anastasius I	399	Marinus I	882	Innocent IV	1243
St Innocent I	401	St Adrian III	884	Alexander IV	1254
St Zosimus	417	Stephen V (VI)	885	Urban IV	1261
St Boniface I	418	Formosus	891	Clement IV	1265
St Celestine I	422	Boniface VI	896	Gregory X	1271
St Sixtus III	432	Stephen VI (VII)	896	Innocent V	1276
St Leo I (the Great)	440	Romanus	897	Adrian V	1276
St Hilary	461	Theodore II	897	John XXI	1276
St Simplicius	468	John IX	898	Nicholas III	1277
St Felix III	483	Benedict IV	900	Martin IV	1281
St Gelasius I	492	Leo V	903	Honorius IV	1285
Anastasius II	496	Sergius III	904	Nicholas IV	1288
St Symmachus	498	Anastasius III	911	St Celestine V	1294
St Hormisdas	514	Landus	913	Boniface VIII	1294
St John I	523	John X	914	Benedict XI	1303
St Felix IV	526	Leo VI	928	Clement V	1305
Boniface II	530	Stephen VII (VIII)	928	John XXII	1316
John II	533	John XI	931	Benedict XII	1334
St Agapetus I	535	Leo VII	936	Clement VI	1342
St Silverius	536	Stephen VIII (IX)	939	Innocent VI	1352
Vigilius	537	Marinus II	942	Urban V	1362
Pelagius I	556	Agapetus II	946	Gregory XI	1370
John III	561	John XII	955	Urban VI	1378
Benedict I	575	Leo VIII	963	Boniface IX	1389
Pelagius II	579	Benedict V	964	Innocent VII	1404
St Gregory I (the Great)	590	John XIII	965	Gregory XII	1406
Sabinianus	604	Benedict VI	973	Martin V	1417
Boniface III	607	Benedict VII	974	Eugene IV	1431
St Boniface IV	608	John XIV	983	Nicholas V	1447
St Deusdedit	615	John XV	985	Callistus III	1455
(Adeodatus I)		Gregory V	996	Pius II	1458
Boniface V	619	Sylvester II	999	Paul II	1464

Sixtus IV	1471	Innocent IX	1591	Clement XIII	1758
Innocent VIII	1484	Clement VIII	1592	Clement XIV	1769
Alexander VI	1492	Leo XI	1605	Pius VI	1775
Pius III	1503	Paul V	1605	Pius VII	1800
Julius II	1503	Gregory XV	1621	Leo XII	1823
Leo X	1513	Urban VIII	1623	Pius VIII	1829
Adrian VI	1522	Innocent X	1644	Gregory XVI	1831
Clement VII	1523	Alexander VII	1655	Pius IX	1846
Paul III	1534	Clement IX	1667	Leo XIII	1878
Julius III	1550	Clement X	1670	St Pius X	1903
Marcellus II	1555	Innocent XI	1676	Benedict XV	1914
Paul IV	1555	Alexander VIII	1689	Pius XI	1922
Pius IV	1559	Innocent XII	1691	Pius XII	1939
St Pius V	1566	Clement XI	1700	John XXIII	1958
Gregory XIII	1572	Innocent XIII	1721	Paul VI	1963
Sixtus V	1585	Benedict XIII	1724	John Paul I**	1978
Urban VII	1590	Clement XII	1730	John Paul II	1978
Gregory XIV	1590	Benedict XIV	1740		

*The original Stephen II died before consecration, and was dropped from the list of popes in 1961; Stephen III became Stephen II and the numbers of the other popes named Stephen were also moved up.
**John Paul died after only 33 days as Pontiff.

HOLY ROMAN EMPERORS

FRANKISH KINGS AND EMPERORS (CAROLINGIAN)

Charlemagne	800–814
Louis I, the Pious	814–840
Lothair I	840–855
Louis II	855–875
Charles II, the Bald	875–877
Throne vacant	877–881
Charles III, the Fat	881–887
Throne vacant	887–891
Guido of Spoleto	891–894
Lambert of Spoleto (co-emperor)	892–898
Arnulf (rival)	896–901
Louis III of Provence	901–905
Berengar	905–924
Conrad I of Franconia (rival)	911–918

SAXON KINGS AND EMPERORS

Henry I, the Fowler	918–936
Otto I, the Great	936–973
Otto II	973–983
Otto III	983–1002
Henry II, the Saint	1002–1024

FRANCONIAN EMPERORS (SALIAN)

Conrad II, the Salian	1024–1039
Henry III, the Black	1039–1056
Henry IV	1056–1106
Rudolf of Swabia (rival)	1077–1080
Hermann of Luxembourg (rival)	1081–1093
Conrad of Franconia (rival)	1093–1101
Henry V	1106–1125
Lothair II	1125–1137

HOHENSTAUFEN KINGS AND EMPERORS

Conrad III	1138–1152
Frederick I Barbarossa	1152–1190
Henry VI	1190–1197
Otto IV	1198–1215
Philip of Swabia (rival)	1198–1208
Frederick II	1215–1250

Henry Raspe (rival)	1246–1247
William of Holland (rival)	1247–1256
Conrad IV	1250–1254
The Great Interregnum	1254–1273

RULERS FROM DIFFERENT HOUSES

Richard of Cornwall (rival)	1257–1272
Alfonso X of Castile (rival)	1257–1273
Rudolf I, Habsburg	1273–1291
Adolf I of Nassau	1292–1298
Albert I, Habsburg	1298–1308
Henry VII, Luxembourg	1308–1313
Louis IV of Bavaria	1314–1347
Frederick of Habsburg (co-regent)	1314–1325
Charles IV, Luxembourg	1347–1378
Wenceslas of Bohemia	1378–1400
Frederick III of Brunswick	1400
Rupert of the Palatinate	1400–1410
Sigismund, Luxembourg	1410–1437

HABSBURG EMPERORS

Albert II	1438–1439
Frederick III	1440–1493
Maximilian I	1493–1519
Charles V	1519–1558
Ferdinand I	1558–1564
Maximilian II	1564–1576
Rudolf II	1576–1612
Matthias	1612–1619
Ferdinand II	1619–1637
Ferdinand III	1637–1657
Leopold I	1658–1705
Joseph I	1705–1711
Charles VI	1711–1740
Charles VII of Bavaria	1742–1745

HABSBURG-LORRAINE EMPERORS

Francis I of Lorraine	1745–1765
Joseph II	1765–1790
Leopold II	1790–1792
Francis II	1792–1806

HISTORIC ASSASSINATIONS

Victim	Details of assassination	Date
Philip II, king of Macedonia	Pausanias, young noble with a grudge	336
Julius Caesar, Roman dictator	Stabbed by Brutus, Cassius et al. in Senate	44
St Thomas à Becket, English archbishop	Slain by four knights in cathedral	29.12.11
Albert I, German king	By nephew, John 'the Parricide'	1.5.13
James I of Scotland	Plot: Sir Robert Graham et al.	21.2.14
David Beaton, Scottish chancellor/cardinal	Band of Protestant nobles in St Andrews Castle	29.5.15
Lord Darnley, husband of Mary Queen of Scots	Blown up; plot	10.2.15
William the Silent, Prince of Orange	Shot by Balthasar Gérard	10.7.15
Henry III of France	Stabbed by fanatic monk (Jacques Clément)	2.8.15
Henry IV of France (de Navarre)	Stabbed by fanatic (François Ravaillac)	14.5.16
Albrecht von Wallenstein, Austrian general	Irish and Scottish officers	25.2.16
Gustavus III of Sweden	Plot: shot by Johan Ankarström	29.3.17
Jean Marat, French revolutionary	Stabbed in bath by Charlotte Corday	13.7.17
Jean Baptiste Kléber, French general	By Turkish fanatic, in Cairo	14.6.18
Abraham Lincoln, US president	Shot by actor, J Wilkes Booth, in theatre	14.4.18
Alexander II, emperor of Russia	Nihilist bomb	13.3.18
James Garfield, US president	Shot at station by Charles Guiteau (grudge)	2.7.18
Sadi Carnot, French president	Stabbed by anarchist	24.6.18
Antonio Cánovas del Castillo, Spanish premier	Shot by anarchist	8.8.18
Elizabeth, empress of Austria	By Italian anarchist at Geneva	10.9.18
Humbert I, king of Italy	By anarchist at Monza	29.7.19
William McKinley, US president	Shot by anarchist, Leon Czolgosz, at Buffalo	6.9.19
Pyotr Stolypin, Russian premier	Shot by revolutionary, Dmitri Bogrov	14.9.19
George I, king of Greece	At Salonika	18.3.19
Francis Ferdinand, archduke of Austria	Alleged Serbian plot: shot in car by Gavrilo Princip at Sarajevo (sparked World War I)	28.6.19
Jean Jaurès, French socialist	By nationalist, in café	31.7.19
Rasputin, powerful Russian monk	By Russian noblemen	31.12.19
Walter Rathenau, German foreign minister	By reactionaries	24.6.19
Michael Collins, Irish Sinn Fein leader	Ambushed and shot	22.8.19
'Pancho' Villa, former Mexican bandit/rebel	Ambushed in car	20.7.19
Alvaro Obregón, Mexican president	Shot while dining, by José Toral	17.7.19
Paul Doumer, French president	Shot by mad Russian émigré, Paul Gorgoulov	6.5.19
Anton Cermak, mayor of Chicago	By anarchist Joseph Zangara, with bullet intended for president-elect F D Roosevelt	15.2.19
Engelbert Dollfuss, Austrian chancellor	Shot by Nazis in chancellery	25.7.19
Alexander I of Yugoslavia ⎫ Jean Louis Barthou, French foreign minister ⎬ Sergei Kirov, Russian political leader ⎭	By Macedonian terrorist at Marseille	9.10.19
	By young party member, Leonid Nikolayev	1.12.19
Huey Long, corrupt American politician	By Dr Carl Austin Weiss	8.9.19
Armand Calinescu, Romanian premier	By pro-Nazi Iron Guards	21.9.19
Leon Trotsky, exiled Russian communist leader	Axed in Mexico by Ramon del Rio	21.8.19
Jean Darlan, French admiral/political leader	In N. Africa; anti-Vichy motive	24.12.19
Mahatma Gandhi, Indian nationalist leader	Shot by Hindu fanatic, Nathuran Godse	30.1.19
Count Folke Bernadotte, Swedish diplomat	Ambushed in Jerusalem by Jewish extremists	17.9.19
Abdullah ibn Hussein, king of Jordan	In Jerusalem mosque	20.7.19
Liaquat Ali Khan, Pakistani premier	By fanatics at Rawalpindi	16.10.19
Anastasio Somoza, Nicaraguan president	Shot by Rigoberto López Pérez, in León	21.9.19
Carlos Castillo Armas, Guatemalan president	By one of own guards	26.7.19
Faisal II of Iraq	Military coup in Baghdad	14.7.19
SWRD Bandaranaike, Ceylonese premier	By Buddhist monk in Colombo	25.9.19
Patrice Lumumba, deposed Congolese premier	Katanga secessionist regime	Jan/Feb 19
Rafael Trujillo Molina, Dominican Republic dictator	Car machine-gunned	30.5.19
Sylvanus Olympio, Togolese president	Army coup	13.1.19
Ngo Dinh Diem, S. Vietnamese president	By generals in coup	2.11.19
John F. Kennedy, US president	Shot in car, in Dallas, Texas‡‡	22.11.19
Malcolm X (Little), US Black Muslim leader	Shot at rally	21.2.19
Sir Abubakar Tafawa Balewa, Nigerian premier	Army coup	15.1.19
Hendrik Verwoerd, South African premier	Stabbed by parliamentary messenger, Dimitri Tsafendas (later ruled mentally disordered)	6.9.19
Rev. Martin Luther King Jr., US Negro Civil Rights leader	Shot on hotel balcony by James Earl Ray, in Memphis, Tennessee	4.4.19
Robert F. Kennedy, US senator	Shot by Arab immigrant, Sirhan Sirhan, in Los Angeles (Hotel Ambassador)	5.6.19
Tom Mboya, Kenyan economics minister	In Nairobi	5.7.19
Abdirashid Ali Shermarke, Somalian president	Shot by security guard, Yussuf Ismail	15.10.19
Wasfi Tal, Jordanian premier	By Palestinian guerrillas, in Cairo	28.11.19
Louis Carrero Blanco, Spanish premier	Explosion under car, Basque terrorists (ETA)	20.12.19
Mrs Park (Yook Young Soo), wife of South Korean president Park Chung Hee	By Mun Se Kwang (member of youth organization) with bullet intended for president	15.8.19

Above: Mahatma Gandhi, who led a non-violent campaign to free India from British rule. He was assassinated shortly after Indian independence by a Hindu fanatic.

Above right: Archbishop Thomas à Becket, struck down in Canterbury Cathedral in 1170 after quarrelling with King Henry II.

Right: Robert Kennedy, US presidential candidate, lies fatally wounded in the lobby of a Los Angeles hotel.

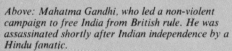

Lalit Mishra, Indian railways minister	Bomb explosion at inauguration of new line	2.1.1975*
King Faisal of Saudi Arabia	Shot by nephew Prince Faisal ibn Masaed	25.3.1975
Ngarta Tombalbaye, Chad president	Military coup	13.4.1975
General Murtala Mohammed, Nigerian head of state	Unsuccessful coup	13.2.1976
Christopher Ewart-Biggs, British ambassador to Republic of Ireland	Car blown up by landmine planted by IRA	21.7.1976
Aldo Moro, president of Italy's Christian Democrats and five times prime minister of Italy	Kidnapped by 'Red Brigade' terrorists (16.3.78) and later found dead	9.5.1978
Sir Richard Sykes, British ambassador in The Hague	Shot by IRA	22.3.1979
Airey Neave, British Conservative MP and Northern Ireland spokesman	Explosion under car while leaving House of Commons car park; IRA	30.3.1979
Lord Mountbatten, uncle of Duke of Edinburgh	Explosion in sailing boat off coast of Ireland; IRA	27.8.1979
Park Chung Hee, president of South Korea	Shot in restaurant by chief of Korean Central Intelligence Agency	26.10.1979
Roman Catholic archbishop Oscar Romeroy Galdamez of El Salvador	Shot by right-wing gunmen while saying mass in San Salvador	24.3.1980
Anastasio Somozoa Debayle, president of Nicaragua	Shot by revolutionaries during Sandinista coup	17.9.1980
John Lennon, musician/songwriter and ex-Beatle	Shot in street in New York by Mark David Chapman	8.12.1980
William R. Tolbert, president of Liberia	Executed by army during coup led by Master-Sergeant Samuel K Doe	12.4.1980
Ziaur Rahman, president of Bangladesh	Shot by army officers during abortive military takeover	30.5.1981
Anwar al-Sadat, president of Egypt	Shot by rebel soldiers while reviewing military parade	6.10.1981
Indira Gandhi, prime minister of India	Assassinated by Sikh bodyguards	31.10.1984

*Died next day.   † Died 19 Sep.   ‡ Died 14 Sep.   § Died 18 Sep.   ¶ Died 6 Mar.   ** Died 10 Sep.   †† Died 29 Sep.
‡‡ Accused. Lee Harvey Oswald, himself shot by Jack Ruby (24 Nov.) while awaiting trial.

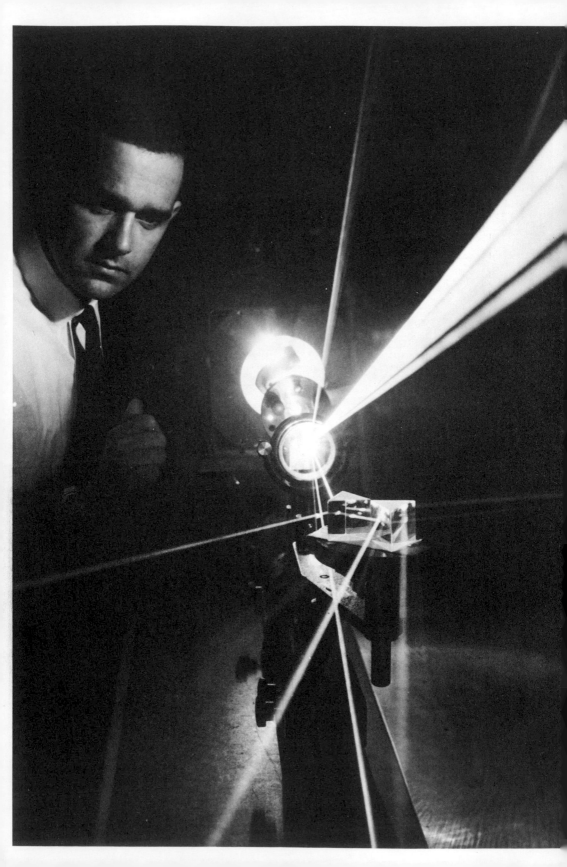

Science and Technology

GLOSSARY OF SCIENCE

Aberration Distortion of image due to imperfections in construction of lens or mirror; chromatic aberration distorts colour; spherical aberration distorts shape.

Absolute temperature Temperature related to ABSOLUTE ZERO. See KELVIN.

Absolute zero Lowest temperature possible in theory; zero on absolute scale is −273.15°C. See also KELVIN.

Absorption Penetration of substance into body of another, e.g. a gas dissolving in liquid. See also ADSORPTION.

Acceleration Rate of change of VELOCITY.

Acid Chemical substance that produces free hydrogen ions in solution. Reacts with BASE to form SALT.

Acoustics Science that deals with sounds.

Actinium (Ac) Rare radioactive metal found in uranium ores, such as pitchblende, resulting from the decay of uranium-235. First of the actinide series of elements.

Adhesion Force making different substances stick together, by attraction between their molecules.

Adiabatic process Physical or chemical process that takes place with no gain or loss in heat.

Adsorption Phenomenon by which a gas or liquid becomes concentrated on surface of a solid. See also ABSORPTION.

Aerodynamics Branch of MECHANICS that deals with forces acting on objects moving through air.

Affinity Chemical attraction between ELEMENTS or COMPOUNDS.

Alcohols Class of organic compounds having characteristic hydroxyl group, —OH. Names end in -ol, e.g. ethanol (ethyl alcohol).

Aldehydes Class of organic compounds having characteristic group —CHO.

Algebra Branch of mathematics in which letters are used to stand for unknown quantities.

Alkali BASE consisting of a soluble metal hydroxide. Alkali metals, such as sodium and potassium, form caustic alkalis.

Alkaline earths Group of metallic elements that form weakly basic (alkaline) oxides; Group II of the Periodic Table; includes magnesium, calcium, strontium, and barium.

Alkaloid Varied group of naturally occurring organic compounds derived from plants; includes morphine and nicotine.

Allotropy Property of an element of existing in more than one physical form, called *allotropes*.

ALLOYS	
Name	Composition
Aluminium bronze	90% Cu, 10% Al
Manganese bronze	95% Cu, 5% Mn
Gun Metal Bronze	90% Cu, 10% Sn
Red brass	90% Cu, 10% Zn
Naval brass	70% Cu, 29% Zn, 1% Sn
Yellow brass	67% Cu, 33% Zn
Nickel silver	55% Cu, 18% Ni, 27% Zn
Steel	99% Fe, 1% C
Stainless steel	Fe with 0.1–2.0% C, up to 27% Cr or 20% W or 15% Ni and lesser amounts of other elements
18-carat gold	75% Au, 25% Ag & Cu
Palladium, or white gold	90% Au, 10% Pd
Sterling silver	92.5% Ag, 7.5% Cu
US silver	90% Ag, 10% Cu
Britannia metal	90% Sn, 10% Sb
Dentist's amalgam	70% Hg, 30% Cu
Type metal	82% Pb, 15% Sb, 3% Sn
Pewter	91% Sn, 7.5% Sb, 1.5% Cu

Alloy Metal composed of more than one element.

Alpha-rays (α-rays) Streams of helium nuclei emitted by some radioactive elements.

Alternating current Electric current flow that rapidly decreases from maximum in one direction, through zero, to maximum in other direction.

Alum Double salt of a trivalent metal sulphate (such as aluminium, chromium, or ferric iron sulphates) and the sulphate of an alkali metal of ammonium; crystallizes with 24 molecules of water. Common 'alum' is potassium aluminium sulphate.

Aluminium (Al) Strong, lightweight, corrosion-resistant metal of the boron group, second in importance only to iron. Most abundant metal in the Earth's crust comprising 8 per cent, but its only important ore is bauxite, containing the oxide alumina.

Amalgam Alloy of mercury.

Americium (Am) Artificial transuranic radioactive element made in 1944 by bombarding plutonium with neutrons.

Ammeter Electrical instrument for measuring current.

Amorphous Non-crystalline.

231

Ampere (A) Unit of electric current; defined as current that, in ELECTROLYSIS of silver nitrate, deposits 0.001118g of silver per second on cathode; equivalent to flow of 6×10^{18} electrons per sec.

Analytical geometry Same as COORDINATE GEOMETRY.

Anhydride Compound that reacts chemically with water to form its parent substance, a HYDRATE.

Anode Positive electrode through which electric current enters electrolysis cell or vacuum tube.

Antimony (Sb) Hard, brittle element of weak metallic character belonging to the nitrogen family. It is added to some alloys (such as type metal) to harden them.

Aqua regia Mixture of hydrochloric and nitric acids able to dissolve noble metals, such as gold.

Arab numerals Number characters (digits) normally used in Western countries; e.g. 1, 2, 3.

Archimedes' principle When a body is immersed or partly immersed in a liquid, apparent loss in weight is equal to weight of liquid displaced.

Argon (Ar) The most abundant of the inert, or rare, gases, making up about 1 per cent of the atmosphere. Obtained by fractional distillation of liquid air, it is used to fill light bulbs and Geiger counters.

Armature Rotating part of electric motor or dynamo, consisting of coils of wire.

Arsenic (As) A feebly metallic element of the nitrogen family, many of whose compounds are deadly poisons. It occurs widely in compounds, such as the sulphide realgar, As_2S_3, and the mixed sulphide with iron, mispickel, FeSAs.

Assaying Methods, mostly chemical, of estimating the amounts of particular substances, e.g. of metals in ores and of ingredients in drugs.

Astatine (At) The rarest naturally-occurring element, which has about 20 known isotopes, none of them stable. It is produced during radioactive decay of uranium, thorium and actinium. It is the heaviest member of the halogen series, and its properties resemble those of iodine.

Atom Smallest fragment of an element that can take part in a chemical reaction. Consists of central nucleus (made up of PROTONS and NEUTRONS) surrounded by orbiting ELECTRONS. Number of protons (equal to number of electrons) is called *atomic number*. Total mass of all subatomic particles is called atomic *mass*. See also ISOTOPE.

Atom smasher General name for any machine, such as CYCLOTRON, that accelerates particles to sufficiently high speeds to split atoms.

Atomic number See ATOM.

Atomic weight Alternative name for atomic mass. See ATOM.

Avogadro's hypothesis Equal volumes of all gases contain equal numbers of molecules.

Avogadro's number Number of atoms in grammeatom, or molecules in grammemolecule (*mol*); approx 6×10^{23}.

Avoirdupois System of weights, formerly used in English-speaking countries, based on units ounce, pound, stone, ton.

Bakelite Thermosetting plastic originally made from phenol and formaldehyde.

Ballistics Study of paths taken by projectiles, such as bullets and rockets.

Barium (Ba) A heavy alkaline-earth metal which

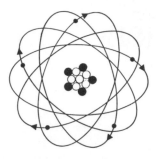

An atom of boron with five protons (dark) and six neutrons (light) in its nucleus. Five electrons orbit the nucleus.

occurs in Nature as the sulphate, barytes or heavy spar, $BaSO_4$; or as the carbonate witherite $BaCO_3$. It can burst into flame on contact with moist air and decompose water.

Barometer Instrument for measuring pressure of atmosphere.

Base Substance that reacts chemically with an ACID to form a SALT and water.

Battery Device that converts chemical energy into electrical energy; an electric cell, a source of DIRECT CURRENT.

Bel Ten DECIBELS.

Berkelium (Bk) Artificial radioactive element obtained by bombarding americium with helium ions; the fifth transuranium element.

Bernoulli's principle When a fluid flows through a tube, at any point the sum of the potential, kinetic, and pressure energies is constant.

Beryllium (Be) A lightweight alkaline-earth metal with a relatively high melting point (1283°C). Strong, hard and elastic, it is used in alloys to confer these properties on other metals. It is highly transparent to X-rays. Its main source is the mineral beryl, beryllium aluminium silicate $(Be_3Al_2Si_6O_{18})$.

Bessemer process Method of making steel quickly in fairly small batches, involving blowing air through molten iron to oxidize excess carbon and other impurities.

Beta-rays (β-rays) Stream of electrons emitted by some radioactive elements.

Betatron Machine that accelerates ELECTRONS in circular magnetic field to produce continuous beam of high-energy particles.

Bevatron Machine that accelerates PROTONS in circular magnetic field.

Bicarbonate of soda Sodium bicarbonate ($NaHCo_3$).

Binary system Number system with only two digits, 0 and 1.

Binomial theorem A mathematical formula for writing out the expansion of any binomial (2-term) expression. E.g. $(a+b)^2 = a^2 + 2ab + b^2$.

Biochemistry Chemistry of processes that take place in living organisms.

Bismuth (Bi) A brittle metal with a reddish tinge, belonging to the nitrogen family. It forms low-melting point, fusible alloys with lead, tin and cadmium. Bismuth salts are used in soothing

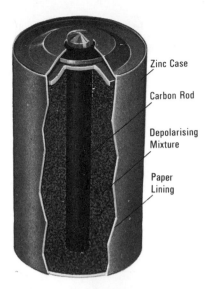

A dry cell electrical battery. The carbon rod is the positive electrode and the zinc case is the negative electrode, so that electrons flow from case to rod.

A lead-acid accumulator electrical battery. This is a true 'battery' because it has a number (6 in this case) of cells. These are wet cells connected in series. Unlike the dry cell, the accumulator can be recharged and reused repeatedly.

medicines for digestive disorders. Bismuth is rarely found native; its chief sources are the sulphide bismuthite or bismuth glance, Bi_2S_3, and the trioxide bismite, B_2O_3.

Bleaching Removing colour or making white; generally achieved with sunlight or a chemical oxidizing agent, such as chlorine, sulphur dioxide (SO_2), or hydrogen peroxide (H_2O_2).

Block and tackle A pulley (or pulleys) and the rope or chain that works it.

Boiling point Temperature at which liquid freely turns into vapour; vapour pressure of liquid then equals external pressure on it.

Bond Chemical link between two atoms in a MOLECULE.

Boolean algebra Type of logic, which uses symbols of algebra, applied to computer programs and operations.

Boron (B) A semi-metallic element in the same family as aluminium whose most familiar compound is borax, disodium tetraborate $Na_2B_4O_7 \cdot 10H_2O$. Boron can take two forms – a brown amorphous powder and a black, lustrous crystalline material. The latter is an important semiconductor. Boron is used in control rods for atomic reactors since it readily absorbs neutrons.

Boyle's law At constant temperature the volume of a gas is inversely proportional to the pressure exerted on it.

British thermal unit (BTU) Quantity of heat needed to raise temperature of 1 pound of water at its maximum density through 1 degree F. 1 BTU = 252 calories = 1055 joules. See also CALORIE.

Bromine (Br) A dark red liquid element of the halogen family, whose vapour is pungent and irritates the eyes and respiratory system. Bromine is extracted from sea water. It is highly reactive and forms useful bromides with metals and organic substances. Among the most important

is light-sensitive silver bromide, which is used in photographic emulsions.

Bubble chamber Apparatus in which paths of charged atomic particles are revealed as row of tiny bubbles in chamber of liquid.

Cadmium (Cd) A soft metal of the zinc group, which, like tin, crackles when deformed. It is obtained mainly as a by-product in lead and zinc smelting and refining. Its main use is for plating metals and alloys to protect them from corrosion. It is used in making control rods for nuclear reactors because it readily absorbs neutrons. Some cadmium compounds are poisonous and have been responsible for serious water pollution in some industrial regions.

Caesium (Cs) A very soft alkali metal, which resembles sodium and potassium and reacts explosively with water. It loses electrons when struck by light and finds ready application in photoelectric devices.

Calcium (Ca) A reactive alkaline-earth metal whose compounds are widespread in Nature, including the carbonate, $CaCO_3$ (*chalk* and *limestone*); the hydrated sulphate, $CaSO_4 \cdot 2H_2O$ (*gypsum*); and the phosphate, $Ca_3(PO_4)_2$ (bones and teeth and the mineral *apatite*). It has many other industrially important compounds.

Calculus Branch of mathematics that deals with rates of change of variable quantities; divided into differential calculus and integral calculus.

Californium (Cf) Artificial radioactive transuranic element produced by bombarding curium with helium ions. One isotope (Cf^{252}) is an intense neutron emitter.

calorie Unit of heat equal to amount needed to raise temperature of 1 gram water through 1 degree C at $14.5°$–$15.5°C$. 1 calorie = 4.2 joules; kilocalorie (=1000 calories) written Calorie (capital C), used for food values.

Candela (cd) Unit of luminous intensity, replacing candle power.

Candlepower Luminous intensity of light source in given direction, expressed in CANDELAS.

Capacitance Property of CONDENSER that enables it to store electric charge; numerical value of charge, measured in Farads.

Capillarity Phenomenon that makes LIQUID rise up narrow space, as in fine-bore tube or between two sheets of glass; caused by forces of attraction between MOLECULES in surface of liquid and molecules in glass surface. See also SURFACE TENSION.

Carbide Chemical compound of carbon and another element, such as calcium.

Carbon (C) A non-metallic element whose atoms have the ability to link with each other in long and complex structures and molecules to form a larger number of compounds than all the other elements put together. Study of these compounds forms the basis of organic chemistry. Carbon occurs native in the Earth's crust as soft, flaky graphite and as hard, crystalline diamond, and in compounds with metals and oxygen as carbonates ($-CO_3$). The atmosphere contains traces of carbon dioxide (CO_2), resulting from plant and animal respiration and from combustion of carbon-containing materials, such as wood and fossil fuels. Partial combustion of carbon yields poisonous carbon monoxide CO. The radioactive isotope carbon-14 is formed in Nature, and provides a means of dating archaeological specimens.

Carbonate Salt of carbonic acid.

Catalyst A substance that speeds up a chemical reaction but which is left more or less unchanged after the reaction, and so can be used many times for the process of catalysis.

Cathode Negative ELECTRODE through which electric current leaves an electrolysis cell or vacuum tube.

Cathode rays Electrons flowing from cathode of discharge tube or valve.

Cellophane Transparent plastic, generally film or thin sheet, made from cellulose.

Celluloid Early thermoplastic material made from cellulose nitrate and camphor.

Celsius See CENTIGRADE.

Centigrade Temperature scale on which 0°C is the melting point of ice and 100°C is boiling point of water; same as Celsius.

Centrifugal force Force that acts outwards on an object moving in circular path.

Centrifuge Machine that rotates at high speeds and makes use of CENTRIFUGAL FORCE to separate solids from liquids or to separate liquids of different densities.

Centripetal force Force that acts inwards as reaction to CENTRIFUGAL FORCE.

Cerium (Ce) One of the rare-earth metals, which is quite plentiful in the Earth's erust, occurring in the minerals cerite and monazite, for example. Mischmetal, in which cerium is mixed with lesser amounts of other rare earth metals and iron, is used in making lighter flints.

cgs system Metric system of units based on centimetre, gram, and second; now replaced by SI UNITS.

Charles' law At constant pressure, the volume of a gas is proportional to its ABSOLUTE TEMPERATURE.

NAMES OF CARBON COMPOUNDS

Common name	IUPAC name	Common name	IUPAC name
Acetaldehyde	Ethanal	Formic acid	Methanoic acid
Acetic acid	Ethanoic acid	Fumaric acid	Transbutenedioic acid
Acetophenone	Phenyl ethanone	Iodoform	Triodomethane
Acetone	Propanone	Maleic acid	Cisbutenedioic acid
Acetonitrile	Ethanonitrile	Malonic acid	Propanedioic acid
Acetylene	Ethyne	Methyl alcohol	Methanol
Aniline	Phenylamine	Methyl chloride	Chloromethane
Benzaldehyde	Benzenecarbaldehyde	Methyl cyanide	Ethanonitrile
Benzonitrile	Benzenecarbonitrile	Methylene chloride	Dichloromethane
Butyl alcohol	Butanol	Methylene iodide	Diiodomethane
Butylene	Butene	Oxalic acid	Ethanedioic acid
Carbon tetrachloride	Tetrachloromethane	Phenol	Benzenol
Carbon tetrafluoride	Tetrafluoromethane	Phenyl cyanide	Benzenecarbonitrile
Chloral	Trichloroethanal	Phenyl isocyanide	Benzene isocarbonitrile
Chloroform	Trichloromethane	Phosgene	Carbonyl chloride
Diethyl ether	Ethoxyethane	Polyethylene	Polyethene
Ethane	Ethane	Polypropylene	Polypropene
Ethyl acetate	Ethyl ethanoate	Propionic acid	Propanoic acid
Ethyl alcohol	Ethanol	Succinic acid	Butanedioic acid
Ethyl chloride	Chloroethane	Toluene	Methylbenzene
Ethylene	Ethene	Trichlorethylene	Trichlorethene
Ethylene tetrafluoride	Tetrafluoroethane	Urea	Carbamide
Formaldehyde	Methanal	Vinyl chloride	Chloroethene
		Vinylidene chloride	Dichloroethane

Carbon compounds were originally given names as they were discovered, and these are now their common names. More recently many of these names were changed by international agreement. These IUPAC (International Union of Pure and Applied Chemistry) names are intended to describe the compound more accurately.

Chemical change Change in type, number, or arrangement of atoms in substance, resulting in change in its chemical composition.

Chemical equivalent Weight of an element that will combine with or replace 1 g of hydrogen or 8 g of oxygen. Of an acid, the weight containing 1 g of replaceable hydrogen.

Chemical reaction Process involving two or more substances (*reactants*) in which chemical change takes place.

Chloride Salt of hydrochloric acid.

Chlorine (C1) Industrially the most important of the halogens, chlorine is a poisonous yellowish-green gas that irritates the eyes and respiratory system. Chlorine combines with both metals and non-metals. It and its compounds are excellent bleaching agents.

Chromatography Techniques of separating and identifying the various ingredients of a mixture. The separation may be carried on a paper strip (paper chromatography) or in a column, through which the mixture is carried in a liquid or a gas.

Chromium (Cr) A hard, white metal which takes a high polish and finds widespread application in chromium plating. It confers strength and corrosion resistance to steel. It was called chromium (colour) because of the colour exhibited by many of its compounds; the red of the ruby and the green of the emerald are due to chromium compounds.

Coal gas Fuel gas produced by destructive distillation of coal; consists mainly of carbon monoxide (CO), methane (CH_4), and hydrogen (H_2) with various impurities.

Cobalt (Co) A metal used in high-temperature and magnetic alloys, such as *alnico* (with aluminium and nickel). It resembles iron in its chemistry, but physically it is heavier, stronger, and harder than iron. It forms more complex ions than any other metal except platinum. The radio-active isotope Co^{60} is widely used as a source of gamma (γ) rays in radiation therapy.

Cohesion Force of attraction between molecules that holds liquid or solid together.

Colloid Substance in colloidal state – a system of particles in a medium with different properties from true solution because of larger size of particles.

Combustion (burning) Chemical reaction in which a substance combines with oxygen and gives off heat and light.

Compound Substance consisting of two or more ELEMENTS in chemical combination.

Concentration Amount of a substance present in a given space or quantity of other substance; concentrations of chemical solutions generally expressed in moles/litre³.

Condensation Change of VAPOUR into LIQUID that takes place when pressure is applied to it or temperature is lowered.

Condenser 1) Apparatus for cooling vapour into liquid during distillation. 2) Circuit element, consisting of arrangement of conductors and insulators, that can store electric charge when voltage is applied across it; also called capacitor.

Conductor Substance that offers little resistance to flow of electricity.

Coordinate geometry Branch of mathematics that deals with lines, curves, and geometrical figures in terms of algebraic expressions that stand for them; also called analytical geometry.

Copper (Cu) A reddish-brown metal widely used on account of its high electrical and thermal conductivity and its ability to form strong, corrosion-resistant alloys, such as bronze (with tin), brass (with zinc) and cupronickel (with nickel). Found native and in sulphides, oxides and carbonates, copper is widely distributed.

Corrosion Slow chemical breakdown, often OXIDATION of metals, by action of water, air or chemicals.

Cosine Trigonometrical ratio, given (for an angle) in right-angled triangle by length of the side adjacent to the angle divided by the length of the hypotenuse.

Cosmic rays High-energy radiation, mainly charged particles, striking the Earth from outer space.

Cosmotron Machine that accelerates PROTONS in the field of a large ring magnet.

Coulomb (C) Unit of quantity of electricity, defined as quantity transferred by 1 ampere in 1 second.

Cracking Process in petroleum industry, using a CATALYST, in which heavy oil products are split to form lighter ones, such as petrol.

Critical temperature Temperature above which a gas cannot be liquefied, no matter how great the pressure.

Cryotron Switch using SUPERCONDUCTIVITY, consisting of superconducting coil of wire wound round another superconducting wire kept at temperature close to ABSOLUTE ZERO; current passed through the coil controls conductivity and hence resistance of wire.

Crystalline dimorphism Property of substance existing in two different crystal forms. See CRYSTALLINE POLYMORPHISM.

Crystalline polymorphism Phenomenon in which chemical substance occurs more than two crystallite forms. See CRYSTALLINE DIMORPHISM.

Crystallization Process in which a regular solid substance (crystal) forms from molten mass or solution. See also HYDRATE.

Curie Measure of RADIOACTIVITY, defined as the amount of a radioisotope that decays at rate of 3.7×10^{10} disintegrations per second.

Curium (Cm) Artificial, highly radioactive transuranium element made by bombarding plutonium with accelerated helium ions.

Current, electric Flow of electrons along a conductor. Measured in AMPERES.

Cyclotron Machine for accelerating atomic particles to high speeds; particles follow spiral path in magnetic field between two D-shaped electrodes.

Dalton's law of partial pressures In a mixture of gases, the pressure of a component gas is the same as if it alone occupied the total volume. See PARTIAL PRESSURE.

Decibel Unit for comparing power levels or sound intensities; tenth of a BEL.

Decimal system Number system using the base 10, i.e. using the digits 1 to 9 and zero.

Delta rays (δ-rays) Electrons knocked out of atoms by high-energy charged particles.

Density Mass of unit volume of a substance. See SPECIFIC GRAVITY.

Desiccation Drying.

Diffraction Splitting of white light into spectrum of

235

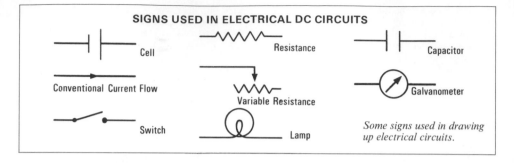

SIGNS USED IN ELECTRICAL DC CIRCUITS

Cell

Resistance

Capacitor

Conventional Current Flow

Variable Resistance

Galvanometer

Switch

Lamp

Some signs used in drawing up electrical circuits.

colours by passing it through narrow slit or past edge of obstacle. More generally, any type of electromagnetic wave can be diffracted.

Diffusion Phenomenon by which gases mix together. See GRAHAM'S LAW.

Dimensions Power to which fundamental unit (length, mass, or time) is raised to describe a physical quantity; e.g. area (length^2) has 2 dimensions of length.

Direct current Electric current that always flows in the same direction.

Dissociation Temporary decomposition of chemical compound, into component molecules or groupings, that reverses when conditions causing it are removed.

Distillation Technique of purifying or separating liquids by heating to boiling point and condensing vapour produced back to liquid.

Doppler effect Apparent change in frequency of sound or light caused by movement of source with respect to observer. Frequency rises for approaching sources, falls for receding ones.

Double decomposition Chemical reaction between two compounds in which reactants form two new compounds; e.g. AB reacts with CD to form AD and CB.

Dry ice Solid carbon dioxide (CO_2).

Ductility Property of a metal that allows it to be drawn out into wire.

Dynamics Branch of MECHANICS that deals with action of forces on objects in motion. See also STATICS.

Dynamo Device for converting mechanical energy into electrical energy essentially consisting of armature rotating between poles of powerful electromagnet.

Dyne Unit of FORCE; imparts acceleration of 1 cm/sec/sec to mass of 1 gm; equivalent to 10^{-5} newton.

Dysprosium (Dy) One of the rare-earth metals, whose compounds are sometimes used as catalysts. It has interesting magnetic properties. At very low temperatures it becomes ferromagnetic and superconductive.

Earthing Connecting an electrical conductor to Earth, or to metal connected to Earth.

Efficiency Of a machine, ratio of energy output to energy input, generally expressed as percentage.

Effusion Movement of gas under pressure through small hole.

Einsteinium (Es) Artificial, short-lived, radioactive transuranium element made by irradiating U^{238} with neutrons. It was first discovered in the debris

from the first thermonuclear (H-bomb) explosion in 1952, and was synthesized two years later.

Elasticity Property of a material that makes it readopt its original shape after a force deforming it is removed; if stressed beyond elastic limit, material does not return to its original shape. See also HOOKE'S LAW.

Electrical energy See ENERGY.

Electric field Region surrounding electric charge in which a charged particle is subjected to a force.

Electrochemical series List of metals in order of their electrode potentials. Each metal will displace from their salts those metals lower down in series; the most noble, unreactive metals, such as gold, appear at bottom of list. Also called electromotive series.

Electrode Metal rod or plate through which electric

ELECTROCHEMICAL SERIES	
Element	Electrode potential (volts)
Lithium	−3.04
Potassium	−2.92
Barium	−2.90
Calcium	−2.87
Sodium	−2.71
Magnesium	−2.37
Aluminium	−1.66
Manganese	−1.18
Zinc	−0.76
Chromium	−0.74
Iron	−0.44
Cobalt	−0.28
Nickel	−0.25
Tin	−0.14
Lead	−0.13
Hydrogen	0.00
Copper	+0.34
Mercury	+0.78
Silver	+0.80
Gold	+1.50

current enters or leaves electrolysis cell, battery, or vacuum tube.

Electrolysis Conduction of electricity between two electrodes, through solution or molten mass (electrolyte) containing ions accompanied by chemical changes at electrodes.

Electromagnet Magnet consisting of iron core surrounded by coil of wire carrying electric current.

Electromagnetic units (emu) System based on unit magnetic pole.

Electromagnetism Magnetism produced by flowing

Very powerful electromagnets are used for picking up and transferring steel scrap.

electric current; also the science that studies this phenomenon.

Electromotive force (emf) Force that drives electric current along a conductor; measured in VOLTS. See also POTENTIAL DIFFERENCE.

Electron Small, negatively charged subatomic particle; every electrically neutral atom has as many orbiting electrons as PROTONS in nucleus. See also CURRENT, ELECTRIC.

Electron microscope Instrument that uses beam of electrons to produce magnified images of extremely small objects, beyond range of optical (light) microscope.

Electron-volt (eV) Small unit of energy equal to work done on electron when it passes through potential of 1 volt; 1 ev $= 1.6 \times 10^{-19}$ joule.

Electroplating Production of thin adherent coating of one metal on another using ELECTROLYSIS.

Electrostatic units (esu) System based on force exerted between two electric charges.

Element Substance made up of exactly similar ATOMS (all with same atomic number).

CHEMICAL ELEMENTS

Name	Symbol	Atomic number	Atomic weight	Valency	Melting point °C	Boiling point °C
Actinium	Ac	89	(227)		1230	3200
Aluminium	Al	13	26.98154	3	660.4	2350
Americium	Am	95	(243)	3,4,5,6	990	2600
Antimony	Sb	51	121.75	3,5	630.7	1640
Argon	Ar	18	39.948	0	−189.4	−185.9
Arsenic	As	33	74.9216	3,5	613 solid sublimes	
Astatine	At	85	(210)	1,3,5,7	300	350
Barium	Ba	56	137.34	2	710	1640
Berkelium	Bk	97	(247)	3,4	986	
Beryllium	Be	4	9.01218	2	1285	2470
Bismuth	Bi	83	208.9804	3,5	271.4	1650
Boron	B	5	10.81	3	2030	3700
Bromine	Br	35	79.904	1,3,5,7	−7.1	58.9
Cadmium	Cd	48	112.40	2	321.1	770
Caesium	Cs	55	132.9054	1	28.6	686
Calcium	Ca	20	40.08	2	840	1490
Californium	Cf	98	(251)			
Carbon	C	6	12.011	2,4	3700 solid sublimes	
Cerium	Ce	58	140.12	3,4	800	3000
Chlorine	Cl	17	35.453	1,3,5,7	−101	−34.0
Chromium	Cr	24	51.996	2,3,6	1860	2600
Cobalt	Co	27	58.9332	2,3	1494	2900
Copper	Cu	29	63.546	1,2	1084.5	2580
Curium	Cm	96	(247)	3	1340	
Dysprosium	Dy	66	162.50	3	1410	2600
Einsteinium	Es	99	(254)			
Erbium	Er	68	167.26	3	1520	2600
Europium	Eu	63	151.96	2,3	820	1450
Fermium	Fm	100	(257)			
Fluorine	F	9	18.99840	1	−219.6	−188.1
Francium	Fr	87	(223)	1	30	650
Gadolinium	Gd	64	157.25	3	1310	3000
Gallium	Ga	31	69.72	2,3	29.8	2070
Germanium	Ge	32	72.59	4	959	2850
Gold	Au	79	196.9665	1,3	1064.4	2850
Hafnium	Hf	72	178.49	4	2230	5300
Hahnium	Ha	105				
Helium	He	2	4.00260	0	3.5 K	4.22 K
Holmium	Ho	67	164.9304	3	1470	2300

Name	Symbol	Atomic number	Atomic weight	Valency	Melting point °C	Boiling point °C
Hydrogen	H	1	1.0079	1	−259.2	−252.8
Indium	In	49	114.82	3	156.6	2050
Iodine	I	53	126.9045	1,3,5,7	113.6	184
Iridium	Ir	77	192.22	3,4	2447	4550
Iron	Fe	26	55.847	2,3	1540	2760
Krypton	Kr	36	83.80	0	−157.3	−153.4
Lanthanum	La	57	138.9055	3	920	3450
Lawrencium	Lr	103	(260)			
Lead	Pb	82	207.2	2,4	327.5	1760
Lithium	Li	3	6.941	1	180	1360
Lutetium	Lu	71	174.97	3	1700	3400
Magnesium	Mg	12	24.305	2	650	1100
Manganese	Mn	25	54.9380	2,3,4,6,7	1250	2120
Mendelevium	Md	101	(258)			
Mercury	Hg	80	200.59	1,2	−38.9	356.6
Molybdenum	Mo	42	95.94	3,4,6	2620	4830
Neodymium	Nd	60	144.24	3	1024	3100
Neon	Ne	10	20.179	0	−248.6	−246.0
Neptunium	Np	93	237.0482	4,5,6	640	
Nickel	Ni	28	58.70	2,3	1455	2150
Niobium	Nb	41	92.9064	3,5	2425	5000
Nitrogen	N	7	14.0067	3,5	−210	−195.8
Nobelium	No	102	(255)			
Osmium	Os	76	190.2	2,3,4,8	3030	5000
Oxygen	O	8	15.9994	2	−218.8	−182.9
Palladium	Pd	46	106.4	2,4,6	1554	3000
Phosphorus	P	15	30.97376	3,5	44.2 (yellow)	280.4
Platinum	Pt	78	195.09	2,4	1772	3720
Plutonium	Pu	94	(244)	3,4,5,6	640	3200
Polonium	Po	84	(209)		254	960
Potassium	K	19	39.098	1	63.2	777
Praseodymium	Pr	59	140.9077	3	935	3000
Promethium	Pm	61	(145)	3	1000	2700
Protactinium	Pa	91	231.0359		1200	4000
Radium	Ra	88	226.0254	2	700	1500
Radon	Rn	86	(222)	0	−71	−62
Rhenium	Re	75	186.207		3180	5600
Rhodium	Rh	45	102.9055	3	1963	3700
Rubidium	Rb	37	85.4678	1	38.8	705
Ruthenium	Ru	44	101.07	3,4,6,8	2310	4100
Rutherfordium	Ru	104				
Samarium	Sm	62	105.4	2,3	1060	1600
Scandium	Sc	21	44.9559	3	1540	2800
Selenium	Se	34	78.96	2,4,6	220	685
Silicon	Si	14	28.086	4	1410	2620
Silver	Ag	47	107.868	1	961.9	2160
Sodium	Na	11	22.98977	1	97.8	900
Strontium	Sr	38	87.62	2	770	1380
Sulphur	S	16	32.06	2,4,6	115	444.7
Tantalum	Ta	73	180.9479	5	3000	5400
Technetium	Tc	43	(97)	6,7	2200	4600
Tellurium	Te	52	127.60	2,4,6	450	990
Terbium	Tb	65	158.9254	3	1360	2500
Thallium	Tl	81	204.37	1,3	304	1460
Thorium	Th	90	232.0381	4	1700	4500
Thulium	Tm	69	168.9342	3	1550	2000
Tin	Sn	50	118.69	2,4	231.9	2720
Titanium	Ti	22	47.90	3,4	1670	3300
Tungsten (Wolfram)	W	74	183.85	6	3387	5420
Uranium	U	92	238.029	4,6	1135	4000
Vanadium	V	23	50.9414	3,5	1920	3400
Xenon	Xe	54	131.30	0	−111.9	−108.1
Ytterbium	Yb	70	173.04	2,3	824	1500
Yttrium	Y	39	88.9059	3	1510	3300
Zinc	Zn	30	65.38	2	419.6	913
Zirconium	Zr	40	91.22	4	1850	4400

Notes: The atomic weights (at. wt.) are based on the exact number 12 as assigned to the atomic mass of the principal isotope of carbon, carbon-12, and are provided through the courtesy of the International Union of Pure and Applied Chemistry (IUPAC) and Butterworths Scientific Publications.

Values in parentheses are for certain radioactive elements whose atomic weights cannot be quoted precisely without knowledge of origin; the value given in each case is the atomic mass no. of the isotope of longest known half-life.

NB: Gold and platinum occur in the earth as elements. Cadmium compounds are found in zinc ores.

PRINCIPAL ELEMENTARY PARTICLES
(excluding antiparticles)

Name	Charge	Mass compared with electron	Lifetime (seconds)
Proton	+	1836	stable
Neutron	none	1838	1010
Hyperons			
Xi-zero	none	2570	2.9×10^{-10}
Xi-minus	−	2580	1.7×10^{-10}
Sigma-plus	+	2320	8.1×10^{-11}
Sigma-zero	none	2330	less than 10^{-14}
Sigma-minus	−	2340	1.66×10^{-10}
Lambda	none	2160	2.5×10^{-10}
Omega-minus	−	3280	1.1×10^{-10}
Leptons			
Electron	−	1	stable
Neutrino	none	0	stable
Muon	−	207	2.2×10^{-6}
Mesons			
Eta	none	1070	unknown
K1-zero	none	970	10^{-10}
K2-zero	none	970	2.8×10^{-8}
K-minus	−	960	1.2×10^{-8}
K-plus	+	960	1.2×10^{-8}
Pi-plus	+	273	2.6×10^{-8}
Pi-zero	none	264	10^{-16}
Pi-minus	−	273	2.6×10^{-8}

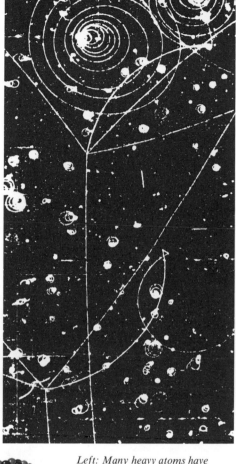

Right: A photograph of tracks in a bubble chamber, produced by the movements of elementary particles. Below: A diagram of the same events, identifying the elementary particles taking place in the collisions. One easily observed fact is that the electron and the positron, having opposite electrical charges, spiral in opposite directions.

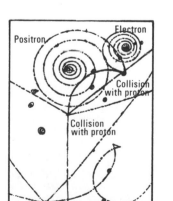

Left: Many heavy atoms have unstable nuclei, which break down spontaneously in radioactive decay. As it breaks down, this heavy nucleus is emitting an alpha particle, which comprises two protons and two neutrons and is the same thing as a helium nucleus.

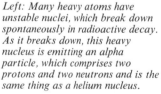

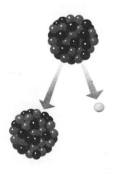

Right: In this case, the heavy, unstable nucleus, in breaking down, emits a beta particle, which is identical with an electron. This form of radiation is more penetrating than alpha-particle radiation. More penetrating still is gamma radiation.

Ellipse Plane figure formed by slicing through circular cone at angle to base.

Emulsion Colloidal suspension of minute droplets of one liquid dispersed in another. See COLLOID.

Energy Capacity for doing work; examples include: chemical energy (possessed by substance in its atoms or molecules, and released in chemical reaction), ELECTRICAL ENERGY (associated with electric charges), HEAT (possessed by body because of motion of its atoms or molecules – form of kinetic energy), KINETIC ENERGY (possessed by body because of its motion), and POTENTIAL ENERGY (possessed by body because of its position). In presence of matter, any one form of energy can be converted into another.

Entropy A quantity in THERMODYNAMICS which measures the degree of disorder of any system, or, what is the same thing, the amount of energy not available for doing useful work. In all irreversible change, entropy increases.

Epsom salts Magnesium sulphate $MgSO_4 \cdot 7H_2O$.

Erbium (Er) One of the rare-earth elements, many of whose compounds are pink. At very low temperatures it is ferromagnetic and superconductive.

Erg Absolute unit of work in CGS SYSTEM, defined as work done by force of 1 dyne acting through 1 cm; 1 erg $= 10^{-7}$ joule.

Esters Class of organic compounds formed by chemical reaction between acids and alcohols.

Europium (Eu) The lightest and softest of the rare-earth elements, it is also one of the least abundant. Many of its salts are coloured. It readily absorbs neutrons and has potential applications in the nuclear energy field.

Evaporation Phenomenon in which liquid turns into vapour, without necessarily boiling. Occurs because fast-moving molecules escape from surface of liquid. See also BOILING POINT.

Fahrenheit Temperature scale on which melting point of ice is $32°F$ and the boiling point of water is $212°F$.

Falling bodies, laws of Distance an object falls under gravity given by $s = \frac{1}{2}gt^2$, where s is distance, g is acceleration due to gravity, and t is time taken. Its final velocity is given by $v = u + gy$, where u is initial velocity.

Fallout General term for radioactive fragments and isotopes that fall to Earth from atmosphere after nuclear explosion.

Farad (F) Unit of electrical CAPACITANCE, defined as that which requires a charge of 1 coulomb to raise its potential by 1 volt.

Faraday's law In an electrical circuit, any induced electromotive force is proportional to rate at which magnetic lines of force cut circuit.

Fermium (Fm) Artificial, radioactive transuranium element, obtained by bombarding U^{238} with neutrons. Like einsteinium, it was first discovered in the debris from the first H-bomb, and subsequently synthesized.

Ferromagnetism The type of magnetism shown by the metals iron, cobalt, nickel and their alloys. It is far stronger than other types of magnetism.

Filtration Process for separating solids from suspension in liquid by straining them off, using special paper or other filter medium; pure liquid that drips through is *filtrate*.

Flame test Technique in chemical analysis in which element is identified by characteristic colour it imparts to gas flame.

Flexibility Property of substance, such as rubber or plastic, that allows it to bend easily without breaking.

Flotation Method of separating solids in which one solid is made to float on detergent-produced froth in tank of liquid.

Fluid State of matter (liquid or gas) that can flow, and takes on shape of part or all of containing vessel.

Fluorescence Emission of light of one wavelength (colour) after absorption of another wavelength; ceases when light source is removed (unlike PHOSPHORESCENCE).

Fluorine (F) A greenish-yellow poisonous gas which is the first member of the halogen family and the most reactive of all the elements. It combines with every other element except the rare gases helium, neon, and argon to form fluorides. It occurs widely in mineral compounds, including *fluorite* (*fluorspar*) CaF_2; *apatite*, $CaF \cdot 3Ca_3(PO_4)_2$; and *cryolite*, sodium aluminium fluoride, Na_3AlF_6. Sodium fluoride is added to drinking water (fluoridation) to help reduce tooth decay.

Foot-candle Unit of illumination equal to 1 lumen/ft². See PHOT.

Foot-pound Unit of work, defined as work done by force of 1 lb acting throught 1 ft.

Force Agency that can make stationary body move, or moving body change speed or direction.

Francium (Fr) Rare radioactive element which is the heaviest of the alkali metals. It occurs transiently during radioactive decay of actinium. Only a few grams are present in the Earth's crust at any moment. Its properties resemble those of caesium.

Freezing point Temperature at which liquid changes to solid. Same as MELTING POINT of solid.

Frequency Of a wave motion, number of vibrations or waves per second, equal to 1 divided by period (time taken for one vibration). See WAVELENGTH.

Friction Force that resists sliding or rolling of one surface on another.

Gadolinium (Gd) A rare-earth metal found with many others in the mineral *monazite*. Its salts and solutions are colourless. It becomes ferromagnetic at temperatures of $17°C$ and below, and at very low temperatures becomes superconductive. It absorbs neutrons more readily than any other element.

Gallium (Ga) A soft metal of the boron group which melts at just above room temperature (at $29.8°C$). Once called eka-aluminium, it has somewhat similar chemical properties to aluminium. Its compounds occur sparsely in Nature.

Gamma-rays (γ-rays) Penetrating electromagnetic radiation of shorter wavelength than X-rays.

Gas Fluid that, no matter how little there is, always takes up whole of vessel containing it. See also VAPOUR.

Gas constant (R) in fundamental gas equation $pV = RT$, where p = pressure, V = volume, T = absolute temperature, R = 8.31 joules/kelvin/mole. See also VAN DER WAAL'S EQUATION.

Gauss (G) Unit (cgs system) of magnetic induction, defined as induction produced in substance with unit magnetic permeability placed in magnetic field of 1 oersted.

Gay-Lussac's law When gases react, they combine in volumes that bear simple numerical ratio to each other and to volume of product.

Geiger counter Instrument for detecting and measuring radioactivity.

Geissler tube Electric discharge tube that glows when high voltage current flows between metal plates sealed into it.

Germanium (Ge) A rare semi-metallic element which, like its sister element silicon, has valuable semiconductor properties. Among its important compounds are the oxide, GeO_2, and the tetrachloride, $GeCl_4$. Germanium is extracted from certain ores, such as *germanite*.

Glauber's salt Crystalline sodium sulphate $Na_2SO_4 \cdot 10H_2O$.

Gold (Au) Bright yellow, unreactive precious metal, the most malleable and ductile of all metals. It occurs native and is widely mined. One of its important industrial uses is for plating contacts in printed circuits and semiconductors.

Graham's law Velocity of diffusion of a gas is inversely proportional to square root of its density.

Gram-molecular weight See MOLE.

Gravimetric analysis Chemical analysis made ultimately by weighing substances.

Gravitation Force of attraction between any two objects caused by their masses.

Gravity, centre of Point at which all of an object's weight appears to act.

Haber process Industrial method of making ammonia from nitrogen and hydrogen in presence of catalyst.

Hafnium (Hf) Metal closely resembling zirconium in chemical properties. It is hard, malleable and ductile, and has excellent corrosion resistance. One of its main uses is in control rods for nuclear reactors. It occurs naturally as the oxide in zirconium minerals such as zircon and cyrtolite.

Hahnium (Ha) A short-lived radioactive transuranium element, whose most stable isotope has a half-life of only a few seconds.

Halogens Elements of Group VII of Periodic Table; fluorine, chlorine, bromine, iodine, and astatine.

Heat A form of ENERGY.

Heavy water Deuterium oxide, D_2O; the oxide of deuterium or 'heavy hydrogen', isotope of hydrogen having atomic mass of 2.

Helium (He) The lightest element after hydrogen and first member of the inert gases. It has the lowest boiling point of any element ($-269°C$), and in liquid form displays the phenomenon of superfluidity. It was discovered first in the Sun's atmosphere. After hydrogen, it is probably the most common element in the universe.

henry (H) Unit of electrical INDUCTANCE, defined as that producing induced electromotive force of 1 volt for a current change of 1 ampere/second.

Henry's law Weight of gas dissolved by liquid is proportional to gas pressure.

Hess's law Sum of quantities of heat evolved in each stage of multistage chemical reaction is equal to total amount of heat evolved when overall reaction proceeds in one stage.

Holmium (Ho) One of the least abundant of the rare earth metals, which forms yellowish-brown salts. It becomes ferromagnetic at very low temperatures (below $-253°C$).

Homogenation Process for making mixture uniform (homogeneous).

Hooke's law Within elastic limit, extension (stress) is proportional to force (strain) producing it. See ELASTICITY.

Horsepower (hp) Unit of power, equal to work performed at rate of 550 ft-lb/sec; 1 hp = 745.7 watts. See also WATT.

Hydrate Compound containing chemically combined water molecules; many SALTS are hydrated by water of crystallization.

Hydraulics Science that studies flow of fluids.

Hydrocarbon Chemical compound of hydrogen and carbon.

Hydrogen (H) The simplest and lightest of all elements, and the most abundant element in the universe. Chemically it bears certain resemblances to both the alkali metals and the halogens. With carbon it forms an enormous range of organic compounds.

Hydrogenation Chemical combination of a substance with hydrogen.

Hydrolysis Decomposing substance chemically by making it react with water.

Hydrostatics Branch of mechanics that deals with fluids at rest.

Hydroxide Chemical compound containing the hydroxyl group —OH.

Hygrometer Instrument for measuring relative humidity of the air.

Hyperbola Curve traced by moving point whose distance from fixed point (focus) is always in same ratio, greater than 1, to its distance from fixed straight line (directrix). See also PARABOLA.

Ignition point Temperature above which substance will burn.

Imaginary number Square root of a negative number; square root of —1 is imaginary number i.

Impact (collision) See MOMENTUM.

Incandescence Giving off light at high temperatures.

Inclined plane Simple machine consisting of smooth plane sloping upwards at angle to horizontal.

Indicator Substance that changes colour to indicate end of a chemical reaction or to indicate the pH (acidity or alkalinity) of a solution. See pH.

Indium (In) Rare metal of the boron family, which is soft and plastic and like tin emits a 'cry' when bent. It was named after the indigo blue colour displayed by its compounds in the flame test. Its most important use is in the manufacture of semiconductor devices.

Inductance Property of electrical circuit to resist change in rate or direction of current; in single circuit called self-inductance, between two circuits mutual inductance; symbol of inductance: L; unit: henry.

Induction coil High voltage generator that makes use of electromagnetic induction between a (primary) coil of wire with few turns and a (secondary) coil with thousands of turns.

Induction, electric In electromagnetic induction, a moving or changing magnetic field induces an electric current in a conductor. In electrostatic induction, a charge on a conductor induces an opposite charge on a nearby uncharged conductor.

Inertia Property of object that makes it resist being moved or change in its motion.

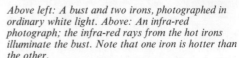

Above left: A bust and two irons, photographed in ordinary white light. Above: An infra-red photograph; the infra-red rays from the hot irons illuminate the bust. Note that one iron is hotter than the other.

Infra-red rays Electromagnetic radiation of wavelengths just longer than those of visible light; invisible heat rays.

Inorganic chemistry Branch of chemistry that deals with all compounds other than those of carbon; a few carbon compounds, such as carbides, carbonates, carbon dioxide, and metallic cyanides, are also studied in inorganic chemistry. See also ORGANIC CHEMISTRY.

Insulation Use of an insulator, a substance that is a poor conductor of heat, sound, or electricity, to prevent their passage.

Insulator, electric Substance that does not conduct electricity; a non-conductor.

Interference Phenomenon caused by combination of waves; spectral colours produced in thin films and by DIFFRACTION are examples.

Interferometer Instrument that produces INTERFERENCE using two halves of a split, single light beam.

Iodine (I) Soft, dark grey crystalline solid belonging to the halogen family. It sublimes at room temperature to give a deep violet, irritating vapour. It occurs naturally in salt deposits and brine, and can also be extracted from seaweeds. Tincture of iodine – iodine dissolved in potassium iodide, Kl, water and alcohol – is an excellent bactericide. Iodine combines with most metals and non-metals.

Ion Atom or group of atoms carrying an electrical charge; positively charged ions are called cations, negatively charged ions anions. During electrolysis, anions migrate towards the ANODE (positive electrode) and cations migrate towards the CATHODE (negative electrode).

Ionization Production of charged IONS from electrically neutral ATOMS or molecular fragments; generally achieved by electrical or chemical processes.

Iridium (Ir) Rare brittle metal of the platinum group which is one of the hardest and densest pure metals known (relative density 22). It finds its greatest use in alloys with platinum, and gives that metal greater chemical resistance.

Iron (Fe) When pure, a soft, easily corroded metal that can be transformed by the addition of small amounts of alloying materials, particularly carbon, into our most important metal, steel. It is the fourth most abundant element and the second most abundant metal (after aluminium) in the Earth's crust, where it occurs as oxides, such as haematite (Fe_2O_3) and magnetite (Fe_3O_4); sulphides, such as pyrites (FeS); and carbonates, such as siderite ($FeCO_3$). One of iron's most distinctive properties is its magnetism.

Isomerism Phenomenon in which two or more compounds exist with same chemical formula, but with different structures (arrangements of atoms in space).

Isomorphous Having similar crystalline forms, and often similar chemical composition.

Isotope One of two or more forms of an element with same atomic number (i.e. number of protons in nucleus), but different atomic masses (due to different numbers of neutrons in nucleus). See also ATOM.

joule (J) Unit of work or energy; defined as work done in 1 sec by current of 1 ampere flowing through resistance of 1 ohm; $1 J = 10^7$ ergs.

kelvin (K) Unit of temperature interval; Kelvin or absolute temperature scale based on absolute zero as 0K; on this scale, the melting point of ice is 273.15K. To convert from Kelvin to centigrade (or Celsius), subtract 273.15 from temperature.

Ketones Class of organic compound containing the characteristic group = CO. See also ALDEHYDES.

Kilowatt A thousand WATTS.

Kinematics Branch of mechanics that deals with movement independent of forces or masses.

Kinetic energy See ENERGY.

Krypton (Kr) One of the inert gases; found in small traces (about one part per million) in the atmosphere. It is used to fill some electric tubes and fluorescent lamps.

Lanthanum (La) The first member of the lanthanide series of rare-earth metals. Lanthanum is found with other rare earths in monazite and other minerals. The alloy, mischmetal, which is used for lighter flints, contains 25 per cent lanthanum.

Laser Type of MASER that produces intense beam of light that is monochromatic (single colour) and

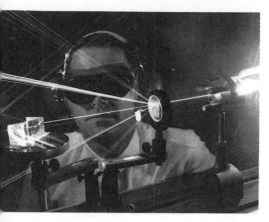

An argon ion laser, one form of gas laser, in operation. It can be used in processing computer information, determining target distances, and carrying voice and television signals.

coherent (all its waves are in step); abbreviation for *l*ight *a*mplification by *s*timulated *e*mission of *r*adiation.

Latent heat Heat absorbed without temperature rise to change substance from solid to liquid or liquid to gas.

Lawrencium (Lw) The eleventh transuranium element, named after the inventor of the cyclotron, Ernest Lawrence. It is made by bombarding californium with accelerated boron ions.

Lead (Pb) A soft, heavy metal related to tin. Easy to shape and resistant to corrosion, it has been used for making water pipes for thousands of years. Today its greatest use is in car batteries, though it is widely used elsewhere in numerous alloys. Its soluble compounds are poisonous.

Lenz's law When a wire moves in a magnetic field, the electric current induced in the wire generates a magnetic field that tends to oppose the movement. See INDUCTION.

Lever Simple machine consisting of rigid beam pivoted at one point, called the fulcrum; effort applied at one point on beam can lift load at another point.

Linear equation Algebraic equation of first power; in coordinate geometry, it represents straight line.

Liquid Fluid that, without changing its volume, takes up shape of all or lower part of vessel containing it.

Lithium (Li) The first of the alkali-metal group and the lightest of all solid elements (relative density 0.53). A soft, silvery white metal of low melting point (180°C), it is used in some lightweight alloys. Like all the alkali metals, it decomposes water, liberating hydrogen.

Litmus Chemical INDICATOR, vegetable dye that is red in acid solutions and blue in alkaline solutions.

Logarithm Of a number, power to which a base must be raised to equal the number; if $A = B^n.n$ is the logarithm of A expressed to the base B.

Lumen (lm) Unit of luminous flux equal to amount of light emitted by source of 1 candela/sec through unit solid angle.

Luminescence Emission of light at low temperatures; FLUORESCENCE and PHOSPHORESCENCE are examples.

Luminosity Brightness.

Lutetium (Lu) Heaviest member of the rare-earth metals, of which it is the hardest and densest and has the highest melting point. It is of little use.

Lux (lx) Unit of illumination equal to 1 lumen/m².

Magnesium (Mg) A light alkaline-earth metal, it is widely used in the aerospace industries in alloys with aluminium and other metals. It burns brilliantly in air to form pure white magnesium oxide. It occurs widely, for example as the carbonate magnesite and the double carbonate with calcium, dolomite.

Magneto High-voltage electric generator in which permanent magnet is spun inside coil; gives only short pulses of current; used for starting petrol engines. See also DYNAMO.

Malleability Property of a metal that allows it to be beaten into thin sheet.

Manganese (Mn) A hard heavy metal, whose main use is in steelmaking. Manganese absorbs impurities from the steel and strengthens it. High manganese steel has exceptional hardness and wear resistance. Important manganese compounds include the oxide, which is a good catalyst, and potassium permanganate ($KMnO_4$), an excellent oxidizing agent.

Maser Microwave amplifier that uses energy changes within atoms or molecules; abbreviation for *m*icrowave *a*mplification by *s*timulated *e*mission of *r*adiation. See also LASER.

Mass Amount of matter in an object; SI unit, kg. See also WEIGHT.

Mass action, law of Speed of chemical reaction is proportional to active masses (concentrations) of reactants.

Mass spectroscopy Technique of identifying or analysing mixture of elements by measuring masses of their atoms.

maxwell Unit of magnetic flux (cgs system), defined as flux through each square centimetre at right-angles to magnetic field of 1 gauss intensity; 1 maxwell = 10^{58} weber.

Mean Mathematical average of group of numbers, given by their sum divided by the number of them.

Mechanics Branch of science that deals with behaviour of matter under action of force.

Melting point Temperature at which solid turns to liquid; equal to FREEZING POINT of the liquid.

Mendelevium (Md) Artificial radioactive element of the actinide series, obtained by bombarding einsteinium with helium ions. Relatively short-lived, its most stable isotope has a half-life of only two months.

Mercury (Hg) The only metal that is liquid at room temperature, mercury is related to zinc and cadmium. Once called quicksilver, mercury is used in barometers and thermometers; and as vapour in discharge tubes and vacuum pumps (mercury diffusion pumps). It forms alloys called amalgams with most metals (but not iron); silver and gold amalgams are used to fill teeth.

Meson One of a group of unstable subatomic particles with masses between those of ELECTRON and PROTON.

METALS AND THEIR ORES

Metal	Ores	Metal	Ores
Aluminium	bauxite, AL_2O_3	Magnesium	magnesite, dolomite, both
Antimony	stibnite, Sb_2S_3		$MgCO_3$; kieserite,
Beryllium	beryl, $3BeO.Al_2O_3.6SiO_2$;		$MgSO_4.H_2O$; carnallite,
	chrysoberyl, $BeAl_2O_4$		$KCl.MgCl_2.6H_2O$
Bismuth	bismuth glance (bismuthinite),	Manganese	pyrolusite, MnO_2; hausman-
	Bi_2S_3; bismite, Bi_2O_3		nite, Mn_3O_4
Calcium	limestone, marble, chalk, all	Mercury	cinnabar, HgS
	$CaCO_3$; gypsum, alabaster,	Nickel	millerite, NiS; pentlandite,
	both $CaSO_4$; fluorspar, CaF_2;		(Fe, Ni) S; garnierite,
	rock phosphate, $CaPO_4$		(Ni; Mg) $SiO_3.xH_2O$
Chromium	chromite, $FeCr_2O_4$	Potassium	carnallite, $KCl.MgCl_2.6H_2O$;
Cobalt	smaltite, $CoAs_2$; cobaltite,		saltpetre, KNO_3
	CoAsS	Silver	silver glance (argentite),
Copper	copper pyrites (chalcopyrite),		AgS_2; horn silver, AgCl
	$CuFeS_2$; copper glance	Sodium	rock salt, NaCl; Chile
	(chalcocyte), Cu_2S; cuprite,		saltpetre, $NaNO_3$
	Cu_2O; bornite, Cu_5FeS_4	Strontium	strontianite, $SrCO_3$; celestine,
Iron	haematite, Fe_2O_3; magnetite,		$SrSO_4$
	Fe_3O_4; siderite, $FeCO_3$;	Tin	tinstone (cassiterite), SnO_2
	(iron pyrites, FeS_2)	Titanium	rutile, TiO_2; ilmenite, $FeO.TiO_2$
Lead	galena, PbS; cerussite. $PbCO_3$;	Uranium	pitchblende (uraninite), UO_2
	massicot, PbO	Zinc	zinc blende (sphalerite), ZnS;
Lithium	spodumene, $LiAl (SiO_3)_2$		calamine, $ZnCO_3$

Metal Element or alloy that is a good conductor of heat and electricity, has a high density, often has characteristic lustre, and can generally be 'worked' by beating or drawing into wire.

Metalloid Element with properties of both metals and non-metals.

Micron (μm) Unit of length equal to 10^{-6} metre.

Microwaves Short-wavelength radio waves (electromagnetic radiation) having wavelengths of approximately 0.1 to 30 cm.

Mixture More than one element or compound together, but not in chemical combination; components can be separated by physical means.

mks system Metric system of units based on metre, kilogram, second; superseded by SI UNITS based on mks.

Mole (mol) Basic unit of amount of substance; weight of substance equal to its molecular weight in grams (e.g. 1 mole H_2O has mass 18.015 g); molar solution contains 1 mol in 1 litre of solution.

Molecular weight Sum of the ATOMIC WEIGHTS of the elements in one molecule of a compound.

Molecule Smallest particle of a chemical substance that can exist alone; made up of one or more atoms.

Molybdenum (Mo) A hard, white metal which is alloyed with steel to impart high-temperature strength. It has a high melting point (2620°C) and retains its hardness and strength at high temperatures. One of its most useful compounds is the disulphide MoS_2, which has a layered structure (like graphite), and is a lubricant.

Momentum Of moving object, product of mass and velocity. According to principle of conservation of momentum, when two or more perfectly elastic objects collide, total momentum before impact equals total momentum after impact.

Monomer Type of chemical compound, having small molecules, capable of undergoing POLYMERIZATION.

THE EQUATIONS OF MOTION

Three equations explain the motion of any object that is accelerating at the same rate. They are

$$v = u + at$$
$$s = ut + \tfrac{1}{2}at^2$$
$$v^2 = u^2 + 2as$$

where a = acceleration
  t = time for which acceleration takes place
  u = velocity at start of acceleration
  v = velocity at end of acceleration
  s = distance travelled during acceleration

In the case of a falling body, a is the acceleration due to gravity (g), which is equal to 9.8 metres/sec/sec.

Metal parts for a Rolls-Royce Olympus engine made from electroslag remelted steel.

Motion (movement) See NEWTON'S LAWS OF MOTION.

Neodymium (Nd) The third most plentiful of the rare-earth metals. Found in the mineral monazite, it is a constituent of the alloy, mischmetal (for lighter flints), and is used to colour ceramic glazes and glasses.

Neon (Ne) One of the most useful of the rare gases, neon is used in discharge tubes. Neon tubes emit a brilliant orange-red light. Neon is obtained by distilling liquid air.

Neptunium (Np) An artificial radioactive element following uranium (which it resembles) in the Periodic Table. It is obtained by bombarding uranium with slow neutrons. Its most stable isotope has a half-life of more than 2 million years.

Neutralization Combining acid and alkali so that resulting solution is neutral (neither acid nor alkaline). See also INDICATOR.

Neutron Uncharged subatomic particle found in the nuclei of all atoms except hydrogen.

newton (N) Unit of force, defined as that imparting acceleration of 1 m/sec/sec to mass of 1 kg.

Newton's laws of motion (1) A stationary object remains still or a moving object continues to move in a straight line unless acted on by an external force. (2) Force producing acceleration in an object is proportional to the product of the object's mass and its acceleration. (3) Every action has an equal and opposite reaction.

Newton's rings INTERFERENCE bands produced in thin film of air, as between convex lens and plane mirror.

Nickel (Ni) A tough, hard silvery white metal, which has excellent corrosion resistance. Its alloy with copper, cupronickel, is used for our 'silver' coinage. It is widely used for plating, in stainless steels, and as a catalyst. Being ferromagnetic, nickel is a major ingredient of magnet alloys.

Niobium (Nb) A soft, ductile metal closely related to tantalum with which it occurs in ores such as columbite. (It was once called columbium.) A major use is in superconductors.

Nitrogen (N) A colourless, tasteless, and odourless gas, nitrogen (N_2) is the major constituent of air (78 per cent by volume). It is an important constituent of living matter. It occurs in Nature as nitrates; and ammonium compounds, and forms a whole series of oxides, including laughing gas, N_2O.

Nobelium (No) An artificial radioactive element made by bombarding curium with carbon ions. The most stable isotope has a 3-month half-life.

Noble metals Chemically unreactive metals such as gold, silver, and platinum.

Nuclear fission Nuclei of heavy atoms split and release vast quantities of energy; this is energy generating process of atomic bombs and nuclear reactors.

Nuclear Fusion Nuclei of light atoms join together, with the release of vast amounts of energy; this is process that occurs in hydrogen bombs and in stars, such as Sun.

Nylon Plastic material of polyamide type.

Oersted Unit of magnetic field strength, defined as force in dynes experienced by unit magnetic pole in the field.

Ohm (Ω) Unit of electrical resistance, given by potential difference across conductor in volts divided by current in amperes flowing through conductor.

Ohm's law Voltage (V) in volts between ends of a conductor equals product of current (I) in amps flowing through it and its resistance (R) in ohms, i.e. $V = IR$.

Organic chemistry Branch of chemistry that deals with the many compounds of carbon; a few carbon compounds are studied under INORGANIC CHEMISTRY.

Oscillograph OSCILLOSCOPE fitted with camera for photographing the 'trace'.

Oscilloscope Electronic instrument in which electric signal, or anything that can be reduced to an electric signal, is displayed as 'trace' by spot of light moving on cathode ray tube screen.

Osmium (Os) A hard, brittle metal that has a greater density (relative density 22.5) than any other. One of the platinum metals, it has an exceptionally high melting point ($3000°C$). It is used chiefly as a hardener in platinum alloys.

Osmosis In solutions, flow of water or other solvent through semipermeable membrane on either side of which is a substance dissolved at different concentrations, so as to equalize the concentrations.

Osmotic pressure The pressure which must be applied to a solution to prevent flow of a solvent, as defined in OSMOSIS.

Oxidation Making substance combine with oxygen; removing hydrogen from substance; or raising oxidation number of an element (i.e. making it lose electrons). See REDUCTION.

Oxide Chemical compound of oxygen and another element.

Oxidizing agent Substance that causes OXIDATION.

Oxygen (O) The life-giving gas (O_2) in air, of which it makes up 21 per cent by volume. It is the most abundant element in the Earth's crust, of which it makes up 46.6 per cent. It combines with most other elements to form oxides, such as water (H_2O), carbon dioxide (CO_2), silicon dioxide (SiO_2), iron oxides (Fe_2O_3, Fe_3O_4) and aluminium oxide, bauxite (Al_2O_3). Liquid oxygen, obtained by distilling liquid air, is used as a rocket propellant and explosive.

Ozone Allotrope of oxygen containing three atoms in each molecule; O_3.

Palladium (Pd) A ductile, corrosion-resistant metal similar to platinum. It is used as a catalyst, and to make jewellery and electrical contacts.

Parabola Curve formed by slicing circular cone parallel to one of its sloping sides; may be traced by point that is always equidistant from fixed point F (*focus*) and fixed straight line AB (*directrix*). See also HYPERBOLA.

Partial pressure Fraction of total pressure of mixture of gases exerted by one of component gases. See DALTON'S LAW OF PARTIAL PRESSURES.

pascal (Pa) Unit of pressure; 1 Pa = 1 newton/m².

Pascal's law In a fluid, pressure applied at any point is transmitted equally throughout it.

Passivity of metals Chemical unreactivity of metals due to protective surface film, e.g. oxide, nitride.

Pasteurization Prolonged heating of milk, to temperature sufficient to kill most bacteria in it; partial sterilization.

Pendulum Device consisting of weight (bob) swinging at end of rigid or flexible support; *period* (time of one swing) of simple pendulum, which has flexible support such as length of cord, is independent of weight of bob, depending only on length of cord.

Periodic Table Organized arrangement of the chemical elements, in order of increasing atomic number; elements with similar chemical properties fall in vertical columns called Groups.

Permutation (in mathematics) Arrangement of set of specified number of different objects; number of permutations of three objects *a*, *b*, *c* is 6; *abc*, *acb*, *bac*, *bca*, *cab*, *cba*. 'Permutations' used in football pools are COMBINATIONS, not permutations.

Petrochemicals Range of chemicals derived from petroleum (natural gas and crude oil).

pH Measure of acidity or alkalinity of a liquid; pH of 7 is neutral, lower numbers are acidic, higher numbers alkaline; pH number is the negative logarithm of the hydrogen ion concentration.

Pharmacology Science that deals with drugs and their action on animals and man.

Phon Unit of loudness.

Phosphate Salt of phosphoric acid.

Phosphorescence Emission of 'cold' light from an object or organism. It is caused by the previous absorption of radiation but appears after a delay. See FLUORESCENCE.

Phosphorus (P) A waxy, solid element of the nitrogen family which glows in the dark. It bursts into flame on contact with air. An essential ingredient in living matter, phosphorus occurs in teeth and bones as calcium phosphate. There are four allotropes of phosphorus – white, red, violet and black, in order of reactivity.

Phot Unit of illumination equal to 1 lumen/cm². See FOOT-CANDLE.

Photon Quantum (packet of energy) of electromagnetic radiation, such as light.

Physical change Change of form, as in melting, as opposed to chemical change.

Physical chemistry Branch of chemistry that deals with physical changes accompanying chemical reactions, and the way chemical composition affects physical properties.

Planck's constant (*h*) Constant relating frequency (*v*) of radiation with energy (*E*): $E = hv$; $h = 6.62 \times 10^{-34}$ joule second.

Platinum (Pt) A heavy, soft, ductile and corrosion-resistant metal with high melting point (1769°C). Its main use is in jewellery, as a catalyst and in the platinum resistance thermometers.

Plutonium (Pu) An artificial radioactive element made by bombarding U^{238} with neutrons. It is the most important of the transuranic elements because its isotope Pu^{239} is fissile, and can therefore be used as fuel in nuclear reactors. Plutonium wastes from nuclear reactors pose a serious pollution threat because they are deadly poisons and they have a long half-life (24,000 years).

Pneumatic Operated by air pressure.

Polarized light Light in which electric and magnetic vibrations are restricted to two planes at right-angles, instead of being possible in all planes.

Polonium (Po) A naturally-occurring radioactive metal found in traces in pitchblende and other uranium minerals. The most common isotope has a half-life of 138 days.

Polymer High-molecular-weight chemical compound obtained by POLYMERIZATION; most plastics are polymers. See also MONOMER.

Polymerization Chemical process in which many molecules of MONOMER join together to give a POLYMER.

Porosity Property of a solid substance that allows gases or liquids to pass through it.

Potassium (K) One of the soft, reactive alkali metals, closely resembling sodium in chemical properties. It was the first metal to be isolated by electrolysis (by Humphry Davy, 1807).

Potential difference Exists between two points of differing electric potential; if connected, current flows between them; measured by work done moving unit charge between them; unit, VOLT. See also ELECTROMOTIVE FORCE.

Potential energy See ENERGY.

Power Rate of doing work, generally expressed in watts or horsepower.

PHYSICAL CONSTANTS

c	speed of light	2.997925×10^8 m/s
G	gravitational constant	6.670×10^{-11} N m²/kg²
g	acceleration due to gravity	9.80665 m/s²
π	circum/diam. circle	3.14159265
e	base of natural logarithms	2.71828
R	gas constant	8.3143 J/K mol
N_A	Avogadro's constant	6.02252×10^{23} per mole
h	Planck's constant	6.6256×10^{-34} J s
F	Faraday's constant	9.64870×10^4 C/mol
e	charge of electron	1.60210×10^{-19} C
m_e	rest mass of electron	9.1091×10^{-31} kg
r_e	radius of electron	2.81777×10^{-15} m
m_p	rest mass of proton	1.67252×10^{-27} kg
m_n	rest mass of neutron	1.67482×10^{-27} kg
	speed of sound at sea level at 0°C	331.7 m/s (742 mph)
	standard temperature and pressure	0°C and 1.01325×10^5 Pa
	standard atmosphere	101,325 N/m²
	melting point of ice	0°C or 273.15 K

Right: The radioactivity of many ores and minerals provides a means for their detection in nature. Here, a prospector employs a radiation detector to search for a radioactive mineral. Most likely, the radioactive elements present in the mineral will be at such low concentrations that the prospector will be at no risk from the radioactivity. His detector, however, will pick up even the smallest amount of radioactive emission.

Praseodymium (Pr) A yellowish rare-earth metal which forms greenish salts. It is used to colour ceramics, in lighter flints, and in some lightweight alloys.

Precipitation Formation and throwing out of solution of insoluble compound as *precipitate*, often achieved by DOUBLE DECOMPOSITION.

Pressure Force per unit area, measured in newtons/m^2 or dynes/cm^2.

Probability (likelihood) In mathematics, if an event can happen in a ways and not happen in b ways, the probability that it will happen is $a/(a + b)$ and that it will not happen is $b/(a + b)$; the sum of the various probabilities is always 1.

Progression Mathematical series of terms; in *arithmetical progressions*, each term bears common difference to preceding term; in *geometrical progressions*, each term is larger than preceding term by constant factor.

Promethium (Pm) A radioactive rare-earth element produced during nuclear fission of uranium and by bombarding neodymium with neutrons. It has typical rare-earth properties, and most of its compounds are pink.

Protactinium (Pa) A very rare naturally occurring radioactive metal preceding uranium in the Periodic Table. Traces of it occur in all uranium ores. The most stable of its 12 isotopes has a half-life of 33,000 years.

Proton Positively charged subatomic particle found in nuclei of all atoms.

Pulley Grooved wheel round which rope or chain runs.

Pythagorean theorem In a right-angled triangle, the square on the hypotenuse (longest side) is equal to the sum of the squares on the other two sides.

Quadratic equation Algebraic expression of the second (square) power, which has two possible solutions.

Quantum theory Theory that light and other forms of energy are given off as discrete packets (quanta) of energy.

rad Unit of absorbed dose of ionizing radiation, equal to energy absorption of 100 ergs/gram of substance irradiated. See REM.

Radical Any characteristic group of atoms (e.g. the ammonium ion, NH_4^+).

Radioactive decay Breakdown of a chemical element into elements of lower atomic weight, by the spontaneous and random disintegration of its atoms, with the emission of one or more kinds of radiation.

Radioactivity Emission of radiation, such as ALPHA-RAYS, BETA-RAYS, and GAMMA-RAYS, from unstable elements by spontaneous splitting of their atomic nuclei.

Radium (Ra) A heavy, rare, radioactive alkaline-earth metal, first isolated in 1910 by Madame Curie. It results from the decay of uranium, and is found in uranium ores such as pitchblende. The penetrating rays given off by radium are used in cancer therapy. The most stable radium isotope has a half-life of 1600 years.

Radon (Rn) The heaviest of the inert rare gases, which is formed when radium decays. Like radium, it is radioactive. Traces of radon appear in the air, but in hardly detectable concentrations. Even the most stable of its 17-odd isotopes has a half-life of only 4 days.

Rare earths Series of metallic elements, beginning with lanthanum, of atomic numbers 57 to 71, and having very similar chemical properties; also called *lanthanides*.

Reagent Chemical compound or solution used in carrying out chemical reactions.

Reducing agent Substance that reacts chemically to remove oxygen or add hydrogen to another substance. See REDUCTION; OXIDIZING AGENT.

Reduction Making a substance react with hydrogen, removing oxygen from a substance, or lowering an element's oxidation number (i.e. making it accept electrons). See OXIDATION.

Reflection Return or bouncing back of sound wave or electromagnetic radiation, such as a light ray, after it strikes a surface.

Refraction Bending of a light ray as it crosses boundary between two media of different optical density.

Relativity Einstein's theory that it is impossible to measure motion absolutely, but only within a given frame of reference, which also always involves time, as *spacetime*.

Reluctance In a magnetic circuit, the magnetomotive force divided by the flux that generates it.

rem Abbreviation for Roentgen equivalent mean, dose of ionizing radiation that has same effect as 1 roentgen of X-rays. See RAD; ROENTGEN.

Resistance Property of electrical conductor that makes it oppose flow of current through it. See OHM'S LAW.

Reversible reaction Chemical reaction that can go in either direction. See also DISSOCIATION.

Rhenium (Re) A very rare and expensive metal with exceptional hardness and resistance to wear and corrosion. It also has a very high density (relative density 21) and its melting point (3180°C) is the highest of all metals except tungsten. It is found naturally in the molybdenum ore, molybdenite, and in other sulphide ores.

Rheostat Device providing variable electrical resistance.

Rhodium (Rh) One of the precious platinum family of metals. Ductile and corrosion-resistant, it is often plated on to silver to prevent tarnishing. It is added to platinum as a hardener.

Roentgen Quantity of X-rays or gamma rays that will produce ions carrying 1 electrostatic unit of electricity in 1 cm^3 of air.

Rubidium (Rb) A soft alkali metal of similar properties to sodium, which will burn in air and decompose water. Two isotopes occur in Nature. One, Ru^{87}, is radioactive, with a 50,000 million year half-life; it decays to Sr^{87}. One form of radiometric dating uses the rubidium-strontium decay.

Ruthenium (Ru) A hard, brittle metal of high melting point related to platinum. It is alloyed with platinum to harden it.

Rutherfordium (Ru) The name suggested for the transuranium element 104 by American physicists. Russian physicists, who claim to have made it in 1964, five years before the Americans, call it kurchatovium.

Salt Chemical compound formed, with water, when a BASE reacts with an ACID; a salt is also formed, often with production of hydrogen, when a metal reacts with an acid. *Common salt* is sodium chloride.

Samarium (Sm) A rare-earth metal, obtained from the mineral monazite. It has uses in ceramics and electronics and as a catalyst in the chemical industry. Its salts are red to yellow.

Saturated solution Solution that will take up no more solute (dissolved substance).

Scandium (Sc) A rare-earth metal first identified in Scandinavian ores containing other rare earths. Traces of scandium are also found in tin and tungsten ores. Many stars, including the Sun, contain appreciable amounts of scandium.

Selenium (Se) A metalloid belonging to the oxygen family of elements and, related chemically to sulphur and tellurium. It often occurs as the selenide with the sulphide ores of lead, silver, and copper. Of its many different forms, the most important is the metallic. The metallic form is used in *photoelectric devices* because it emits electrons when light strikes it.

Semiconductor Substance, such as germanium and gallium arsenide, in which electrical resistance falls as its temperature rises. Used for making diodes and transistors.

Semi-permeable membrane Membrane that allows some substances to pass through it but not others; see OSMOSIS.

Set theory Branch of mathematics that deals with objects as collections, called sets, and their inter-relationships.

Silicon (Si) The most abundant element (27.7 per cent) in the Earth's crust after oxygen, silicon is a non-metal closely related to carbon. It occurs almost everywhere in the crust as silicates, such as feldspar, $KAlSi_3O_8$; or as the dioxide, silica

or crystalline quartz, SiO_2. Pure silicon is a hard, metallic-looking solid with the crystal structure of diamond. Minute silicon chips form the basis of the large-scale integrated (LSI) circuits used in many solid-state electronic devices, such as pocket calculators. Silicon is also used to make the solar cells which provide spacecraft with electricity.

Silicones Group of synthetic rubbery substances with molecular backbone of silicon atoms linked to carbon atoms.

Silver (Ag) A precious metal related to copper and gold. Its beautiful whiteness, the ease with which it can be shaped, and its resistance to most corrosion led to its use in jewellery, for coins, and for expensive tableware. The scientist prizes it because it conducts heat and electricity better than any other element. Many of its salts are light-sensitive.

Simple machines Six devices fundamental to all machinery: lever; wheel and axle; pulley; inclined plane; wedge; and screw.

Sine Trigonometrical ratio given (for an angle) in right-angled triangle by length of the side opposite the angle divided by the hypotenuse (longest side).

SI units (Système International d'Unites) Internationally agreed system built round seven basic units and replacing cgs and mks systems for scientific purposes.

SI UNITS		
Basic units	**Symbol**	**Measurement**
metre	m	length
kilogram	kg	mass
second	s	time
ampere	A	electric current
kelvin	K	thermodynamic temperature
mole	mol	amount of substance
candela	cd	luminous intensity
Derived units*		
hertz	Hz	frequency
newton	N	force
pascal	Pa	pressure, stress
joule	J	energy, work, quantity of heat
watt	W	power, radiant flux
coulomb	C	electric charge, quantity of electricity
volt	V	electric potential, potential difference, emf
farad	F	capacitance
ohm	Ω	electric resistance
siemens	S	conductance
weber	Wb	magnetic flux
tesla	T	magnetic flux density
henry	H	inductance
lumen	lm	luminous flux
lux	lx	illuminance
Supplementary units		
radian	rad	plane angle
steradian	sr	solid angle

*These have special names; there are other derived units, such as m^2 (area). mol/m^3 (concentration), m^3/kg (specific volume), etc.

Soda Washing soda is sodium carbonate Na_2CO_3; baking soda is sodium bicarbonate $NaHCO_3$; caustic soda is sodium hydroxide NaOH.

Sodium (Na) A soft, alkali metal which is the sixth most abundant (2.80 per cent) element in the

SELECTED SPECIFIC GRAVITIES

Substance	S.G.	Substance	S.G.
Alcohol	0.8	Pitch	1.1
Aluminium	2.7	Plaster of Paris	1.8
Asbestos	2.4	Platinum	21.9
Benzene	0.7	Polystyrene	1.06
Borax	1.7	Polythene	0.93
Butter	0.9	PVC	1.4
Charcoal	0.4	Sand	1.6
Copper	8.9	Silver	10.5
Cork	0.25	Steel (stainless)	7.8
Corundum	4.0	Talc	2.8
Diamond	3.5	Tar	1.0
Gold	19.3	Tin	7.3
Granite	2.7	Tungsten	19.3
Ice (at 0°C)	0.92	Turpentine	0.85
Iridium	22.42	Uranium	19.0
Lead	11.3	Water	1.0
Limestone	2.6	sea water	1.03
Marble	2.7	Wood:	
Milk	1.03	balsa	0.2
Nylon	1.14	bamboo	0.4
Olive oil	0.9	beech	0.75
Osmium*	22.57	boxwood	1.0
Paraffin oil	0.8	cedar	0.55
Perspex	1.2	mahogany	0.8
Petroleum	0.8	teak	0.9

*Densest of all measurable elements

Earth's crust. One of the most widespread sodium compounds is the chloride, common salt (NaCl). One of the most reactive of all elements, sodium decomposes water to yield sodium hydroxide, or caustic soda (NaOH), which is a strong alkali.

Solder Alloy, generally of tin and lead, having low melting point, used for joining metals.

Solenoid Coil consisting of many turns of wire wound on hollow tube; behaves as magnet when carrying electric current. Used for relays, switches, brakes etc.

Solid State of matter that has definite shape and resists having it changed; crystalline solid melts to a liquid on heating above its melting point.

Solid state physics Branch of physics that deals with matter in the solid state, particularly SEMI-CONDUCTORS.

Solubility Quantity of substance (solute) that will dissolve in solvent to form solution.

Solvent Liquid component of a solution.

Specific gravity Ratio of density of a substance to that of water at 4°C; equals density when density is expressed in g/cm³.

Specific heat Quantity of heat needed to raise temperature of unit mass of a substance by 1 degree; in SI units, joules/kg/kelvin.

Spectrograph Instrument for producing and photographing spectra. See SPECTRUM.

Spectroscope Instrument for splitting the various wavelengths (colours) from a single light source into a spectrum, using glass prism or diffraction grating.

Spectrum Any series of bands and lines observed through a SPECTROGRAPH, when light or other radiation is diffracted. See DIFFRACTION.

Spectrum analysis Method of identifying elements by means of their spectra, produced when the element is heated to incandescence.

Speed Distance travelled by moving object divided by time taken. Speed in a particular direction is VELOCITY.

Standard temperature and pressure (STP) Temperature of 0°C and pressure of 760 mm of mercury, under which volumes of gases are compared; also called normal temperature and pressure (NTP).

Static electricity Electricity involving charges at rest.

Statics Branch of mechanics that deals with the action of forces on stationary objects.

Strontium (Sr) An alkaline-earth metal whose compounds colour a flame a characteristic crimson. It occurs in minerals such as the carbonate strontianite ($SrCO_3$) and the sulphate celestite ($SrSO_4$). It closely resembles calcium.

Sublimation Phenomenon in which a substance, on heating, changes directly from solid to gas or vapour without first melting to liquid.

Sulphate Salt of sulphuric acid.

Sulphide Chemical compound of sulphur and another element.

Sulphur (S) A non-metallic element related to oxygen, sulphur is one of the few elements that can be found native in the Earth's crust. It also occurs in the form of metal sulphides – those of iron (FeS), lead (Pbs), and zinc (ZnS), for example; and as sulphates, such as gypsum ($CaSO_4 \cdot 2H_2O$). The most important chemical made from sulphur is sulphuric acid, H_2SO_4.

Superconductivity Phenomenon, occurring at very low temperatures (approaching ABSOLUTE ZERO), in which a metal continues to conduct an electric current without application of external electromotive force; the metal's resistance is effectively zero.

Superfluidity Condition in which liquid at very low temperatures, notably helium below 2.2K, flows without friction.

Supersaturation Ability of some undisturbed solutions of being able to hold more dissolved substance (solute) than normal SATURATED SOLUTION.

Surface tension Property of the surface of a liquid that makes it behave as though it were covered with a thin elastic skin; caused by forces of attraction between molecules in the surface. See also CAPILLARITY.

Suspension System consisting of very fine solid particles evenly dispersed in liquid.

Synchrocyclotron Cyclotron in which accelerating electric field is pulsed to give particles of very high energies.

Synchrotron Cyclotron with pulsed magnetic field, but constant-frequency electric field.

Tangent (1) Straight line touching curve at a point. (2) Trigonometrical ratio given (for an angle) in right-angled triangle by length of the side opposite the angle divided by length of the adjacent side.

Tantalum (Ta) A very hard, acid-resisting heavy metal with an extremely high melting point (3000°C). It is closely related to niobium. Its main uses are in capacitors and in corrosion-resistant chemical equipment.

Technetium (Tc) A radioactive element, not occurring naturally but produced synthetically by nuclear bombardment. Large quantities of technetium are now produced in nuclear reactors as products of nuclear fission.

Tellurium (Te) A metalloid in the oxygen group which closely resembles selenium. It is obtained as a by-product of lead, gold and copper refining, occurring in the ores as a telluride. It is occasionally used in alloys, and in semiconductors.

Temperature Degree of heat of an object referred to an arbitrary zero (see CENTIGRADE, FAHRENHEIT) or to absolute zero (see KELVIN).

Terbium (Tb) One of the rarest of the rare-earth metals, it is sometimes used in lasers and semiconductors.

Thallium (Tl) A soft metal whose physical properties closely resemble those of lead, which follows it in the Periodic Table. Its compounds are very poisonous.

Thermocouple Device consisting of two dissimilar metals joined together, that generates small electric current when junction is heated; used for measuring temperature.

Thermodynamics Branch of physics that deals with processes in which energy is conserved but heat changes take place.

Thermoelectricity Electricity generated by means of heat, as from a THERMOCOUPLE.

Thermostat Control device, sensitive to changes in temperature, that maintains temperature in an enclosure within narrow, predetermined range.

Thorium (Th) A naturally occurring radioactive metal of the actinide series. Occurring in such minerals as monazite and thorite, thorium is three times more abundant than uranium. In breeder reactors the isotope Th^{232} will change into U^{233}, which is fissile.

Thulium (Tm) A rare-earth metal. Its short-lived radioactive isotope, Tm^{170}, is sometimes used as a portable X-ray source since it emits soft gamma-radiation resembling X-rays.

Tin (Sn) A soft, ductile corrosion-resistant metal of the carbon family. It is widely used as plating on mild steel, as tinplate, and in many alloys, including solder, bronze, type metal and pewter. It occurs in two allotropic forms – white and grey. The familiar form is white which, when pure, changes into the powdery grey form at low temperatures. Impure commercial tin does not usually undergo such a change.

Titanium (Ti) A strong, lightweight metal which has excellent corrosion resistance. It is widely used in the aerospace industries. It is also used in surgical aids. The ninth most abundant element, it is found in the minerals, ilmenite and rutile.

Torque Turning moment produced about an axis by force acting at right-angles to a radius from the axis.

Transformer Electrical machine for converting alternating-current voltage to higher or lower voltage.

Transistor Semiconductor device that can amplify electric current.

Transmutation of elements Changing of one element into another; impossible by chemical processes, but can be achieved in nuclear reactors and by using atom smashing machines, such as CYCLOTRON.

Trigonometry Branch of mathematics based on properties of the triangle, particularly various relationships between lengths of sides and size of angles.

Tungsten (W) Also called wolfram; a very strong metal which has the highest melting point among metals (3380°C). It is incorporated in steel to increase high-temperature strength. Tungsten wire is used for electric light bulb filaments. Tungsten carbide is used for making very hard, tough tools and dies.

UHF Ultra-high frequency radio waves.

Ultrasonic waves 'Sound' waves beyond range of human hearing.

Ultraviolet rays Electromagnetic radiation of wavelengths just shorter than those of visible light.

Uranium (U) A naturally occurring radioactive heavy metal of the actinide series. Natural uranium is made up mainly of the isotope U^{238}, but with traces of U^{235} and U^{234}. U^{235} has the property of undergoing fission, which makes possible commercial nuclear power.

Vacuum Ideally, region in which gas pressure is zero; in practice, region in which pressure is considerably less than atmospheric pressure.

Valency Number of hydrogen atoms (or their equivalent) with which an atom can combine.

Vanadium (V) A rare metal whose main use is in alloy steels. It improves the steel's hardness, strength and shock resistance. It was named after the Scandinavian goddess of beauty, for solutions of its compounds display beautiful colours.

Van der Waal's equation Equation of state for gases taking into account mutual attraction of molecules: $(p + alv^2)(v - b) + RT$, where a and b are constants for particular gas, and R is the gas constant. See GAS CONSTANT.

Vapour Gas that can be turned into liquid by compressing it without cooling.

Vapour density Density of gas or vapour, generally with respect to that of hydrogen; equal numerically to half molecular weight of gas.

Vector Physical quantity that needs direction as

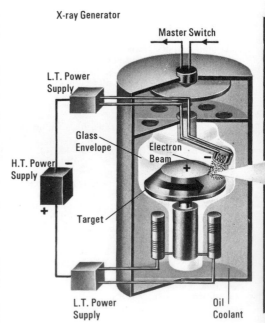

X-ray Generator

Master Switch

L.T. Power Supply

Glass Envelope

Electron Beam

H.T. Power Supply

Target

L.T. Power Supply

Oil Coolant

well as magnitude to define it (e.g. velocity).

Velocity Rate of change of position, equal to SPEED in a particular direction.

VHF Very high frequency radio waves.

Vinyl Organic radical, CH_2CH, derived from ethylene.

Viscosity Property of fluid (liquid or gas) that makes it resist internal movement; sticky or thick liquids are highly viscous.

Volt (V.) Unit of electromotive force and potential difference, defined as potential difference between two points on conductor with current of 1 ampere when power dissipated between points is 1 watt.

Volumetric analysis Method of chemical analysis using only liquids and their volumes.

Water of crystallization One or more molecules of water included in crystals of substances called HYDRATES.

watt (W) Unit of electrical power, defined as the rate of work done in JOULES per second; equal to product of current (A) and potential difference in volts (V), $W = AV$.

Wavelength Of a wave motion, distance between crests (or troughs) of two consecutive waves; equal to velocity of wave divided by its frequency.

Waves Regular disturbances that carry energy. Particles of a medium may vibrate; e.g. air molecules vibrate when sound waves pass, and water molecules vibrate when ripples cross water; or electromagnetic vectors may be displaced, as when light waves pass.

weber (Wb) Unit of magnetic flux, equal to 10^8 MAXWELLS.

Weight Force of attraction (due to gravity) between an object and Earth; in gravitational units, weight is numerically equal to MASS.

Wheatstone bridge Electrical circuit for measuring resistance, consisting of battery, galvanometer, three known resistances, and resistance to be measured.

Wilson cloud chamber Apparatus in which charged particles leave miniature vapour trails that reveal their paths.

Wolfram See TUNGSTEN.

Work Done by a moving force; equal to the product of the force and distance it moves along its line of action; measured in JOULES, ERGS, etc.

Xenon (Xe) A very rare inert gas, more than four times as heavy as air. It is used in high-intensity flash lamps. It was the first inert gas to be made to combine chemically with other elements.

X-rays Very short wavelength electromagnetic waves produced when stream of high-energy electrons bombards matter.

Young's modulus For stretched wire, ratio of cross-sectional stress to longitudinal strain.

Ytterbium (Yb) A soft rare-earth metal which forms pale green or white salts. It is scarce, expensive and little used.

Yttrium (Y) An abundant rare-earth metal found in such rare-earth ores as xenotime and gadolinite. Yttrium compounds are used in ceramics, in lasers, and in red phosphors for colour television.

Zinc (Zn) A common metal related to cadmium and mercury. Mixed with copper, it forms the important alloy brass; it is coated on steel to prevent rusting (galvanizing). It is the negative pole in dry batteries. Its most important commercial ore is zinc blende, or sphalerite, ZnS.

Zirconium (Zr) A soft, ductile, corrosion-resistant transition metal related to titanium. Its major use is for cladding fuel rods in nuclear reactors. It has low neutron absorption, and remains strong at high temperatures.

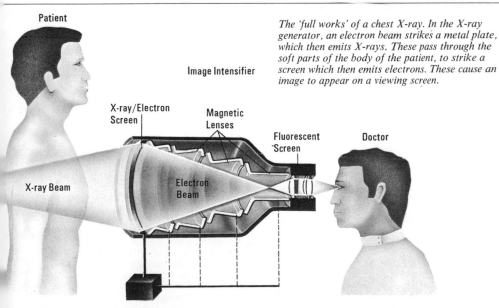

Patient

Image Intensifier

X-ray/Electron Screen

Magnetic Lenses

Fluorescent Screen

Doctor

X-ray Beam

Electron Beam

Lead Shielding

H.T. Power Supply

The 'full works' of a chest X-ray. In the X-ray generator, an electron beam strikes a metal plate, which then emits X-rays. These pass through the soft parts of the body of the patient, to strike a screen which then emits electrons. These cause an image to appear on a viewing screen.

COMPUTER TERMS

Accumulator Intermediate storage area where arithmetic results can be formed.

Address *Characters* or *bits* identifying a specific location.

ALGOL *ALGO*rithmic (or *ALG*ebraic *O*riented) *L*anguage: programming and publication language, devised 1958. Internationally used, similar to Fortran.

Analog(ue) Representation of numerical or physical quantities by means of physical variables such as voltage or resistance.

Base Number of *characters* applied to each digital position (i.e. 10 in the decimal system); also called *radix*.

BASIC *B*eginners *A*ll-purpose *S*ymbolic *I*nstruction *C*ode; simple computing language, widely adopted for home computing and in schools.

Binary Number system with base of two, using the *marks* 0 and 1.

Bit Numeral in binary notation, i.e. 0 or 1; from binary digit.

Block Single unit of computer instruction.

Bug Error in coding causing failure of program.

Byte Eight bits, the usual length of a coded character, and the unit of measurement for computer storage.

Call Transferring of control to *subroutine*.

Central processing unit (CPU) Part of system comprising memory, arthmetic, and control units.

Character One of set of symbols recognized by computer, usually A–Z, 0–9, and other special symbols.

Character recognition Machine-reading of characters designed for easy recognition by users; e.g. *magnetic ink character recognition* (MICR) and, for normal printing ink, *optical character recognition* (OCR).

COBOL *CO*mmon *B*usiness *O*riented *L*anguage: programming language designed for solution of commercial problems and for general use.

Coding Writing programming language statements.

CAL *C*omputer *A*ided *L*earning, programmed teaching of students through computer.

Compiler Software which translates programming language such as Basic into bit-codes readable by the computer.

Console Unit by which operator communicates directly with computer.

Core storage Form of high-speed storage that makes use of tiny magnetic cores, each representing one of two states, symbolized by binary digits 0 and 1.

CPU See *central processing unit*.

Dataa General term for basic elements of information for processing in computer.

Data base Collection of information stored in a computer.

Data processing What a computer does – receiving, processing, and producing a result from data.

Debug Locate and correct errors in computer program.

Digital Concerned with representation of data in numerical form.

Disks or **discs** Used to store data on magnetized surface. Hard discs hold more information, cost more than floppy discs (which look like single records).

Down time Period when computer is not in use owing to mechanical defects.

Field Specific set of characters treated as a whole, or recording area used for particular kind of data.

File Organized collection of records, such as payslips.

Flowchart Diagram ashowing main steps in program.

FORTRAN *FO*mula *TRAN*slation: programming language for scientific use based on mathematical notation.

Hardware Physical working units of computer system.

Housekeeping Administrational operations necessary to maintain control of process.

Input Section of computer that translates information into code. Formerly done by punched tape and cards. Now by keyboard, magnetic tape, discs, optical scanners reading bar codes (on shop goods, for instance).

Instruction Coded program step that defines single operation to be performed by computer.

Language Defined set of characters, etc., for communication with computer.

Lap top computer Computer designed to be used while travelling.

Light pen Photosenstive device that can communicate instructions to computer via the screen of its terminal.

Line printer Output device that prints entire line of data at a time.

Loop Repeated execution of series of instructions up to terminal condition.

Mainframe Largest-sized computer.

Mark Symbol used in number system (e.g. binary system has two, 0 and 1).

Memory Storage or *core storage* in particular.

Memory chip silicon chip which holds information.

Microcomputer Smallest kind of computer, for home and desk use.

Microprocessor Central processing unit which does the actual computing work inside a microcomputer.

Minicomputer Medium-sized computer, between mainframe and microcomputer.

Mouse Remote control device for moving about the computer screen.

Operations research Analytical study of human activities as aid to management.

Output Usually takes the form of a TV display or high speed paper printout; but can take other forms – such as instructions to a robot.

Overflow Production of arthmetical result greater than capacity of result field.

Printout Output of *line printer*.

Program Complete sequence of instructions for steps for job to be performed by computer.

Programmer One who prepares programs for computer.

Radix Same as *base*.

Retrieve Find and select specific record from storage.

Run Complete performance of computer program.

Silicon chip Wafer of silicon bearing miniaturized circuits.

Software Library of programs available with computer to simplify programming and operations.

Storage Any device – mechanical, electrical, electronic – capable of recording data and retaining it for future use.

Systems analysis Examination of business procedure to determine optimum method of operation, usually with view to computerization.

Terminal A keyboard connected to a *mainframe* computer for remote input or output of data.

Time sharing Many users, each with a terminal, sharing a large computer facility.

Translate Change information from one form to another without altering meaning.

User friendly Making computers more 'human' and less daunting for inexperienced users, e.g. by giving them soothing voices

Videotext TV-based information system broadcasting 'pages' of data on to viewers' screens (examples are BBC *Ceefax*, ITV *Oracle*).

Viewdata Information system which uses telephone link to central computer, with data displayed on TV screen (example is British Telecom *Prestel*).

Word Set of *bits* or *characters* treated by computer as logical unit.

The central microchip, about 3mm across, stores as much information as the older magnetic core memory section behind it.

Word processor Computer-based system used to store and manipulate information; in simplest form, the electronic typewriter with memory.

Write Record data on output device, e.g. magnetic tape.

Zero suppression Elimination of non-significant zeros on output.

CHRONOLOGY OF INVENTIONS AND DISCOVERIES

INVENTION

4000–3000 BC Bricks – in Egypt and Assyria
*c.*3000 BC Wheel – in Asia
*c.*3000 BC Plough – in Egypt and Mesopotamia
*c.*500 BC Abacus – the Chinese
*c.*300 BC Geometry – Euclid (Gk.)
200s BC Screw (for raising water) – Archimedes (Gk.)
AD 105 Paper (from pulp) – Ts'ai Lun (Chin.)
AD 250 Algebra – Diophantus (Gk.)
*c.*1000 Gunpowder – the Chinese
*c.*1100 Magnetic compass – the Chinese
*c.*1100 Rocket – the Chinese
*c.*1440 Printing press (movable type) – Johannes Gutenberg (Ger.)
1520 Rifle – Joseph Kotter (Ger.)
1589 Knitting machine – William Lee (Eng.)
*c.*1590 Compound microscope – Zacharias Janssen (Neth.)
1593 Thermometer – Galileo (It.)
1608 Telescope – Hans Lippershey (Neth.)
1614 Logarithms – John Napier (Scot.)
1636 Micrometer – William Gascoigne (Eng.)
1637 Co-ordinate geometry – René Descartes (Fr.)
1640 Theory of numbers – Pierre de Fermat (Fr.)
1642 Calculating machine – Blaise Pascal (Fr.)
1643 Barometer – Evangelista Torricelli (It.)
1650 Air pump – Otto von Guericke (Ger.)
1656 Pendulum clock – Christian Huygens (Neth.)
1665–75 Calculus – Sir Isaac Newton (Eng.) & Gottfried Leibniz (Ger.) independently

1675 Pressure cooker – Denis Papin (Fr.)
1698 Steam pump – Thomas Savery (Eng.)
1712 Steam engine – Thomas Newcomen (Eng.)
1714 Mercury thermometer – Gabriel Fahrenheit (Ger.)
1725 Stereotyping – William Ged (Scot.)
1733 Flying shuttle – John Kay (Eng.)
1735 Chronometer – John Harrison (Eng.)
1752 Lightning conductor – Benjamin Franklin (US)
1764 Spinning jenny – James Hargreaves (Eng.)
1765 Condensing steam engine – James Watt (Scot.)
1768 Hydrometer – Antoine Baumé (Fr.)
1783 Parachute – Louis Lenormand (Fr.)
1785 Power loom – Edmund Cartwright (Eng.)
1790 Sewing machine – Thomas Saint (Eng.)
1793 Cotton gin – Eli Whitney (US)
1796 Lithography – Aloys Senefelder (Ger.)
1800 Electric battery – Count Alessandro Volta (It.)
1800 Lathe – Henry Maudslay (Eng.)
1804 Steam locomotive – Richard Trevithick (Eng.)
1815 Miner's safety lamp – Sir Humphry Davy (Eng.)
1816 Metronome – Johann Mälzel (Ger.)
1816 Bicycle – Karl von Sauerbronn (Ger.)
1817 Kaleidoscope – David Brewster (Scot.)
1822 Camera – Joseph Niepce (Fr.)

1823 Digital calculating machine – Charles Babbage (Eng.)
1824 Portland cement – Joseph Aspdin (Eng.)
1825 Electromagnet – William Sturgeon (Eng.)
1826 Photograph (permanent) – Joseph Niepce (Fr.)
1827 Match – John Walker (Eng.)
1828 Blast furnace – James Neilson (Scot.)
1831 Dynamo – Michael Faraday (Eng.)
1834 Reaping machine – Cyrus McCormick (US)
1836 Revolver – Samuel Colt (US)
1837 Telegraph – Samuel F B Morse (US)
1839 Vulcanized rubber – Charles Goodyear (US)
1844 Safety match – Gustave Pasch (Swed.)
1846 Sewing machine – Elias Howe (US)
1849 Safety pin – Walter Hunt (US)
1852 Gyroscope – Léon Foucault (Fr.)
1853 Passenger lift – Elisha Otis (US)
1855 Celluloid – Alexander Parkes (Eng.)
1855 Bessemer converter – Henry Bessemer (Eng.)
1855 Bunsen burner – Robert Bunsen (Ger.)
1858 Refrigerator – Ferdinand Carré (Fr.)
1858 Washing machine – Hamilton Smith (US)
1859 Internal combustion engine – Etienne Lenoir (Fr.)
1861 Linoleum – Frederick Walton (Eng.)
1862 Rapid-fire gun – Richard Gatling (US)
1865 Cylinder lock – Linus Yale Jr (US)
1866 Dynamite – Alfred Nobel (Swed.)
1867 Typewriter – Christopher Sholes (US)
1870 Margarine – Hippolyte Mège-Mouriés (Fr.)
1873 Barbed wire – Joseph Glidden (US)
1876 Telephone – Alexander Graham Bell (Scot.)
1876 Carpet sweeper – Melville Bissell (US)
1877 Phonograph – Thomas Edison (US)
1878 Microphone – David Edward Hughes (Eng./ US)
1879 Incandescent lamp – Thomas Edison (US)
1879 Cash register – James Ritty (US)
1884 Fountain pen – Lewis Waterman (US)
1884 Linotype – Ottmar Mergenthaler (US)
1885 Motorcycle – Edward Butler (Eng.)
1885 Vacuum flask – James Dewar (Scot.)
1885 Electric transformer – William Stanley (US)
1886 Electric fan – Schuyler Wheeler (US)
1886 Halftone engraving – Frederick Ives (US)
1887 Gramophone – Emile Berliner (Ger./Us)
1887 Monotype – Tolbert Lanston (US)
1887 Motor-car engine – Gottlieb Daimler & Karl Benz (Ger.), independently
1888 Pneumatic tyre – John Boyd Dunlop (Scot.)
1888 Kodak camera – George Eastman (US)
1890 Rotogravure – Karl Klic (Czech.)
1892 Zip fastener – Whitcomb Judson (US)
1895 Wireless – Guglielmo Marconi (It.)
1895 Photoelectric cell – Julius Elster & Hans Geitel (Ger.)
1895 Safety razor – King C. Gillette (US)
1897 Diesel engine – Rudolf Diesel (Ger.)
1898 Submarine – John P Holland (Ire./US)
1899 Tape recorder – Valdemar Poulsen (Den.)
1901 Vacuum cleaner – Cecil Booth (Eng.)
1902 Radio-telephone – Reginald Fessenden (US)
1903 Aeroplane – Wilbur & Orville Wright (US)
1904 Diode – John Fleming (Eng.)
1906 Triode – Lee De Forest (US)
1908 Bakelite – Leo Baekeland (Belg./US)
1908 Cellophane – Jacques Brandenberger (Switz.)

1911 Combine harvester – Benjamin Holt (US)
1913 Geiger counter – Hans Geiger (Eng.)
1914 Tank – Ernest Swinton (Eng.)
1915 Tungsten filament lamp – Irving Langmuir (US)
1918 Automatic rifle – John Browning (US)
1925 Television (working system) – John Logie Baird (Scot.) & others
1925 Frozen food process – Clarence Birdseye (US)
1926 Rocket (liquid fuel) – Robert H. Goddard (US)
1928 Electric shaver – Jacob Schick (US)
1929 Television (electronic system, adopted as standard) – Vladimir Zworykin (US)
1930 Jet engine – Frank Whittle (Eng.)
1931 Cyclotron – Ernest Lawrence (US)
1935 Nylon – Wallace Carothers (US)
1935 Parking meter – Carlton Magee (US)
1935 Radar – Robert Watson-Watt (Scot.)
1939 Electron microscope – Vladimir Zworykin and other (US)
1939 Betatron – Donald Kerst (US)
1944 Automatic digital computer – Howard Aiken (US)
1946 Electronic computer – J Presper Eckert & John W Mauchly (US)
1947 Polaroid camera – Edwin Land (US)
1948 Transistor – John Bardeen, Walter Brattain and William Shockley (US)
1948 Xerography – Chester Carlson (US)
1948 Long-playing record – Peter Goldmark (US)
1954 Maser – Charles H Townes (US)
1954 Solar battery – D Pearson, C Fuller, G Pearson (US)
1955 Hovercraft – Christopher Cockerell (Eng.)
1955 Contraceptive pill – Gregory Pincus and others (US)
1956 Videotape recording – A Poniatoff (US)
1959 Fuel cell – Francis Bacon (Eng.)
1960 Laser – Theodore Maiman (US)
1965 Holography (an idea conceived in 1947 and subsequently developed using laser) – D Gabor (Hung./GB).
1971 EMI-Scanner – Godfrey Hounsfield (Eng.) (developed from his invention of computed tomography in 1967)

Radio 1895

Telephone 1876

Electronic computer 1946

DISCOVERY

1543 Sun as centre of solar system – Copernicus (Pol.)
1590 Law of falling bodies – Galileo (It.)
1609–19 Laws of planetary motion – Johannes Kepler (Ger.)
1662 Relation between gas pressure and volume – Robert Boyle (Eng./Ire.)
1669 Phosphorus – Hennig Brand (Ger.)
1675 Measurement of speed of light – Olaus Römer (Dan.)
1678 Wave theory of light – Christian Huygens (Dut.)
1687 Laws of gravitation and motion – Isaac Newton (Eng.)
1751 Nickel – Axel Cronstedt (Swe.)
1755 Magnesium – Sir Humphry Davy (GB)
1766 Hydrogen – Henry Cavendish (GB)
1772 Nitrogen – Daniel Rutherford (GB)
1774 Oxygen – Joseph Priestly (GB); Karl Scheele (Swe.)
1774 Chlorine – Karl Scheele (Swe.)
1781 Uranus (planet) – William Herschel (GB)
1783 Tungsten – Fausto and Juan José de Elhuyar (Sp.)
1789 True nature of combustion – Antoine Lavoisier (Fr.)
1797 Chromium – Louis Vauquelin (Fr.)
1803 Atomic structure of matter – John Dalton (GB)
1811 Molecular hypothesis – Amadeo Avogadro (It.)
1817 Cadmium – Friedrich Stromeyer (Ger.)
1820 Electromagnetism – Hans Christian Oersted (Dan.)
1824 Silicon – Jöns Berzelius (Swe.)
1826 Bromine – Antoine Balard (Fr.)
1826 Laws of electromagnetism – André Ampère (Fr.)
1827 Law of electric conduction – Georg Ohm (Ger.)
1827 Aluminium – Hans Christian Oersted (Dan.)
1831 Electromagnetic induction – Michael Faraday (GB); discovered previously, but not published, by Joseph Henry (US)
1839 Ozone – Christian Schönbein (Ger.)
1841 Uranium – Martin Klaproth (Ger.)
1846 Neptune (Planet) – Johann Galle (Ger.), from predictions of others
1864 Electromagnetic theory of light – James Clerk Maxwell (GB)
1868 Helium – Sir William Ramsay (GB)
1869 Periodic arrangement of elements – Dmitri Mendeleev (Russ.)
1886 Electromagnetic waves – Heinrich Hertz (Ger.)
1886 Fluorine – Henri Moissan (Fr.)
1894 Argon – Sir William Ramsay and Baron Rayleigh (GB)
1895 X-rays – Wilhelm Roentgen (Ger.)
1896 Radioactivity – Antoine Bacquerel (Fr.)
1897 Electron – Sir Joseph Thomson (GB)
1898 Radium – Pierre and Marie Curie (Fr.)
1900 Quantum theory – Max Planck (Ger.)
1905 Special theory of relativity – Albert Einstein (Swi.)
1910 Russell-Hertzsprung diagram (star pattern) – Henry Russell and Eijnar Hertzsprung (US)
1913 Atomic number – Henry Moseley (GB)
1915 General theory of relativity – Albert Einstein (Swi.)
1919 Proton – Ernest Rutherford (GB)
1924 Wave nature of electron – Louis de Broglie (Fr.)
1926 Wave mechanics – Erwin Schrödinger (Aus.)
1927 Uncertainty principle – Werner Heisenberg (Ger.)
1930 Pluto (planet) – Clyde Tombaugh (US), from prediction by Percival Lowell (US) in 1905
1931 Possibility of neutrino (massless atomic particle) predicted by Wolfgang Pauli (Ger.)
1931 Deuterium (heavy hydrogen) – Harold Urey (US)
1932 Neutron – James Chadwick (GB)
1932 Positron – Carl Anderson (US)
1935 Mesons (subatomic particle) – predicted by Hideki Yukawa (Jap.)
1940 Plutonium – G T Seaborg and others. (US)
1948 Theory of continuous creation of matter – Fred Hoyle (GB)
1950 Unified field theory – Albert Einstein (Swi./US)
1953 DNA/double helix – F Crick, J Watson, M Wilkins (Eng.)
1955 Antiproton – Emilio Segré and Owen Chamberlain (US)
1958 Radiation belts surrounding earth – James Van Allen (US)
1963 Quasars – Thomas Matthews and Allan Sandage (US)
1964 Omega particle – Brookhaven Laboratory, New York (US)
1967 Pulsars – Radio Astronomy Group, University of Cambridge (GB)
1974 Psi particle – discovered independently by two US laboratories
1977 Chiron: distant asteriod orbiting between Saturn and Uranus – Charles Kowal (USA)

Marie Curie with her husband Pierre Curie. She isolated and purified radium, but died, at the age of 67, from leukemia caused by the radiation she had received.

The Living World

BIOLOGICAL TERMS

Abdomen (1) Region of the body of a vertebrate that contains the digestive, excretory and reproductive organs. (2) Hindmost group of segments that form the body of an arthropod.

Acellular Not divided into cells; unicellular (single-celled).

Acoelomate (of an animal) Having no COELOM.

Adaptation Any characteristic of a living organism that improves its chances of survival in a particular environment or improves its ability to perform a particular function (e.g. flying).

Adrenaline Hormone produced by the adrenal gland (situated on the kidney) of a vertebrate that stimulates part of the nervous system and results in increased heart-rate and increased blood supply to heart, muscles and brain.

Adventitious (of roots or buds) Arising in unusual positions, e.g. roots growing out of stems or leaves and buds growing out of roots.

Aestivation Process in which some animals undergo a period of dormancy during dry summer months.

Algae Simple plant without stem, leaves or roots. Algae range from tiny single-celled plants to giant seaweeds.

Alimentary canal Tube that runs from mouth to anus. Concerned with the passage, digestion and absorption of food.

Alternation of generations Process, during the life cycles of certain animals and plants, in which a generation having sexual reproduction alternates with a generation that reproduces asexually. Examples of organisms that show alternation of generations include jellyfish, tapeworms and mosses.

Amino acid Organic acid containing an amino group, made up of one nitrogen and two hydrogen atoms ($-NH_2$). There are 21 different amino acids and they are the building blocks of proteins.

Anatomy Study of the internal structure of living organisms.

Angiosperm Member of the subdivision Angiospermae; a flowering plant; a plant that produces ovules enclosed in ovaries.

Animal Member of the animal kingdom; a living organism chiefly distinguished by the fact that it cannot manufacture its own food. Most animals can move, and advanced animals have complicated nervous and muscular systems. Simple animals, however, are often hard to distinguish from simple plants and these organisms are sometimes classified together in a separate kingdom – Protista.

Annual plant Plant that grows from seed, flowers, produces seeds and dies within a single year.

Annual ring Ring formed by one year's growth of the secondary XYLEM in the trunk or branch of a tree. The ring appears because the xylem cells produced towards the end of summer are much smaller than those produced the following spring.

Antenna Sensory appendage on the head of an arthropod.

Anterior Of a region, organ or part of an organ near or towards the head of an animal.

Anther Of a flower, club-shaped end of a stamen containing pollen in two pairs of pollen sacs.

Antibody Protein produced by white blood cells when a foreign substance (antigen) invades the body of a vertebrate. Antibodies form a major part of the body's defence mechanism (known as the immune system) which protects the animal against disease and infection. For example, bacteria and viruses carry antigens which are recognized by the immune system and stimulate the production of antibodies. These combine with the antigens and cause the immobilization or destruction of the invading body.

Anus Opening of the alimentary canal to the outside.

Aquatic Living in water.

Arachnid Member of the class Arachnida; an arthropod normally with four pairs of walking legs, no antennae and a pair of grasping appendages on the head. E.g. spiders, scorpions.

Arctogaea Largest of the world's three zoogeographical realms, consisting of the NEARCTIC,

Above: A section of a tree trunk or branch, showing the annual rings by which the tree can be aged. These rings are the result of the wood laid down in summer being darker than that formed in spring.

PALAEARCTIC, ETHIOPIAN and ORIENTAL REGIONS.

Artery Blood vessel that carries blood away from the heart.

Arthropod Member of the phylum Arthropoda; an animal with a hard exoskeleton and jointed limbs. Arthropods form the largest phylum in the animal kingdom, having more than one million species.

Asexual reproduction Any process of reproduction that does not involve sex cells, or GAMETES. Forms of asexual reproduction in the animal kingdom include fission (division and separation of cells) and budding (growth of a new individual on the surface of an existing one). Plants such as fungi reproduce asexually by producing SPORES. Many flowering plants have methods of VEGETATIVE REPRODUCTION.

Auditory Concerned with hearing.

Aural Concerned with the ear.

Australasian region (Notogaea) One of the world's six zoogeographical regions. It includes Australia, Tasmania, New Zealand and New Guinea.

Backbone see VERTEBRAL COLUMN.

Biennial plant Plant that grows from seed, flowers and produces seed within a period of two years. During the first year the plant grows and stores food, which is used up during the second year, when the plant flowers. E.g. beets, parsnips.

Binocular vision Type of vision that is achieved when both eyes are focused on an object at the same time. Each eye sees the object from a slightly different angle. The images received by the eyes are transmitted to the brain, which interprets them as a single, stereoscopic image.

Biome Major community of plants and animals, characterized by a particular type of vegetation (e.g. Savanna, rain forest) and climate.

Biological control Control of pests by use of natural predators or diseases; e.g. use of bacteria to control grain weevils and use of fish to control mosquitoes.

Biology Study of living organisms.

Biosphere That part of the Earth and atmosphere which is inhabited by living organisms.

Blood Fluid (plasma), containing several types of cells, that flows all round the body of vertebrates through the blood vessels. Pumped by the heart, the blood carries nourishment to different parts of the body and carries away waste products. There are three different types of cell. The red cells, or corpuscles, contain haemoglobin, which gives blood its red colour. They carry oxygen from the lungs to the tissues of the body. The white corpuscles act primarily as fighters of disease by destroying microbes that enter the body (see ANTIBODY). The platelets play an important part in the clotting of blood.

Bone Main mechanical tissue in vertebrates which supports the body, protects many delicate tissues and organs, and enables the body to move by acting as levers controlled by muscle action. Bones are made up of organic material and inorganic substances such as calcium.

Botany Study of plants.

Buccal Of the mouth.

Cambium Layer of dividing cells found mainly between PHLOEM and XYLEM in the stem of a seed-bearing plant. In most woody plants it forms a cylinder around the xylem (wood). Each year it produces new xylem cells on the inside, thus leading to the formation of ANNUAL RINGS.

Carbohydrate Chemical compound composed of carbon, hydrogen and oxygen, e.g. sugars, starch and cellulose.

Carbon cycle Series of reactions in which carbon is continuously circulated between living organisms and their surroundings. During PHOTOSYNTHESIS, plants use carbon dioxide gas from the air to make various other carbon compounds. Animals eat the plants, or else eat other animals that have eaten plants. The carbon compounds in this food are broken down in the animals' bodies during respiration and as a result, energy is released and carbon dioxide produced. The carbon dioxide is returned to the air when the animals breathe out, thus completing the cycle. Carbon dioxide is also released when dead organisms decay and when certain fuels are burnt.

Carpel Female reproductive part of a flower, consisting of an OVARY and a STIGMA, which is often on the end of a long stalk, or style.

Carnivore (1) Flesh-eating animal. (2) Member of the mammal order Carnivora, which includes cats, dogs, bears, weasels and seals.

Carrion Flesh of a dead animal.

Cartilage Soft material that forms part of the skeleton of vertebrates. The skeletons of sharks and rays consist entirely of cartilage.

Caste Highly specialized subgroup of a colony of social insects, e.g. bees, which have three castes – queens (fertile females), workers (sterile females) and drones (fertile males).

Caterpillar Soft-bodied larva that is a stage in the development of certain kinds of insect, e.g. moths and butterflies.

Cell Basic unit of living organisms, often highly specialized to perform different functions. Consists of PROTOPLASM including an enclosing plasma membrane. Plants have an additional cell wall made of cellulose.

Cell differentiation Developmental process by which cells become specialized for particular functions.

Cellulose Carbohydrate substance made up of long chains of glucose molecules; main constituent of plant cell walls.

Central nervous system See NERVOUS SYSTEM.

Chitin Long-chain carbohydrate substance containing nitrogen; forms the exoskeletons of arthropods.

Chlorophyll Green pigment contained in the chloroplasts of green plants. Responsible for conversion of light energy into chemical energy during PHOTOSYNTHESIS.

Chloroplast Small, CHLOROPHYLL-containing organelle in cytoplasm of green plant cells.

Chordate Member of the phylum Chordata; animal that has a NOTOCHORD, a nerve cord and gill slits at some stage of its development.

Chromosome Minute thread-like structure, several of which occur in a cell nucleus. Consists largely of DNA and protein and contains the GENES (hereditary instructions).

Cilium Fine thread protruding from surface of a cell which acts like an oar to help propel a unicellular organism through water or, in a multicellular organism, causes liquid to flow over the cell. Usually, many cilia act together.

Class Grouping used in the classification of animals and plants. In the animal kingdom similar classes are grouped together in a phylum; in the plant kingdom they are grouped together in a division. A class is divided into orders.

Classification The way in which animals and plants are divided into groups and sub-groups – pages 265–271.

Climax community Stable community of animals and plants; the end product of a SUCCESSION.

Coelenterate Member of the phylum Coelenterata; animal with more or less radially symmetrical body that consists basically of two layers of cells. Gut has only one opening to the outside and the animal has no blood system or central nervous system (the nervous system is a diffuse network).

Coelom Fluid-filled cavity formed by a middle layer of embryonic cells in animals whose bodies consist of or are derived from three layers of cells. Forms the main body cavity in which the organs are suspended.

Coelomate (of an animal) Having a coelom.

Coral Tiny marine coelenterate, called a polyp, which forms a cup-shaped limestone skeleton around itself. The majority of corals live in colonies; the skeletons become fused and these can eventually form coral reefs.

Cotyledon Seed leaf; the first leaf, or pair of leaves, of the embryo plant in a seed, often providing a food store. See MONOCOTYLEDON, DICOTYLEDON.

Cranial Concerned with the head.

Cytoplasm Jelly-like watery substance and various organelles contained within a cell, excluding the nucleus.

Deciduous (of a plant) Shedding all its leaves at a certain time of the year.

Dicotyledon Flowering plant that has two COTYLEDONS (seed leaves) in its seeds. Dicotyledons are also distinguished by their net-veined leaves and other structural features. E.g. daisy, oak.

Digestion Process of breaking down food materials into chemicals that can be absorbed and used by the body.

Digit Finger or toe.

Dioecious (of a flowering plant) Bearing male and female flowers on separate plants.

Division Grouping used in the classification of plants. The plant kingdom is divided into several divisions, which are, in turn, divided into classes.

DNA Deoxyribonucleic acid; chemical compound in e.g. CHROMOSOMES of a cell that contains the genetic code of the organism (see also GENE). A DNA molecule is a polymer of compounds called nucleotides. Usually, two such strands are linked parallel to each other and coiled into a double helix.

Dormancy Resting condition in which an organism (or part of an organism, such as a spore, seed or egg) is alive although its metabolism is relatively slow.

Dorsal Of or close to the back of an animal.

Echinoderm Member of the phylum Echinodermata; more or less radially symmetrical animal with hard plates in the skin that form a skeleton. Also present are a water vascular system and tube feet. E.g. starfish, sea urchin.

Ecology Study of the relationships of plants and animals to their surroundings and to each other.

Ecosystem Community of organisms and the habitat in which they live.

Ectothermic Poikilothermic; 'cold-blooded'.

Embryo (1) Young plant that has developed from an ovum (egg cell); in seed-bearing plants the embryo is contained within the seed. (2) Animal in the process of developing from an ovum, but not yet recognizably similar to the adult form; usually refers to unborn or unhatched offspring.

Endocrine gland Ductless gland; gland that produces hormones directly into the blood stream.

Endoplasmic reticulum Complicated system of membrane-lined channels present in the CYTOPLASM of a cell. On the surface of some of these membranes are tiny, granular bodies (ribosomes), consisting largely of RNA. Endoplasmic reticulum and ribosomes are together concerned with making proteins.

Endoskeleton Skeleton that lies inside the body; e.g. the skeleton of a vertebrate.

Endosperm Food material inside a seed that nourishes the developing embryo until the first leaves begin to manufacture food.

Endothermic Homoiothermic; 'warm-blooded'.

Entomology Study of insects.

Environment Conditions in which an organism lives; factors involved include light, temperature, water availability, chemical concentrations and the presence of other plants and animals.

Enzyme Protein that acts as a catalyst, i.e. that helps a chemical reaction to take place without itself being used up in the reaction.

Epidermis The outer layer of cells of a plant or animal. The epidermis of a plant or invertebrate is one cell thick and is often covered by a protective layer called the cuticle. The epidermis of a vertebrate consists of several layers of cells and forms the outer part of the skin (the inner part is called the dermis).

Epiphyte Plant that grows on another plant without taking any nourishment from it, e.g. many lichens and mosses and a few flowering plants.

Epithelium Layer of thin-walled cells that lines a tube or cavity or the outer layer of the skin.

Ethiopian region One of the world's six zoogeographical regions. Consists of Africa south of the Sahara desert and the southern half of the Arabian peninsula. Forms part of the zoogeographical realm ARCTOGAEA.

Evolution Process by which higher forms of life are believed to have developed from more primitive forms through a series of very slow, gradual changes.

Excretion Expulsion of waste products, such as water, carbon dioxide and nitrogen-containing chemicals, from the system of both plants and animals.

Exocrine gland Gland that produces a substance onto a surface (inside or outside the body) via a duct, e.g. sweat gland, digestive gland.

Exoskeleton Skeleton that covers the outside of the body, e.g. skeleton of an insect.

Extinct (of a group of animals or plants) No longer in existence.

Family Grouping used in the classification of animals and plants. Similar families are grouped together in an order. A family is divided into genera (*singular*: genus).

Fat Substance used by animals and plants for storing energy-rich food. Many substances are referred to as fats, but a true fat is a chemical combination of glycerol and fatty acids.

Fauna Animal population of a particular area or period in time.

Fertile Able to produce functional gametes.

Fertilization Fusion of two sex cells, or GAMETES, during sexual reproduction, resulting in a single cell, or ZYGOTE.

Flagellum Fine thread protruding from the surface of a cell. Has the same structure as a CILIUM, but is much longer and has a lashing or wave-like movement. Many single-celled animals and swimming sex cells have flagella, which are used for propulsion. Usually only one or a few are present, but some bacteria, algae and protozoans have many.

Flora (1) Plant population of a particular area or period in time. (2) List of the plants found in a particular area, together with a key to help in identifying them.

Foetus Unborn mammal that has completed the embryo stage and has developed features recognizably similar to those of the adult animals.

Food chain Chain of animals and plants in any natural community along which energy, in the form of food, is transferred. At one end of the chain are the green plants, which manufacture their own food. These are eaten by herbivorous animals, which, in turn, are preyed on by carnivores or their remains are eaten by carrion-feeders. Bacteria and fungi also form an essential part of a food chain, breaking down the tissues of dead animals and plants.

Fossil Remains or evidence of the former existence of an animal or plant. Fossils are generally found in rock.

Fungus Member of the division Mycophyta. Fungi are either single-celled or made up of long filaments called hyphae. They lack chlorophyll and therefore cannot manufacture their own food. They feed either as SAPROPHYTES or PARASITES. Fungi produce masses of spores during reproduction and some of the higher fungi grow large fruiting bodies e.g. mushrooms and toadstools, which produce the spores.

Gamete Sex cell; reproductive cell that contains half the normal number of chromosomes. As a result, when it fuses with another gamete the normal number of chromosomes is made up. Gametes are usually differentiated into male and female gametes. Female gametes are mostly immobile and generally have large amounts of cytoplasm. Male gametes usually move to the female gametes by means of flagella.

Gametophyte Gamete-producing stage in the life-cycle of a plant that shows ALTERNATION OF GENERATIONS. All the cells of the gametophyte, including the gametes, contain the 'half number' of chromosomes. The gametophyte of a moss is the adult plant; in ferns it is the tiny heart-shaped prothallus from which the adult plant grows. Seed-bearing plants have tiny male gametophytes, which develop inside the pollen grains, and a female gametophyte inside each ovule. See SPOROPHYTE.

Gastric Concerned with the stomach.

Gene Short length of a CHROMOSOME that forms a hereditary unit. It contains coded information for the production of a specific protein influencing a particular characteristic. The whole system of information is referred to as the genetic code and is passed on from one generation to the next.

Genetics Study of heredity and how inherited characteristics can vary from one generation to the next.

Genus (*plural*: genera) Grouping used in the classification of living organisms. Similar genera are grouped together in a family. A genus is divided into species.

Gestation period Time taken from fertilization of an egg cell to birth of active young. In man this is about 266 days.

Gill (1) Thin-walled organ of an aquatic animal through which it takes oxygen from water. (2) One of the many blade-like, spore-bearing structures on the underside of the cap of a gill fungus, such as a mushroom.

Gland Organ that produces a particular chemical substance either onto the surface of or into the body of an animal or plant.

Golgi apparatus Small organelle in the cytoplasm of a cell, consisting of membranes folded into small sacs. Probable function is to export substances from the cell.

Gonad Organ of an animal that produces GAMETES.

Growth Increase in size; achieved in an animal or plant by the division and multiplication of cells. Usually accompanied by CELL DIFFERENTIATION.

Gymnosperm (meaning 'naked seed') Member of the subdivision Gymnospermae, which includes the conifers. Plant that bears its ovules and seeds exposed, most often in cones, instead of having flowers.

Habitat Local surroundings in which a plant or animal lives. Each habitat has a particular ENVIRONMENT.

Haemoglobin Iron-containing pigment found in red blood cells of vertebrates. It combines with oxygen and transports it from the lungs or gills to tissues of the body.

Heart Muscular organ that pumps blood around the body. In a mammal, it consists of four chambers – two auricles, which receive blood from the veins, and two ventricles, which pump blood into the arteries.

Above: Dolphins are mammals that have gone back to life in water, and have adapted to become as streamlined as fast-swimming fishes. Left: Edward Drinker Cope (1840–1897) was a notable fossil hunter of the American midwest, where he discovered, in rivalry with Othniel Marsh (1831–1899), a whole range of dinosaur fossils.

Herbaceous plant (herb) Plant that does not grow a woody stem.

Herbivore Plant-eating animal.

Heredity Transmission of characteristics from one generation to another.

Hermaphrodite (1) Having both male and female organs on the same individual animal. (2) Having both male and female organs in the same flower.

Hibernation Process in which some animals undergo a period of dormancy during winter.

Histology Study of tissues.

Homoiothermic (of animals) 'Warm-blooded'; able to control the body temperature independently of the temperature of the surroundings. Heat is produced by body's metabolic process. Amount of heat retained or lost is largely controlled by structures in the skin, e.g. hair, sweat glands, blood capillaries.

Hormone Organic chemical messenger produced in an organism and having a particular effect on some aspect of the organism's growth or function.

Hybrid Plant or animal produced as a result of the mating of genetically unalike parents i.e. of different species or varieties. Hybrids between species are usually sterile, e.g. mule.

Inflorescence Shoot bearing one or more flowers. Types of inflorescence vary according to how the flowers are arranged on the shoot.

Insect Member of the class Insecta; type of arthropod, with one pair of antennae, six legs and a body divided into three parts – head, thorax and abdomen.

Insectivore (1) Member of the mammal order Insectivora. (2) Insect-eating animal.

Intestine Part of the alimentary canal that links the stomach and the anus. The organ of the body where assimilation mainly occurs. In vertebrates, it is divided into the duodenum, small intestine and large intestine (colon).

Invertebrate Animal without a backbone.

Kidney Organ in a vertebrate used for excretion of waste nitrogen compounds and for regulating amount of water in the blood.

Kingdom Largest grouping used in the classification of living organisms. Traditionally, two kingdoms are used – the animal kingdom and the plant kingdom. But some scientists place all the simple organisms (bacteria, fungi, protozoa and single-celled algae) in a third kingdom – the Protista. The plant kingdom is divided into divisions; the animal kingdom is divided into phyla.

Larva Form, completely different from the adult, in which certain animals hatch from their eggs. Usually incapable of sexual reproduction, a larva becomes an adult by undergoing METAMORPHOSIS. Examples of larvae include the tadpole of a frog or a salamander and the caterpillar of a butterfly. Many invertebrate animals hatch out as larvae.

Lichen Organism formed from the close symbiotic association of an alga and a fungus.

Life cycle Series of stages through which an organism passes from fertilization to the death of the gamete-producing adult. After fertilization, the ZYGOTE may develop directly into a fertile adult. In other cases the organism may pass through one or more different forms before reaching the adult stage. Often there are phases of asexual reproduction during the life cycle and in a few cases no sexual reproduction occurs.

Liver Large organ of a vertebrate that has a number of functions including: regulation of the amount of carbohydrates, fats and proteins in the blood; production of bile (used in the digestion of fats); removal of poisons and worn-out red blood cells from the blood; and storage of iron and vitamins.

Living fossil Animal or plant that has remained almost unchanged for millions of years.

Living organism Entity that shows the six characteristics of feeding, growth, respiration, reproduction, movement and sensitivity.

Lung Breathing organ found in man and many other vertebrates; usually paired. It has thin, moist internal walls lined with tiny blood vessels (capillaries) that allow oxygen to pass into the blood and carbon dioxide to pass from the blood into the lungs for exhalation.

Mammal Member of the class Mammalia; warm-blooded vertebrate with a larger brain and therefore greater intelligence than any other type of animal. All mammals suckle their young and have a covering of hair.

Marsupial Member of the subclass Metatheria; mammal in which female has very simple PLACENTA and produces young in a very early state of development. Young complete their development inside their mother's pouch.

Meiosis Reduction division of a cell to produce GAMETES. The cell divides twice, but the chromosomes divide only once, resulting in the daughter cells (the gametes) having only half the normal number of chromosomes.

Mesozoan Member of the subkingdom Mesozoa, a group of parasitic, multicellular animals. The body of a mesozoan consists of a single central cell surrounded by a layer of ciliated cells.

Metabolism The chemical processes that occur within an organism. This includes catabolism –

261

the breaking down of complex chemicals into simple chemicals, with the release of energy – and anabolism – the building up of complex body chemicals from simple chemicals.

Metamorphosis Change into an adult from a completely different larval form. The metamorphosis of a frog, for example, occurs when the tadpole grows legs and loses its gills and tail. The dramatic metamorphosis of a butterfly occurs inside the chrysalis, or pupa.

Metazoan Member of the subkingdom Metazoa; any multicellular animal other than a mesozoan or parazoan (sponge).

Mitochondria (*singular*: mitochondrion) Microscopic cell organelles that act as the powerhouses of the cell. Respiration, with the consequent production of energy, takes place in the mitochondria.

Mitosis Simple cell division in which all parts of the cell divide once, including the chromosomes.

Monocotyledon Flowering plant that has only one seed leaf in each seed. Monocotyledons are also distinguished by their parallel-veined leaves and other structural features. See also COTYLEDON.

Monoecious (of a flowering plant) Having both male and female flowers on the same plant.

Monotreme Member of the subclass Prototheria. An egg-laying mammal with other reptilian features. E.g. platypus, echidna.

Muscle Animal tissue consisting of cells that are capable of contracting to produce movement.

Mutation Sudden change in the DNA of a gene or genes. When mutations occur in a sex cell, the resulting offspring may have characteristics that differ from those of the parent.

Natural selection Selection of inherited characteristics of organisms that are best suited to the habitat in which the organisms live. Organisms with the most suitable characteristics stand the best chance of surviving and reproducing, thus passing on the beneficial characteristics to their offspring. This is the process by which EVOLUTION occurs.

Nearctic region One of the world's six zoogeographical regions. Consists of Greenland and North America down to Central Mexico. Forms part of the zoogeographical realm ARCTOGAEA.

Neogaea One of the world's three zoogeographical realms; the Neotropical region.

Neoteny Retention of larval characteristics in a sexually mature animal, e.g. in the Mexican axolotl, a salamander with external gills.

Nerve Bundle of nerve fibres and associated tissues. Each fibre consists of a greatly elongated cell which carries electrical impulses between the muscles or organs of a body and the central NERVOUS SYSTEM.

Nervous system System of NERVES that runs throughout the body. In vertebrates it consists of three main parts. The central nervous system (CNS) comprises the brain, and the great bundle of nerves leading to the brain called the spinal cord. This is the control centre of the system. (Some emergency actions, called reflexes, are controlled in the spinal cord and not in the brain.) Second, there are the peripheral nerves. These take messages to the CNS from all parts of the body, and take back the orders that control the body's actions. Third, there is the autonomic nervous system, which is rather separate. It governs the automatic functions of the body, like the heartbeat, that are not under complete conscious control.

Nitrogen cycle Circulation of the element nitrogen through the biosphere. Plants take in nitrates from the soil and build up organic nitrogen compounds. The plants die and decay, or are eaten by animals which return the nitrogen compounds to the soil as waste products in their urine and faeces. The animals too are either eaten, or die and decay, and bacteria in the soil recycle all the nitrogen compounds.

Notochord Solid rod, composed of large, fluid-filled cells, that lies between the central nervous system and the alimentary canal. Forms the skeleton at early stage in the development of every vertebrate, but is later replaced by the vertebral column.

Notogaea One of the world's three zoogeographical regions; the Australasian region.

Nucleus Body in a cell that contains the chromosomes and coordinates most functions of the cell.

Nymph Young insect that recognizably resembles the adult, but is sexually immature and has no or incompletely developed wings.

Oesophagus Part of the alimentary canal that links the stomach with the pharynx.

Optic Concerned with the eye.

Oral Concerned with the mouth.

Order Grouping used in the classification of plants and animals. Similar orders are grouped together in a class. An order is divided into families.

Organ Many-celled part of an animal or plant that forms a structural unit and has a particular function. Examples include the liver and kidney of an animal and a leaf of a plant.

Organelle Body in a cell that has a specialized function; e.g. chloroplast, mitochondrion.

Oriental region One of the world's six zoogeographical regions. Includes India, southern China, southeast Asia and the islands of Borneo, Java and Sumatra. Forms part of the zoogeographical realm ARCTOGAEA.

Osmosis Movement of water from a weak solution of a chemical (e.g. sugar) to a strong solution through a semi-permeable membrane.

Otic Concerned with the ear.

Ovary (1) Organ of an animal that produces ova, or eggs. (2) Hollow region in the base of the CARPEL of a flowering plant that contains one or more ovules.

Oviparous (of an animal) Laying eggs.

Ovoviviparous (of an animal) Producing eggs but retaining them in the body until they hatch and giving birth to active young.

Ovule Structure in a seed-bearing plant that contains the egg cell and which develops into the seed after fertilization.

Ovum (*plural*: ova) Egg cell that has not been fertilized.

Palaearctic region One of the world's six zoogeographical regions. Consists of Europe, most of Asia and North Africa. Forms part of the zoogeographical realm ARCTOGAEA.

Parasite Organism that lives on or in another organism (the host), taking nourishment from it

262

and doing the host more or less harm. Some parasites are able to live separately from their hosts; others cannot live independently.

Parthenogenesis Production of young from an egg cell without involving a male sex cell or meiosis.

Perennial plant Plant that continues to grow from year to year.

Petals Parts of a flower that lie just inside the sepals. Often brightly coloured and are collectively known as the corolla.

Pharynx Part of the alimentary canal that links the mouth with the oesophagus.

Phloem Living conducting tissue of a plant that transports chemicals, such as sugars, proteins and dissolved gases to all parts of the plant.

Photosynthesis Process in which a plant converts carbon dioxide and water into food sugars and oxygen, using light energy trapped by the green pigment chlorophyll.

Phylum (*plural*: phyla) Grouping used in the classification of animals. The animal kingdom is divided into a number of phyla, which in turn are divided into classes.

Pistil All the CARPELS of a flower.

Placenta (1) Organ through which nourishment is provided for an unborn placental mammal or marsupial. Consists of a union between a modified part of the uterus and embryonic membranes. The blood supplies of mother and young are held closely together, without the two blood streams actually mixing. (2) Part of a flowering plant's ovary wall on which the ovules are borne.

Placental mammal Member of the subclass Eutheria; mammal that produces relatively well-developed young and prior to birth nourishes its young via a highly efficient placenta.

Plankton Small animals and plants found in seas or lakes that drift with the currents, mostly near the surface of the water.

Plant Member of the plant kingdom; living organism that manufactures its own food by PHOTOSYNTHESIS. Exceptions are some parasitic flowering plants and all fungi, which have no chlorophyll. Unlike higher animals, higher plants show no locomotion but they do have a fairly wide range of movements.

Poikilothermic (of animals) 'Cold-blooded'; having a body temperature that varies with the temperature of the surroundings.

Pollen Spores of a seed plant that contain the male reproductive cells. Produced in anthers.

Pollination Process by which the fertilization of flowering plants occurs; the transfer of pollen from an anther to a stigma. Achieved by wind, by animals (usually insects, but sometimes birds or mammals) or, rarely, by water.

Posterior Of a region, organ or part of an organ near or towards the hind end or tail of an animal.

Predator Animal that kills and feeds on other animals.

Primate Member of the order Primates, which includes monkeys, apes and man. Features of primates include the presence of five distinct fingers and toes, with nails rather than claws, and hands (and often feet) that can be used for grasping. Primates mostly have flattened faces and their eyes point forwards, giving BINOCULAR VISION.

Protein Complicated chemical compound consisting of one or more long, folded chains of AMINO ACIDS.

Protoplasm All the contents of a cell; the nucleus and the cytoplasm containing various organelles such as the MITOCHONDRIA, the ENDOPLASMIC RETICULUM and the GOLGI APPARATUS.

Pulmonary Concerned with the lung.

Pupa Stage between the larva and adult in the development of some insects. Feeding and growth cease, but inside the pupal case, the body of the insect is completely reorganized.

Reproduction Process by which a new living organism is produced by one or two parents.

Respiration Process by which aerobic organisms obtain energy from their food, using oxygen from their surroundings. Air-breathing animals take in oxygen via a lung or similar structure; water-living animals take in dissolved oxygen via gills or some other surface; plants take in oxygen via the stomata (pores) on the undersides of their leaves.

Ribosome See ENDOPLASMIC RETICULUM.

RNA Ribonucleic acid; the chemical compound in the cell concerned with making proteins. Similar in structure to DNA.

Saprophyte Organism that feeds on organic matter released by the tissues of dead and decaying plants and animals.

Seed Structure that results from the development of a fertilized ovule. Consists of an embryo enclosed in one or more protective coats. Endospermic seeds have endosperm (food reserves) outside their cotyledons. Non-endospermic seeds have endosperm contained within the cotyledons.

Seed plant Member of the division Spermatophyta; plant that produces seeds; angiosperm (flowering plant) or gymnosperm.

Sepals parts of a dicotyledon flower that form the outer ring. Usually green, they are collectively known as the calyx. Function is to protect the unopened flower-bud.

Sexual reproduction Reproduction that involves the fusion of two gametes, or sex cells.

Species Smallest grouping used in the classification of living organisms. Members of the same species can breed with each other, whereas members of different species are not normally able to breed successfully.

Sperm Spermatozoon; small male gamete that swims with the aid of a FLAGELLUM.

Spinal cord Part of the central nervous system of a vertebrate that lies within the vertebral column. It passes through each vertebra via a spinal canal.

Spore Single-celled reproductive body which grows into a new plant without any form of sexual union.

Sporophyte Spore-producing stage in the life-cycle of a plant that shows ALTERNATION OF GENERATIONS. All the cells of a sporophyte have the full number of chromosomes. The sporophyte of a moss consists of a capsule and its long stalk; the sporophyte of a fern is the adult plant; the sporophyte of a seed plant is also the adult plant, which produces two kinds of spore – male microspores, or pollen grains, and female megaspores inside the ovules.

Stamen Male reproductive organ of a flowering plant. Consists of an anther on the end of a long stalk, or filament.

Sterile Unable to produce functional gametes.

Stigma (1) Pollen-receiving surface of a carpel, situated either on the surface of the carpel or on the end of a long stalk, or style. (2) Eye-spot of a flagellated alga or protozoan.

Stomach Part of the alimentary canal that links the oesophagus and the intestine. Prepares food for assimilation in the intestine.

Symbiosis Association between two dissimilar living organisms from which both partners benefit.

Taxonomy Study of the classification of living organisms.

Terrestrial Living on land.

Testis Organ of an animal that produces sperms.

Thorax (1) Chest region of a vertebrate, containing the heart and lungs. In mammals it is separated from the abdomen by the diaphragm. (2) The three segments behind the head of an insect. They bear the legs and wings.

Tissue Collection of cells, mostly of the same or similar type, generally having the same function.

Transpiration Loss of water by evaporation from the pores (stomata) on the undersides of the leaves of a plant. Responsible for the flow of water (transpiration stream) up the xylem of the plant and hence the uptake of water and dissolved minerals from the soil.

Tropism Plant movement made in response to a stimulus, such as light or gravity.

Uterus Womb; muscular chamber in a female mammal in which the young develop.

Vacuole Fluid-filled space in the cytoplasm of some cells. The pressure of the fluid in the vacuole helps to keep the cell rigid. In plants loss of this fluid pressure results in wilting.

Vascular bundle Long strand of conducting tissue (XYLEM and PHLOEM) in a seed plant.

Vegetative reproduction Form of plant asexual reproduction in which a part of the plant, other than a seed or spore, becomes detached and develops into a new plant. E.g. bulb, tuber.

Vein (1) Blood vessel that carries blood towards the heart. (2) VASCULAR BUNDLE of a leaf. (3) Fine tube forming part of the network that supports the wing of an insect.

Ventral Of or close to the under surface of an animal.

Vertebral column Backbone; chain of small bones or cartilages (vertebrae) that lie along the back of a vertebrate animal.

Vertebrate Animal with a backbone.

Virus Organism that infects plants or animals and can only reproduce itself within a living cell. Consists of a nucleic acid (either DNA or RNA) inside a mainly protein coat. Viruses frequently cause disease.

Viviparous (of an animal) Giving birth to active young without the production of eggs.

Xylem Wood; conducting tissue of a plant that provides support and through which water passes up to the leaves.

Zoogeography Study of the geographical distribution of animals.

Zoology Study of animals.

Zygote Cell that results from the fusion of two gametes; a fertilized egg before it begins to divide.

*Speeds of up to 177 kph (110 mph) have been recorded with strong following winds.
†Official record, over 0.4 Km ($\frac{1}{4}$-mile) course: 69.62 kph (43.26 mph).
‡Fastest recorded: 67.14 kph (41.72 mph).
§World sprint records average nearly 37 kph (23 mph).

ANIMALS: LONGEVITY AND SPECIALIZED NAMES

	Avg. Life span (years)	Male	Female	Young	Group
Antelope	10	buck	doe	fawn	herd
Bear	15–50	boar	sow	cub	sleuth
Cat	15	tom	queen	kitten	cluster
Cattle	20	bull	cow	calf	herd
Deer	10–20	buck, hart, stag	doe, hind	fawn	herd
Dog	12–15	dog	bitch	puppy	kennel
Donkey	20	jack	jenny	foal	herd
Duck	10	drake	duck	duckling	team
Elephant	60	bull	cow	calf	herd
Fox	10	dog-fox	vixen	cub	skulk
Giraffe	10–25	bull	cow	calf	herd
Goat	10	billy-goat	nanny-goat	kid	herd
Goose	25	gander	goose	gosling	skein, gaggle
Hippopotamus	30–40	bull	cow	calf	herd
Horse	20–30	stallion	mare	foal	herd
Kangaroo	10–20	buck	doe	joey	mob
Lion	25	lion	lioness	cub	pride
Ostrich	50	cock	hen	chick	flock
Pig	10–15	boar	sow	piglet	drove
Rabbit	5–8	buck	doe	kit	warren
Rhinoceros	25–50	bull	cow	calf	crash
Sheep	10–15	ram	ewe	lamb	flock
Tiger	10–25	tiger	tigress	cub	
Whale	20	bull	cow	calf	school, pod
Zebra	20–25	stallion	mare	foal	herd

ANIMAL SPEED RECORDS

	km/h	mph
Peregrine falcon	290	180
Spine-tailed swift	170	106
Sailfish	109	68
Cheetah	105	65
Pronghorn antelope	97	60
Racing Pigeon*	97	60
Lion	80	50
Gazelle	80	50
Hare	72	45
Zebra	64	40
Racehorse†	64	40
Shark	64	40
Greyhound‡	63	39
Rabbit	56	35
Giraffe	51	32
Grizzly bear	48	30
Cat	48	30
Elephant	40	25
Sealion	40	25
Man§	32	20
Bee	18	11
Pig	18	11
Chicken	14	9
Spider	1.88	1.17
Tortoise	0.8	
	0.05	0.03

The speeds shown are maximum speeds over a short distance.

CLASSIFICATION OF PLANTS

Main group	Principal types, common names	No. of species
1. True plants: many-celled organisms, usually possessing chlorophyll.		
Angiosperms	Flowering plants: *monocotyledons* include grasses, lilies, orchids and palms *dicotyledons* include many herbaceous plants and shrubs and most kinds of trees	About 250,000
Gymnosperms	Conifers, yews, cycads and gingko (maidenhair tree); gnetales (desert plants)	About 1,000
Pteridophytes	Ferns, horsetails, clubmosses (small creeping plants); quillworts (small water plants); psilotes or whisk ferns (primitive land plants)	About 10,000 (mostly ferns)
Bryophytes	Mosses, liverworts and hornworts	A few thousand
Chlorophytes	Green algae or seaweeds (some are single-celled algae)	About 6,000
Phaeophytes	Brown algae or seaweeds	About 1,000
Rhodophytes	Red algae or seaweeds (some are single-celled algae)	About 2,500
Charophytes	Stoneworts (lime-encrusted freshwater algae)	About 250
2. Fungi: single- or many-celled plant-like organisms, never possessing chlorophyll.		
Basidiomycetes	Mushrooms, toadstools, puffballs, stinkhorns, jelly fungi, smuts and rusts (plant parasites)	Many thousands
Ascomycetes	Sac fungi: morels, truffles, green and black moulds including *Penicillium*, single-celled yeasts	Many thousands
Deuteromycetes	Imperfect fungi, so-called because they lack a perfect or sexual phase. Related to above groups	Many thousands
Phycomycetes	Pin moulds, downy mildews, tiny water moulds	Many thousands

Main group	Principal types, common names	No. of species
Myxomycetes	Slime moulds: organisms showing a creeping or flowing movement, resembling both fungi and protozoa	Some
3. Protista: single-celled or few-celled plant-like organisms with or without chlorophyll		
Euglenophytes	*Euglena* and related species: tiny, green, motile water organisms	Some hundreds
Xanthophytes	Yellow-green algae	Many hundreds
Bacillariophytes	Diatoms: silica-shelled algae	Many hundreds
Chrysophytes	Golden algae	Many hundreds
Pyrrophytes	Dinoflagellates and related algae	Many hundreds
Lichenes	Lichens: symbiotic plant-like organisms which contain a single-cell green or blue green alga in association with a fungus	More than 15,000
Cyanophytes	Blue green algae: more closely related to the bacteria than to other algae	Many thousands
Bacteriophytes	Bacteria: microscopic single-celled organisms, some of which have a form of chlorophyll	Many thousands

The Scots pine is classified as a gymnosperm, or naked-seed plant. This distinguishes it from angiosperms, or flowering plants, which bear their seeds in fruits.

265

CLASSIFICATION OF ANIMALS

INVERTEBRATES: animals without backbones

Phylum	Common name, if any	No. of species
Protozoa	Single-celled animals	More than 30,000
Porifera	Sponges	About 5,000
Coelenterata	Jellyfish and relatives	About 9,500
Ctenophora	Comb jellies	About 100
Platyhelminthes	Flatworms	About 15,000
Nemertina	Ribbonworms	750
Nematoda	Roundworms	10,000
Nematomorpha	Horsehair worms	200
Priapulida	Priapulid worms	8
Rotifera	Rotifers	2,000
Gastrotricha	Hairy backs	175
Kinorhyncha	None	100
Acanthocephala	Thorny-headed worms	300
Bryozoans	Moss animals	4,000
Phoronida	Phoronid worms	15
Brachiopoda	Lamp shells	260
Annelida	Earthworms and relatives	About 7,000
Sipunculoidea	Peanut worms	250
Echiuroidea	Echiurid worms	60
Pentastomida	Tongue worms	70
Tardigrada	Water bears	180
Mollusca	Molluscs	More than 46,000
Chaetognatha	Arrow worms	50
Pogonophora	Beard worms	About 80
Echinodermata	Starfish and relatives	About 5,500
Hemichordata	Acorn worms and relatives	90
Chordata	Chordates	About 1,300 plus all the species of back-boned animals

Phylum Arthropoda: 'joint-legged animals'

Order	Common name, if any	No. of species

Class Insecta: Insects: six-legged arthropods

A: Apterygote insects

Thysanura	Silverfish and relatives	550
Diplura	Two-pronged bristletails	600
Protura	None	Over 200
Collembola	Springtails	1,500

B: Exopterygote insects

Ephemeroptera	Mayflies	2,000
Odonata	Dragonflies, etc.	5,000
Plecoptera	Stoneflies	1,700
Grylloblattodea	None	16
Orthoptera	Grasshoppers and relatives	17,000

Order	Common name, if any	No. of species
Phasmida	Stick-insects and leaf-insects	2,500
Dermaptera	Earwigs	1,200
Embioptera	Web-spinners	over 300
Dictyoptera	Cockroaches and mantises	5,300
Isoptera	Termites	2,000
Zoraptera	None	22
Psocoptera	Booklice	1,600
Mallophaga	Biting lice	2,800
Siphunculata	Sucking lice	300
Hemiptera	True bugs	50,000
Thysanoptera	Thrips	5,000

C: Endopterygote insects

Neuroptera	Lacewings, alder flies, etc.	4,000
Coleoptera	Beetles	330,000
Strepsiptera	Styploids	370
Mecoptera	Scorpion flies	300
Siphonaptera	Fleas	1,400
Diptera	True flies	85,000
Lepidoptera	Butterflies and moths	100,000
Trichoptera	Caddis flies	5,000
Hymenoptera	Ants, bees, wasps, sawflies, etc.	100,000

Class Crustacea: water-dwelling arthropods

Subclass

Cephalocarida	None	4
Branchiopoda	Water fleas	1,200
Ostracoda	Mussel shrimps	20,000
Copepoda	Copepods	4,500
Mystacocarida	None	3
Branchiura	Fish lice	75
Cirripedia	Barnacles, etc.	800
Malacostraca	Crabs and relatives	18,000

Class Pycnogonida

	Sea spiders	About 500

Class Merostomata

	King crabs, or horsehoe crabs	5

Class Arachinida: eight-legged land arthropods

Araneae	Spiders	20,000
Solifugae	Sun spiders	570
Acarina	Mites, ticks	10,000
Ricinulei	None	About 15
Opiliones	Harvestmen	2,400
Scorpionida	Scorpions	600
Pseudo-scorpionida	False scorpions	1,100
Uropygi	Whip scorpions	105
Palpigradi	Micro-whip scorpions	21

Class Pauropoda

	None	60

Class Diplopoda

	Millipedes	8,000

The water spider (above left) is classified together with all other spiders, in the class Arachnida. Arachnids make up one class of the phylum Arthropoda. Another class is Diplopoda, made up of by the many-legged millipedes (left). Arthropods are all invertebrates or animals without backbones. The plaice (above) is a vertebrate. It belongs to the phylum Chordata and the class Osteichthyes, or bony fishes.

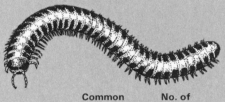

Order Class	Common name, if any	No. of species
Class Chilopoda	Centipedes	2,000
Class Symphyla	None	120
Class Onychophora	Velvet worms	About 120

VERTEBRATES: animals with backbones

Order	Common name, if any	No. of species
Class Agnatha: jawless fishes		
Cyclostomata	Lampreys and hagfishes	45
Class Chondrichthyes: fishes with a cartilage skeleton		
Lamniformes	Sharks	200
Rajiformes	Rays and skates	350
Chimeriformes	Chimeras	25
Class Sarcopterygii: fishes with fleshy fins		
Crossopterygii	Coelacanth	1
Dipnoi	Lungfishes	5
Class Actinopterygii: Fishes with ray fins		
Polypteriformes	Bichirs	12
Acipenseriformes	Sturgeons	22
Amiiformes	Bowfin	1
Semionotiformes	Garpikes	7
Elopiformes	Tarpons	12
Anquilliformes	Eels	300
Notacanthiformes	Spiny eels	20
Clupeiformes	Herring and relatives	350
Osteoglossiformes	Bony tongues	16
Mormyriformes	Mormyrids	150
Salmoniformes	Salmon, trout	500

Class Actinopterygii: Fishes with a bony skeleton

Order	Common name, if any	No. of species
Myctophiformes	Lantern fish	300
Ctenothrissiformes	Macristed fish	1
Gonorhynchiformes	Milk fish	15
Cypriniformes	Carp and relatives	350
Siluriformes	Catfishes	200
Percopsiformes	Pirate perch	10
Batrachoidiformes	Toadfishes	10
Gobiesociformes	Clingfishes	100
Lophiiformes	Anglerfishes	150
Gadiformes	Cod and relatives	450
Beryciformes	Whalefishes, squirrelfishes	150
Atheriniformes	Flying fishes, Killifishes	600
Zeiformes	John Dory, etc	60
Lampridiformes	Ribbonfish, etc.	50
Gasterosteiformes	Seahorses and relatives	150
Channiformes	Snakeheads	5
Synbranchiformes	Swamp eels and cuchias	7
Scorpaeniformes	Gurnards and relatives	700
Dactylopteriformes	Flying gurnards	6
Pegasiformes	Sea moths, dragonflies	4
Tetraodontiformes	Triggerfishes, puffer fishes	250
Pleuronectiformes	Flatfishes	500
Perciformes	Perch and relatives, e.g. mackerel, tuna, sea bass	6,500

VERTEBRATES

The tree frog is a member of the Order Anura, or tailless amphibians. Frogs and toads are rather specialised amphibians, whose bodies have become adapted for hopping or climbing.

Above; The gavial or gharial is a close relative of the crocodiles and alligators, but it has a much narrower snout, for catching fishes. Above right: The tuatara is an even more ancient sort of reptile, whose ancestors predate the dinosaurs. It lives only in islands off the coast of New Zealand. Right: This python, although a rather primitive sort of snake, is a much more modern type than the other two reptiles.

Class Amphibia: vertebrates which spend their lives between land and water. Most have tadpole-like young

Family	Common name	No. of species
Order Anura: Frogs and toads		
Ascaphidae	Hochstetter's frog, etc.	4
Pipidae	Clawed toads	15
Discoglossidae	Midwife toad	10
Rhynophrynidae	Mexican burrowing toad	1
Pelobatidae	None	54
Bufonidae	Toads	300
Ranidae	Frogs	More than 300
Hylidae	Tree frogs	600
Leptodactylidae	None	650
Atelopodidae	Arrow-poison frogs, etc.	About 90
Rhacophoridae	None	Over 200
Microphylidae	None	Over 200
Order Urodela: newts and salamanders		
Hynobiidae	Asiatic land salamanders	30
Cryptobranchidae	Giant salamanders	3
Ambystomidae	Axolotl, etc.	32
Salamandridae	Newts, etc.	42
Amphiumidae	Lamper eels	3
Plethodontidae	Lungless salamanders	183
Proteidae	Mud puppy, etc.	6
Sirenidae	Sirens	3
Order Apoda: Limbless, wormlike amphibians		
Cecilidae	Cecilians or apodans	About 170

Class Reptilia: cold-blooded land vertebrates that lay thick-shelled eggs

Family	Common name	No. of species
Order Chelonia: turtles and tortoises		
Testudinidae	Tortoises, terrapins	115
Chelydridae	Snappers etc.	23
Dermatemydidae	The Central American river turtle	1
Cheloniidae	Marine turtles	5
Dermochelyidae	Leathery turtle	1
Trionychidae	Soft-shells	22
Carettochelidae	The New Guinea pitted-shelled turtle	1
Pelomedusidae	Side-necks	14
Chelidae	Snake-necks	31
Order Crocodilia: crocodiles, alligators and gavial		
Crocodylidae	Crocodiles and alligators	20
Gavialidae	Gavial	1
Order Rhynchocephalia: an ancient group of reptiles with one survivor.		
Sphenodontidae	Tuatara	1
Order Squamata: lizards and snakes		
Lacertidae	Lizards	150
Teiidae	Tegus	200
Gekkonidae	Geckos	400
Chameleontidae	Chameleons	85
Iguanidae	Iguanas	700
Agamidae	Agamids	300
Pygopodidae	Flap-footed lizards	13

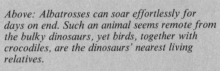

Above: Albatrosses can soar effortlessly for days on end. Such an animal seems remote from the bulky dinosaurs, yet birds, together with crocodiles, are the dinosaurs' nearest living relatives.

Family	Common name	No of species
Scincidae	Skinks	700
Feyliniidae	Limbless skinks	4
Dibamidae	Burrowing lizards	4
Anguidae	Slow worms	40
Anniellidae	Californian legless lizard	2
Amphisbenidae	Worm lizards	120
Xantusiidae	Night lizards	11
Gerrosauridae	Plated lizards	25
Cordylidae	Girdle-tailed lizards	23
Xenosauridae	Crocodile lizards and relatives	4
Helodermatidae	Poison lizards	2
Lanthanotidae	Earless monitor	1
Varanidae	Monitors	24
Boidae	Constricting snakes	70
Typhlopidae	Blind snakes	150
Anomalepidae	None	20
Leptotyphlopidae	Thread snakes	40
Uropeltidae	Indian shield-tailed snakes	43
Aniliidae	Pipe snakes	10
Xenopeltidae	Sunbeam snake of Asia	1
Acrochordidae	Asian sea snakes	2
Colubridae	Colubrids	1,100
Elapidae	Cobra family	200
Viperidae	Vipers	100

Class Aves: birds

Order	Common name	No of species
Passeriformes	Perching birds; passerines	5,000
Piciformes	Woodpeckers and relatives	400
Coraciiformes	Kingfishers and relatives	190
Coliiformes	Mousebirds	6
Trogoniformes	Trogons	36
Apodiformes	Swifts and relatives	387
Caprimulgiformes	Nightjars and relatives	94
Strigiformes	Owls	130
Cuculiformes	Cuckoos and relatives	147
Psittaciformes	Parrot family	315
Columbiformes	Pigeons and relatives	305
Charadriiformes	Gulls and relatives (mainly waders)	295
Gruiformes	Cranes and relatives	197
Galliformes	Game birds	151
Falconiformes	Birds of prey	271
Anseriformes	Ducks and relatives	148
Ciconiiformes	Storks and relatives	120
Pelecaniformes	Pelicans and relatives	59
Procellariiformes	Albatrosses and relatives	91
Sphenisciformes	Penguins	18
Gaviiformes	Divers	5
Podicipediformes	Grebes	21
Tinamiformes	Tinamous	50
Casuariiformes	Emu and cassowaries	4
Rheiiformes	Rheas	2
Struthioniformes	Ostrich	1
Dinornithiormes	Kiwis	1

Class Mammalia: mammals

Family	Common name	No. of species
Order Monotremata: egg-laying mammals		
Tachyglossidae	Echidnas	5
Ornithorhyn-chidae	Platypus	1

Order Marsupialia: pouched mammals that give birth to little-developed young

Family	Common name	No. of species
Caenolestidae	Rat opossums	7
Didelphidae	True opossums	65
Dasyuridae	Native cats, Native mice	45
Notoryctidae	Marsupial moles	2
Myrmecobiidae	Numbat	1
Peramelidae	Bandicoots	19
Phalangeridae	Koala and relatives	45
Vombatidae	Wombats	2
Macropodidae	Kangaroos and wallabies	52

Order Insectivora: insect- and worm-eating mammals; rather primitive

Family	Common name	No. of species
Soricidae	Shrews	200
Macroscelididae	Elephant shrews	14
Potamogalidae	Otter shrews	3
Solenodontidae	Solenodons	2
Tenrecidae	Tenrecs	20
Erinaceidae	Hedgehogs	15
Talpidae	Moles, desmans	19
Chrysochloridae	Golden moles	20

Order Chiroptera: bats: flying mammals

Family	Common name	No. of species
Pteropodidae	Fruit bats, flying foxes	130
Vespertilionidae	Typical small bats	275
Myzopodidae	Madagascar disc-winged bat	1
Thyropteridae	South American disc-winged bats	2
Furipteridae	Smoky bats	2
Natalidae	Funnel-eared bats similar to above	15
Rhinopomatidae	Mouse-tailed bats	4
Emballonuridae	Sheath-tailed bats	50
Noctilionidae	Bulldog bats	2
Nycteridae	Slitfaced bats	10
Rhinolophidae	Horseshoe bats	50
Hipposideridae	Leaf-nosed bats	100
Phyllostomatidae	American leaf-nosed bats	100
Desmodontidae	Vampires	3

Family	Common name	No. of species
Megadermatidae	False vampires	5
Mystacinidae	New Zealand short-tailed bat	1
Molossidae	Matiff or free-tailed bats	80

Order Primates: tree shrews, lemurs, tarsiers, monkeys, apes, man

Family	Common name	No. of species
Tupaiidae	Tree shrews	20
Lemuridae	Lemurs	19
Daubentoniidae	Aye-aye	1
Lorisidae	Bush babies and relatives	11
Tarsiidae	Tarsiers	3
Callitrichidae	Marmosets and relatives	21
Cebidae	New World monkeys	26
Cercopithecidae	Old World monkeys	60
Pongidae	Apes	9
Hominidae	Human beings	1

Order Edentata: anteaters, armadillos and sloths

Family	Common name	No. of species
Myrmecophagidae	Anteaters	3
Dasypodidae	Armadillos	20
Bradypodidae	Sloths	7

Order Pholidota: pangolins

Family	Common name	No. of species
Manidae	Pangolins	7

Order Dermoptera: Colugos or flying lemurs

Family	Common name	No. of species
Cynocephalidae	Flying lemurs	2

Order Rodentia: rodents, gnawing mammals

Family	Common name	No. of species
Aplodontidae	Sewellel or mountain beaver	1
Sciuridae	Squirrels	250
Geomyidae	Pocket gophers	30
Heteromyidae	Pocket mice, etc.	70
Castoridae	Beaver	1
Anomaluridae	Scaly-tailed squirrels	9
Pedetidae	Springhaas	1
Muridae	Rats, mice	500
Gliridae	Dormice	13
Zapodidae	Jumping mice	11
Dipodidae	Jerboas	25

Family	Common name	No. of species
Cricetidae	Hamsters, etc.	570
Spalacidae	Mediterranean mole rats	3
Rhizomyidae	Bamboo rats and African mole rats	18
Hystricidae	Old World porcupines	20
Erethizontidae	New World porcupines	23
Caviidae	Guineapigs, etc.	23
Hydrochoeridae	Capybara	1
Dinomyidae	Pacarana	1
Dasyproctidae	Agoutis, acuchis and pacas	30
Chinchillidae	Chinchillas, viscachas	6
Capromyidae	Coypus, etc.	10
Octodontidae	Degu, etc.	8
Ctenomyidae	Tuco-tucos	26
Abrocomidae	Chinchilla rats	2
Echimyidae	Spiny rats	75
Thryonomyidae	Cane rats	6
Petromyidae	Rock rat	1
Bathyergidae	African mole rats	50
Ctenodactylidae	Gundis, etc.	8

Order Lagomorpha: rabbits, hares and pikas

Leporidae	Rabbits and hares	50
Ochotonidae	Pikas	14

Order Cetacea: whales, including dolphins and porpoises

Platanistidae	River dolphins	4
Ziphiidae	Beaked whales	15
Monodontidae	White whales	2
Delphinidae	Dolphins and porpoises. Killer whale	50
Physeteridae	Sperm whales	2
Balenopteridae	Rorquals or fin whales	6
Balenidae	Right whales	3
Eschrichtiidae	Californian grey whale	1

Order Carnivora: flesh-eating mammals

Mustelidae	Weasel family	70
Viverridae	Civets and relatives	75
Hyaenidae	Hyaenas	4
Felidae	Cats	34
Canidae	Dogs, etc.	37
Ursidae	Bears	7
Procyonidae	Pandas and racoons, etc.	18

Order Pinnipedia: seals and walrus, closely related to carnivores

Phocidae	Seals	18
Otariidae	Sea lions	13
Odobenidae	Walrus	1

Order Artiodactyla: hoofed mammals with an even number of toes

Suidae	Pigs	8
Tayassuidae	Peccaries	2
Hippopotamidae	Hippopotamus	2
Camelidae	Camels	3
Cervidae	Deer	40
Tragulidae	Chevrotains	4
Bovidae	Cattle and antelopes	110
Antilocapridae	Pronghorn	1
Giraffidae	Giraffe, okapi	2

Order Perissodactyla: hoofed mammals with an odd number of toes.

Tapiridae	Tapirs	4
Rhinocerotidae	Rhinoceroses	5
Equidae	Horses and zebras	6

Order Sirenia: sea cows, water mammals not closely related to whales, seals, etc.

Trichechidae	Manatees	3
Dugongidae	Dugong	1

Order Tubulidentata: the aardvark

Orycteropodidae	Aardvark	1

Order Hyracoidea: hyraxes or dassies

Procaviidae	Hyraxes, dassies	6

Order Proboscidea: elephants

Elephantidae	Elephants	2

Mammals come in many shapes and sizes. The opossum (far left) is a marsupial, carrying its young in a pouch. Next come the insectivorous hedgehog and the bush baby, a tiny primate; the massive Brown bear is one of the biggest carnivores; zebras (below) are closely related to the horse.

271

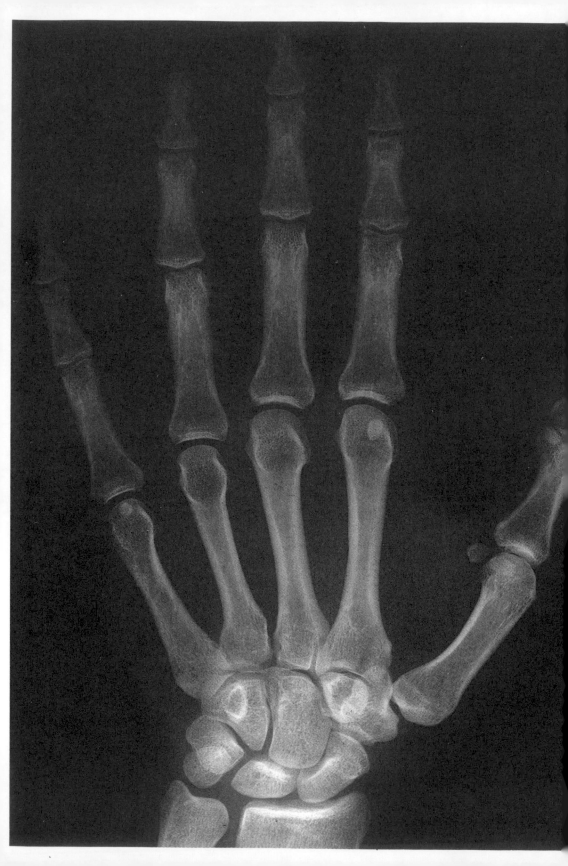

Medicine

MEDICAL TERMS

Abortion Premature ending of pregnancy, resulting in death of foetus. In modern terminology, an artificial termination is usually referred to as an abortion, and an accidental or spontaneous one as a miscarriage.

Abrasion Area where skin has been scraped, rubbed or grazed, allowing blood or clear plasma to ooze out.

Abscess Localized collection of pus, due to bacterial infection from a wound or disease.

Accident proneness Predisposition to have a significantly higher number of accidents than average.

Acidity Burning feeling connected with stomach disorders and indigestion.

Acidosis Condition connected with kidney diseases and severe diabetes, in which the body uses up its reserves of alkali, necessitating adjustment to the diet.

Acne Infection of sweat glands (sebaceous glands) of the skin by bacteria, causing inflammation, pimples and blackheads.

Acupuncture Treatment of illness, originating in China, by inserting and vibrating needles at specific points in the skin which appear to bear no relationship to the area of pain or disease.

Acute illness One of rapid onset and short duration.

Addiction Uncontrollable craving for a drug, leading to increased tolerance of it and physical dependence on it.

Addison's disease Form of anaemia due to deficiency of aldosterone normally produced by adrenal glands.

Adenoids Pads of tissue in the upper part of the throat behind nasal passages; part of the body's defence mechanism. Enlargement caused by small repeated infections leads to snoring, mouth breathing and sometimes deafness.

Adhesions Sticking together of tissues which should normally be movable, following inflammation.

Agoraphobia Irrational fear of open spaces.

AIDS stands for Acquired Immune Deficiency Syndrome; it reduces the body's ability to fight off other diseases, and is usually fatal.

Albinism Inherited condition caused by non-formation of normal body pigment owing to an enzyme deficiency. Albinos have white hair, pale skin and pink eyes.

Alcoholism Over-dependence on alcohol, leading to deterioration of physical and mental health and personal relationships.

Allergy Over-susceptibility to external substances or foods such as pollen, house dust, eggs, etc. Symptoms include sneezing, rashes and inflamed and running eyes.

Alopecia Baldness. Can be a normal process of ageing or a symptom of disease or strain.

Amenorrhoea Absence of menstruation during a woman's reproductive years.

Amnesia Sudden complete loss of memory.

Amniocentesis Taking a specimen of the fluid surrounding an unborn baby for the detection of abnormalities.

Amphetamine Addictive stimulant such as benzedrine or dexedrine, formerly used to combat depression or as a slimming aid. Now seldom prescribed.

Amputation Surgical removal of part of the body.

Anaemia Lack of haemoglobin, the oxygen-carrying pigment in red blood cells, leading to pallor, tiredness and weakness.

Anaesthetic Substance producing loss of sensation in part of the body while patient remains awake (local anaesthetic) or total unconsciousness (general anaesthetic).

Analgesic Type of pain-relieving drug that does not produce unconsciousness.

Aneurysm Bulge in arterial wall, usually at a weak point.

Angina pectoris Severe spasmodic pain in chest, due to diseased heart arteries. Occurs during or after exercise and normally stops after rest.

Ankylosis Loss of joint movement, due to prolonged immobilization, injury or arthritis.

Anorexia nervosa Potentially dangerous neurotic illness, usually of young women, in which the patient rejects food while persuading herself that she eats well.

Antacid Type of drug which counteracts excess stomach acid, e.g. sodium bicarbonate or magnesium trisilicate.

Anthrax Bacterial disease of cattle and sheep that can be passed on to man. Symptoms include fever, swelling of lymph glands (nodes) and pneumonia.

Antibiotic Type of drug obtained chiefly from fungi, used to combat disease bacteria.

Anticoagulant Type of drug which reduces the tendency of the blood to form clots.

Antihistamine Type of drug used to reduce symptoms of allergy and travel sickness. Can cause drowsiness, so should not be taken before driving.

Antipyretic Type of drug which reduces fever.

Antiscorbutic Food or preparation containing vitamin C, which prevents scurvy.

Antiseptic Chemical preparation which can be applied to the body to destroy bacteria.

Antitoxin Antidote produced naturally by the body to combat bacterial poisons.

Left: An X-ray of the human hand. X-rays are invaluable for revealing lesions of harder internal parts of the body – and softer parts too if these can be appropriately densified. But being penetrating radiation, X-rays must not be overused as they can damage the body.

273

Antitussive Type of drug used to suppress coughing.

Anxiety Normal reflex response of body to danger. 'Anxiety state' is *abnormal* persisting fear when there is no obvious reason for it.

Aphasia Loss, or partial loss, of the ability to speak.

Appendicitis Acute inflammation or abscess of appendix, necessitating abdominal surgery.

Arteriosclerosis Narrowing, hardening and roughening of artery walls caused by fatty and mineral deposits.

Arthritis Acute or chronic inflammation of joints.

Artificial insemination Artificial introduction of male semen into the female genital tract in order to achieve pregnancy.

Artificial respiration Any method of introducing air into the lungs when natural breathing has stopped (i.e. kiss of life, iron lung).

Aspergillosis Chest infection caused by fungus.

Asphyxia Suffocation caused by interference with normal breathing.

Asthma Disorder of bronchial tubes due to infection, allergy or emotional disturbance.

Astigmatism Inability to focus the whole of an image correctly, caused by cornea of eye not being uniformly curved.

Ataxia Lack of co-ordination in muscles required to perform a specific movement.

Athlete's foot Fungus infection of skin between toes.

Atrophy Wasting or shrinkage of tissue, limb or organ.

Autism Mental disorder starting in childhood in which patient seems cut off from his surroundings and fails to respond to outside stimuli.

Autopsy Examination of body after death (post-mortem).

Backache Common symptom of many conditions related to the spine and pelvis.

Barbiturate Type of sedative drug which reduces activity of central nervous system and is used in tranquillizers and sleeping pills.

BCG vaccine (bacille Calmette-Guérin) Vaccine, called after a French bacteriologist and a French surgeon, is a preventive against tuberculosis.

Bedwetting This can occur after a child becomes dry at night normally (around the age of three), owing to kidney or bladder disease or emotional disturbance.

Bell's palsy Paralysis of facial nerve, giving the face a lop-sided appearance.

Benign Medical term distinguishing a relatively mild or harmless form of disease from a malignant or dangerous one.

Beriberi Disease caused by lack of vitamin B_1, which results in swelling of the body, heart weakness and numbness of the legs.

Bilharzia Tropical disease caused by parasitic fluke worms which invade the body, enter the circulatory system and settle in organs or tissue.

Biliousness Nausea, vomiting and stomach discomfort associated with illness or over-eating.

Biopsy Removal of small piece of tissue for examination under a microscope.

Birth control (contraception) Deliberate prevention of conception by artificial or natural means.

Birthmark Congenital skin blemish such as mole, strawberry mark or port-wine stain.

Blackhead Characteristic inflamed spot with a black centre formed by plug of greasy material in opening of sebaceous gland.

Blackwater fever Rare complication of malaria where red blood cells are destroyed and black or brown urine is produced.

Blindness Absence of useful sight, caused by injury or disease. More common in people over 65.

Blister Raised area of skin, with fluid underneath. Usually caused by friction or heat.

Blood pressure The pressure at which the heart pumps blood into the major arteries, measurable by using a sphygmomanometer.

Blue baby Newly-born infant whose skin looks bluish. Usually indicates a congenital heart defect which prevents its blood from being oxygenated properly.

Boil Pus-filled abscess forming in hair root or sweat gland, and usually caused by a staphylococcus.

Botulism Dangerous though rare type of food poisoning caused by bacterial contamination.

Brain tumour Condition, sometimes cancerous, which destroys tissue or causes pressure, resulting in headaches, personality changes, fits or paralysis.

Bronchitis Acute or chronic inflammation of the bronchi, or air tubes of the lungs, with fever and cough. Caused by virus and bacterial infection.

Brucellosis Bacterial infection caused mainly by milk from infected cattle. Symptoms include fever, weakness, aches and pains.

Bruise Discoloration of skin caused by a blow.

Bunion Deformity of big toe joint with tender, fibrous tissue over the protrusion. Usually caused by wearing ill-fitting shoes.

Burn Injury to tissue caused by excessive dry heat or flames.

Caesarean Delivery of baby through surgical incision in wall of abdomen and womb.

Cancer (general) Abnormal growth of cells, resulting in malignant tumour.

... of the blood (leukaemia): affection of bone marrow, preventing maturity of white cells.

... of the breast: often starts with a painless lump or slight change in breast. Self-examination and early detection give good hope of cure.

... of the cervix (neck of womb): examination of cells from the cervix ('smear test') can ensure early detection and eradication.

... of the lung: this has enormously increased due to smoking. Routine chest x-rays can aid early detection.

... of the pancreas: diagnosis is difficult, but surgery can be carried out in some cases.

... of the prostate gland: an enlarged prostate gland in men does not necessarily mean cancer, but if it does, hormone treatment or removal of the gland is usually effective.

... of the skin: this is usually noticed at an early stage and treatment is always more effective if started quickly.

... of the stomach: loss of appetite, abdominal discomfort or indigestion symptoms should be investigated early, to aid diagnosis of this common form of cancer.

Carbuncle Bacterial skin infection similar to boil but larger and deeper, usually found at back of neck. Infection can spread round body.

Carcinogen Any substance which may help to cause cancer.

Stunting is one result of an inadequate diet. Among peoples such as those of Europe, who have enjoyed a steady improvement in their diet over the past century, a steady increase in average height and weight has also been observed.

CALORIFIC VALUE OF FOODS

Average portion	Calories
Apple (1) 5 oz (142 g)	70
Bacon (fried) 2 oz (57 g)	250–320
Banana (1) 5 oz (142 g)	110
Beans, green (boiled) 4 oz (113 g)	10
Beef (roast) 3 oz (85 g)	325
Beef steak (grilled) 6 oz (170 g)	520
Beer (bitter) 1 pint (0.6 l)	180
Bread (white, 1 slice) 1 oz (28 g)	73
Butter $\frac{1}{2}$ oz (14 g)	110
Cabbage (boiled) 5 oz (142 g)	15
Carrots (boiled) 4 oz (113 g)	24
Celery (raw) 4 oz (113 g)	8
Cheese (cheddar) 1 oz (28 g)	112
Cheese (cottage) 1 oz (28 g)	29
Chicken (roast) 4 oz (113 g)	220
Chocolate (milk) 2 oz (57 g)	300
Cod (grilled) 4 oz (113 g)	170
Coffee (white, no sugar) 6 fl oz (170 ml)	25
Corn flakes 1 oz (28 g)	100
Cream (double) $\frac{1}{2}$ oz (14 g)	64
Egg (boiled, 1) 2 oz (57 g)	90
Grapefruit ($\frac{1}{2}$) 7 oz (198 g)	42
Honey $\frac{1}{2}$ oz (14 g)	41
Lamb (roast) 3 oz (85 g)	250
Lettuce 2 oz (57 g)	5
Magarine $\frac{1}{2}$ oz (14 g)	110
Melon (1 slice) 5 oz (142 g)	30
Milk (cup) 6 fl oz (170 ml)	110
Orange (1) 6 oz (170 g)	60
Peanuts 2 oz (57 g)	330
Potatoes (fried) 4 oz (113 g)	270
(boiled, baked) 4 oz (113 g)	90
Rice (boiled) 6 oz (170 g)	600
Sardines (tinned) 3 oz (85 g)	240
Sausages (pork, 2) 4 oz (113 g)	400
Spinach (boiled) 1$\frac{1}{2}$ oz (43 g)	10
Spirits (measure) 1 fl oz (28 ml)	63
Strawberries 5 oz (142 g)	35
Sugar 2 oz (57 g)	215
1 teaspoon	25
Tea (cup, no sugar) 6 fl oz (170 ml)	15
Tomato (1) 3 oz (85 g)	12
Wine, dry (glass) 4 fl oz (114 ml)	84
sweet (glass) 4 fl oz (114 ml)	128

CALORIES NEEDED PER DAY

Age		Both sexes	
0–1		800	
1–2		1,200	
2–3		1,400	
3–5		1,600	
5–7		1,800	
7–9		2,100	
	Male	Female	
9–12	2,500	2,300	
12–15	2,800	2,300	
15–18	3,000	2,300	
		2,200 (normal life)	
18–35	2,700 (normal life)	2,500 (very active)	
	3,600 (very active)	2,400 (pregnant)	
		2,700 (breast feeding)	
35–65	2,600	2,200	
65–75	2,300	2,100	
75 on	2,100	1,900	

As foods, the body's fuel, vary in the amount of energy they liberate when 'burnt' or metabolized, it is convenient to express their value in units of heat or Calories. A Calorie is the amount of heat needed to warm a kilogram of water by 1 °C.

Carcinoma Generally applied to cancers which arise in covering and lining tissues of body.
Cataract Clouding of the lens of the eye which causes dimness or loss of vision.
Catarrh Inflammation of mucous membrane (usually of the nose) accompanied by excessive discharge of mucus.
Cellulitis Inflammation of cellular tissue, usually that under skin, due to infection.
Chancroid Type of venereal disease.
Chickenpox Common virus disease of children, with itchy rash turning to inflamed blisters. Incubation period about 2 weeks. Same virus causes herpes zoster (shingles) in adults.
Chilblain Inflamed, swollen and itchy condition of hands and feet, caused by cold weather.
Chlorpromazine Powerful tranquillizer used to treat mental illness.
Choking Suffocation, partial or complete, caused by foreign body in windpipe, spasm of the larynx or excessive secretions from the lungs.
Cholera Serious disease caused by bacterium in food or water contaminated by human faeces. Can rapidly become epidemic in unsanitary conditions.
Cholesterol Fat-like substance found in most tissues.

Chorea (St. Vitus's dance) Characteristics are jerky, twitching movements of limbs or body. Cause is unknown but may sometimes be connected with rheumatic fever.

Chronic illness A disease of long duration.

Circumcision Surgical removal of part of the foreskin of the penis.

Cirrhosis Liver disease sometimes caused by alcoholism. Cells are destroyed and replaced by fatty or fibrous tissue.

Claustrophobia Irrational fear of confined spaces.

Cleft palate Gap along middle line of roof or mouth.

Club foot Congenital foot deformity due to faulty development before birth.

Colic Pain, often severe, in internal organs. Can be caused by irritants in the bowel. In infants, may be due to swallowing air.

Colitis Chronic or acute inflammation of the colon.

Colostomy An operation which makes an artificial opening in the intestine to allow evacuation of faeces.

Colour blindness Condition more common in men than women,· characterized by inability to distinguish between colours, in particular, red and green.

Coma State of deep unconsciousness.

Concussion Shaking of brain caused by a fall or blow, sometimes leading to unconsciousness for a long or short time.

Congenital defect Disorder present from birth.

Conjunctivitis Inflammation of delicate membrane covering the eye.

Constipation Retention of solid matter in bowel and inability to pass it without difficulty.

Contagious disease One that is transmitted by direct contact.

Contusion Bruise.

Convulsion Violent involuntary contraction of muscles, sometimes with loss of consciousness. In children, a convulsion often accompanies a rapid rise in temperature.

Corn Area of dead, horny skin on foot, usually caused by pressure of shoe.

Cortisone Steroid hormone produced by adrenal glands; can be manufactured for medical use.

Cramp Painful spasm of the muscles.

Cretinism Congenital deficiency of thyroid hormone, leading to mental and physical retardation.

Croup Respiratory infection with harsh coughing and characteristic strained breathing, usually in children. Caused by allergy or virus or bacterial infection.

Cyst Abnormal swelling which contains fluid.

Cystic fibrosis Hereditary disease affecting numerous glands, leading to digestive disorders, breathing difficulties and lung infections.

Cystitis Inflammation of the bladder, more common in women than men.

Dandruff Scaly dead skin on the scalp, which falls off in small flakes.

Deficiency diseases Those caused by prolonged lack of essential vitamins or minerals in the diet.

Delirium tremens Mental disorder with frightening hallucinations due to heavy drinking.

Dental caries Tooth decay.

Depressant Type of drug that slows down a mental or physical activity.

Depression Long-lasting lowering of spirits, impairing mental and physical functions, out of proportion to the possible causes.

Dermatitis Inflammation of the skin, or eczema.

Dexedrine An amphetamine; inhibits appetite.

Diabetes mellitus Disorder in which body cannot control amount of sugar in the blood and an excessive amount of urine is produced. Caused by lack of insulin, hormone secreted by pancreas.

Diarrhoea Frequent passing of watery bowel motions, usually due to inflammation of the intestines.

Digitalis Drug, originally obtained from foxgloves, valuable for treating heart problems.

Diphtheria Acute infectious disease, with inflammation of larynx. Incubation period 2–7 days. Now less common owing to immunization of children.

Dropsy Accumulation of fluid in the tissues, symptom of certain heart, kidney or liver conditions.

Duodenal ulcer Ulcer of small intestine, causing pain and tenderness in stomach two to four hours after meals.

Dysentery Infection of the intestine, due to bacteria or amoebae, causing pain, diarrhoea and bleeding.

Dyslexia Persistent difficulties with learning to read and write, in which child may, for example, write letters backwards or upside-down. Cause uncertain.

Dyspepsia Difficulty in digesting and discomfort after meals, sometimes due to overeating.

Dysphagia Difficulty in swallowing.

Ectopic pregnancy The development of an embryo which takes place in a Fallopian tube or elsewhere and not in the womb.

Eczema Form of dermatitis with patches of scaly red skin and itching.

Electrocardiogram Record of electrical changes in heart muscle recorded by a sensitive machine (electrocardiograph).

Electroencephalogram Record of electrical patterns in the brain recorded on an electroencephalograph.

Embolism Blocking of artery by a bloodclot or air bubble.

Emetic Substance given to induce vomiting.

Emphysema Lung condition in which the dividing walls between air spaces are destroyed so that exchange of oxygen and carbon dioxide cannot take place effectively.

Encephalitis Inflammation of the brain.

Endemic A disease which is always present in a given location.

Endocarditis Inflammation of the heart lining, especially the valves.

Enema Liquid injection into the rectum, to clear the bowel or introduce fluid or nutrients.

Enteritis Inflammation of intestines, usually with abdominal pain and diarrhoea, caused by bacterial or virus infection, food poisoning, too much food or alcohol.

Epilepsy Periodic loss of consciousness, sometimes with convulsions, caused by brain damage or excessive disturbance in one part of the brain.

Erysipelas Severe, highly contagious infection of the skin, usually on the face.

Expectorant Type of drug that aids coughing up of sputum.

Fainting Sudden temporary loss of consciousness due to lowering of blood supply to the brain.

Fever Raised body temperature, or a condition in

which temperature is raised above normal.

Fibroid Non-malignant tumour of the womb.

Fibrositis Pain and stiffness in muscles, sometimes called 'muscular rheumatism'.

Fistula Wound or ulcer which creates an abnormal channel between two organs or between the skin and a hollow organ.

Flatulence Accumulation of gas in the stomach or intestines.

Food poisoning Acute illness with vomiting and/or diarrhoea and abdominal pain. Usually caused by eating food contaminated by bacteria.

Fracture Break in a bone.

Frigidity A woman's lack of pleasurable physical response during sexual intercourse.

Fringe medicine Types of treatment (such as acupuncture, homeopathy, osteopathy) which are outside the scope of orthodox medicine.

Frostbite Injury to skin and sometimes tissues by freezing temperatures.

Frozen shoulder Stiffness and pain in shoulder caused by inflammation.

Gallstones Stones composed of such substances as cholesterol or calcium and bile pigment, which form in the gall bladder.

Ganglion 1) Cyst or swelling, usually painless, on a joint capsule or tendon sheath. 2) Nerve junction.

Gangrene Death and decay of part of the body tissue. Mortification.

Gastrectomy Surgical removal of part or all of the stomach.

Gastric ulcer Eroded sore in the wall of the stomach.

Gastritis Inflammation of the stomach lining.

Gastro-enteritis Inflammation of the stomach and intestines with diarrhoea, vomiting, high temperature and dehydration.

Geriatrics Study and medical care of old people.

German measles Common infectious virus disease, with rash and enlargement of glands behind ears. Incubation period 2–3 weeks. Should be avoided in early pregnancy as it can cause defects in the unborn baby.

Glandular fever Fever, with sore throat, swollen lymph glands and enlarged spleen; exact cause unknown, but can be diagnosed by examination of white blood cells.

Glaucoma Eye disorder due to increased pressure of eyeball fluid; can lead to blindness.

Goitre Enlargement of the thyroid gland, commonly caused by iodine deficiency.

Gold treatment Preparations of gold sometimes used to treat rheumatoid arthritis.

Gonorrhoea Commonest form of veneral disease, transmitted by sexual contact. If untreated can cause serious disease of genito-urinary system and risk of sterility.

Gout Inflammation of joints due to disorder of body chemistry resulting in excessive uric acid in the blood.

Graft Transfer of skin or bone by surgery from one part of body to another, to repair injury.

Gravel Small deposits of mineral salts in kidneys or bladder.

Gripes Spasmodic pain caused by excessive contractions of the intestines.

Gumboil Abscess on the gums, associated with tooth decay.

Gynaecology Branch of medicine dealing with the female reproductive system.

Haematoma Swelling caused by blood leaking into the tissues.

Haemophilia Inherited disease (nearly always male) in which one of the factors needed for normal blood clotting is missing.

Haemorrhage Severe bleeding.

Haemorrhoids (piles) Enlarged, inflamed veins at lower end of the rectum and anal canal.

Hallucination Feeling of having heard or seen something which has no physical origin.

Hallucinogen Type of drug which causes hallucinations.

Hay fever Common allergic reaction to pollen, causing sneezing, conjunctivitis and asthmatic symptoms.

Headache Pain in the head, which can be a symptom of many conditions.

Heartburn Chest pain, symptom of indigestion.

Heart failure Inability of heart to work efficiently, sometimes, but not always, resulting in death. Common cause of a heart attack or acute heart failure is a coronary thrombosis, when the blood supply to the heart muscle is stopped by a clot.

Heart-lung machine Device which takes over heart and lung functions and maintains circulation and oxygen supply to the blood.

Heart murmur Abnormal sound heard by listening to heart through a stethoscope. May or may not be significant.

Hemiplegia Paralysis affecting only one side of body.

Hepatitis Inflammation of liver, usually due to virus infection, but can be caused by certain drugs.

Hermaphrodite Person having both male and female sex organs.

Hernia Bulging of an organ or part of an organ through a weak spot in the wall of surrounding muscle tissue.

Heroin Dangerous addictive drug derived from morphine.

Herpes Inflamed blisters usually found round mouth and nose and associated with colds.

Herpes zoster (shingles) Caused by same virus as chickenpox, and characterized by painful blisters and fever.

Hiccough Sudden spasms of diaphragm, often caused by drinking or eating too quickly.

Histamine Substance produced by breakdown of histidine, an amino-acid, in all parts of the body, causing allergic symptoms.

Hives Allergic reaction to certain foods, causing red, itchy patches on the skin.

Hodgkin's disease Rare disease of spleen and lymph nodes, causing anaemia and fever.

Homosexuality Sexual attraction between members of the same sex. Between women it is known as lesbianism.

Huntington's chorea Hereditary illness, with progressive mental deterioration and jerky muscular movements, usually arising when patient is 35–50.

Hydrocephalus Abnormal enlargement of head, due to accumulation of cerebro-spinal fluid.

Hyperpyrexia Very high fever, with dangerously raised body temperature.

Hypnosis Type of trance induced in a willing patient by a skilled practitioner. Can be used for medical or psychiatric treatment.

Hypochondria Abnormal preoccupation with one's real or imaginary illnesses.

Hypothermia Lowering of body temperature. Can be medically induced or may occur in babies or old people in cold conditions.

Hysterectomy Surgical removal of the womb.

Hysteria Type of neurosis in which symptoms mimicking physical illness are often produced or there are violent outbursts of emotion.

Immunity Being proof against or having protection against infection.

Immunization Artificial production of immunity, often by injection (i.e. vaccination against smallpox).

Impetigo Contagious skin disease caused by staphylococci.

Impotence A man's inability to get an erection.

Incontinence Inability to control emptying of the bladder and/or rectum.

Incubation period Period of time between infection and appearance of symptoms.

Indigestion Discomfort arising from the stomach and related to the eating of food.

Induction Usually used of artificial starting of childbirth.

Infarction Blockage of a blood vessel, with death and scarring of affected tissue.

Infectious disease One caused by invasion of body by microscopic organisms, very often spread by droplet infection in coughs, sneezes etc. of person carrying the disease.

Infertility Inability to procreate children.

Inflammation Defensive reaction to injury or irritation, characterized by swelling, redness, heat and pain.

Influenza Infectious virus disease, with fever, headache and pains. Can be dangerous and lead to bacterial lung infections.

Inoculation Introduction of mild form of a disease to the body, to confer immunity.

Insomnia Inability to sleep.

Insulin Hormone produced by pancreas which controls metabolism of sugar.

Itching Sensation of skin, leading to desire to scratch. Cause includes parasites, skin infections and certain other diseases.

Jaundice Yellowing of skin as a result of excessive bile pigment in blood; causes include hepatitis or gallstones.

Kidney machine Machine which extracts waste products from the body when kidneys have failed through disease.

Kidney stone Accumulation of calcium or uric acid in the kidney, sometimes requiring surgery.

Kiss of life Mouth-to-mouth (or nose) resuscitation in which the operator blows air from his own mouth into the patient's nose to start his breathing again.

Kleptomania Overwhelming desire to steal when there is no apparent reason to do so.

Laryngitis Inflammation of larynx and vocal cords, with cough and temperature.

Lassa fever Serious infectious virus disease first identified in Nigeria; symptoms include high temperature and exhaustion.

Laudanum Alcoholic extract of opium, formerly used as pain-killing drug.

Legionnaires' disease Serious bacterial illness, similar in symptoms to pneumonia.

Leprosy Disease of long progression which produces ulcers and nodules in skin and tissues and damages nerves. Now found mainly in tropics.

Lesbianism Homosexual relationship between women.

Lesion Disease or wound anywhere in body.

Leucotomy Brain operation in which nerve fibres are severed to cut links between certain stimuli and responses.

Lice Small insects which cause itching of head or body.

Lumbago Term generally used to describe persistent pain in lower back, but specifically is fibrositis in lumbar region of back just below the waist.

Lumbar puncture Insertion of needle into space between spinal cord and covering membrane to draw off fluid for examination.

Malaria Tropical fever caused by minute parasite transmitted by mosquito bite.

Malignant Severe or progressive form of a disease (i.e. a malignant tumour is cancerous and can invade other tissues).

Manic depression Mental illness in which periods of extreme elation alternate with moods of deep depression.

Masochism Deviation in which person enjoys being hurt or abused by their sexual partner.

Mastectomy Surgical removal of breast.

Mastitis Inflammation of the breast, usually due to infection.

Masturbation Satisfaction of sexual urges by self-manipulation.

Measles Infectious virus disease with rash, sore eyes and throat. Incubation period 10 days.

Meningitis Inflammation of membranes covering brain.

Menopause Cessation of menstruation in women, usually taking place between ages of 45 and 50.

Menstruation Periodic monthly bleeding in women of childbearing age.

Metastasis Spread of disease round body by blood stream or lymphatic system.

Migraine Severe headache with vision disturbances, nausea and vomiting.

Mole Conglomeration of pigment cells on skin.

Mongolism (Down's syndrome) Congenital disorder due to chromosome abnormality, leading to retarded growth and mental development.

Morning sickness Nausea on rising experienced by some women in early stages of pregnancy.

Morphine Addictive pain-killer derived from opium.

Multiple sclerosis Chronic disease in which small areas of brain and spinal cord degenerate, leading to weakness, paralysis and lack of co-ordination.

Mumps Virus disease with fever and painful swelling of neck glands. Incubation period 2–4 weeks.

Myocarditis Inflammation of the heart muscle.

Myopia Short sightedness.

Narcotic Any pain-killing drug that produces stupor and sleep.

Nausea Feeling of impending vomiting.

Nephritis Inflammation of the kidney.

Nervous breakdown Emotional illness which makes the sufferer unable to cope with normal life.

Nettle rash Rash resulting from nettle stings, now often applied to allergic condition giving rise to itching blisters and weals.

Neuralgia Sharp pain, usually along nerves of the face.

Neurasthenia Neurosis, with irritability, weakness and depression.

Neuritis Inflammation of a nerve.

Neurosis Psychological abnormality in which the patient manifests abnormal but not psychotic behaviour.

Obstetrics Branch of medicine dealing with pregnancy and childbirth.

Oedema Accumulation of fluid in the tissues or body cavities.

Oedipus complex Attraction of boys to their mother, accompanied by jealousy of their father.

Ophthalmia Inflammation of the eye or eyelid lining.

Orgasm Pleasurable culmination of the sexual act.

Orthodontics Dental techniques concerned with correcting bad positioning of teeth.

Orthopaedics Surgery of bones and joints.

Osteoarthritis Degeneration of joints, with loss of cartilage and formation of bony outgrowths.

Osteomyelitis Abscess formation in bone marrow, with inflammation, pain and tenderness.

Osteoporosis Weakening and increased brittleness of the bones, usually occurring in old people.

Otosclerosis Deafness due to hardening and thickening of bones of the middle ear.

Ovariectomy Surgical removal of one or both ovaries.

Pacemaker The part of the heart from which originate contractions of the heart muscles. If it fails to work, an artificial pacemaker can be inserted.

Palpitation Strong, irregular or rapid heartbeats.

Pandemic Epidemic disease that spreads to many countries.

Paralysis Loss of voluntary power of movement caused by damage to nervous system or muscular mechanism.

Paraplegia Paralysis of lower part of body and legs.

Parasite Organism living in or on another creature, known as the host and causing discomfort or disease.

Parkinson's disease Common nervous disease with muscular tremors, weakness and stooping, usually found in older people. The mind is not affected.

Pellagra Form of malnutrition caused mainly by a deficiency of niacin, a B-group vitamin.

Penicillin Antibiotic obtained from a mould or fungus – the first one ever to be used.

Pericarditis Inflammation of the membraneous sac containing the heart.

Peritonitis Inflammation of the membrane lining the abdominal cavity.

Pernicious anaemia Severe progressive anaemia.

Perversion Form of sexual gratification other than by ordinary intercourse with partner of opposite sex.

Pharyngitis Inflammation of the throat.

Phenobarbitone Sedative barbiturate drug.

Phenylketonuria Hereditary disease caused by absence of special enzyme. Can easily be detected in infants and the condition remedied.

Phlebitis Inflammation of a vein, often associated with blockage by a blood clot.

Physiotherapy Treatment of illness by massage, heat and exercises.

Placebo A medicine which has no direct action on a disease, but which gives the patient confidence that it is being treated.

Plastic surgery Surgical repairs and reconstructions of parts of the body after injury or for cosmetic reasons.

Pleurisy Inflammation of the membranes covering the lungs and lining the chest cavity.

Pneumoconiosis Disease of the lungs caused by inhaled dust.

Pneumonia Bacterial or virus infection of the lungs which become inflamed and filled with fluid so they can no longer function properly.

Poliomyelitis Virus infection of the central nervous system resulting in temporary or permanent paralysis.

Polyp Tumour (usually benign) attached to membrane by a 'stalk'.

Pregnancy Period of gestation from conception to birth – about 39 weeks in human beings.

Premenstrual tension Emotional disturbances, headaches, etc. experienced in the few days before menstruation.

Prickly heat Itchy rash caused by blockage of the sweat glands in humid tropical conditions.

Prognosis Prediction of future course and outcome of a disease.

Prolapse Downward displacement of organ; usually applied to rectum or womb.

Prosthesis Artificial substitute for missing part of body (i.e. dentures, artificial limb).

Psittacosis Severe virus infection transmitted by parrots and other birds.

Psoriasis Common inherited skin disease. Red patches covered with scales appear, usually on back, arms and scalp.

Psychopath Person who feels no guilt about destructive anti-social behaviour.

Psychosis Severe mental disorder in which the patient is totally out of touch with reality.

Psychosomatic illness One in which mental stress or disturbance causes physical symptoms.

Pus Yellowish fluid produced by the body against bacterial infection; it consists of blood serum, white blood cells, bacteria and damaged tissue.

Pyelitis Inflammation of the central part of the kidney.

Pyloric stenosis Narrowing of outlet from stomach, usually in infants rather than adults. Characterized by 'projectile vomiting' and loss of weight.

Pyorrhoea Discharge of pus, but usually used to describe infection of the gums.

Quarantine Period during which people who have been in contact with an infectious disease have to be isolated so they do not pass on the infection.

Quinine Antimalarial drug obtained from bark of the cinchona tree.

Quinsy Abscess found on the tonsil.

Rabies Severe virus infection, usually the result of a bite from an infected dog, with fever, delirium, muscles spasms and eventual death.

Radiotherapy Treatment using X-rays, radium or other radioactive substances.

Rash Temporary eruption on the skin.

Resolution Successful repair of damaged tissue without formation of ulcers or pus.

Resuscitation Restorative measures to revive a

person who is apparently dead as a result of drowning, heart attack, etc.

Rheumatic fever Inflammation of lining and valves of heart and connective tissues of larger joints.

Rheumatism Pain in joints, muscles and bones, not directly due to injury or infection.

Rheumatoid arthritis Chronic inflammation of joint linings, particularly affecting hands or feet. More common in women than men.

Rickets Disease of children caused by vitamin D deficiency, in which bones do not develop properly.

Rigor Severe shivering attack.

Ringworm Fungus infection of the skin.

Rodent ulcer Type of skin cancer, usually on face or scalp.

Roundworm Common parasite found in the intestine.

Sarcoma Cancer originating in connective tissue such as muscles.

Scabies Skin infection caused by a small parasite.

Scald Tissue damage caused by moist heat.

Scarlet fever Sore throat caused by a streptococcus, with accompanying rash. Incubation period is 4 days.

Schizophrenia Serious mental illness characterized by delusions or hallucinations.

Sciatica Severe pain in sciatic nerve running from lower back into legs. Caused by inflammation or pressure on nerve roots.

Sclerosis Hardening of any tissue.

Scurvy Deficiency disease, with swollen bleeding gums, dizziness and weakness, caused by lack of vitamin C.

Seborrhoea Over-production of oily substance by sebaceous oil glands of skin, often associated with acne, eczema and dandruff.

Sedative Type of drug which acts on nervous system and reduces tension and excitement.

Septicaemia Blood poisoning caused by entry of bacteria into bloodstream and their multiplication there.

Shock Failure of circulatory system to maintain flow of blood, caused by injury or acute illness.

Silicosis Inflammation of lungs, caused by rock dust.

Sinusitis Inflammation of the mucous membrane lining the sinuses, head cavities linked to the nose.

Sleeping sickness Tropical infectious disease transmitted by tsetse fly.

Slipped disc Cracking or displacement of cartilaginous disc between spinal vertebrae, so that it presses on a nerve, causing pain.

Smallpox Highly infectious virus disease, with rash which can leave pock marks in skin. Incubation period about 12 days.

Somnambulism Sleep walking.

Soporific Any drug used to induce sleep.

'Spare part' surgery Replacement of parts of the body with artificial parts.

Spastic paralysis Loss of voluntary movement in muscles, with tautness or spasms.

Spina bifida Congenital defect of the vertebrae where spinal cord is pinched in a gap in the backbone with resulting possible mental and physical handicap.

Spondylitis Inflammation of the vertebrae.

Sprue Chronic diarrhoea, leading to weight loss and anaemia.

Squint Faulty alignment of the eyes.

Stammering Hesitant speech due to spasms or lack of muscular co-ordination.

Sterilization Surgical operation rendering it impossible to conceive or father children.

Steroids Group of natural or synthetic compounds, including hormones, often used to combat inflammation.

Stimulant Type of drug that temporarily speeds up mental or physical activity.

Stroke Interference with blood circulation in part of the brain, usually due to blockage or rupture of artery and generally causing permanent damage.

Stye Boil in skin glands of the eyelid.

Sulphonamides Group of drugs which stop bacteria multiplying and allow body's defence mechanisms to destroy the invaders.

Suppository Small cone of glycerine containing antiseptic or drugs which is inserted into the rectum or vagina.

Syphilis Venereal disease of slow development, transmitted by close contact, which can eventually cause madness and death.

Systemic Affecting the whole body, not local (i.e. injected drug circulated throughout the body).

Tachycardia Unduly quick heartbeat.

Tapeworm Parasitic worm, usually caught from eating undercooked meat, which attaches itself by hooks on the head to the intestines. It produces reproductive segments which break off and are passed in the faeces.

Temperature (variation in) 'Normal' body temperature varies according to time of day and part of the body. Average mouth temperature of human beings is 36–37.2°C (97–99°F).

Temper tantrums Uncontrollable fit of rage in a child.

Tetanus Serious disease with spasms, often of the jaw muscles, caused by introduction of the tetanus bacillus through a deep, dirty wound.

Threadworm Common intestinal parasite in the large intestine.

Thrombosis Clotting of blood in artery or vein, with blocking of the circulation.

Thrush Infection of mucous membrane, usually in mouth, by a yeast-like fungus.

Tic Repeated rapid twitching movement.

Tongue tie Restriction of tongue movement by malformation of the fold of skin underneath it.

Tonsillitis Inflammation of the tonsils, the two masses of tissue at the back of the mouth which protect the throat from bacteria.

Toxaemia Presence of, or illness caused by, poisons in bloodstream.

Tracheotomy Operation in which opening is made through the neck into the windpipe (trachea).

Trance State of sleep or altered consciousness from which arousal is difficult.

Tranquillizer Type of drug that calms without impairing alertness.

Transfusion Transfer of blood from a healthy individual to an ill one.

Transplant Tissue or organ transferred by surgery from one person to another.

Tuberculosis Disease caused by bacillus which can affect many parts of the body, but usually the lungs. Symptoms include cough, sometimes with blood, glandular swelling and weight loss.

Tumour Abnormal growth or swelling which can be benign or malignant.

Typhoid Fever caused by bacterium (Salmonella typhi) found in food or water contaminated by someone suffering from the disease or harbouring it without symptoms.

Typhus Fever caused by bacteria (Rickettsia) and prevalent during famines, war or natural disasters where people are crowded together.

Ulcer Persistent inflamed open sore on skin or membrane, where surface cells and underlying membranes are gradually destroyed.

Umbilical hernia Protrusion of part of the intestine through the abdominal wall near the navel.

Uraemia Blood poisoning due to kidneys not moving toxic waste efficiently.

Urethritis Inflammation of the tube (urethra) carrying urine away from the bladder.

Vaccination Technique of producing immunity by injecting a preparation containing live, weakened or dead germs.

Vasectomy Form of male sterilization involving cutting or tying the duct which carries sperm.

Venereal diseases Diseases of the genitals, usually transmitted through sexual contact.

Verruca Type of wart found on the foot.

Vertigo Dizziness or unsteadiness resulting from disturbance of balancing mechanism in ear.

Vomiting Emptying of stomach, preceded by nausea.

Warts Small, rough growths on the skin, usually caused by a virus.

Wasserman test Blood test used to diagnose syphilis.

Wasting Loss of weight and muscle shrinkage.

Whiplash reaction Injury caused by neck jerking violently backwards and forwards, often caused by car crash.

Whooping cough Acute infectious illness, usually in children, with fever, paroxysms of coughing, 'whooping' noise and vomiting. Incubation period variable, usually about 7 days.

Worms General term for infections with worm-like parasites.

X-rays Short wavelength rays which can penetrate soft tissue and register on photographic film.

Yaws Infectious tropical disease with lesions of the skin and bones.

Yellow fever Tropical virus disease, with fever and jaundice, transmitted by type of mosquito.

Zoonosis Infections of animals that may affect man.

VITAMINS		
Vitamin	Chief source	Needed for
Vitamin A	Carotene (which body can convert to Vit. A) in carrots, egg yolks, butter, yellow or orange fruits, vegetables	growth; prevention of dry skin; formation of visual purple, which aids vision in dim light; lack of Vit. A can lead to atrophy of white of eyeball
Vitamin B$_1$ (thiamine)	wheat germ, bread, pork, liver, potatoes, milk	prevention of beri-beri
Vitamin B$_2$ (riboflavine)	milk, eggs, liver	lack may result in skin disorders, inflammation of tongue, and cracked lips
Biotin	liver, yeast, milk, butter	probably concerned with healthy skin
Folic acid	many green vegetables, liver, yeast, mushrooms	prevention of one form of anaemia
Nicotinic acid (niacin)	yeast, liver, bread, wheat germ, kidney, milk	prevention of pellagra
Pantothenic acid	many foods, but abundant in liver, yeast, and eggs	lack may play part in skin disorders
Vitamin B$_6$ (pyridoxine)	meat, fish, milk, yeast	lack can lead to convulsions in babies or anaemia in adults
Vitamin B$_{12}$ (cyanocobalamin)	liver, kidney, eggs, fish	formation of red blood cells, healthy nerve tissue
Vitamin C	fresh fruit and vegetables	prevention of scurvy
Vitamin D	margarine, fish, oils, eggs, butter; also formed in skin exposed to sunlight	formation of bones; lack causes rickets in children
Vitamin E	most foods	little known but may affect fertility and ageing
Vitamin K	green vegetables; also formed by bacteria in intestine	clotting of blood

Prominent People

Abelard, Peter (1079–1142); French scholar, philosopher, and theologian, taught that man's reasoning power was divine and should be used to understand God. Condemned as heretic; finally became monk. Tragic romance with Héloise resulted in his castration by her uncle.

Abruzzi, Duke of the (Luigi Amadeo; 1873–1933); Italian naval officer, Arctic explorer, mountain climber; expedition farthest north (86°33′); mountain-climbing firsts in Alaska and Himalaya; commander Italian fleet World War I.

Adam, Robert (1728–92); Scottish architect, worked closely with his brother, **James Adam** (1730–94) in designing buildings in elegant Neo-Classic style. London's Adelphi Terrace. Furniture design.

Adams, John (1735–1826); Second President of the United States. Envoy to Paris, 1782, later envoy to Britain and Vice-President under Washington. President 1796–1800; defeated by Jefferson.

Adams, Will (1575?–1620); English navigator, sailed with Dutch to East Indies and spent 20 years in Japan as adviser to the *Shogun* Iyeyasu.

Addison, Joseph (1672–1719); English essayist and classical scholar, contributed to *Tatler* and *Spectator*. Member of Kit-Cat Club founded by leading Whigs, including STEELE and CONGREVE. MP for Malmesbury from 1708 until death.

Adenauer, Konrad (1876–1967); German statesman and lawyer; imprisoned by Nazis; chancellor of West Germany, 1949–63; led country's economic recovery.

Adler, Alfred (1870–1937); Austrian psychiatrist, disagreed with Freud's theories of infantile sexuality and proposed that power, not sex, was key. Introduced idea of inferiority complex.

Aeschylus (525–456 BC) Greek tragic dramatist said to have served in the Athenian armies in the Persian wars. Of his many plays, only 7 survive.

Aga Khan Hereditary title carried by spiritual head of Nizari Ismaili sect of Muslims. First holder was Persian religious leader **Ali Shah Hasan** (1800–81).

Agricola, Georgius (George Bauer; 1494–1555); German mineralogist, wrote *De Re Metallica*, which summarized all practical knowledge gained by Saxon miners.

Akbar the Great (1542–1605); Greatest Mughal emperor of India, succeeded father, Humayun, 1555; expanded empire.

Alaric (370?–410); King of the Goths who first served the Roman emperor Theodosius, then turned against Roman rule, twice invading Italy and sacking Rome in 410.

Albee, Edward (b.1928) American playwright best known for *Who's Afraid of Virginia Woolf* (1962).

Albert of Saxe-Coburg-Gotha, Prince (1819–61); Husband of Queen Victoria (*m.*1840), won public acclaim for his encouragement of science and art, helping to set up the Great Exhibition of 1851.

Alexander, Harold Rupert Leofric George, 1st Earl (1891–1969); British general, directed Dunkirk and Burma evacuations; C-in-C North Africa, 1942; minister of defence, 1952–54.

Alexander the Great (356–323 BC); King of Macedonia from 336 BC, set out to conquer world, and by 323 BC ruled empire stretching from Greece to Indus River Valley. Conquered Persia and Egypt. Died possibly of malaria when about to invade Arabia.

Alfred the Great (849–899); Became King of Wessex 871. After many defeats led Saxons to victory over Danish invaders; divided England with Danes. Revived scholarship and literature in England.

Allenby, Edmund Henry Hynman, 1st Viscount (1861–1936); British field marshal who captured Jerusalem from the Turks in 1917.

Ampère, André Marie (1775–1836); French mathematician and physicist, discovered electrodynamics and laws of electromagnetism. Found relation between magnetic field and electric current producing it. Invented solenoid.

Amundsen, Roald (1872–1928); Norwegian explorer, made first voyage through North-West Passage, 1903–06. In 1911 led first expedition to South Pole. Disappeared while searching for missing aviator in Arctic.

Anaxagoras (*c.*500–*c.*428 BC); Greek philosopher, accurately explained phases of Moon and eclipses of Sun and Moon. Proposed seed theory of formation of Earth, Sun, and all heavenly bodies.

Andersen, Hans Christian (1805–75); Danish author; novelist, but main claim to fame his *Fairy Tales*, including *The Ugly Duckling*, and *The Red Shoes*.

Anderson, Elizabeth Garrett (1836–1917); British doctor who pioneered women's roles in medical and thus other professions. In 1866 opened special hospital for women in London, later named after her.

Anouilh, Jean (1910–1987); French playwright; *La Sauvage* (1935), *Le Voyageur Sans Bagages* (1936), *L'Invitation au Château* (1947; translated as *Ring Round the Moon*).

Anson, George, Baron (1697–1762); British admiral who sailed around the world, 1740–44 and defeated the French at Cape Finisterre, 1747. Improved efficiency of the Royal Navy.

Left: John Adams was the second President of the United States. He helped to guide the young country through some of its most serious troubles, but made enemies through bluntness and impatience. His son, John Quincy Adams, became sixth President the year before his father died.

Archimedes (*c*.287–*c*.212 BC); Greek mathematician and engineer, discovered principles of buoyancy and the lever, founded science of statics. Possibly invented a screw pump and planetarium. Calculated accurate value of pi. His devices prolonged Roman siege of Syracuse.

Ariosto, Ludovico (1474–1533); Italian poet and diplomat; main work, epic poem *Orlando Furioso* (1516).

Aristarchus (*c*.320–*c*.250 BC); Greek astronomer, first proposed Sun-centred idea of solar system, not accepted until after time of COPERNICUS.

Aristophanes (*c*.445–*c*.385 BC); Greatest Greek comedy writer; works include *The Wasps*, *The Birds*, *The Clouds*, *The Frogs*, *Lysistrata*, *Plutus*.

Aristotle (384–322 BC); Greek philosopher, studied under PLATO, taught in Athens as head of Peripatetic school. Believed that happiness stems from human reason; ideal political state an enlightened monarchy. His works (*Ethics*, *Politics*, *Metaphysics*, etc.) have had a profound effect on thinkers through the ages.

Armstrong, (Daniel) Louis (1900–71); American Negro jazz trumpeter, band-leader, and vocalist, did more to popularize jazz internationally than any other single person.

Armstrong, Neil (b.1930); American astronaut, first man to set foot on Moon, 1969. Naval pilot, he became astronaut in 1962, and made first space flight in *Gemini 8*, 1966.

Arnold, Benedict (1741–1801); Colonial general in American War of Independence; went over to British, 1780.

Arnold, Matthew (1822–88); English poet and critic; inspector of schools 1851–86; professor of poetry, Oxford, 1857–67; *Essays in Criticism* (1865–88).

Arrhenius, Svante August (1859–1927); Swedish chemist, 1903 Nobel chemistry prize for theory of ionic dissociation of electrolytes in solution. Also began work on molecular biology, proposed that life began on Earth due to spores travelling in space; suggested greenhouse effect of carbon dioxide in atmosphere.

Assurbanipal (d. *c*.626 BC); Last great king of Assyria. Completed Assyrian conquest of Egypt (669–662 BC) and overran Babylon (652). Empire was breaking up by time he died.

Astaire, Fred (Frederick Austerlitz, 1899–1987); American actor/dancer who after a stage career with his sister Adele, 1916–32, achieved even greater success in movies, notably with Ginger Rogers.

Astor, John Jacob (1763–1848); American financier, born in Germany. Emigrating to the US in 1784 he made fortunes from fur trade, land deals and government loans.

Astor, Viscountess Nancy (1879–1964); American by birth, Lady Astor was the first woman MP to take her seat in the House of Commons, where she campaigned vigorously on behalf of the poor, and women in particular.

Attila (*c*.406–453); Joint king of Huns with brother Bleda, 433; killed Bleda 445. Invaded Gaul 451; defeated at Châlons-sur-Marne by Romans; ravaged Italy, but forced to retreat by plague.

Attlee, Clement Richard, 1st Earl (1883–1967); British statesman, leader of Labour Party 1935–51, deputy prime minister during World War II and prime minister 1945–51.

Auden, Wystan Hugh (1907–73); British-American poet; emigrated to US in 1939, returned to England shortly before death; poems, plays, essays; Pulitzer prizewinner. Wrote with ardent moral passion.

Audubon, John James (1785–1851); French-American ornithologist, completed large and beautiful collection of paintings of natural history studies. Initiated studies of bird migrations.

Augustine, St. (354–430); Numidian theologian, Bishop of Hippo in N. Africa (396–430). Author of *Confessions* (autobiography) and *City of God*, statement of idealism in Christian doctrine.

Augustine, St (d. 604); Italian-born Christian missionary to the English, 596, who baptized Ethelbert, King of Kent and became the first archbishop of Canterbury.

Augustus (63 BC–AD 14); First Roman emperor, named Gaius Octavianus (Octavian), great-nephew and heir of JULIUS CAESAR. Master of Roman Empire from 30 BC; Senate voted him Augustus – exalted – 27 BC; finally consul for life. Made Rome strong after century of civil war.

Austen, Jane (1775–1817); English novelist. In spite of completely uneventful life, produced six great novels: *Sense and Sensibility*, *Pride and Prejudice*, *Mansfield Park*, *Emma*, *Northanger Abbey*, and *Persuasion*, published (1811–18).

Avogadro, Amedeo (1776–1856); Italian physicist, first propounded hypothesis that equal volumes of different gases contain equal numbers of particles.

Baade, Walter (1893–1960); German-American astronomer, calculated size and distance of Andromeda galaxy.

Babbage, Charles (1792–1871); English mathematician, inventor of earliest computer, a mechanical one.

Baber (1483–1530); Descendant of GENGHIS KHAN, ruler of Kabul, Afghanistan, at 21; invaded India 1525–27 and set up Mughal (Mongol) Empire.

Bach, Johann Sebastian (1685–1750); German composer and organist, most famous of renowned Bach family and one of world's greatest musicians. Wrote 3 passions (including *St. Matthew Passion*), 5 masses, over 200 church cantatas, 29 concerti, 48 preludes and fugues.

Bacon, Francis, Baron Verulam of Verulam, Viscount St. Albans (1561–1626); English statesman (MP) and philosopher, wrote *Advancement of Learning*. Stressed importance of experiment and scientific induction to further understanding of nature. Thought by some to have written plays attributed to SHAKESPEARE.

Bacon, Roger (1220–*c*.1292); English scholar with ideas far in advance of his time. Believed Earth round; pointed out defects of Julian calendar; constructed magnifying glasses; believed in experimentation and mathematics as essentials to scientific advance.

Baden-Powell, Lord (Robert Stephenson Smyth Baden-Powell; 1857–1941); British soldier; defended Mafeking in Boer War; founded Boy Scout movement, 1980.

Baer, Karl Ernst von (1792–1896); Estonian embryologist, founded study of embryology and

Left: Johann Sebastian Bach, the greatest of a large and distinguished family of German musicians.
Right: In 1963 fame came to the pop group called The Beatles, when they were voted No. 1 in both Britain and the United States. Between 1962 and 1970, 30 of their songs topped disc sales of one million.

proposed theory of germ layer formation. Believed animal relationships to be shown by their embryos; not in favour of Darwinism.

Baffin, William (1584–1622); English navigator who in seeking the North-West Passage discovered Baffin Bay and reached a northernmost latitude of 77°45″.

Baker, Sir Samuel (1821–1893); English explorer who journeyed up the Nile River and discovered Lake Albert, 1864.

Bakst, Leon Nikolaevich (Leon Rosenberg, 1866 – 1924); Russian painter who designed sets for DIAGHILEV's ballets.

Bakunin, Mikhail (1814–76); Russian anarchist and revolutionary, who collaborated for a time with MARX and ENGELS and promoted the Nihilist creed.

Balboa, Vasco Núñez de (*c.*1475–1517); Spanish conquistador, first European to see Pacific Ocean, 1513. Executed on trumped-up charge of treason.

Baldwin, Stanley, 1st Earl Baldwin of Bewdley (1866–1947); British statesman, Conservative prime minister 1923–24, 1924–29, 1935–37.

Balfour, Arthur James, 1st Earl of Balfour (1848–1930); British statesman, Conservative prime minister 1902–05, foreign secretary 1916–19. Remembered for his declaration that Britain favoured a Palestinian national home for Jews.

Balzac, Honoré de (1799–1850); French author; major work a series of novels under the title *La Comédie Humaine*; also *Les Chouans* (1829); short stories; plays.

Banting, Sir Frederick Grant (1891–1941); Canadian physiologist; 1923 Nobel prize, with John Macleod, for isolation of insulin for treatment of diabetes.

Barbirolli, Sir John (1899–1970); English conductor and cellist, resident conductor Hallé Orchestra 1943–68.

Barnard, Christiaan Neethling (b. 1922); South African surgeon, performed first successful heart transplant.

Barnum, Phineas Taylor (1810–91); American showman who in 1871 opened the Greatest Show on Earth. In 1881 he joined forces with James A Bailey to form Barnum and Bailey's Circus.

Barrie, Sir James Matthew (1860–1937); Scottish novelist and dramatist. Works include *The Admirable Crichton* (1902), *Peter Pan* (1904), and *Dear Brutus* (1917).

Barrymore, Maurice (1847–1905); American actor

and father of Lionel (1878–1954), Ethel (1879–1959) and John (1882–1942), who formed one of the most celebrated theatrical families.

Bartók, Béla (1881–1945); Hungarian composer and violinist, strongly influenced by Hungarian folk music. Original compositions sounded too modern for most of contemporaries. Wrote opera *Bluebeard's Castle*, mime play *The Miraculous Mandarin*, and piano and violin concertos.

Bateson, William (1861–1926); English biologist who supported the ideas of MENDEL and was one of the pioneers of modern genetics.

Baudelaire, Charles (1821–67); French poet, regarded in his day as decadent; drug addict; *Les Fleurs du Mal* (1857) condemned as immoral in court.

Beadle, George Wells (1903–1989); American geneticist, shared 1958 Nobel prize for discovery of how genes work.

Beale, Dorothea (1831–1906); English educator, principal of Cheltenham Ladies' College, (1858–1906) and a champion of education for girls.

Beardsley, Aubrey Vincent (1872–98); English artist and book illustrator, known for his work on the *Yellow Book* and other books of the Aesthetic movement.

Beatles, The Britain's most successful pop group; their new style of singing and playing swept world of popular music in 1960s: **John Lennon** (1940–80), **Paul McCartney** (b. 1942), **George Harrison** (b. 1943), **Ringo Starr** (b. 1940).

Becket See THOMAS À BECKET.

Beckett, Samuel (1906–1989); Irish author, writing in French and living in France; play *Waiting for Godot* (1952); novels *Molloy* (1951), *Malone Dies* (1951), *The Unnamable* (1953); Nobel prize 1969.

Becquerel, Antoine Henri (1852–1908); French physicist, shared 1903 Nobel prize with CURIES for discovery of natural radioactivity.

Bede, the Venerable (673–735); English monk, scholar, and historian. Wrote *History of the English Church and People*, important source work later translated into Old English by ALFRED THE GREAT; many other works.

Beecham, Sir Thomas (1879–1961); English conductor, founded Royal Philharmonic Orchestra. Fervent admirer of Richard Strauss and Delius.

Beerbohm, Sir Henry Maximillian (Max) (1872–1956); English writer, caricaturist, and wit. Only novel, *Zuleika Dobson* (1911), satirical tale of Oxford undergraduate.

285

Beethoven, Ludwig van (1770–1827); German composer whose musical genius, especially in his 9 symphonies, has never been surpassed. Also wrote an opera, 2 masses, 16 string quartets, many songs and piano solos, and much orchestral music. In spite of increasing deafness, later works embody some of his most advanced ideas.

Belisarius (?505–565); Illyrian soldier who became a general of the Roman Empire, under Justinian I, and defended Italy against barbarian invaders.

Bell, Alexander Graham (1847–1922); Scottish-American inventor of telephone.

Bellini, Giovanni (c.1430–1516); Venetian artist, profoundly influenced classical painting; pupils included TINTORETTO, TITIAN, Giorgione. Many altar-pieces and Madonnas noted for composition and original colouring.

Belloc, Hilaire (Joseph Hilary Pierre Belloc, 1870–1953); British writer of essays, verse, novels, biography and criticism.

Ben-Gurion, David (1886–1973); Polish Jew, became leading Zionist in 1919; first prime minister of Israel, 1948–1953, 1961–63; guided country through early days of war, 1948–49.

Bennett, Enoch Arnold (1867–1931); English novelist, much of his work dealing with life in the Potteries; *Anna of the Five Towns*, etc.

Bentham, Jeremy (1748–1832); English philosopher and legal theorist, exponent of utilitarianism; *Principles of Morals and Legislation* (1789).

Benton, Thomas Hart (1889–1975); American painter, notably of life in the Middle West farm lands.

Bering, Vitus (1680–1741); Danish navigator exploring on behalf of the Russian Tsar, after whom the Bering Sea and Strait are named.

Berkeley, George (1685–1753); Irish philosopher, who claimed that material things exist only in as much as they are perceived to do so.

Berlin, Irving (1888–1989); American composer of popular songs and musicals, born Israel Baline, in Russia. Hits include *Alexander's Ragtime Band*, *I'm Dreaming of a White Christmas*, musical *Call Me Madam*.

Bernadotte, Count Folke (1895–1948); Swedish diplomat, nephew of Gustavus V; mediator in both world wars; assassinated while negotiating cease-fire in Israel, 1948, on behalf of UN.

Bernard, Claude (1813–78); French physiologist, discovered that main part of digestion occurs in small intestine; that body temperature controlled by dilation and constriction of blood vessels; that red blood corpuscles carry oxygen.

Bernhardt, Sarah (Henriette Rosine Bernard; 1844–1923); French actress; tragic roles, particularly Phèdre, earned her title Divine Sarah; continued on stage after leg amputation 1915; silent films.

Bernini, Giovanni Lorenzo (1598–1680); Italian baroque sculptor, architect, and painter, worked mainly in Vatican. Trevi Fountain; sculptures *Apollo and Daphne, David*.

Bernoulli Family of Swiss mathematicians: **Jacques Bernoulli** (1654–1705) worked on finite series, calculus, trigonometry, and theory of probability (invented Bernoulli numbers); **Jean Bernoulli** (1667–1748), Jacques' brother, worked on calculus and complex numbers; **Daniel Bernoulli** (1700–82), Jean's son, developed science of hydrodynamics

and stated Bernoulli's principle (higher the velocity of fluid, lower its pressure); worked on differential equations, trigonometry, calculus, and probability.

Bernstein Leonard (1918–1990); American conductor, composer, and pianist, became first American musical director of New York Philharmonic Orchestra; wrote score for musical *West Side Story*.

Berzelius, Jöns Jakob (1779–1848); Swedish chemist, originated modern system of chemical symbols and formulae. Responsible for discovery of cerium, selenium, and thorium, and for isolating calcium, silicon, and tantalum.

Bessel, Friedrich Wilhelm (1784–1846); German astronomer, in 1838 first determined distance of a star (61 Cygni) by parallax measurement.

Bismarck, Prince Otto von (1815–98); Prussian statesman, prime minister from 1862. By diplomacy created united German Reich, 1871; German chancellor, 1871–90; dismissed by Wilhelm II; known as Iron Chancellor.

Bizet, Georges (1838–75); French composer, mainly remembered for opera *Carmen*; also wrote other operas and incidental music to *l'Arlesienne*.

Björnson, Björnsterne (1832–1910); Norwegian writer; also editor and theatre director; novels include *Arne* (1859), *In God's Way* (1889); plays *Geography and Love* (1885); Nobel prize 1903.

Black, Joseph (1728–99); Scottish chemist, showed carbon dioxide could be formed by decomposition of calcium carbonate and is component of air. Discovered latent heats of melting and evaporation, and specific heats of substances.

Top left: Ludwig van Beethoven's life as a composer was overshadowed by increasing deafness. Left: Sarah Bernhardt, the brilliant but temperamental French actress. Above: Tycho Brahe, the Danish astronomer, in his observatory.

Blackbeard (Edward Teach; d. 1718); British pirate; terrorized American shipping; killed after battle with two naval sloops from Virginia.

Blackstone, Sir William (1723–80); English judge, famous for *Commentaries on the Laws of England* (1765–69), influential legal work.

Blake, William (1757–1827); English poet, engraver, painter, and mystic. His faith in spirit of love pervades his works, which include *Songs of Innocence* (1789), *The Marriage of Heaven and Hell* (1790), and *Songs of Experience* (1794).

Blériot, Louis (1872–1936); French aviator, made first aeroplane flight across English Channel, 1909, winning £10,000.

Blücher, Gebhard Leberecht von, Marshal (1742–1819); Prussian military commander who fought against Napoleon and assisted Wellington at the victory of Waterloo, 1815.

Boabdil (?–c.1533); Last Moorish ruler in Europe, also known as Abu-Abdullah, called El Chico (the little), ruled as Muhammad XI, king of Granada (1482–83, 1486–92), driven out by Ferdinand and Isabella.

Boadicea (Boudicca; d. AD 62); Queen of Iceni tribe of Britons, led rebellion against Romans; defeated and took poison.

Boccaccio, Giovanni (1313–75); Italian writer of prose, famous for his collection of stories, the *Decameron* (1353).

Bohr, Niels (1885–1962); Danish physicist, won 1922 Nobel prize for work on atomic structure. His basic theory of atom suggested shell orbital structure and attributed radiation of energy to electrons jumping from orbit to orbit.

Bolivar, Simón (1783–1830); South American patriot, b. Venezuela. With rebel army liberated Bolivia, Colombia, Ecuador, Peru, Venezuela from Spanish rule; president of Colombia 1819–30; known as El Libertador, the Liberator.

Bonaparte Family name of NAPOLEON I and brothers **Joseph** (1768–1844), King of Naples and later of Spain; **Louis** (1778–1846), King of Holland; **Jerome** (1784–1860), King of Westphalia. Also of Napoleon III, Louis's son.

Boone, Daniel (1734–1820); American frontiersman who explored Kentucky, Virginia and Missouri, guiding settlers and founding forts.

Booth, William (1829–1912); English religious leader and evangelist, founded Christian Mission (1865), renamed Salvation Army (1878); known as General Booth.

Borgia Spanish-Italian noble family: **Alfonso** (1378–1458), pope as Callistus III from 1455; nephew **Rodrigo** (c.1431–1503), pope as Alexander VI from 1492; Alexander's children: **Cesare** (c.1475–1507), tried to conquer kingdom in central Italy; failed; killed in battle; **Lucrezia** (1480–1519), renowned for beauty; patroness of the arts.

Borodin, Alexander Porfirevich (1833–87); Russian composer and professor of chemistry, one of nationalist group known as The Five. Remembered mainly for opera *Prince Igor*, symphonic poem *In the Steppes of Central Asia*, and *B Minor Symphony*.

Boswell, James (1740–95); Scottish writer, biographer, and libertine. Under pseudonym The Hypochondriak wrote for *London Magazine*. Books include *Journal of a Tour to the Hebrides* (1785), *Life of Samuel Johnson* (1791), and *Boswell's London Journal* (pub. 1950).

Botticelli, Sandro (Alessandro dei Filipepi; c.1444–1510); Italian painter; delicate colouring seen at best in mythological pictures, e.g. *The Birth of Venus*.

Bougainville, Louis Antoine de (1729–1811); French navigator who circumnavigated the world, 1766–69, explored the Pacific and also took part in the American Revolution.

Boult, Sir Adrian Cedric (1889–1983); English conductor, formed BBC Symphony Orchestra, conducting it 1930–49. Until 1957, principal conductor London Philharmonic Orchestra. Knighted 1937.

Bourbon Name of royal house of France 1589–1792, 1814–48. First Bourbon king HENRY IV, followed by LOUIS XIII, LOUIS XIV, LOUIS XV, LOUIS XVI, LOUIS XVIII, CHARLES X, LOUIS PHILIPPE.

Boyle, Robert (1627–91); Irish-born scientist, noted for work on compression and expansion of gases, and Boyle's Law. Invented compressed air pump. Pioneer of fresh attitude to scientific methods.

Bragg English physicists, father and son. **Sir William Henry Bragg** (1862–1942) measured distance travelled by alpha particles; 1915 Nobel prize, with son **William Laurence Bragg** (1890–1971), for work on X-ray wavelengths and crystal structure.

Brahe, Tycho (1546–1601); Danish astronomer, rejected Copernican system and corrected values of basic astronomical tables; observations provided basis for much of his assistant KEPLER's later work.

Brahms, Johannes (1833–97); German composer and pianist, leading Romantic-Classical symphony composer of his time. Wrote more than 2000 songs, 4 symphonies, piano and violin concertos, much choral and orchestral music. Close friend of SCHUMANN; also helped by Joachim and LISZT.

Brandt, Willy (1913–92); German politician; mayor of West Berlin, 1957–66; chancellor of West Germany, 1969–74; resigned following spy scandal.

Braque, Georges (1882–1963); French painter, leading Fauvist; with PICASSO, founder of Cubism; specialized in still lifes.

Braun, Wernher Magnus Maximillian von (1912–1977); German rocket engineer, built first true missile, V-2 rocket, in 1942. Went to US after war and led group that put America's first satellite in orbit.

Breakspear, Nicholas (?1100–59); Only Englishman to become Pope (1154–59).

Breasted, James Henry (1865–1935); American historian and archaeologist, leading authority on history of Near East and Egypt. Founded Oriental Institute of University of Chicago. Books include *The Conquest of Civilization* (1926).

Brecht, Berthold (1898–1956); German writer and theatre producer; in US during Nazi period; plays include *The Threepenny Opera* (1928), *The Caucasian Chalk Circle* (1948).

Brezhnev, Leonid Ilyich (1906–1982); Soviet Comunist leader; president of USSR, 1960–64; First Secretary of Communist party from 1964.

Britten, Benjamin (1913–1976); British composer, gift for marrying words and music; operas include *Peter Grimes* and *Billy Budd*; symphonic work *The Young Person's Guide to the Orchestra*.

Bromfield, Louis (1896–1956); American novelist; in France during 1920s, settled as farmer in Ohio, 1933; novels include *Early Autumn* (1926), *The Strange Case of Miss Annie Spragg* (1928), *The Rains Came* (1937), *Mrs Parkington* (1943).

Brontë Three English novelists and poets, sisters: **Charlotte** (Currer Bell; 1816–55) wrote *Jane Eyre*; **Emily** (Ellis Bell; 1818–48) wrote *Wuthering Heights*; **Anne** (Acton Bell; 1820–49) wrote *The Tenant of Wildfell Hall*. Together they produced a book of poems under their pseudonyms.

Brooke, Rupert (1887–1915); English poet; died serving in World War I; *1914 and Other Poems* (1915).

Browning English poets, husband and wife. **Elizabeth Barrett** (1806–61), was an invalid from age of 15; *Sonnets from the Portuguese* (1850); recovered health after marriage to **Robert** (1812–89); travelled widely; dramas including *Pippa Passes*; many poems, long and short; *The Ring and the Book* (1869), his masterpiece.

Brueghel, Pieter (c.1525–69); Flemish painter, specialized in Flemish landscapes and peasant scenes in bright colours; *The Peasant Wedding*. Sons **Pieter the Younger**, **Jan the Elder**, and Jan's sons also painters.

Brunel, Sir Marc Isambard (1769–1849) and **Isambard Kingdom** (1806–59); Engineers. M I Brunel was French, but worked mostly in Britain, building the Thames Tunnel, 1825–43; his son I K Brunel built railways, bridges, tunnels and steamships, notably the *Great Western*, *Great Britain* and *Great Eastern*.

Buchan, John, 1st Baron Tweedsmuir (1875–1940); Scottish author and statesman, governor-general of Canada. Wrote adventure stories and thrillers, including *Prester John* (1910), *The Thirty-nine Steps* (1915), and *Greenmantle* (1916).

Buchman, Frank Nathan Daniel (1878–1961); American evangelist, founded Oxford Group (1921), leading to Moral Rearmament movement (MRA) in 1930s. Adherents pledged to absolute honesty, purity, unselfishness, and love.

Buddha (Siddhartha Gautama; c.563–c.483 BC); Founder of Buddhism, well-born Indian who renounced worldly pleasures and sat under bodhi tree until mysteries of life were unfolded to him. *Buddha* title meaning *The Enlightened One*.

Buffalo Bill (William Frederick Cody; 1846–1917); American scout for Kansas cavalary; buffalo hunter; showman from 1872.

Bunche, Ralph Johnson (1904–71); American Negro statesman; negotiated armistice between Israel and Arab neighbours, 1949; Nobel peace prize, 1950.

Bunsen, Robert Wilhelm (1811–99); German chemist, inventor of gas burner with intense flame for laboratory use.

Bunyan, John (1628–88); English non-conformist preacher; author of *Pilgrim's Progress*, an exciting moral allegory. Imprisoned several times for outspoken preaching.

Burke, Edmund (1729–97); Irish-born British statesman, orator, writer; criticized French Revolution; supported American colonists; led attack on WARREN HASTINGS; MP 1765–97.

Burke, Robert O'Hara (1821–61); Irish-Australian explorer, led first expedition to cross Australia south to north (1860–61). Let down by support party, he died on way back.

Burney, Fanny (1752–1840); English writer and diarist, married French general d'Arblay and lived some years in Paris.

Burns, Robert (1759–96); Scottish poet; farmer, later exciseman; national poet of Scotland; many dialect poems and songs including *Auld Lang Syne*, *Holy Willie's Prayer*, *The Cotter's Saturday Night*, *To a Mouse*.

Burton, Sir Richard (1821–90); Eccentric British traveller, explored Arabia and Africa, and with John Speke discovered Lake Tanganyika. Wrote more than 50 books.

Bush, George Herbert Walker (b. 1924); A Republican from Massachusetts, 41st president of the USA 1989–1992; his term in office saw the end of the cold war with the Soviet Union.

Butler, Samuel (1612–80); English satirist; poem *Hudibras*, burlesque satire on puritanism, found great favour with Charles II.

Butler, Samuel (1835–1902); English author, painter, and musician, started working life as sheepfarmer in New Zealand, setting for satirical romance *Erewhon* (1872); works of scientific controversy against Darwinism.

Byrd, Richard Evelyn (1888–1957); American naval airman, made the first flights over both North and South poles. Led expeditions to Antarctica in 1928, 1933–35, and 1939–41. Commanded 4000-strong party in 1946–47, mapping coast.

Byron, Lord (George Gordon Byron; 1788–1824); English romantic poet; born lame; left England 1816; went to help Greeks rebel against Turks, but died in Greece; poems include *Childe Harold's Pilgrimage* (1812), *The Giaour* (1813), *Manfred*, *Don Juan*.

Cabot, John (*c*.1450–*c*.1499); Italian navigator, discovered mainland of North America on behalf of Henry VII of England, in 1497.

Caesar, (Gaius) Julius (100–44 BC); Roman statesman and general, joined with Crassius and Pompey in First Triumvirate to rule Rome, 60 BC; conquered Gaul and invaded Britain. Ordered by Senate to disband army, crossed River Rubicon and invaded Italy; dictator from 49 BC; assassinated by political rivals who feared his power. Orator and writer; masterly accounts of Gallic wars and civil war.

Calamity Jane (Martha Jane Canary; *c*.1852–1903); American frontierswoman and expert marksman; lived in mining camps and at Deadwood, S Dakota. Married name, Burke.

Calderon de la Barca, Pedro (1600–81); Spanish dramatist and poet, soldier and priest, author of over 200 works.

Caligula (Gaius Julius Caesar Germanicus; AD 12–41); Succeeded great-uncle Tiberius as Roman emperor, 37. Became mentally ill and ruled cruelly. Nickname Caligula means little boots, a childhood name, Murdered by own guard.

Callas, Maria (1923–1977); Greek-born American coloratura soprano; thrilling voice and fine acting made her leading prima donna of 1950s and 1960s.

Calvin, John (1509–64); French religious leader and theologian, a pioneer of Reformation. Established centre for preaching of his austere brand of Protestantism in Geneva. Doctrine of predestination and rejection of papal authority set forth in *Institutes of the Christian Religion*.

Camoes, (Camoens) Luiz Vaz de (1524–80); National poet of Portugal, author of *Os Lusiadas*, an epic poem about Portuguese history.

Camus, Albert (1913–60); Algerian-born French dramatist, novelist, philosopher; in French Resistance World War II; plays *Caligula* (1938), *Le Malentendu* (1945); novels *L'Etranger* (1942), *La Peste* (1947), *La Chute* (1956); Nobel prize 1957. Killed in car accident.

Canaletto, Antonio (1697–1768); Italian (Venetian) painter, known primarily for his views of Venice (particularly canals), In England mid-1700s, painting views of Thames and Richmond, Surrey.

Canning, George (1770–1827); British statesman and orator, supporter of PITT, foreign secretary twice, prime minister in 1827, fought duel with CASTLEREAGH. Promoted British support of liberal movements abroad.

Canute (Cnut; *c*.994–1035); Son of Sweyn Forkbeard of Denmark. King of England from 1016; of Denmark 1018; of Norway 1028. Married Emma, widow of Saxon king Ethelred II. Restored order to England.

Čapek, Karel (1890–1938); Czech author and journalist; plays include *R.U.R.* (*Rossum's Universal Robots*, 1920), *The Insect Play* (with brother Josef, 1921), *The Makropoulos Secret* (1922); novels; short stories.

Carlyle, Thomas (1795–1881); Scottish author of

The French Revolution (1837). Translated German literature. Attacked corruptions of modern society and exerted much influence on religious, political, and ethical beliefs of time.

Carnegie, Andrew (1835–1919); Scottish-born American philanthropist, made fortune in steel; gave millions of dollars to schools, universities, and for public libraries.

Carnot, Nicolas Léonard Sadi (1796–1832); French physicist, calculated how to obtain maximum efficiency from steam engine. Founded study of thermodynamics.

Carroll, Lewis (Charles Lutwidge Dodgson; 1832–98); English writer for children, and mathematician. Wrote *Alice's Adventures in Wonderland* (1865) and *Through the Looking Glass* (1872); also *Euclid and his Modern Rivals* (1879).

Carter, James Earl (b. 1924); A Democrat peanut farmer from Georgia and former governor of that state, he was USA's 39th president 1977–81.

Cartier, Jacques (1491–1557); French explorer of North America; sailed up St. Lawrence River to site of present-day Montreal.

Cartier-Bresson, Henri (b. 1908); French photographer of outstanding international events, turned photographic reportage into work of art.

Caruso, Enrico (1873–1921); Italian operatic tenor, the leading singer of his day.

Casals, Pablo (1876–1973); Spanish master cellist and conductor, renowned for playing of Bach's unaccompanied cello suites. Lived in voluntary exile in Puerto Rico when Franco came to power.

Casanova, Giovanni Jacopo (1725–98); Italian adventurer and traveller, living by his wits and for his amatory escapades, about which he wrote.

Cassini, Giovanni Domenico (1625–1714); French-Italian astronomer who discovered four of Saturn's moons and the gap in the outer and middle rings (the Cassini division).

Castlereagh, Robert Stewart, Viscount (1769–1822); British statesman, rival of CANNING, and foreign secretary 1812–22. Committed suicide as a result of stress and overwork.

Castro, Fidel (b. 1927); Cuban Marxist, overthrew President Batista, 1959, and became prime minister.

Catherine II, the Great (1729–96); Deposed her mad husband, Tsar Peter III of Russia, and became empress (1762). Strengthened power of nobility; captured Crimea, Black Sea coast, and much of Poland.

Catullus, Gaius Valerius (*c*.84–*c*.54 BC); Roman lyrical poet; bitterly attacked JULIUS CAESAR; wrote many epigrams.

Cavell, Edith (1865–1915); English nurse in Brussels in World War I; shot by Germans for helping Allied soldiers to escape.

Cavendish, Henry (1731–1810); English scientist, experimented with hydrogen, water, and air. Calculated mass and density of Earth using lead balls and Newton's Law of gravitation. Eccentric and secretive.

Caxton, William (1422–91); First English printer, set up press at Westminster (1476).

Cellini, Benvenuto (1500–71); Florentine sculptor and goldsmith; largest surviving sculpture *Nymph of Fontainebleau*, in Louvre. Sensational autobiography.

Celsius, Anders (1701–44); Swedish astronomer, the first to describe the centigrade thermometer scale, 1742.

Cervantes (Saavedra), Miguel de (1547–1616); Spanish writer; fought at Lepanto, 1571; prisoner of Turks, 1575–80; many plays; eloquent short poems; novel *Don Quixote* (1605–15), and many others.

Cetewayo (1834–84); Zulu chief who rebelled against British rule; but was captured and exiled to England.

Cézanne, Paul (1839–1906); French painter, greatly influenced Impressionists; used pure colour and distorted perspectives to achieve certain effects. Painted portraits, landscapes, still lifes; *Bathers*.

Chadwick, Sir James (1891–1974); English physicist; 1955 Nobel prize for discovery of neutron.

Chaghall, Marc (1887–1985); Russian painter, first Surrealist. Left Russia after 1917 to work mainly in Europe and US. Russian Jewish influence evident in book illustrations, stage sets, mosaics, tapestries, and glass designs.

Chain, Ernst Boris (1906–79); German-English biochemist, shared 1945 Nobel prize with FLEMING and FLOREY for work on penicillin.

Chamberlain Family of British politicians: **Joseph** (1836–1914), Liberal; colonial secretary. **Sir Austen** (1863–1937), elder son of Joseph; Conservative; foreign secretary, 1924–29; Nobel peace prize. **Neville** (1869–1940), second son of Joseph; Conservative; prime minister 1937–40; followed appeasement policy towards Nazis at Munich, 1938; forced to resign, 1940.

Chaplin, Sir Charles Spencer (Charlie) (1889–1977); English/American film star, director, and producer. Role as baggy-trousered little tramp of silent screen endeared him to millions. Starred in *The Gold Rush*, *City Lights*, *Modern Times*, etc.

Charlemagne (Charles the Great; 742–814); King of Franks from 771, extended territory into Germany and Italy. Crowned Emperor of the West in Rome by Pope Leo III, 800; great patron of learning and subject of many legends.

Charles I (1600–49); King of England and Scotland, kept short of money by Parliament, tried to rule without it. Parliament revolted against unjust taxation, and in Civil War (1642–45) defeated Charles. Executed after trial on charge of treason.

Charles V (1500–58); Holy Roman Emperor from 1519; king of Spain as Charles I from 1516. Ruled over more of Europe than any other HABSBURG. Abdicated 1554.

Charles XII (1682–1718); King of Sweden from 1697. Brilliant general; led armies to victory in Northern Wars of 1700–21; but defeated by Russians at Poltava, 1709; killed in battle.

Charles, Prince (Full name Charles Philip Arthur George; b. 1948); Eldest son and heir of Queen ELIZABETH II; Duke of Cornwall; created Prince of Wales 1958; invested at Caernarvon 1969; served in Royal Navy; married Lady Diana Spencer 1981.

Charles Martel (c.688–741); The Hammer, Frankish ruler of Austrasia (715–41), halted Muslim advance into western Europe at Battle of Tours (732).

Chateaubriand, François René de, Vicomte (1768–1848); French author and diplomat. Went to America 1791 to escape Revolution, wrote about American Indians.

Chatham, Earl of (William Pitt the Elder, 1708–78); British statesman. As war minister, organized victory in Seven Years War. Supported American colonies in struggle for freedom.

Chaucer, Geoffrey (c.1340–1400); English poet, merchant, and diplomat. Translated part of *Le Roman de la Rose*, wrote *The Parlement of Foules*, *Troilus and Criseyde*, and *Canterbury Tales*. Buried in Westminster Abbey – first occupant of Poet's Corner.

Chekhov, Anton Pavlovich (1860–1904); Russian writer and physician; plays *The Seagull* (1896), *Uncle Vanya* (1897), *The Cherry Orchard* (1904); short stories.

Chesterton, Gilbert Keith (1874–1936); British writer; poet, novelist and critic among whose works are the detective stories featuring the priest Father Brown.

Chiang Kai-shek (1887–1975); Chinese statesman and general, succeeded SUN YAT-SEN as leader of Kuomintang (Nationalist) party, 1928; commander-in-chief from 1932. President 1943. Ejected from China by Communists, 1949; established government in Taiwan (Formosa).

Chippendale, Thomas (1718–79); English furniture-maker, used dark mahogany without inlays; often embodied Chinese designs in Queen Anne and Georgian styles.

Chopin, Frédéric François (1810–49); Polish composer and pianist, settled in France, and for a time lived with novelist GEORGE SAND. Wrote studies, mazurkas, polonaises, and nocturnes, almost wholly for solo piano.

Chou En-lai (Zhou Enlai; 1898–1976); Chinese Communist statesman, active in Red Army from 1931; prime minister from 1949.

Christ See JESUS CHRIST.

Christie, Agatha Mary Clarissa (1891–1976); English detective-story writer, created Belgian detective Hercule Poirot. Plays include *Witness for the Prosecution* and record-breaking *The Mousetrap*.

Churchill, Sir Winston Leonard Spencer (1874–1965); British soldier, statesman, author, First Lord of Admiralty, 1911–15; Chancellor of Exchequer, 1924–29; First Lord of Admiralty, 1939–40; prime minister, 1940–45, and 1950–55; led Britain through World War II. Nobel prize for literature, 1953.

Cicero, Marcus Tullius (106–43 BC); Roman statesman, philosopher; tried to preserve the Republic; supported murder of JULIUS CAESAR; killed on orders from Octavian (AUGUSTUS).

Clark, William (1770–1838); American explorer who with LEWIS crossed the continent overland, 1804–06.

Claudius I (Tiberius Claudius Drusus Nero Germanicus, 10 BC–54 AD); Roman emperor who succeeded Caligula in 41 AD, sent an army to Britain, and was poisoned by his niece Agrippina.

Clausewitz, Karl von (1780–1831); Prussian general; books on art of war.

Clemenceau, Georges (1841–1929); French statesman; premier 1906–09, 1917–20; headed Versailles Peace Conference; nicknamed Tiger because of his toughness.

Cleopatra VII (69–30 BC); Macedonian queen of

Egypt, joint ruler with brother, Ptolemy XII, in 51 BC; with Ptolemy XIII from 48 BC. Mistress of JULIUS CAESAR, 49–44 BC; of MARK ANTONY from 41 BC. Murdered Ptolemy XIII 44 BC. Committed suicide after defeat by Octavian (AUGUSTUS).

Clinton, William Jefferson (b. 1946); 42nd president of the USA, inaugurated in 1993. A Democrat from Arkansas, he was the first member of his party to be elected president since 1976.

Clive, Robert (1725–74); British soldier. Victory at Plassey (1757) gave British control of India; governor of Bengal, 1764–67; censored for misgovernment; committed suicide. Created baron, 1762.

Cobden, Richard (1804–65); English statesman and economist who advocated free trade and minimal government intervention.

Cockcroft, Sir John Douglas (1897–1967); English physicist; 1951 Nobel prize for devising voltage-multiplier for accelerating protons.

Cocteau, Jean (1889–1963); French dramatist, poet, critic, and film director; pioneered many literary and artistic (Cubism, surrealism) experiments, created ballets and mimes for DIAGHILEV. Wrote *Les Parents Terribles* (play 1938, film 1948), *Les Enfants Terribles* (novel 1930, film 1950).

Coleridge, Samuel Taylor (1772–1834); English poet and critic, author of *The Rime of the Ancient Mariner* (1798), *Christabel* (1816), and *Kubla Khan* (1816).

Colet, John (1467 –1519); English scholar and churchman, influenced by ERASMUS, founder of St. Paul's School, first lay school in England.

Colette (Sidonie-Gabrielle Colette; 1873–1954); French author, one-time dancer; books include *Cheri* (1920), *Gigi* (1944).

Collins, Michael (1890–1922); Irish revolutionary who took part in the Easter Rising, 1916, became a leader of Sinn Fein and died during the civil war.

Columbus, Christopher (1451–1506); Genoese navigator, discovered New World 1492 while seeking westward route to Indies. Voyages were sponsored by Spain. Made four trips to West, but never realized he had found a new continent.

Compton, Arthur Holly (1892–1962); American physicist, shared 1927 Nobel physics prize with Charles Wilson for discovery of Compton effect, which led to idea of dual wave-particle nature of light. Research on nature of cosmic rays.

Confucius (c.551 479 BC); Chinese philosopher and reformer, his name being Latinized form of K'ung Fu-tzu. In his *Analects* (collected sayings) he outlined man's duty to his fellow man in terms of absolute justice and moderation. Confucianism has influenced Chinese thinking more deeply than any other doctrine.

Congreve, William (1670–1729); English writer of polished comedies; *Love for Love* (1695), *The Way of the World* (1700).

Conrad, Joseph (Teodor Josef Konrad Korzeniowski, 1857–1924); Polish novelist and short-story writer who settled in England and wrote in English after seafaring career. Novels include *Lord Jim* (1900) and *Chance* (1914); short stories: *Youth*, *Typhoon* (1902).

Constable, John (1776–1837); English landscape painter, specialized in Suffolk scenes. Deeply in-

Top: Comedian Charles Chaplin, in his most famous 'little tramp' role.
Above: The Genoese Christopher Columbus, who discovered the New World of the Americas in 1492. To the end of his life, he believed that he had found a westward route to the Spice Islands.

fluenced Delacroix, and foreshadowed Impressionists; *The Hay Wain, Salisbury Cathedral*.

Constantine I, the Great (c.274–337); First Christian Emperor of Rome. Defeated Emperor Maxentius and assumed power in West, 312; defeated Emperor Licinius and took power in East, 324. Founded new capital, Constantinople. Helped spread of Christianity.

Cook, James (1728–79); British navigator, was first person to sail south of Antarctic Circle. Explored Pacific, charting coasts of New Zealand and Australia and visiting many islands. Died in a scuffle in Hawaii.

Copernicus, Nicolas (1473–1543); Polish astronomer, favoured Sun-centred idea of solar system; worked it out in mathematical detail.

Copland, Aaron (1900–1990); American composer; orchestral and chamber music shows distinct traces of jazz. *Appalachian Spring*, popular ballet music.

Corbusier, Le (Charles Edouard Jeanneret; 1887–1965); Swiss architect, applied functionalism to all his designs; defined house as a machine for living in; UN Building (New York), Pavillon Suisse (Paris).

Corday, Charlotte (1768–93); French patriot; killed MARAT because she was horrified at his ruthlessness; guillotined.

Corneille, Pierre (1606–84); French dramatist and poet, regarded as the father of French tragedy.

Corot, Jean Baptiste Camille (1796–1875); French classical landscape painter, early work distinguished by large artificial landscapes for formal exhibition; later work more subtle and natural; also figures and portraits.

Correggio, Antonio Allegri da (*c.*1494–1534); Italian painter, master of illusion by means of foreshortening. Human figures delicately modelled and painted with gentle tones. One of his masterpieces *Assumption of the Virgin*, fresco in Parma Cathedral.

Cortés, Hernando (1485–1547); Greatest Spanish conquistador, conquered Mexico in 1519–21, with force of only 550 men. Ruled as governor until 1530.

Coubertin, Pierre, Baron de (1863–1937); French educator and sportsman who revived the Olympic Games in Greece (1894) and was first president of the International Olympic Committee, 1894–1925.

Cousteau, Jacques-Yves (b. 1910); French oceanographer, inventor of Aqualung. Made underwater films and designed structures for underwater living.

Coverdale, Miles (1488–1568); English translator and Puritan preacher, converted Reformer; edited Great Bible (1539). Appointed Bishop of Exeter under Edward VI; fled to Switzerland when Mary I came to the throne, and worked on Geneva Bible (1557–59). Returned to England on ELIZABETH I's accession.

Coward, Sir Noël (1899–1973); British actor, director, playwright, composer; master of the sparkling dialogue; plays include *Hay Fever* (1925), *Private Lives* (1930); musicals *Bitter Sweet* (1929), *Pacific 1860* (1946); films *In Which We Serve*, *Brief Encounter*; 280 songs; knighted 1970.

Cowper, William (1731–1800); English poet, author of *The Ballad of John Gilpin*, whose work led English poetry away from the artificiality of classicism.

Cranach, Lucas (the Elder) (1472–1553); German artist celebrated for portraits and animal pictures. Designed religious woodcuts for LUTHER.

Cranmer, Thomas (1489–1556); English reformer, archbishop of Canterbury; promoted Reformation in England in reigns of HENRY VIII and Edward VI. Chief author *39 Articles* (1552); *First Prayer Book* (1549), etc. Imprisoned on succession of Roman Catholic Mary I (1553); burned at stake.

Crick, Francis Harry Compton (b. 1916); English biochemist, shared 1962 Nobel prize with WATSON and Wilkins for discovery of structure of DNA molecule.

Crockett, Davy (1786–1836); American scout, soldier, pioneer, politician, and folk hero. Frontiersman; Congressman from Tennessee, 1827–31, 1833–35; killed at Alamo.

Croesus (d. 546 BC); King of Lydia in Asia Minor, renowned for his vast wealth and the subject of many legends.

Cromwell, Oliver (1599–1658); Lord Protector of England 1653–58. Country gentleman; M.P. from 1628; brilliant cavalry general in Civil War. Massacred garrisons of Drogheda and Wexford, Ireland, 1649. Dissolved parliament 1653; made Lord Protector; declined offer of crown.

Crookes, Sir William (1832–1919); English physicist, experimented with radiation and behaviour of objects in vacuum. Invented radiometer and devised improved vacuum tube, Crooke's tube.

Curie Family of scientists: **Pierre Curie** (1859–1906), French chemist, discovered piezoelectric effect in crystals; discovered critical temperature (Curie point) at which metal loses magnetism; married **Marie Sklodowska** (1867–1934), Polish chemist, who coined term *radioactivity*. They discovered polonium and radium, and shared 1903 Nobel physics prize with BECQUEREL for discovery of radioactivity. Marie Curie received 1911 Nobel chemistry prize for isolation of pure radium from

pitchblende. Daughter **Irene Joliot-Curie** (1897–1956) studied atomic structure with husband Frédéric Joliot by bombarding elements with alpha-particles. They shared 1935 Nobel chemistry prize for production of radioisotope of nitrogen.

Curtiss, Glenn Hammond (1878–1930); American aviation pioneer who made first public flight in US (1908) and set up his own aircraft company.

Custer, George Armstrong (1839–76); US army officer, killed by Indians with 225 men at Battle of Little Big Horn (Custer's Last Stand).

Cuvier, Georges Léopold Chrétien Frédéric Dagobert, Baron (1769–1832); French anatomist, founder of comparative anatomy; introduced phyla into classification. Studied fossils and founded palaeontology; believed in catastrophism rather than evolution.

Cyrus (?600–529 BC); King of Persia and founder of the Persian Empire, overthrowing CROESUS and conquering Babylon, freeing the Jews from captivity there.

Da Gama, Vasco (*c.*1460–1524); Portuguese navigator, made first voyage from Europe to India round Cape of Good Hope.

Daguerre, Louis Jacques Mandé (1787–1851); French painter who invented the daguerreotype, a forerunner of the photographic process.

Daimler, Gottlieb Wilhelm (1834–1900); German inventor, first to construct high-speed engine. Built first motorcycle. Founded Daimler motor company.

Dali, Salvador (1904–1989); Spanish surrealist artist; beautifully finished and meticulously detailed works usually expression of irrational dream world and seem designed to shock.

Dalton, John (1766–1844); English chemist, proposed atomic theory and prepared table of atomic weights. This resulted from early studies of gases (Dalton's law of partial pressures).

Dampier, William (1652–1715); English sailor and pirate, who explored the coasts of Australia, New Guinea and New Britain.

D'Annunzio, Gabriele, Prince of Monte Nevoso (1863–1938); Italian writer and patriot; led capture of Fiume (Rijeka), 1919; novel *Il Fuoco* (1900) described his love for actress Eleonora Duse; plays; poems.

Dante Alighieri (1265–1321); Italy's greatest poet; magistrate of Florence 1300; exiled 1302; main work *Divina Commedia* (*Inferno, Purgatorio, Paradiso*); *Vita Nuova*.

stories and novels about life in southern France.

Daumier, Honoré (1808–79); French artist known for his satirical drawings of contemporary politicians and social figures, who died in poverty, his talent unrecognized.

David (d. 962 BC); Second king of Israel, in succession to Saul. In uniting the Israelites and making Jerusalem their capital, he set an ideal of kingship esteemed beyond Judaism.

David ap Gruffud (d. 1283); Last native Prince of Wales, Succeeding his brother Llewellyn as ruler of Gwynedd, he led the last Welsh resistance to English rule.

David, Jacques Louis (1748–1825); French painter, founder of French classical school. Court painter first to LOUIS XVI, then NAPOLEON.

Davies, Emily (1830–1921); British educator and pioneer of women's education and emancipation. Founded Girton College, Cambridge.

Davis, Jefferson (1808–89); American statesman, who was President of the Confederacy during the American Civil War, 1861–65.

Davis, William Morris (1850–1934); American geographer and geologist, father of geomorphology, conceived idea of cycle of erosion of land masses.

Davy, Sir Humphry (1778–1829); English chemist,

Danton, Georges Jacques (1759–94); French lawyer and revolutionary; helped organize Reign of Terror, but was himself guillotined by order of ROBESPIERRE.

Darby, Abraham (?1678–1717); English ironmaster who first smelted iron ore using coke as fuel (instead of charcoal as formerly). His grandson, Abraham, built the world's first iron bridge at Coalbrookdale in Shropshire, 1779.

Dario, Ruben (Felix Ruben Garcia Sarmiento, 1867–1916); Nicaraguan poet, journalist and diplomat whose influence on Spanish literature spread far beyond his native land.

Darnley, Henry Stewart, Lord (1545–67); English second husband of MARY, QUEEN OF SCOTS and father of King James I of England (VI of Scotland). He was murdered, possibly on the orders of the Earl of Bothwell, Mary's third husband.

Darwin, Charles Robert (1809–82); English naturalist, proposed theory of evolution by natural selection in *The Origin of Species* (1859) after nearly 20 years spent building up evidence; caused bitter controversy.

Daudet, Alphonse (1840–97); French writer of short

Above: Sir Humphry Davy, the English chemist and inventor, who is best remembered for his invention of the miners' safety lamp.
Opposite left: Oliver Cromwell, Lord Protector of the Commonwealth of England.
Left: The Italian poet Dante Alighieri; the Tuscan dialect in which he wrote became Italy's standard language.

inventor of miners' (Davy) lamp, and electric arc lamp. Isolated, by electrolysis, potassium, sodium, barium, strontium, and magnesium. Proved chlorine to be an element.

Debussy, Claude Achille (1862–1918); French Impressionist composer; works include orchestral music (*l'Après midi d'un faune*), piano music (*Clair de lune*), opera (*Pelléas et Mélisande*).

Defoe, Daniel (*c.*1660–1731); English author. Involved in Monmouth rebellion. Wrote political pamphlets, and novels including *Robinson Crusoe* (1719) and *Moll Flanders* (1722).

De Forest, Lee (1873–1961); American inventor of triode and tetrode valves.

Degas, (Hilaire Germaine) Edgar (1834–1917); French Impressionist painter and sculptor, concentrated on human figure; free use of colour and composition had strong influence on GAUGUIN and PICASSO.

De Gaulle, Charles (1890–1970); French general and statesman; formed Free French movement after fall of France, 1940; president 1945–46; retired from politics; president with new constitution 1959–69; ended war in Algeria, 1962.

Delacroix, Eugène (1798–1863); French painter of romantic and exotic subjects, inspired by contemporary events.

De la Mare, Walter (1873–1956); English novelist and poet, whose work appeals to adults and children. Wrote *Songs of Childhood* (1902), *Collected Rhymes and Verses* (1944). Anthology *Come Hither* appeared in 1923.

Delius, Frederick (1862–1934); English composer, largely self-taught; impressionistic style owed much to DEBUSSY. Operas, choral works, orchestral music; tone poem *On Hearing the First Cuckoo in Spring*.

Democritus (*c*.470–*c*.380 BC); Greek philosopher, first to propose that matter consisted of tiny indivisible particles.

Demosthenes (*c*.385–322 BC); Athenian orator; in *Philippics*, attacked Philip II of Macedon.

De Quincey, Thomas (1785–1859); English essayist; slave to opium; his *Confessions of an English Opium Eater* (1821) won him fame; work published mostly in magazines.

Descartes, René (1596–1650); French philosopher and mathematician, invented system of plotting curves represented by algebraic equations – analytic geometry.

De Valéra, Eamon (1882–1975); Irish patriot and revolutionary; in Easter Rebellion, 1916, prime minister 1937–48, 1951–54, 1957–59; president 1959–73. Born New York City.

De Vries, Hugo Marie (1848–1935); Dutch botanist, rediscovered and publicized MENDEL's laws of inheritance; proposed theory of mutations, thus completing DARWIN's theory of evolution.

Diaghilev, Sergei Pavlovich (1872–1929); Russian ballet impresario; great talent lay in exploiting to full talent of others. Founded Ballets Russes, 1908; from then many great composers, painters, and dancers contributed to their success.

Dias, Bartolomeu (*c*.1450–1500); Portuguese sailor, first European to round Cape of Good Hope (1487–88).

Dickens, Charles (1812–70); English novelist, most popular of 19th century; his 15 novels include *Pickwick Papers* (1837), *A Christmas Carol* (1843), *David Copperfield* (1850), *A Tale of Two Cities* (1859), *Great Expectations* (1861); at first journalist, then theatrical manager; lecture tour of America, 1867–68.

Dickinson, Emily (1830–86); American poet; led retired life; poems published after her death, 1890–1936.

Diderot, Denis (1713–84); French philosopher, author, and encyclopedist. Chief editor of multi-volume *Encyclopédie*.

Diogenes (d. *c*.320 BC); Greek philosopher of the Cynic school; stoic and austere, he was reputed to have gone in search of an honest man in broad daylight holding a lantern.

Dirac, Paul Adrien Maurice (1902–1984); English physicist; shared 1933 Nobel prize for work on wave mechanics and theory of antiparticles.

Disney, Walt (Walter Elias; 1901–66); American cartoon film maker whose characters Micky Mouse and Donald Duck are known world over; *Snow White and the Seven Dwarfs* (1938) was first ever full length animated cartoon film.

Disraeli, Benjamin, 1st Earl of Beaconsfield (1804–81); British statesman, twice prime minister (Conservative), 1868, 1874–80; bought share in Suez Canal for Britain. Also wrote novels, including *Coningsby* (1844). Made peer 1876.

Dominic, St (Domingo de Guzman; *c*.1170–1221); Spanish priest and scholar who founded a preaching order of mendicant friars.

Donatello (Donato di Niccolò di Betto Bardi; *c*.1386–1466); Italian painter and sculptor; bold, original style brought new dimension to sculpture; *Gattemalata*, famous bronze equestrian statue.

Donizetti, Gaetano (1797–1848); Italian composer of opera, including *Lucia di Lammermoor* and *Don Pasquale*.

Donne, John (*c*.1571–1631); English poet and clergyman; Dean of St. Paul's, 1621; leader of metaphysical school; early work passionate love poems; later work religious; *Divine Poems* (1607), *Holy Sonnets* (1618), *Of the Progress of the Soul* (1633).

Doppler, Christian (1803–53); Austrian astronomer and physicist who predicted the Doppler effect, the apparent change in wavelength when the wave source and the observer are in relative motion.

Dostoyevsky, Fyodor Mikhailovich (1821–81); Army officer, 1841–44; sent to Siberia for conspiracy, 1849–54; founded two reviews; novels include *Crime and Punishment* (1866), *The Idiot* (1869), *The Brothers Karamazov* (1880).

Right: Oliver Twist asks for more – an illustration to one of Charles Dickens's most famous books. Dickens was a crusader against the appalling conditions in which the poor lived.

Far right: Albert Einstein, whose general theory of relativity published in 1929 superseded Newton's gravitational theory.

Dowland, John (1562?–1626); English (possibly Irish) musician, who travelled widely absorbing new influences; many of his compositions are for the lute.

Doyle, Sir Arthur Conan (1859–1930); British doctor and author, b. Edinburgh; knighted for medical services in Boer War, 1902; created Sherlock Holmes; also wrote science fiction, historical romances, and about spiritualism.

Drake, Sir Francis (c.1543–96); English adventurer, plundered Spanish settlements in America. Sailed round world in 1577–80. Burned a Spanish fleet at Cadiz in 1587, and helped to defeat Spanish Armada in 1588. Died in West Indies.

Dreyfus, Alfred (1859–1935); French Jewish officer falsely accused of spying and jailed for life, 1894; acquitted 1906 after two more trials and great scandal.

Dryden, John (1631–1700); English poet and dramatist; poet laureate 1668–88; political satires *Absolom and Achitophel* (1681), *The Medal* (1682); plays *The Indian Emperor* (1665), *Marriage-à-la-Mode* (1673).

Dubček, Alexander (b. 1921); Czech Communist leader whose reforms were suppressed in 1968; restored to power 1990.

Duccio di Buoninsegna (d. 1318?); Italian painter who founded the Sienese school, merging classical Byzantine and religious Gothic styles; greatest achievement is the altarpiece of Siena Cathedral.

Dufy, Raoul (1877–1953); French artist whose bright colours and calligraphic style of drawing make instant appeal to casual glance; much work for book illustration.

Dulles, John Foster (1888–1959); American diplomat, Secretary of State 1953–59; energetic and dedicated; inflexible in policy towards Russia.

Dumas French writers, father and son: **Alexandre the Elder** (1802–70); hundreds of novels of adventure with aid of assistants, including *The Three Musketeers* and *The Count of Monte Cristo*. **Alexandre the Younger** (1824–95); *La Dame aux Camélias* (1848) and plays.

Dunlop, John Boyd (1840–1921); Scottish inventor of the pneumatic rubber tyre, which he made originally for his son's tricycle (the principle had already been patented).

Duns Scotus, John (c.1265–1308); Scottish scholastic philosopher, known as Subtle Doctor. Opposed doctrines of Aquinas, teaching that God is ultimate Truth and that faith is separate from reason.

Dürer, Albrecht (1471–1528); German artist; pencil drawings, woodcuts, and copper-plate engravings; also first-rate watercolour painter. Engravings *Knight, Death, and the Devil*.

Duse, Eleonora (1858–1924); Italian actress famous for her playing of Ibsen (*Hedda Gabler*) and contemporary French writers; married Gabriele D'ANNUNZIO.

Dvořák, Antonín (1841–1904); Czech composer and violinist, much influenced by Czech folk music and Negro spirituals. Wrote operas, songs, symphonies (*From the New World*, etc.), cello concerto, and set of *Slavonic Dances*.

Dylan, Bob (Robert Zimmerman; b. 1941); American folk singer, originally influenced by Woody Guthrie, later a major force on popular music styles and themes through his own songs.

Earhart, Amelia (1898–1937); American aviator, first woman to fly Atlantic Ocean alone (1932); vanished on round-world flight.

Eastman, George (1854–1932); American inventor, patented first photographic film (first made from paper, then celluloid, and finally cellulose acetate) and Kodak camera.

Eddington, Sir Arthur Stanley (1882–1944); English astronomer and physicist, made theoretical investigations into interior of stars.

Eddy, Mary Baker (1821–1910); American religious leader, founded Christian Science movement. Her doctrine, based on the one reality of Mind, God, and Good (matter and evil being unreal) incorporates spiritual healing; expounded in her book *Science and Health with Key to the Scriptures*.

Eden, (Robert) Anthony, 1st Earl of Avon (1897–1977); British statesman; resigned as foreign secretary in 1938 in protest at appeasement of ADOLF HITLER, served as foreign secretary 1940–45 during the war, and succeeded CHURCHILL as prime minister, 1955, resigning in the aftermath of the Suez crisis in 1956.

Edinburgh, Duke of See PHILIP, PRINCE.

Edison, Thomas Alva (1847–1931); American inventor, patented nearly 1300 inventions, including phonograph, electric light bulb, and electricity generating station. Also invented a motion picture.

Edward, the Black Prince (1330–76); Son of Edward III of England. Successful general; won Battle of Poitiers (1356).

Edward VIII (1894–1972); Succeeded his father, George V, as king of Great Britain in January 1936. Abdicated December 1936 to marry American, Wallis Simpson (1896–1986), twice married previously. Given title Duke of Windsor.

Ehrlich, Paul (1854–1915); German bacteriologist, shared 1908 Nobel prize for work on immunity and serum therapy.

Eijkman, Christiaan (1858–1930); Dutch physician, first discovered cause of beri beri, later established as vitamin deficiency disease.

Einstein, Albert (1879–1955); German-born theoretical physicist, made greatest scientific advances since NEWTON over 200 years earlier. In 1905 used quantum theory to explain photoelectric effect, produced famous $E = mc^2$ equation relating mass

to energy, explained Browning movement thus confirming atomic theory of matter, and expounded special theory of relativity; published general theory of relativity in 1916 (superseded Newton's gravitational theory); unified field theory 1929. Became Swiss citizen 1901, American 1940 (as a Jew could not work in Germany in 1930s). Reluctantly persuaded President ROOSEVELT to begin atomic research 1939. Fought for world peace. Nobel physics prize 1921.

Eisenhower, Dwight David (1890–1969); American soldier and statesman, C-in-C, Allied forces North Africa 1942; in western Europe 1943–45. Served as 34th president, 1953–61.

Eisenstein, Sergey (1898–1948); Latvian-born master of Soviet cinema, director of the classic films *Potemkin, Alexander Nevsky* and *Ivan the Terrible*.

Elgar, Sir Edward (1857–1934); English composer, most prolific period in early 1900s; orchestral set of *Enigma Variations*, 5 *Pomp and Circumstance Marches*; oratorio, *The Dream of Gerontius*.

Eliot, George (Mary Ann Evans; 1819–80); English author; novels include *Adam Bede* (1859), *The Mill on the Floss* (1860), *Silas Marner* (1861), *Middlemarch* (1872); poems.

Eliot, Thomas Stearns (1888–1965); American-born British poet; main poems *The Waste Land* (1922), *Ash Wednesday* (1930), *Four Quartets* (1944); plays *Murder in the Cathedral* (1935), *The Cocktail Party* (1950); Order of Merit, 1948; influenced many other writers.

Elizabeth I (1533–1603); Became queen of England 1558 at time of turmoil, and by wise statecraft made England stronger than it had ever been. Her people fought off Spanish invasion (1588) and began expansion overseas. Never married; great scholar and talented musician.

Elizabeth II (b. 1926) Succeeded her father GEORGE VI as British sovereign and Head of Commonwealth in 1952. Married Lieut. Philip Mountbatten, PRINCE PHILIP 1947.

Engels, Friedrich (1820–95); German Socialist, collaborated with MARX to write *Communist Manifesto* (1848). Revolutionary activities led him to flee to England, where he edited Marx's works.

Epstein, Sir Jacob (1880–1959); American-born British sculptor; highly individual style scandalized critics and spectators whenever statues unveiled. Most of work powerful and larger than life, carved with rugged simplicity. Busts: Maugham, Shaw, Einstein, etc.

Erasmus, Desiderius (c.1466–1536); Dutch Renaissance scholar, theologian, philosopher, and Augustinian monk. Sympathetic with aims of Reformation, but dislike of violence prevented his openly joining reformers. Published first Greek edition of New Testament (1516).

Eratosthenes (c.276–c.194 BC); Greek astronomer, worked out system for determining prime numbers. Made map of known world. Calculated size of Earth.

Ericson, Leif See LEIF ERICSON.

Ernst, Max (1891–1976); German painter and sculptor, originally a student of psychiatry, a founder of the Surrealist movement and an exponent of free association of images from the mind and the external world of objects.

Essex, Robert Devereux, 2nd Earl of (1566?–1601); English courtier who replaced the Earl of Leicester as favourite of ELIZABETH I. A rash but vigorous soldier, helped sack Cadiz in 1596, but failed to suppress rebellion in Ireland. Led abortive rebellion (1601) in London; executed for treason.

Euclid (c.300s BC); Greek mathematician, founder of modern geometry. Codified mathematical knowledge into *The Elements*.

Eugène of Savoy, Prince (1663–1736); Austrian general; with DUKE OF MARLBOROUGH won victories over French in War of Spanish Succession; also won victories against Turks. Born in France.

Euler, Leonhard (1707–83); Swiss mathematician, one of the most prolific mathematical writers of all time.

Euripides (c.480–406 BC); Greek tragic playwright; plays include *Medea, Iphigenia in Tauris, Helen, Orestes, Iphigenia in Aulis, The Trojan Women*.

Evans, Sir Arthur John (1851–1941); British archaeologist, excavated Palace of Minos at Knossos, Crete; discovered early type of Greek script.

Evelyn, John (1620–1706); English government official, author; secretary of Royal Society; books on architecture, trees, commerce, travels; his *Diary* (1640–1705), a major source book for his time.

Eyre, Edward John (1815–1901); British administrator and explorer, discovered Lakes Torrens and Eyre, S. Australia. Crossed Nullarbor Plain, 1840. Lieutenant-governor, New Zealand, 1846–53; governor, Jamaica, 1864–66.

Fahrenheit, Gabriel Daniel (1686–1736); German-Dutch physicist, made first mercury thermometer and worked out Fahrenheit scale of temperature.

Faisal I (1885–1933); Arab statesman who led Arab revolt against Turkish rule, 1916, and after peace became king of Iraq, 1921; his ability to unite diverse interests made him a notable architect of Arab nationalism.

Faraday, Michael (1791–1867); English scientist, founder of science of electromagnetism. Assisted and then succeeded DAVY at Royal Institution 1833. Pioneered cryogenics, discovered benzene, proposed laws of electrolysis. Devised simple electric motor, discovered induction, and invented first generator.

Farquhar, George (1678–1707); Irish playwright, whose social comedies include *The Recruiting Officer* and *The Beaux Stratagem*.

Faulkner, William (1897–1962); American novelist; works include *The Sound and the Fury* (1929), *As I Lay Dying* (1930); Pulitzer prizewinner; Nobel prize for literature, 1949.

Fawkes, Guy (1570–1606); English conspirator; caught trying to blow up Houses of Parliament, 5 November 1605; executed for treason.

Ferdinand II of Aragon (1452–1516); Husband of ISABELLA OF CASTILE, became king of Aragon 1479, uniting almost all Spain under one rule; established Inquisition in Spain, and expelled Jews.

Fermat, Pierre de (1601–65); French mathematician, founded theory of probability (with BLAISE PASCAL) and theory of numbers.

Fermi, Enrico (1901–54); Italian-American physicist, won 1938 Nobel prize for work on neutron bombardment. Built first nuclear reactor, called atomic pile.

Fielding, Henry (1707–54); English novelist, with RICHARDSON, generally credited with founding the novel in English; turned from plays to ironic picaresque novels, notably *Tom Jones* (1749).

Fields, W C (William Claude Dukenfield; 1880–1946); American film actor; cynical, drunken, anti-sentimental roles endeared him to the discerning in such films as *David Copperfield* and *Never Give a Sucker an Even Break.*

FitzGerald, Edward (1809–83); British poet, known mainly for translation of *Rubáiyát* of OMAR KHAYYÁM (1859).

Fitzgerald, F Scott (1896–1940); American writer; life ruined by alcohol; novels include *This Side of Paradise* (1920), *The Great Gatsby* (1925); mirrored Depression years and age of jazz.

Flamsteed, John (1646–1719); English astronomer, produced first great star map.

Flaubert, Gustave (1821–80); French novelist; *Madame Bovary* (1857), *Trois Contes* (1877).

Fleming, Sir Alexander (1881–1955); Scottish bacteriologist, discovered lysosomes and penicillin. Shared Nobel prize 1945.

Florey, Lord (Howard Walter Florey; 1898–1968); Austrian–British pathologist, worked out chemical structure of penicillin with ERNEST CHAIN. Shared Nobel prize 1945.

Foch, Ferdinand (1851–1929); French marshal; outstanding general World War I; allied C-in-C, 1918.

Fonteyn, Dame Margot (Margaret Hookham; b. 1919); English ballerina, *Prima ballerina assoluta* of Royal Ballet. Made world tours, starring especially in such roles as Giselle; partnered Nureyev in 1960s.

Ford, Gerald Rudolph (b. 1913); American statesman, nominated by RICHARD NIXON to replace Spiro Agnew as vice-president, 1973; succeeded Nixon as 38th president, 1974–76; withdrew US forces from Vietnam.

Ford, Henry (1863–1947); American car manufacturer; introduced mass production methods to make cheap cars.

Forster, Edward Morgan (1879–1970); British novelist and critic, who wrote of the tensions between personal and social, notably in *The Longest Journey, Howards End* and *A Passage to India.*

Foster, Stephen (1826–64); American composer of popular songs and ballads, including *Swanee River, Camptown Races* and *Beautiful Dreamer.*

Foucault, Jean Bernard Léon (1819–68); French physicist, calculated velocity of light using rotating mirror method. Demonstrated rotation of Earth using large pendulum that gradually altered its plane of oscillation.

Fox, Charles James (1749–1806); British politician, arch opponent of George III, rival to PITT, and one of the few British parliamentarians to support the French Revolution.

Fox, George (1624–91); English religious leader, who founded the Society of Friends, widely known as Quakers, in protest against established Church.

France, Anatole (Jacques Anatole François Thibault; 1844–1924); French novelist, satirist; *Le Crime de Sylvestre Bonnard* (1881), *Thaïs* (1890),

Les Dieux Ont Soif (1912); member of French Academy; Nobel prize for literature 1921.

Francesca, Piero della (1420?–92); Italian painter, born in Umbria, who was also a mathematician; noted for his frescoes.

Francis of Assisi, St (*c.*1182–1226); Italian friar, founded Franciscan Order of friars; love of animals proverbial.

Franco, Francisco (1892–1975); Led rebellion in Spain during Civil War of 1936–39; head of state (El Caudillo) and dictator from 1939.

Franklin, Benjamin (1706–90); American statesman and scientist, one of founding fathers of American nation. Invented an improved stove and bifocal glasses. Experimented with static electricity and lightning; invented lightning conductor. Suggested use of positive and negative terms in electricity.

Benjamin Franklin, the American statesman whose inventions included the lightning conductor, experiments with a kite during a thunderstorm.

Frederick II, the Great (1712–86); King of Prussia from 1740; brilliant general; fought MARIA THERESA in War of Austrian Succession; skilled flautist.

Freud, Sigmund (1856–1939); Austrian psychiatrist, proposed idea of conscious and subconscious mind. Began psychoanalysis and interpretation of dreams. Proposed theories of infantile sexuality and their effects on adult life.

Frobisher, Sir Martin (*c.*1535–94); English explorer, made three attempts to find North West Passage. Commanded part of fleet that defeated Spanish Armada, 1588. Fatally wounded at siege of Brest.

Froebel, Friedrich (1782–1852); German founder of the kindergarten system for preschool children; worked for a time under the Swiss educational reformer Johann PESTALOZZI.

Frost, Robert Lee (1874–1963); American poet, author of *A Boy's Will, New Hampshire, From Snow to Snow,* etc.

Fry, Elizabeth (1780–1845); A Quaker who lived in Norwich, she became an active reformer of English prisons; she was also requested by King Louis Philippe of France to inspect and report on French prisons, which led to prison reforms in France. She was involved in other fields of reform such as improving standards of nursing and education.

Fulton, Robert (1765–1815); American engineer who built the first commercially successful steamship, the *Clermont*, 1807.

Gabor, Dennis (1900–79); Hungarian phycisist, 1971 Nobel prizewinner for invention of holography, or three-dimensional photography; worked in England from 1933.

Gagarin, Yuri (1934–68); Russian cosmonaut, made first human space flight, in Vostok I, 1961. Died in plane crash.

Gainsborough, Thomas (1727–88); English painter, portraits and landscapes, strongly influenced by RUBENS; much sought after by society clients; *The Blue Boy, Mrs. Siddons*.

Galileo (1564–1642); Italian scientist, first to combine theory and experiment in modern scientific manner. Discovered principle of pendulum and of falling bodies. Invented telescope and made astronomical observations that finally established Copernican theory of universe, but not before he was imprisoned for his 'heretical' views.

Galsworthy, John (1867–1933); English novelist and playwright; main novels *The Forsyte Saga* and its sequels (1906–28); plays include *The Silver Box* (1906), *The Skin Game* (1920); Order of Merit 1929; Nobel prize for literature 1932.

Galton, Sir Francis (1822–1911); English scientist, cousin of DARWIN; anthropologist, studied heredity and first applied statistical methods to biology; founded eugenics. Also pioneered weather chart and devised fingerprint identification.

Galvani, Luigi (1737–98); Italian anatomist, discovered electricity produced by metals in contact, but believed it came from living tissue – animal electricity.

Gandhi, Mohandas Karamchand (1869–1948); Indian lawyer, ascetic, and Hindu spiritual leader; worked for independence from Britain, largely by non-violent civil disobedience; jailed several times; assassinated by Hindu fanatic because he preached peace with Muslims. Known as *Mahatma*, great soul.

Garbo, Greta (Greta Gustafsson; b. 1905); Swedish-born American film star. Cultivated well-publicized dislike of publicity. Starred in *Camille*, *Ninotchka*, etc.

Garibaldi, Giuseppe (1807–82); Italian patriot; with 1000 men (Red-shirts) conquered Kingdom of Two Sicilies 1860; after proclamation of Kingdom of Italy, 1861, twice tried to conquer Rome (1862, 1867); fought for France, 1870–71; member of Italian parliament, 1874.

Garrick, David (1717–79); English actor-manager, managed London's Drury Lane Theatre from 1747, pioneered use of naturalistic backdrops and concealed lighting; popular Shakespearean actor.

Gauguin, (Eugène Henri) Paul (1848–1903); French Post-Impressionist painter, abandoned 'civilization' to live and paint in Tahiti. Tremendous influence on other Post-Impressionists.

Gauss, Johann Karl Friedrich (1777–1855); German mathematician, worked out method of least squares, and theories of planetary perturbations. Did much work in all branches of mathematics including theory of numbers. Worked on terrestrial magnetism, and devised system of units.

Gay-Lussac, Joseph Louis (1778–1850); French chemist, showed different gases expand by equal amounts with increased temperature. Stated laws of combining volumes of gases. Isolated boron (jointly); showed iodine to be element.

Genghis Khan (c.1162–1227); Tribal leader from Mongolia, named Temujin; conquered most of central Asia to form empire stretching from Pacific coast to River Dniepr. Took title Genghis Khan – Ruler of All Men – 1206.

George VI (1895–1952); Second son of George V of Britain, succeeded brother, EDWARD VIII, 1936. Served Royal Navy, World War I; married Lady Elizabeth Bowes-Lyon, 1923. Succeeded by ELIZABETH II.

Gershwin, George (1898–1937); American composer, originally specialized in jazz and musicals, later wrote 'serious' music with jazz flavour; *Rhapsody in Blue*, Negro opera *Porgy and Bess*.

Gibbon, Edward (1737–94); English historian, wrote *Decline and Fall of the Roman Empire* (1776–88). Became MP (1774–83); served as commissioner of trade and plantations.

Gide, André (1869–1951); French writer; founded magazine *La Nouvelle Revue Française* (1909); novels *Les Nourritures Terrestres* (1897), *Les Faux Monnayeurs* (1926); essays; Nobel prize for literature 1947.

Gilbert, William (1544–1603); English physician and physicist, perhaps the earliest true experimenter. Discovered magnetic dip of Earth. Made early experiments with attractive force, now known as electrostatic attraction. Had advanced ideas on structure of universe.

Gilbert, Sir William Schwenk (1836–1911); English writer, with SIR ARTHUR SULLIVAN (1842–1900), English composer, the creator of famous series of comic operas, including *HMS Pinafore*, *Iolanthe*, *The Mikado*, and *The Gondoliers* for the D'Oyly Carte Company.

298

Giotto (di Bondone) (*c*.1266–1337); Florentine painter, first Italian artist to break with flat Byzantine tradition in favour of more naturalistic and emotional approach; magnificent religious frescoes in Florence, Padua, and Assisi.

Gladstone, William Ewart (1809–98); British Liberal statesman; four times prime minister (1868–74, 1880–85, 1886, 1892–94); tried but failed to secure home rule for Ireland.

Goddard, Robert Hutchings (1882–1945); American physicist, first to develop rocketry.

Goebbels, Joseph Paul (1897–1945); German Nazi propaganda chief; close personal friend of HITLER; committed suicide in Berlin with Hitler.

Goering, Hermann (1893–1946); German Nazi politician. Air ace, World War I; close supporter of HITLER; head of German air force, World War II; condemned for war crimes, but took poison.

Goethe, Johann Wolfgang von (1749–1832); German poet, playwright, statesman, scientist, chief minister of Weimar, 1775–88; plays *Götz von Berlichingen* (1773), *Egmont* (1788), *Torquato Tasso* (1790); *Faust* (1808–32); novels *The Sorrows of Young Werther* (1774), *Wilhelm Meister's Apprenticeship* (1796); scientific works; founder of modern German literature.

Gogol, Nikolai Vasilievich (1809–52); Russian writer; government clerk and teacher; lived in exile from 1836; comedy *The Inspector-General* (1836); novel *Dead Souls* (1842).

Goldsmith, Oliver (1728–74); Irish-born British author; worked as a book reviewer, living beyond his means; main works, poem *The Deserted Village* (1770); novel *The Vicar of Wakefield* (1766); play *She Stoops to Conquer* (1773).

Gorbachev, Mikhail Sergeevich (b. 1931); became Soviet Communist party secretary in 1985; initiated policy of *glasnost* (openness) and *perestroika* (restructuring); negotiated treaty with US to limit nuclear missiles; became president 1989.

Gorki, Maxim (Alexei Maximovich Peshkov; 1868–1936); Russian writer and revolutionist; in exile (1905–13, 1921–28); novels *Foma Gordeyev* (1899), *Mother* (1907); short stories; plays *The Lower Depths* (1903), *The Judge* (1924); Nizhni Novgorod now named *Gorki* for him.

Far left: Yuri Gagarin, the Russian cosmonaut who became the first man in space in 1961.
Above left: A self-portrait by the artist Thomas Gainsborough, renowned for his portraits and for his landscapes.
Right: Greta Garbo, who gave up acting at the height of her career, in 1941, without explanation.

Gounod, Charles (1818–93); French composer and conductor, wrote *Ave Maria* based on Bach prelude; 2 operas, *Faust* and *Romeo and Juliet.*

Goya (y Lucientes), Francisco José de (1746–1828); Spanish painter and etcher; realistic style included royalty, bullfights, everyday portraits. Grim etchings, *The Disasters of War*, powerful pacifist propaganda. *La Maja Desnuda* one of most famous nudes in art.

Graham, Billy (William Franklin) (b. 1918); American evangelist; revivalist meetings drew huge crowds in most English-speaking countries after World War II.

Graham, Thomas (1805–69); Scottish physical chemist, studied diffusion of gases and discovered rate of diffusion inversely proportional to molecular weight. Discovered colloids, osmosis, and dialysis.

Grant, Ulysses Simpson (1822–85); American general and statesman; Union general in Civil War; Union C in-C, 1864. Served as 18th president, 1869–77.

Graves, Robert Ranke (1895–1985); British poet, novelist, critic, son of Irish poet Alfred Percival Graves; novels include *I, Claudius* (1934), *Sergeant Lamb of the Ninth* (1940); essays; collections of poems; autobiographies; translations of classics; lived in Majorca from 1929.

Gray, Thomas (1716–71); English poet; *Elergy Written in a Country Churchyard* (1751).

Greco, El (Domenicos Theotocopoulos; *c*.1541–1614); Cretan-born painter, lived and worked in Spain. Highly original style, involving vivid colours and unnatural, twisted, elongated shapes, did not always please Spanish religious hierarchy; *View of Toledo.*

Grieg, Edvard Hagerup (1843–1907); Norwegian composer, intensely nationalistic; inspired by country's folk music. Incidental music to Ibsen's *Peer Gynt*, *Piano Concerto in A Minor*, several songs.

Grimm, the Brothers German collectors of fairy tales (1812–15), and philologists; **Jacob** (1785–1863) and **Wilhelm** (1786–1859) began compiling the *German Dictionary* (1854); Jacob also wrote *German Grammar* (1819–37).

Gropius, Walter (1883–1969); German architect, founder and designer of Bauhaus. Industrial architecture; felt that art should subserve function. Later years in US.

Grotius, Hugo (Huig de Groot; 1583–1645); Dutch lawyer, founder of international law; jailed for opposing Calvinism; Swedish ambassador to France, 1635–45.

Gustavus II Adolphus (1594–1632); King of Sweden from 1611. Reformed government, aided by chief minister, Axel Oxenstierna; intervened in Thirty Years War, 1630; killed at Lützen.

Gutenberg, Johannes (1400?–68); German inventor of printing with movable type (in the 1440s), made first printed Bible.

Haber, Fritz (1868–1934); German chemist, won 1918 Nobel prize for invention of process for making ammonia cheaply by combining nitrogen and hydrogen.

Habsburg Name of family that held title of Holy Roman Emperor almost continuously 1273–1806; emperors of Austria 1806–1918. Founded by Albert, Count of Habsburg, 1153. First emperor Rudolf III. Members include CHARLES V; MARIE ANTOINETTE. Also spelt Hapsburg.

Hahn, Otto (1879–1968); German physical chemist, won 1914 Nobel prize for discovery of fission of uranium atoms.

Haig, Douglas, 1st Earl Haig (1861–1928); Leading British general, World War I; created earl 1919.

Haile Selassie (1892–1975); King of Ethiopia 1928; emperor 1930; deposed 1974. In exile 1936–41. Original name Ras Taffari; regent 1916–1928.

Haldane, John Burdon Sanderson (1892–1964); English geneticist, estimated rate of mutation of human gene. Noted for explaining science to laymen.

Halley, Edmund (1656–1742); English astronomer, renowned for studies of comets, particularly that of 1682 (Halley's) predicting its 75-year cycle. Encouraged, financed, and published NEWTON's *Principa* (1687). First magnetic survey of oceans; first map of global winds. Astronomer royal 1720–42.

Hals, Frans (*c*.1580–1666); Dutch portrait painter whose brushwork lent air of liveliness and spontaneity to faces of his sitters. *Laughing Cavalier*, one of the world's most popular paintings.

Hamilton, Alexander (1757–1804); First US treasury secretary, 1789–95; killed in duel with vice-president Aaron Burr. Trained as lawyer.

Hammarskjöld, Dag (1905–61); Swedish economist and statesman; second secretary-general of UN from 1953; killed in air crash while trying to end civil war in Congo (now Zaire).

Hammurabi (d. 1686 BC); King of Babylon from 1728 BC; drew up code of laws, and enforced them rigidly.

Handel, George Frideric (1685–1759); German-born composer, became naturalized Briton 1726. Superb oratorios (*Messiah*, *Israel in Egypt*, etc.). Revered by composers such as BEETHOVEN, HAYDN, MOZART. Vast output included 27 oratorios, 41 operas, organ, orchestral (*Water Music*), and chamber music.

Hannibal (247–183 BC); Carthaginian statesman and general. In 2nd Punic War with Rome (218–201 BC) led army over Alps into Italy, winning many victories; recalled to defend Carthage; defeated at Zama, 202 BC; headed government of Carthage; exiled 196 BC; committed suicide.

Hapsburg See HABSBURG.

Hardy, Thomas (1840–1928); English novelist, poet, architect; created fictional 'Wessex'; novels include *Far from the Madding Crowd* (1874), *The Return of the Native* (1878), *Tess of the D'Urbervilles* (1891); epic play *The Dynasts* (1908).

Harun al-Rashid (764?–809); Caliph of Baghdad, ruler of Middle East and North Africa; communicated with CHARLEMAGNE and with China, warred against the Byzantines, and is idolized in the *Arabian Nights* as the ideal ruler.

Harvey, William (1578–1657); English physician, studied heart and blood vessels of dissected animals; discovered one-way circulation of blood.

Hastings, Warren (1732–1818); British statesman; first governor-general of India, 1773–85; impeached for cruelty and dishonesty, but acquitted after 7-year trial.

Hawthorne, Nathaniel (1804–64); American author, diplomat, customs inspector; *The Scarlet Letter* (1850); *Tangle wood Tales* (1853) for children; short stories.

Haydn, Franz Joseph (1732–1809); Austrian composer; vast output based on new symphonic form, earned him title 'Father of the Symphony'. Wrote 104 symphonies (*The Suprise*, *The Drum-Roll*, *The Clock*, etc.), 20 operas, over 80 string quartets, and sparkling oratorios.

Heath, Edward (b. 1916) First elected leader of; British Conservative party, 1965; prime minister 1970–74; took Britain into European Economic Community.

Hegel, Georg Wilhelm Friedrich (1770–1831); German philosopher, advocate of supreme human consciousness (to 'absolute' knowledge) and a systematically whole universe; influence on Existentialism, Marxism and Positivism.

Heifetz, Jasha (1901–1988); Russian-born US virtuoso violinist, child prodigy during World War I. Various composers, including Walton, wrote works for him.

Heine, Heinrich (1797–1856); German poet and critic; poems include *The Lorelei*, *On Wings of Song*; *Der Salon* (art criticism, 1835–40); from 1831 in Paris; paralyzed for last years of life.

Heisenberg, Werner Karl (1901–1976); German physicist, won 1932 Nobel prize for Uncertainty Principle (impossible to determine both position and momentum of any body at same time). Much work on quantum theory.

Helmholtz, Hermann Ludwig Ferdinand von (1821–94); German physicist and physiologist, invented ophthalmoscope. Proposed theory of hearing mechanism. Measured speed of nerve impulse. Worked on theory of conservation of energy.

Above: George Frideric Handel, the German-born composer who spent most of his working life in England. His best known work is the oratorio Messiah. *Right: The Carthaginian leader Hannibal leads his army, elephants and all, across the Alps.*

Hemingway, Ernest (1898–1961); American author, journalist, traveller; books based on his experiences; novels include *A Farewell to Arms* (1929), *Death in the Afternoon* (1932), *To Have and Have Not* (1937), *For Whom the Bell Tolls* (1940), *The Old Man and the Sea* (1952); short stories; Pulitzer prizewinner; Nobel prize for literature, 1954.

Henry, Joseph (1797–1878); American physicist, originally developed telegraph, discovered induction and self-induction; built electric motors.

Henry IV (1553–1610); First Bourbon king of France, leader of Huguenots and King of Navarre. Succeeded Henry III in 1589 after years of rebellion. Became Roman Catholic, but issued Edict of Nantes, giving political rights to Huguenots. Restored France's finances; assassinated.

Henry VIII (1491–1547); King of England from 1509, broke with Church of Rome in order to divorce first wife, Catherine of Aragon, and remarry so he could have son. Later marriages were to Anne Boleyn, Jane Seymour, Anne of Cleves, Catherine Howard, Catherine Parr. Ordered dissolution of monasteries.

Henry the Navigator (1394–1460); Portuguese prince, built observatory and navigation school, and pioneered study of navigation that began Age of Exploration.

Hepplewhite, George (d. 1786); English cabinetmaker; winged easy chairs with delicate, heart-shaped backs.

Hepworth, Dame Barbara (1903–75); English sculptor, work resembles HENRY MOORE's; abstract forms in wood, metal, stone.

Herodotus (*c*.484–*c*.424 BC); Greek traveller and writer, called the Father of History. Recorded customs, manners, and traditions of peoples in places he visited.

Herophilus (*c*.300 BC); Greek anatomist, described sensory and motor nerves, retina of eye, liver, spleen and genital system. Named prostate gland and duodenum.

Herschel, Sir William (1792–1871); German-English astronomer, made telescopes, studied double stars, star clusters, and nebulae. Discovered Uranus.

Hertz, Heinrich Rudolph (1857–94); German physicist, confirmed usefulness of JAMES MAXWELL's equations in electromagnetic theory. Produced electromagnetic radiation and detected its wave nature.

Hesiod (8th century BC); Greek poet; major surviving work *Works and Days*; *Theogony*; originator of didactic (instructive) verse.

Hess, (Walther Richard) Rudolf (1894–1987); German Nazi leader, friend of Adolf Hitler; flew to Scotland, 1941, to try to negotiate peace in World War II; jailed for life for war crimes, 1946.

Hillary, Sir Edmund (b. 1919); New Zealand explorer, one of first two men to climb Everest (1953). Reached South Pole with Commonwealth Transantarctic Expedition, 1958. Explored Himalayas 1960.

Himmler, Heinrich (1900–45); German Nazi leader; Gestapo chief from 1936; organized mass killings; captured 1945, committed suicide.

Hindenburg, Paul von (1847–1934); German general and statesman; C-in-C German armies World War I, 1916–18; president of German republic, 1925–34; made ADOLF HITLER chancellor, 1933.

Hipparchus (*c*.190–*c*.120 BC); Greek astronomer, measured size of Moon by parallax method. Made first accurate star map. First observed precession of equinoxes. Divided stars into groups according to magnitude. Devised method for calculating positions of planets.

Hippocrates (460–*c*.370 BC); Greek physician, supposed to have written 50 books, but these most likely written by members of Hippocratic school. This school believed disease to result from imbalance of vital fluids ('humours'). Hippocratic ethics are reflected in oath taken by modern doctors.

Hitchcock, Sir Alfred Joseph (1899–1980); British film director, master of suspense tinged with relieving humour in films such as *The Man Who Knew Too Much* (1934), *Dial M for Murder* (1954), *Psycho* (1960).

Hitler, Adolf (1889–1945); Austrian politician, became German dictator. Corporal World War I; leader National Socialist (Nazi) Party from 1920; chancellor of Germany 1933; Führer from 1934. Annexed Austria 1938. Began World War II by invading Poland, 1939. Committed suicide, 1945, in ruins of Berlin. Married Eva Braun just before death.

Hobbes, Thomas (1588–1679); English political theorist and philosopher; believed that social order should be based on human co-operation rather than ruling authority; *Leviathan* (1651).

Ho Chi Minh (1892–1969); Vietnamese statesman, original name *Nguyen Ai Quoc*; became Communist; led independence movement in Indochina; head of state of North Vietnam, 1954–69.

Hogarth, William (1699–1764); English satirical painter and engraver, specialized in 'modern moral subjects'. Exaggerated human weaknesses in series of engravings, *The Rake's Progress*, *Marriage à la Mode*; painting *The Shrimp Girl*.

Hohenzollern German royal family, founded in 11th century. Included kings of Prussia from 1701; Kaiser WILHELM II; kings Carol II and Michael of Romania.

Holbein, Hans (the Younger) (*c*.1497–1543); German artist, court painter to HENRY VIII. Established reputation with illustrations for LUTHER'S Bible. Famous series of woodcuts: *Dance of Death* and *Alphabet of Death*; portrait *The Ambassadors*.

Holland, John Philip (1840–1914); Irish-American inventor of the prototype of the modern submarine (1881).

Holmes, Oliver Wendell (1809–94); American essayist and anatomist; *The Autocrat of the Breakfast-Table* (1858); other essays; novels; poems; son **Oliver Wendell Holmes Jr** (1841–1935), Leading American judge.

Holst, Gustave Theodore (1874–1934); English composer, deeply influenced by English folk music. Operas include *The Perfect Fool*, and orchestra music *The Planets* suite.

Homer, Legendary Greek poet; traditionally author of *The Iliad* and *The Odyssey*; lived possibly 850 BC, according to HERODOTUS.

Hooke, Robert (1635–1703); English physicist, studied action of springs, and derived Hooke's law. Made microscopic observations and drawings, including those of insects, feathers, and fish scales.

Hopkins, Gerard Manley (1844–89); English poet and Jesuit priest; used compound words and sprung rhythm; poems not published until 1918; had great influence.

Horace (Quintus Horatius Flaccus; 65–8 BC); Roman poet; helped by Maecenas, a rich patron; *Odes*, *Epodes*, *Epistles*, *Satires*; criticism.

Hounsfield, Godfrey Newbold (b. 1919); Scientist and inventor of body scanner with ability to detect tumours by computer tomography; received Nobel prize for physiology and medicine for this invention in 1979.

Hoyle, Sir Frederick (b. 1915); English astronomer and writer, suggested scheme for nuclear reactions inside stars; exploding star theory of Solar System (1946); later suggested, with W K Wickramsinghe, that life on Earth may have originated from deep space; writings include *Nature of the Universe*, *Lifecloud*, and science fiction, *The Black Cloud*.

Hubble, Edwin Powell (1889–1953); American astronomer. Discovered that some nebulae, later realized to be galaxies, were outside our galaxy. Classified galaxies according to shape, calculated their real velocities. Put forward idea of expanding universe.

Hudson, Henry (d. 1611); English navigator, tried to find route to China through Arctic Ocean. Found and named Hudson River, 1609. On last voyage his mutinous crew set him and eight others adrift in Hudson Bay.

Hugo, Victor Marie (1802–85); French Romantic writer; opposed Napoleon III as emperor and spent 19 years in exile; senator 1876; plays include *Ruy Blas* (1838); novels *Notre-Dame de Paris* (1831), *Les Misérables* (1862); poems lyrical and epic; essays.

Humboldt, Friedrich Wilhelm Heinrich Alexander, Baron von (1769–1859); German naturalist and explorer, travelled in S. America, Europe, and Asia. Made important contributions to geography, meteorology, and climatology.

Hume, David (1711–76); Scottish philosopher and historian, took Berkeley's ideas (who replaced material objects with mind forms) and denied mind too. Attitude one of scepticism allowing only impressions to remain; *Treatise of Human Nature* (1739).

Huss, Jan (*c*.1370–1415); Bohemian religious reformer, foreshadowed Reformation in Europe. With followers, attacked abuses and privileges within Church; condemned for heresy and burnt at Constance.

Hutton, James (1726–97); Scottish scientist, founder of modern geology. Maintained uniformitarian principle, that there has been slow evolution of rock structure. Earlier studied medicine and chemistry, and died working on book that anticipated DARWIN's theory of evolution by 60 years.

Huxley Distinguished English family of scientists and writers: **Thomas Henry Huxley** (1825–95), zoologist, popularizer of science, spread DARWIN's theory of evolution; invented word 'agnostic' to describe own religious beliefs. **Sir Julian Sorell Huxley** (1887–1975), biologist and writer, grandson of T H, helped establish UNESCO (1st director-general, 1947); prominent conservationist. **Aldous Leonard Huxley** (1894–1963), author, brother of Julian, wrote witty satires of 1920s England, e.g. *Antic Hay* (1923), the brilliant science fiction satire *Brave New World* (1932), books on mysticism. **Andrew Fielding Huxley** (b. 1917), physiologist, half-brother of Julian and Aldous, shared 1963 Nobel prize for work on nerve impulses.

Huygens, Christiaan (1629–95); Dutch physicist and astronomer, developed improved lenses for telescopes. Discovered Orion Nebula, Titan (Saturn moon), and ring round Saturn. Invented working pendulum clock.

Ibsen, Henrik (1828–1906); Norwegian dramatist; dealt with contemporary society and situations; plays include *Peer Gynt* (1867), *A Doll's House* (1879), *The Wild Duck* (1884), *Hedda Gabler* (1890), *The Master Builder* (1892).

Imhotep (*c.*2970 BC); Egyptian scholar, probable architect of earliest step pyramid.

Ingres, Jean Auguste Dominique (1780–1867); Leading French Classicist painter, pupil of DAVID. Paintings endowed with innate sensuality seen equally in nudes and historical portraits; *La Source.*

Irving, Washington (1783–1859); American author; lived in Europe, 1815–32; *Knickerbocker's History of New York* (1809); short stories, including *Rip Van Winkle* (1820).

Isabella of Castile (1451–1504); Wife of FERDINAND II OF ARAGON; marriage united Spain. Financed voyage of CHRISTOPHER COLUMBUS, leading to discovery of Americas.

Ivan IV, the Terrible (1530–84); First tsar of all Russia. Became ruler 1533; assumed personal power 1546. Vicious and cruel; had many people murdered and tortured; developed religious mania; murdered eldest son, repented and became monk on deathbed.

Jackson, 'Stonewall' Thomas Jonathan (1824–63); Leading Confederate general in American Civil War. Accidentally shot by own men at Battle of Chancellorsville.

James, Henry (1843–1916); American novelist; lived in England from 1876; *The American* (1877), *What Maisie Knew* (1897), *The Turn of the Screw* (1898), *The Golden Bowl* (1904); short stories; biographies.

Jeans, Sir James Hopwood (1877–1946); English mathematician and astronomer, studied behaviour of spinning bodies, and proposed 'catastrophic' origin of Solar System.

Jefferson, Thomas (1743–1826); American lawyer, inventor, architect, and statesman. Drafted Declaration of Independence; Secretary of State 1789; president 1801–09; bought Louisiana territory from France, 1803.

Jenner, Edward (1749–1823); English physician, father of immunology, developed smallpox vaccine made from cowpox germs.

Jesus Christ (*c.*4 BC–*c.*AD 29); Founder of Christianity; Jesus Hebrew for Saviour, Christ from Greek Christos, anointed one or Messiah. Born Bethlehem, said to be miraculously conceived by mother Mary. Believed by followers to be son of God; preached Word of God and healed sick. Crucified by Pontius Pilate. Christians believe he physically rose from dead and ascended into heaven.

Jinnah, Mohammed Ali (1876–1948); Led Muslim demand for independence from India, and became first governor-general of new country of Pakistan, 1947.

Joan of Arc (1412–31); French national heroine, first came to notice as peasant girl who 'heard voices'. Later led French armies and helped

Henrik Ibsen, Norwegian dramatist.

Above: Thomas Jefferson drafted the American Declaration of Independence. Below: Edward Jenner, pioneer of immunology.

Dauphin to victory against English in Hundred Years War. Captured by English and burnt as witch; canonized in 1920.

John III (Jan Sobieski; 1624–96); Polish military hero, elected king 1674; defeated Turks 1683.

Johnson, Lyndon Baines (1908–73); 36th president of United States. Texas schoolteacher; senator 1948; vice-president to KENNEDY 1960; succeeded as president 1963; re-elected 1964; retired 1969.

Johnson, Samuel (1709–84); English writer and lexicographer; immortalized in biography by BOSWELL; *Dictionary* (1755), *The Lives of the Poets* (1779–81); essays; poems; renowned as a wit.

Jones, Inigo (1573–1672); English architect, introduced Italian classicism into English building; banqueting house in Whitehall and Queen's House, Greenwich.

Jonson, Ben (c.1573–1637); English poet and dramatist; saw army service in Flanders; leader of literary circles in London; plays include *Every Man in His Humour* (1598), *Volpone* (1606), *The Alchemist* (1610).

Joule, James Prescott (1818–89); English physicist, determined accurate mechanical equivalent of heat. Discovered temperature drop of expanding gas (Joule-Thomson effect), and magnetostriction.

Joyce, James (1882–1941); Irish novelist; from 1904 lived in Zurich, Trieste, Paris; *A Portrait of the Artist as a Young Man* (1916), *Ulysses* (1922); *Finnegans Wake* (1939; full of difficult passages and invented words).

Jung, Carl Gustav (1875–1961); Swiss psychiatrist, popularized terms 'introvert' and 'extrovert'. Interpreted deeper conscious levels in terms of mythology.

Justinian I (Flavius Petrus Sabbatius Justinianus; 483–565); Last great Roman emperor. Emperor of the East, 527; reconquered much of Italy from barbarians. Codified Roman law.

Juvenal (Decimus Junius Juvenalis; c.60–c.140); Roman lawyer and satirist attacked morals and attitudes of time.

Kafka, Franz (1883–1924); Austrian writer; three novels: *The Trial* (1925), *The Castle* (1926), *Amerika* (1927); short stories.

Kandinsky, Vassily (1866–1944); Russian painter, traditionally originator of abstract art. With Franz Marc founded *Blaue Reiter* (Blue Rider) group, Munich pioneers of German expressionism; taught at Bauhaus school until closed by HITLER; moved to Paris.

Kant, Immanuel (1724–1804); German philosopher and author, had deep and widespread influence on 19th-century philosophy. Propounded theories in *Critique of Pure Reason* (1781), *Foundations of the Metaphysics of Ethics* (1785).

Karajan, Herbert von (1908–89); Austrian conductor and opera producer, prominently associated with Berlin Philharmonic Orchestra, Vienna State Opera, La Scala (Milan), New York Metropolitan Opera.

Keats, John (1795–1821); English Romantic poet; studied medicine; died of tuberculosis; poems include *Endymion, Ode to a Nightingale, The Eve of St. Agnes.*

Kelvin, Lord (William Thomson; 1824–1907); Scottish mathematician and physicist, developed absolute temperature scale. Worked with JOULE

on Joule-Thomson effect. Invented improved electric cables and galvanometers; several navigational aids.

Kemal Atatürk (1881–1938); Turkish general and statesman; commander at Gallipoli, 1915; overthrew sultan, founded republic of Turkey, 1923; president, 1923–38, introduced sweeping reforms.

Kennedy, John Fitzgerald (1917–63); 35th and youngest president of United States, and first Roman Catholic, Took office 1961; dealt firmly with Cuban crisis 1962; assassinated.

Kepler, Johannes (1571–1630); German astronomer and mathematician, devised system of heavens based on BRAHE's observations, with planets having elliptical orbits round Sun.

Kerensky, Alexander (1881–1970); Russian revolutionary; prime minister after first revolution of 1917; overthrown by Bolsheviks; in France until 1940, then in United States.

Keynes, John Maynard, 1st Baron (1883–1946); British economist; books on money and prices have influenced all modern economists; created baron 1942.

Khrushchev, Nikita Sergeyevich (1894–1971); Became premier of Soviet Union 1955; denounced rule of JOSEPH STALIN. Also First Secretary of Communist party. Ousted 1964 by ALEXEI KOSYGIN and LEONID BREZHNEV.

Kierkegaard, Søren Aabye (1813–55); Danish philosopher, rejected organized religion as useless in man's personal approach to God or Truth. Works, such as *Stages on Life's Way* (1845), influenced later Existentialists.

King, Martin Luther (1929–68); American Negro clergyman and civil rights leader, advocated passive resistance in demonstrations against segregation of blacks. Nobel peace prize, 1964, assassinated Memphis, Tennessee.

Kipling, Rudyard (1865–1936); Indian-born English writer; journalist; novels *Kim* (1902), *The Light That Failed* (1891); many volumes of short stories; children's books: *The Jungle Books* (1894–95); *Just So Stories* (1901); *Stalky and Co* (1899); *Puck of Pook's Hill* (1906); much poetry.

Kissinger, Henry (b. 1923); German-born American professor of government; adviser to NIXON, 1969; Secretary of State, 1973; Nobel peace prize, 1973, for Vietnam cease-fire.

Kitchener, Horatio Herbert, 1st Earl (1850–1916); Governor-general Sudan, recapturing Khartoum from Muslim fanatics; C-in-C South Africa, 1900; secretary of state for war, 1914; drowned when ship hit mine.

Klee, Paul (1879–1940); Swiss artist, co-founder of the Blue Four movement, expressed the workings of the subconscious mind in paintings.

Knox, John (c.1505–72); Scottish divine, established Church of Scotland. Converted to Protestantism; exiled to Geneva and came under influence of CALVIN. After Civil War, started Presbyterianism in Scotland.

Koch, Robert (1843–1910); German bacteriologist, developed anthrax vaccine. Isolated several disease-causing bacteria, including tubercle and cholera bacilli; Nobel prize for work on tuberculosis, 1905.

Kokoschka, Oscar (1886–1980); Austrian painter, leading Expressionist artist of portraits and landscapes, often tortured and imaginative; forced to flee to England in 1938 following Nazi invasion.

Kosygin, Alexei Nikolayevich (1904–80); Soviet leader, economic administrator, premier of USSR from 1964–80, though playing a subordinate role to L I BREZHNEV.

Kublai Khan (1216–94); Grandson of GENGHIS KHAN and greatest Mongol emperor, completed Mongol conquest of China and founded Yüan dynasty there. His empire reached to Poland and south to Vietnam.

Lafayette, Marquis de (1757–1834); French soldier and statesman, fought for colonists in American War of Independence; leader in French Revolution; joined in revolution of 1830.

Lagrange, Joseph Louis (1736–1813); Italian-French astronomer and mathematician, worked out algebraic systematization of mechanics, and laws governing motions of systems containing more than two bodies.

Lamarck, Jean Baptiste Pierre Antoine de Monet (1744–1829); French naturalist, proposed theory of evolution by inheritance of acquired characteristics.

Lamartine, Alphonse de (1790–1869); French poet, orator, and politician; *Méditations Poétiques* (1820).

Lamb, Charles (1775–1834); English author; worked as a clerk; *Essays of Elia* (1823); plays; *Tales from Shakespeare* (1807), in collaboration with sister, **Mary** (1764–1847).

Langley, Samuel Pierpoint (1834–1906); American astronomer and aviation pioneer, successfully flew models but failed in two full-scale trials (1903) shortly before Wright brothers' historic flight.

Langmuir, Irving (1881–1957); American chemist and inventor. Extended life of tungsten filament in electric light bulbs; developed atomic blow torch and high-vacuum tubes, later used in radios. Nobel prize for work in surface chemistry, 1932.

Lao-tze (*c*.604–531 BC); Chinese philosopher, founder of Taoism. Taught that man has lost the 'way' (Tao); in order to recover it and live in harmony with it, man must live simply and humbly.

Laplace, Pierre Simon (1749–1827); French astronomer and mathematician, refined work of NEWTON and LAGRANGE on motions of planetary bodies. Gave modern form to calculus.

La Salle, Robert Cavalier, Sieur de (1643–87); Wealthy French fur trader, explored Mississippi River in 1681. Became governor of Louisiana in 1684. Shot by one of his followers after landing at remote bay in Texas.

Laue, Max Theodore Felix von (1879–1960); German physicist, Nobel prize (1914) for development of X-ray diffraction technique; enabled wavelength of X-rays to be calculated and crystal structure to be studied.

Lavoisier, Antoine Laurent (1743–94); French chemist, disproved phlogiston theory, and maintained air to consist of two gases, oxygen and azote (later called nitrogen). Established law of conservation of mass. Helped devise system of chemical names.

Lawrence, David Herbert (1885–1930); English novelist and poet; influenced many other writers; novels include *The Rainbow* (1915), *Women in Love* (1920), *Lady Chatterley's Lover* (1928: banned for many years for obscenity); poems; essays; letters.

Lawrence, Ernest Orlando (1901–58); American physicist, Nobel prize for development of cyclotron, 1939.

Lawrence, Thomas Edward (1888–1935); British archaeologist, soldier, and author; helped to organize Arab revolt against Turks, World War I; sought obscurity in RAF, changing name to T E Shaw; wrote *Seven Pillars of Wisdom* (1928); *The Mint* (1935).

Leakey, Louis Seymour Bazett (1903–72); British anthropologist and palaeontologist, discovered remains of early Man in East Africa, more than 1 million years older than previously believed. Also zoologist, handwriting expert. His son **Richard Leakey** (b. 1944) also an anthropologist, has made significant discoveries of early man.

Lear, Edward (1812–88); English book illustrator and writer of nonsense verses; specialized in bird pictures; *A Book of Nonsense* (1846) and other collections of light verse; popularized the limerick.

Le Chatelier, Henri Louis (1850–1936); French chemist, proposed principle governing changes in equilibrium. Used thermocouple to measure high temperatures; invented optical pyrometer.

Lee, Robert Edward (1807–70); American career soldier; C-in-C Confederate forces in Civil War, 1862; surrendered at Appomatox, 1865.

Leeuwenhoek, Anton van (1632–1723); Dutch biologist; observed through simple, but excellent, microscopes fine structure of many living tissues. First discovered protozoa; first described spermatozoa. Described organisms that were probably bacteria.

Leibniz, Gottfried Wilhelm, Baron von (1646–1716); German philosopher and mathematician, devised calculating machine that could add, subtract, multiply, divide. Recognized importance of binary system of numbers, and law of conservation of energy. First suggested aneroid barometer.

Leif Ericson (*c*.970–?); Viking explorer, sailed westwards in *c*.1000 and found 'Woodland' and 'Vinland', probably Newfoundland and Maryland.

Lenin, Vladimir (1870–1924); Russian revolutionary, founded Communist party (originally Bolsheviks). Exiled 1895–1917; returned to Russia to join February revolution; assumed power in October revolution. Became ill and lost control of government 1922. Name originally Vladimir Ulyanov

Leonardo da Vinci (1452–1519); Italian artist, architect, engineer, inventor, scientist, and mathematician, epitomized 'the complete man' of Renaissance. *Mona Lisa* and *The Last Supper* fresco; advanced studies in anatomy, circulation of blood, weaponry, flying machines, submarines, meteorology, and hydraulics.

Leoncavallo, Ruggiero (1858–1919); Italian composer of opera, including *I Pagliacci* (1892) and *La Bohème* (1897).

Lewis, Meriwether (1774–1809); American explorer, with William Clark, led expedition to explore the newly acquired lands of the Louisiana purchase, west of the Mississippi; reached Pacific Ocean.

Lewis, Sinclair (1885–1951); American author and journalist; portrayed American life; novels *Main Street* (1920), *Babbitt* (1922); *Elmer Gantry* (1927); Nobel prize for literature, 1930 (first US winner).

Lie, Trygve (1896–1968); Norwegian lawyer; first secretary-general of UN, 1946–1953; resigned because of Russian opposition to his views.

Liebig, Justus von (1803–73); German chemist, helped discover organic isomers. Developed methods of organic analysis. Studied biochemistry and established that energy in living organisms is derived from fats and carbohydrates.

Lincoln, Abraham (1809–65); Lawyer, became 16th president of United States, 1861; led Union through civil war; declared all slaves free, 1863; re-elected 1864; assassinated by John Wilkes Booth.

Lindbergh, Charles Augustus (1902–74), American aviator; made first solo flight across Atlantic Ocean, 1927. Eldest son kidnapped and killed, 1932.

Linnaeus, Carolus (Carl von Linné; 1707–78); Swedish botanist, established methodical classification of living things and began binomial nomenclature.

Lister, Lord Joseph (1827–1912); English surgeon, began antiseptic surgery, using carbolic acid to prevent infection.

Liszt, Franz (1811–86); Hungarian pianist and composer, arguably greatest pianist of all time. Invented tone poem; works include *Hungarian Rhapsodies*.

Livingstone, David (1813–73); Scottish missionary doctor, explored Africa. After crossing Kalahari Desert and travelling down River Zambesi, he sought sources of Congo (Zaïre) and Nile rivers. Feared lost, he was found by STANLEY (1871). Died still exploring.

Livy (Titus Livius; 59 BC–AD 17); Roman historian, spent 40 years writing history of Rome up to 9 BC, *Annals of the Roman People*. AUGUSTUS was his patron.

Lloyd George, David, 1st Earl of Dwyfor (1863–1945); British Liberal statesman. Sponsored old-age pensions, 1908; coalition prime minister in World War I, 1916; resigned 1922; created peer, 1945.

Locke, John (1632–1704); English philosopher and empiricist; in *Essay Concerning Human Understanding* (1690), abjured philosophical speculation in favour of sense experience as source of knowledge.

Lockyer, Sir Joseph Norman (1836–1920); English astronomer, observed spectra of solar prominences, and shared discovery of new element with French astronomer Pierre Janssen; named it helium. Founded and edited journal *Nature*, 1869–1920.

Lomonosov, Mikhail Vasilievich (1711–65); Founder of Russian science; ahead of his time with anti-phlogistic and atomist views; suggested law of conservation of mass and wave theory of light; first to record freezing of mercury; first observed atmosphere of Venus (1761), some 150 years before Western scientists. Also wrote important poems, dramas, grammar (reformed Russian language); first history and first accurate map of Russia. Two centuries later, birthplace Denisovka changed name to Lomonosov; crater on Moon named after him; still largely unrecognized in West.

London, Jack (1876–1916); American writer, sailor and tramp, author of *The Call of the Wild* (1903) and 42 other books.

Longfellow, Henry Wadsworth (1807–1882); American poet; professor of modern languages, 1835–54; poems include *The Wreck of the Hesperus*, *The Song of Hiawatha*, *The Courtship of Miles Standish*, *Evangeline*.

Lorca, Federico García (1898–1936); Spanish poet and playwright; killed in Spanish Civil War; *Romancero Gitano* (1928).

Lorentz, Hendrik Antoon (1853–1928); Dutch physicist, postulated that volume of electron decreases to zero, mass increases to infinity as it reaches speed of light; 1902 Nobel prize.

Louis XIV (1638–1715); King of France from 1643, had longest reign of any European monarch. Held magnificent court at Versailles and ruled as complete autocrat. Persecution of Huguenots led 400,000 to flee country.

Louis XVI (1754–93); Became king of France 1774. Country was poor and torn by class hatred. Under influence of nobility and his wife, MARIE ANTOINETTE, Louis antagonized the people. Revolution broke out 1789; Louis guillotined for treason.

Louis Philippe (1773–1850); Last king of France. In 1830 rebellion placed him on throne in place of Charles X. His repressive measures led to new revolt in 1848 and he abdicated.

Lovell, Sir Alfred Charles Bernard (b. 1913); English astronomer, built 250-ft dish radio telescope at Jodrell Bank.

Low, Sir David Alexander Cecil (1891–1963); New Zealand-born cartoonist, creator of the wartime character Colonel Blimp, and noted political satirist.

Lowell, Percival (1855–1916); American astronomer, studied Mars and began 'intelligent life' cult. Predicted discovery of Pluto.

Loyola, St. Ignatius (*c.*1491–1556); Basque nobleman, soldier, and theologian. After being wounded in battle, experienced religious conversion that led to his founding Society of Jesus (Jesuits).

Luther, Martin (1483–1546); German reformer, Bible scholar, and writer, initiated Protestant Reformation. Nailed 95 Theses to door of church in Wittenburg in protest at Church decadence; refused to retract at Diet of Worms and was excommunicated. Translated Bible into contemporary German; hymns and prose works.

MacArthur, Douglas (1880–1964); American general, C-in-C Allied forces, south-west Pacific, World War II; headed military government of Japan, 1945–51. C-in-C UN forces in Korea, 1950–51; dismissed for controversial statements.

Macaulay, Thomas Babington, 1st Baron Macaulay (1800–59); British historian and statesman, wrote *History of England*, covering 1685–1702; *Lays of Ancient Rome*; essays. Barrister and MP; secretary for war, 1839–41.

MacDonald, Flora (1722–90); Scottish Jacobite; helped Prince Charles Edward to escape after Culloden, 1746.

Mach, Ernst (1838–1916); Austrian physicist, discovered sudden change in airflow over object as

306

Abraham Lincoln was brought up on the wild Indiana frontier. As American president he led his country through the Civil War and abolished slavery before his assassination.

Marie Antoinette, the ill-fated Queen of France whose extravagance and frivolity contributed to the monarchy's unpopularity and to the French Revolution.

it nears speed of sound; speed of sound in air called Mach 1.

Machiavelli, Niccolò (1467–1527); Influential Italian statesman and author, claimed in *The Prince* that all rulers should aim for welfare of state, regardless of methods. Name became byword for devious plotting.

McMillan, Edwin Mattison (1907–91); American physicist, developed synchro-cyclotron. Discovered elements neptunium and plutonium; shared Nobel chemistry prize 1951.

Macmillan, Harold (1894–1987); British Conservative prime minister, 1957–63; created Earl of Stockton, 1984; spoke of 'wind of change' in Africa, 1960.

Magellan, Ferdinand (1480–1521); Portuguese navigator, found route to Pacific Ocean round south of America. Forcing way through Magellan Strait, he entered Pacific 1520. Was killed in skirmish in Philippines. Remaining ship and 18 men completed first voyage round world.

Mahler, Gustav (1860–1911); Bohemian composer and conductor; 9 symphonies, songs. Director Vienna State Opera (1897–1907); conductor New York Philharmonic Orchestra (1908–11).

Major, John (b. 1943); Conservative Prime Minister; held office 1990–92 due to mid-term leadership change; retained office in Conservative victory at general election of 1992.

Malphighi, Marcello (1628–94); Italian physiologist, first to discover, through microscope, number of fine structures in living tissue, including blood capillaries.

Malthus, Thomas (1766–1834); British economist; believed population grew faster than food supplies.

Manet, Édouard (1832–83); French Impressionist painter, refused to exhibit with Impressionists. Everyday, somewhat sentimental, subjects – *Washing Day* – handled in oils with light, soft touch.

Mann, Thomas (1875–1955); German novelist: *Buddenbrooks* (1901), *Joseph and his Brothers* (1934–44); opposed Nazism and went into exile, 1933; American citizen, 1944; Nobel prize, 1929.

Mao Tse-tung (Mao Zedong; 1893–1976); Chinese Communist ruler. He led the Communists to power in China. After quarrelling with CHIANG KAI-SHEK, formed government in Yenan 1927. Assumed power 1949. *Thoughts of Mao Tse-tung* required reading in China until revision of Mao's ideas under his successors, when the Maoist notion of continuous cultural revolution was rejected.

Marat, Jean Paul (1743–93); French physician and revolutionary; whipped up mob violence; leading Jacobin; stabbed in bath by CHARLOTTE CORDAY.

Marconi, Marchese Guglielmo (1874–1937); Italian electrical engineer, inventor of radio; shared Nobel physics prize 1909.

Marcus Aurelius (Antoninus) (121–180); Roman emperor and philosopher, born Marcus Annius Verus. Epigrammatic *Meditations* dispensed Stoic philosophy.

Maria Theresa (1717–80); Empress of Holy Roman Empire from 1740; defended right to throne in War of Austrian Succession, 1740–48; husband, Francis of Lorraine, recognized as emperor, 1748.

Marie Antoinette (1755–93); Queen of France and wife of LOUIS XVI; daughter of Empress MARIA THERESA of Austria. Interfered in politics, hated by French people. Tried and guillotined for treason.

Mark Antony (Marcus Antonius; c.83–30 BC); Roman general and supporter of JULIUS CAESAR. Shared power with Octavian (AUGUSTUS) and Lepidus as triumvir 43 BC; became lover of Cleopatra 41 BC; quarrelled with Octavian and defeated by him 30 BC; committed suicide.

Marlowe, Christopher (1564–93); Elizabethan English playwright, second only to WILLIAM SHAKESPEARE; *Doctor Faustus, Tamburlaine the Great, Edward II, The Jew of Malta;* killed in tavern brawl.

Marvell, Andrew (1621–78); English poet, supporter of Cromwell, defended MILTON following Restoration, attacked government in satires and pamphlets; most quoted poem is *To His Coy Mistress.*

Marx, Karl Heinrich (1818–83); German philosopher, radical leader, and theorist of socialism, laid foundations of Communism. With ENGELS, published *Communist Manifesto* (1848) and later wrote *Das Kapital* (1867). Doctrine of dialectical materialism revolutionized much of political thinking of 20th century. Exile in London from 1849.

Mary, Queen of Scots (1542–87); Succeeded father, James V, at age of one week. In 1558 married French dauphin, later King Francis II (d. 1560). Married cousin, LORD DARNLEY, 1565; he was murdered 1567. Married Earl of Bothwell 1567; forced to abdicate and fled to England 1568; prisoner of Elizabeth I; executed for treason.

Masaryk Two Czech statesmen: **Tomás** (1850–1937), first president of Czechoslovakia, 1918–35. **Jan** (1886–1948), son of Tomás; foreign minister, 1945–48; opposed Communists; died either by suicide or murder.

Mascagni, Pietro (1863–1945); Italian composer and conductor, remembered only for world-famous opera *Cavalleria Rusticana*.

Masefield, John (1878–1967); English poet and novelist; ran away to sea, 1891; works include many sea ballads; and novels *Sard Harker* (1924), *Dead Ned* (1938); poet laureate 1930–67; Order of Merit, 1935.

Mata Hari (1876–1917); Dutch dancer, born *Margaretha Gertrud Zelle*; executed as German spy by French.

Matisse, Henri (1869–1954); French painter and sculptor, leader of 'Fauves', used colour in art as he felt light functioned in nature; *Joy of Life* and *Large Red Interior*.

Maugham, W Somerset (1874–1965); English novelist and playwright; master short-story writer (stories collected as *The World Over*, 1951); novels include *Of Human Bondage* (1916), *The Moon and Sixpence* (1919), *The Razor's Edge* (1944); plays include *The Constant Wife* (1927).

Maupassant, Guy de (1850–93); Leading French short-story writer (*Boule de Suif*, 1880), and novelist (*Bel-Ami*, 1885).

Mauriac, François (1885–1970); French writer; verse *Les Mains Jointes* (1909); novels *Le Baiser au Lépreux* (1922), *Le Fin de la Nuit* (1939); essays; plays; Nobel prize for literature 1952.

Maximilian (Ferdinand Maximilian Joseph; 1832–67); Brother of Emperor Franz Joseph of Austria, offered throne of Mexico (1864) under French auspices; surrendered after defeat in civil war and executed by forces of Juarez.

Maxwell, James Clerk (1831–79); Scottish mathematician and physicist, revolutionized fundamental physics. Developed electromagnetic theory, predicting existence of electromagnetic waves (1864); used statistical methods on kinetic theory of gases.

Mazarin, Jules (1602–61); Italian-French cardinal and statesman, succeeded RICHELIEU as prime minister, laid base for foreign policy successes of LOUIS XIV; also built a huge personal fortune and library.

Mazzini, Giuseppe (1805–72); Italian patriot, lawyer and revolutionary leader of Young Italy movement, helped organize expedition led by GARIBALDI, refused office under newly established Italian monarchy following independence from Austrian rule, remaining an ardent republican.

Mead, Margaret (1901–1979); American anthro-

Above: Lorenzo de' Medici, ruler of Renaissance Florence, was known as 'the Magnificent' by his admirers. He was a man of many ideas who encouraged learning in both the arts and the sciences. Right: Michelangelo's marble sculpture of Lorenzo de' Medici, who had been his patron. The statue was not intended as a portrait, but as a personification of the reflective man, and was made for the Medici tomb.

pologist, studied culture of Pacific Islands. Wrote *Coming of Age in Samoa* (1928), etc.

Mechnikov, Ilya Ilich (also known as Elie Metchnikoff; 1845–1916); Russian-French bacteriologist, shared 1908 Nobel prize for work on white blood corpuscles.

Medici Name of ruling family of Florence, Italy. Founder **Giovanni de' Medici** (1360–1429), wealthy merchant. Sons **Cosimo** (banker); **Lorenzo** ('the Magnificent'), ruler of Florence (1449–92). **Marie de Médicis** (1573–1642) married HENRY IV of France.

Meir, Golda (1898–1978); Prime minister of Israel, 1970–74; born Kiev as Golda Mabovitch; brought up in United States; emigrated to Palestine 1921; minister to Moscow, 1948–49; foreign minister, 1956–65; retired; brought back to restore peace to Israeli Labour Party.

Melville, Herman (1819–91); American author; bank clerk, teacher, whaler, customs official; *Moby Dick* (1851); *Billy Budd* (1924).

Mendel, Gregor Johann (1822–84); Austrian botanist and monk, discovered principles of heredity; studied breeding of pea plants and proposed two laws of inheritance, ignored for 30 years.

Mendeleyev, Dmitri Ivanovich (1834–1907); Russian chemist, devised Periodic Table of elements, arranged according to atomic weight and valence.

Mendelssohn (Bartholdy), (Jacob Ludwig) Felix (1809–47); German composer and conductor,

classic experiment showing no measurable motion of Earth through ether. Worked on accurate measurement of speed of light. Suggested use of red line of cadmium spectrum as new standard of length (adopted 1925).

Mies van der Rohe, Ludwig (1886–1969); German architect, pioneered design of glass-walled skyscrapers. Director of Bauhaus (1930–33); emigrated to US when HITLER came to power.

Mill, John Stuart (1806–73); English philosopher and economist, convinced Utilitarian; advanced theories in widely studied *Principles of Political Economy* (1848).

Millais, Sir John Everett (1829–96); English painter who, with Holman Hunt and D G ROSSETTI, founded the Pre-Raphaelite Movement. His unconventional *Christ in the House of His Parents* aroused a storm of controversy.

Milne, Alan Alexander (1882–1956); English novelist and playwright; created the *Pooh* books for children.

Milton, John (1608–74); English poet, classical scholar, and a staunch Puritan; Latin secretary under Commonwealth; became blind 1652; major poems: *Paradise Lost* (1667), *Paradise Regained* (1671); *Samson Agonistes* (1671); many political pamphlets.

Miró, Joán (1893–1984); Spanish painter; with Dali pioneered Surrealism. Free style and bright colours; murals of UNESCO building, Paris.

Mohammed See MUHAMMAD.

Molière (Jean Baptist Poquelin; 1622–73); French dramatist; became an actor, 1643; plays include *Tartuffe* (1664), *Le Misanthrope* (1666), *Le Bourgeois Gentilhomme* (1670), *Le Malade imaginaire* (1673).

Monet, Claude (1840–1926); French Impressionist painter; open-air subjects – *Rouen Cathedral* – characterized by special lighting effects achieved by use of broken colour.

Montaigne, Michel de (1533–92); French writer; created the essay; strongly influenced French philosophers.

Montesquieu, Baron de (Charles Louis de Secondat; 1689–1755); French philosopher; wrote *The Spirit of Laws* (1748).

Montessori, Maria (1870–1952); First woman medical graduate of Rome University; became a famous educator. Her teaching methods of 'free discipline', where children move freely from task to task in the classroom, using simple but stimulating apparatus, apply to children of 3–10 years old and are outlined in the two handbooks she wrote.

Monteverdi, Claudio (1567–1643); Italian composer of madrigals, opera, motets, masses and religious music; innovative and reforming.

Montezuma II (1466–1520); Last Aztec emperor of Mexico, surrendered to Spanish adventurer CORTÉS; killed by stone while pacifying mob.

Montgolfier French brothers who invented first balloons capable of carrying men into air. First manned flight 1783. **Joseph Michel** (1740–1810) and **Jacques Étienne** (1745–99), born Vidalonlez-Annonay.

Montgomery, Bernard Law, 1st Viscount (1887–1976); Commanded British Eighth Army, 1942; spearheaded Normandy invasion, 1944. Victories included Battle of Alamein, 1942.

child prodigy, became favourite musician of Victorian England. Works include violin concerto, oratorio *Elijah*, *Scottish* and *Italian* symphonies.

Menuhin, Sir Yehudi (b. 1916); American-born British violinist and conductor; renowned for his playing of Bach, Beethoven and Elgar.

Menzies, Sir Robert Gordon (1894–1978); Australian statesman; prime minister 1939–41, 1949–66; knighted 1963.

Mercator, Gerardus (Gerhard Kremier; 1512–94); Flemish geographer, made first cylindrical projection map of world to show round surface on flat paper.

Metternich, Prince Clemens von (1773–1859); Austrian foreign minister, 1809–48; tried to keep status quo in Europe and resisted change; resigned after revolution of 1848; lived in retirement.

Michelangelo (Buonarroti) (1475–1564); Italian sculptor, painter, and poet, one of greatest figures of Renaissance. Covered vast ceiling of Sistine Chapel with awesome Biblical scenes. Other masterpieces include sculpture (*Pietà* in Rome), huge statues *David*, *Moses*. Appointed chief architect of St. Peter's, Rome (1547).

Michelson, Albert Abraham (1852–1931); German-born American physicist, won 1907 Nobel prize for work in optics. Devised interferometer, and made first accurate measurement of star's diameter. With Edward Williams Morley, conducted

Moore, Henry (1898–1986); English sculptor; he worked in wood, stone and bronze; advocate of direct carving. His massive statues, often reclining, decorate buildings world-wide.

More, Sir Thomas (1478–1535); English lawyer, statesman, and scholar, became Lord Chancellor under HENRY VIII. After king's divorce, More refused to recognize him as head of Church and was executed for treason. Wrote *Utopia*, describing ideal political state.

Morgan, Sir Henry (*c*.1635–88); Welsh pirate, arrested 1672, pardoned and made lieutenant-governor of Jamaica, 1672–83.

Morris, William (1834–96); English artist, poet, printer, and designer, one of Pre-Raphaelite Brotherhood. Founded firm of furniture-makers, and Kelmscott Press (high-class printers and publishers) to revive fine craftsmanship. Writings, e.g. *A Dream of John Ball*, reflect socialist views.

Mountbatten, Lord Louis (1900–79); Formerly prince; related to British royal family; distinguished naval career; Supreme Allied Commander, South-East Asia, 1943–1946; last viceroy of India, 1947; first governor-general, 1947–48; created Earl Mountbatten of Burma 1947. Murdered by IRA.

Mozart, Wolfgang Amadeus (1756–91); Austrian composer, child prodigy, became one of world's greatest musicians. Mastery of melody, phrasing and rhythm unique. Wrote over 40 symphonies (*Linz, Prague, Jupiter*, etc.), 21 piano concertos, several operas (*The Marriage of Figaro, Don Giovanni, The Magic Flute*, etc.), 24 string quartets, etc. Died in poverty.

Muhammad (*c*.570–632); Arab prophet and founder of Islam. With fanatical followers, conquered Mecca and laid foundations of Islamic Empire. Sayings revealed to him by Allah (God) embodied in *Koran*.

Muhammad Reza Pahlavi (1919–80); Ruler of Iran as shah, succeeding his father in 1941; introduced widespread industrialization and modernization based on oil revenues but ruled autocratically. Deposed by Islamic revolution, died in exile in Egypt shortly afterwards.

Müller, Paul (1899–1965); Swiss chemist; Nobel medicine and physiology prize (1948) for discovery of insecticidal use of DDT.

Murat, Joachim (1767?–1815); French soldier, cavalry leader under NAPOLEON, whose sister he married; king of Naples (1808); captured and executed (1815).

Musset, Alfred de (1810–57); French writer, lover of GEORGE SAND; poems *Tales of Spain and Italy* (1830); plays collected in *Comédies et Proverbes* (1840).

Mussolini, Benito (1883–1945); Dictator of Italy from 1922. At first schoolmaster and journalist; founded Fascist party, 1919; conquered Ethiopia (Abyssinia), 1935–36; took Italy into World War II in support of ADOLF HITLER, 1940; overthrown 1943; shot by resistance fighters.

Mussorgski, Modest Petrovich (1839–81); Russian composer, one of 'The Five' and, like BORODIN, not a professional musician. Realistic approach evident in opera *Boris Godunov*, orchestral pieces *Night on the Bare Mountain* and *Pictures from an Exhibition*.

Nansen, Fridtjof (1861–1930); Norwegian zoologist and statesman, made first crossing of Greenland, 1888, and tried to reach North Pole, 1895. Later Norway's ambassador to London; won Nobel peace prize 1922.

Napier, John (1550–1617); Scottish mathematician, invented logarithms and decimal point.

Napoleon I (1769–1821); Corsican soldier, made himself emperor of French 1804, already holding supreme power. Conquered Italy, Spain, Egypt, Netherlands, most of central Europe. Invasion of Russia failed (1812). Defeated Leipzig (1813), abdicated 1814. Returned to power 1815, defeated at Waterloo, exiled to St. Helena. Family name BONAPARTE.

Nash, Ogden (1902–71); American writer of humorous verse; *Hard Lines* (1931).

Nasser, Gamal Abdel (1918–70); Egyptian revolutionary and army officer; helped depose King Farouk, 1952; president from 1956; tried to modernize country; nationalized Suez Canal, 1956.

Nehru, Jawahalal (1889–1964); Indian statesman, worked for Indian independence, 1919–47; India's first prime minister, 1947–64.

Nelson, Horatio (1758–1805); British naval hero, lost eye and arm in battle; destroyed French fleet at Battle of Nile, 1798; won Battle of Copenhagen, 1801; destroyed another French fleet at Trafalgar, 1805, dying in moment of victory. Created viscount, 1801; liaison with Emma, Lady Hamilton, a public scandal.

Nero (Nero Claudius Drusus Germanicus; 37–68); Roman emperor. Feared plots, and had many people murdered, including mother, Agrippina. Undeservedly vain of powers as singer and actor. Committed suicide when army revolted.

Newman, John Henry (1801–90); English cardinal and leader of the so-called Oxford Movement which sought to move the Anglican Church closer to Catholicism; became a Roman Catholic (1845).

Newton, Sir Isaac (1642–1727); English scientist, made fundamental and far-reaching contributions to physics, mathematics, and astronomy. In 18 months (1665–67) he derived law of universal gravitation from his laws of motion, he discovered secrets of light and colour (particulate theory of light), and invented calculus. Thanks largely to HALLEY, works published in famous *Mathematical Principles of Natural Philosophy* (1687), known as *Principia*.

Ney, Michel (Marshal) (1769–1815); French soldier under NAPOLEON, marshal of France (1804), ennobled by Louis XVIII after the restoration of the monarchy (1814) but returned to his old Bonapartist allegiance during the Hundred Days; executed for treason after Waterloo.

Nicholas II (1868–1918); Last tsar of Russia; succeeded 1894; corruption of ministers led to revolutions in 1905, 1917; abdicated; killed by Communists 1918.

Niemeyer, Oscar (b. 1907); Brazilian architect, planned city of Brasilia.

Nietzsche, Friedrich Wilhelm (1844–1900); German philosopher, claimed that driving force of human endeavour was thirst for power. Elaborated ideas in *Thus Spake Zarathustra* (1880).

Nightingale, Florence (1820–1910); English reformer, became nurse; against much opposition organized sanitary barrack hospitals in Crimean War (1854–56), saving thousands of lives; known as 'lady with the lamp'. System adopted worldwide.

Nijinsky, Vaslav (1890–1950); Russian ballet dancer, danced with DIAGHILEV's Ballets Russes; grace, strength, and prodigious leaps revitalized male dancing in western Europe; insanity cut short career in 1917.

Nixon, Richard Milhous (b. 1913); Vice-president of United States, 1953–61; 37th president, 1969–74; resigned to avoid impeachment over Watergate conspiracy scandal.

Nobel, Alfred Bernhard (1833–96); Swedish inventor of dynamite and blasting gelatine, left his fortune to establish annual prizes for peace, literature, physics, chemistry, and physiology and medicine.

Oates, Titus (1649–1705); English conspirator; invented 'Popish plot' to assassinate Charles II; gave much false evidence; flogged and jailed for perjury.

O'Casey, Sean (1880–1964); Irish playwright and major influence in Irish literature; plays *Shadow of a Gunman* (1923), *Juno and the Paycock* (1924), *The Plough and the Stars* (1926); autobiography.

Oersted, Hans Christian (1777–1851); Danish physicist, first showed connection between electricity and magnetism.

Offenbach, Jacques (1819–80); German-born French composer, wrote more than 90 popular light operas: *Orpheus in the Underworld, La Belle Hélène*, etc.; one serious opera, *Tales of Hoffmann*.

O'Higgins, Bernardo (1778–1842); Chilean patriot, son of Irish father, led Chilean rebellion against Spaniards, 1814; fled to Argentina; with SAN

MARTIN won victory, 1817; became dictator of Chile; forced to resign, 1823.

Oistrakh, David (1908–74); Russian violinist and conductor, toured Western cities from 1950s. Russian composers such as PROKOFIEV composed for him. Son **Igor Oistrakh** (b. 1931) also violin virtuoso.

Olivier, Laurence Kerr, Lord Olivier of Brighton (1907–89); English actor, director, and theatre manager. Director of National Theatre; also made outstanding contribution to British acting at Old Vic; directed and starred in films *Henry V, Hamlet, Richard III*.

Omar Khayyám (d. c.1123); Persian poet, astronomer, mathematician; poem the *Rubáiyát* (Collection of Quatrains) freely translated by FITZGERALD (1859).

O'Neill, Eugene (1888–1953); American playwright; *Emperor Jones* (1921), *Mourning Becomes Electra* (1931), *Long Day's Journey into Night* (1957); Pulitzer prize-winner, Nobel prize for literature 1936.

Oppenheimer, J Robert (1904–67); American physicist, after early work on subatomic particles, headed development of atomic bomb at Los Alamos; opposed development of hydrogen bomb. Controversially labelled 'not a good security risk' by Atomic Energy Commission as McCarthyism' swept US.

Orwell, George (Eric Arthur Blair; 1903–50); English satirical novelist, b. Bengal. Independent radical thinker; fought in Spanish Civil War; main works: *The Road to Wigan Pier* (1937), *Animal Farm* (1945), *Nineteen Eighty-Four* (1949).

Osborne, John (b. 1929); British playwright, actor, and producer; plays include *Look Back in Anger* (1956); *The Entertainer* (1957); one of group of

Isaac Newton, the English scientist who discovered the laws of motion and gravity, examined the nature of light, and invented the branch of mathematics called calculus.

Below: Tsar Nicholas II of Russia with his family, all of whom were killed during the Russian Revolution. His only son, the Tsarevich, suffered from the terribly painful illness haemophilia, inherited through his German mother. Right: The dancer Nijinsky in Le Spectre de la Rose, *one of his most famous roles. His brilliant career was curtailed by his insanity.*

1950's writers, known popularly as angry young men.

Ovid (Publius Ovidius Naso; 43 BC–*c*. AD 17); Roman poet; narrative poem *Metamorphoses*; elegies; love poems.

Owen, Robert (1771–1858); Welsh social reformer, established in textile mills at New Lanark, Scotland, model co-operative industrial community with ideal housing and working conditions.

Owen, Wilfred (1893–1918); English war poet of the Western Front, killed in action; his poems edited by fellow poet Siegfried Sassoon (1920).

Owens, Jesse (James Cleveland Owens; 1913–80); Black American athlete who won four gold medals at the 1936 Berlin Olympics, thus contraverting the Nazi myth of white supremacy.

Paderewski, Ignace Jan (1860–1941); Polish virtuoso pianist and statesman, became Poland's first prime minister (1919). Works include *Minuet in G*.

Paganini, Niccolo (1782–1840); Italian violinist and composer, possibly greatest of all violinists; 24 caprices for solo violin.

Paine, Thomas (1737–1809); British-born agitator and writer; wrote *Common Sense* (1776) supporting American colonists; *Rights of Man* (1792), supporting French Revolution; fought in American War of Independence; member of French National Convention 1792–93; died in poverty in America.

Palestrina, Giovanni Pierluigi da (*c*.1525–94); Italian composer, hailed as 'Prince of Music'. Set rigid standards for composition of sacred music in which his contrapuntal skill for unaccompanied voices was of highest order.

Palladio, Andrea (1518–80); Italian architect, pioneered modern Italian architecture.

Palmerston, Viscount (Henry John Temple; 1784–1865); British statesman. War secretary, 1809–28; foreign secretary 1830–41, 1846–51; home secretary 1853–55; prime minister 1855–57, 1859–65. Known for aggressive policies.

Pankhurst, Emmeline (1858–1928); English suffragette, helped obtain vote for British women. With daughters **Christabel** and **Sylvia,** encouraged militant action by followers, including arson, chaining themselves to railings, and hunger strikes during imprisonment.

Papin, Denis (1647–1712?); French physicist, credited with being first to use steam to raise a piston; also built paddle boat driven by water power and invented 'steam digester' (pressure cooker).

Paracelsus, Philipus Aureolus (Theophrastus Bombastus von Hohenheim, 1493?–1541); Swiss alchemist and doctor, opposed medieval idea of body humours and advocated specific causes for specific diseases; and treatment based on observation and experience.

Parnell, Charles Stewart (1846–91); Irish nationalist member of Parliament who campaigned for Irish Home Rule; discredited following charge of adultery and ensuing divorce suit.

Pascal, Blaise (1623–62); French scientist, philosopher, and writer. Wrote treatise on conic sections at 16, invented calculating machine at 18. Founded, with FERMAT, theory of probability, formulated laws of hydraulics (Pascal's Law relating to pressures in vessel) and atmospheric pressure. Became Jansenist monk (1654), wrote *Provincial Letters* (1656–57), brilliant reply to Jesuits in defence of Jansenism.

Pasternak, Boris Leonidovich (1890–1960); Russian writer; main novel *Doctor Zhivago* (1957); declined 1958 Nobel prize for literature because of political pressure.

Pasteur, Louis (1822–95); French chemist, established bacteriology as science; devised method of gentle heating (pasteurization) to kill microorganisms in wine and beer; showed air to contain spores of living organisms; proposed germ theory of disease; developed inoculation of animals against anthrax and rabies.

Patrick, St (*c*.385–461); Patron saint of Ireland; born in Wales and sold into slavery in Ireland. After escaping, returned and evangelized Irish.

Patton, George Smith (1885–1945); American general World War II; reckless and outspoken.

Paul, St (d. *c*.AD 64); Christian missionary and apostle, originally Saul, Jewish nationalist and Roman citizen who persecuted Christians. After sudden conversion to Christianity, made many missionary journeys in Mediterranean regions. Author of major epistles in New Testament.

Pauli, Wolfgang (1900–58); Austrian-American physicist, 1945 Nobel prize for earlier discoveries about structure and nature of atoms; exclusion principle of quantum theory, 1925. Postulated existence of new particle (neutrino) in 1931 (detected 1956).

Pauling, Linus Carl (b. 1901); American chemist, revolutionized ideas of structure of molecules and nature of chemical bonds; 1954 Nobel chemistry prize and 1963 Nobel peace prize for work towards nuclear disarmament.

Pavlov, Ivan Petrovich (1849–1936); Russian physiologist, established idea of conditioned reflexes ('Pavlov's dogs'); 1904 Nobel prize for discovery of details of digestion and establishing importance of autonomic system.

Pavlova, Anna Matveyevna (1885–1931); Russian ballerina, danced for DIAGHILEV's Ballets Russes in Paris. Fokine created role of *The Dying Swan* for her.

Peary, Robert Edwin (1856–1920); American polar explorer and sailor, reached North Pole (1909) after previous failures.

Peel, Sir Robert (1788–1850); British statesman, prime minister 1834, 1841–46; founded London police force, 1829.

Penn, William (1644–1718); English Quaker leader, founder of Pennsylvania and Philadelphia.

Pepys, Samuel (1633–1703); English civil servant, organizer of modern British naval service; famous for his *Diary* (1660–69); secretary to the Admiralty.

Pericles (*c*.495–429 BC); Athenian statesman, led government of Athens 460–430 BC; known as 'father of democracy'.

Perón, Juan Domingo (1895–1974); Twice president of Argentina; in power 1946–55, supported by wife **Eva** (1919–52); exiled; again president, 1973–74; succeeded by second wife, **Maria Estela Isabel,** who was vice-president.

Pestalozzi, Johann Heinrich (1746–1827); Swiss educational reformer, set up schools for poor children, practised principles of ROUSSEAU, influenced teaching methods later used throughout Europe and America.

Pétain, Henri Philippe (1856–1951); French soldier and statesman; hero of World War I for defence of Verdun; recalled to be premier, 1940, on fall of France in World War II; headed Vichy government, 1940–44; tried and jailed for treason, 1945.

Peter I, the Great (1672–1725); Tsar of Russia 1689. Toured western Europe, then modernized Russia. Defeated CHARLES XII of Sweden, 1709. Founded St Petersburg (Leningrad). Enforced law harshly.

Petrarch (Francesco Petrarcha; 1304–74); Italian scholar and poet; perfected the sonnet; *Rime* (poems in Italian); many works in Latin; rediscovered the classics.

Petrie, Sir Flinders (1853–1942); British Egyptologist, excavated many Egyptian sites, also sites in Palestine and Stonehenge. Professor of Egyptology, London, 1892–1933.

Phidias (*c*.500–432 BC); Greek sculptor and architect, constructed Parthenon and gold and ivory *Athene*; *Zeus*, at Olympia.

Philip II of Spain (1527–98); Son of Emperor Charles V and Isabella of Portugal, married four times, second wife being Mary I of England, ruled huge empire in Europe and New World in the name of Roman Catholicism, warred with Elizabeth I of England (1587–89), built Escorial mausoleum but weakened Spanish economy.

Philip, Prince (b. 1921); Consort of ELIZABETH II. Son of Prince Andrew of Greece; brought up in England. Served Royal Navy, 1939–50; renounced Greek titles 1947 to marry Elizabeth; created Duke of Edinburgh.

Picasso, Pablo (1881–1973); Spanish artist; strongly influenced many 20th-century movements in art. With BRAQUE, pioneered Cubism. Later turned to pottery and sculpture.

Pindar (*c*.522–443 BC); Greek lyric poet; invented Pindaric ode; many odes and fragments of other poems survive.

Pitt, William, the Elder. See CHATHAM.

Pitt, William, the Younger (1759–1806); British statesman; son of EARL OF CHATHAM. Prime minister 1783–1801, 1804–06; organized opposition to NAPOLEON I; introduced income tax, 1799.

Pizarro, Francisco (*c*.1474–1541); Spanish conquistador, settled in Panama 1513; visited Peru 1524; conquered it with 180 men, 1528. Assassinated.

Planck, Max Karl Ernst Ludwig (1858–1947); German physicist, revolutionized physics with quantum theory; 1918 Nobel prize.

Plantagenet Surname of House of Anjou, which ruled England 1154–1399. Founded by Geoffrey, Count of Anjou, who married Matilda, daughter of Henry I of England. First Plantagenet king Henry II; last Richard II. After Richard, split into Houses of York and Lancaster.

Plato (*c*.427–347 BC); Greek philosopher, pupil of SOCRATES and teacher of ARISTOTLE. Teachings contained in written *Dialogues*: *Republic* deals with justice and ideal statesman; *Apology* describes trial of Socrates. Platonism, stressing idea of the good rather than material appearances, has influenced philosophic thought ever since.

Pliny Two Roman authors. **Pliny the Elder** (Gaius Plinius Secundus; 23–79) wrote on history and science; **Pliny the Younger** (Gaius Plinius Caecilius Secundus; *c*.61–*c*.113), his nephew, wrote *Letters* recording life of Rome.

Plutarch (*c*.46–*c*.120); Greek biographer and teacher, wrote *Parallel Lives of Illustrious Greeks and Romans*, important historical source work.

Poe, Edgar Allan (1809–49); American writer, with fascination for morbid and mysterious. Poetry *The Raven and Other Poems* (1845); novels *The Murders in the Rue Morgue* (1841); stories *Tales of the Grotesque and Arabesque* (1840).

Polo, Marco (*c*.1254–1324); Venetian merchant, travelled with father and uncle to court of emperor KUBLAI KHAN in Cathay (China). Served as travelling envoy for Kublai Khan, returning to Venice 1295, after 24-year absence, a wealthy man.

Pompey the Great (Gnaeus Pompeius Magnus; 106–48 BC); Roman general and statesman, cleared the Mediterranean of pirates; member of First Triumvirate with JULIUS CAESAR and Crassus (60 BC); opposed Caesar 48 BC; defeated; fled to Egypt, where he was murdered.

Pope, Alexander (1688–1744); English poet and satirist, noted for polished heroic couplets; poems include *The Rape of the Lock* (1712), *Dunciad* (1728); *Essay on Man* (1733–34).

Porter, Cole (1893–1964); American jazz and light music composer; hits included *Night and Day*.

Pound, Ezra (1885–1972); American poet; influenced many other poets; lived mostly in London, Paris, Italy; charged with treason after radio broadcasts during World War II on behalf of Italians; in mental hospital 1945–58.

Praxiteles (4th cent. BC); Athenian sculptor, only surviving work marble statue of *Hermes with the Infant Dionysius*. Copies of *Aphrodite of Cnidus* and other works show superb technique of flowing lines and balanced light and shadow.

Presley, Elvis Aaron (1935–77); American singer, who to a country and western background added black rhythm and blues to create a world-sweeping sound for which he was dubbed King of Rock 'n' Roll; first hit *Heartbreak Hotel* (1956). Energetic stage act earned him the nickname Elvis the Pelvis, and helped launch him to a fame equalled by few if any popular entertainers.

Priestley, Joseph (1733–1804); English chemist and religious thinker; discoverer of oxygen, ammonia, carbon monoxide, sulphur dioxide, hydrogen chloride, oxides of nitrogen. Accepted 'phlogiston' theory, and discovered 'dephlogisticated air', later called oxygen by LAVOISIER; shared discovery with SCHEELE. One of founders of Unitarian Society. Persecuted for political views; lived in US after 1794.

Prokofiev, Sergei Sergeyevich (1891–1953); Russian composer and pianist, broke new ground with satirical innovations in rhythm and harmony. Children's musical fairytale *Peter and the Wolf*; ballet *Romeo and Juliet*.

Proust, Marcel (1871–1922); French novelist; introspective, asthmatic; wrote seven-volume masterpiece *A la Recherche du Temps Perdu* (*Remembrance of Things Past*, 1913–27).

Ptolemy (*c*. AD 100); Greek astronomer, proposed Earth-centred idea of Universe. Also studied optics and geography.

Puccini, Giacomo (1858–1924); Italian operatic composer; gift for theatrical effect made works immensely popular; *La Bohème, Tosca, Madame Butterfly*.

Purcell, Henry (1659–95); English composer and organist, widely regarded as greatest English musical figure. Wrote many beautiful songs, opera *Dido and Aeneas*, much unsurpassed stage music.

Pushkin, Aleksander Sergeyevich (1799–1837); Russian writer and civil servant; play *Boris Godunov* (1826); narrative poems; *Eugene Onegin* (1833), *The Bronze Horseman* (1833); novels *The Queen of Spades* (1834); mortally wounded in duel.

Pythagoras (*c*.582–*c*.497 BC); Greek philosopher, founder of Pythagorean cult. Discovered relationship between length of vibrating string and pitch of note emitted. Calculated theorem of right-angled triangles.

Quisling, Vidkun Abraham Lauritz (1887–1945); Norwegian politician and traitor, collaborated with German invaders of Norway, 1940–45; executed for treason at liberation.

Rabelais, François (*c*.1494–1553); French satirist and monk; wrote *Pantagruel* (1533), *Gargantua* (1535), full of broad, racy 'Rabelaisian' humour.

Rachmaninov, Sergei Vasilievich (1873–1943); Russian composer and pianist lived in US after Russian Revolution. *Rhapsody on a Theme by Paganini, Prelude in C Minor*, piano concertos.

Racine, Jean Baptiste (1639–99); French playwright, produced seven tragic masterpieces, including *Plèdre* (1677).

Raleigh, Sir Walter (*c*.1552–1618); English soldier and courtier, established first colony in Virginia. Explored Guiana region of S. America. Jailed for treason by James I, he was freed to find gold, but failed. James had him executed.

Ramsay, Sir William (1852–1916); Scottish chemist, discovered argon (with RAYLEIGH), helium, neon, krypton, and xenon, and calculated atomic weight of radon; 1904 Nobel prize.

Ranjit Singh (1780–1839); Indian maharaja, founder of Sikh kingdom and known as the 'Lion of the Punjab'; an ally of the British in India.

Ranke, Leopold von (1795–1886); German historian, founded modern objective method of writing history based on research rather than legend or tradition. Professor of history, Berlin, 1825–71.

Raphael (Raffaello Sanzio; 1483–1520); Italian painter, influenced by work of LEONARDO and MICHELANGELO, painted numerous Madonnas with soft colouring and outline that went perfectly with their dignified pose; *School of Athens* fresco in papal apartments.

Rasputin, Grigori Yefimovich (1871–1916); Russian monk and mystic; gained influence over family of Tsar Nicholas II; murdered by Russian nobles.

Ravel, Maurice (1875–1937); French composer; logical, clear-cut approach to music set new standards in piano composition and orchestration. Works include *Bolero, Le Tombeau de Couperin*, suite *Mother Goose*, and ballet *Daphnis and Chloë*.

Ray, John (1627?–1705); English naturalist, made systematic collections of plants and animals; divided flowering plants into dicotyledons and monocotyledons, and attemped classification of species; assisted by pupil Francis Willoughby (1635–1672).

Rayleigh, Lord (John William Strutt; 1842–1919); English physicist, 1904 Nobel prize for contribution towards discovery of argon in air; studied wave motions of all types.

Reagan, Ronald Wilson (b. 1911); elected 40th president of the US, 1979, the oldest man ever elected; re-elected 1983 for second term; film actor, 1937–64; became a Republican politician, 1964; governor of California, 1967–75. Signed nuclear missile limitation treaty with the Soviet Union, 1987.

Rembrandt (Harmensz van Rijn) (1606–69); Dutch artist, master of light, colour, and mood, particularly in portraiture; *The Night Watch, The Anatomy Lesson*, many self-portraits and fine etchings.

Renoir, Pierre Auguste (1841–1919); French Impressionist painter; pure colour and subtle lighting used mainly for female nude; painted about 6000 pictures.

Revere, Paul (1735–1818); American silversmith and patriot; rode from Boston to Lexington to warn of British troop movements, 1755.

Reynolds, Sir Joshua (1723–92); English portrait painter, and the most fashionable artist of his day; painted many leading figures (Garrick, Johnson, Sarah Siddons); also much-admired studies of women and children.

Rhodes, Cecil John (1853–1902); British statesman, made fortune from diamonds in South Africa, and became premier of Cape Colony, 1890. Masterminded white settlement of Rhodesia, 1890–95. Disgraced over Jameson Raid on Transvaal, 1896.

Ribbentrop, Joachim von (1893–1946); German Nazi leader, ambassador to Britain, 1936–38; foreign minister, 1939–45; executed as war criminal.

Richardson, Samuel (1689–1761); English novelist, author of *Pamela* (1740), *Clarissa Harlowe* (1748), *Sir Charles Grandison* (1753).

Richelieu, Cardinal (Armand Jean du Plessis; 1585–1642); Chief minister of Louis XIII, 1624–42, and virtual ruler of France; cardinal from 1622; broke power of Huguenots and curbed that of nobles.

Riemenschneider, Tilman (*c*.1460–1531); German sculptor, leader of late Gothic style, remembered mainly for superbly carved church decorations.

Rimsky-Korsakov, Nikolai Andreyevich (1844–1908); Russian composer, one of 'The Five' with BORODIN, MUSSORGSKY, etc. Works include *Flight of the Bumblebee*, suite *Scheherazade*, opera *The Golden Cockerel*.

Robbia, della; Family of Italian sculptors working in Florence; **Luca** (1400–1482), nephew **Andrea** (1437–1528), Andrea's sons **Giovanni** (1469–1529) and **Girolamo** (1488–1566).

Robert I, the Bruce (1274–1329); Crowned king of Scotland in 1306, when throne was vacant. After many defeats in wars with English, won resounding victory at Bannockburn (1314); forced English to recognize Scottish independence (1328).

Robespierre, Maximilien (1758–94); French lawyer and revolutionary; leader of Jacobins; voted for death of LOUIS XVI; supported Reign of Terror, but himself fell victim to it.

Robin Hood (*c*.1200s); Legendary English folk-hero; may have basis in fact.

Above: Maximilien Robespierre, leader of the Reign of Terror during the French Revolution, and the guillotine on which so many perished on his orders and on which he himself was executed.
Right: Jean Jacques Rousseau, one of the most versatile and influential Frenchmen of the mid-18th century.

Rob Roy (Robert MacGregor; 1671–1734); Scottish Highland outlaw and cattle thief; captured by English but pardoned, 1727.

Rochester, John Wilmot, 2nd Earl (1647–80); English courtier and poet, dissolute companion of Charles II, author of elegant and erotic lyrics, biting satires.

Rockefeller Family of American businessmen and philanthropists; **John Davison** (1839–1937) became world's richest man through oil; began Rockefeller Foundation; **Nelson Aldrich** (1908–1979); became US vice-president to GERALD FORD, 1974.

Rodgers, Richard (b. 1902); American composer of musicals; partnership with Oscar Hammerstein yielded such hits as *The King and I* and *The Sound of Music*.

Rodin, Auguste (1840–1917); French sculptor, worked in bronze and marble; *The Thinker*, *The Kiss*.

Roentgen, Wilhelm Konrad (1845–1923); German physicist; 1901 Nobel prize for discovery of X-rays.

Romanov Name of Russian dynasty, descended from German nobleman. Romanovs were tsars of Russia 1613–1730 in direct male line, to 1917 in female line. Tsars included PETER I, THE GREAT; NICHOLAS II.

Rommel, Erwin (1891–1944); German field-marshal; commanded Afrika Korps World War II, 1941–43; commanded army in Normandy, 1944; ordered to commit suicide for opposing ADOLF HITLER.

Ronsard, Pierre de (1524–85); French lyric poet; leader of *La Pléide*, new poetic movement following the classics.

Roosevelt, Franklin Delano (1884–1945); 32nd president of United States, 1933–45; elected for four terms. Began 'New Deal' reforms to help end 'Great Depression'; led country through World War II; helped draft Atlantic Charter, 1941.

Ross, Sir Ronald (1857–1932); English physician, showed that malarial parasite is carried by mosquito; 1902 Nobel prize.

Rossetti (English brother and sister of Italian parentage): **Dante Gabriel** (1828–82); poet and painter, helped found Pre-Raphaelite Brotherhood (1848). **Christina Georgina** (1830–94); short lyric poems, especially for children.

Rossini, Gioacchino Antonio (1792–1868); Italian composer, mainly operatic; vigour, humour, and gift for melody ensured immediate success of his operas: *The Barber of Seville*. *La Cenerentola*; also wrote lovely *Stabat Mater* and 15 cantatas.

Rothschild Jewish family of bankers. Founder **Mayer Amschel** (1743–1812), in Frankfurt-am-Main; his five sons opened banks in London, Paris, Vienna, Naples. **Lionel Walter** (1858–1937), distinguished zoologist; **Nathaniel**, third baron (b. 1910); biologist and bomb-disposal expert.

Rousseau, Henri 'Douanier' (1844–1910); French 'primitive' painter who worked as a customs official. No formal art training. Best known for fantasy paintings.

Rousseau, Jean Jacques (1712–78); French writer, philosopher, composer; champion of liberty; works include novel *Emile* (1762), *The Social Contract* (1762), opera *Les Muses Galantes* (1747), autobiography *Confessions* (1782). In later years became partly insane.

Rubens, Sir Peter Paul (1577–1640); Flemish painter commissioned by several European courts. Vast output only maintained by establishing 'workshop' in which other artists were employed. Rich, sensuous colours and textures characterized his paintings; masterpiece, triptych *Elevation of the Cross* (Antwerp Cathedral). Successful diplomat, knighted by Charles I.

Rupert, Prince (1619–82); Son of Elector Palatine Frederick V and grandson of James I of Britain; dashing army commander who served as general of horse to Charles I during Civil War; later dismissed in disgrace but restored to favour at Restoration as Admiral of the Fleet; experimented with munitions and alloys.

Ruskin, John (1819–1900); English art critic, reformer, philanthropist; *Modern Painters* (1843–60), *Seven Lamps of Architecture* (1849), *Stones of Venice* (1851–53), *Sesame and Lilies* (1865); seeker of beauty in all things, profoundly influenced contemporaries.

Russell, Bertrand, (third Earl Russell; 1872–1970); English mathematician, philosopher, pacifist, social reformer; *Principles of Mathematics* (1903), *The ABC of Relativity* (1925), *History of Western Philosophy* (1945); Nobel prize for literature 1950.

Rutherford, Ernest, Baron Rutherford of Nelson (1871–1937); New Zealand-born British physicist, first to 'split' atom, 1919. Named and studied alpha- and beta-rays, and discovered gamma-rays. Studied radioactive decay, discovered half-life and proposed idea of isotopes. Discovered nature of alpha-particles, and, using them, evolved theory of nuclear atom for which he received 1914 Nobel chemistry prize.

Saint-Saëns, (Charles) Camille (1835–1921); French composer; opera *Samson and Delilah*, orchestral pieces *Danse Macabre* and *Carnival of the Animals*.

Saladin (1138–93); Arab soldier and statesman, sultan of Egypt and Syria, driving Christians from Holy Land; captured Jerusalem, fought against and eventually repelled the Third Crusade, led by Richard I (Lionheart) of England and Philip II of France. Widely respected for his chivalry and honour.

Sand, George (Amandine Aurore Lucie Dupin, Baronne Dudevant; 1804–76); French novelist; mistress of Alfred de Musset and CHOPIN; pioneer of 'women's lib'; novels *Indiana* (1831), *The Miller of Angibault* (1845).

San Martin, José de (1778–1850); Argentinian general, great leader in cause of S. America's struggle for independence against Spain.

Sappho (*c.*600 BC); Greek lyric poet; she wrote nine books of poems, of which one ode survives; headed religious cult.

Sargent, Sir (Harold) Malcolm (1895–1967); British conductor and organist, largely responsible for success of Promenade concerts as conductor-in-chief.

Sartre, Jean-Paul (1905–81); French philosopher and novelist, leader of Existentialist movement, claiming that man creates a meaning for his existence by taking responsibility for own destiny.

Savonarola, Girolamo (1452–98); Italian priest who denounced the corruption of Florentine society, led a rebellion against Pope Alexander VI, captured and executed for sedition and heresy.

Scarlatti, Alessandro (1659–1725); Italian composer, helped to develop Italian opera, wrote much church music. Son **(Giuseppe) Domenico** (1685–1757), harpsichord virtuoso, composed about 600 harpsichord sonatas.

Scheele, Karl Wilhelm (1742–86); Swedish chemist, prepared and discovered remarkable number of new substances, including several acids, inorganic gases, chlorine (did not recognize it as element), manganese, barium, tungsten, nitrogen, and, most important of all, oxygen, but did not carry work

Walter Scott, the Scottish writer who qualified as a lawyer before becoming famous as a poet. He then turned to novels, at first published anonymously for fear of damaging his literary reputation. They remained popular well into the 20th century.

far enough (in case of oxygen, published too late) and others usually got credit.

Schiller, Friedrich von (1759–1805); German poet and playwright; army surgeon, later professor of literature; plays: *Wallenstein* (1799), *Maria Stuart* (1800), *Wilhelm Tell* (1804); books on history and art.

Schliemann, Heinrich (1822–90); German archaeologist, discovered remains of ancient Troy; also ancient Mycenae. Born poor, made fortune as trader; retiring in 1863 to study archaeology. Spoke 13 languages.

Schoenberg, Arnold (1874–1951); Austrian composer, created a new method of composition using a 12-tone series, pioneered atonal music, taught Berg and Webern.

Schopenhauer, Arthur (1788–1860); German philosopher, combined German idealism with Oriental fatalism. Taught negation of human will and claimed that strife arose only from conflict of wills; *The World as Will and Idea* (1819).

Schrödinger, Erwin (1887–1961); Austrian physicist, shared 1933 Nobel prize for work on wave (quantum) mechanics; 'Schrödinger equation' put quantum theory on mathematical basis.

Schubert, Franz Peter (1797–1828); Austrian composer, astonishing gift for melody; produced over 600 well-loved songs (*Ave Maria, The Erl King*, etc.). Established German *lieder* ('songs') tradition; numerous chamber works, 2 symphonies including *The Unfinished*. Died of typhus.

Schumann, Robert Alexander (1810–56); German composer and pianist, leader of German Romantic school. Turned to composition only after injuring hand through over-zealous piano practice. Wrote piano pieces *Papillons, Carnival*, etc.; cello concerto, 4 symphonies.

Schweitzer, Albert (1875–1965); Alsatian theologian, physician, philosopher, missionary and

musician, devoted life to caring for sick in French Equatorial Africa (Lambaréné); raised funds with organ recitals in Europe; Nobel peace prize 1952. Regarded by many as noblest figure of 20th century.

Scipio Name of two Roman generals, father and son. **Publius Scipio the Elder** (*c*.236–*c*.184 BC) defeated HANNIBAL. **Publius Scipio the Younger** (185–129 BC) besieged and captured Carthage.

Scott, Robert Falcon (1868–1912); English naval officer, led an expedition to South Pole in 1911. Hampered by bad weather, Scott reached Pole in January 1912, to find AMUNDSEN had beaten him to it. Scott's party died on return trip.

Scott, Sir Walter (1771–1832); Scottish poet and novelist, became lawyer, won fame with *The Lay of the Last Minstrel* (epic poem; 1805); first novel *Waverley* (1814), instant success; from 1825 worked unceasingly to pay off creditors of firm he had shares in; created baronet 1820.

Scriabin, Alexander Nikolayevich (1872–1915); Russian composer and pianist, a Romantic writer of piano pieces and architect of massive tone poems such as *Prometheus*.

Segovia, Andrés (1893–1987); Spanish guitarist; revived art of classical guitar and pioneered its use as a concert instrument. Many composers wrote for him, and he transcribed earlier instrumental works for the guitar.

Seneca (Lucius Annaeus Seneca; *c*.4 BC–AD 65); Roman statesman, writer, and playwright. Copious essays, including *Moral Letters* urging man's Stoical resignation to divine wisdom. Nero's tutor.

Shackleton, Sir Ernest Henry (1874–1922); British naval officer, led two expeditions to Antarctica, in 1907–08 and 1915–16. Died of heart failure while travelling to lead third expedition.

Shaftesbury, Anthony Ashley Cooper, 7th Earl (1801–85); English philanthropist, urged reform of child labour regulations, campaigned for abolition of female labour in mines, use of small children as chimney sweeps, helped set up ragged schools.

Shakespeare, William (1564–1616); Greatest English dramatist; actor from *c*.1590; poems *Venus and Adonis, Sonnets*; plays include come-

William Shakespeare, and the Globe Theatre at which many of his plays were first produced. He is acknowledged to be the greatest playwright of the English language. Much of his life is still the subject of speculation.

dies, histories, tragedies; outstanding are *Hamlet, Macbeth, Othello, King Lear, Romeo and Juliet, A Midsummer Night's Dream, The Tempest, Henry V, Julius Caesar.*

Shapley, Harlow (1885–1972); American astronomer, compiled picture of galaxy that gave relatively true idea of real size, placing Solar System towards edge instead of in centre.

Shaw, George Bernard (1856–1950); Irish-born dramatist, critic, and active Socialist; music and drama critic for newspapers; member of Fabian Society; main plays include *Caesar and Cleopatra* (1901), *Major Barbara* (1905), *Pygmalion* (1912; as a musical, *My Fair Lady* 1956), *St. Joan* (1923).

Shelley, Percy Bysshe (1792–1822); English Romantic poet; rebel against tyranny and convention; poems include *Prometheus Unbound* (1820), *Adonais* (1821); drowned near Leghorn, Italy. Married as second wife **Mary Wollstonecraft Godwin** (1797–1851; author of *Frankenstein*, 1818).

Sheraton, Thomas (1751–1806); English furniture designer; simple lines and elegant proportions.

Sheridan, Richard Brinsley (1751–1816); British playwright and politician; born in Ireland; theatre manager from 1776; MP 1780–1812; led impeachment of WARREN HASTINGS; plays *The Rivals* (1775), *The School for Scandal* (1777), *The Critic* (1779).

Sherman, William Tecumseh (1820–91); American general, on Union side in Civil War; laid waste much of Georgia, S Carolina.

Shostakovitch, Dmitri (1906–1975); Russian composer; symphonies, operas, and ballets. Weathered repeated Soviet disapproval without compromising his musical standards.

Sibelius, Jean Julius Christian (1865–1957); Finnish composer, one of leading symphonists of 20th century. Works, inspired by Finnish legends, include tone poem *Finlandia*, 7 symphonies, violin concerto.

Sidney, Sir Philip (1554–86); English soldier, statesman, poet. Mortally wounded at Battle of Zutphen, Netherlands. Poems: *Astrophel and Stella*.

Sikorsky, Igor (1889–1972); Russian aircraft designer, built world's first four-engined aeroplane (1913) and designed first commercially successful helicopter (1939).

Sinatra, Frank (b. 1917); American singer and film actor; worldwide following built up through radio and records. Starred in *From Here to Eternity*.

Smetana, Friedrich (1824–84); Czech composer, shaped Czech national school of music. Works include tone poem *Ma Vlast*, charming Mozartian opera *The Bartered Bride*.

Smith, Adam (1723–90); Scottish economist, author of *The Wealth of Nations* (1776), seen by many as the starting point for modern economic theory.

Smith, Joseph (1805–44); American religious leader, claimed to have translated *Book of Mormon* from ancient language written on golden plates. Murdered by mob in Illinois; his followers established Church of Jesus Christ of Latter-Day Saints (Mormons).

Smollett, Tobias George (1721–71); Scottish novelist and surgeon, author of the picaresque works *The Adventures of Roderick Random* (1748), *The Adventures of Peregrine Pickle* (1751); last and best novel is *The Expedition of Humphrey Clinker* (1770).

Smuts, Jan Christiaan (1870–1950); South African soldier and statesman, Boer general in war of 1899–1902; fought for Britain, World War I; prime minister South Africa, 1919–24, 1939–48.

Snorri Sturluson (1179–1241); Icelandic poet and historian; head of legislature; wrote *Heimskringla*, poetic chronicles, and *Prose Edda*, textbook of Norse mythology.

Socrates (469–399 BC); Greek philosopher, taught by method of question and answer; acknowledgment of one's own ignorance is beginning of wisdom. Among his pupils were PLATO and Xenophon. Died of hemlock self-poisoning, after being condemned to death for unpopular political ideas.

Soddy, Frederick (1877–1956); English chemist, 1921 Nobel prize for discovery of isotopes.

Solon (*c*.638–*c*.559 BC); Athenian archon (chief magistrate) and lawmaker; reorganized constitution, law courts, and economic affairs of Athens.

Solzhenitsyn, Alexander Isayevich (b. 1918); Russian author; expelled from Russia 1974 for publication in West of *The Gulag Archipelago*, a denunciation of Russian labour camps; Nobel prize for literature 1970; other major works *One Day in the Life of Ivan Denisovich* (1963), *The First Circle* (1968), *Cancer Ward* (1968), *August 1914* (1972).

Sophocles (*c*. 496–*c*.406 BC); Greek tragic playwright; served as treasurer of Athens and army commander; wrote 123 plays, of which 7 survive: *Oedipus Rex, Oedipus at Colonus, Antigone, Electra, Philoctetes, Ajax, Maidens of Trachus*.

Sousa, John Philip (1854–1932); American composer and bandleader, 'march king of the USA'; *Blaze Away, Under the Double Eagle, El Capitan,* *The Stars and Stripes Forever, Washington Post*.

Southey, Robert (1774–1843); English poet and biographer, friend of COLERIDGE, proponent of idealized colony – pantisocracy – in America; became Poet Laureate (1813), but today esteemed more for his prose writings and biographies than for his poetry.

Speke, John Hanning (1827–64); English explorer, travelled with BURTON in search of source of Nile River, discovered Lakes Tanganyika and Victoria, announcing the latter as the Nile source.

Spence, Sir Basil Urwin (1907–1976); Scottish architect, designed the new Coventry cathedral; is also known for his innovative approach in modern university building.

Spencer English family tracing ancestry from Robert Despenser, steward to William the Conqueror. The present Princess of Wales (b. 1961) traces her lineage through her father, the 8th Earl, to James I.

Spender, Stephen (b. 1909); English poet and critic, originally political like most of his contemporaries of the 1930s, later more personal; critical work appeared in *Horizon* and *Encounter* magazines. Spent some years in Germany with fellow-writer Christopher Isherwood.

Spengler, Oswald (1880–1936); German historian and philosopher, drew convincing analogy between birth, growth, and death of civilizations and human life-cycles. Doctrine first expounded in famous 2-volume work *Decline of the West* (1918–22).

Spenser, Edmund (1552–99); English poet; *The Shepheardes Calender* (1579), dedicated to SIDNEY, *Astrophel* (1586) on Sidney's death, and *Faerie Queene* (six books, 1590–96).

Spinoza, Benedict or Baruch (1632–77); Dutch-Jewish philosopher, equated God with Nature as basic substance of universe; published ideas in *Ethics* (1677).

Stahl, Georg Ernst (1660–1734); German chemist, proposed phlogiston theory of combustion.

Stalin, Joseph (1879–1953); Russian revolutionary, succeeded LENIN as ruler of Soviet Union, 1924. Purged political opponents, 1930s. Led country during German invasion of World War II. Name originally *Iosif Dzhugashvili*.

Stanley, Sir Henry Morton (1841–1904); American-British journalist, explored Africa. Sent to find LIVINGSTONE 1871. Explored Lakes Victoria and Tanganyika, 1874, then sailed down Congo (Zaire). Rescued Emin Pasha in Sudan, 1888.

Stavisky, Serge Alexandre (*c*. 1886–1934); Russian-born French swindler, sold millions of worthless bonds to workers; ensuing scandal revealed widespread political corruption and brought downfall of two ministries.

Steele, Sir Richard (1672–1729); Irish-born British writer and editor; founded successively the *Tatler, Spectator, Guardian, Englishman*; wrote many essays, commenting on affairs of day.

Stein, Gertrude (1874–1946); American writer, resident in France where she entertained visiting expatriates and fellow writers; wrote *The Autobiography of Alice B Toklas* and other books.

Steinbeck, John (1902–68); American novelist and journalist; main works *Of Mice and Men* (1937), *The Grapes of Wrath* (1939), *East of Eden* (1952),

The Australian soprano Joan Sutherland, who with the encouragement of her conductor husband Richard Bonynge gained international fame.

The Winter of Our Discontent (1961); Nobel prize for literature 1962.

Steiner, Rudolf (1861–1925); Austrian writer, philosopher and teacher, founder of the anthroposophical movement.

Stendhal (Marie Henri Beyle; 1783–1842); French novelist and soldier; *Le Rouge et le Noir* (1831), *La Chartreuse de Parme* (1839).

Stephenson, George (1781–1848); English inventor of steam locomotive; built Stockton–Darlington Railway (1821–25). Also developed miner's lamp and alarm clock. Son **Robert** (1803–59) built bridges, viaducts, and railways.

Sterne, Laurence (1713–68); Irish-born novelist; clergyman from 1738; main work *The Life and Opinions of Tristram Shandy* (1760–67, unfinished).

Stevenson, Robert Louis (1850–94); Scottish poet and novelist; travelled in search of health; lived in Samoa from 1888; novels include *Treasure Island* (1883), *Dr. Jeykll and Mr. Hyde* (1886).

Stowe, Harriet (Elizabeth) Beecher (1811–96); American novelist, author of *Uncle Tom's Cabin*, which with its antislavery sentiments, inspired abolitionists.

Stradivari, Antonio (1644–1737); Italian musical instrument-maker; superb violins most coveted of all instruments today. With sons set up workshop at Cremona; also made cellos.

Strafford, Thomas Wentworth, 1st Earl (1593–1641); English statesman, supporter of Charles I against Parliamentary opposition, Lord Lieutenant of Ireland and virtual ruler of Britain as chief adviser to king; was impeached for treason, abandoned by Charles, and beheaded.

Strauss, Johann (the elder, 1804–49; the younger, 1825–99); Austrian composers, father and most famous of 3 sons. Elder wrote *Radetzky March*. Younger known as 'Waltz King'; *The Blue Danube*, operettas such as *Die Fledermaus* (*The Bat*).

Strauss, Richard (1864–1949); German composer and conductor, work influenced early by BRAHMS and later by WAGNER. Wrote instrumental and ballet music, operas (*Der Rosenkavalier*), symphonic poems (*Don Juan*).

Stravinsky, Igor Fedorovich (1882–1971); Russian-born American composer; his new music full of dissonances and strange rhythms alienated critics at first. Ballets *The Fire-Bird*, *Petrouchka*, and *Rite of Spring*; opera *The Rake's Progress*.

Strindberg, August (1849–1912); Swedish writer; also teacher, librarian; plays include *The Father* (1887), *Miss Julie* (1888), *The Ghost Sonata* (1907); novels.

Stuart Name of Scottish royal house from 1371 to 1714; of English royal house 1603–1714. Founder Walter FitzAlan, High Steward (Stewart, Stuart) of Scotland. First King **Robert II** (1316–90). Notable members: James VI (I of England); CHARLES I, Charles II; James VII and II; MARY QUEEN OF SCOTS.

Stuart, Charles Edward (1720–88); Known as the Young Pretender to the British crown; son of James Edward Stuart, and grandson of James II. Led the unsuccessful 1745 invasion of Scotland in an attempt to bring about a Jacobite rebellion against the Hanoverian dynasty. Defeated at Culloden (1746), lived rest of his life in exile.

Sturt, Charles (1795–1869); British army officer, discovered Darling, Murray, and Murrumbidgee rivers, Australia.

Suetonius (Gaius Suetonius Tranquillus; *c*.69–140); Roman biographer; wrote *Lives of the Caesars*, valuable source book.

Suleiman I, the Magnificent (*c*.1494–1566); Sultan of Ottoman Empire from 1520, conquered Belgrade, Rhodes, part of Hungary, eastern Turkey, Syria; known as *Kanuni*, the Lawgiver, because of reforms.

Sulla, Lucius Cornelius (138–78 BC); Successful Roman general, crushed rivals and made himself dictator, 82 BC.

Sullivan, Sir Arthur (1842–1900); English composer, wrote *The Lost Chord* and *Onward Christian Soldiers*. Gained undying fame through collaboration with W S GILBERT which produced the Savoy operas (*The Mikado*, *The Pirates of Penzance*, etc.).

Sun Yat-sen (1866–1925); Chinese revolutionary and statesman; headed Kuomintang (Nationalist) party; president of China 1912, 1921–25.

Sutherland, Graham (1903–80); British painter of landscapes, portraits, war-torn cities; designed the tapestry *Christ in Glory* for Coventry Cathedral (1962).

Sutherland, Joan (b. 1926); Australian operatic coloratura soprano, nicknamed 'La Stupenda' by La Scala audiences. Joined Covent Garden Opera Company (1952) and gained overnight fame for portrayal of Lucia in *Lucia di Lammermoor*. CBE in 1961.

Swedenborg, Emanuel (1688–1772); Swedish scientist, theologian, philosopher, and mystic, writings influenced BLAKE, BALZAC, and others. Followers organized Church of the New Jerusalem after his death.

Swift, Jonathan (1667–1745); Irish-born satirist; clergyman from 1694, Dean of St. Patrick's, Dublin, from 1713; main work *Gulliver's Travels* (1726).

Swinburne, Algernon Charles (1837–1900); English writer of lyric and romantic poetry and drama of uneven quality.

Synge, John Millington (1871–1909); Irish dramatist; helped to found Abbey Theatre, Dublin; plays include *Riders to the Sea* (1904), *The Playboy of the Western World* (1907).

Tacitus, Cornelius (*c*.55–*c*.120); Roman historian, wrote *Annals*, Roman history from Tiberius to Nero; *Historiae*, continuing history up to Domitian; works describing life in Germany and Roman Britain.

Tagore, Rabindranath (1861–1941); Indian poet, awarded Nobel prize for literature (1913), resigned his knighthood (1919) in protest at British policy in Punjab.

Talleyrand (Charles Maurice de Talleyrand-Périgord, Prince de Bénévent; 1754–1838); French statesman and cleric, revolutionary; foreign minister 1796–1807; adviser to LOUIS PHILIPPE.

Tallis, Thomas (1510?–85); English organist and composer, who established English cathedral music; with William Byrd granted royal monopoly warrant to print music (1575).

Tamerlane (1336–1405); Mongol chieftain from Samarkand, conquered empire in eastern Asia stretching from Turkey to India and north to Moscow, in Europe. Name means 'Timur the Lame'.

Tasman, Abel Janszoon (*c*.1603–*c*.1659); Dutch trader, discovered Tasmania, New Zealand, Tonga, and Fiji (1642–43).

Tasso, Torquato (1544–95); Italian poet; taught astronomy and mathematics; became deranged, 1577; main works *Gerusalemme Liberata* (1575), *Aminta* (1573).

Tchaikovsky, Piotr Ilyich (1840–93); Russian Romantic composer, most popular of all Russian composers with Western audiences. Fantasy overture *Romeo and Juliet, 1812 Overture, Piano Concerto No. 1*; ballets *Swan Lake, Sleeping Beauty, The Nutcracker.*

Teilhard de Chardin, Pierre (1881–1955); French explorer, palaeontologist and theologian who made important finds of early man in eastern Asia; major philosophical work is *The Phenomenon of Man* (1939, not published until 1955).

Telford, Thomas (1757–1834); Scottish engineer, who built the Caledonian Canal and the Menai Strait suspension bridge, plus numerous roads and road bridges.

Tenniel, Sir John (1820–1914); English caricaturist and cartoonist, illustrated *Alice's Adventures in Wonderland* and *Through the Looking Glass*; long-time illustrator for *Punch*.

Tennyson, Alfred, first Lord Tennyson (1809–92); English poet laureate from 1850; poems include *Idylls of the King* (1859), *Locksley Hall, In Memoriam*; plays.

Terence (Publius Terentius Afer; 185–159 BC); Roman playwright; born in Carthage; at first a slave, but freed; his six surviving plays are *Andria, Heautontimoroumenos, Eunuchus, Phormio, Hecyra, Adelphi.*

Tereshkova, Valentina Vladimirova (b. 1937); The first woman in space. Formerly a Russian textile worker, she was launched in the spacecraft *Vostok 6* in June 1963, and returned to Earth three days later after completing 48 orbits.

Thackeray, William Makepeace (1811–63); English novelist and satirist, b. Calcutta; novels include *Vanity Fair* (1848), *Henry Esmond* (1852), *The Newcombes* (1855).

Thant, U (1909–75); Burmese diplomat; UN secretary-general 1961–71.

Thatcher, Margaret Hilda (b. 1925); first woman prime minister of Great Britain; led Conservative Party to power in general election of 1979, and won general elections of 1983 and 1987. She failed to win re-election as party leader in 1990 and resigned as prime minister.

Thomas, Dylan (1914–53); Welsh poet; outstanding work *Under Milk Wood* (1954), a play for radio; novel *Portrait of the Artist as a Young Dog* (1940); lecturer, broadcaster; tempestuous life, early death due to alcoholism.

Thomas à Becket, St. (1118–70); Archbishop of Canterbury; murdered in Canterbury Cathedral at instigation of former friend and patron Henry II. The two quarrelled repeatedly over respective jurisdiction of Church and State.

Thomas à Kempis (*c*.1380–1471); German theologian, believed to be author of *The Imitation of Christ*, one of most widely read Christian devotional works.

Thomas Aquinas, St. (1225–74); Catholic theologian and philosopher, became a Dominican and later taught at Paris. Systemized Catholic theology and published doctrine of Thomism in *Summa Theologica.*

Thomson, Sir Joseph John (1856–1940); English physicist, studied cathode rays and thus discovered electron. Measured its mass-to-charge ratio; 1906 Nobel prize.

Thoreau, Henry David (1817–62); American writer; *A Week on the Concord and Merrimack Rivers* (1849); *Walden* (1854); 20-vol. collection of writings published 1906.

Thurber, James (1894–1961); American humorist and artist; collections of sketches *The Owl in the Attic* (1931), *My Life and Hard Times* (1934), *Let Your Mind Alone* (1937).

Tiglath Pileser III (d. 728 BC); Originally named Pul, usurped throne of Assyria 745 BC. Occupied most of Israel (734 BC), and annexed Babylon.

Tintoretto (Jacopo Robusti; 1518–94); Italian painter; elongated figures, impressionistically exaggerated, are feature of his many religious subjects; *Paradise*, painted for Doge's Palace.

Titian (Tiziano Vecellio; *c*.1487–1576); Italian painter, greatest of Venetian painters of High Renaissance; early influenced by work of Giorgione. Pictures, mythological and religious, characterized by rich, warm colour.

Tito (Josip Broz; 1892–1980); Yugoslav partisan, led Communist resistance in Yugoslavia during World War II; prime minister 1945–53; president from 1953.

Tolstoy, Leo Nicolayevich, Count Tolstoy (1828–1910); Russian writer, philosopher, and reformer; in 1890 gave up his wealth and worked as peasant; novels include *War and Peace* (1866), *Anna*

Karenina (1877); other works; *What I Believe* (1884).

Torricelli, Evangelista (1608–47); Italian physicist, invented first barometer (1643); first proposed atmosphere to be finite and space to be a vacuum.

Toscanini, Arturo (1867–1957); Italian conductor, became best known of all conductors. Musical director at La Scala, Milan; left fascist Italy, settled in US, where NBC Symphony Orchestra was created specially for him.

Toulouse-Lautrec, Henri de (1864–1901); French painter of Parisian life; excelling in posters and lithographs.

Toussaint L'Ouverture, Pierre Dominique (1743–1803); Haitian liberator, born of African slave parents, became leader of French republican rebels, gained control of island and ruled well until overthrown by French military intervention (1802).

Townes, Charles Hard (b. 1915), American physicist, shared 1964 Nobel prize for invention and development of maser and laser.

Townshend, Charles (1674–1738); English politician, Whig supporter of George I, but overshadowed by WALPOLE; after resignation (1730) spent his time farming, improving cultivation of turnips and crop rotation.

Trevithick, Richard (1771–1833); English inventor, built steam locomotives, though not as successfully as STEPHENSON.

Trotsky, Leon (Lev Davidovich Bronstein; 1879–1940); Russian revolutionary, Minister under LENIN, 1917; organized Red Army, civil war of 1918–21; opposed STALIN; exiled 1929; assassinated by a Stalin agent in Mexico.

Truman, Harry S (1884–1972); Succeeded Franklin D Roosevelt as 33rd president of the United States, 1945; took decision to drop atomic bomb on Japan; sent US troops to fight in Korean War, 1950; retired 1953. Vice-president 1945.

Tudor Name of family that ruled England 1485–1603. Founder Owen Tudor, Welsh gentleman who married Catherine of France, widow of Henry V of England. Sovereigns: Henry VII, HENRY VIII, Edward VI, Mary I, ELIZABETH I.

Tull, Jethro (1674–1741); English farmer; invented drill for sowing seed.

Turgenev, Ivan Sergeyevich (1818–83); Russian novelist; gave up civil service to travel; novels include *On the Eve* (1860), *Fathers and Sons* (1862); plays *A Month in the Country* (1850), *A Provincial Lady* (1851).

Turner, Joseph Mallord William (1775–1851); England's greatest painter, specialized in watercolour landscapes; mastery of light, achieved with broken colour, foreshadowed art of Impressionists; *The Fighting Temeraire* and *Rain, Steam, and Speed.*

Twain, Mark (Samuel Langhorne Clemens; 1835–1910); American author, printer, river pilot, journalist; *The Adventures of Tom Sawyer* (1876), *Adventures of Huckleberry Finn* (1885), *A Connecticut Yankee at King Arthur's Court* (1889); travel papers, sketches.

Tyler, Wat (d. 1381); English rebel, leader of the Peasants' Revolt which sought redress of economic distress from Richard II; killed by Lord Mayor Walworth.

Tyndale, William (1492?–1536); English preacher and scholar who first translated New Testament into English (from Greek) in an attempt to combat what he saw as corruption in the Church; visited LUTHER, advocated principles of Reformation, and for this was arrested in Antwerp and burned by the Spanish Inquisition.

Uccello, Paolo (Paolo di Dono; 1397–1475); Italian painter, working in Florence, known for his experiments with perspective, paintings include *Battle of San Romano, St. George and the Dragon.*

Ulanova, Galina (b. 1910); Russian prima ballerina. ballet mistress of Bolshoi Theatre. Début in *Les Sylphides* (1928); starred particularly in *Giselle* with Bolshoi Ballet in 1950s.

Valentino, Rudolph (Rodolpho d'Antonguolla; 1895–1926); Italian-born American film star of silent screen; object of hysterical female adulation; best known for romantic lead in *The Sheik.*

Vanderbilt American family prominent in finance and transport; fortune founded by **Cornelius** (1794–1877) in shipping and railways.

Van Dyke, Sir Anthony (1596–1641); Flemish painter to the court of Charles I of England, best known for royal portraits.

Van Gogh, Vincent (1853–90); Dutch painter, specialized in vivid, colourful landscapes and portraits with simple form and passionate use of colour. Suffered intermittent periods of insanity; finally committed suicide.

Vaughan Williams, Ralph (1872–1958); English composer, collector of folk and Tudor music. Wrote 6 symphonies, ballad opera *Hugh the Drover, Fantasia on a Theme by Thomas Tallis,* ballet music, many songs.

Vega, Lope de (1562–1635); One of Spain's greatest writers; created Spanish national drama; 470 surviving plays; many poems; sailed with Spanish Armada, 1588; later became a priest.

Velázquez, Diego Rodriguez de Silva y (1599–1660); Spanish artist, court painter to Spanish royal family. Experimented with properties of light; *Rokeby Venus* and *Las Meniñas.*

Verdi, Giuseppe (1813–1901); Italian operatic composer; sense of theatre and gift for melody established new era in Italian opera. Operas *Rigoletto, Il Trovatore,* and *La Traviata;* superb *Requiem.*

Vermeer, Jan (1632–75); Dutch painter; calm, peaceful interiors typified by *Young Woman with a Water Jug* and *The Lady Standing at the Virginals.*

Verne, Jules (1828–1905); French science fiction writer; novels include *Voyage to the Centre of the Earth* (1864), *Twenty Thousand Leagues under the Sea* (1870), *Around the World in Eighty Days* (1873).

Vesalius, Andreas (1514–64); Flemish anatomist, wrote *De Corporis Humani Fabrica* (1543), most accurate and well illustrated book on anatomy until then.

Vespucci, Amerigo (1451–1512); Florentine merchant, made several voyages to New World, exploring coast of South America, claiming to be first to sight it. It was named after him.

Victor Emmanuel II (1820–78) King of Sardinia, leader in war against Austria and struggle for Italian unification; first King of Italy (from 1861), guided by Cavour, his chief minister.

Victoria (1819–1901); Became queen 1837 and had longest reign of any British monarch. After death of husband, Prince Albert, in 1861, became partial recluse. High moral tone she and Albert set helped restore people's confidence in monarchy.

Villa, Pancho (Doroteo Arango; 1877–1923); Mexican bandit and revolutionary, brutal killer; assassinated.

Villon, François (1431–c.1463); French lyric poet; led wild life, in and out of jail; condemned to death for murder but reprieved; main work *Grand Testament* (1461).

Virgil (Publius Vergilius Maro; 70–19 BC); Major Roman poet; wrote epic *The Aeneid*; *Eclogues*; *Georgics*.

Volta, Alessandro Giuseppe Antonio Anastasio, Count (1745–1827); Italian physicist, invented electrophorus (basis of electrical condenser) and first battery, 'Voltaic pile' (1800); *volt* named after him.

Voltaire (François Marie Arouet; 1694–1778); French author, philosopher and acidulous critic; attacked organized religion, oppression, and civil injustices with wit and scorn; admired English liberalism. *Candide* (1759), famous satirical novel; tragedies, poems, histories.

Voroshilov, Kliment Efremovich (1881–1969); Russian soldier and statesman, commissar for defence (1925–40), command of Leningrad front 1941 and with ZHUKOV broke German siege 1943; president USSR 1953–60.

Wagner, Wilhelm Richard (1813–83); German operatic composer and conductor, regarded his monumental Romantic operas as 'music dramas'. Built Festival Opera at Bayreuth, Bavaria, to stage own productions. Works include *The Flying Dutchman*, *Tannhaüser*, *Ring of the Nibelung* (4-opera cycle).

Waldheim, Kurt (1918–92); Austrian politician; foreign minister 1968–70; as UN secretary-general 1972–80; elected Austrian president in 1986.

Wallis, Sir Barnes Neville (1887–1979); British scientist and inventor who made numerous important contributions in the field of aviation design, including swing-wing aircraft; developed the famous 'bouncing bomb' that breached the Ruhr dams in World War II.

Walpole, Sir Robert (1676–1745); Britain's first prime minister (1721–42); served under George I and George II; created Earl of Orford, 1742.

Warwick the Kingmaker (Richard Neville, Earl of Warwick; 1428–71); leading Yorkist in Wars of Roses, supporting Edward IV; later supported Lancastrian Henry VI; killed in battle.

Washington, George (1732–99); Commanded colonial armies during American War of Independence (1755–83); elected country's first president, 1789; retired 1797.

Watson, James Dewey (b. 1928); American biochemist, shared 1962 Nobel prize for discovery of structure of DNA molecule.

Watson-Watt, Sir Robert Alexander (1892–1973); Scottish electronics engineer, developed the reflection of radio waves into practical 'radar' system (mid-1930s), decisive 'weapon' in Battle of Britain. Knighted 1942.

Watt, James (1736–1819); Scottish engineer, invented steam engine more efficient than previous ones, and which transferred longitudinal motion of piston into rotary motion of wheel. Also invented centrifugal governor to control speed of engine automatically.

Weber, Karl Maria Friedrich Ernst von, Baron (1786–1826); German composer of opera (*Oberon*, 1826, and others) and instrumental works; cousin of Mozart's wife Constanze.

Wedgwood, Josiah (1730–95); English potter, developed new processes in Staffordshire industry with blue or black unglazed ware decorated with white relief designs.

Wegener, Alfred Lothar (1880–1930); German geologist, first proposed continental drift theory.

Weizmann, Chaim (1874–1952); Russian-born Jewish research chemist; Zionist leader from 1898; first president of Israel, 1948–52.

Wellington, Duke of (Arthur Wellesley; 1769–1852); British soldier and statesman, defeated French in Peninsular War, 1808–14; defeated NAPOLEON I at Battle of Waterloo, 1815; prime minister, 1828–30.

Wells, Herbert George (1866–1946); English writer; radical campaigner; works include science fiction *The Invisible Man* (1897), the far-sighted *The War of the Worlds* (1898), and novels *Kipps* (1905) and *The History of Mr. Polly* (1910).

Wesley, John (1703–91); English theologian, evangelist, and founder of Methodism; travelled many thousands of miles preaching in open his message of salvation through faith in Christ. Brother Charles Wesley (1707–88) wrote over 6000 hymns.

Whistler, James Abbott McNeill (1834–1903); American artist, lived in Paris and London. Won farthing damages in famous lawsuit against RUSKIN. Best known painting *The Artist's Mother*.

White, Patrick (1912–90); Australian writer; *The Tree of Man* (1956), *Voss* (1957), *The Eye of the Storm* (1973); Nobel prize for literature 1973.

Whitman, Walt (1819–92); American poet; his free verse caused a sensation; poems published under title *Leaves of Grass* (1855–92).

Whittington, Richard 'Dick' (c.1358–1423); English merchant, three times lord mayor of London; subject of legends.

Wilberforce, William (1759–1833); English MP, reformer, and philanthropist, campaigned ceaselessly against slavery and slave trade. Achieved abolition and emancipation throughout British colonies by 1834.

Wilde, Oscar Fingal O'Flahertie Wills (1854–1900); Irish poet, dramatist, wit; loved beauty for its own sake; jailed for homosexual crimes, 1895–97; plays include *Lady Windermere's Fan* (1892), *The Importance of Being Earnest* (1895); poems *The Ballad of Reading Gaol*; novels *The Picture of Dorian Gray* (1891).

Wilhelm II (1859–1941); Third and last Kaiser of Germany. Arrogant and tactless; allowed army leaders to run country. Deposed 1918 after World War I; died in exile.

William I, the Conqueror (c.1027–87); Inherited dukedom of Normandy 1035, and in 1066 invaded and conquered England. Brought strong rule to England, and had first national survey made (*Domesday Book*, 1086).

William III of Orange (1650–1702); Stadtholder of

Netherlands 1671; king of England (jointly with wife, Mary II) by invitation of Parliament from 1689, deposing Roman Catholic father-in-law James II.

Wilson, (James) Harold (b. 1916); British Labour politician; prime minister 1964–70 and 1974–76; created a life peer, 1983.

Windsor, Duke of See EDWARD VIII.

Wolfe, James (1727–59); British soldier. Victory over French at Quebec, at which he was killed, won Canada.

Wolsey, Thomas (c.1475–1530); English cleric and statesman, minister to Henry VII and HENRY VIII; archbishop of York, 1514, cardinal 1515, lord chancellor 1515; failed to secure Henry's divorce from Catherine of Aragon; fell from power 1529; died before trial for treason.

Woolf, (Adeline) Virginia (1882–1941); English novelist: *Mrs. Dalloway* (1925), *To the Lighthouse* (1925), *Between the Acts* (1941); and essayist; born Virginia Stephen, married Leonard Woolf (1912); leader of 'Bloomsbury Group'; committed suicide.

Wordsworth, William (1770–1850); Major English poet, settled in Lake District after European travels, 1813; poet laureate 1843; *The Prelude* (1805), *The Excursion* (1814), many shorter poems and sonnets.

Wren, Sir Christopher (1632–1723); English architect, astronomer, and mathematician. St. Paul's Cathedral one of more than 50 churches he built in London.

Wright, Frank Lloyd (1869–1959); American architect, pioneered use of new materials (e.g. reinforced concrete) in building; aimed always to integrate buildings with environment.

Wright (brothers): **Orville** (1871–1948) and **Wilbur** (1866–1919); American inventors, built and flew first man-carrying aeroplane (1903).

Wycliffe, John (c.1328–84); English reformer, accepted authority of Scriptures implicitly and rejected much of teachings of Church. Began first translation of Bible into English.

Xavier, St. Francis (1506–52); Spanish RC missionary, helped to found Jesuits. Called 'Apostle to the Indies'; made missionary journeys to India, E. Indies, China, and Japan.

Xerxes I, the Great (c.519–465 BC); King of Persia. Attacked Greece, 480 BC, won victory at Thermopylae, burned Athens; fleet defeated at Salamis, Murdered.

Yeats, William Butler (1865–1939); Irish poet and dramatist; led Irish literary revival; founded Abbey Theatre, Dublin; plays include *The Countess Cathleen* (1892), essays include *Celtic Twilight* (1893). Nobel prize for literature 1923.

Young, Brigham (1801–77); American religious leader, replaced murdered JOSEPH SMITH as head of Mormons. Led followers through many hardships to final settlement at Salt Lake City.

Zhukov, Georgi Konstantinovich (1896–1974); Russian general in World War II, led defence of Moscow and Stalingrad, broke German siege of Leningrad, led armies through Poland into Germany; captured Berlin; accepted German surrender, 1945.

Zola, Émile (1840–1902); French novelist; *Les Rougon-Macquart* (20 volumes); intervened in DREYFUS case with *J'Accuse* (1898).

Top: George Washington, who led 13 British colonies in North America to independence as the United States, and became first American president. He served two terms before retiring to run his Virginia estates. One of his officers described him as 'First in war, first in peace, and first in the hearts of his countrymen'.

Above: The American poet Walt Whitman.

Zoroaster (Zarathustra) (c.600s BC); Persian religious leader, founded Zoroastrianism; said to have written its sacred book, *Avesta*.

Zwingli, Ulrich (1484–1531); Swiss religious leader, prominent in Swiss Reformation. In *Concerning True and False Religion*, attacked monasticism and idolatry. Killed in attack on Zurich by citizens of anti-Protestant cantons.

Sport

PERSONALITIES IN SPORT

Ali, Muhammad (b. 1942); American boxer, controversial, colourful character who won world heavyweight title (as Cassius Clay) in 1964 (beating Sonny Liston), defended it successfully 9 times before losing it for refusing to join Army, and regained it from George Foreman in 1974. Reigned until 1978, after which he allowed his career to tail off in anticlimax. With a tongue as quick as fists or feet, he nevertheless proved himself an outstanding champion in the ring.

Bannister, Sir Roger (b. 1929); English athlete, first man to run mile in under 4 min (1954). Chairman Sports Council 1972–74.

Beamon, Bob (b. 1946); American long-jumper, put himself into the history books with one leap – a monstrous 8.90 m (29 ft 2½ in) which won him 1968 Olympic title, beating previous world record by 55 cm (1 ft 9½ in).

Best, George (b. 1946); Irish footballer whose brilliant career was brought to premature end by his inability to handle off-field pressures that menace modern folk heroes. European and English Footballer of Year 1968, when he won European Cup medal with Manchester United.

Borg, Björn (b. 1956); Swedish tennis player, won the Wimbledon singles title 5 times running (1976–80), a record in modern times. With his speed, his two-fisted backhand, and his topspin forehand, he reigned supreme until succumbing to John McEnroe in the 1981 final.

Botham, Ian (b. 1955); English cricketer, famed for his exploits with bat and ball that sensationally turned the 1981 Test series against Australia. With his mighty hitting and deadly swing bowling, he joined the select band with 2000 runs and 200 wickets in Tests, and he was still only 26.

Brabham, Jack (b. 1926); Australian racing driver, first to win world championship in own car. Won championship in 1959 and 1960 in Coopers, and again in 1966 in a Brabham, also winning constructor's championship. Retired from track in 1970, having started in record 127 grands prix.

Bradman, Sir Donald (b. 1908); Australian cricketer, outstanding batsman of all time. Averaged 99.94 in 52 Tests (1928–48) and 95.14 in all matches. Captained Australia in 5 series; became leading administrator.

Budge, Donald (b. 1916); American tennis player, first to complete 'Grand Slam' of the four major titles in one year (1938).

Busby, Sir Matt (b. 1909); Scottish international footballer who became Manchester United manager, surviving Munich air crash to build first English side to win European Cup (1968).

Left: Bjorn Borg, the Swedish tennis player who won the Wimbledon singles title a record 5 times running, as well as gaining many other international titles.

Charlton, Bobby (b. 1937); English footballer, scored record 49 goals in a then record 106 internationals. Exemplary career with Manchester United, captaining them to European Cup success in 1968. European and English Footballer of Year in 1966, when he won World Cup medal.

Clark, Jim (1936–68); Scottish racing driver, ranked with Fangio as greatest of all. Driving only for Lotus, he won 25 grands prix (including a record 7 in 1963) and World Driver's Championship in 1963 and 1965, before sliding off track at Hockenheim and receiving fatal injuries.

Coe, Sebastian (b. 1956); English athlete, won the 1980 Olympic 1500 m title after finishing second to his great rival Steve Ovett in the 800 m. Set world records from 800 m to 1 mi.

Compton, Denis (b. 1918); English cricketer/footballer. Record 3816 runs and 18 centuries in season (1947), and fastest 300 (181 min); played 78 Tests. Won FA Cup medal with Arsenal (1950); played wartime soccer for England.

Connolly, Maureen (1934–69); American tennis player, 'Little Mo', first woman to complete 'Grand Slam' of four major titles in one year (1953); ranked by many as best ever. Only 1.57 m (5 ft 2 in), she perfected a 'clock work' baseline game and was unbeaten 1951–54. Horse-riding accident ended career.

Court, Margaret (b. 1942); Australian tennis player, née Smith, second woman to achieve 'Grand Slam' (1970). Won record 22 major singles and 58 titles in all.

Cruyff, Johan (b. 1947); Dutch footballer, transferred from Ajax to Barcelona for world record £922,300 in 1973. Won 3 European Cup medals with Ajax; twice European Footballer of Year (1971, 1973).

Davis, Joe (1901–78); English billiards and snooker player, turned snooker into a world game in 1930s. Only man to hold world billiards and snooker titles simultaneously, he reigned supreme at snooker 1927–46, when he retired from championship play. To record maximum 147 (1955).

Davis, Steve (b. 1957); English snooker player. No relation to Joe, but his performances in 1981, when he won the world title and every other major tournament he entered, suggested he might rival his illustrious namesake in snooker history. In January 1982, he made the first televised maximum break (147).

Dempsey, Jack (1895–1983), U.S. boxer, an aggressive, powerful puncher, won world heavyweight title 1919. Lost it to Gene Tunney 1926, narrowly failing to regain it in 1927 return ('Battle of Long Count').

Didrikson, Mildred 'Babe' (1914–56); all-round American sportswoman. Excelled at numerous sports, winning 1932 Olympic hurdles and javelin titles and later becoming champion golfer (Mrs. Zaharias).

325

Di Stefano, Alfredo (b. 1926); perhaps the most complete footballer of all time. Capped for Spain as well as his native Argentina; star of all-conquering Real Madrid who won first 5 European Cups (1946–50), scoring record 49 in this competition. European Footballer of Year 1957 and 1959.

Fangio, Juan Manuel (b. 1911); Argentinian racing driver, record 5 times world champion. Came to fore in his late 30s and, whether driving Alfa-Romeos, Maseratis, Mercedes, or Ferraris, bestrode grand prix scene (24 wins) in 1950s.

Finney, Tom (b. 1922); English footballer, fine sportsman and brilliant winger for Preston and England (30 goals in 76 games). Famed for body swerve and two-footed accuracy. English Footballer of Year 1954 and 1957.

Fraser, Dawn (b. 1937); Australian swimmer, won 3rd consecutive 100 m free-style title at 1964 Olympics at 27 – old for swimmer. Career noted also for frequent clashes with authority. First woman to break minute for 100 m (1962).

Grace, William Gilbert (1848–1915); English all-round cricketer, dominated cricket in late 1800s. Amassed 54,904 runs, 126 centuries, 2876 wickets in career that continued into his 60s. Doctor of medicine.

Hagen, Walter (1892–1969); American golfer, the man who did most to make golf a respectable profession. A great champion, he won 4 British Opens, 2 US Opens, and 5 US PGA titles.

Henie, Sonja (1912–69); Norwegian ice-skater, became Hollywood star and brought much glamour to the sport. Won 10 successive world (1927–36) and 3 Olympic (1928–36) titles.

Hobbs, Sir Jack (1882–1963); English cricketer, prolific opening batsman. Scored 61,237 runs, including 5410 in 61 Tests, and a record 197 centuries, 98 after his 40th birthday.

Hutton, Sir Len (1916–1990), English cricketer. Opening batsman; captained England in 23 of his 79 Tests, scoring 6971 runs, including 364 not out against Australia in 1938, a record that lasted 20 years.

James, Alex (1902–53); Scottish footballer, legendary character in baggy shorts who, from a goalscorer with Preston, became greatest goalmaker in the game and mainspring of great Arsenal side of 1930s.

John, Barry (b. 1945); Welsh rugby fly-half. Retired 1972 after climaxing career in New Zealand with British Lions, scoring 180 points and earning nickname 'The King'. Scored record 90 points for Wales in 25 games. Capitalized on perfect service from scrum-half Gareth Edwards, his elusive running and accurate touch- and goal-kicking a delight to watch.

King, Billie Jean (b. 1943); American tennis player, diminutive but fiercely competitive. Six times Wimbledon champion and first sportswoman to win £100,000 in one year.

Laker, Jim (1922–86); England and Surrey cricketer (right-arm off-spinner), took world record 19 wickets (for 90) in a Test against Australia, Old Trafford 1956.

Laver, Rod (b. 1938); Australian tennis player, only man to achieve 'Grand Slam' of four major titles twice – as amateur in 1962 and pro in 1969. Leading pro in latter 1960s, first to win $1 million.

Law, Denis (b. 1940); Scottish footballer, perhaps the most exciting post-war striker. Starred for both Manchester clubs, named European Footballer of Year 1964 when with United. Won 55 Scottish caps, scoring record 30 goals.

Lenglen, Suzanne (1899–1938); French tennis player, virtually unbeatable 1919–26. Fast, accurate, powerful, and a great crowd-puller, she turned pro in 1926 having won 6 Wimbledon singles. Regarded by older experts as all-time No. 1.

Lillee, Dennis (b. 1949); Australian cricketer, devastatingly fast bowler, set a new record for Test wickets when he took his 310th in December 1981. His occasionally offensive on-field behaviour has marred his cricketing reputation, however.

Louis, Joe (1914–81); American boxer, 'Brown Bomber', won world heavyweight title 1937. Retired 1949 after record 25 successful defences. Made abortive comeback because of back-taxes owed.

McBride, Willie John (b. 1940); Irish rugby second-row forward. Captained British Lions to historic triumph in South Africa 1974 – his 5th tour (a record) – having previously set world record 57 caps for Ireland.

Marciano, Rocky (1923–69); American boxer, tough and aggressive all-action puncher. Won world heavyweight title 1952; retired unbeaten in 49 fights (43 inside distance), including 6 title defences, in 1956. Died in plane crash.

Matthews, Sir Stanley (b. 1915); English footballer, first to be knighted. 'Wizard of Dribble', mesmeric right-winger with dazzling ball control and speed off mark. Starred for Blackpool and Stoke. European Footballer of Year 1956; English – remarkably – 1948 and 1963.

Meads, Colin (b. 1936); New Zealand rugby lock-forward, massively built, yet fast with a fine rugby brain. Known as 'Pinetree', won 55 caps. Only second player sent off in rugby international (1967).

Moody, Helen Wills (b. 1905); American tennis player, 'Little Miss Poker Face', dominated game 1922–38, winning 19 major singles (8 Wimbledon), losing only twice in major competition.

Moore, Bobby (b. 1941); English footballer, capped record 108 times. Constructive second stopper. Captained England to World Cup victory 1966, West Ham to European Cup-Winners' Cup success 1965.

Moss, Stirling (b. 1929); English racing driver, best never to win world championship (4 2nds, 3 3rds). Won 16 grands prix. Near-fatal crash at Goodwood ended career in 1962, but he remained symbol of British motor racing.

Nicklaus, Jack (b. 1940); American golfer won record 17 'big four' titles by 1982. Big hitter, he emerged as world's leading golfer in late 1960s.

Nurmi, Paavo (1897–1973); Finnish athlete, foremost of 'Flying Finns'. Almost unbeatable over 1500–10,000 m, he set record 22 world records and won record 9 Olympic medals (1920–28).

Ovett, Steve (b. 1955); English athlete, won the 1980 Olympic 800 m title. A master tactician, he ran up a record 42 straight wins in 1500 m and mile races from 1977 to 1980.

Owens, Jesse (1913–80); American athlete, set 5 word records – 100 yd (equal), long jump, 220 yd/200 m (same race), 220 yd hurdles – in one afternoon (25.5.35). A Negro, he embarrassed Nazi Germany at 1936 Olympics, winning 4 gold medals.

Palmer, Arnold (b. 1929); American golfer. His charisma helped make golf growth sport of 1960s. Followed by massive band of supporters – 'Arnie's Army' – he won 2 British Opens, 1 US Open, and 4 US Masters 1956–64, and continued to attract crowds and win big money well into 1970s.

Pelé (b. 1940); Brazilian footballer, ranked by many as world's greatest. Over 1200 goals for Santos and Brazil (90 goals in 110 games); starred in 1958 and 1970 World Cups (injury kept him out of 1962 final). Allied supreme ball control with brilliantly inventive footballing brain. Full name Edson Arantes do Nascimento.

Perry, Fred (b. 1909); English tennis/table tennis player, only man to lead world at both. World table tennis champion 1929; brought off first Wimbledon treble (1934–36) since World War I.

Piggott, Lester (b. 1935); English jockey, ranked by many as all-time No. 1. Amassed 25 English classic winners (8 Derbies) and 10 jockey championships by early 1980s.

Player, Gary (b. 1935); South African golfer, dedicated, painstaking perfectionist, only 1.70 m (5 ft 7 in), who took on – and beat – Americans on their own courses. First non-American to win all 4 major golf titles. Won his 1st 'big four' title, the British Open, in 1959, and his 8th, the US Masters, 18 years later, in 1978.

Puskas, Ferenc (b. 1927); Hungarian footballer, enjoyed two quite separate careers with two of greatest sides in soccer history, Hungary and Real Madrid. Deadly left-foot shot, he scored 83 goals in 84 internationals before 1956 Uprising. Joined Real Madrid to contribute to classic 1960 European Cup triumph, scoring 4 of their 7 goals in final.

Ramsey, Sir Alf (b. 1920); English footballer and manager, knighted after masterminding England's 1966 World Cup triumph.

Rhodes, Wilfred (1877–1973); English cricketer, took record 4187 wickets (slow left-arm), scored 39,722 runs. Did 'double' (1000 runs/100 wickets in season) 16 times. Played in 58 Tests.

Richards, Sir Gordon (1904–86); English jockey, dominated British racing for quarter of a century. Champion jockey 26 times (1925–53), he won record 4870 races, including record 269 in 1947. Rode 14 classic winners, climaxing career with his only Derby success, on Pinza in 1953.

Robinson, Sugar Ray (b. 1920); American boxer, world champion at welter and middle. Regarded by many as finest boxer, pound for pound, of all. Won middleweight title 5 times.

Rono, Henry (b. 1952); Kenyan athlete, rewrote the record books in four events in 1978, the 3000 m, 5000 m, 10,000 m, and steeplechase, but was denied Olympic honours because of his country's boycott of the 1976 and 1980 Games.

Ruth, George Herman 'Babe' (1895–1948); American baseball player. Legendary figure who revolutionized baseball in 1920s with prolific big-hitting for New York Yankees. Set numerous batting records, including 60 home runs in season (1927) and 714 in career.

Pele of Brazil, probably the greatest footballer of all time.

Kenyan runner Henry Rono holds world records for 3000 m, 10,000 m and 3000 m steeplechase.

327

Left: Gary Sobers, the West Indian cricketer who scored six sixes in an over.
Below: Mark Spitz of the USA won seven Olympic gold medals for swimming in the 1972 Olympics.

Sobers, Sir Gary (b. 1936); West Indian cricketer, scored record 8032 runs in 93 Tests, including record 365 not out against Pakistan in 1958. Took 235 Test wickets (left-arm fast-medium or spin); struck record 6 sixes in one over for Notts against Glamorgan in 1968.

Spitz, Mark (b. 1950); American swimmer, won unprecedented 7 gold medals at 1972 Olympics, 4 individual (2 freestyle, 2 butterfly) and 3 team – all world records.

Stewart, Jackie (b. 1939); Scottish racing driver, won 3 world championships and record 27 grands prix before retiring in 1973. Amassed fortune on and off track. Responsible for revolutionizing safety precautions.

Surtees, John (b. 1934); English motor-cyclist/racing driver, only man to win world championship in both sports, on MV Agustas (late 1950s) and in a Ferrari (1964).

Thorpe, Jim (1888–1953); American athlete, arguably the outstanding all-round sportsman of all time. Won pentathlon and decathlon at 1912 Olympics, but later lost medals on a technicality. Half Indian, he later played major league baseball and was outstanding footballer (American).

Tilden, William Tatem (1893–1953); American tennis player. 'Big Bill', tall, stylish, dominated men's tennis in 1920s, unbeaten 1920–25. Ranked No. 1 of all time by leading experts.

Trueman, Fred (b. 1931); England and Yorkshire cricketer (fast bowler), took a record 307 Test wickets.

Weissmuller, Johnny (1904–84); American swimmer known for his screen portrayal of 'Tarzan'. Arguably greatest swimmer of all time, winning 5 Olympic golds (1924–28), setting 24 world records.

Zatopek, Emil (b. 1922); Czech athlete, finest postwar middle- and long-distance runner. Set 18 world records and won 4 Olympic titles, including unique treble of 5000 and 10,000 m and marathon in 1952.

OLYMPIC GAMES		WINTER OLYMPICS	COMMONWEALTH GAMES
1896 Athens	1976 Montreal	1924 Chamonix, France	1930 Hamilton, Canada
1900 Paris	1980 Moscow	1928 St Moritz, Switzerland	1934 London, England
1904 St Louis	1984 Los Angeles	1932 Lake Placid, USA	1938 Sydney, Australia
1908 London	1988 Seoul, S. Korea	1936 Garmisch, Germany	1950 Auckland, New Zealand
1912 Stockholm	1992 Barcelona, Spain	1948 St Moritz, Switzerland	1954 Vancouver, Canada
1920 Antwerp		1952 Oslo, Norway	1958 Cardiff, Wales
1924 Paris		1956 Cortina, Italy	1962 Perth, Australia
1928 Amsterdam		1960 Squaw Valley, USA	1966 Kingston, Jamaica
1932 Los Angeles		1964 Innsbruck, Austria	1970 Edinburgh, Scotland
1936 Berlin		1968 Grenoble, France	1974 Christchurch, New Zealand
1948 London		1972 Sapporo, Japan	1978 Edmonton, Canada
1952 Helsinki		1976 Innsbruck, Austria	1982 Brisbane, Australia
1956 Melbourne		1980 Lake Placid, USA	1986 Edinburgh, Scotland
1960 Rome		1984 Sarajevo, Yugoslavia	1990 Auckland, New Zealand
1964 Tokyo		1988 Calgary, Canada	1994 Victoria, Canada
1968 Mexico City		1992 Albertville, France	
1972 Munich		1994 Lillehammer, Norway	

ASSOCIATION FOOTBALL

World Cup Finals

1930	Montevideo, Uruguay	Uruguay..............4	Argentina..............2
1934	Rome, Italy	Italy..................2	Czechoslovakia..........1
1938	Paris, France	Italy..................4	Hungary..............2
1950	Rio de Janeiro, Brazil	*Uruguay..............2	Brazil..............1
1954	Berne, Switzerland	W. Germany...........3	Hungary..............2
1958	Stockholm, Sweden	Brazil................5	Sweden..............2
1962	Santiago, Chile	Brazil................3	Czechoslovakia..........1
1966	Wembley, England	England..............4	W. Germany...........2
1970	Mexico City, Mexico	Brazil................4	Italy..............1
1974	Munich, W. Germany	W. Germany...........2	Netherlands..........1
1978	Buenos Aires, Argentina	Argentina..............3	Netherlands..........1
1982	Madrid, Spain	Italy..................3	W. Germany...........1
1986	Mexico City	Argentina..............3	W. Germany...........2
1990	Rome	W. Germany...........1	Argentina..............0

European Cup Finals

1959	Stuttgart	Real Madrid(Spain)..........2	Stade de Reims (France)..........0
1960	Glasgow	Real Madrid (Spain)..........7	Eintracht Frankfurt (W. Ger.)......3
1961	Berne	Benfica (Portugal)..............3	Barcelona (Spain)..............2
1962	Amsterdam	Benfica (Portugal) 5	Real Madrid (Spain)..............3
1963	Wembley	AC Milan (Italy)..............2	Benfica (Portugal)..............1
1964	Vienna	Internazionale (Italy)..........3	Real Madrid (Spain)..............1
1965	Milan	Internazionale (Italy)..........1	Benfica (Portugal)..............0
1966	Brussels	Real Madrid (Spain)..........2	Partizan Belgrade (Yug.)..........1
1967	Lisbon	Celtic (Scotland)..............2	Internazionale (Italy)..............1
1968	Wembley	Manchester U (England)..........4	Benfica (Portugal)..............1
1969	Madrid	AC Milan (Italy)..............4	Ajax (Netherlands)..............1
1970	Milan	Feyenoord (Netherlands)..........2	Celtic (Scotland)..............1
1971	Wembley	Ajax (Netherlands)..............2	Panathinaikos (Greece)..........0
1972	Rotterdam	Ajax (Netherlands)..............2	Internazionale (Italy) 0
1973	Belgrade	Ajax (Netherlands)..............1	Juventus (Italy)..............0
1974	Brussels	Bayern Munich (W. Ger.)..........1	Atlético Madrid (Spain)..........1
	Replay		
1975	Paris	Bayern Munich (W. Ger.)..........2	Leeds United (England)..........0
1976	Glasgow	Bayern Munich (W. Ger.)..........1	St Etienne (France)..............0
1977	Rome	Liverpool (England)..............3	B. Mönchengladbach (W. Ger.).....1
1978	Wembley	Liverpool (England)..............1	FC Bruges (Belgium)..............0
1979	Munich	Nottingham Forest (England)......1	Malmö (Sweden)..............0
1980	Madrid	Nottingham Forest (England)......1	SV Hamburg (W. Ger.)..............0
1981	Paris	Liverpool (England)..............1	Real Madrid (Spain)..............0
1982	Rotterdam	Aston Villa (England)..............1	Bayern Munich (W. Ger.)..........0
1983	Athens	Hamburg (W. Ger.)..............1	Juventus (Italy)..............0
1984	Rome	Liverpool (England)..............1	AS Roma (Italy)..............1
		(Liverpool won 4–2 on penalties)	
1985	Brussels	Juventus (Italy)..............1	Liverpool (England)..............0
1986	Seville	Steaua Bucharest (Romania).......0	Barcelona (Spain)..............0
		(Steaua Bucharest won 2–0 on penalties)	
1987	Vienna	Porto (Portugal)..............2	Bayern Munich (W. Ger.)..........1
1988	Stuttgart	PSV Eindhoven (Netherlands)......0	Benfica (Portugal)..............0
		(Eindhoven won 6–5 on penalties)	
1989	Barcelona	AC Milan (Italy)..............4	Steaua Bucharest (Romania)..........0
1990	Vienna	AC Milan (Italy)..............1	Benfica (Portugal)..............0
1991	Bari	Red Star Belgrade (Yug.)..........0	Marseille (France)..............0
		(Red Star Belgrade won 5–3 on penalties)	
1992	Wembley	Barcelona (Spain)..............1	Sampdoria (Italy)..............0

Facts

Ball – circum. 27–28 in (68–71 cm)
weight 14–16 oz (400–450 gm)
Duration of game – 90 min (2×45) plus 2×15 min
extra in certain cup games
Number per side – 11 (1 or 2 substitutes, depending
on competition)
Ruling body – Fédération Internationale de Football
Association (FIFA)

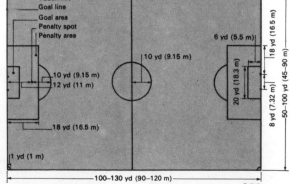

ATHLETICS

Ruling body – International Amateur Athletic Federation (IAAF)

MEN'S WORLD RECORDS

100 metres	9.92s	Carl Lewis (USA)	24.9.88
200 metres	19.72s	Pietro Mennea (Italy)	12.9.79
400 metres	43.29s	Butch Reynolds (USA)	17.8.88
800 metres	1m 41.72s	Sebastian Coe (GB)	10.6.81
1,000 metres	2m 12.18s	Sebastian Coe (GB)	11.7.81
1,500 metres	3m 29.46s	Saïd Aouita (Morocco)	23.8.85
1 mile	3m 46.32s	Steve Cram (GB)	27.8.85
2,000 metres	4m 50.81s	Saïd Aouita (Morocco)	16.7.87
3,000 metres	7m 29.45s	Saïd Aouita (Morocco)	20.8.89
5,000 metres	12m 58.38s	Saïd Aouita (Morocco)	22.7.87
10,000 metres	27m 08.23s	Arturo Barrios (Mexico)	18.8.89
Marathon*	2hr 06m 50s	Belayneh Dinsamo (Ethiopia)	17.5.88
110 metres hurdles	12.92s	Roger Kingdom (USA)	16.8.89
400 metres hurdles	47.02s	Ed Moses (USA)	31.8.83
3,000 metres steeplechase	8m 5.35s	Peter Koech (Kenya)	4.7.89
4 × 100 metres relay	37.83s	United States	11.8.84
4 × 200 metres relay	1m 20.26s	United States	30.8.89
High jump	2.44m (8ft)	Javier Sotomayor (Cuba)	29.7.89
Pole vault	6.06m (19ft 10¼in)	Sergey Bubka (USSR)	10.7.88
Long jump	8.9m (29ft 2½in)	Bob Beamon (USA)	18.10.68
Triple jump	17.97m (58ft 11½in)	Willie Banks (USA)	16.6.85
Shot put	23.12m (75ft 10¼in)	Randy Barnes (USA)	20.5.90
Discus throw	74.08m (243ft)	Jürgen Schult (E. Germany)	6.6.86
Hammer throw	86.74m (274ft 7in)	Yuriy Sedykh (USSR)	30.8.86
Javelin throw†	89.58m (293ft 10in)	Steven Backley (GB)	2.7.90

†With the new javelin; the record with the old javelin was 104.8m (343ft 10in) by Uwe Hohn (East Germany).

WOMEN'S WORLD RECORDS

100 metres	10.49s	Florence Griffith Joyner (USA)	16.7.88
200 metres	21.34s	Florence Griffith Joyner (USA)	29.9.88
400 metres	47.6s	Marita Koch (E. Germany)	6.10.85
800 metres	1m 53.28s	Jarmila Kratochilova (Czechoslovakia)	26.7.83
1,000 metres	2m 30.6s	Tatyana Providokhina (USSR)	20.8.78
1,500 metres	3m 52.47s	Tatyana Kazankina	13.8.80
1 mile	4m 15.61s	Paula Ivan (Romania)	10.7.89
2,000 metres	5m 28.68s	Maricica Puica (Romania)	11.7.86
3,000 metres	8m 22.62s	Tatyana Kazankina	26.8.84
5,000 metres	14m 37.33s	Ingrid Kristiansen (Norway)	5.8.86
10,000 metres	30m 13.74s	Ingrid Kristiansen (Norway)	5.7.86
Marathon*	2hr 21m 6s	Ingrid Kristiansen (Norway)	31.4.85
100 metres hurdles	12.26s.	Yordanka Donkova (Bulgaria)	7.9.86
400 metres hurdles	52.94s	Marina Styepanova (USSR)	17.9.86
4 × 100 metres relay	41.37s	East Germany	6.10.85
4 × 400 metres relay	3m 15.92s	East Germany	3.6.84
High jump	2.08m (6ft 9¾in)	Stefka Kostadinova (Bulgaria)	31.5.86
Long jump	7.52m (24ft 8¼in)	Galina Chistyakova (USSR)	11.6.88
Shot put	22.63m (74ft 3in)	Natalya Lisovskaya (USSR)	7.6.87
Discus throw	76.8m (252ft)	Gabriele Reinsch (E. Germany)	9.7.88
Javelin throw	80m (262ft 5in)	Petra Felke (E. Germany)	9.9.88
Heptathlon	7,291 points	Jacqueline Joyner-Kersee (USA)	23–24.9.88

*World best time (no official world record because of variation in courses).

BADMINTON

Court – 44×20 ft (13.4×6.1 m). singles – 44×17 ft (13.4×5.2 m)
Height of net – 5 ft 1 in (1.55 m)
Weight of shuttlecock – 4.73–5.50 gm
Scoring – best of 3 or 5 15-pt. games, men; best of 3 11-pt. games, women
Ruling body – International Badminton Federation (IBF)
World team championships – Thomas Cup (men); Uber Cup (women)
Major individual competitions – World championships; All-England Championships

BASEBALL

Pitching distance – 60 ft 6 in (18.4 m)
Side of 'diamond' – 90 ft (27.4 m)
Max. length of bat – 3 ft 6 in (1.07 m)

Diameter of ball – 2¾ in (7 cm)
Weight of ball – 5–5¼ oz (149–156 gm)
Number per side – 9 (substitutes allowed)
No. of innings – 9 or more (played to finish)

BASKETBALL

Court – 85×46 ft (26×14 m)
Height of baskets – 10 ft (3.05 m)
Diameter of baskets – 18 in (45 cm)
Circumference of ball – 29½–30½ in (75–78 cm)
Weight of ball – 21–23 oz (600–650 gm)
Duration – 40 min actual play (2×20) plus periods of 5 min until result is obtained
No. per side – 5 (usually up to 5 substitutes)
Ruling body – Fédération Internationale de Basketball Amateur (FIBA)
Major competitions – World championships (men and women) and Olympic Games

BILLIARDS AND SNOOKER

Table – 12 ft×6 ft 1½ in (3.50×1.75 m)
Diameter of balls – 2 1/16 in (5.25 cm)
Billiards – red, white, spot white
Billiards scoring – pot or in-off red 3, white 2; cannon 2
Snooker balls (value) – black (7), pink (6), blue (5), brown (4), green (3), yellow (2), 15 reds (1 each), white (cue-ball)
Ruling body – Billiards and Snooker Control Council
Major competitions – World championships (for both snooker and billiards, professional and amateur)

BOWLS (flat green)

Rink (max.) – 132×19 ft (40.2×5.8 m)
Bowls – diam. (max.) 5¾ in (14.6 cm) biased, weight (max.) 3½ lb (1.59 kg), black or brown, made of wood, rubber, or composition
Jack – diam. 2½ in (6.35 cm), weight 8–10 oz (227–284 gm)
Ruling body – International Bowling Board
Events – singles (4 bowls each, 21 SHOTS up), pairs (2–4 bowls each, 21 ENDS), triples (2 or 3 bowls each, 18 ENDS), fours (2 bowls each, 21 ENDS)
World championships – every 4 years

BOXING

Professional

Ring – 16–20 ft (4.88–6.10 m) square
Gloves – 6 oz (170 gm) fly to welter-weight, 8 oz (227 gm) light-middleweight and above
Duration – 6, 8, 10, 12, or 15 (title) 3-min rounds
Ruling body – World Boxing Council (WBC)

Amateur

Ring – 12–20 ft (3.66–6.10 m) square
Gloves – 8 oz (227 gm)
Duration – three 3-min rounds (seniors)
Ruling body – Amateur International Boxing Association (AIBA)

Weight limits

division	WBC st-lb	WBC kg	AIBA st-lb	AIBA kg
Light-fly	—	—	7–07	48.0
Fly	8–00	50.80	8–00	51.0
Bantam	8–06	53.52	8–07	54.0
Feather	9–00	57.15	9–00	57.0
Junior light	9–04	58.97	—	—
Light	9–09	61.24	9–07	60.0
Junior welter	10–00	63.50	10–00	63.5
Welter	10–07	66.68	10–08	67.0
Junior middle	11–00	69.85	11–02	71.0
Middle	11–06	72.58	11–11	75.0
Light-heavy	12–07	79.38	12–10	81.0
Heavy	no limit		14–03	91.0

CHESS

Ruling body – International Chess Federation

World Champions

1866–94	Wilhelm Steinitz (Austria)
1894–1921	Emanuel Lasker (Germany)
1921–27	Jose R. Capablanca (Cuba)
1927–35	Alexander A. Alekhine (USSR*)
1935–37	Max Euwe (Netherlands)
1937–46	Alexander A. Alekhine (USSR*)
1948–57	Mikhail Botvinnik (USSR)
1957–58	Vassily Smyslov (USSR)
1958–59	Mikhail Botvinnik (USSR)
1960–61	Mikhail Tal (USSR)
1961–63	Mikhail Botvinnik (USSR)
1963–69	Tigran Petrosian (USSR)
1969–72	Boris Spassky (USSR)
1972–75	Bobby Fischer† (USA)
1975–1985	Anatoli Kharpov (USSR)
1985–	Gary Kasparov (USSR)

*Took French citizenship
†Karpov won title when Fischer defaulted.

Top: Sebastian Coe (wearing 717) with a field of international runners. Coe and his great rival Steve Ovett, also of Great Britain, battled for world records in the early 1980s.
Above: Ian Botham, the English cricketer who seems set to become one of the great record holders, having achieved 2000 runs and 200 Test wickets at the age of only 26.

CRICKET

Pitch – wicket to wicket 22 yd (20 m), bowling crease 8 ft 8 in (2.64 m) long
Stumps – 28 in (71.1 cm) high, 9 in (22.9 cm) overall width
Bat (max.) – 38 in (96.5 cm) long, 4¼ in (10.8 cm) wide
Ball – circum, 8 13/16–9 in (22.4–22.9 cm), weight 5½–5¾ oz (156–163 gm)
No. per side – 11 (subs. only for fielding)
Ruling body – International Cricket Conference (ICC)

331

Cricket records – Test matches

Highest innings – 365* G S Sobers, W Indies (v Pakistan, Kingston, 1958)
Most runs in series – 974 D G Bradman, Australia (v England, 1930) in career – 8,090 G Boycott, England
Most hundreds – 34 Sunil Gavaskar, India
Best bowling in match – 19–90 J C Laker, England (v Aus., Old Trafford, 1956) in innings – 10–53 J C Laker, England (v Australia, Old Trafford, 1956)
Most wickets in series – 49 S F Barnes, England (v S Africa, 1913–14) in career – 315 Lillee, Australia
Highest partnership – 451 (2nd wkt) W H Ponsford (266) & D G Bradman (244), Australia (v England, Oval, 1934)
Highest total – 903 (for 7) England (v Australia, Oval, 1938)
Most wicket-keeping dismissals in career – 290 R W Marsh, Australia
Most Test appearances – 114 M C Cowdrey, England

Cricket records – all matches

Highest innings – 499 Hanif Mohammad, Karachi (v Bahawalpur, 1958–59)
Most runs in season – 3.816 D C S Compton, England and Middlesex, 1947; in career – 61.237 J B Hobbs, England and Surrey
Most hundreds in career – 197 J B Hobbs, England and Surrey
Most runs in over – 36 G S Sobers, Notts (v Glamorgan, Swansea, 1968)
Best bowling in innings – 10–10 H Verity, Yorks (v Notts, Leeds, 1932)
Most wickets in season – 304 A P Freeman, England and Kent, 1928; in career – 4,187 W Rhodes, England and Yorks
Highest partnership – 577 (4th wkt) V S Hazare (288) and Gul Mahomed (319), Baroda (v Holkar, Baroda, 1947)
Highest total – 1,107 (all out) Victoria (v NSW, Melbourne, 1926)
Most wicket-keeping dismissals in career – 1,649 R. W. Taylor, England and Middlesex   *not out

CROQUET

Court – 35×28 yd (32×25.6 m)
Players – 2 or 4
Balls – 4 (blue and black v red and yellow), diam. $3\frac{5}{8}$ in (9.2 cm), weight 1 lb (454 gm)
Hoops – 6 (twice each) plus PEG; diam. $3\frac{3}{4}$ in (9.5 cm)
International team competition – MacRobertson Shield

CYCLE RACING

Ruling body – Union Cycliste Internationale
Major competitions: ROAD RACING – Tour de France, Olympic 100-km (62-mile) race
TRACK RACING – Olympics and world championships (sprint, pursuit, 1-km time trial, motor-paced)
Other cycle sports – six-day racing, cyclo-cross, cycle speedway, bicycle polo, time trials

EQUESTRIAN SPORTS

Ruling body – Fédération Equestre Internationale (FEI)
Major competitions: SHOW JUMPING – world championships (men's and women's) every 4 years, alternating with Olympics; President's Cup (world team championship) based on Nations Cup results; 2-yearly European Championships (men's and women's); King George V Gold Cup; Queen Elizabeth II Gold Cup
THREE-DAY EVENT (1 Dressage, 2 Endurance or Cross-country, 3 Show jumping) – 4-yearly world championships and Olympics; 2-yearly European Championships; Badminton Horse Trials
DRESSAGE – Olympics and world championships

FENCING

Ruling body – Fédération Internationale d'Escrimé (FIE)
Events – foil, épée, sabre (men); foil (women)

Major competitions – annual world championships (including Olympics)
Duration of bout – first to 5 hits (or 6 min) men; 4 hits (or 5 min) women

FOOTBALL, AMERICAN

Pitch – 360×160 ft (110×49 m)
Goals – 20 ft (6 m) high, $18\frac{1}{2}$ ft (5.6 m) wide, 10 ft (3 m) off ground, amateur; 30 ft (9 m), prof.
Ball – length 11 in (28 cm), short circum. $21\frac{1}{4}$ in (54 cm), weight 14–15 oz (397–425 gm)
Duration – 60 min (4×15) playing time
No. per side – 11 (unspecified no. of subs.)
Scoring – TOUCHDOWN 6 pts., EXTRA POINT 1, FIELD GOAL 3, SAFETY 2

FOOTBALL, AUSTRALIAN RULES

Pitch – oval 135–185 m (148–202 yd) by 110–155 m (120–170 yd)
Goal posts – 6.4 m (21 ft) wide, BEHIND POSTS 6.4 m either side of goal posts
Ball – short circum. 57 cm ($22\frac{1}{2}$ in), long circum. 74 cm (29 in), weight 450–500 gm (16–17 oz)
Duration – 100 min (4×25)
No. per side – 18 (2 substitutes)
Scoring – GOAL 6 pts., BEHIND 1

FOOTBALL, GAELIC

Pitch – 140–160 yd (128–146 m) by 84–100 yd (77–91 m)
Goal posts – 21 ft (6.4 m) wide, 16 ft (4.9 m) high, crossbar at 8 ft (2.4 m)
Ball – circum. 27–29 in (69–74 cm), weight 13–15 oz (369–425 gm)
Duration – 60 min (2×30)
No. per side – 15 (3 substitutes)
Scoring – GOAL 3 pts., BALL OVER CROSSBAR 1
Ruling body – Gaelic Athletic Association
Major competition – All Ireland Championship (Sam Maguire Trophy) for counties

GOLF

Ball – max. weight 1.62 oz (46 gm), min. diam. UK 1.62 in (4.11 cm), US 1.68 in (4.27 cm)

Three types of weapon are used in fencing. These are the foil (left), the épée (centre), and the sabre (right). The target areas are shown shaded. Women only fence with the foil.

Hole – diam. $4\frac{1}{4}$ in (10.8 cm)
No. of clubs carried – 14 maximum
Ruling body – Royal and Ancient Golf Club of
  St Andrews; United States Golf Association
Major competitions: Individual – Open, US
  Open, US Masters, US PGA
Team – World Cup (international teams of 2,
  annual), Eisenhower Trophy (world amateur, teams
  of 4, 2-yearly), Ryder Cup (US v Europe, 2-yearly)
Golf Records
Lowest round – 55 A E Smith (GB) 1936
36 holes – 122 Sam Snead (US) 59–63, 1959
72 holes – 255 Peter Tupling (GB) 1981
Most 'Big Four' titles – 17 Jack Nicklaus (US)
Most British Opens – 6 Harry Vardon (GB)
Most US Opens – 4 Willie Anderson (US), Bobby
  Jones (US), Ben Hogan (US), Jack Nicklaus (US)
Most US Masters – 5 Jack Nicklaus (US)
Most US PGA's – Walter Hagen (US), Jack Nicklaus
  (US)
Golf Terms
BIG FOUR The major individual tournaments:
  Open and US Open, Masters, and PGA.
BIRDIE One under par for hole.
BOGEY One over par for hole.
DORMIE In match play, leading by numbers of holes
  left.
DOUBLE BOGEY Two over par for hole.
EAGLE Two under par for hole.
FAIRWAY Smooth turf between tee and green.
FOURBALL Match in which pairs score their 'better ball'
  at each hole.
FOURSOME Match in which pair play same ball,
  alternately.
GREEN Specially prepared surface in which hole is
  situated.
MATCH PLAY In which player or pair play each other
  and winner is determined by holes won.
MEDAL PLAY In which number of strokes taken
  determines winner.
PAR Standard score (assessed on first-class play) for
  hole or holes.
ROUGH Unprepared part of course.
STROKE PLAY Medal play.
TEE Starting place for hole, or peg on which ball is
  placed.

GYMNASTICS
Ruling body – Fédération Internationale de
  Gymnastique
Events: men's – floor exercises, rings, parallel bars,
  pommel horse, vault (lengthwise), horizontal bar;
  overall; team; women's – floor exercises (to music),
  vault, asymmetrical bars, beam; overall; team
Major competitions – World and Olympic
  championships, alternately every 4 years

HANDBALL (team)
Court – 40 m (131 ft) by 20 m (65.6 ft)
Goals – 3 m (9.8 ft) wide, 2 m (6.6 ft) high
Ball – circum. 58–60 cm (23–24 in) men's, 54–56 cm
  (21–22 in) women's; weight 425–475 gm (15–16$\frac{3}{4}$
  oz) men's, 325–400 gm (11$\frac{1}{2}$–14 oz) women's
Duration – 60 min (2×30) men's, 50 min (2×25)
  women's; in tournaments 2×15 and 2×10,
  respectively, without the 10-min interval
No. per side – 7 (max. 12 on team)
Ruling body – International Handball Federation

HOCKEY
Goals – 12 ft (3.66 m) wide, 7 ft (2.13 m) high
Ball – circum. 9 in (23 cm), weight 5$\frac{1}{2}$–5$\frac{3}{4}$ oz
  (156–163 gm), made of cork and twine covered in
  leather
Duration of game – 70 min (2×35)
No. per side – 11 (2 subs. in men's game)
Ruling bodies: men's – Fédération Internationale de

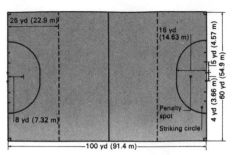

The layout of a hockey pitch.

Hockey (FIH); women's – Women's International
Hockey Rules' Board
Major competitions – Olympic Games and World Cup
  (4-yearly)

HORSE RACING
Major races
England – Derby, Oaks, St Leger, 1,000 and 2,000
  Guineas (the 5 Classics), King George VI & Queen
  Elizabeth Stakes, Ascot Gold Cup; Grand National
  (steeplechase), Cheltenham Gold Cup ('chase),
  Champion Hurdle
Ireland – Irish Sweeps Derby
France – Prix de l'Arc de Triomphe
Australia – Melbourne Cup, Caulfield Cup
South Africa – Durban July Handicap
USA – Kentucky Derby, Preakness Stakes, Belmont
  Stakes (Triple Crown); Washington International

LACROSSE
Pitch – 110×60 yd (100×54 m) men; 120×70 yd
  (110×64 m) preferred for women's international
  matches
Goals – 6×6 ft (1.8×1.8 m)
Ball – circum. 7$\frac{3}{4}$–8 in (19.7–20.3 cm), weight
  5–5$\frac{1}{4}$ oz (141–149 gm) men; 4$\frac{3}{4}$–5$\frac{1}{4}$ oz (135–
  149 gm) women
Duration – 60 min (4×15) men, 50 min (2×25)
  women
No. per side – 10 (13 subs.) men, 12 (1 sub.) women

MODERN PENTATHLON
Order of events – riding, fencing, shooting, swimming,
  running
Ruling body – Union Internationale de Pentathlon
  Moderne et Biathlon
Major competitions – annual world championships
  (including Olympics)

MOTOR SPORT
Ruling body – Fédération Internationale de
  l'Automobile (FIA)
Major events and competitions: Formula One – World
  Drivers Championship (based on points gained in
  individual grands prix: 9, 6, 4, 3, 2, 1 for first 6
  Sports car racing – Le Mans
  Rally driving – Monte Carlo Rally
Other motor sports – drag racing, karting, hillclimbing,
  trials, autocross, rallycross, autotests, stock-car
  racing, vintage-car racing
Records
World Drivers Championship – 5 J M Fangio (1951,
  1954–57)
Championship GP wins – 27 Jackie Stewart
  (1965–73)
GP wins in season – 7 Jim Clark 1963
Land Speed Record – 1,016.1 km/h (631.4 mph) Gary
  Gabelich (US) IN THE BLUE FLAME, 1970
Water Speed Record – 514.4 km/h (319.6 mph) Ken
  Warby (Aus) in SPIRIT OF AUSTRALIA, 1978

MOTOR SPORT – WORLD CHAMPIONSHIP

1950	Giusepe Farine (Italy)	
1951	Juan Manuel Fangio (Argentina)	
1952	Alberto Ascari (Italy)	
1953	Alberto Ascari (Italy)	
1954	Juan Manuel Fangio (Argentina)	
1955	Juan Manuel Fangio (Argentina)	
1956	Juan Manuel Fangio (Argentina)	
1957	Juan Manuel Fangio (Argentina)	
1958	Mike Hawthorn (England)	
1959	Jack Brabham (Australia)	
1960	Jack Brabham (Australia)	
1961	Phil Hill (USA)	
1962	Graham Hill (England)	
1963	Jim Clark (Scotland)	
1964	John Surtees (England)	
1965	Jim Clark (Scotland)	
1966	Jack Brabham (Australia)	
1967	Denis Hulme (New Zealand)	
1968	Graham Hill (England)	
1969	Jackie Stewart (Scotland)	
1970	Jochen Rindt (Austria)	
1971	Jackie Stewart (Scotland)	
1972	Emerson Fittipaldi (Brazil)	
1973	Jackie Stewart (Scotland)	
1974	Emerson Fittipaldi (Brazil)	
1975	Niki Lauda (Austria)	
1976	James Hunt (England)	
1977	Niki Lauda (Austria)	
1978	Mario Andretti (USA)	
1979	Jody Scheckter (South Africa)	
1980	Alan Jones (Australia)	
1981	Nelson Piquet (Brazil)	
1982	Keke Rosberg (Finland)	
1983	Nelson Piquet (Brazil)	
1984	Niki Lauda (Austria)	
1985	Alain Prost (France)	
1986	Alain Prost (France)	
1987	Nelson Piquet (Brazil)	
1989	Alain Prost (France)	
1990	Ayrton Senna (Brazil)	

MOTORCYCLING SPORT

Ruling body – Fédération Internationale Motorcycliste (FIM)

Classes – 50 cc, 125 cc, 250 cc, 350 cc (junior), 500 cc (senior), 750 cc, unlimited; sidecar

Major competitions – world championships (based on points gained in individual grands prix), including Isle of Man TT

NETBALL

Court – 100×50 ft (30.5×15.2 m)

Net – 10 ft (3.05 m) high; ring diam. 15 in (38 cm)

Ball – as for soccer

Duration of game – 60 min (4×15)

No. per side – 7 (subs. for injuries)

Ruling body – International Federation of Netball Associations

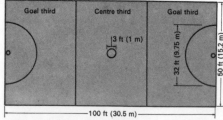

The layout of a netball court.

ROWING

Ruling body – Fédération Internationale des Sociétés d'Aviron (FISA)

International events: men – eights, fours and pairs (both coxed and coxless), single, double, and quadruple sculls; women – eights, coxed fours, single, double, and quadruple sculls

Major competitions – World championships every 4 years, alternating with Olympics; Henley Regatta (including Grand Challenge Cup and Diamond Sculls)

Standard course – men 2,000 m (2,187 yd), boys 1,500 m (1,640 yd), women 1,000 m (1.094 yd)

Terms

BOW Front part of boat.

CATCH A CRAB Feather blade in water, usually disrupting boat.

COX or COXSWAIN One who sits at stern, facing oarsmen, and steers.

COXLESS Without cox, steered by one of the oarsmen.

FEATHERING Turning blade flat between strokes to reduce air resistance.

REPECHAGE Race in which losing crews in heats have second chance to qualify for next round

SCULLS Boats in which each oarsman (sculler) has two oars.

STERN Rear end of boat.

STROKE Oarsman nearest stern (with back to others) who sets rhythm and rate; complete cycle of rowing action.

RUGBY LEAGUE

Pitch (max.) – 75 yd (68 m) wide, 110 yd (100 m) between goals, 6–12 yd (6–11 m) behind goals

Goal posts – as for rugby union

Ball – length $10\frac{1}{2}$–$11\frac{1}{2}$ in (27–29 cm), short circum. $22\frac{3}{4}$–24 in (58–61 cm)

Duration of game – 80 min (2×40)

No. per side – 13 (2 substitutes)

Scoring – TRY 3 pts., CONVERSION 2, PENALTY GOAL 2, DROPPED GOAL 2 (1 in internationals)

Ruling body – Rugby Football League International Board

Major competition – World Cup

Records

Team score – 119 Huddersfield (1914) in Test – 56 Australia (v France, 1960)

Test appearances – 46 Mick Sullivan (GB)

 tries – 43 Mick Sullivan (GB)

 goals – 93 Neil Fox (GB)

Tries: career – 834 Brian Bevan (1946–64)

 season – 80 Albert Rosenfeld (Huddersfield, 1913–14)

 match – 11 'Tich' West (Hull Kingston Rovers, 1905)

Goals: career – 2,955 Jim Sullivan (1921–46)

 season – 221 David Watkins (Salford, 1972–73)

 match – 22 Jim Sullivan (Wigan, 1925)

Points: career – 6,220 Neil Fox

 season – 496 Lewis Jones (Leeds, 1956–57)

 match – 53 'Tich' West (Hull Kingston Rovers, 1905)

Attendance – 102,569 Odsal Stadium, Bradford (Warrington v Halifax, Challenge Cup final replay, 5.5.54)

RUGBY UNION

Pitch (max.) – 75 yd (69 m) wide, 110 yd (100 m) between goals, 25 yd (22 m) behind goals

Goal posts – $18\frac{1}{2}$ ft (5.6 m) wide, no height limit, crossbar 10 ft (3 m) above ground

Ball – length 11 in (28 cm), short circum. $22\frac{3}{4}$–$24\frac{1}{2}$ in (58–62 cm), weight 14–$15\frac{1}{2}$ oz (400–440 gm)

Duration of game – 80 min (2×40)

No. per side – 15 (2 subs. for injury only)

Scoring – TRY 4 pts., CONVERSION 2, PENALTY GOAL 3, DROPPED GOAL 3

Ruling body – International Rugby Football Board

Major competitions – Five Nations Championship

Right: A Rugby football ground, and (below) an international squash court.

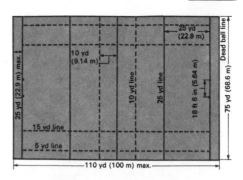

(England, France, Ireland, Scotland, Wales), Ranfurly Shield (New Zealand), Currie Cup (South Africa)

Records

Team score: touring side – 125 New Zealand (v Northern New South Wales, 1962)
in international – 92 France (v Spain, 1979)
in International Championship – 69 England (v Wales, 1881)
Individual score: any first-class match – 80 Jannie van der Westhuizen, Carnarvon (v Williston, 1972)
international – 24 Fergie McCormick, New Zealand (v Wales, 1969)
international career – 249, Andy Irvine (Scotland)
international tries – 23 Ian Smith (Scotland)

SPEEDWAY

Track – 4 laps of 300–450 yd (274–411 m)
surface – red shale or granite dust
Meeting – 20 races, 4 riders in race, each getting 5 rides
Scoring – 1st 3 pts., 2nd 2, 3rd 1
Machines – Brakeless 500 cc motorcycles
Ruling body – Fédération Internationale de Motorcycliste (FIM)
Major competitions – World Championship (individual), World Team Cup, World Pairs Championship

SPEEDWAY WORLD CHAMPIONSHIPS	
1951	Jack Young (Australia)
1952	Jack Young (Australia)
1953	Freddie Williams (Wales)
1954	Ronnie Moore (New Zealand)
1955	Peter Craven (England)
1956	Ove Fundin (Sweden)
1957	Barry Briggs (New Zealand)
1958	Barry Briggs (New Zealand)
1959	Ronnie Moore (New Zealand)
1960	Ove Fundin (Sweden)
1961	Ove Fundin (Sweden)
1962	Peter Craven (England)
1963	Ove Fundin (Sweden)
1964	Barry Briggs (New Zealand)
1965	Bjorn Knuttsson (Sweden)
1966	Barry Briggs (New Zealand)
1967	Ove Fundin (Sweden)
1968	Ivan Mauger (New Zealand)
1969	Ivan Mauger (New Zealand)
1970	Ivan Mauger (New Zealand)
1971	Ole Olsen (Denmark)
1972	Ivan Mauger (New Zealand)
1973	Jerry Szczakiel (Poland)
1974	Anders Michanek (Sweden)
1975	Ole Olsen (Denmark)
1976	Peter Collins (England)
1977	Ivan Mauger (New Zealand)
1978	Ole Olsen (Denmark)
1979	Ivan Mauger (New Zealand)
1980	Michael Lee (England)
1981	Bruce Penhall (United States)
1982	Bruce Penhall (United States)
1983	Egon Müller (W. Germany)
1984	Eric Gundersen (Denmark)
1985	Eric Gundersen (Denmark)
1986	Hans Nielsen (Denmark)
1987	Hans Nielsen (Denmark)
1988	Erik Gundersen (Denmark)
1989	Hans Neilsen (Denmark)
1990	Peter Jonsson (Sweden)

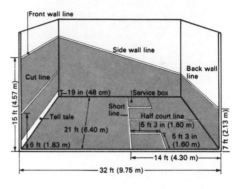

SQUASH

Ball – diam. 39.5–41.5 mm (1.56–1.63 in), weight 23.3–24.6 gm (0.82–0.87 oz), made of matt-surface rubber
Racket (max.) – length 27 in (68.6 cm), head $8\frac{1}{2}$ in (21.6 cm) long by $7\frac{1}{4}$ in (18.4 cm) wide
Scoring – best of 5 9-up games
Ruling body – International Squash Rackets Federation (ISRF)
Major competitions – World Open, Women's Open

SWIMMING AND DIVING

Standard Olympic pool – 50 m (54.7 yd) long, 8 lanes
Ruling body – Fédération Internationale de Natation Amateur (FINA)
Competitive strokes – freestyle (usually front crawl), backstroke, breaststroke, butterfly; individual medley (butterfly, backstroke, breaststroke, freestyle), medley relay (backstroke, breaststroke, butterfly, freestyle)
Diving events – men's and women's springboard at 3 m ($9\frac{3}{4}$ ft), highboard at 10 m (33 ft) (lower boards also used)
Major competitions – Olympics and world championships
Major long-distance swims – English Channel, Cook Strait (NZ), Atlantic City Marathon (US)

TABLE TENNIS

Table – 9×5 ft (2.74×1.52 m), $2\frac{1}{2}$ ft (76 cm) off floor
Net – height 6 in (15.2 cm), length 6 ft (1.83 m)
Ball – diam. 1.46–1.50 in (37–38 mm), weight 2.40–2.53 gm (0.085–0.089 oz), made of celluloid-type plastic, white or yellow
Bat surface – max. thickness 2 mm (0.08 in) pimpled rubber or 4 mm (0.16 in) sandwich rubber
Scoring – best of 3 or 5 21-pt games
Ruling body – International Table Tennis Federation
Major competitions – world championships, Swaythling Cup (men's team), Corbillon Cup (women's team), all two-yearly

335

WIMBLEDON CHAMPIONSHIPS (since 1953)

	men	women		men	women
1953	Victor Seixas (US)	Maureen Connolly (US)	1974	Jimmy Connors (US)	Chris Evert (US)
1954	Jaroslav Drobny (Cz)	Maureen Connolly (US)	1975	Arthur Ashe (US)	Billie Jean King (US)
			1976	Bjorn Borg (Swed)	Chris Evert (US)
1955	Tony Trabert (US)	Louise Brough (US)	1977	Bjorn Borg (Swed)	Virginia Wade (GB)
1956	Lew Hoad (Aus)	Shirley Fry (US)	1978	Bjorn Borg (Swed)	Martina Navratilova (Cz)
1957	Lew Hoad (Aus)	Althea Gibson (US)	1979	Bjorn Borg (Swed)	Martina Navratilova (Cz)
1958	Ashley Cooper (Aus)	Althea Gibson (US)	1980	Bjorn Borg (Swed)	Evonne Cawley† (Aus)
1959	Alex Olmedo (Peru)	Maria Bueno (Brazil)	1981	John McEnroe (US)	Chris Evert-Lloyd (US)
1960	Neale Fraser (Aus)	Maria Bueno (Brazil)	1982	Jimmy Connors (US)	Martina Navratilova (US)
1961	Rod Laver (Aus)	Angela Mortimer (GB)			
1962	Rod Laver (Aus)	Karen Susman (US)	1983	John McEnroe (US)	Martina Navratilova (US)
1963	Chuck McKinley (US)	Margaret Smith (Aus)			
1964	Roy Emerson (Aus)	Maria Bueno (Brazil)	1984	John McEnroe (US)	Martina Navratilova (US)
1965	Roy Emerson (Aus)	Margaret Smith (Aus)	1985	Boris Becker (W Ger)	Martina Navratilova (US)
1966	Manuel Santana (Sp)	Billie Jean King (US)			
1967	John Newcombe (Aus)	Billie Jean King (US)	1986	Boris Becker (W Ger)	Martina Navratilova (US)
1968	Rod Laver (Aus)	Billie Jean King (US)	1987	Pat Cash (Aus)	Martina Navratilova (US)
1969	Rod Laver (Aus)	Ann Jones (GB)			
1970	John Newcombe (Aus)	Margaret Court* (Aus)	1988	Stefan Edberg (Swe)	Steffi Graf (W Ger)
			1989	Boris Becker (W Ger)	Steffi Graff (W Ger)
1971	John Newcombe (Aus)	Evonne Goolagong (Aus)	1990	Stefan Edberg (Swe)	Martina Navratilova (US)
1972	Stan Smith (US)	Billie Jean King (US)			
1973	Jan Kodes (Cz)	Billie Jean King (US)			

*Formerly Margaret Smith. †Formerly Evonne Goolagong.

A tennis court. The dimensions given are those for a doubles match; for singles, the inner sidelines are used with the posts placed 3 feet outside them.

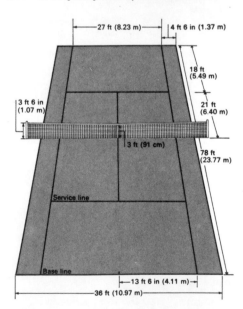

27 ft (8.23 m)
4 ft 6 in (1.37 m)
18 ft (5.49 m)
3 ft 6 in (1.07 m)
21 ft (6.40 m)
3 ft (91 cm)
78 ft (23.77 m)
Service line
Base line
13 ft 6 in (4.11 m)
36 ft (10.97 m)

TENNIS

Ball – diam. $2\frac{1}{2}$–$2\frac{5}{8}$ in (6.35–6.67 cm), weight 2–$2\frac{1}{16}$ oz (56.7–58.5 gm), made of wool-covered rubber, white or yellow

Rackets – no limits, wood or metal frames, strung with lamb's gut or nylon

Scoring – best of 3 or 5 6-up sets, with tiebreaker at 6–6 (or first to lead by 2); games of 4 pts. (15, 30, 40, game), 40–40 being DEUCE and 2-pt. lead

required; tiebreaker game usually first to 7 pts. with 2-pt. lead

Ruling body – International Lawn Tennis Federation (ILTF)

Major competitions – Wimbledon, Australian Open, US Open, French Open (the four constituting 'Grand Slam'), Davis Cup (world team championship), Federation Cup (Women's World Cup), Wightman Cup (US v GB women)

TENPIN BOWLING

Lane – 60 ft (18.3 m) long, $3\frac{1}{2}$ ft (1.07 m) wide

Pins – $1\frac{1}{4}$ ft (38 cm) high, of maple wood, standing in 3 ft (91 cm) triangle

Bowls – circum. 27 in (68.6 cm) max., weight (max.) 16 lb ($7\frac{1}{4}$ kg)

Scoring – 10 FRAMES of 2 bowls: STRIKE (10 pins down with 1st bowl) scores 10 plus score with next 2 bowls, SPARE (10 down with 2 bowls) scores 10 plus score with next bowl; max. game score 300 (12 strikes)

Ruling body – Fédération Internationale des Quilleurs (FIQ)

Major competition – world championships

VOLLEYBALL

Court – 18×9 m (59×$29\frac{1}{2}$ ft)

Net height – 2.43 m (7 ft 11.7 in) for men, 2.24 m (7 ft 4 in) for women

Ball – circum. 65–67 cm (25.6–26.4 in), weight 260–280 gm (9–10 oz)

No. per side – 6 (6 substitutes)

Scoring – best of 3 or 5 15-pt. sets

Ruling body – Fédération Internationale de Volleyball (FIVB)

Major competitions – Olympics and world championships, alternately every 4 years (men and women)

WATER POLO

Pool – 20–30 m (22–33 yd) by 8–20 m ($8\frac{3}{4}$–22 yd); min. depth 1 m (1.8 m for international competition)

Goals – 3×0.9 m (9¾×3 ft) for depths over 1.5 m (4 ft 11 in); for shallower pool, crossbar 2.4 m (7 ft 10 in) above bottom
Ball – circum. 68–71 cm (26¾–28 in), weight 400–450 gm (14–16 oz)
Duration of game – 28 min (4×7)
No. per side – 7 (6 substitutes)
Ruling body – FINA (see SWIMMING)
Major competitions – as for SWIMMING

WATER SKIING
Ruling body – World Water Ski Union
Events – slalom, jumping, figures (free-style tricks), and overall title
World championships – every 2 years
Record jumps:
  men – 59.4 m (194 ft) M. Hazlewood (GB) 1980
  women – 39.25 m (129 ft) D. Brush (USA) 1979

WEIGHTLIFTING
Ruling body – International Weightlifting Federation (IWF)
Lifts – SNATCH (bar pulled overhead in one movement) and (CLEAN AND) JERK (bar raised to shoulders first, then driven aloft as legs are straightened); (non-Olympic) BENCH PRESS, SQUAT, DEAD LIFT
World championships – annual (including Olympics)
Classes – flyweight (52 kg/114½ lb limit), bantam (56 kg/123¼ lb), feather (60 kg/132½ lb), light (67.5 kg/148¾ lb), middle (75 kg/165¼ lb), light-heavy 82.5 kg/181¾ lb), middle-heavy (90 kg/198¼ lb), heavy (110 kg/242½ lb), super-heavy (over 110 kg)

WINTER SPORTS
Ice Skating
Ruling body – International Skating Union (ISU)
World championships – annual (including Olympics)
Figure skating events – men's, women's single, pairs, (pairs) dancing (all with compulsory and 'free' sections); two sets of marks, for technical merit and artistic impression
Speed skating events (on oval 400-m circuits) – men's 500, 1,500, 5,000, and 10,000 m; women's 500, 1,000, 1,500, and 3,000 m; overall titles in world and international events

Ice Hockey
Rink – max. 200×100 ft (61×30 m)
Surround – max. 4 ft (1.22 m) high boards
Goals – 6×4 ft (1.83×1.22 m)
Puck – diam. 2 in (7.62 cm), thickness 1 in (2.54 cm), weight 5½–6 oz (156–170 gm), made of vulcanized rubber or similar material
Duration – 60 min (3×20) playing time
No. per side – 6 (max. 18 on team)
Ruling body – International Ice Hockey Federation
Major competitions (amateur) – annual world championships (incl. Olympics)

Curling
Rink – 138×14 ft (42×4.27 m)
Houses (targets) – diam. 12 ft (3.66 m), dist. between centres 114 ft (34.75 m)
Stones (max.) – circum. 36 in (91.4 cm), thickness 4½ in (11.4 cm), weight 44 lb (20 kg), made of granite or similar
No. per team – 4 (2 stones each)
No. of HEADS (or ENDS) – 10 or 12 (or time limit)
Ruling body – Royal Caledonian Curling Club
World championships – Silver Broom Trophy (annual)

Bobsleigh
Course – min. length 1,500 m (1,640 yd), with at least 15 banked turns; agg. time for 4 descents
Events – 2- and 4-man bobs
Ruling body – International Bobsleigh Federation
World championships – annual (including Olympics)

Luge Tobogganing
Course – 1,000–1,500 m (1,094–1,640 yd); agg. time for 4 descents
Events – 1- and 2-man luge, 1-woman luge; ridden in sitting position
Ruling body – International Luge Federation
World championships – annual (including Olympics)

Cresta Run
Course – unique to St Moritz, 1,213 m (1,326.6 yd); agg. time for 3 descents
Event – single seater, ridden face down
Ruling body – St Moritz Tobogganing Club
Major competitions – Grand National (full course, from Top), Curzon Cup (from Junction, 888 m or 971 yd); Olympic event (full course) 1928 and 1948

Alpine Ski Racing
Events – downhill, slalom, giant slalom, combined
Downhill – vert. drop 800–1,000 m (2,625–3,281 ft) men; 500–700 m (1,640–2,297 ft) women
Slalom – 55–75 gates men, 40–60 gates women; alternate gates (pairs of poles 4–5 m, 13–16 ft, apart) have blue or red flags and are 0.75–15 m (2.5–49 ft) apart
Giant slalom – min. 33 gates 4–8 m (13–26 ft) wide, at least 10 m (32 ft) apart
Ruling body – Fédération Internationale de Ski (FIS)
Major competitions – 2-yearly world championships (including Olympics, which has no combined title), annual World Cup (men's and women's, individuals scoring in 15 of 21 top international events, first 10 scoring 25, 20, 15, 11, 8, 6, 4, 3, 2, 1 pts.), annual Arlberg-Kandahar

Ski-Bob Racing
Events – downhill, giant slalom, special slalom, combined
Ruling body – Fédération Internationale de Skibob (FISB)
World championships – two-yearly (men's and women's)

Nordic Ski Competition
Events – 15, 30, 50 km (9.3, 18.6, 31 miles) men's, 5, 10 km (3.1, 6.2 miles) women's; 4×10 km relay (men), 3×5 km relay (women); nordic combination (15 km cross-country and ski jumping, men's); men's 70 and 90 m (230 and 295 ft) ski jumping (points awarded for style and distance)
Ruling body – Fédération Internationale de Ski (FIS)
Major competitions – 2-yearly world championships (including Olympics); 90-m ski jumping and biathlon, annually

Biathlon
Course – 20 km (12.4 miles), with 4 stops for target shooting men; 10 km (6.2 mi), with 3 stops, women.
Events – men's individual and relay (4×7.5 km)
Scoring – on time, with 2-min penalties for shots missing target, 1-min penalty for hit in outer ring of target

YACHT RACING
Ruling body – International Yacht Racing Union
Major competitions – annual world championships (various classes), Olympics (classes for 1984: Flying Dutchman, Finn, Soling, Star, Sailboard, Tornado, 470), America's Cup (12-metre yachts, best of 7 races, held every few years between holders, New York YC, and challengers), Admiral's Cup (2-yearly international ocean-racing team competition at Cowes, points gained in 4 races: Channel Race, Britannia Cup, New York YC Cup, Fastnet Race), Southern Cross (ocean-racing series in Australia, including Sydney-Hobart race), Little America's Cup (International Catamaran Challenge Trophy)

General Information

NOBEL PEACE PRIZE

1901	Henri Dunant (Swiss) & Frédéric Passy (French)
1902	Elie Ducommun and Albert Gobat (Swiss)
1903	Sir William Cremer (British)
1904	Institute of International Law
1905	Baroness Bertha von Suttner (Austrian)
1906	Theodore Roosevelt (American)
1907	Ernesto Moneta (Italian) & Louis Renault (French)
1908	Klas Arnoldson (Swedish) & Fredrik Bajer (Danish)
1909	Auguste Beernaert (Belgian) & Paul d'Estournelles (French)
1910	Permanent International Peace Bureau
1911	Tobias Asser (Dutch) & Alfred Fried (Austrian)
1912	Elihu Root (American)
1913	Henri La Fontaine (Belgian)
1914–16	*No award*
1917	International Red Cross
1919	*No award*
1919	Woodrow Wilson (American)
1920	Léon Branting (French)
1921	Karl Branting (Swedish) & Christian Lange (Norwegian)
1922	Fridtjof Nansen (Norwegian)
1923–24	*No award*
1925	Sir Austen Chamberlain (British) & Charles Dawes (American)
1926	Aristide Briand (French) & Gustav Stresemann (German)
1927	Ferdinand Buisson (French) & Ludwig Quidde (German)
1928	*No award*
1929	Frank Kellog (American)
1930	Nathan Söderblom (Swedish)
1931	Jane Addams & Nicholas Butler (American)
1932	*No award*
1933	Sir Norman Angell (British)
1934	Arthur Henderson (British)
1935	Carl von Ossietzky (German)
1936	Carlos de Saavedra Lamas (Argentina)
1937	Viscount Cecil of Chelwood (British)
1938	Nansen International Office for Refugees
1939–43	*No award*
1944	International Red Cross
1945	Cordell Hull (American)
1946	Emily Balch & John Mott (American)
1947	Friends Service Council (British) & American Friends Service Committee
1948	*No award*
1949	Lord John Boyd Orr (British)
1950	Ralph Bunche (American)
1951	Léon Jouhaux (French)
1952	Albert Schweitzer (Alsatian)
1953	George C. Marshall (American)
1954	Office of the UN High Commission for Refugees
1955–56	*No award*
1957	Lester Pearson (Canadian)
1958	Dominique Georges Pire (Belgian)
1959	Philip Noel-Baker (British)
1960	Albert Luthuli (South African)
1961	Dag Hammarskjöld (Swedish)
1962	Linus Pauling (American)
1963	International Red Cross & League of Red Cross Societies
1965	UNICEF (UN Children's Fund)
1966–67	*No award*
1968	René Cassin (French)
1969	International Labour Organization
1970	Norman Borlaug (American)
1971	Willy Brandt (West German)
1972	*No award*
1973	Henry Kissinger (American); Le Duc Tho (North Vietnamese) – declined
1974	Sean MacBride (Irish) & Eisaku Sato (Japanese)
1975	Andrei Sakharov (Russian)
1976	Betty Williams & Mairead Corrigan (British)
1977	Amnesty International
1978	Mohammed Anwar El Sadat (Egyptian & Menachem Begin (Israeli)
1979	Mother Teresa of Calcutta (Indian)
1980	Adolfo Pérez Esquivel (Argentinian)
1981	Office of the UN High Commissioner for Refugees
1982	Alva Myrdal (Swedish) & Alfonso Robles (Mexican)
1983	Lech Walesa (Polish)
1984	Bishop Desmond Tutu (South African)
1985	International Physicians for the Prevention of Nuclear War
1986	Elie Wiesel (American)
1987	President Oscar Arias Sánchez (Costa Rican)
1988	UN peacekeeping forces
1989	The Dalai Lama (Tibetan)
1990	Mikhail Gorbachev (Russian)

ECONOMICS

1969	Ragnar Frisch (Norwegian) and Jan Tinbergen (Dutch)
1970	Paul Samuelson (American)
1971	Simon Kuznets (American)
1972	Kenneth Arrow (American) and Sir John Hicks (British)
1973	Wassily Leontief (American)
1974	Gunnar Myrdal (Swedish) and Fridrich von Hayek (Austrian)
1975	Leonid Kantorovich (Russian) & Tjalling Kiipmans (Dutch)
1976	M. Friedman (American)
1977	J. E. Meade (British) & B. Ohlin (Swedish)
1978	H. A. Simoni (American)
1979	Theodore W. Schultz and Arthur Lewis (American)
1980	Lawrence Klein (American)
1981	James Tobin (American)
1982	George Stigler (American)
1983	Gerard Debreu (American)
1984	Sir Richard Stone (British)
1985	Franco Modigliani (American)
1986	James Buchanan (American)
1987	Robert Solow (American)
1988	Maurice Allais (French)
1989	Trygve Haavelmo (Norwegian)
1990	Harry Markowitz, Merton Miller & William Sharpe (American)

Right: Anwar El Sadat of Egypt and Menachem Begin of Israel, who were jointly awarded the Nobel Peace Prize in 1978 for their efforts to establish a lasting peace between their countries.

PHYSIOLOGY AND MEDICINE

1901	Emil Von Behring (German)
1902	Sir Ronald Ross (British)
1903	Niels Finset (Danish)
1904	Ivan Pavlov (Russian)
1905	Robert Koch (German)
1906	Camillo Golgi (Italian) & Santiago Ramón y Cajal (Spanish)
1907	Charles Laveran (French)
1908	Paul Ehrlich (German) & Elie Mechnikoff (Russian/French)
1909	Emil Theodor Kocher (Swiss)
1910	Albrecht Kossel (German)
1911	Allvar Gullstrand (Swedish)
1912	Alexis Carrel (French)
1913	Charles Richet (French)
1914	Robert Bárany (Austrian)
1915–18	*No award*
1919	Jules Bordet (Belgian)
1920	August Krogh (Danish)
1921	*No award*
1922	Archibald Hill (British) & Otto Meyerhof (German)
1923	Sir Frederick Banting (Canadian) & John Macleod (British)
1924	Willem Einthoven (Dutch)
1925	*No award*
1926	Johannes Fibiger (Danish)
1927	Julius Wagner-Jauregg (Austrian)
1928	Charles Bicolle (French)
1929	Christiaan Eijkman (Dutch) & Sir Frederick Hopkins (British)
1930	Karl Landsteiner (American)
1931	Otto Warburg (German)
1932	Edgar Adrian & Sir Charles Sherrington (British)
1933	Thomas H. Morgan (American)
1934	George Minot, William P. Murphy, & George Whipple (American)
1935	Hans Spemann (German)
1936	Sir Henry Sale (British) & Otto Loewi (German/Austrian)
1937	Albert Szent-Györgyi (Hungarian)
1938	Corneille Heymans (Belgian)
1940–42	*No award*
1943	Henrik Dam (Danish) & Edward Doisy (American)
1944	Joseph Erlanger & Herbert Gasser
1945	Sir Alexander Fleming, Howard Florey, & Ernst Chain (British)

1946	Hermann Muller (American)
1947	Carl and Gerty Cori (American) & Bernardo Houssay (Argentinian)
1948	Paul Muller (Swiss)
1949	Walter Hess (Swiss) & Antonio Moniz (Portuguese)
1950	Philip Hench & Edward Kendall (American), Tadeus Reichstein (Swiss)
1951	Max Theiler (S. African/American)
1952	Selman Waksman (American)
1953	Fritz Lipmann (German/American) & Hans Krebs (German/British)
1954	John Enders, Thomas Weller, & Frederick Robbins (American)
1955	Hugo Theorell (Swedish)
1956	Andre Cournand & Dickinson Richards Jr (American) and Werner Forssman (German)
1957	Daniel Bovet (Italian)
1958	George Beadle, Edward Tatum, & Joshua Lederberg (American)
1959	Severo Ochoa & Arthur Kornberg (American)
1960	Sir Macfarlane Burnet (Australian) & Peter Medawar (British)
1961	George von Bekesy (Hungarian/American)
1962	Francis Crick & Maurice Wilkins (British) & James Watson (American)
1963	Alan Hodgkin & Andrew Huxley (British) & Sir John Eccles (Australian)
1964	Konrad Bloch (German/American) & Feodor Lynen (German)
1965	Francois Jacob, Andre Lwoff, & Jacques Monod (French)
1966	Charles Huggins & Francis Peyton Rous (American)
1967	Ragnar Granit (Swedish) & Haldan Hartline & George Wald (American)
1968	Robert Holley, Hara Gobind Khorana, & Marshall Nirenberg (American)
1969	Max Delbruck, Alfred Hershey, & Salvador Luri (American)
1970	Sir Bernard-Katz (British), Ulf von Euler (Swedish), & Julius Axelrod (American)
1971	Earl Sutherland Jr (American)
1972	Rodney Porter (British) & Gerald Edelman (American)
1973	Karl von Frisch & Konrad Lorenz (Austrian) & Nikolaas Tinbergen (Dutch)
1974	Albert Claude & Christian de Duve (Belgian) & George Palade (Romanian-American)
1975	David Baltimore & Howard Temin (American), Renato Dulbecco (Italian)
1976	B. S. Blumberg & D. G. Gajdusek (American)
1977	Rosalyn Yallow, R. Guillemin & A. Schally (American)
1978	W. Arber (Swiss), D. Nathans & H. Smith (American)
1979	Godfrey Newbold Hounsfield (British) & Allen McLeod Cormack (American)
1980	George Snell (American), Jean Dausset (French) & Barui Benacerra (Venezuelan)
1981	David Hubel, Rober Sperry (American) & Torsten Wiesel (Swedish)
1982	Sune Bergstroen, Bengt Samuelson (Swedish) & John Vane (British)
1983	Barbara McClintock (American)
1984	César Milstein (British), Geroge Köhler (West German) & Niels Jerne (Danish)
1985	Michal Brown & Joseph Goldstein (American)
1986	Rita Levi-Montalcini (American and Italian) & Stanley Cohen (American)
1987	Susumu Tonegawa (Japanese)
1988	Sir James Black (British) & Gertrude Elion & George Hitchings (American)
1989	J. Michael Bishop & Harold E. Varmus (American)
1990	Joseph Murray & Donald Thomas (American)

LITERATURE

1901	René Sully Prudhomme (French)
1902	Theodor Mommsen (German)
1903	Björnstjerne Björnson (Norwegian)
1904	Frédéric Mistral (French) and José Echegaray (Spanish)
1905	Henryk Sienkiewicz (Polish)
1906	Giosuè Carducci (Italian)
1907	Rudyard Kipling (English)
1908	Rudolf Eucken (German)
1909	Selma Lagerlöf (Swedish)
1910	Paula von Heyse (German)
1911	Maurice Maesterlinck (Belgian)
1912	Gerhart Hauptmann (German)
1913	Sir Rabindranath Tagore (Indian)
1914	*No award*
1915	Romain Rolland (French)
1916	Verner von Heidenstam (Swedish)
1917	Karl Gjellerup and Henrik Pontoppidan (Danish)
1918	*No award*
1919	Carl Spitteler (Swiss)
1920	Knut Hamsun (Norwegian)
1921	Anatole France (French)
1922	Jacinto Benavente (Spanish)
1923	William Butler Yeats (Irish)
1924	Wladyslaw Reymont (Polish)
1925	George Bernard Shaw (Irish)
1926	Grazia Deledda (Italian)
1927	Henri Bergson (French)
1928	Sigrid Undset (Norwegian)
1929	Thomas Mann (German)
1930	Sinclair Lewis (American)
1931	Erik Karlfeldt (Swedish)
1932	John Galsworthy (English)
1933	Ivan Bruin (Russian)
1934	Luigi Pirandello (Italian)
1935	*No award*
1936	Eugene O'Neill (American)
1937	Roger Martin du Gard (French)
1938	Pearl S. Buck (American)
1939	Frans Eemil Sillanpää (Finnish)
1940–43	*No award*
1944	Johannes V. Jensen (Danish)
1945	Gabriela Mistral (Chilean)
1946	Hermann Hesse (Swiss)
1947	André Gide (French)
1948	Thomas Stearns Eliot (Anglo-American)
1949	William Faulkner (American)
1950	Bertrand Russell (English)
1951	Pär Lagerkvist (Swedish)
1952	François Mauriac (French)
1953	Sir Winston Churchill (English)
1954	Ernest Hemingway (American)
1955	Halldór Laxnes (Icelandic)
1956	Juan Ramón Jimenez (Spanish)
1957	Albert Camus (French)
1958	Boris Pasternak (Russian) – declined
1959	Salvatore Quasimodo (Italian)
1960	Saint-John Perse (Alexis Saint-Léger) (French)
1961	Ivo Andric (Yugoslavian)
1962	John Steinbeck (American)
1963	George Seferis (Giorgios Seferiades) (Greek)
1964	Jean-Paul Sartre (French) – declined
1965	Mikhail Sholokhov (Russian)
1966	Shmuel Yosef Agnon (Israeli) and Nelly Sachs (Swedish)
1967	Miguel Angel Asturias (Guatemalan)
1969	Yasunari Kawabata (Japanese)
1969	Samuel Becket (Irish)
1970	Alexander Solzhenitsyn (Russian)
1971	Pablo Neruda (Chilean)
1972	Heinrich Böll (W. German)
1973	Patrick White (Australian)
1974	Eyvind Johnson and Harry Edmund Martinson (Swedish)
1975	Eugenio Montale (Italian)
1976	Saul Bellow (American)
1977	V. Aleixandre (Spanish)
1978	Isaac Bashevis Singer (American)
1979	Odysseus Alepoudhelis (Greek) – known as Odysseus Elytis
1980	Czeslaw Milosz (American)
1981	Elias Canetti (Bulgarian)
1982	Gabriel Garcia Marquez (Colombian)
1983	William Golding (British)
1984	Jaroslav Seifert (Czechoslovakian)
1985	Claude Simon (French)
1986	Wole Soyinka (Nigerian)
1987	Joseph Brodsky (Russian)
1988	Naguib Mahfouz (Egyptian)
1989	Camilo José Cela (Spanish)
1990	Octavio Paz (Mexico)

CHEMISTRY

1901	Jacobus van't Hoff (Dutch)
1902	Emil Fischer (German)
1903	Svante Arrhenius (Swedish)
1904	Sir William Ramsay (British)
1905	Adolf von Baeyer (German)
1906	Henri Moissan (French)
1907	Eduard Buchner (German)
1908	Ernest Rutherford (New Zealand/British)
1909	Wilhelm Ostwald (German)
1910	Otto Wallach (German)
1911	Marie Curie (French)
1912	Victor Grignard & Paul Sabatier (French)
1913	Alfred Werner (Swiss)
1914	Theodore Richards (American)
1915	Richard Willstätter (German)
1916–17	*No award*
1918	Fritz Haber (German)
1919	*No award*
1920	Walther Nernst (German)
1921	Frederick Soddy (British)
1922	Francis Aston (British)
1923	Fritz Pregl (Austrian)
1924	*No award*
1925	Richard Zsigmondy (German)
1926	Theodore Svedberg (Swedish)
1927	Heinrich Wieland (German)
1928	Adolf Windaus (German)
1929	Arthur Harden (British) & Hans von Euler-Chelpin (German/Swedish)
1930	Hans Fischer (German)
1931	Carl Bosch & Friedrich Bergius (German)
1932	Irving Langmuir (American)
1933	*No award*
1934	Harold Urey (American)
1935	Frédéric and Irène Joliot-Curie (French)
1936	Peter Debye (Dutch)
1937	Walter Haworth (British) & Paul Karrer (Swiss)
1938	Richard Kuhn (German)
1939	Adolf Butenandt (German) & Leopold Ružička (Swiss)
1940–42	*No award*
1943	Georg von Hevesy (Hungarian/Swedish)
1944	Otto Han (German)
1945	Atturi Virtanen (Finnish)
1946	James Sumner, John Northrop, & Wendell Stanley (American)
1947	Sir Robert Robinson (British)
1948	Arne Tiselius (Swedish)
1949	William Giauque (American)
1950	Otto Diels & Kurt Alder (German)
1951	Glen Seaborg & Edwin McMillan (American)
1952	Archer Martin & Richard Synge (British)
1953	Hermann Staudinger (German)
1954	Linus Pauling (American)
1955	Vincent du Vigneaud (American)

1956	Sir Cyril Hinshelwood (British) & Nikolai Semenov (Russian)
1957	Sir Alexander Todd (British)
1958	Frederick Sanger (British)
1959	Jaroslav Heyrovsky (Czechoslovakian)
1960	Willard Libby (American)
1961	Melvin Calvin (American)
1962	Max Perutz & John Kendrew (British)
1963	Karl Ziegler (German) & Giulio Natta (Italian)
1964	Dorothy Crowfoot Hodgkin (British)
1965	Robert Woodward (American)
1966	Robert Mulliken (American)
1967	Ronald Norrish & George Porter (British) & Manfred Elgen (German)
1968	Lars Onsager (American)
1969	Derek Barton (British) & Odd Hassel (Norwegian)
1970	Luis Leloir (Argentinian)
1971	Gerhard Herzberg (Canadian)
1972	Christian Anfinsén, Stanford Moore, & William Stein (American)
1973	Ernst Otto Fischer (West German) & Geoffrey Wilkinson (British)
1974	Paul Florey (American)
1975	John Cornforth (Australian) & Vladmir Prelog (Swiss)
1976	W. N. Lipscomb (American)
1977	L. Prigogine (Belgian)
1978	Peter Mitchell (British)
1979	Herbert C. Brown (American) & George Witting (German)
1980	Paul Berg, Walter Gilbert (American) & Frederick Sanger (British)
1981	Kenichi Fukui (Japanese) & Roald Hoffman (American)
1982	Aaron Klug (British)
1983	Henry Taube (American)
1984	Bruce Merrifield (American)
1985	Herbert Hauptman & Jerome Karle (American)
1986	Dudley Herschbach & Yuan Lee (American) & John Polyani (Canadian)
1987	Charles Pedersen & Donald Cram (American)
1988	Johann Deisendorfer, Robert Huber & Hartmut Michel (West German)
1989	Thomas R. Cech (American) & Sidney Altman (Canadian)
1990	Elias J. Corey (American)

PHYSICS

1901	Wilhelm Roetgen (German)
1902	Hendrik Lorentz & Pieter Zeeman (Dutch)
1903	Pierre and Marie Curie & Henri Becquerel (French)
1904	Lord Rayleigh (British)
1905	Philipp Lenard (German)
1906	Sir Joseph Thomson (British)
1907	Albert Michelson (American)
1908	Gabriel Lippmann (French)
1909	G. Marconi (Italian) & F. Braun (German)
1910	Johannes van der Waals (Dutch)
1911	Wilhelm Wien (German)
1912	Nils Gustav Dalén (Swedish)
1913	Heike Kamerlingh-Onnes (Dutch)
1914	Max von Laue (German)
1915	Sir William H. Bragg & William L. Bragg (British)
1916	No award
1917	Charles Barkia (British)
1918	Max Planck (German)
1919	Johannes Stark (German)
1920	Charles Guillaume (Swiss)
1921	Albert Einstein (German/Swiss)
1922	Niels Bohr (Danish)
1923	Robert Millikan (American)
1924	Karl Siegbahn (Swedish)
1925	James Franck & Gustav Hertz (German)
1926	Jean Perrin (French)
1927	A. Compton (American) & C. T. R. Wilson (British)

1928	Owen Richardson (British)
1929	Prince Louis Victor de Broglie (French)
1930	Sir Chandrasekhara Raman (Indian)
1931	No award
1932	Werner Heisenberg (German)
1933	Erwin Schrodinger (Austrian) & Paul Dirac (British)
1934	No award
1935	James Chadwick (British)
1936	Victor Hess (Austrian) & Carl Anderson (American)
1937	C. Davisson (American) & G. Thomson (British)
1938	Enrico Fermi (Italian)
1939	Ernest O. Lawrence (American)
1940–42	No award
1943	Otto Stern (American)
1944	Isidor Isaac Rabi (American)
1945	Wolfgang Pauli (Austrian)
1946	Percy Bridgman (American)
1947	Sir Edward Appleton (British)
1948	Patrick M. S. Blackett (British)
1949	Hideki Yukawa (Japanese)
1950	Cecil Frank Powell (British)
1951	Sir John Cockcroft (British) & Ernest Walton (Irish)
1952	Edward Purcell & Felix Bloch (American)
1953	Frits Zernike (Dutch)
1954	Max Born (German/British) & W. Bothe (German)
1955	Polykarp Kusch & Willis Lamb Jr (American)
1956	W. Shockley, W. Brattain & J. Bardeen (American)
1957	Tsung Dao Lee & Chin Ning Yang (Chinese/American)
1958	Pavel Cherenkov, Ilya Frank & Igor Tamm (Russian)
1959	Emilio Segre & Owen Chamberlain (American)
1960	Donald Glaser (American)
1961	R. Hofstadter (American) & R. Mossbauer (German)
1962	Lev Landau (Russian)
1963	Eugene Wigner (American), Marie Goeppert-Mayer (German/American) & Hans Jensen (German)
1964	Charles Townes (American) & Nikolai Basov & Alexandr Prokhorov (Russian)
1965	Richard Feynman & Julian Schwinger (American) & Schinichiro Tomonaga (Japanese)
1966	Alfred Kastler (French)
1967	Hans Bethe (American)
1968	Luis Alvarez (American)
1969	Murray Gell-Mann (American)
1970	Hannes-Allfven (Swedish) & Louis Neel (French)
1971	Dennis Gabor (British)
1972	J. Bardeen, L. Cooper, & J. Schrieffer (American)
1973	Ivar Glaever (American), Leo Esaki (Japanese) & Brian Josephson (British)
1974	Sir Martin Ryle & Anthony Hewish (British)
1975	James Rainwater (American), Aage Bohr & Benjamin Mottelson (Danish)
1976	B. Richter (American) & G. Ting (American)
1977	Sir Nevill Mott (British), J. Van Vleck (American) & P. Anderson (American)
1978	P. J. Kapitsa (Russian), A. A. Penzias (American) & R. W. Wilson (American)
1979	Sheldon Glashow (American), Abdus Salam (Pakistan), & Stephen Weinberg (American)
1980	James Cronin & Val Fitch (American)
1981	Kai Siegbahn (Swedish), Nicholaas Bloembergon & Arthur Schawlaw (American)
1982	K. G. Wilson (American)
1983	Subramanyan Chandrasekhar & William Fowler (American)
1984	C. Rubbia (Italian) & Simmon van der Meer (Dutch)
1985	Klaus von Klitzing (West German)
1986	Ernst Ruska & Gerd Binnig (West German) & Heinrich Rohrer (Swiss)
1987	K. Müller (Swiss) & J. Bednorz (West German)
1988	Leon Lederman, Melvin Schwartz & Jack Steinberger (American)
1989	Norman F. Ramsey & Hans G. Dehmelt (American) & Wolfgang Paul (West German)
1990	Jerome I. Friedman & Henry W. Kendall (American)

TRANSPORT AND ENGINEERING

CIVIL AIRCRAFT MARKINGS: INTERNATIONAL PREFIXES

Prefix	Country	Prefix	Country	Prefix	Country
A2–	Botswana	PI–	Philippines	YI–	Iraq
A40–	Oman	PJ–	Netherlands Antilles	YJ–	New Hebrides
A7–	Qatar	PK–	Indonesia	YK–	Syria
AN–	Nicaragua	PP– PT–	Brazil	YR–	Romania
AP–	Pakistan	PZ–	Surinam	YS–	El Salvador
B–	Taiwan (Formosa)	S2–	Bangladesh	YU–	Yugoslavia
C–	Canada	SE–	Sweden	YV–	Venezuela
C2–	Nauru	SP–	Poland	ZA–	Alabania
CC–	Chile	ST–	Sudan	ZK–, ZL–,	
CCCP–	USSR	SU–	Egypt	ZM–	New Zealand
Cf–	Canada	SX–	Greece	ZP–	Paraguay
CN–	Morocco	TC–	Turkey	ZS–, ZT–	
CP–	Bolivia	TF–	Iceland	ZU–	South Africa
CS–	Portugal	TG–	Guatemala	3A–	Monaco
CU–	Cuba	TI–	Costa Rica	3B–	Mauritius
CX–	Uruguay	TJ–	Cameroon	3C–	Equatorial Guinea
D–	Germany	TL–	Central African	3D–	Swaziland
DQ–	Fiji		Empire	3X–	Guinea
EC–	Spain	TN–	Congo	4R–	Sri Lanka
EI, EJ–	Republic of Ireland	TR–	Gabon	4W–	Yemen
EL–	Liberia	TS–	Tunisia	4X–	Israel
EP–	Iran	TT–	Chad	5A–	Libya
ET–	Ethiopia	TU–	Ivory Coast	5B–	Cyprus
F–	France, colonies and	TY–	Benin	5H–	Tanzania
	protectorates	TZ–	Mali	5N–	Nigeria
G–	Great Britain,	VH–	Australia	5R–	Malagasy Republic
	Gibraltar	VP–B	Bahamas	5T–	Mauritania
HA–	Hungary	VP–F	Falkland Islands	5U–	Niger
HB–	Switzerland	VP–H	Belize	5V–	Togo
	Liechtenstein	VP–L	Antigua	5W–	Western Samoa
HC–	Ecuador	VP–P	Western Pacific	5X–	Uganda
HH–	Haiti		High Commission	5T–	Kenya
HI–	Dominican Republic	VP–V	St Vincent	6O–	Somalia
HK–	Columbia	VP–X	Gambia	6V–, 6W–	Senegal
HL–	South Korea	VP–Y,		6Y–	Jamaica
HP–	Panama	VP–W	Malawi, and	7P–	Lesotho
HR–	Honduras		Zimbabwe	7QY–	Malawi
HS–	Thailand	VQ–G	Grenada	7T–	Algeria
HZ–	Saudi Arabia	VQ–H	St Helena	8P–	Barbados
I–	Italy	VQ–L	St Lucia	8R–	Guyana
JA–	Japan	VQ–S	Seychelles	9G–	Ghana
JY–	Jordan	VR–	Bermuda	9H–	Malta
LN–	Norway	VR–H	Hong Kong	9J–	Zambia
LQ– LV–	Argentina	VR–O	Sabah (Malaysia)	9K–	Kuwait
LX–	Luxembourg	VR–U	Brunei	9L–	Sierra Leone
LZ–	Bulgaria	VR–W	Sarawak (Malaysia)	9M–	Malaysia
N–	United States	VT–	India	9N–	Nepal
OB–	Peru	XA–, XB–,		9Q–	Zaire
OD–	Lebanon	XC–	Mexico	9U–	Burundi
OE–	Austria	XT–	Burkina Faso	9B–	Singapore
OH–	Finland	XU–	Cambodia	9XR–	Rwanda
OK–	Czechoslovakia	XV–	Vietnam	9Y–	Trinidad and
OO–	Belgium	XW–	Laos		Tobago
OY–	Denmark	XY–, XZ–	Myanmar (Burma)		
PH–	Netherlands	YA–	Afghanistan		

The first motor-powered, heavier-than-air flight was made in 1903 by the American brothers Orville and Wilbur Wright. It took place at Kitty Hawk, North Carolina, and covered a distance of 37 metres. Right: A motor club meeting in England in 1905.

MOTORCARS: INTERNATIONAL IDENTIFICATION LETTERS

A	Austria	GR	Greece	RCB	Congo
AFG	Afghanistan	GUY	Guyana	RCH	Chile
AL	Albania			RH	Haiti
AND	Andorra	H	Hungary	RI	Indonesia
AUA	Australia	HK	Hong Kong	RIM	Mauritania
		HKJ	Jordan	RL	Lebanon
B	Belgium			RM	Malagasy Republic
BD	Bangladesh	I	Italy	RMM	Mali
BDS	Barbados	IL	Israel	RO	Romania
BG	Bulgaria	IND	India	ROK	South Korea
BH	Belize	IR	Iran	ROU	Uruguay
BR	Brazil	IRL	Ireland, Republic of	RP	Philippines
BRN	Bahrain	IRQ	Iraq	RSM	San Marino
BRU	Brunei	IS	Iceland	RU	Burundi
BS	Bahamas			RWA	Rwanda
BUR	Myanmar (Burma)	J	Japan		
		JA	Jamaica	S	Sweden
C	Cuba			SD	Swaziland
CDN	Canada	K	Cambodia	SF	Finland
CH	Switzerland	KWT	Kuwait	SGP	Singapore
CI	Ivory Coast			SME	Surinam
CL	Sri Lanka	L	Luxembourg	SN	Senegal
CO	Columbia	LAO	Laos	SU	USSR
CR	Costa Rica	LAR	Libya	SY	Seychelles
CS	Czechoslovakia	LB	Liberia	SYR	Syria
CY	Cyprus	LS	Lesotho		
				T	Thailand
D	Germany	M	Malta	TG	Togo
DK	Denmark	MA	Morocco	TN	Tunisia
DOM	Dominican Republic	MAL	Malyasia	TR	Turkey
DY	Benin	MC	Monaco	TT	Trinidad and Tobago
DZ	Algeria	MEX	Mexico		
		MS	Mauritius	USA	United States
E	Spain (including provinces)	MW	Malawi		
EAK	Kenya			V	Vatican City
EAT	Tanazania	N	Norway	VN	Vietnam
EAU	Uganda	NA	Netherlands Antilles		
EC	Ecuador	NIC	Nicargua	WAG	Gambia
ES	El Salvador	NIG	Niger	WAL	Sierra Leone
ET	Egypt	NL	Netherlands	WAN	Nigeria
		NZ	New Zealand	WD	Dominica
F	France (including overseas			WG	Grenada
	departments and territories)	P	Portugal (including overseas	WL	St Lucia
FJI	Fiji		territories)	WS	Western Samoa
FL	Leichtenstein	PA	Panama	WV	St Vincent
FR	Faroe Islands	PAK	Pakistan		
		PE	Peru	YU	Yugoslavia
GB	Great Britain	PL	Poland	YV	Venezuela
GBA	Alderney	PNG	Papua New Guinea		
GBG	Guernsey Channel Islands	PY	Paraguay	Z	Zambia
GBJ	Jersey			ZA	South Africa
GBM	Isle of Man	RA	Argentina	ZRE	Zaire
GBZ	Gibraltar	RB	Botswana	ZW	Zimbabwe
GCA	Guatemala	RC	Taiwan (Formosa)		
GH	Ghana	RCA	Central African Republic		

NOTABLE AIR DISASTERS

Date	Aircraft and nature of accident	Deaths
24.8.21	ZR-2 dirigible (GB) broke in two, near Hull	62
3.9.25	*Shenandoah* dirigible (US) broke up, Caldwell, Ohio	14
4.4.33	*Akron* dirigible (US) crashed, New Jersey coast	73
6.5.37	*Hindenburg* zeppelin (Ger.) burned at mooring, Lakehurst, NJ	36
23.8.44	UA Air Force B-24 hit school, Freckelton, England	76*
28.7.45	US Army B-25 hit Empire State Building, NY, in fog	19*
4.5.49	Italian airliner crashed at Superga, Turin	31†
1.11.49	DC-4 airliner (US) rammed by Bolivian P-38 fighter, Wash., DC	55
20.12.52	US Air Force C-124 fell and burned, Washington	87
18.6.53	US Air Force C-124 crashed and burned near Tokyo	129
30.6.56	Super-Constellation and DC-7 airliners collided over Grand Canyon	128
6.2.58	Elizabethan airliner (GB) crashed on take-off at Munich, W. Germany	23‡
16.12.60	DC-8 Super-Constellation airliners collided over New York	134*
15.2.61	Boeing 707 (Belgian) crashed near Brussels	73§
3.6.62	Boeing 707 (French) crashed on take-off, Paris	130
22.6.62	Boeing 707 (French) crashed in storm, Guadeloupe	113
20.5.65	Boeing 720B (Pak.) crashed at Cairo airport	121
24.1.66	Boeing 707 (Indian) crashed on Mont Blanc (France)	117
4.2.66	Boeing 727 (Jap.) plunged into Tokyo Bay	133
5.3.66	Boeing 707 (GB) crashed on Mt Fuji (Japan)	124
20.4.67	Britannia turboprop (Swiss) crashed at Nicosia (Cyprus)	126
16.3.69	DC-(Venez.) crashed on take-off Maracaibo	155*
30.7.71	Boeing 727 (Jap.) collided with F-86 fighter, Japan	162
14.8.72	Ilyushin-62 (E. Ger.) crashed on take-off, Berlin	156
13.10.72	Illyushin-62 (USSR) crashed near Moscow	176
4.12.72	Spanish charter jet airliner crashed on take-off, Canary Is.	155
22.1.73	Boeing 707 (chartered) crashed on landing at Kano, Nigeria	176
3.6.73	TU-144 (USSR) exploded in air, Goussainville, France	14¶
3.3.74	DC-10 (Turk.) crashed in forest, Ermenonville, France	346
10.9.76	British Trident 3 and Yugoslavian DC-9 collided in mid-air near Zagreb (Yugoslavia)	176
27.3.77	Two Boeing 747s (American and Dutch) collided on ground at Los Rodeos airport	582
1.1.78	Boeing 747 (Indian) crashed into the sea off Bombay (India)	213
15.11.78	DC-8 (Iceland) crashed while attempting to land, Sri Lanka	262
14.3.79	Trident (China) crashed near Peking	200
24.5.79	DC-10 (US) crashed near Cicago	273
25.4.80	British chartered Boeing 727 crashed in Canary Islands	146
7.7.80	Airliner (USSR; type unspecified) crashed on take-off, Alma-Ata	163
19.8.80	Lockheed Tristar (Saudi) destroyed by fire after emergency landing, Riyadh	301
1.12.81	DC-9 (Yugoslav.) crashed ian Corsica	174
13.1.82	Boeing 737 (US) crashed shortly after take-off, Washington, DC	78
12.8.85	Jumbo jet crashed into Mount Osutaka, Japan	520
6.11.86	Helicopter crashed in North Sea	45
21.12.88	US Boeing 747 blown up by bomb over Scotland	270
8.1.89	British Boing 737 crashed on motorway in England	47
19.7.89	US jetliner crashed at Sioux City, Iowa	119

* Total includes deaths on ground or in buildings.
† Including the entire team of Italian footbal champions Torino.
‡ Mostly players (8) and officials (3) of England football champions Manchester United, and 8 journalists.
§ Including skaters (17) and officials of US world championships team.
¶ First supersonic airliner crash.

NOTABLE SEA DISASTERS

Birkenhead (1852), British troopship, ran aground off Port Elizabeth (S Africa) and broke in two on rocks; 455 perished, 193 survived.

Sultana (1865), Mississippi river steamer, blew up (boiler explosion); 1,450 died.

Mary Celeste (1872), American half-brig, found abandoned in Atlantic with no sign of life; great mystery of the sea.

General Slocum (1904), an excursion steamer, burned in New York harbour; 1,021 died.

Titanic (1912), British liner, struck iceberg in N Atlantic; about 1,500 died, 705 survived.

Empress of Ireland (1914), Canadian steamer, sank after collision in St Lawrence River; 1,024 died.

Lusitania (1915), British liner, torpedoed by German submarine off Ireland; 1,198 died.

Thetis (1939), British submarine, sank in Liverpool Bay; 99 perished.

Curacao (1942), British cruiser, sank after collision with liner *Queen Mary*; 335 died.

Wilhelm Gustloff (1945), German liner, torpedoed by Russian submarine off Danzig; about 7,700 died.

Toya Maru (1954), Japanese ferry, sank in Tsugaru Strait; 1,172 died.

Andrea Doria (1956), Italian liner, collided with Swedish liner *Stockholm* off Nantucket (NY) in fog; 51 died, about 1,655 rescued.

Thresher (1963), American nuclear submarine, sank in N Atlantic; 129 died.

Scorpion (1968), American nuclear submarine, sank in N Atlantic; 99 died.

Herald of Free Enterprise (1987), Cross-Channel ferry capsized off Zeebrugge, 193 passengers died.

Dona Paz (1987). Philippines ferry collided with tanker *Victor* off Marinduque island; over 1,500 died.

NOTABLE RAIL DISASTERS

1876 Dec. 29: Passenger train derailed as iron bridge collapsed in snowstorm, Ashtabula River, Ohio, USA; 91 died.
1879 Dec. 28: Tay Bridge, Dundee, Scotland, blown down taking train with it; 73 drowned.
1881 June 2: Train fell into river near Cuartla, Mexico; about 200 died.
1915 May 22: Two passenger trains and troop train collided at Quintins Hill, Dumfriesshire, Scotland; 227 died.
1917 Dec. 12: Troop train derailed near mouth of Mt Cenis tunnel, Modane, France; 543 died.
1944 Jan. 16: Train wrecked inside tunnel, Leon Province, Spain; 500–800 died.
1944 Mar. 2: Train stalled in tunnel near Salerno, Italy; 521 suffocated.
1953 Dec. 24: express plunged into stream near Waiouru, New Zealand; 155 died.
1955 Apr. 3: Train plunged into canyon near Guadalajara, Mexico; about 300 died.
1957 Sept. 1: Train plunged into ravine near Kendal, Jamaica; about 175 died.
1957 Sept. 29: Express train crashed into

stationary oil train in W. Pakistan; nearly 300 died.
1962 May 3: Three trains collided in Tokyo; 163 died.
1963 Nov. 9: Two trains hurtled into derailed train near Yokohama, Japan; over 160 died.
1970 Feb. 4: Express train crashed into stationary commuter train near Buenos Aires; 236 died.
1970 Feb. 16: Train crashed in northern Nigeria; about 150 killed in crash and another 52 injured survivors killed in road crash on way to hospital.
1972 Oct 6: Train carrying religious pilgrims derailed and caught fire near Saltillo, Mexico; 204 died, over 1,000 injured.
1980 Aug. 8: Passenger and freight trains collided near Torun, Poland; 62 died.
1981 June 6: Crowded train fell of bridge into river in Bihar State India; 268 died.
1988 Dec. 12: Three trains collided at Clapham, London; 34 died.
1989 June 4: Spark ignited a gas leak in the USSR, destroying two passing trains; 460 died.
1990 Jan 4: Two trains collided at Sanghi Pakistan; nearly 300 died.

LONGEST BRIDGE SPANS

*Under construction

	location	longest span (m)	longest span (ft)	opened
Suspension				
Akashi-Kaiko	Japan	1,980	6,496	*
Humber Estuary	England	1,410	4,626	1980
Verrazano Narrows	NY, USA	1,298	4,260	1964
Golden Gate	Calif., USA	1,280	4,200	1937
Cantilever				
Quebec Railway	Canada	549	1,800	1917
Forth Rail	Scotland	518	1,700	1890
Steel Arch				
New River Gorge	W. Va., USA	518	1,700	1977
Bayonne	NJ, USA	504	1,652	1931
Sydney Harbour	Australia	503	1,650	1932
Cable-Stayed				
Vancouver	Canada	465	1,526	1986
St Nazaire	Loire, France	404	1,325	1975
Sunshine Valley	St Petersburg, Fla.	366	1,200	1986
Continuous Truss				
Astoria	Oregon, USA-	376	1,232	1966
Concrete Arch				
Gladesville	Australia	305	1,000	1964
Longest bridge (total length)				
Pontchartrain Causeway	Louisiana, USA	38.4 km	23.9 mi	1969

TALLEST STRUCTURES

The world's tallest building is the 110-storey 1,454 ft (443 m) Sears Tower in Chicago, USA. With TV antennae, it reaches 1,559 ft (475.2 m). The world's tallest structure is the 2,120 ft (646 m) mast of Warszawa Radio at Konstantynow, near Plock, in Poland. Made of galvanized steel, it was completed in July 1974.

The highest structures of ancient times were the pyramids of Egypt. The Great Pyramid of Cheops, at el-Gizeh, built in about 2580 BC, reached a height of 480.9 ft (146.6 m). It was another 4,000 years before this was surpassed – by the central tower of Lincoln Cathedral, England, which was completed in 1548 and stood 525 ft (160 m) before it toppled in a storm.

LONGEST TUNNELS

Railway	km	miles:yds	opened
Eurotunnel			Due to
(England/France)	49.94	31.53	open 1993
Seikan (Japan)	53.9	33:862	1988
Simplon II			
(Switz./It.)	19.923	12.559	1922
Road			
St Gotthard (Swit.)	16.32	10:246	1980
Arlberg (Austria)	14.0	8:1232	1978
Mont Blanc			
(France/Italy)	11.585	7:352	1965
Underwater			
Seikan (Japan)*	23.3	14:880	1988
Shin Kammon	18.7	11:1073	1974

*Length of the sub-acqueous section of the Seikan railway tunnel.

COOKING TERMS

Anglaise Garnish of boiled vegetables such as turnips, carrots, and celery hearts, used with boiled salt beef.

Au bain marie Cook by standing container of food in hot-water bath to protect from fierce heat; can also be used to keep food warm.

Au beurre Cooked with butter, either by itself or in sauce.

Au gratin Cooked with crumbed bread or cheese on top, then browned under grill.

Bake Cook in enclosed space using dry heat only.

Bake blind Bake pastry case having filled it completely with dried beans to keep it from rising.

Bard Cover fatless meat or game with large piece of fat or bacon to keep it moist in cooking.

Baste Spoon hot fat or liquid over food being roasted or poached.

Bat Flatten (with heavy object) fillet of sole, lamb cutlet, or veal escalope.

Beat Mix using strong implement and steady regular stroke.

Béchamel White sauce made from roux of butter and flour, mixed with milk, sometimes with herbs and diced vegetables.

Beurre manié Kneaded butter used for thickening soups and sauces.

Beurre noisette Butter cooked to nut-brown colour, with herbs and lemon juice then added; served with fish or meat.

Blanch Put food, usually onions or some meats, into cold water, bring to boil, and remove. Or put green vegetables into boiling water for $\frac{1}{2}$ minute, drain, and refresh with cold water.

Bind Hold together and solidify mixture by adding another ingredient, usually eggs.

Blanquette Dish cooked with white sauce, e.g. blanquette de veau – white veal stew.

Blend Mix ingredients together to form homogeneous mixture.

Boil Cook food in boiling water or water-based liquid.

Bonne femme Garnish of bacon lardons, button onions, button mushrooms, and small potatoes.

Bouchée Small vol-au-vent.

Bouillon Broth.

Bouquet garni Parsley, bayleaf, and thyme with other herbs, all tied together. Used to flavour stews and casseroles; removed after cooking.

Bourguignon Sauce containing red burgundy, button mushrooms, and small onions; served with beef.

Braise Cook slowly to tenderness in oven.

Brochettes Pieces of meat cooked with herbs on skewers.

Broil Cook meat directly over fire.

Brunoise Garnish of root vegetables; as julienne, but very finely diced before cooking.

Canapés Fried bread, cheese, or short-crust pastry cut into small shapes and covered with savoury mixture.

Casserole Cook meat, game, or poultry, and sometimes vegetables, together in an enclosed container in an oven.

Chasseur Sautéed mushrooms added to sauté of game, chicken, or veal.

Clarify Clean out impurities in butter by heating, or in broth by using the white of an egg.

Colbert Sauce containing meat or fish glaze, light stock, softened butter, lemon juice, Madeira, and parsley.

Compote Fruit poached in sugar syrup.

Concasser Skin and seed tomatoes and cut into thin strips.

Consommé Strong, clear bouillon.

Court bouillon Slightly acid stock made from water, root vegetables, and white wine or vinegar.

Cream Beat ingredients to a cream-like consistency.

Croûtes Pieces of fried bread used as base for savouries, tournedos, or eggs.

Croûtons Very small cubes of fried bread served with soups.

Cuisson Natural cooked juices from fish, chicken, or meat.

Cut and fold Cut to bottom of air-containing mixture and fold over so as to mix in other ingredients without losing the air.

Deglaze Scrape down meat juices from roasting tin with metal spoon.

Degorger Remove unwanted substances from certain foods; e.g. salt from anchovies by soaking in milk; bitter juices from aubergines by sprinkling with salt.

Demi-glace Brown sauce made from mirepoix, tomato purée, mushrooms, and bouquet garni.

Depouiller Remove fat from sauce by dropping in cold liquid to solidify fat, which can then be skimmed off.

Dice Cut food into small, neat cubes.

Doria Garnish of cucumber.

Dredge Sprinkle liberally with flour or sugar.

Dripping Beef fat that is left after roasting beef.

Dropping consistency Consistency of a mixture that, when lifted up on a spoon, drops easily back into the bowl.

Dubarry Cauliflower flowerets coated with mornay sauce and cooked au gratin.

Duxelles Finely chopped mushrooms and shallots, often used in stuffings.

Escalope Slice of veal, $\frac{1}{4}$–$\frac{1}{2}$ in (6–13 mm) thick, preferably cut across best part of leg. Can also be taken from neck or loin and well beaten.

Flamande Garnish of red cabbage and glazed small onions; used with pork or beef.

Flamber Set light to, using brandy or fortified wine.

Florentine Garnish of spinach. Also old name for apple pie.

Fricassée Pieces of cooked white meat reheated in creamy white sauce.

Frit Fried.

Fry Cook in hot fat in open pan over heat.

Fumet Strong stock made from fish or game and well reduced.

Garni Garnished.

Garnish Decorate with complementary foodstuffs.

Glaze Brush with liquid substance that cooks or dries to shiny finish.

Grate Reduce to small particles by rubbing against rough surface.

Grill Cook underneath direct heat.

Sage
Lemon Verbena
Bay
Rosemary
Marjoram
Basil

A few of the many herbs commonly used in cooking. Lamb is traditionally cooked with rosemary and pork with sage, for instance, but many cooks love to experiment with different flavours.

USEFUL MEASURES

Imperial

2 teaspoons	=	1 dessertspoon
2 dessertspoons	=	1 tablespoon
16 tablespoons	=	1 cup
2 cups	=	1 pint
1 pint	=	20 fl. oz

American

1 Amer. pint	=	16 fl. oz
1 Amer. cup	=	8 fl. oz

Metric (working) equivalents

1 teaspoon	=	5 ml
1 Amer. teaspoon	=	4 ml
1 pint	=	$\frac{1}{2}$ litre (approx.)
1 litre	=	$1\frac{3}{4}$ pints (approx.)
1 lb	=	$\frac{1}{2}$ kilo (approx.)

Level tablespoons per oz (approx.)

Breadcrumbs (dry)	3–4
Cheese (grated)	3–4
Flour	2
Gelatine	2
Raisins, etc.	2
Rice	2
Sugar (granulated)	1

Hollandaise Hot emulsified sauce containing egg yolks, butter, and lemon juice.

Indienne Mayonnaise seasoned with curry and chopped chives.

Jardinière Groups of different vegetables, or a macedoine, used to garnish meat dishes, usually with demi-glace sauce.

Joinville Garnish of sliced truffles, crayfish tails, and mushrooms, with a sauce Nantua.

Julienne Vegetables cut into very thin strips and cooked slowly in butter.

Knead Work and blend moist dough to homogeneous consistency.

Lard Thread strips of fat through fatless meat to moisten it in cooking.

Lardons Approximately finger-sized strips of bacon used for flavouring.

Liaison Thickening and enriching agent added to soup or sauce towards end of cooking time.

Lyonnaise Garnish of fried onions.

Macedoine Mixture of vegetables or fruit cut into large dice.

Macerer Soak fruit in liqueur or syrup.

Marinate Soak food for some hours in suitable liquid; e.g. meat in red wine with herbs and spices; fruit in sugar and liqueur syrup.

Mayonnaise Cold emulsified sauce made with egg yolks, oil, and a little vinegar, and/or lemon juice and seasoning.

Meunière Finish of beurre noisette with lemon juice.

Milanese Pasta with tomato sauce, shredded ham, and mushrooms.

Mirepoix Selection of $\frac{1}{4}$-in (6-mm) diced vegetables in equal quantities, including carrots, turnips, onions, and celery.

Mornay Béchamel sauce flavoured with cheese.

Nantua Garnish of prawns, lobster, or crayfish, and sometimes tomato.

Napolitaine Garnish or sauce of tomatoes and parmesan cheese. Also a 3-coloured ice cream.

Navarin Brown lamb or mutton stew with root vegetables.

Noisette Best end of neck of lamb or mutton, boned, seasoned, tied into a roll, and cut into $1\frac{1}{2}$-in (4-cm) thick slices.

Normande Garnish of cider, apples, butter, and cream. Or, with sole, garnish of mussels, oysters, shrimps, and mushrooms.

Panade Very thick white sauce, or bread crumbs soaked in milk and beaten smooth.

Parboil Partially cook by boiling.

Pickle Soak for long time in strong preservative liquid.

Poach Cook very gently in shallow pan in water-based liquid at 170°–186°F (77°–86°C).

Portuguese Rich tomato sauce, or garnish of tomatoes.

Pot au feu Beef broth, possibly thickened with rice or pasta, or served as clear consommé. Or the boiled beef that has been used in making the former.

APPROXIMATE OVEN TEMPERATURES

Description	Electric °F	°C	Gas no.*
very cool	225°	107°	$\frac{1}{4}$ (240°)
	250°	121°	$\frac{1}{2}$ (265°)
cool	275°	135°	1 (290°)
	300°	149°	2 (310°)
warm	325°	163°	3 (335°)
moderate	350°	177°	4 (355°)
fairly hot	375°	191°	5 (375°)
	400°	204°	6 (400°)
hot	425°	218°	7 (425°)
very hot	450°	232°	8 (450°)
	475°	246°	9 (470°)

*Temperature equivalents of the gas numbers are given in °F in parentheses.

Pot roast Cook very slowly in covered pan with fat, herbs and onion.

Princesse Denotes use of chicken.

Pulses Seeds of leguminous plant that can be eaten, e.g. peas, beans, lentils.

Purée Boil food substance to pulp, and strain.

Ragoût Brown stew in which meat is cut into large pieces, with some fat left on, and cooked with vegetables.

Revenir Pass vegetables through hot oil to glaze, but not to cook them.

Ribbon, beat to the Beat until mixture, when lifted up on a spoon, forms a long continuous ribbon-like stream without dropping directly back into the bowl.

Rissoler Brown slowly in fat.

Roast Cook in enclosed space using fat; French roast by using small quantity of liquid to provide extra moisture.

Robert Usually denotes use of mustard.

Rôti Roast.

Roux Mixture of flour and fat used as base for sauce or soup.

St. Germain Garnish of peas and sometimes

pommes noisette. Also a cream of pea soup.

Salpicon Savoury filling of largish pieces of sliced vegetables, meat, or fish.

Sauté Cook in small quantity of fat in open pan; fat is absorbed completely into food.

Scald Bring milk or cream to near boiling point.

Sear Brown and seal outside of meat very quickly.

Sift Shake dry ingredients through fine mesh to remove lumps.

Simmer Cook in liquid at temperature of about $185°–200°F$ ($85°–93°C$) so that liquid shows slight movement but does not actually boil.

Slake Mix, usually arrowroot or cornflour, with small amount of cold water before using as thickening for sauce, soup, or gravy.

Soubise Onion purée, often mixed with white sauce.

Steam Cook slowly by exposing food to concentrated steam.

Suprême Of chicken breast.

Tournedos Fillet of beef, $1–1\frac{1}{2}$ in (25–40 mm) thick, cut from heart of fillet.

Valentino Denotes asparagus and sometimes cheese.

Whip Mix thoroughly and quickly with whisk to include as much air as possible into mixture.

WINE GLOSSARY

Alsace Province of eastern France between Vosges and Rhine, best known for white wines named after grape (Riesling, Sylvaner, etc.).

Amontillado Pale, medium-dry Sherry.

Amoroso Golden, fairly rich, dessert Sherry.

Appellation Contrôlée Term used on labels of superior French wines, indicating registered trade name and that wine conforms with description on label. See VDQS.

Asti Spumante Sparkling, white Italian wine, made in Piedmont; highly scented and usually medium-sweet.

Barsac Luscious French white wine, nearly as sweet as Sauternes (in which district it lies); some labelled Sauternes.

Beaujolais Large district in Burgundy, producing light, fresh, and fruity wines. Most of vast output is red.

Bordeaux Major wine-producing area in south-western France: red Bordeaux (claret) includes wine from major districts Médoc, St. Emilion, Pomerol, Graves; white Bordeaux from Sauternes, Graves, Entre Deux Mers, etc. Least distinguished Bordeaux sold simply as Bordeaux rouge or Bordeaux blanc.

Bouquet Perfume given off by wine.

Bourgeois Term for high-quality wine, not quite in top bracket.

Brut Of Champagne, etc., very dry.

Burgundy Former province of eastern France, famous for the red wines of the Côte d'Or, Beaujolais, Mâcon, etc., and white wines of Côte d'Or (Côte de Beaune), Chablis, etc.

Chambré Brought to room temperature.

Champagne Former province of northern France where the famous sparkling wine is produced (mostly white, but also rosé). Méthode Cham-

penoise puts sparkle in by inducing second fermentation in bottle.

Château In Bordeaux, a wine-producing estate or farm, seldom with a castle.

Chianti Italian red wine from Tuscany; young medium-bodied kind in familiar wicker-covered fiascos or matured full-bodied kind.

Claret Term often used in Britain for red Bordeaux.

Corky Spoilt by diseased cork.

Demi-sec Of Champagne, sweet.

Dry Unsweetened.

Extra-sec Of Champagne, very dry.

Fino Pale, dry, delicate Sherry.

Fortified wines Strengthened at some stage of production with brandy or spirit (e.g. Sherry, Port, Madeira).

Graves Large district in Bordeaux area, producing mainly white wines, the best being dry. The finest Graves are red, and include Haut-Brion.

Hock Term often used in Britain for German Rhine wines.

Kabinett German label term indicating high-quality wine (made without added sugar).

Liebfraumilch Name permitted by law for any indeterminate Hock of QbA standard.

Loire Major wine-producing area extending from Bay of Biscay to central France; mostly white wines.

Madeira Fortified wines of island of Madeira: Sercial, Verdelho, Bual, Malmsey.

Manzanilla Very pale, tart Sherry, with distinctive nutty taste.

Marsala Dark brown fortified wine of Sicily, with burnt-caramel flavour.

Médoc Major district of Bordeaux, producing many great red wines.

Moselle Name commonly given in Britain to

German Mosel-Saar-Ruwer wines, mostly delicate white (pale greenish), made from Riesling grape, with deliciously fresh acidity (e.g. Piesporter).

Mousseux French sparkling wines, mostly white, but some red and rosé.

Oloroso Full-bodied, dark, sweet Sherry.

Orvieto White Italian wines, dry (secco) or full-flavoured medium-sweet (abboccato).

Port Fortified wine of Portugal, mostly red, but some white (used for blending or drunk as apéritif); Wood Port is blended and matures in wood; Vintage Port is from one good vintage, and after 2 years in wood is matured in bottle for further 10–20; Ruby Port is young Wood Port, sweet, fruity, full-bodied, and brilliant purple; Tawny Port is a paler, russet colour (as result of age or blending), with lighter body and subtle taste, drier and nuttier.

QbA (Qualitätswein bestimmter Anbaugebiete) Good-quality German wine made to standard laid down by law.

Qualitätswein mit Prädikat Highest quality German wine.

Red wine Made by leaving skin and juice together during fermentation; colour comes from pips and skins. Usually served at room temperature.

Retsina Greek wine with turpentine flavour caused by addition of resin.

Rhine (Rhein) Area in Germany that produces Hock, in valleys of Rhine and some of its tributaries.

Rhône Major wine-producing area of France, stretching from Lyon to Avignon, particularly noted for red wines (Côtes du Rhône, Châteauneuf du Pape, etc.); also rosé (the dry, fruity Tavel Rosé) and white.

Riesling Type of grape from which many fine German wines are made (most Moselles, some Hocks); also used in Alsace, Yugoslavia, etc.

Rosé Made like red wine, but juice run off sooner, giving it lighter colour and taste; usually served chilled.

Sauternes Major district of Bordeaux, producing rich, sweet wines, made from grape with high sugar content encouraged by growth of mould the 'noble rot'.

Sec Of Champagne, etc., dry.

Sekt German sparkling wines, usually made by

ALCOHOL CONTENT PROOF SYSTEMS

°Proof		%
GB	US	alcohol
175	200	100
100	114.3	57.1
87.5	100	50
85	97.1	48.6
80	91.4	45.7
75	85.7	42.9
70	80	40
65	74.3	37.1
60	68.6	34.3
52.5	60	30
50	57.1	28.6
35	40	20
26.3	30	15
21	24	12
17.5	20	10

WORLD CONSUMPTION

Wine consumption	(litres per head)*
France	93
Italy	90
Portugal	86
Argentina	77
Spain	70
W. Germany	24
Australia	16

Beer consumption	(litres per head)*
W. Germany	145
Czechoslovakia	140
E. Germany	134
Australia	134
Belgium	126
Ireland	122
UK	122

*Figures for 1976

WINE: VINTAGE GRADINGS

	Claret (Red Bordeaux)	White Bordeaux	Red Burgundy	White Burgundy	Rhone	Loire	Rhine	Moselle
1945	10	9	6	–	9	–	–	–
1946	1	1	1	–	4	–	–	–
1947	7	7	6	–	9	6	–	–
1948	7	7	6	–	6	–	–	–
1949	9	9	7	–	9	–	–	–
1950	6	9	1	–	7	–	–	–
1951	0	1	0	–	3	–	–	–
1952	6	7	7	4	9	–	–	–
1953	7	9	6	4	9	–	9	7
1954	4	1	3	1	4	–	1	–
1955	7	10	6	4	9	–	6	6
1956	0	1	0	0	4	–	–	–
1957	6	6	7	6	9	–	4	4
1958	6	6	3	4	6	–	4	4
1959	9	9	9	6	9	–	9	9
1960	6	4	0	0	9	–	1	1
1961	10	10	7	7	10	–	7	6
1962	9	9	7	9	9	–	4	4
1963	1	0	1	1	3	–	3	3
1964	7	4	9	9	9	6	9	9
1965	0	0	0	0	3	–	1	0
1966	10	6	9	10	9	6	9	7
1967	9	7	6	9	9	7	7	6
1968	1	0	1	3	3	1	4	3
1969	7	7	10	10	7	10	9	9
1970	10	10	7	10	7	9	7	6
1971	7	9	10	10	7	9	10	10
1972	4	4	6	6	7	9	1	1
1973	6	6	4	4	6	9	6	7
1974	5	0	3	8	6	9	5	3
1975	10	10	3	6	3	9	10	10
1976	7	7	10	8	9	9	10	10
1977	4	3	3	5	6	5	6	5
1978	9	8	9	8	9	8	5	5
1979	9	9	7	8	8	7	7	7
1980	6	8	6	7	7	6	6	6
1981	8	9	6	7	7	9	7	7
1982	6-7	–	5	5	6	6	4	4

Types of wine glasses. The tulip (1) is a general purpose glass; the balloon (2) is used for good Burgundies and brandy. Champagne may be drunk from a flute (3), and Port from the small glass (4). The copita (5) is used for Sherry and the Roemer (6) for German wines such as Hock and Moselle. Most people make do with general purpose glasses, often shaped like the Port glass only larger.

WHICH WINE? – A ROUGH GUIDE

Food	Type of wine*
Hors d'oeuvre	dry white or dry Sherry
Soup (clear)	dry Sherry or Madeira
Pasta	light red
Egg dishes	medium quality dry wine†
Seafood ‡	dry white
Fish	dry or medium white, sparkling, or rosé
Red meat, liver, kidney, game §	full-bodied red
Poultry	dry white or light red¶
Veal, pork	white
Curry, goulash, etc.	full-flavoured (or, preferably, beer)
Puddings	Champagne or sweet white
Dessert (fresh fruit, nuts)	sweet white or sweet fortified
Cheese	red or Port

*Dry Champagne or a white Burgundy will go with anything.
†Red, white, or rosé, depending on what is cooked with the eggs.
‡Rosé possible with shellfish; Sherry with lobster; classic wine to drink with oysters is Chablis.
§Dry white wines suitable with cold game.
¶For roast birds with rich sauce or stuffing, red is preferable.

méthode Champenoise.

Sherry Famous fortified wine of Spain (imitated in Cyprus, South Africa, etc.); cream is smooth, sweet blend; brown, sweet with rich, full flavour. See Amontillado, Fino, Manzanilla, Oloroso.

Sparkling wines 'Sparkle' results from presence of free carbon dioxide, either from second fermentation (méthode Champenoise) or artificially introduced. They include French Champagnes and Mousseux, Italian Asti Spumantes, Sekt (German), Perelada (Spanish), Vinho Verdes (Portuguese).

Spätlese High-quality German wines made from late-picked (hence more delicate and fruity) grapes.

Tokay Rich Hungarian wines of high quality; Aszu, a sweet dessert wine, golden orange with a 'bready' flavour; Szamorodni, golden wine, dry or sweet.

VDQS wines (Vins Délimités de Qualité Supérieure) French wines not quite up to Appellation Controlée standard; guarantee of origin and quality.

Vermouth A wine 'manufactured' in Italy and France, not quite a fortified wine; 'French' is dry, 'Italian' or 'It' sweetish and red (rosso); bianco is sweet white; complex mixture of herbal ingredients with filtered white wine, fortified with grape brandy; drunk as apéritif, alone or in cocktails.

vin de pays (du pays) Ordinary but identified wine, more respectable than vin ordinaire.

vin ordinaire Term used in Britain to denote everyday table wine; in France, anonymous wine usually priced according to alcoholic strength.

Vinho Verdes Light and fresh medium-dry Portuguese wines, red or white, with slight sparkle to tongue.

vintage wine One made entirely from grapes picked from 'vintage' (harvest) of single year.

white wines Made without pips and by removing skins before fermentation.

Picked grapes are carefully divided into different varieties and qualities. Some will be made into simple vin ordinaire; *others will go to make the finest vintage wines.*

GENERAL INFORMATION

TRADITIONAL ANNIVERSARY NAMES

Year	Name
1	paper
2	cotton
3	leather
4	fruit, flowers
5	wood
6	iron, sugar
7	wool, copper
8	bronze
9	pottery
10	tin, aluminium
11	steel
12	silk, fine linen
13	lace
14	ivory
15	crystal
20	china
25	silver
30	pearl
35	coral
40	ruby
45	sapphire
50	golden
55	emerald
60	diamond
75	diamond

BIRTHSTONES

Month	Hebrew (Biblical)	Present day
January	garnet	garnet
February	amethyst	amethyst
March	jasper	aquamarine
		bloodstone
April	sapphire	diamond
May	chalcedony	emerald
	carnelian	chrysoprase
	agate	
June	emerald	pearl
		moonstone
		alexandrite
July	onyx	ruby
		carnelian
August	carnelian	peridot
		sardonyx
September	chrysolite	sapphire
		lapis lazuli
October	aquamarine	opal
	beryl	tourmaline
November	topaz	topaz
December	ruby	turquoise
		zircon

SEVEN WONDERS OF THE WORLD*

*Originally compiled by Antipater of Sidon, a Greek poet, in the 100s BC.

Pyramids of Egypt Oldest and only surviving 'wonder'. Built in the 2000s BC as royal tombs, about 80 are still standing. The largest, the Great Pyramid of Cheops, at el-Gizeh, was (147 m) 481 ft high.

Hanging Gardens of Babylon Terraced gardens adjoining Nebuchadnezzar's palace said to rise from (23-91 m) 75 to 300 ft. Supposedly built by the king about 600 BC to please his wife, a princess from the mountains, but they are also associated with the Assyrian Queen Semiramis.

Statue of Zeus at Olympia Carved by Phidias, the (12-m) 40-ft statue marked the site of the original Olympic Games in the 400s BC. It was constructed of ivory and gold, and showed Zeus (Jupiter) on his throne.

Temple of Artemis (Diana) at Ephesus Constructed of Parian marble and more than (122 m) 400 ft long with over 100 columns (18 m) 60 ft high, it was begun about 350 BC and took some 120 years to build. Destroyed by the Goths in AD 262.

Mausoleum at Halicarnassus Erected by Queen Artemisia in memory of her husband King Mausolus of Caria (in Asia Minor), who died 353 BC. It stood (43 m) 140 ft high. All that remains are a few pieces in the British Museum and the world 'mausoleum' in the English language.

Colossus of Rhodes Gigantic bronze statue of sun-god Helios (or Apollo); stood about (36 m) 117 ft high, dominating the harbour entrance at Rhodes. The sculptor Chares supposedly laboured for 12 years before he completed it in 280 BC. It was destroyed by an earthquake in 244 BC.

Pharos of Alexandria Marble lighthouse and watchtower built about 270 BC on the island of Pharos in Alexandria's harbour. Possibly standing (122 m) 400 ft high, it was destroyed by an earthquake in 1375.

The great pyramid of Cheops at Gizeh.

CHESS NOTATION

Below: The chessboard with pieces positioned for the start of a game. The bottom right-hand square must be a white one. Bottom: There are two systems of chess notation: descriptive has different square names for white and black (shown within the board), and algebraic (a1 etc.) is shown outside the board. Most English-speaking countries use the descriptive system.

BLACK

WHITE

♔	King, K
♕	Queen, Q
♖	Rook, R
♗	Bishop, B
♘	Knight, Kt or N
♙	Pawn, P
x	takes
ch	check
O-O	castles on King's side
O-O-O	castles on Queen's side
!	fine move, 'brilliancy'
?	questionable move, mistake

BLACK

a b c d e f g h

WHITE

PRINCIPAL LANGUAGES OF THE WORLD

Language	Speakers (millions)	Where spoken
Mandarin	575	China (north and east central)
English	360	UK and Commonwealth, Ireland, South Africa, USA
Hindi	170	India (north central)
Great Russian	170	USSR
Spanish	140	Spain, Central and South America (not Brazil)
German	100	Germany, Austria, Switzerland
Japanese	100	Japan
Bengali	90	Bangladesh, India (east)
Arabic	80	Middle East, North Africa
French	80	France and French Community, Canada
Malay/Indonesian*	80	Malaysia, Indonesia
Portuguese	80	Portugal, Brazil
Urdu	80	Pakistan
Italian	60	Italy
Cantonese	50	China (south)
Min	50	China (south and east)
Wu	50	China (east)
Javanese	45	Java
Telugu	45	India (south-east)
Ukranian	41	USSR
Bihari	40	India (north-east)
Marathi	40	India (west)
Tamil	40	India (south-east), Sri Lanka
Korean	37	Korea
Punjabi	35	India (north)
Polish	33	Poland
Turkish	28	Turkey

*Officially called *Bahasa Indonesia* in Indonesia.

DERIVATION OF DAYS AND MONTHS

Day/Month	Named after
Sunday	the Sun
Monday	the Moon
Tuesday	Tiu, Norse god of war
Wednesday	Woden, Anglo-Saxon chief of gods
Thursday	Thor, Norse god of thunder
Friday	Frigg, Norse goddess
Saturday	Saturn, Roman god of harvests
January	Janus, Roman god of doors and gates
February	Februa, Roman period of purification
March	Mars, Roman god of war
April	aperire, Latin 'to open'
May	Maia, Roman goddess of spring and growth
June	Juno, Roman goddess of marriage
July	Julius Caesar
August	Augustus, first emperor of Rome
September	septem, Latin 'seven'
October	octo, Latin 'eight'
November	novem, Latin 'nine'
December	decem, Latin 'ten'

ALPHABETS

Greek			Hebrew			Russian		
Letter	Name	Transliteration	Letter	Name	Transliteration	Letter		Transliteration
Α α	alpha	a	א	aleph	'	А	а	a
Β β	beta	b	ב	beth	b	Б	б	b
Γ γ	gamma	g	ג	gimel	g	В	в	v
Δ δ	delta	d	ד	daleth	d	Г	г	g
Ε ε	epsilon	e	ה	heh	h	Д	д	d
Ζ ζ	zeta	z	ו	wāw	w	Е	е	e, ye
Η η	eta	ē	ז	zayin	z	Ж	ж	zh
Θ θ	theta	th	ח	heth	ḥ	З	з	z
Ι ι	iota	i	ט	teth	ṭ	И	и	i
Κ κ	kappa	k	י	yod	y	Й	й	i
Λ λ	lambda	l	כ ך	kaph	k, kh	К	к	k
Μ μ	mu	m	ל	lamed	l	Л	л	l
Ν ν	nu	n	מ ם	mem	m	М	м	m
Ξ ξ	xi	x (ks)	נ ן	nun	n	Н	н	n
Ο ο	omicron	o	ס	samekh	s	О	о	o
Π π	pi	p	ע	ayin	'	П	п	p
Ρ ρ	rho	r	פ ף	peh	p, ph	Р	р	r
Σ σ,ς*	sigma	s	צ ץ	sadhe	ṣ	С	с	s
Τ τ	tau	t	ק	qoph	q	Т	т	t
Υ υ	upsilon	u, y	ר	resh	r	У	у	u
Φ φ	phi	ph	שׁ	shin	sh	Ф	ф	f
Χ χ	chi	kh, ch	שׂ	sin	ś	Х	х	kh
Ψ ψ	psi	ps	ת	taw	t	Ц	ц	ts
Ω ω	omega	o				Ч	ч	ch
						Ш	ш	sh
						Щ	щ	shch
							ы	i
							ь	'
						Э	э	e
						Ю	ю	yu
						Я	я	ya

ABBREVIATIONS

A Associate; Academician
a are (metric measure)
AAM air-to-air missile
AB Able-bodied seaman; *Artium Baccalaureus*, Bachelor of Arts
Abb Abbess; Abbot; Abbey
abd. abdicated
abl. ablative
Abp. Archibishop
abr. abridged
abs, absol. absolutely
abs, abstr. abstract
AC Aircraftman; *ante Christum*, Before Christ; alternating current
a.c. alternating current
acc. acount (also **a/c**); accusative (also **accus.**); according
ACT Australian Capital Territory
act. active
ACTH adrenocorticotrophin
ACW Aircraftwoman
AD *anno Domini*, in the year of the Lord
a.d. after date; *ante diem*, before the day
ad. advertisement
ADC Aide-de-camp
adj. adjective; adjourned; adjustment
adjt. Adjutant
ad lib. *ad libitum*, at pleasure
ad loc. *ad locum*, at the place
Adm. Admiral.
a.d.p. automatic data processing
adv. advent; adverb; *adversus*, against; advocate; advisory
ad val. *ad valorem*, according to value
advt. advertisement
a.f. audio frequency
AFC Air Force Cross
AFM Air Force Medal
AG Aktiengesellschaft (Ger.), limited liability company
agr., agric. agriculture
Agt. Agent
AID artificial insemination donor
Ala. Alabama
Alas. Alaska
Alba. Alberta
Ald. Alderman
alg. algebra
alt. alternate; altitude; alto
a.m. *ante meridiem*, before noon
AM amplitude modulation
Am., Amer. America; American
amt. amount
anal. analysis; analogy
anat. anatomy; anatomical
anc. ancient
anon. anonymous
ans. answer
AP Associated Press
Apoc. Apocalypse; Apocrypha, Apocryphal
app. Appendix; apparently; apprentice
appro. approval, approbation
AQ achievement quotient
aq. *aqua*, water
Ar., Arab. Arabic

arch. archaic; architecture
Archd. Archdeacon; Archduke
Ariz. Arizona
Ark. Arkansas
arr. arranged; arrival
art. article; artificial
ASM air-to-surface missile
Ass., Assoc. Association
Asst. Assistant
AST Atlantic Standard Time
astr., astron. astronomer; astronomy
atm. atmosphere
at. no., at. numb. atomic number
a.t.s. anti-tetanic serum
Att. Attic (Greek); Attorney
Att.-Gen. Attorney-General
attrib. attribute (d); attributive
Atty. Attorney
at. wt. atomic weight
Aufl. *Auflage* (Ger.), edition
Auth. Ver., A.V., AV Authorised Version
av. (and **ave.**) avenue; average
AWOL absent without official leave

B. Baron; British; Bachelor
B (on lead pencils) black
b. born; book; breadth
BA *Baccalaureus Artium*, Bachelor of Arts
B Agr(ic) Bachelor of Agriculture
BAI *Baccalaureus in Arte Ingeniaria*, Bachelor of Engineering
bal. balance
B and B. bed and breakfast
BAOR British Army of the Rhine
Bap., Bapt. Baptist
bap., bapt. baptised
Bar. Barrister
B Arch Bachelor of Architecture
Bart. Baronet
bat, batt battalion; battery
BB (on lead pencils) double, or very, black
bb. books
BBB (on lead pencils) triple black
BBC British Broadcasting Corporation
BC Before Christ; British Columbia
b.c.g. bacillus of Calmette and Guérin, used for inoculation against tuberculosis
B Ch *Baccalaureus Chirurgiae*, Bachelor of Surgery
BCL Bachelor of Civil Law
B Com(m) Bachelor of Commerce
BD Bachelor of Divinity
bd. bound
Bde. Brigade
BDS Bachelor of Dental Surgery
BE Bachelor of Engineering
b.e. bill of exchange
B Ed Bachelor of Education.
Beds Bedfordshire
bef. before
Belg. Belgian, Belgic
BEM British Empire Medal

B Eng Bachelor of Engineering
Berks Berkshire
bet. between
bf brought forward
bhp brake horsepower
B Hy Bachelor of Hygiene
Bib. Bible
Bibl. Biblical
bibliog. bibliographer; bibliography
biog. biographer; biography, biographical
biol. biology; biological
bk book; bank
bkg. banking
BL Bachelor of Law; Bachelor of Letters
bl. barrel; bale
b.l. bill of lading
bldg. building
B Lit(t) *Baccalaureus Lit(t)erarum*, Bachelor of Literature or Letters
Blvd. Boulevard
BM Bachelor of Medicine; British Museum
B Mus Bachelor of Music
Bn. Baron
bn. battalion
b.o. branch office; buyer's option
Boh. Bohemia
Bol. Bolivia
bor. borough
bot. botany; botanical; bought
Boul. Boulevard
Bp. Bishop
BP British Pharmacopoeia; British Petroleum
b.p. boiling-point (or **bp**); bills payable; birthplace (also **b.pl.**)
B Pharm Bachelor of Pharmacy
B Phil *Baccalaureus Philosophiae*, Bachelor of Philosophy
Br., Bro. Brother
br. Branch; brig; brown
Braz. Brazil; Brazilian
b. rec. bills receivable
Brig. Brigadier
Brig.-Gen. Brigadier-General
Brit. Britain; Britannia; British; Briton
Bro. Brother
Bros. Brothers
b.s. bill of sale
BS Bachelor of Science or of Surgery
B Sc Bachelor of Science
BSI British Standards Institution
BST British Summer Time; British Standard Time
Bt. Baronet
Btu British Thermal Unit
bu., bus. (or **bush.**) bushel (s)
Bucks Buckinghamshire
Bulg. Bulgaria; Bulgarian
BVM(&)S Bachelor of Veterinary Medicine & Surgery

C. Conservative
°C degree (s) Celsius, centigrade
c. *caput*, chapter; cent; centime;
C circa, about

ca. circa. about
Cal., Calif. California
Cam., Camb. Cambridge
Cambs Cambridgeshire
Can. Canon; Canto
Cant. Canterbury; Canticles
Cantab. *Cantabrigiensis,* of Cambridge
cap. *caput,* chapter; capital
caps capitals
Capt. Captain
CAR Central African Republic
car. carat
Card. Cardinal
CARD Campaign Against Racial Discrimination
Cards Cardiganshire
CARE Co-operative for American Relief to Everywhere
carp. carpentry
cat. catechism; catalogue
Cath. Catholic
CB Companion of the Order of the Bath
CBE Commander of the Order of the British Empire
CBS Columbia Broadcasting System
CC County Council; Cricket Club; closed circuit (transmission)
cc. *capita,* chapters
cc cubic centimetre(s)
CD *Corps Diplomatique,* Diplomatic Corps; Civil Defence; Contagious Disease(s)
Cdr. Commander
CDSO Companion of the Distinguished Service Order
CE Christian Endeavour; Council of Europe
Celt. Celtic
cen. central; century
C Eng Chartered Engineer
cent., cent *centum,* a hundred; century; central
CENTO Central Treaty Organization
CERN *Conseil* (now *Organization*) *Européen pour la Recherche Nucléaire,* European Organization for Nuclear Research
cert. certainty; certificate; certified
CET Central European Time
cf. *confer,* compare; calf (bookbinding)
c.f.i. cost, freight, and insurance
cg centigram(s)
c.g. centre of gravity
CGS, cgs centimetre-gramme-second unit, or system; Chief of the General Staff
CH Companion of Honour
Ch. Chief; China; Church; Champion
ch. chapter; child
c.h. central heating
Chamb. Chamberlain
Chanc. Chancellor; Chancery
Chap. Chaplain; Chapter
Chas. Charles
Ch B *Chirurgiae Baccalaureus,* Bachelor of Surgery
chem. chemistry; chemical
Chin. China; Chinese
Ch M *Chirurgiae Magister,* Master of Surgery

Chr. Christ; Christian
Chron. Chronicles
chron. chronicle; chronology; chronological
CI Channel Islands
CIA Central Intelligence Agency (USA)
CID Criminal Investigation Department
Cie (Fr.) *Compagnie,* Company
c.i.f. cost, insurance, freight
C.-in-C. Commander-in-Chief
cir., circ. *circa, circiter, circum,* about
cit. citation; citizen
civ. civil; civilian
cl centilitre(s)
cl. class; clause
class. classical; classification
C Litt Companion of Literature
CM *Chirurgiae Magister,* Master of Surgery
cm centimetre(s)
CND Campaign for Nuclear Disarmament
CNR Canadian National Railway
CNS central nervous system
CO Commonwealth Office; Commanding Officer, conscientious objector
Co. Company; County
c/o care of
c.o.d. cash (or collect) on delivery
C of E Church of England; Council of Europe
C of I Church of Ireland
C of S Chief of Staff; Church of Scotland
cog. cognate
c.o.g. centre of gravity
COL Computer-oriented language
Col. Colonel; Colorado; Colossians
col. column
coll. college; colleague; collector; colloquial
collat. collateral; collaterally
colloq. colloquial; colloquially
Coloss. Colossians
Com. Commander; Commodore; Committee; Commissioner; Commonwealth; Communist
com. common; comedy; commerce; committee
Comdr Commander
Comdt Commandant
COMECON Council for Mutual Economic Aid, or Assistance (Communist Nations)
comm. commentary; commander
commn. commission
comp. comparative; compositor; compare; compound
Com. Ver. Common Version
Con. Consul
con. *contra,* against; conclusion
conc. concentrated; concentration
Cong. Congress; Congregation
conj. conjunction; conjunctive
Conn. Connecticut
conn. connection; connected; connotation
cons. consonant
con. sec. conic section
cont., contd. continued
contr. contracted; contraction
conv. conventional

co-op. co-operative
Cop., Copt. Coptic
Cor. Corinthians; Coroner
Corn. Cornish; Cornwall
corol., coroll. corollary
Corp. Corporation; Corporal
corr. corrupted; corruption; correspond
cosmog. cosmography
cp. compare
CP Carriage Paid; Cape Province (S Africa)
Cpl. Corporal
CPR Canadian Pacific Railway
C.R. *Carolus rex,* King Charles
cr credit; creditor; crown
cres., cresc. crescendo; crescent
CRO cathode-ray oscillograph
CRT cathode-ray tube
CS Civil Service; Christian Science
c/s cycles per second (hertz)
CSI Companion of the Order of the Star of India (not conferred since 1947).
CSIRO Commonwealth Scientific and Industrial Research Organization.
CST Central Standard Time
ct cent; carat
Ct. Connecticut
cu., cub. cubic
cur., curt current (this month)
cusec cubic feet per sec
c.v. *curriculum vitae,* course of life
c.v.a. cerebrovascular accident (i.e. a stroke)
CVO Commander of the (Royal) Victorian Order.
c.w.o. cash with order.
cwt hundredweight(s)

d. *dele,* delete; dead; died; *denarius* or *denarii,* penny or pence (old); duke
d day; diameter
DA District Attorney; Diploma of Art
Dan. Daniel; Danish
dat. dative
dau. daughter
DBE Dame Commander of the Order of the British Empire
DC *Da capo* (It.), return to the beginning (*mus.*); District of Columbia; direct current; District Commissioner
d.c. direct current
DCL Doctor of Civil Law
DCM Distinguished Conduct Medal
DCVO Dame Commander of the (Royal) Victorian Order
DD *Divinitatis Doctor,* Doctor of Divinity
d.d., D/D, d/d days after date; day's date
DDS Doctor of Dental Surgery
DDT Dichlorodiphenyltrichloroethane
Dec. December
dec. deceased
dec., decl. declaration; declension
D Ed Doctor of Education
def. definition; (or **deft.**)
defendant
deg. degree(s)
Del. Delaware

del. delegate; (or **delt.**) *delineavit*, drew it (put after draughtsman's name)

demon., demons. demonstrative

D Eng Doctor of Engineering

dent. dental; dentist; dentistry

dep., dept. department; deputy

dep. deposed

der., deriv. derivation; derived

Deut. Deuteronomy

DEW Distant Early Warning

D.F. Defender of the Faith; Dean of the Faculty

DFC Distinguished Flying Cross

DFM Distinguished Flying Medal

dft. defendant; draft

DG *Dei gratia*, by the grace of God

dial. dialect

diam. diameter

dict. dictator; dictionary

diff. different; difference

dil. dilute

D Ing *Doctor Ingeniariae*, Doctor of Engineering.

Dip. Diploma

Dir. Director

dis. discontinued

disc. discount; discoverer

diss. dissertation

dist. distance; distinguish; district; distilled

div. divide; division; divine; divorced

DIY Do-it-yourself

D.J., DJ 'dee-jay, disc-jockey

D Lit(t) *Doctor litterarum* or *litteraturae*, Doctor of Letters or Literature

DM Deutsche Mark

D Mus Doctor of Music

DNA deoxyribonucleic acid

do. *ditto* (It.), the same (aforesaid)

DOA dead on arrival

dols. dollars

Dom. *Dominus*; Dominion

dom. domestic

Dor. Doric

doz. dozen

DP Displaced Person; data processing

d.p. duly performed (work of the class)

D Ph, or **D Phil** *Doctor Philosophiae*, Doctor of Philosophy

dpm disintegrations per minute

dpt. department

Dr Debtor; Doctor; Driver

dr. dram; drawer

d.r. dead reckoning

d.s., D/S. days after sight

D Sc *Scientiae Doctor*, Doctor of Science

DSC Distinguished Service Cross

DSM Distinguished Service Medal

DSO Distinguished Service Order

dsp *decessit sine prole*, died without issue

DT data transmission

DT's, dt's delirium tremens

D Th *Doctor Theologiae*, Doctor of Theology

DV *Deo volente*, God willing

d.v.p. *decessit vita patris*, died in father's lifetime

dwt pennyweight – *denarius*, and *wt* for weight

E. East; English

E. and O.E. errors and omissions excepted

e.a.o.n. except as otherwise noted

Ebor. *Eboracum*, York

EC East Central; Established Church

Eccl., Eccles. Ecclesiastes; Ecclesiastical

ECE Economic Commission for Europe

ECG electrocardiogram (-graph)

ECSC European Coal and Steel Community

ECT Electroconvulsive therapy

ECU English Church Union

Ed. Editor

ed., edit. edited; edition

Ed. B., Ed B Bachelor of Education

EDC European Defence Community

EDF European Development Fund

Edin. Edinburgh

E.E. Errors Excepted

EEC European Economic Community

EEG electroencephalogram (-graph)

EFTA European Free Trade Association

e.g., eg, ex. gr. *exempli gratia*, for example

EI East Indies

elec., elect. electric; electricity

EMA European Monetary Agreement

Emp. Emperor, Empress

Ency., Encyc. Encyclopaedia

Eng. England; English

eng. engineer; engraver; engraving

Ens. Ensign

E.N.T. Ear, Nose and Throat

ent., entom. entomology

e.o.d. every other day

Ep. Epistle

EP Extended play

EPA European Productivity Agency

Eph. Ephesians

Epiph. Epiphany

Epis., Episc. Episcopal

EPNS electroplated nickel silver

EPU European Payments Union

ER *Elizabetha Regina*, Queen Elizabeth

ESN Educationally subnormal

esp., espec. especially

ESP extra-sensory perception

Esq., Esqr. Esquire

est. established; estimated

EST Eastern Standard Time

Esth. Esther

ESU English Speaking Union

ETA (or **D**) Estimated time of arrival (or departure)

et al. *et alibi*, and elsewhere; *et alii, aliae,* or *alia,* and others

etc., &c. *et ceteri* or *cetera,* and the others, and so forth

et seq. *et sequens,* and the following

ety., etym. etymology; etymological

Euratom European Atomic Energy Community

Ex., Exod. Exodus

ex. examined; example; exception; executive; export

Exc. Excellency

exc. except; exception

ex. div. *extra dividendum,* without dividend

exp. export; exponential

exr. executor, **exrx.** executrix

ext. extension; externally; extinct; extra; extract

Ez. Ezra

Ezek. Ezekiel

F Fahrenheit; farad; fellow

f following; feminine; fathom; forte

Fa. Florida

FA Football Association

fam. familiar; family

f.a.o. for the attention of

FAO Food and Agriculture Organization

f.a.s. free alongside ship

FBI Federal Bureau of Investigation (US)

FC Football Club

FCO Foreign and Commonwealth Office

fcp., fcap. foolscap

F.D. *Fidei Defensor,* Defender of the Faith

fem. feminine

ff. folios; following; fortissimo

FH Fire hydrant

Fid. Def. *Fidei Defensor,* Defender of the Faith

FIDO Fog Investigation and Dispersal Operation

fig. figure; figuratively

fin. *ad finem,* at the end

fl. *floruit,* flourished

Fla, Flor. Florida

fl. oz. fluid ounce

fm fathom

F.M. Field-Marshal

FM frequency modulation

F.O. Field-Officer; Flying Officer

fo., fol. folio

f.o.b. free on board

FOE Friends of Europe

f.o.r. free on rail

FP former pupil; Free Presbyterian

fp forte-piano

f.p. freezing-point

Fr. Father; France; French; Friar; Friday

fr. fragment; franc; frequently

FRCP Fellow of the Royal College of Physicians

FRCS Fellow of the Royal College of Surgeons

FRS Fellow of the Royal Society

ft foot, feet; fort

fur. furlong(s)

fut. future

fz. forzando or forzato

g gram(s); gravity, acceleration due to gravity

Ga. Georgia

GA General Assembly

Gael. Gaelic

Gal. Galatians

gal, gall gallon(s)

GATT General Agreement on Tariffs and Trade

gaz. gazette; gazetteer

GB Great Britain
g.b.h. grievous bodily harm
GC George Cross
GCM General Court-martial;
(also **gcm**) greatest common
measure
Gdns. Gardens
Gen. Genesis; (or **Genl.**) General
gen. gender; genitive; genus
gent. gentleman
Geo. Georgia
geog. geography
geol. geology
geom. geometry
Ger. German
ger. gerund
GHQ General Headquarters
GI (US Army) government (or
general) issue; hence, common
soldier.
Gib. Gibraltar
Gk Greek
Glam. Glamorganshire
GLC Greater London Council
Glos. Gloucestershire
GM George Medal
gm gram
GMT Greenwich Mean Time
G.O.C. General Officer
Commanding
Gov. Governor; Government
(also **Govt.**)
GP General Practitioner; Gallup
Poll
GPI general paralysis of the insane
Gr. Greek
gr. grain; grammar; gross; gunner
GR *Georgius Rex*; George, King
GS General Staff
gs guineas
G.S.O. General Staff Officer
GT gran turismo
guin. guinea

H Hydrant; hospital; hard (on
lead pencils)
h hour; height
h.a. *hoc anno*, this year
ha hectare
Hab. Habakkuk
hab. habitat
Hag. Haggai
h and c hot and cold (water
laid on)
Hants Hampshire
Hb haemoglobin
HB hard black (on lead pencils)
HC House of Commons; Holy
Communion
HCF Honorary Chaplain to the
Forces; highest common factor
(also **hcf**)
HE His Excellency; His Eminence;
High Explosive
Heb., Hebr. Hebrew; Hebrews
HEH His (or Her) Exalted
Highness
her. heraldry; *heres*, heir
Herts Hertfordshire
hf. half
HF high frequency
HG His (or Her) Grace
HGV Heavy goods vehicle
HH His (or Her) Highness; very
hard (on lead pencils)
Hi-Fi, hi-fi high fidelity
nist. historian; history

HM His (or Her) Majesty
HMAS His (or Her) Majesty's
Australian Ship
HMC His (or Her) Majesty's
Customs
HMI His (or Her) Majesty's
Inspector, Inspectorate
HMS His (or Her) Majesty's Ship
or Service
HMSO His (or Her) Majesty's
Stationery Office
ho. house
Hon. Honourable, Honorary
hor. horizon; horology
hort, hortic. horticulture;
horticultural
Hos. Hosea
HP High Priest; half-pay; hire-
purchase; horsepower (also **h.p.**)
HQ headquarters
HR House of Representatives;
Home Rule
Hr Herr
hr hour
HRE Holy Roman Emperor or
Empire
HRH His (or Her) Royal
Highness
HSH his (or Her) Serene
Highness
ht. height
HT High tension
Hunts Huntingdonshire
HWM high water mark
Hz hertz (cycles per second)

Ia. Iowa
IAEA International Atomic
Energy Agency
ib., ibid. *ibidem*, in the same
place
IBRD International Bank for
Reconstruction and Development
(World Bank)
i/c in charge
ICAO International Civil Aviation
Organization
ICBM Intercontinental ballistic
missile
ich., ichth. ichthyology
ICI Imperial Chemical Industries
ICJ International Court of Justice
icon. iconography, iconographic
id. *idem*, the same
ID Intelligence Department
Id. Idaho
IDA International Development
Association
i.e., ie *id est*, that is
IFC International Finance
Corporation
III. Illinois
ill. illustration; illustrated
ILO International Labour
Organization
ILP Independent Labour Party
IMCO Inter-Governmental
Maritime Consultative
Organization
IMF International Monetary Fund
imit. imitative
Imp. Imperial; *imperator*, Emperor
imp. (also **imperf.**) imperfect;
(also **imper.**) imperative; (also
impers.) impersonal
in inch(es)
inc.. incorp., Inc. incorporated

incl. including; included
incog. *incognito* (It.), unknown,
avoiding publicity
Ind. Indiana; Independent
ind., indic. indicative
indecl. indeclinable
indef. indefinite
indic. indicative
indiv. individual
inf. *infra*, below; infantry;
infinitive
infra dig. *infra dignitatem*,
beneath one's dignity
init. *initio*, in the beginning
in loc. cit. *in loco citato*, in the
place cited
inst. instant — the present month;
institute (also **Inst.**)
int. interest; interior; interpreter;
international; integral
interrog. interrogation;
interrogative
in trans. *in transitu*, in transit
intrans. intransitive
intro., introd. introduction
inv. *invenit*, designed it;
inventor; invented; invoice
IOM Isle of Man
IOU I owe you
IOW Isle of Wight
IQ Intelligence Quotient
i.q. *idem quod*, the same as
IRA Irish Republican Army
IRBM intermediate range ballistic
missile
Irel. Ireland
Is., Isa. Isaiah
ISBN International Standard Book
Number
Is(I). island
ISO Imperial Service Order;
International Organization for
Standardization
It Italian; Italian vermouth
ita initial teaching alphabet
ital. italic; Italian
ITO International Trade
Organization
ITU International Telecommunica-
tions Union
IUPAC International Union of
Pure and Applied Chemistry
IUPAP International Union of
Pure and Applied Physics
IW Isle of Wight
IWW Industrial Workers of the
World

J. Judge, Justice
Jas. James
JC Jesus Christ; Justice Clerk
J.C.D., JCD *Juris Civilis Doctor*,
Doctor of Civil Law
Jer. Jeremiah
Jo. Joel
Josh. Joshua
JP Justice of the Peace
Jr., Jun., Junr. Junior
JUD *Juris Utriusque Doctor*,
Doctor of both Canon and
Civil Law
Jud., Judg. Judges
Junc. Junction
jurisp. jurisprudence

K Kelvin (thermometer scale)
Kan. Kansas

357

KB Knight of the Bath; Knight Bachelor; King's Bench
KBE Knight Commander of the Order of the British Empire
KC King's Counsel
kc kilocycle(s)
KCB Knight Commander of the Bath
KCVO Knight Commander of the Royal Victorian Order
Ken. Kentucky
kg kilogram(s)
KG Knight of the Order of the Garter
KGB Komitet Gosudarstvennoi Bezopasnosti (Russian Committee of State Security)
KGCB Knight of the Grand Cross of the Bath
kilo kilogram; kilometre
KKK Ku Klux Klan
KLM Koninklijke Luchtvaart Maatschappij (Royal Dutch Airlines)
KM Knight of Malta
km kilometre(s)
kn knot
KO, ko knock out
kr. krone
Ks. Kansas
Kt Knight
kW kilowatt
Ky. Kentucky

L Lake; Latin; Liberal; learner (driver); *libra*, pound
l. latitude; league; left; length; long; *libra*, pound
l litre
La. Louisiana
LA Law Agent; Los Angeles
Lab. Labour
lab. laboratory
Lam. Lamentations
Lancs Lancashire
lang. language
Lat. Latin
lat. latitude
lb. *libra*, pound
lbw leg before wicket (in cricket)
lc lower-case (in printing); letter of credit
L Ch (or **L Chir**) *Licentiatus Chirurgiae*, Licentiate in Surgery
LCJ Lord Chief Justice
LCM, lcm least common multiple
Ld Lord
Ldp, Lp Lordship
LEA Local Education Authority
lect. lecture
leg. legal; legate; legislature
Leics Leicestershire
Lev., Levit. Leviticus
lex. lexicon
LF low frequency
LGP liquefied petroleum gas
l.h. left hand
LHD *Litterarum Humaniorum Doctor*, Doctor of Letters
LI Light Infantry
lib. *liber*, book
Lieut. Lieutenant
Lincs Lincolnshire
Linn. Linnaean, Linnaeus
liq. liquid
lit. literally; literature

lith., litho., lithog. lithograph; lithography
Lit Hum. *litterae humaniores*, humane letters, the humanities
Lit(t)D *Litterarum Doctor*, Doctor of Letters
LJ Lord Justice
LLB *Legum Baccalaureus*, Bachelor of Laws
LLD *Legum Doctor*, Doctor of Laws
LLM *Legum Magister*, Master of Laws
loc. cit. *loco citato*, at the place quoted
log logarithm
lon., long. longitude
LP Lord Provost; long-playing; low pressure
LSD lysergic acid diethylamide; *librae, solidi, denarii*, pounds, shillings, pence
LSE London School of Economics.
Lt. Lieutenant
Lt.-Col. Lieutenant-Colonel
Ltd. Limited
Lt-Gen. Lieutenant-General

M Member
M. *Monsieur* (Fr.), Mr (pl. MM.)
M. or **m.** *mille*, a thousand
m. married; masculine; *meridiem*, noon
m metre; mile
MA *Magister Artium*, Master of Arts
Mac., Macc. Maccabees
mach. machinery
Mad. Madam
mag. magazine
Maj. Major
Mal. Malachi
Man., Manit. Manitoba
marg. margin; marginal
Marq. Marquis
mas., masc. masculine
Mass. Massachusetts
math., maths mathematics
Matt. Matthew
max. maximum
MB *Medicinae Baccalaureus*, Bachelor of Medicine
MBE Member of the Order of the British Empire
MC Member of Congress; Master of Ceremonies; Member of Council; Military Cross
MCC Marylebone Cricket Club
M Ch *Magister Chirurgiae*, Master of Surgery
MCP(A) methyl-chloro-phenoxyacetic acid (methoxone; weedkiller)
Mc/s megacycles per second
Md. Maryland
MD *Medicinae Doctor*, Doctor of Medicine; mentally deficient
Mdm Madam
MDS Master of Dental Surgery
M.E. Most Excellent; Middle English.
Me. Maine
mech. mechanic; mechanical
med. medical; medicine; medieval; *medius*, middle
Mem. Member
memo. memorandum

Messrs *Messieurs* (Fr.), Sirs, Gentlemen
met., metaph. metaphysics; metaphor
met., meteor. meteorology
metal., metall. metallurgy
meth(s). methylated spirits
Mex. Mexico; Mexican
mfd manufactured
MFH Master of Foxhounds
mfrs manufacturers
mg milligram(s)
Mgr Monseigneur; Monsignor
M.H.G. Middle High German
MI Military Intelligence; **MI5** Security Services **MI6** Secret Intelligence Service
Mi. Mississippi
Mic. Micah
Mich. Michigan
MIDAS Missile Defence Alarm System
Middx Middlesex
mil., milit. military
min minute
min. mineralogy; minimum
Min. Ministry
Minn. Minnesota
misc. miscellaneous; miscellany
Miss. Mississippi
MIT Massachusetts Institute of Technology
MK (on cars) mark
MKS, mks metre-kilogram-second unit or system
ml millilitre(s)
Mlle (pl. **Mlles**) *Mademoiselle* (Fr.) (pl. *Mesdemoiselles*)
MM. *Messieurs* (Fr.), Gentlemen or Sirs
MM Military Medal
mm millimetre(s)
Mme (pl. **Mmes**) *Madame* (Fr.) (pl. *Mesdames*)
MN Merchant Navy
Mo. Missouri
MO Medical Officer
mo. month
mod. modern; moderato
MOH Medical Officer of Health
mol wt molecular weight
Mon. Monmouthshire; Monday
Monsig. Monsignor
Mont. Montana; Montgomeryshire
Mor. Morocco
mp mezzo-piano (rather soft)
m.p. melting point
MP Member of Parliament; Military Police
mpg miles per gallon
mph miles per hour
M Pharm Master of Pharmacy
MR Master of the Rolls
Mr Master or Mister
MRA Moral Rearmament
Mrs Mistress
MS (MSS) manuscript (manuscripts)
MS Master of Surgery; multiple sclerosis
Ms Miss, Mrs
M Sc Master of Science
Mt, mt mount
mth month
M Th Master of Theology
Mts, mts mountains
mus. music; museum

Mus B(ac) Bachelor of Music
Mus D, Doc Doctor of Music
Mus M Master of Music
mv merchant vessel; motor vessel
MW medium wave
Mx Middlesex
myth. mythology

N. North, Northern
n. name; noun; *natus*, born; neuter; noon
N.A. North America
Nah. Nahum
N and Q Notes and Queries
Nap. Napoleon
NASA National Aeronautics and Space Administration (USA)
nat. *natus*, born
Nat. National
nat. hist. natural history
NATO North Atlantic Treaty Organization
Nat. Phil. Natural Philosophy
Nat. Sci. Natural Science(s)
naut. nautical
nav. naval; navigation
NB New Brunswick; North Britain; North British
NB, nb *nota bene*, note well, or take notice
N.C. North Carolina
NC New Church
NCO non-commissioned officer
NCR No carbon required
n.c.v. no commercial value
N.D., N. Dak. North Dakota
n.d. no date, not dated
Neb., Nebr. Nebraska
NEB New English Bible
neg. negative
Neh. Nehemiah
nem. con. *nemine contradicente*, no one contradicting
nem. diss. *nemine dissentiente*, no one dissenting
Nep. Neptune
Neth. Netherlands
neut. neuter
Nev. Nevada
NF, Nfd. Newfoundland
N.H. New Hampshire
NI Northern Ireland
NIBMAR No Independence Before Majority Rule
N.J. New Jersey
N.M., N. Mex. New Mexico
N.O. New Orleans; natural order
No., no. *numero*, number
nom., nomin. nominative
noncom. noncommissioned
Noncon. Nonconformist
non seq. *non sequitur*, it does not follow
n.o.p. not otherwise provided
Northants Northamptonshire
Northumb. Northumberland
Nos., nos. numbers
Notts Nottinghamshire
NP Notary Public; New Providence; (also **n.p.**) new paragraph
nr near
NS New Style; Nova Scotia
n.s. not specified
NSW New South Wales
NT New Testament; Northern Territory

ntp normal temperature and pressure
Num., Numb. Numbers
NV New Version
n.v.d. no value declared
NWT North-west Territory (Canada)
NY New York (city or state)
NYC New York City
NZ New Zealand

O. Ohio
OAS On active service; Organization of American States
OAU Organization of African Unity
ob. *obiit*, died
Ob., Obad. Obadiah
OBE Officer of the Order of the British Empire
obj. object; objective
obl. oblique; oblong
obs. observation; obsolete
o/c overcharge
OC Officer Commanding
oct. octavo
OD Ordinary Seaman
O.E. Old English
OECD Organization for Economic Co-operation and Development
OED Oxford English Dictionary
O.F. Old French
off. offical
O.F.S. Orange Free State
O.H.G. Old High German
O.H.M.S. On His (or Her) Majesty's Service
Okla. Oklahoma
Old Test. Old Testament
OM Order of Merit; Old Measurement
o.n.o. or near offer
Ont. Ontario
Op. Opera; *Opus*, work
O.P. opposite prompt (*theat.*)
o.p. out of print
op. opposite; *opus*; operation
op. cit. *opere citato*, in the work cited
opp. opposed; opposite
Ops Operations; Operations Officer; Operations room
opt. optative; *optime*, very well indeed
Or., Ore., Oreg. Oregon
ord. ordained; order; ordinary; ordnance
orig. origin; original; originally
OS Old Style; Ordinary Seaman; outsize
osp *obiit sine prole*, died without issue
OT Old Testament; occupational therapy
Oxf. Oxford
Oxon. *Oxonia*, Oxford; *Oxoniensis*, of Oxford
oz ounce(s)

P. President; Prince; pedal
P parking
p. page, participle
p new penny; new pence; piano
pa. past
Pa. (or **Penn.**) Pennsylvania
p.a. per annum; participial adjective

PA Press Association
paint. painting
Pal. Palestine
pam. pamphlet
Pan. Panama
P. & O. Peninsular and Oriental (Steamship Company)
pa. p. past participle
par. paragraph; parallel; parish
PAS para-amino-salicylic acid, used for TB
pass. passive
pa. t. past tense
PC Privy Councillor; Police Constable
pc postcard
pd. paid
PE physical education
ped. pedal
PEI Prince Edward Island
Pen. Peninsula
Penn. Pennsylvania
Pent. Pentecost
per. period; person
per an. *per annum*, per year, by the year
per cent *per centum*, by the hundred
perf. perfect
perh. perhaps
per pro. *per procurationem*, by the agency (of)
Pers. Persian
pers. person; personal
pf piano-forte
Pg Portugal; Portuguese
PG paying guest
Phar., Pharm. pharmaceutical; pharmacopoeia; pharmacy
Ph. B., Ph B *Philosophiae Baccalaureus*, Bachelor of Philosophy
Ph. D., Ph D *Philosophiae Doctor*, Doctor of Philosophy
Phil. Philippians; Philemon; Philadelphia; philology; philosophy
phon., phonet. phonetics
phot. photography
phr. phrase
phys. physiology; physics; physician
pinx. *pinxit*, painted it
PL Poet Laureate
PLA Port of London Authority
PLP Parliamentary Labour Party
plu., plur. plural
plup. pluperfect
PM Past Master; (also **p.m.**) *post meridiem*, after noon; Postmaster; *post mortem*, after death; Prime Minister
PMG Postmaster-General
Pmr. Paymaster
p.n. promissory note
P.O. post-office (also **PO**); Petty Officer; Pilot Officer
p.o.d. pay on delivery
Pol. Econ. Political Economy
pop. population; popular
pos., posit. positive
POW prisoner of war
PP parish priest; present pupil; past President
Pp pages
pp pianissimo
p.p. past participle

359

pp. pages; *per procurationem*, by proxy, for and on behalf of
PPI Plan Position Indicator
PPS *post postscriptum*, additional postscript; Parliamentary Private Secretary
Pr. Prince; priest
pr. pair; per; present; price
PR proportional representation; *Populus Romanus*, the Roman people
Preb. Prebend; Prebendary
pref. preface
prep. preparation; preparatory; preposition
Pres. President
Pret. preterite
Prin. Principal
Pro. Professional
PRO Public Relations Officer
prob. probably
Prof. Professor
prop. proper; properly; proposition; property
Prot. Protestant
pro tem. *pro tempore*, for the time being
Prov. Proverbs; Provincial; Provost
prox. *proximo* (*mense*), next (month)
PS *post scriptum*, written after; a postscript
Ps., Psa. Psalm(s)
pseud. pseudonym
PST Pacific Standard Time
pt part; pint(s)
PT physical training; purchase tax
p.t. post-town
PTA Parent/Teacher Association
Pte. private (military)
PTFE polytetrafluoroethylene
PTO Please turn over
pty, Pty proprietary
pwt pennyweight
pxt *pinxit*, painted it

Q (or **Qu.**) query, question; (or **Que.**) Quebec; Queensland
q. *quadrans*, farthing; query
QB Queen's Bench
QC Queen's Counsel
q.e. *quod est*, which is
Q.E.D. *quod erat demonstrandum*, which was to be demonstrated
Q.E.F. *quod erat faciendum*, which was to be done
Q.E.I. *quod erat inveniendum*, which was to be found
q.l. *quantum libet*, as much as you please
Q.M. Quartermaster
Q.M.S. Quartermaster-Sergeant.
Qq. (or **qq.**) quartos
qq. v *quae vide*, which (pl.) see (sing. *q.v.*)
qr. quarter
QSO quasi-stellar object (quasar)
qt. quantity; quart(s)
q.t. quiet
qto. quarto
qty. quantity
Qu. Queen; question
qu., quar. quart; quarter; quarterly
q.v. *quod vide*, which see

R. *rex, regina*, King, Queen; rand
r. right; radius; *recipe*, take

RA Royal Academy or Academician; Royal Artillery; Rear Admiral
RAAF Royal Australian Air Force
Rabb Rabbinical
Rad. Radical
rad. *radix*, root
rad radian
RAF Royal Air Force
RAN Royal Australian Navy
R and A Royal and Ancient (Golf Club), St Andrews
RC Roman Catholic; Red Cross
RCAF Royal Canadian Air Force
RD Rural Dean; refer to drawer
Rd. Road
Rec. *recipe*, take
recd. received
recpt. receipt
Rect. Rector; Rectory
ref. referee; reference
regt. regiment
rel. relating; relation; relative
Rep. representative; republic; report
retd. returned; retired
Rev. revise; revision; Revelation; (or **Revd.**) Reverend
rev revolution
Rev. Ver. Revised Version
RF radio frequency
RFC Rugby Football Club
Rgt. Regiment
Rh rhesus
RH Royal Highness
r.h. right hand
rhet. rhetoric
RI Rhode Island
R.I.P. *requiescat in pace*, may he (or she) rest in peace
Rly, rly railway
RM Royal Marines; resident magistrate; riding master
RMA Royal Military Academy, Sandhurst
RN Royal Navy
RNA ribonucleic acids
RNZAF Royal New Zealand Air Force
RNZN Royal New Zealand Navy
Ro. *recto*, on the right-hand page
Rom. Romans
Rom. Cath. Roman Catholic
rpm, rps revolutions per minute, second
RR Right Reverend
Rs Rupees
RSFSR Russian Soviet Federated Socialist Republic
RSG Regional Seats of Government
RSM Regimental Sergeant-Major
RSO railway sorting office; rural sub-office
RSV Revised Standard Version
RSVP *répondez s'il vous plait* (Fr.), reply if you please
Rt Hon Right Honourable
Rt Rev. Right Reverend
RU Rugby Union
RV Revised Version
R.W. Right Worthy
Ry, ry railway

S. South; Sabbath; Saint; society; sun

S square
s second(s)
SA South Africa; South America; South Australia; Salvation Army; sex-appeal; *Société Anonyme* (Fr.), limited liability company
SAA South African Airways
SABENA (*Société anonyme belge d'exploitation de la navigation aérienne*) Belgian national airline
s.a.e. stamped addressed envelope
SALT Strategic Arms Limitation Talks
SAM surface-to-air missile
Sam. Samuel
SARAH Search and rescue and homing
SAS Scandinavian Airlines System
Sask. Saskatchewan
Sat. Saturday
SBN Standard Book Number
S.C. South Carolina
SC Special Constable; Supreme Court; Staff College; Staff Corps
sc, s. caps, sm. caps small capitals
Sc B *Scientiae Baccalaureus*, Bachelor of Science
Sc D *Scientiae Doctor*, Doctor of Science
sci. fi. science fiction
Scot. Scotland; Scottish
Script. Scripture
sculp., sculpt. sculpture; sculptor
SD *salutem dicit*, sends greeting; standard deviation
S.D., S. Dak. South Dakota
s.d. *sine die*, without a day (fixed)
SDP Social Democratic Party
SEATO South-East Asia Treaty Organization
Sec., Secy Secretary
sec. second; section
sec secant
sec. leg. *secundum legem*, according to law
sec. reg. *secundum regulam*, according to rule
sect. section
Sem. seminary; Semitic
Sen. Senator; senior
seq. *sequens*, following
ser. series; sermon
Serg., Sergt Sergeant
Serj., Serjt Serjeant
Sess. Session
S.F. Sinn Fein; science fiction; (or **SF**) signal frequency
SFA Scottish Football Association
sfz. sforzando
SG Solicitor-General
s.g. specific gravity
SHAEF Supreme Headquarters of the Allied Expeditionary Force
SHAPE Supreme Headquarters Allied Powers Europe
SI Système International (d'Unités), International system of units
sig. signature
sing. singular
sld sailed
s.l.p. *sine legitima prole*, without lawful issue

S.M. Sergeant-Major
s.m.p. *sine mascula prole*, without male issue
s.n. *secundum naturam*, according to nature
SNP Scottish National Party
s.o. seller's option
SO Staff Officer; Signal Officer; standing order
Soc. Society
sol. solution
Sol., Solr. Solicitor
Sol.-Gen. Solicitor-General
sop. soprano
sp. spelling; species
s.p. *sine prole*, without issue
SPCK Society for Promoting Christian Knowledge
sp. gr. specific gravity
sport. sporting
SPQR *Senatus Populusque Romanus*, the Senate and People of Rome
s.p.s. *sine prole superstite*, without surviving issue
spt seaport
sp. vol. specific volume
sq., Sq. square; *sequens*, following
squ squadron
Sr senior; Sir; Senor
SRI *Sacrum Romanum Imperium*, Holy Roman Empire
SS or S.S. *Schutzstaffel* (Hitler's bodyguard)
S.S. Sunday (or Sabbath) School
SS Saints
s.s. steamship; screw steamer
SS. D. *Sanctissimus Dominus*, Most Holy Lord (the Pope)
SSM surface-to-surface missile
SST supersonic transport
St Saint; Strait; Street
st. stone (weight)
Staffs Staffordshire
STD subscriber trunk dialling
std standard
Ste *Sainte* (Fr.), Fem. of *Saint*
stg. sterling
STOL Short Take-Off and Landing
stp standard temperature and pressure
str steamer
str. strong
sub. subject
subj. subject; subjunctive
subst. substitute; substantive
suf., suff. suffix
sup. superfine; superior; superlative; supreme; *supra*; supine; supplement
superl. superlative
supp., suppl. supplement
Supt Superintendent
Surg. surgeon; surgery
SW Shortwave
sym. symbol
syn. synonym
synop. synopsis
syst. system

t tonne; time
tal. qual. *talis qualis*, just as they come; average quantity
Tam. Tamil
TB tuberculosis
TBD torpedo-boat destroyer

TCP trichlorophenylmethyl-iodosalicyl
tech. technical; technology
tel., teleg. telegram, telegraph
temp. temporal; *tempore*, in the time of; temperature; temporary
Ten., Tenn. Tennessee
ten. tenor; tenuto
Ter., Terr. Territory; terrace
term. termination
Test. Testament
Teut. Teutonic
Tex. Texas
Text. Rec. *textus receptus*, the received text
Th. Thursday
Th D Doctor of Theology
theat. theatrical
theol. theology; theologian
theor. theorem
Thess. Thessalonians
Tho., Thos Thomas
t.i.d. *ter in die*, thrice a day
TIF *Transports Internationaux par Chemin de Fer*, International Rail Transport
Tim. Timothy
TIR *Transports Internationaux Routiers*, International Road Transport
TIROS Television and Infrared Observation Satellite
Tit. Titus
TN trade name
TNT trinitrotoluene
T.O. (or **t.o.**) turn over; Telegraph-office; Transport Officer
Toc H Talbot House
tom. *tomus*, tome or volume
TP Transvaal Province
tp. township; troop
tr. transpose; transactions; translator; trustee
trans. transitive; translated; translation
transf. transferred
treas. treasurer
TRH Their Royal Highnesses
trig. trigonometry
Trin. Trinity
TT teetotal; teetotaller; Tourist Trophy; tuberculin tested
TTL to take leave
Tu., Tues. Tuesday
TUC Trades Union Congress
TV television
TVA Tennessee Valley Authority
typ., typo. typographer; typography

U Unionist; upper-class
UAR United Arab Republic
UCAR Union of Central African Republics
UDC Urban District Council; Universal Decimal Classification
UDI Unilateral Declaration of Independence
UFO unidentified flying object
UHF Ultra high frequency
UJD *Utriusque Juris Doctor*, Doctor of both Canon and Civil Law
UK United Kingdom
ult., ulto. *ultimo*, last; ultimate; ultimately

UN United Nations
UNESCO United Nations Educational, Scientific and Cultural Organization
UNICEF United Nations International Children's Emergency Fund
Unit. Unitarian
Univ. University; Universalist
UNO United Nations Organization
UNRRA United Nations Relief and Rehabilitation Administration
UP United Press
UPU Universal Postal Union
Uru. Uruguay
US United States; Under-secretary
u.s. *ut supra*, as above
USA United States of America; United States Army
USPG United Society for the Propagation of the Gospel
USS United States Ship or Steamer
USSR Union of Soviet Socialist Republics
usu. usually
USW ultrasonic waves; ultrashort waves
Ut. Utah
ut dict. *ut dictum*, as said
ut sup. *ut supra*, as above
UU Ulster Unionist
uv ultraviolet
ux. *uxor*, wife

v velocity; *versus*, against; *vide*, see; verb; verse; volume
V1 *Vergeltungswaffe 1*, German flying bomb
V2 German flying rocket
Va. Virginia
vac. vacuum
val. value
var. variant; variety; variable
VAT Value-added Tax
Vat. Vatican
vb verb
VC Vice-Chancellor; Vice-Consul; Victoria Cross
VD venereal disease(s)
v.d. various dates; vapour density
VE Victory in Europe
veg. vegetable(s)
vel. velocity
Ven. Venerable
VERA Versatile reactor assembly; vision electronic recording apparatus
Vert. Vertebrata
ves. vessel
Vet., Veter. Veterinary
Vot. Surg. Veterinary Surgeon
VF voice frequency; video frequency
v.g. *verbi gratia*, for example; (or **V.G.**) very good
VHF very high frequency
v.i. verb intransitive
Vic. Vicar; Vicarage
Vict. Victoria; Victoria University
vid. *vide*, see
VIP Very Important Person
Vis., Visc. Viscount
viz. *videlicet*, namely
VJ Victory over Japan
VLF very low frequency
Vo. *verso*, on the left-hand page

361

voc. vocative
vocab. vocabulary
Vol. Volunteer
vol volume, vols volumes
VP Vice-President
VR *Victoria Regina*, Queen Victoria
VS Veterinary Surgeon; *volti subito*, turn quickly
Vt. Vermont
v.t. verb transitive
VTO Vertical Take-off (L. and Landing)
Vul., Vulg. Vulgate
vul., vulg. vulgar
vv., ll. *variae lectiones*, various readings
v.y. various years

W. West; Welsh; women(s)
W watt
WA West Africa; Western Australia
Wal. Walloon
Wash. Washington
WC water-closet; Western Central; Wesleyan Chapel

W./Cdr. Wing Commander
Wed. Wednesday
WEU Western European Union
w.f. wrong fount
WFTU World Federation of Trade Unions
WHO World Health Organization
WI West Indies
Wilts Wiltshire
Wis. Wisconsin
wk. week
Wm William
WMO World Meteorological Organization
WNP Welsh Nationalist Party
WO War Office; Warrant Officer
Worcs Worcestershire
Wp., Wpfl. Worshipful
w.p. weather permitting
wpm words per minute
WRAC Women's Royal Army Corps
WRAF Women's Royal Air Force
WRNS Women's Royal Naval Service
wt weight

W. Va. West Virginia
wx women's extra
Wy., Wyo. Wyoming

x. ex (L., without), as in x.d., ex dividend
X. or Xt. Christ
Xm., Xmas. Christmas
Xn., Xtian. Christian

y. year; yard
yd yard
Yeo. Yeomanry
YHA Youth Hostels Association
YMCA Young Men's Christian Association
Yorks Yorkshire
yr. your; younger; year
YWCA Young Women's Christian Association

zB *zum Beispiel* (Ger.), for example
Zech. Zechariah
Zeph. Zephaniah
ZST Zone Standard Time

MEASUREMENT AND NUMBER

CONVERSION FACTORS

1 acre = 0.4047 hectares
1 bushel (imp.) = 36.369 litres
1 centimetre = 0.3937 inch
1 chain = 20.1168 metres
1 cord = 3.62456 cubic metres
1 cubic centimetre = 0.0610 cubic inch
1 cubic decimetre = 61.024 cubic inches
1 cubic foot = 0.0283 cubic metre
1 cubic inch = 16.387 cubic centimetres
1 cubic metre = 35.3146 cubic feet = 1.3079 cubic yards
1 cubic yard = 0.7646 cubic metre
1 fathom = 1.8288 metres
1 fluid oz (apoth.) = 28.4131 millilitres
1 fluid oz (US) = 29.5735 millilitres
1 foot = 0.3048 metre = 30.48 centimetres
1 foot per second = 0.6818 mph = 1.097 km/h
1 gallon (imperial) = 4.5461 litres
1 gallon (US liquid) = 3.7854 litres
1 gill = 0.142 litre
1 gram = 0.0353 ounce = 0.002205 pound = 15.43 grains = 0.0321 ounce (Troy)
1 hectare = 2.4710 acres
1 hundredweight = 50.80 kilograms
1 inch = 2.54 centimetres
1 kilogram = 2.2046 pounds
1 kilometre = 0.6214 mile = 1093.6 yards
1 knot (international) = 0.5144 metres/sec = 1.852 km/h
1 litre = 0.220 gallon (imperial) = 0.2642 gallon (US) = 1.7598 pints (imperial) = 0.8799 quarts
1 metre = 39.3701 in = 3.2808 ft = 1.0936 yd
1 metric ton = 0.9842 long ton = 1.1023 short ton
1 mile (statute) = 1.6093 kilometres
1 mile (nautical) = 1.852 kilometres
1 millimetre = 0.03937 inch

1 ounce = 28.350 grams
1 peck (imperial) = 9.0922 litres
1 pennyweight = 1.555 grams
1 pica (printer's) = 4.2175 millimetres
1 pint (imperial) = 0.5683 litre
1 pound = 0.4536 kilogram
1 quart (imperial) = 1.1365 litres
1 square centimetre = 0.1550 square inch
1 square foot = 0.0929 square metre
1 square inch = 6.4516 square centimetres
1 square kilometre = 0.3860 square mile
1 square metre = 10.7639 square feet = 1.1960 square yards
1 square mile = 2.5900 square kilometres
1 square yard = 0.8361 square metre
1 ton (long) = 1.0160 square metre
1 ton (short) = 0.9072 metric ton (tonne)
1 yard = 0.9144 metre

°Centigrade	°Fahrenheit
100	212
90	194
80	176
70	158
60	140
50	122
40	104
30	86
20	68
10	50
0	32
−10	14
−20	−4
−30	−22
−40	−40
−50	−58

LENGTH

Metric units
millimetre (mm)
10 mm=1 centimetre (cm)
100 cm=1 metre (m)
1000 m=1 kilometre (km)

1 micron $(\mu)=10^{-6}$m (i.e. 1 micrometre)
1 millimicron $(m\mu)=10^{-9}$m (i.e. 1 nanometre)
1 angstrom $(A)=10^{-10}$m (i.e. 100 picometres)

Imperial units
inch (in)
12 in=1 foot (ft)
3 ft=1 yard (yd)
1760 yd=1 mile=5280 ft

1 mil=$\frac{1}{1000}$ in
12 lines=1 in
1 link=7.92 in
100 links=1 chain=22 yd
1 rod, pole, or perch=$5\frac{1}{2}$ yd
4 rods=1 chain
10 chains=1 furlong=220 yd
8 furlongs=1 mile
3 miles=1 league (statute)

AREA

Metric units
square millimetre (mm²)
100 mm²=1 square centimetre (cm²)
10,000 cm²=1 square metre (m²)
100 m²=1 are (a)=1 square decametre
100 a=1 hectare (ha)=1 square hectometre
100 ha=1 square kilometre (km²)

Imperial units
square inch (in²)
144 in²=1 square foot (ft²)
9 ft²=1 square yard (yd²)
4840 yd²=1 acre
640 acres=1 square mile (mile²)

625 square links=1 square rod
16 square rods=1 square chain
10 square chains=1 acre
36 square miles=1 township (US)

VOLUME

Metric units
cubic millimetre (mm³)
1000 mm³=1 cubic centimetre (cm³)
1000 cm³=1 cubic decimetre (dm³)=1 litre
1000 dm³=1 cubic metre (m³)
1,000,000,000 m³=1 cubic kilometre (km³)

Imperial units
cubic inch (in³)
1728 in³=1 cubic foot (ft³)
27 ft³=1 cubic yard (yd³)
5,451,776,000 yd³=1 cubic mile (mile³)

WEIGHT

Metric units
milligram (mg)
1000 mg=1 gram (g)
1000 g=1 kilogram (kg)
100 kg=1 quintal (q)
1000 kg=1 metric ton, or tonne (t)

Imperial units (Avoirdupois)
grain (gr); dram (dr)
7000 gr=1 pound (lb)
16 dr=1 ounce (oz)
16 oz=1 lb
14 lb=1 stone
28 lb=1 quarter
112 lb=1 hundredweight (cwt)
20 cwt=1 (long) ton=2240 lb
2,000 lb=1 short ton (US)

Troy
24 gr=1 pennyweight (dwt)
20 dwt=1 (Troy) ounce=480 gr
12 (Troy) oz=1 (Troy) lb (US)=5760 gr

Apothecaries
20 gr=1 scruple
3 scruples=1 drachm
8 drachms=1 (apoth.) ounce=480 gr
12 (apoth.) oz=1 (apoth.) pound=0.82 lb

CAPACITY

Metric units
millilitre (ml)
1000 ml=1 litre (l)
100 l=1 hectolitre (hl)

Imperial units
gill
4 gills=1 pint
2 pints=1 quart
4 quarts=1 gallon=277.274 in³

Dry
2 gallons=1 peck
4 pecks=1 bushel
8 bushels=1 quarter
36 bushels=1 chaldron

Apothecaries' fluid
minim (min)
60 min=1 fluid drachm (fl. dr.)
8 fl. dr.=1 fluid ounce (fl. oz)
5 fl. oz=1 gill
20 fl. oz=1 pint

US units
1 US gallon (liquid)=0.8327 gallon (imp.)
1 US gallon (dry)=0.9689 gallon (imp.)
60 minims (US)=1 fluid dram (US)
8 fluid drams (US)=1 fluid ounce (US)
1 fluid oz (US)=1.0408 fl. oz (apoth.)

MISCELLANEOUS MEASURES

Nautical
1 span=9 in
8 spans=1 fathom=6 ft
1 cable's length=$\frac{1}{10}$ nautical mile
1 nautical mile (old)=6080 ft
1 nautical mile (international)=6076.1 ft=1.151
 statute miles (=1852 metres)
60 nautical miles=1 degree
3 nautical miles=1 league (nautical)
1 knot=1 nautical mile per hour
1 ton (shipping, UK)=42 cubic feet
1 ton (displacement)=35 cubic feet
1 ton (register)=100 cubic feet

Crude oil (petroleum)
1 barrel=35 imperial gallons
 =42 US gallons

Timber
1000 millisteres=1 stere=1 m³
1 board foot=144 in³ (12×12×1 in)
1 cord foot=16 ft³
1 cord=8 cord feet
1 hoppus foot=4/π ft³ (round timber)
1 Petrograd standard=165 ft³

Paper (writing)
24 sheets=1 quire
20 quires=1 ream=480 sheets

Printing
1 point=$\frac{1}{72}$ in
1 pica=$\frac{1}{6}$ in=12 points

Cloth
1 ell=45 in
1 bolt=120 ft=32 ells

Brewing
9 gallons=1 firkin
4 firkins=1 barrel=36 gallons
6 firkins=1 hogshead=54 gallons
4 hogsheads=1 tun

HISTORICAL UNITS

Old unit	Current equivalent
Cubit (elbow to finger tip)	
Egypt (2650 BC)	52.4 cm (20.6 in)
Babylon (1500 BC)	53.0 cm (20.9 in)
Assyrian (700 BC)	54.9 cm (21.6 in)
Jerusalem (AD 1)	52.3 cm (20.6 in)
Druid England (AD 1)	51.8 cm (20.4 in)
Black Cubit	
(Arabia AD 800s)	54.1 cm (21.3 in)
Mexico (Aztec)	52.5 cm (20.7 in)
Ancient China	53.2 cm (20.9 in)
Ancient Greece	46.3 cm (18.2 in)
England	45.7 cm (18.0 in)
Northern Cubit	
(c.3000 BC–AD 1800s)	67.6 cm (26.6 in)
Foot (length of foot)	
Athens	31.6 cm (12.44 in)
Aegina	31.4 cm (12.36 in)
Miletus	31.8 cm (12.52 in)
Olympia	32.1 cm (12.64 in)
Etruria	31.6 cm (12.44 in)
Rome	29.6 cm (11.66 in)
Northern	33.5 cm (13.19 in)
England (Medieval)	33.5 cm (13.19 in)
France	32.5 cm (12.79 in)
Moscow	33.4 cm (13.17 in)

Ancient Greece
1 digit = 1.84 cm (0.72 in)
100 digits = 1 orguia approx 1.83 m (6 ft)
10 orguias = 1 amma approx 18.3 m (20 yd)
10 ammas = 1 stadion approx 183 m (200 yd)

Ancient Rome
1 digitus = 1.85 cm (0.73 in)
4 digiti = 1 palmus = 7.4 cm (2.9 in)
4 palmi = 1 pes = 29.6 cm (11.7 in)
5 pes = 1 passus = 1.48 m (4.86 ft)
125 passus = 1 stadium = 185 m (202.3 yd)
8 stadia = 1 milliar = 1480 m (0.92 mi)

INTERNATIONAL PAPER SIZES*

A0	841×1189	33.11×46.81
A1	594×841	23.39×33.11
A2	420×594	16.54×23.39
A3	297×420	11.69×16.54
A4	210×297	8.27×11.69
A5	148×210	5.83×8.27
A6	105×148	4.13×5.83
A7	74×105	2.91×4.13
A8	52×74	2.05×2.91
A9	37×52	1.46×2.05
A10	26×37	1.02×1.46

*The sizes are based on a rectangle of area
1 sq metre (A0), with sides in the ratio 1: $\sqrt{2}$.

TIME

second (s, or sec)
60 s = 1 minute (min)
60 min = 1 hour (h. or hr)
24 h = 1 day (d)
7 days = 1 week
365$\frac{1}{4}$ days = 1 year
10 years = 1 decade
100 years = 1 century
1,000 years = 1 millennium
1 mean solar day = 24 h 3 min 56.555 s
1 sidereal day = 23 h 56 min 4.091 s
1 solar, tropical, or equinoctial year =
 365.2422 d (365 d 5 h 48 min 46 s)
1 sidereal year = 365.2564 d
 (365 d 6 h 9 min 9.5 s)
1 synodic (lunar) month = 29.5306 d
1 sidereal month = 27.3217 d
1 lunar year = 354 d = 12 synodic months

364

NUMERATION

Arabic	Roman	Binary*	Arabic	Roman	Binary
1	I	1	128	CXXVIII	10000000
2	II	10	200	CC	11001000
3	III	11	256	CCLVI	100000000
4	IV	100	300	CCC	100101100
5	V	101	400	CD	110010000
6	VI	110	500	D	111110100
7	VII	111	512	DXII	1000000000
8	VIII	1000	600	DC	1001011000
9	IX	1001	900	CM	1110000100
10	X	1010	1000	M	1111101000
11	XI	1011	1024	MXXIV	10000000000
12	XII	1100	1500	MD	10111011100
13	XIII	1101	2000	MM	11111010000
14	XIV	1110	4000	$M\overline{V}$	111110100000
15	XV	1111	5000	$\overline{V}$	1001110001000
16	XVI	10000	10000	$\overline{X}$	10011100010000
17	XVII	10001	20000	$\overline{XX}$	100111000100000
18	XVIII	10010	100000	$\overline{C}$	11000011010100000
19	XIX	10011			
20	XX	10100			
21	XXI	10101			
29	XXIX	11101			
30	XXX	11110			
32	XXXII	100000			
40	XL	101000			
50	L	110010			
60	LX	111100			
64	LXIV	1000000			
90	XC	1011010			
99	XCIX	1100011			
100	C	1100100			

*NR: In the binary system there are just two symbols, 0 and 1. The base of the system is 2 (written 10), just as 10 is the base of the decimal system. And just as 10^3 (10 to the power of 3) is written in the decimal system by a one followed by three zeros, so 2^3 is written 1000 in the binary system. In other words, 8 (which is 2^3) is written 1000. To write a number in the binary system, you break it up into powers of 2. For example, $13=8+4+1$, i.e. 1×2^3, 1×2^2, 0×2^1, 1×2^0; it is written 1101. If you want to double a number in the binary system (i.e. raise it to the power of 2, or the power of '10' in the binary system), just add a zero on the right.

DECIMAL MULTIPLES

Prefix	Symbol		Multiplication factor
tera	T	10^{12}	1,000,000,000,000
giga	G	10^9	1,000,000,000
mega	M	10^6	1,000,000
kilo	k	10^3	1,000
hecto	h	10^2	100
deca	da	10	10
deci	d	10^{-1}	0.1
centi	c	10^{-2}	0.01
milli	m	10^{-3}	0.001
micro	μ	10^{-6}	0.000001
nano	n	10^{-9}	0.000000001
pico	p	10^{-12}	0.000000000001
femto	f	10^{-15}	0.000000000000001
atto	a	10^{-18}	0.000000000000000001

ANGLE

second (")
$60''=1$ minute (')
$60'=1$ degree (°)
$90°=1$ quadrant, or right-angle
4 quadrants=1 circle=360°
1 radian=57.2958°=57°17'44.8"
2π radians=1 circle=360°
$1°=0.017453$ radian

MATHEMATICAL FORMULAE*

*r = radius, h = height.

Circumference
Circle $2\pi r$

Area
Circle πr^2
Surface of sphere $4\pi r^2$
Ellipse, semi-axes a, b πab
Triangle, base b $\frac{1}{2}bh$
Rectangle, sides a, b ab
Trapezium, parallel sides a, c $\frac{1}{2}h(a+c)$
Regular pentagon, side a $1.721a^2$
Regular hexagon, side a $2.598a^2$
Regular octagon, side a $4.828a^2$

Volume
Sphere $\frac{4}{3}\pi r^3$
Cylinder $h\pi r^2$
Cone $\frac{1}{3}h\pi r^2$
Rectangular prism, sides a, b, c abc
Pyramid, base area b $\frac{1}{3}hb$

Algebraic
$a^2-b^2=(a+b)(a-b)$
$a^2+2ab+b^2=(a+b)^2$
$a^2-2ab+b^2=(a-b)^2$
For quadratic equation $ax^2+bx+c=0$,

$$x=\frac{-b\pm\sqrt{b^2-4ac}}{2a}$$

365

Index

In a work of this kind it is not possible to index every entry; otherwise the index would be almost as long as the book itself. For this reason, look at the terms and definitions in the relevant glossaries, such as the Glossary of Astronomy and the Glossary of Musical Terms. They are all alphabetically arranged and index themselves.

ACKNOWLEDGEMENTS

Photographs
Page 2 *top* Japan Tourist Office, *centre* Reg Wilson, *bottom* Zefa; 4 *top* Zefa, *centre* Colorsport, *bottom* Columbia; 5 South African Tourist Office; 6 The Mansell Collection; 7 Colorsport; 8 California Institute of Technology and Carnegie Institute, Washington; 17 *top* RAS; 118 Novosti; 19 *top* California Institute of Technology; 22 NASA; 24 Swiss National Tourist Office; 38 J. Allan Cash Ltd; 46 Zefa; 48 Alan Hutchinson Library; 49 Australian Information Service; 52 Zefa; 53 W.H.O.; 55 Zefa; 58 Anglo-Chinese Educational Institute; 62 Zefa; 63 Finnish Tourist Board; 64 *bottom* Zefa, *top left* French Government Tourist Office, *top right* Zefa; 65/66 Zefa; 67 *top right and left* German Embassy; 69 *left* Dave Collins, *right* Icelandic Tourist Office; 72 Finnish Embassy; 75 *top right* Irish Tourist Board, *centre* Zefa; 76/77 Italian State Tourist Office; 78 *left* Japan Information Centre; 79–81 Zefa; 88 Netherlands National Tourist Office; 89 National Publicity Studios, New Zealand; 90–97 Zefa; 101 South African Tourist Corporation; 103 *left* Zefa, *right* Swiss National Tourist Office; 106 J. Allan Cash Ltd; 107 Novosti; 109 Aerofilms; 110–118 Zefa; 124 John Topham Picture Library; 127 W.H.O.; 128 UN; 137 Sonia Halliday; 138 The Mansell Collection; 141 Sonia Halliday; 142 The Mansell Collection; 143 Michael Holford; 145 National Museum Copenhagen; 152 National Portrait Gallery; 153 Chris Davies; 156/157 Cinema International Corp (UK); 161 Reg Wilson; 163 J. Allan Cash Ltd; 166 *left* The Mansell Collection, *right* Metropolitan Museum of Art; 167 J. Allan Cash Ltd; 170 Giraudon; 172 *left* The Mansell Collection, *right* Michael Holford; 173 Robert Harding, *inset* The Mansell Collection; 174–183 The Mansell Collection; 185 *top* Sonia Halliday; 190 Bibliotheque Nationale, Paris; 191 *right* The Mansell Collection; 193 British and Foreign Bible Society; 197 Bildarchiv, Berlin; 198 Mary Evans Picture Library; 201–209 The Mansell Collection; 211 Mary Evans Picture Library; 212 Imperial War Museum; 213 Novosti; 214 Paul Popper Ltd; 215 *left* Imperial War Museum, *right* Press Association; 217 Paul Popper Ltd; 218 Keystone Press Agency Ltd; 219 Syndication International; 220 Maritime Museum; 223 *top* The Mansell Collection, *2nd* Science Museum, *3rd* The Mansell Collection, *bottom* The Mansell Collection; 224 National Portrait Gallery; 225 Paul Popper Ltd; 229 *left* Radio Times Hulton Picture Library, *top right* The Mansell Collection, *right* Associated Press; 230 Carl Byoir and Associates Inc/Hughes Aircraft Company; 244 Products of River Don and Associated Works Special Steel Division; 247 AEA; 253 IBM; 255 Mary Evans Picture Library; 256 Australian News and Information Bureau; 260 The Mansell Collection; 267 Pat Morris; 268 NHPA; 269 *top left* New Zealand House, *top right* NHPA, *centre* Paul Popper Ltd; 270 *left* Pat Morris, *centre* Natural Science Photos, *right* SATOUR; 272 Middlesex Hospital; 275 FAO; 283–285 The Mansell Collection; 286–287 *top* The Mansell Collection; 291 *top* National Film Board, *centre* Mary Evans Picture Library; 292 National Portrait Gallery; 293 *left* The Mansell Collection, *right* National Portrait Gallery; 294–297 The Mansell Collection; 298 Novosti; 299 *left* National Portrait Gallery, *right* National Film Archives; 301 *left* The Mansell Collection, *right* Mary Evans Picture Library; 303 The Mansell Collection; 307 *left* National Gallery of Art, Washington DC, *right* The Mansell Collection; 308 The Mansell Collection; 309 Italian Institute; 311 The Mansell Collection; 315 *left* The Mansell Collection, *right* Mary Evans Picture Library; 316 The Mansell Collection; 317 *left* The Mansell Collection, *right* National Portrait Gallery; 319 Paul Popper Ltd; 323 *top* National Portrait Gallery, *centre* the Mansell Collection; 324–331 Colorsport; 342 The Mansell Collection; 343 National Motor Museum; 350 C. Sappa; 351 Robert Harding.